Copyright © 2020 by Sophie Summers

All rights reserved. No part of this publication may be reproduced, distributed, or transmitted in any form or by any means, including photocopying, recording, or other electronic or mechanical methods, without the prior written permission of the publisher, except in the case of brief quotations embodied in critical reviews and certain other noncommercial uses permitted by copyright law.

Disclaimer: Some of the recipes in this book include raw eggs. Raw eggs may contain bacteria. It is recommended that you purchase certified salmonella-free eggs from a reliable source and store them in the refrigerator. You should not feed raw eggs to babies or small kids. Likewise, pregnant women, elderly persons, or those with a compromised immune system should not eat raw eggs. Neither the author nor the publisher claims responsibility for adverse effects resulting from the use of the recipes and/or information found within this book.

The information presented is purely to share my experience and for entertainment purposes. As always, check with a doctor before making any fitness or nutrition changes. The author disclaims liability for any damage, mishap, or injury that may occur from engaging in any activities or ideas from this site. All information posted is merely for educational and informational purposes. It is not intended as a substitute for professional advice. Should you decide to act upon any information in this book, you do so at your own risk. The content displayed in the book is the intellectual property of the author. You may not reuse, republish, or reprint such content without our written consent.

TABLE OF CONTENTS

INTRODUCTION **10**
BREAKFAST RECIPES **11**
Hash Brown Breakfast 11
Chicken Paprika Casserole 11
Bacon and Cheese Breakfast 11
Avocado Chicken Burrito 11
Berry Oats 11
Tomato and Bacon Mix 11
Bacon Hash Browns 12
Parmesan Frittata 12
Blackberry Breakfast Mix 12
Paprika Breakfast 12
Cheese and Mushrooms Pie 12
Veggie Breakfast Mix 13
Mozzarella Breakfast Toast 13
Cherry Omelet 13
Cornmeal Cakes 13
Sugary Toasts 13
Creamy Eggs Soufflé 13
Spinach and Mushrooms Mix 14
Worcestershire Muffins 14
Cheddar Peppery Mix 14
Italian Mozzarella Sandwich 14
Cheddar Bread Pudding 14
Greek Potatoes Breakfast 15
Cheddar Dough Rolls 15
Buttermilk Biscuits 15
Corn Cilantro Omelet 15
Artichoke Omelet 15
Parmesan Potato Omelet 16
Cheddar Cheese Toasts 16
Beans Casserole 16
Marine Tortilla 16
Mozzarella Pastry 16
Provolone Tuna Sandwiches 16
Yogurt Peas Omelet 17
Milk Oats 17
Pear and Nuts Oats 17
Milky Almond Pudding 17
Mushrooms Feta Mix 17
Tarragon Omelet 17
Rotisserie Chicken & Parmesan Tortillas 18
English Sandwich 18
Apple Pancakes 18
Quinoa Romanesco Mix 18
Mozzarella Burritos 18
Veggie Casserole 19
Sugary Yam Pudding 19
Creamy Cauliflower Breakfast 19
Nutmeg Fritters 19
Parsley and Tofu Breakfast 19
Feta Peppers 20
Rocket and Lettuce Mix 20
Mozzarella Pie 20
Tomato and Peppers Breakfast 20
Rosemary Tomatoes Mix 20
Milky Pumpkin Oats 21
Cinnamon Breakfast 21
Almond Oats 21
Vanilla Strawberry Oats 21
Pepper Oatmeal 21
Maple Granola 21
Spinach Eggs 22
Parmesan Rolls 22
Chili Soufflé 22
English Fried Sandwich 22
Chipolatas Breakfast 22
Parmesan Muffins 22
Cornmeal Bites 23
Pepper Potatoes 23
Sugary Vanilla Toasts 23
Thyme Potato Hash 23
Creamy Casserole 23
Turkey Casserole 24
Cheddar Breakfast 24
Sausage Casserole 24
Bell Peppers Burrito 24
Broccoli Breakfast Scramble 25
Fruit Casserole 25
Cheese Hash Browns 25
Cinnamon Toasts 25
Smoked Breakfast 25
Roasted Parmesan Frittata 26
Asparagus Omelet 26
Cream Cheese Casserole 26
Mustard Brie Breakfast 26
Paprika Eggs 26
Parmesan Tomatoes 27
Gouda Cheese Quiche 27
Swiss Quiche 27
Tofu Breakfast 27
Cheddar Broccoli Quiche 27
Smoked Paprika Eggs 27
Cheesy Air Fried Toasts 28
Honey Bread Pudding 28
Maple Biscuits 28
Coriander Rolls 28
Corn Omelet 29
Chives Omelet 29
Oregano Frittata 29
Beef Mustard Burger 29
Potatoes Frittata 29
Mozzarella Sausage Frittata 29
Cheddar Sandwich 30
Long Beans Omelet 30
French Beans and Egg Breakfast Mix 30
Breakfast Doughnuts 30
Greek Breakfast Tofu 30
Broccoli Burritos 31
Corn Fish Tacos 31
Spinach Creamy Parcels 31
Monterey Frittata 31
Shrimp Wheat Sandwiches 31
Creamy Pea Tortilla 32
Cheese Rolls 32
Gold Potato Frittata 32
Milk Espresso Oats 32
Gouda Oatmeal 32
Pear Oatmeal 33
Cherries Risotto 33
Rice, Almonds and Raisins Pudding 33
Dates and Millet Pudding 33

LUNCH RECIPES **34**
Greek Sandwiches 34
Chicken Pie 34
Parmesan Pizza Rolls 34
Old Bay Chicken Wings 34

Dijon Hot Dogs	34
Spinach Lunch Cakes	35
Beef Tomato Meatballs	35
Beef Meatball Baguettes	35
Cod and Grapes Salad	35
Turkey Lunch	35
Herbed Meatballs	36
Beef Stew	36
Seafood Pasta	36
Marinara Ravioli	36
Milky Curry	36
Monterey Jack Casserole	37
Cajun Potato Lunch	37
Garlic Beef and Cabbage Mix	37
Corn Bread Pudding	37
Coconut Veggies Mix	37
Chicken and Mushroom Mix	38
Chicken and Mozzarella Bowls	38
Cod and Fennel Mix	38
Chicken and Tomato Bake	38
Sea Bass Stew	38
Colby Jack Lunch Burger	39
Rosemary Lamb	39
Lemon Broccoli Mix	39
Bell Peppers Lunch Stew	39
Zucchini Stew	39
Black Beans and Rice	40
Green Peppers and Quinoa Stew	40
Chickpeas Stew	40
Lentils Ginger Curry	40
Cumin Eggplant Stew	40
Tomatoes Corn Salad	41
Lunch Veggies Casserole	41
Tomato Chicken Mix	41
Sweet Chicken Thighs	41
Butter Baby Carrots	41
Apple and Quinoa Pesto Mix	41
Feta and Quinoa Salad	42
Quinoa and Olives Mix	42
Chicken and Chili Curry	42
Chicken and Beans Mix	42
Leeks Stew	42
Chicken and Quinoa Stew	43
Lunch Mushroom Rolls	43
Goat Cheese Toast	43
Stuffed Mushrooms	43
Quick Lunch Pizzas	43
Lunch Gnocchi	44
Tuna and Zucchini Tortillas	44
Oregano Fritters	44
Basil Croquettes	44
Salsa Pancakes	44
Italian Sandwiches	44
Fresh Chicken Mix	45
Cayenne Chicken	45
Spicy Chicken Pie	45
Macaroni and Mozzarella	45
Chicken Fajitas	46
Lunch Chicken Salad	46
Fish And Chips	46
Hash Brown Mozzarella Fries	46
Beef Cubes with Rice	46
Pasta Peppers	47
Philadelphia Chicken Lunch	47
Beef Cheeseburgers	47
Feta Koftas	47
Honey Kabobs	48
Beef and Cheddar Meatballs	48
Sour-Sweet Chicken Wings	48
Cheesy Hot Dogs	48
Lentils Fritters	48
Bell Pepper and Potato Salad	48
Creamy Corn Swiss Casserole	49
Sauce Sausage Mix	49
Beef Meatballs with Mustard Sauce	49
Beef Meatballs	49
Sirloin Steaks with Veggies	49
Maple Turkey Breast	50
Italian Eggplant Sandwich	50
Thyme Chicken Stew	50
Turkey Cakes	50
Cheese Ravioli and Marinara Sauce	51
Beef Thyme Stew	51
Onion Baguettes with Meatballs	51
Air Fried Red Cabbage Salad	51
Sweet Potato Coconut Casserole	51
Herbed Casserole	52
Chicken and Lime Casserole	52
Turkey and Shallot Burgers	52
Salmon and Asparagus	52
Shiitake and Poultry Lunch	52
Chicken and Coconut Casserole	53
Chicken and Kale Mix	53
Chicken, Jalapeno, Mozzarella Casserole	53

SIDE DISH RECIPES 53

Sour Cream Potatoes	53
Sweet Potato Ginger Salad	53
Garlic Brussels Sprouts	54
Walnut Shallots	54
Italian Parmesan Mix	54
Coriander Eggplant Mix	54
Creole Tomatoes	54
Bread Zucchini Fries	54
Smoked Paprika Peppers	55
Provence Carrots Mix	55
Maple Parsnips Mix	55
Air Fried Beets	55
Cauliflower and Chestnuts Risotto	55
Sumac Eggplants	55
Sesame Cauliflower Mix	56
Salty Rosemary Potatoes	56
Parsnips and Thyme Fries	56
Pepper Tomatoes Mix	56
Yellow Squash and Zucchini Mix	56
Cheesy Mushroom Salad	56
Paprika Corn	56
Spicy Potatoes	57
Rice Chicken Mix	57
Turmeric Quinoa	57
Mushrooms Risotto	57
Nutmeg Pumpkin Rice	57
Milky Sweet Potatoes	58
Saffron Arborio Rice	58
Cherries Rice	58
Chicken Flavored Risotto	58
Parmesan Rice	58
Beans Medley	58
Cumin Beans Mix	59
Pineapple Rice	59
Beans and Peppers Mix	59

Spring Cauliflower Puree 59
Creamy Parsnips 59
Carrot Souffle... 60
Butternut Mash... 60
Cheesy Asparagus 60
Nutmeg Fennel 60
Fresh Peas 60
Lunch Artichokes 60
Orange Cauliflower Mix 60
Garlicky Beets 61
Parsley Fava Beans 61
Applesauce Cabbage 61
Creamy Lettuce Salad 61
Cheesy Spinach 61
Rhubarb with Walnuts 61
Oregano Potatoes 62
Tomato and Cranberry Beans Salad 62
Scallions and Chili Rice Mix 62
Tomato Cabbage Mix 62
Mung Beans Mix 62
Ginger Lentils Mix with Spinach 63
Indian Potatoes with Cilantro 63
Creamy Potato Wedges 63
Mushroom Side Dish 63
Curry Potato Fries 63
Corn with Paprika and Feta 64
Herbed Potatoes 64
Garlic Brussels Sprouts Mix..................... 64
Creamy Air Fried Potato Side Dish 64
Green Beans and Shallots Mix.................. 64
Sugary Air Fried Pumpkin 65
Cracker Mushrooms 65
Parmesan Potatoes 65
Eggplant Pepper Mix................................ 65
Creamy Cheddar Mushrooms................... 65
Eggplant Fries 65
Buttermilk Tomatoes 66
Cauliflower Rice Parmesan Cakes............ 66
Brussels Sprouts with Cream 66
Buttermilk and Cheese Biscuits 66
Crispy Zucchini Fries 66
Thyme Tomatoes 67
Sweet Paprika Peppers 67
Greek Endives.. 67
Provence Carrots 67
Vermouth Mushrooms 67
Maple Parsnips 67
Herbed Risotto.. 68
Sweet Beets.. 68
Chicken and Beer Risotto 68
Soy Rice.. 68
Walnut Carrots Mix 68
Roasted Eggplant 68
Lemony Broccoli...................................... 69
Crispy Onion Rings 69
Parmesan Potato Patties........................... 69
Rosemary Fried Potato Chips................... 69
Avocado Crispy Fries 69
Veggie Fries 70
Green Creamy Cabbage 70
Spicy Paprika Chips 70
Zucchini Croquettes 70
Greek Salty Potatoes 70
Nutmeg Mushroom Cakes 70
Roasted Greek Peppers Dish 71
Herbed Veggie Mix 71
Air Fried Zucchini Mix............................ 71
Ginger Cauliflower 71
Cheddar Cheesy Potatoes 71
Cajun Onion Wedges............................... 72
Farro and Rice Pilaf................................. 72
Cinnamon Rice 72
Herbed Basmati Rice 72
Potato Casserole 73
Air Fried Artichokes 73
Zesty Cauliflower..................................... 73
Garlic Beets.. 73
Fried Red Cabbage 73
Lemony Artichokes Sauce 73
Pine Brussels Sprouts Side Dish............... 74
Crispy Buttered Potatoes 74

SNACK AND APPETIZER RECIPES........74
Peanut Butter Banana Chips.................... 74
Caramel Apple Bites................................. 74
Garlic Zucchini Balls............................... 74
Basil Butter Crackers............................... 74
Balsamic Zucchini Slices 75
Air Fried Turmeric Carrots...................... 75
Radish Chives 75
Paprika Lentils Snack 75
Buttered Corn 75
Air Fried Coconut Shrimps...................... 75
Crunchy Chicken Sticks 76
Cheesy Beef Meatballs.............................. 76
Bell Pepper Feta Rolls 76
Italian Cheesy Sticks 76
Flax Crackers 76
Salty Potato Chips.................................... 76
Garlicky Broccoli Bites............................. 77
Creamy Endives Side Dish 77
Coriander Bites.. 77
Beef Tomatoes Dip................................... 77
Red Lentils with Tomatoes 77
Herbed Dip 77
Onion and Zucchini Spread..................... 78
Veggie Dip.. 78
Salty Mushroom Mix 78
Buttery Cauliflower Side Dish 78
Fast Mango Dip 79
Herbed Party Mix 79
Tomatoes and Sultanas Dip 79
Sweet Chili Salsa 79
Onion Sauce 79
Cranberry Chili Dip 80
Sweet Onion Dip 80
Eggplant and Garlic Spread 80
Coconut Veggie Spread............................ 80
Buttery Cayenne Dip 80
Apple and Dates Dip 80
Fennel and Tomato Dip 81
Creamy Leek Dip 81
Fast Parsley Sauce 81
Chili Scallions Dip 81
Corn and Wine Dip.................................. 81
Crunchy Chicken Bites 81
Buffalo Veggie Snack 82
Sweet Chicken Wings 82
Crunchy Salmon Patties 82
Salty Banana Chips 82
Cabbage Rolls 82

Chives and Radish Chips 83
Air Fried Paprika Pickles 83
Chickpeas Paprika Snack 83
Yogurt Chicken Dip 83
Sugary Popcorn 83
Apple Chips 84
Cinnamon Pastry Sticks 84
Coconut Shrimp 84
Tiger Shrimp Appetizer 84
White Fish Sticks 84
Crunchy Fish Nuggets 84
Shrimp and Mushroom Rolls 85
Seafood Appetizer 85
Salmon Cilantro Meatballs 85
Garlicky Chicken Wings 85
Mozzarella Chicken Rolls 86
Crispy Chicken Breast Sticks 86
Provolone Beef Rolls 86
Beef Empanadas 86
Greek Feta Meatballs 86
Beef and Sage Rolls 87
Beef and Ham Patties 87
Bell Peppers and Feta Rolls 87
Goat Cheese Peppers 87
Parsley Tomatoes Appetizer 87
Creamy Jalapeno Balls 87
Minty Shrimp 88
Cheddar Veggie Patties 88
Stuffed Peppers Medley 88
Mozzarella and Zucchini Snack 88
Creamy Spinach Balls 88
Mushrooms Appetizer 89
Parmesan Wings 89
Cheesy Pepper Sticks 89
Blue Chicken Rolls 89
Basil Flax Crackers 90
Parmesan Chips 90
Pepper Tuna Cakes 90
Seafood Snack 90

FISH & SEAFOOD RECIPES 91
Sweet Cod Fillets 91
Pecan Cod 91
Balsamic Cod 91
Garlic Salmon Fillets 91
Shrimp and Veggie Mix 91
White Fish with Peas and Basil 91
Cod and Chives 92
Paprika Salmon Fillets 92
Thyme Tuna 92
Maple Salmon 93
Balsamic Orange Salmon 93
Crunchy Pistachio Cod 93
Roasted Parsley Cod 93
Salmon with Almonds 93
Pineapple Salmon Fillets 93
Easy Salmon Fillets and Bell Peppers 94
Ginger Air Fried Cod 94
Salmon and Mustard Mix 94
Paella Marinera 94
Parsley Coconut Shrimp 94
Tiger Shrimp Mix 94
Paprika and Tabasco Shrimp Mix 95
Rosemary Shrimps 95
Peppery Salmon 95

Olives Snapper 95
Garlic Trout 95
Cilantro Trout Fillets 96
Rice with Salmon 96
Veggie Salmon 96
Chili Cod 96
Herbed Salmon 96
Garlic Salmon Steak 96
Chinese Trout Bites 96
Crunchy Trout 97
Spicy Mussels 97
Seafood Medley 97
Clams and Potatoes 97
Creamy Clams 97
Parsley Shrimp Mix 98
Red Pepper Shrimps 98
Red Onion Shrimps 98
Shrimp and Tomatoes 98
Tomato Vinegar Shrimp 98
Shrimp and Peas Mix 98
Chili Shrimp Mix 98
Oregano Shrimp and Spaghetti 99
Butter Flounder Fillets 99
Parmesan Shrimp 99
Ginger Squid 99
Shrimp and Mushrooms Mix 99
Mayo Shrimp Salad 100
Trout and Soy Sauce 100
Herbed Baked Cod 100
Lime Baked Salmon 100
Salmon and Berry Dip 100
Shrimp and Tomato Sauce 100
Fried Ginger Cod 101
Paprika Catfish 101
Fennel Cod Fillets 101
Squid and Guacamole 101
Spicy Shrimp 101
Bell Pepper Shrimp Skewers 102
Honey Salmon 102
Herbed Cod Steaks 102
Flavored Air Fried Salmon 102
Salmon with Potatoes 102
Saba Fish 103
Spicy Sweet Halibut 103
Cod and Veggies Medley 103
Seafood Mix 103
Orange Trout 104
Parsley Cod Fillets 104
Thyme and Parsley Salmon 104
Butter Trout and Lemon Sauce 104
Cheddar Salmon 104
Salmon and Peppery Salsa 105
Italian Barramundi and Olives Mix 105
Creamy Shrimp and Veggies 105
Tuna Steak and Arugula 105
Air Fried Shrimps and Cauliflower 106
Mushroom-Stuffed Salmon 106
Maple Salmon 106
Jamaican Salmon with Arugula 106
Swordfish and Spicy Fruit Salsa 107
Salmon and Citric Marmalade 107
Chili Salmon 107
Salmon with Citric Relish 107
Salmon and Coconut Dip 108
Crunchy Salmon 108
Maple Salmon and Chives Medley 108

Cod Fillet and Plum Sauce 108
Sea Bass with Couscous 109
Peanut Cod 109
Cod with Pearl Onions 109
Hawaiian Pineapple Salmon 109
Salmon and Herbed Salad 109
Salmon and Greek Salsa 110
Beets Salmon 110
Spanish Salmon 110
Herbed Salmon 110
Red Snapper with Okra 111
Snapper with Peppers 111
Citric Branzino 111
Lemon Sole with Chard Mix 111
Salmon and Sweet Berry Glaze 112
Oriental Fish 112
French Cod with Tomatoes 112
Worcestershire Catfish Fillets 112
Ginger Tilapia 112
Greek Tilapia 113
Citric Sea Bass 113
Tasty Pollock 113

POULTRY RECIPES 114
Ginger Chicken Legs 114
Rosemary Turkey Breast 114
Salsa Verde Chicken Breast 114
Cheesy Chicken Thighs 114
Soy Chicken 114
Sweet Paprica Chicken Thighs 115
Spicy Chicken 115
Sweet Duck Breast 115
Duck and Cranberries 115
Wine Chicken Wings 115
Turkey and Parsley Pesto 115
Mushroom Chicken Breasts 116
Chicken Drumsticks and Coconut Sauce116
Party Chicken Thighs 116
Chicken Breasts Delight 116
Mozzarella Chicken Mix 117
Chicken and Veggie Medley 117
Sweet and Sour Chicken Thighs 117
Whole Chicken 117
Italian Chicken Thighs 117
Glazed Chicken and Apples 117
Citric Chicken and Zucchini 118
Turkey with Fruit Sauce 118
Garlic and Lemon Pepper Chicken 118
Tarragon Chicken Breasts 118
Chicken Breasts and Pear Jelly 118
Sweet Chicken and Dates Mix 119
Chicken Thighs and Leeks 119
Chicken and Bell Peppers Mix 119
Air Fried Chicken Wings 119
Turkey Breasts and Spring Onions 120
Soy and Ginger Chicken 120
Parmesan Chicken 120
Duck and Gold Potatoes 120
Cheesy Chicken 120
Simple Lemongrass Chicken 120
Herbed Chicken 121
Turkey with Lentils 121
Mexican Turkey and Mushrooms 121
Balsamic Chicken 121
Parmesan Turkey Meatballs 122

Garlic Chicken Breasts 122
Chicken and Smoked Pancetta 122
Turkey Wings with Cranberries 122
Spicy Chicken Mix 122
Honey Wings 123
Chicken and Tomatoes Mix 123
Cajun Chicken with Veggies 123
Sweet Chicken and Green Chilies 123
Chicken Drumsticks and Beer 123
Chicken Creamy Curry 124
Marinara Cheddar Chicken 124
Buffalo Chicken Mix 124
Chicken and Gold Potatoes 124
Carrots Chicken and Chickpeas 124
Chicken Drumsticks and Squash 125
Indian Chicken with Tomatoes 125
Sesame and Soy Sauce Chicken 125
Marjoram Chicken 125
Coconut Chicken 126
Lime Chicken Wings 126
Thyme Chicken 126
Chicken Mozzarella 126
Chicken Verde 126
Chicken and Creamy Rice 127
Italian Chicken with Parmesan 127
Mustard Duck Breasts 127
Sour-Sweet Duck Legs 127
Yum-Stuffed Chicken 127
Easy Chicken Thighs and Baby Potatoes 128
Butter Chicken and Capers 128
Chicken and Oregano Mushrooms 128
Duck Breasts and Beef Sauce 128
Japanese Duck with Honey 129
Mushroom Duck Breasts 129
Duck Breasts with Endives 129
Chicken Breasts with Tomato 129
Rosemary Chicken and Asparagus 129
Maple Chicken in Syrup 130
Oregano Chicken and Maple Sauce 130
Cheddar Chicken and Lentils 130
Mozzarella Fried Chicken 130
Chicken Salad 131
Coconut Chicken and Green Sauce 131
Tomatoes and Chicken Cacciatore 131
Chicken Wings and Mint Sauce 131
Citric Chicken 132
Chicken Breasts and Coconut 132
Garlic Chicken and Black Olives 132
Crispy Crusted Chicken 132
Pepperoni Chicken 132
Chicken and Creamy Mushrooms Mix .. 133
Turkey Quarters and Herbs 133
Chicken and Garlic Sauce 133
Turkey Breasts with Celery 133
Salty Chicken Thighs 133
Chicken Tenders and Paprika 134
Ginger Duck 134
Marjoram Chicken and Apricot Dip 134
Turmeric Chicken and Cauliflower Rice 134
Parsley Chicken and Baby Spinach 135
Balsamic Chicken and Water Chestnuts 135
Rosemary Glazed Chicken 135
Italian Chicken Breasts 135
Zucchini Chicken 135
Red Wine Duck and Orange Sauce 136
Duck with Figs 136

Duck Breasts and Raspberry Sauce 136
Duck and Cherries 136
Lemony Duck Breasts 137
Tea Duck 137
Tarragon Duck Breasts 137
Passion Fruit Chicken 137
BBQ Chicken with Chili 137
Duck with Mango Salsa 138
Milky Chicken Casserole 138
Peach Chicken 138
Black Tea Chicken 138
Chicken and Radish Mix 139

MEAT RECIPES 139
Garlic Pork Chops 139
Broccoli Pork and Soy Sauce 139
Provence Beef Mix 139
Soy Beef and Mushrooms 140
Oregano Pork Chops 140
Crusted Rack of Macadamia Lamb 140
Coconut and Ginger Pork 140
Rosemary Pork and Brussels Sprouts 140
Tarragon Pork and Mustard 140
Beef in Wine 141
Creamy Lamb Chops 141
Sweet Paprika Pork Chops 141
Beef with Grapes 141
Smoked Paprika Pork Mix 141
Garlic Beef Roast 142
Garlic Pork Loin 142
Celery Beef and Tomatoes 142
Sesame Beef Mix 142
Pork and Bell Peppers 142
Lamb and Beans 143
Pork Chops with Pesto 143
Ground Cumin Beef with Peppers 143
Paprika Pork Roast 143
Soy Pork and Cauliflower 143
Pork and Bell Peppers 143
Beef Steaks with Peas 144
Fennel Pork Mix 144
Lamb Meatballs 144
Chorizo Meatloaf 144
Paprika Pork Steaks 144
Rosemary Sausage Mix 144
Cinnamon Pork Mix 145
Tomato Beef with Leeks 145
Loin Roast 145
Pork Chops with Peanuts 145
Ginger Flank Steaks 145
Coconut Lamb 146
Worcestershire Beef 146
Chives Pork Chops 146
Beef in Vinegar 146
Cilantro Beef 146
Tomato Beef Curry 147
Mushrooms Beef 147
Jalapeno Peppers Beef 147
Cumin Beef Mix 147
Lamb and Carrots Mix 147
Pork and Celery Mix 148
Pork and Chives Mix 148
Mozzarella Beef Casserole 148
Beef Steak and Tofu 148
Chuck Roast Beef 148
Pork and Red Cabbage 149
Tomato Pork Chops 149
Salty Lamb Ribs 149
Olive Lamb Chops 149
Creamy Pork Mix 149
Tomato and Garlic Lamb Chops 150
Beef and Plums Mix 150
French Lamb Mix 150
Sugary Rib Eye Steak 150
Sesame Steak and Florets 151
French Pork 151
Beef Strips, Snow Peas and Mushrooms 151
Herbed Lamb Chops 151
Crusty Lamb 151
Indian Pork Dish 152
Creamy Lamb and Sprouts 152
Beef with Mayo 152
Marinated Pepper Beef 152
Sweet Paprika Pork 152
Marinated Cayenne Pork 153
Simple Pork in Wine 153
Oregano Couscous Pork 153
Air Fried Pork 153
Fennel Pork Loin 154
Beef Brisket with Tomatoes 154
Sesame Beef and Onions 154
Garlic Beef 154
Marinated Lamb and Veggies 154
Creamy Lamb 155
Coriander Lamb Shanks 155
Rosemary Lamb Roast 155
Lamb Leg in Herbs 155
Beef Wine Curry 156
Beef Roast with Smoked Paprika 156
Garlic Beef and Cabbage 156
Onion Lamb Shanks and Tomatoes 156
Veggie Lamb Ribs 156
Oriental Lamb 157
Ribs and Wine Sauce 157
Short Ribs in Beer 157
Pork Belly and Apples 157
Citric Pork Steaks 157
Pork and Mushroom Mayo 158
Squash with Beef 158
Greek Beef Salad 158
Beef Patties and Creamy Sauce 158
Worcestershire Beef Casserole 159
Cardamom Lamb and Spinach 159
Lamb and Citric Flavor 159
Lamb and Parsley 159
Fennel Lamb Racks 160
Burgundy Beef and Tomatoes 160
Mexican Beef Mix 160
Cheddar Ham and Cauliflower 160
Portobello Mix 160
Hot Sausage and Peppers 161
Sirloin Steaks and Tomato Sauce 161
Coffee Rib Eye Steaks 161
Filet Mignon and Coconut Sauce 161
Beef and Zucchini Kabobs 162
Mediterranean Scallops 162
Beef Chili Medallions 162
Balsamic Beef 162
Roasted Pork Chops and Paprika 162
Sage Pork Chops and Beans 163
Buttered Pork Chops 163

Onion Ham and Collard Greens 163
Air Fried Ham Mix 163

VEGETABLE RECIPES 164
Creamy Spinach Mix 164
Balsamic Lime Asparagus........................ 164
Cheesy Asparagus..................................... 164
Simple Fennel Mix 164
Beets in Cilantro 164
Sesame Beets 164
Beets and Scallions Mix........................... 164
Cherry Tomato Salad............................... 165
Cauliflower Peanut Mix 165
Broccoli and Scallions 165
Cilantro Brussels Sprouts........................ 165
Cheese Broccoli.. 165
Balsamic Red Cabbage 165
Butter Carrots 166
Garlic Beans Mix 166
Chili Kale Mix 166
Oregano Eggplants Mix 166
Creamy Greek Potatoes........................... 166
Coconut Mix... 166
Spicy Pearl Onions 167
Goat Cheese Sprouts................................ 167
Oregano and Zucchini Mix 167
Artichokes and Parmesan Mayo 167
Artichokes with Coconut 167
Asparagus and Prosciutto....................... 167
Cajun Asparagus 168
Butternut Squash Salad 168
Sour Cream Squash Mix 168
Zesty Carrots 168
Cherry Tomatoes and Feta Salad 168
Green Beans and Chili Salad 168
Bell Peppers and Kale Leaves................. 169
Garlic Parsnips... 169
Florets and Pomegranate 169
Bacon and Cauliflower Mix 169
Lime Broccoli 169
New Potatoes Dish................................... 169
Nutmeg Napa Cabbage........................... 169
Sweet Paprika Cabbage Mix.................... 170
Turmeric Mix 170
Green Cayenne Cabbage......................... 170
Easy Celery Root Mix 170
Maple Corn 170
Dill Buttery Corn 170
Fettucchine Casserole 171
Collard Greens Mix................................. 171
Tomato and Balsamic Greens 171
Lime Endives 171
Nutmeg Endives and Bacon 171
Spinach Milky Pie.................................... 171
Oregano Artichokes 172
Mozzarella Artichokes 172
Artichokes and Coconut Sauce 172
Beet Salad and Capers 172
Blue Beets and Cheese Salad 172
Sweet Beets and Arugula 172
Goat Cheese and Veggies Mix................. 173
Broccoli Florets Salad 173
Green Brussels Sprouts Mix 173
Sprouts and Mustard Sauce.................... 173
Parmesan Brussels Sprouts 173
Spicy Cabbage and Carrots..................... 174
Sugary Baby Carrots 174
Balsamic Greens Mix 174
Garlic Greens and Turkey 174
Herbed Zucchinis and Eggplant Mix..... 174
Parmesan Fennel 174
Okra and Corn Salad 175
Air Fried Leeks 175
Crunchy Gold Potatoes and Parsley 175
Indian Turmeric Salad............................ 175
Simple Mushroom Tomatoes 175
Indian Chili Potatoes 176
Tomatoes and Florets Stew 176
Collard Greens and Tomatoes................ 176
Spicy Mustard Greens 176
Parmesan Radish Hash 176
Swiss Chard and Ricotta 177
Swiss Chard and Pine Nuts Salad 177
Spanish Greens 177
Oregano Air Fried Tomatoes.................. 177
Italian Stew 178
Rutabaga and Veggie Pasta Mix 178
Cheddar and Garlic Tart 178
Zucchini Noodles with Tomato Sauce ... 178
Cherry Tomatoes and Rosemary Sauce . 179
Balsamic Cherry Tomatoes Skewers 179
Spinach and Portobello Mushrooms...... 179
Mexican Salad.. 179
Beef-Stuffed Peppers 179
Stuffed Poblano Peppers......................... 180
Baby Peppers with Shrimp 180
Eggplant and Ginger Sauce 180
Eggplant Tabasco Hash........................... 180
Cinnamon Potatoes Mix 180
Greek Veggies Mix................................... 181
Broccoli Hash... 181
Feta Fried Asparagus............................... 181
Greek Stuffed Eggplants 181
Salty Beans and Parmesan 182
Mozzarella Green Beans.......................... 182
Green Veggies Mix................................... 182
Potatoes and Beans Mix 182
Flavored Green Beans 182
Potatoes and Paprika Mix 182
Baby Balsamic Potatoes.......................... 183
Potatoes and Oregano Sauce 183

DESSERT RECIPES........................... 183
Avocado Cake... 183
Oreo Cheesecake...................................... 183
Cherry and Raisins Pudding 183
Chocolate Amaretto Cream 184
Cinnamon Rolls..184
Sweet and Spicy Pumpkin Pie................ 184
Cinnamon Pears 184
Butter Donuts... 184
Cinnamon Sugar Apples 184
Lemon Chocolate Cake 185
Greek Cake... 185
Zucchini Bread... 185
Cream of Tartar Bread............................ 185
Sweet Orange Cake.................................. 185
Maple Cinnamon Apples 185
Pineapple and Yogurt Cake..................... 186
Rum Sugar Cheesecake 186

Strawberry Cream Cheese 186
Coffee Cream 186
Cream Cheese Vanilla Cookies 186
Walnut and Cocoa Cookies 186
Creamy Vanilla and Blackberry Mix 187
Chocolate Brownies & Chocolate Chips 187
Cream Cheese Cake 187
Creamy Vanilla Cheesecake 187
Greek Cake 187
Banana Bread 188
Pear Bread 188
Citric Cake 188
Maple Pear Dessert 188
Juicy Orange Stew 188
Baked Pears and Wine 188
Heavy Liqueur Chocolate Cream 188
Apricot and Ginger Cake 189
Spiced Banana Pudding 189
Milky Tapioca Pudding 189
Strawberry Ricotta Cheesecake 189
Almond and Ricotta Cake 189
Creamy Orange Pudding 189
Brioche Milk and Raisins Pudding 190
Apple and Wine Sauce 190
Juicy Lemons Stew 190
Milky Rice Pudding 190
Vanilla and Blackberry Pudding 190
Maple Rice Pudding 190
Zesty Orange Marmalade 191
Pound Jam 191
Cranberry and Currant Jam 191
Sugary Plum Stew 191
Cinnamon Apple Jam 191
Honey Banana Cake 191
Cream Cheesecake 191
Doughnuts Pudding 192
Doughy Amaretto Dessert 192
Sugary Rolls and Cheese Dip 192
Spicy Pie 192
Pastry Pears 192
Glazed Donuts 193
Buttery Cocoa Cake 193
Greek Choco Cake 193
Apple Spiced Bread 193
Milky Banana Bread 194
Cocoa Lava Cakes 194
Baked Cinnamon Apples 194
Nuts Cake 194
Ginger Cream Cheesecake 194
Coconut and Strawberry Pie 195
Caramel Cheesecakes 195
Cocoa Cookies 195
Walnut Brownies 195
Berry Scones 196
Chip Cookies 196
Creamy Orange Cake 196
Coconut Macaroons 196
Lime Cheesecake 196
Coconut Granola 196
Fruity Cobbler 197
Milk Tea Cake 197
Lemony Plum Cake 197
Raisin Cookies 197
Lentils and Dates Brownies 198
Applesauce Cupcakes 198
Sweet Rhubarb Pie 198

INTRODUCTION

An air fryer is believed to be one of the most useful kitchen appliances. It can successfully grill, cook, bake, steam, and even roast food. We live in such a hectic and busy world that there's no place for cooking by the end of the day. If you are one of those who can't stand spending time in the kitchen or simply have no time to do it, then this book is the best choice you are about to make!

Being a modern and innovative tool, the air fryer will make cooking fun (probably again) for you. You are going to discover a fair ton of air fryer recipes that will instantly make your life easier and your cooking tastier than it has ever used to be.

You can forget about those pans and pots of yours and you certainly don't have to be an expert cook to use the air fryer. Simply pick the recipe you like, get the ingredients you need and enjoy the meal you have chosen in less time than you can ever expect.

Make this tool your best friend in the kitchen just like millions of people around the world did. If you have decided to buy an air fryer, make sure you get a lot of accessories with it to make your kitchen experience even smoother. This way you will be able to make the greatest variety of delightful dishes.

Air fryer use guarantees that your food will be done faster and in a healthy way. The air inside this appliance reaches up to 400 degrees F, and it allows you to cook perfectly crispy and fat-free food in a few minutes. Catchy deal it is!

Speaking of what you can prepare in a modern air fryer, we thought you could use a cooking manual that will help you get started. The more ideas – the better, that's why there are 1001 of them here! We searched and carefully chose some of the most delicious and rich breakfasts, lunch dishes, side dishes, snacks, appetizers, seafood and fish meals, poultry, meat or vegetable dishes, and even some most amazingly sweet, tangy, chewy and crispy desserts you can cook using only the air fryer.

So, what are you waiting for? Get your new air fryer today, and start cooking the best meals for yourself and all those people you care for.

Let's get started with your new best air fryer cookbook ever!

AIR FRYER BREAKFAST RECIPES

HASH BROWN BREAKFAST
Preparation time: 5 min | Cooking time: 25 min | Servings: 4

INGREDIENTS:

- 1½ pounds hash browns
- 1 red onion, chopped
- 2 tsp vegetable oil
- 1 red bell pepper, chopped
- Salt and black pepper to taste
- 1 tsp thyme, chopped
- 2 eggs

DIRECTIONS:
Heat up your air fryer at 350 degrees F. Then add the oil and heat it up. Add all other ingredients and cook for 25 minutes. Divide between plates and serve

NUTRITION:
calories 241, fat 4, fiber 2, carbs 12, protein 11

CHICKEN PAPRIKA CASSEROLE
Preparation time: 5 min | Cooking time: 25 min | Servings: 4

INGREDIENTS:

- 1 pound chicken meat, ground
- 1 tbsp olive oil
- ½ tsp sweet paprika
- 12 eggs, whisked
- 1 cup baby spinach
- Salt and black pepper to taste

DIRECTIONS:
In a bowl, whisk the eggs with the salt, pepper, and paprika. Then add the spinach and chicken and mix well. Heat up your air fryer at 350 degrees F; add the oil and allow it to heat up. Add the chicken and spinach mix, cover, and cook for 25 minutes. Divide between plates and serve hot.

NUTRITION:
calories 270, fat 11, fiber 8, carbs 14, protein 7

BACON AND CHEESE BREAKFAST
Preparation time: 5 min | Cooking time: 20 min | Servings: 4

INGREDIENTS:

- 4 bacon slices, cooked and crumbled
- A drizzle of olive oil
- 2 cups coconut milk
- 2½ cups cheddar cheese, shredded
- 1 pound breakfast sausage, chopped
- 2 eggs
- Salt and black pepper to taste
- 3 tbsp cilantro, chopped

DIRECTIONS:
In a bowl, mix the eggs with milk, cheese, salt, pepper, and the cilantro, and whisk well. Grease your air fryer with the drizzle of oil, and heat it up at 320 degrees F. Add the bacon, sausage, and the egg mixture, spread, and cook for 20 minutes. Serve hot and enjoy!

NUTRITION:
calories 244, fat 11, fiber 8, carbs 15, protein 9

AVOCADO CHICKEN BURRITO
Preparation time: 5 min | Cooking time: 10 min | Servings: 2

INGREDIENTS:

- 4 chicken breast slices, cooked and shredded
- 1 green bell pepper, sliced
- 2 eggs, whisked
- 1 avocado, peeled, pitted and sliced
- 2 tbsp mild salsa
- Salt and black pepper to taste
- 2 tbsp cheddar cheese, grated
- 2 tortillas

DIRECTIONS:
In a bowl, whisk the eggs with the salt and pepper, and pour them into a pan that fits your air fryer. Put the pan in the air fryer's basket, cook for 5 minutes at 400 degrees, and transfer the mix to a plate. Place the tortillas on a working surface, and between them divide the eggs, chicken, bell peppers, avocado, and the cheese; roll the burritos. Line your air fryer with tin foil, add the burritos, and cook them at 300 degrees F for 3-4 minutes. Serve for breakfast — or lunch, or dinner!

NUTRITION:
calories 329, fat 13, fiber 11, carbs 20, protein 8

BERRY OATS
Preparation time: 10 min | Cooking time: 20 min | Servings: 6
Ingredients:

- 2 cups old fashioned oats
- 1 tsp baking powder
- 1 cup sugar
- 1 tsp cinnamon powder
- 1 cup blueberries
- 1 banana, peeled and mashed
- 2 cups milk
- 2 eggs, whisked
- 2 tbsp butter
- 1 tsp vanilla extract
- Cooking spray

DIRECTIONS:
In a bowl, mix the sugar, baking powder, cinnamon, blueberries, banana, eggs, butter, and vanilla; whisk. Heat up your air fryer at 320 degrees F, and grease with cooking spray. Add the oats, the berries and banana mix; cover, and cook for 20 minutes. Divide into bowls and serve.

NUTRITION:
calories 260, fat 4, fiber 7, carbs 9, protein 10

TOMATO AND BACON MIX
Preparation time: 10 min | Cooking time: 30 min | Servings: 6

INGREDIENTS:
- 1 pound white bread, cubed
- 1 pound smoked bacon, cooked and chopped
- ¼ cup avocado oil
- 1 red onion, chopped
- 30 ounces canned tomatoes, chopped
- ½ pound cheddar cheese, shredded
- 2 tbsp chives, chopped
- ½ pound Monterey jack cheese, shredded
- 2 tbsp chicken stock
- Salt and black pepper to taste
- 8 eggs, whisked

DIRECTIONS:
Add the oil to your air fryer and heat it up at 350 degrees F. Add all other ingredients except the chives and cook for 30 minutes, shaking halfway. Divide between plates and serve with chives sprinkled on top.

NUTRITION:
calories 211, fat 8, fiber 7, carbs 14, protein 3

BACON HASH BROWNS
Preparation time: 10 min | Cooking time: 20 min | Servings: 6

INGREDIENTS:
- 1½ pounds hash browns
- 1 cup almond milk
- A drizzle of olive oil
- 6 bacon slices, chopped
- 8 ounces cream cheese, softened
- 1 yellow onion, chopped
- 1 cup cheddar cheese, shredded
- 6 spring onions, chopped
- Salt and black pepper to taste
- 6 eggs

DIRECTIONS:
Heat up your air fryer with the oil at 350 degrees F. In a bowl, mix all other ingredients except the spring onions, and whisk well. Add this mixture to your air fryer, cover, and cook for 20 minutes. Divide between plates, sprinkle the spring onions on top, and serve.

NUTRITION:
calories 231, fat 9, fiber 9, carbs 8, protein 12

PARMESAN FRITTATA
Preparation time: 10 min | Cooking time: 20 min | Servings: 6

INGREDIENTS:
- 6 ounces jarred roasted red bell peppers, chopped
- 12 eggs, whisked
- ½ cup parmesan cheese, grated
- 3 garlic cloves, minced
- 2 tbsp parsley, chopped
- Salt and black pepper to taste
- 2 tbsp chives, chopped
- 6 tbsp ricotta cheese
- A drizzle of olive oil

DIRECTIONS:
In a bowl, mix the bell peppers with the eggs, garlic, parsley, salt, pepper, chives, and ricotta; whisk well. Heat up your air fryer at 300 degrees F, add the oil, and spread. Add the egg mixture, spread, sprinkle the parmesan on top, and cook for 20 minutes. Divide between plates and serve.

NUTRITION:
calories 262, fat 6, fiber 9, carbs 18, protein 8

BLACKBERRY BREAKFAST MIX
Preparation time: 5 min | Cooking time: 10 min | Servings: 4

INGREDIENTS:
- 3 cups milk
- 1 tbsp sugar
- 2 eggs, whisked
- ¼ tsp nutmeg, ground
- ¼ cup blackberries
- 4 tbsp cream cheese, whipped
- 1½ cups corn flakes

DIRECTIONS:
In a bowl, mix all ingredients and stir well. Heat up your air fryer at 350 degrees F, add the corn flakes mixture, spread, and cook for 10 minutes. Divide between plates, serve, and enjoy.

NUTRITION:
calories 180, fat 5, fiber 7, carbs 12, protein 5

PAPRIKA BREAKFAST
Preparation time: 5 min | Cooking time: 10 min | Servings: 4

INGREDIENTS:
- 4 eggs, whisked
- A drizzle of olive oil
- Salt and black pepper to taste
- 1 red onion, chopped
- 2 tsp sweet paprika

DIRECTIONS:
In a bowl, mix all ingredients and whisk. Heat up your air fryer with the oil at 240 degrees F, add the eggs mixture, stir again, and cook for 10 minutes. Serve right away.

NUTRITION:
calories 190, fat 7, fiber 7, carbs 12, protein 4

CHEESE AND MUSHROOMS PIE
Preparation time: 10 min | Cooking time: 10 min | Servings: 4

INGREDIENTS:
- 1 tbsp olive oil
- 9-inch pie dough
- 6 white mushrooms, chopped
- 2 tbsp bacon, cooked and crumbled
- 3 eggs
- 1 red onion, chopped
- ½ cup heavy cream
- Salt and black pepper to taste
- ½ tsp thyme, dried
- ¼ cup cheddar cheese, grated

DIRECTIONS:
Roll the dough on a working surface, then

press it on the bottom of a pie pan that fits your air fryer and grease with the oil. In a bowl, mix all other ingredients except the cheese, stir well, and pour mixture into the pie pan. Sprinkle the cheese on top, put the pan in the air fryer, and cook at 400 degrees F for 10 minutes. Slice and serve warm as a breakfast or lunch.

NUTRITION:
calories 192, fat 6, fiber 6, carbs 14, protein 7

VEGGIE BREAKFAST MIX
Preparation time: 10 min | Cooking time: 20 min | Servings: 4

INGREDIENTS:

- 1 cauliflower head, stems removed, florets separated, and steamed
- 3 carrots, chopped and steamed
- 2 ounces cheddar cheese, grated
- 3 eggs
- 2 ounces milk
- 2 tsp cilantro, chopped
- Salt and black pepper to taste

DIRECTIONS:
In a bowl, mix the eggs with the milk, parsley, salt, and pepper; whisk. Put the cauliflower and the carrots in your air fryer, add the egg mixture, and spread. Then sprinkle the cheese on top. Cook at 350 degrees F for 20 minutes, divide between plates, and serve.

NUTRITION:
calories 194, fat 4, fiber 7, carbs 11, protein 6

MOZZARELLA BREAKFAST TOAST
Preparation time: 5 min | Cooking time: 8 min | Servings: 3

INGREDIENTS:

- 6 bread slices
- 5 tbsp butter, melted
- 3 garlic cloves, minced
- 6 tsp basil and tomato pesto
- 1 cup mozzarella cheese, grated

DIRECTIONS:
Arrange bread slices on a working surface. In a bowl, mix the butter, pesto, and garlic, and spread on each bread slice. Place them in your air fryer's basket, sprinkle the cheese on top, and cook at 350 degrees F for 8 minutes. Serve right away.

NUTRITION:
calories 187, fat 6, fiber 6, carbs 13, protein 5

CHERRY OMELET
Preparation time: 5 min | Cooking time: 11 min | Servings: 2

INGREDIENTS:

- 1 sausage link, sliced
- 2 eggs, whisked
- 4 cherry tomatoes, halved
- 1 tbsp cilantro, chopped
- 1 tbsp olive oil
- 1 tbsp cheddar cheese, grated
- Salt and black pepper to taste

DIRECTIONS:
Put the tomatoes and sausage in the air fryer's basket and cook at 360 degrees F for 5 minutes. Take a pan that fits your air fryer, grease it with the oil, and then transfer the tomatoes and sausage to the pan. In a bowl, mix all remaining ingredients and stir. Pour this over the sausage and tomato mixture, spread, and place the pan in the air fryer; cook at 360 degrees F for 6 minutes more. Serve warm for breakfast.

NUTRITION:
calories 270, fat 14, fiber 3, carbs 23, protein 16

CORNMEAL CAKES
Preparation time: 10 min | Cooking time: 25 min | Servings: 4

INGREDIENTS:

- 1 cup cornmeal
- 3 cups water
- Salt and black pepper to taste
- 1 tbsp butter, softened
- ¼ cup potato starch
- A drizzle of vegetable oil
- Maple syrup for serving

DIRECTIONS:
Put the water in a pot, heat up over medium heat, add the cornmeal, whisk, and cook for 10 minutes. Add the butter, whisk well again, then take off the heat and allow to cool down. Take spoonfuls of polenta and shape into balls; flatten them, dredge in potato starch, and place them on a lined baking sheet that fits your air fryer. Drizzle with oil. Place the baking sheet in the fryer and cook at 380 degrees F for 15 minutes, flipping them halfway. Serve with maple syrup drizzled on top.

NUTRITION:
calories 170, fat 2, fiber 2, carbs 12, protein 4

SUGARY TOASTS
Preparation time: 5 min | Cooking time: 5 min | Servings: 6

INGREDIENTS:

- 1 stick butter, softened
- 12 bread slices
- ½ cup brown sugar
- 2 tsp vanilla extract

DIRECTIONS:
In a bowl, mix the butter, sugar, and vanilla; stir. Spread mixture over bread slices, put them in your air fryer, and cook at 400 degrees F for 5 minutes.

NUTRITION:
calories 170, fat 6, fiber 5, carbs 11, protein 2

CREAMY EGGS SOUFFLÉ

Preparation time: 5 min | Cooking time: 9 min | Servings: 3

INGREDIENTS:

- 3 eggs
- 2 tbsp heavy cream
- 1 red chili pepper, chopped
- 2 tbsp parsley, finely chopped
- Salt and white pepper to taste

DIRECTIONS:
In a bowl, mix all ingredients, whisk, and pour into 3 ramekins. Place ramekins in your air fryer's basket and cook at 400 degrees F for 9 minutes.

NUTRITION:
calories 200, fat 6, fiber 1, carbs 11, protein 3

SPINACH AND MUSHROOMS MIX

Preparation time: 5 min | Cooking time: 20 min | Servings: 4

INGREDIENTS:

- 8 white mushrooms, sliced
- 1 garlic clove, minced
- 8 cherry tomatoes, halved
- 4 slices bacon, chopped
- 7 ounces spinach, torn
- A drizzle of olive oil
- 4 eggs
- Salt and black pepper to taste

DIRECTIONS:
In a pan greased with oil and that fits your air fryer, mix all ingredients except for the spinach; stir. Put the pan in your air fryer and cook at 400 degrees F for 15 minutes. Add the spinach, toss, and cook for 5 min.

NUTRITION:
calories 160, fat 2, fiber 5, carbs 12, protein 9

WORCESTERSHIRE MUFFINS

Preparation time: 5 min | Cooking time: 15 min | Servings: 4

INGREDIENTS:

- 2 eggs
- 2 tbsp olive oil
- 3 ounces almond milk
- 1 tbsp baking powder
- 4 ounces white flour
- A splash of Worcestershire sauce
- 2 ounces parmesan cheese, grated

DIRECTIONS:
In a bowl, mix the eggs with 1 tbsp of the oil, milk, baking powder, flour, Worcestershire sauce, and the parmesan; stir well. Grease a muffin pan that fits your air fryer with the remaining 1 tbsp of oil, divide the cheesy mix evenly, and place the pan in the air fryer. Cook at 320 degrees F for 15 minutes.

NUTRITION:
calories 190, fat 12, fiber 2, carbs 11, protein 5

CHEDDAR PEPPERY MIX

Preparation time: 5 min | Cooking time: 30 min | Servings: 2

INGREDIENTS:

- 2 eggs
- ½ cup cheddar cheese, shredded
- 2 tbsp red onion, chopped
- A pinch of salt and black pepper
- ¼ cup milk
- ½ cup tomatoes, chopped

DIRECTIONS:
In a bowl, mix all ingredients except for the cheese; stir well. Pour mixture into a pan that fits your air fryer, sprinkle the cheese on top, and place the pan in the fryer. Cook at 350 degrees F for 30 minutes. Divide the mix between plates, serve, and enjoy!

NUTRITION:
calories 210, fat 4, fiber 2, carbs 12, protein 9

ITALIAN MOZZARELLA SANDWICH

Preparation time: 30 min | Cooking time: 25 min | Servings: 2

INGREDIENTS:

- 1 eggplant, sliced
- 2 tsp parsley, chopped
- Salt and black pepper to taste
- ½ cup panko breadcrumbs
- ½ tsp garlic powder
- 2 tbsp coconut milk
- ½ tsp Italian seasoning
- 4 bread slices
- 1 tbsp avocado oil + a drizzle
- ½ cup mayonnaise
- ¾ cup tomato paste
- 2 tbsp cheddar cheese, grated
- 2 cups mozzarella cheese, grated
- 2 tbsp fresh basil, chopped

DIRECTIONS:
Season eggplant slices with salt and pepper and set aside for 30 minutes. Then pat them dry them and brush with mayo and milk. In a bowl, combine the parsley, breadcrumbs, Italian seasoning, garlic powder, salt, and black pepper; stir. Next, dip the eggplant slices in this mix, and place them on a lined baking sheet; drizzle with oil. Place the baking sheet in your air fryer's basket and cook at 400 degrees F for 15 minutes, flipping the eggplant slices halfway. Brush the bread slices with the remaining 1 tbsp of the oil. Then arrange 2 of them on a working surface, and add cheddar, mozzarella, baked eggplant slices, tomato paste, and basil; top with the other 2 bread slices. Grill sandwiches on your grill for 10 minutes.

NUTRITION:
calories 251, fat 11, fiber 4, carbs 8, protein 7

CHEDDAR BREAD PUDDING

Preparation time: 10 min | Cooking time: 1 hour and 15 min | Servings: 6

INGREDIENTS:

- 4 bacon slices, cooked and chopped
- 1 tbsp olive oil
- 2 cups corn
- ½ cup green bell pepper, chopped
- 1 yellow onion, chopped
- ¼ cup celery, chopped
- 1 tsp thyme, chopped
- 2 tsp garlic, grated
- Salt and black pepper
- ½ cup heavy cream
- 1½ cups whole milk
- 3 eggs
- 3 cups bread, cubed
- 3 tbsp parmesan cheese, grated
- 1 cup cheddar cheese, grated

DIRECTIONS:
Heat up the oil in a pan over medium heat. Add the corn, celery, onion, bell pepper, salt, pepper, garlic, and thyme to the pan; stir, sauté for 15 minutes, and transfer to a bowl. To the same bowl, add the bacon, milk, cream, eggs, salt, pepper, bread, and the cheddar cheese. Stir well, then pour into a casserole dish that fits your air fryer. Place the dish in the fryer and cook at 350 degrees F for 30 minutes. Sprinkle the pudding with parmesan cheese, and cook for 30 minutes more. Slice, divide between plates, and serve.

NUTRITION:
calories 251, fat 6, fiber 9, carbs 14, protein 7

GREEK POTATOES BREAKFAST
Preparation time: 5 min | Cooking time: 20 min | Servings: 4

INGREDIENTS:

- 1½ pounds gold potatoes, cubed
- 2 tbsp olive oil
- Salt and black pepper to taste
- 1 tbsp sweet paprika
- 4 ounces Greek yogurt
- 1 tbsp cilantro, chopped

DIRECTIONS:
Put the potatoes in your air fryer, and then add the oil, salt, pepper, and paprika. Stir and cook at 360 degrees F for 20 minutes. Transfer the potatoes to a bowl, and add the yogurt and cilantro. Toss, serve, and enjoy.

NUTRITION:
calories 251, fat 7, fiber 4, carbs 14, protein 7

CHEDDAR DOUGH ROLLS
Preparation time: 10 min | Cooking time: 6 min | Servings: 4

INGREDIENTS:

- 8 crescent roll dough pieces, separated
- 8 small sausages
- 8 cheddar cheese slices

DIRECTIONS:
Unroll the crescent roll pieces on a working surface, and place one sausage and one slice of cheese on each. Wrap the sausage and cheese with each roll, and seal the edges. Place 4 wraps in your air fryer, cook at 380 degrees F for 3 minutes, and transfer to a plate. Repeat with the remaining 4 sausage rolls and serve.

NUTRITION:
calories 181, fat 11, fiber 1, carbs 14, protein 4

BUTTERMILK BISCUITS
Preparation time: 10 min | Cooking time: 8 min | Servings: 12

INGREDIENTS:

- 2 cups white flour
- ¼ tsp baking soda
- ½ tsp baking powder
- 1 tsp sugar
- 5 tbsp butter
- 1 cup buttermilk

DIRECTIONS:
In a bowl, mix the flour, baking soda, baking powder, sugar, 4 tbsp of the butter, and the buttermilk; stir until you obtain a dough. Transfer the dough to a floured working surface, roll, and cut 12 pieces with a cookie cutter. Melt the remaining 1 tbsp of butter, brush the biscuits with it, and place them in your air fryer's cake pan. Cook at 400 degrees F for 8 minutes, serve, and enjoy.

NUTRITION:
calories 202, fat 11, fiber 9, carbs 14, protein 7

CORN CILANTRO OMELET
Preparation time: 5 min | Cooking time: 7 min | Servings: 4

INGREDIENTS:

- 4 eggs, whisked
- ½ pound chorizo, chopped
- ½ cup corn
- 1 tbsp vegetable oil
- 1 tbsp cilantro, chopped
- 1 tbsp feta cheese, crumbled
- Salt and black pepper to taste

DIRECTIONS:
Heat up your air fryer at 350 degrees F, add the oil, and heat it up. Add the chorizo, stir, and cook for 1-2 minutes. In a bowl, mix all remaining ingredients; whisk, and then pour over the chorizo. Cook for 5 minutes, divide between plates, and serve.

NUTRITION:
calories 270, fat 6, fiber 9, carbs 12, protein 7

ARTICHOKE OMELET
Preparation time: 5 min | Cooking time: 15 min | Servings: 6

INGREDIENTS:

- 3 artichoke hearts, canned, drained and chopped
- 2 tbsp avocado oil
- 6 eggs, whisked
- ½ tsp oregano, dried
- Salt and black pepper to taste

DIRECTIONS:

In a bowl, mix all ingredients except the oil; stir well. Add the oil to your air fryer's pan, and heat it up at 320 degrees F. Add the egg mixture, cook for 15 minutes, divide between plates, and serve.

Nutrition:
calories 216, fat 11, fiber 6, carbs 9, protein 4

PARMESAN POTATO OMELET
Preparation time: 5 min | Cooking time: 20 min | Servings: 6

Ingredients:

- 8 eggs, whisked
- 1 tbsp olive oil
- 1 pound small potatoes, chopped
- 2 red onions, chopped
- Salt and black pepper to taste
- 1 ounce parmesan cheese, grated
- ½ cup heavy cream

Directions:
In a bowl, mix all ingredients except the potatoes and oil; stir well. Heat up your air fryer's pan with the oil at 320 degrees F. Add the potatoes, stir, and cook for 5 minutes. Add the egg mixture, spread, and cook for 15 minutes more. Divide the frittata between plates and serve.

Nutrition:
calories 271, fat 11, fiber 7, carbs 14, protein 6

CHEDDAR CHEESE TOASTS
Preparation time: 5 min | Cooking time: 8 min | Servings: 2

Ingredients:

- 4 bread slices
- 4 tsp butter, softened
- 4 cheddar cheese slices

Directions:
Spread the butter on each slice of bread. Place 2 cheese slices each on 2 bread slices, then top with the other 2 bread slices; cut each in half. Arrange the sandwiches in your air fryer's basket and cook at 370 degrees F for 8 minutes. Serve hot, and enjoy!

Nutrition:
calories 200, fat 3, fiber 5, carbs 12, protein 4

BEANS CASSEROLE
Preparation time: 5 min | Cooking time: 10 min | Servings: 4

Ingredients:

- 4 eggs, whisked
- 1 tsp soy sauce
- 1 tbsp olive oil
- 4 garlic cloves, minced
- 3 ounces green beans, trimmed and halved
- Salt and black pepper to taste

Directions:
In a bowl, mix all ingredients except the beans and oil; whisk well. Heat up your air fryer at 320 degrees F, then add the oil and heat it up. Add the beans, stir, and sauté them for 3 minutes. Add the egg mixture over the beans, spread, and cook for 7-8 minutes more. Slice the omelet and serve immediately.

Nutrition:
calories 212, fat 8, fiber 6, carbs 8, protein 6

MARINE TORTILLA
Preparation time: 10 min | Cooking time: 17 min | Servings: 4

Ingredients:

- 4 tortillas
- A drizzle of olive oil
- 1 green bell pepper, chopped
- 1 red onion, chopped
- 1 cup corn
- 4 cod fillets, skinless and boneless
- ½ cup salsa
- A handful of baby spinach
- 4 tbsp parmesan cheese, grated

Directions:
Put the fish fillets in your air fryer's basket, cook at 350 degrees F for 6 minutes, and transfer to a plate. Heat up a pan with the oil over medium heat, add the bell peppers, onions, and corn, and stir. Sauté for 5 minutes and take off the heat. Arrange all the tortillas on a working surface, and divide the cod, salsa, sautéed veggies, spinach, and parmesan evenly between the 4 tortillas; then wrap / roll them. Place the tortillas in your air fryer's basket and cook at 350 degrees F for 6 minutes. Divide between plates, serve, and enjoy!

Nutrition:
calories 230, fat 12, fiber 7, carbs 14, protein 5

MOZZARELLA PASTRY
Preparation time: 10 min | Cooking time: 10 min | Servings: 4

Ingredients:

- 1 puff pastry sheet
- 4 handfuls mozzarella cheese, grated
- 4 tsp mustard
- 8 ham slices, chopped

Directions:
Roll out puff pastry on a working surface and cut it in 12 squares. Divide cheese, ham, and mustard on half of them, top with the other halves, and seal the edges. Place all the patties in your air fryer's basket and cook at 370 degrees F for 10 minutes. Divide the patties between plates and serve.

Nutrition:
calories 212, fat 12, fiber 7, carbs 14, protein 8

PROVOLONE TUNA SANDWICHES
Preparation time: 5 min | Cooking time: 9 min | Servings: 4

Ingredients:

- 16 ounces canned tuna, drained
- ¼ cup mayonnaise
- 2 tbsp mustard
- 1 tbsp lime juice
- 2 spring onions, chopped
- 6 bread slices
- 3 tbsp butter, melted
- 6 provolone cheese slices

DIRECTIONS:
In a bowl, mix the tuna, mayo, lime juice, mustard, and spring onions; stir until combined. Spread the bread slices with the butter, place them in preheated air fryer, and bake them at 350 degrees F for 5 minutes. Spread tuna mix on half of the bread slices, and top with the cheese and the other bread slices. Place the sandwiches in your air fryer's basket and cook for 4 minutes more. Divide between plates and serve.

NUTRITION:
calories 212, fat 8, fiber 7, carbs 8, protein 6

YOGURT PEAS OMELET
Preparation time: 5 min | Cooking time: 10 min | Servings: 8

INGREDIENTS:

- ½ pound baby peas
- 3 tbsp avocado oil
- 1½ cups yogurt
- 8 eggs, whisked
- ½ cup mint, chopped
- Salt and black pepper to taste

DIRECTIONS:
Heat up the oil in a pan that fits your air fryer over medium heat. Add the peas, stir, and cook for 3-4 minutes. In a bowl, mix the yogurt, salt, pepper, eggs, and mint; whisk. Pour yogurt mixture over the peas, toss, and cook at 350 degrees F for 7 minutes. Slice the omelet and serve right away; enjoy!

NUTRITION:
calories 212, fat 9, fiber 4, carbs 13, protein 7

MILK OATS
Preparation time: 5 min | Cooking time: 17 min | Servings: 4

INGREDIENTS:

- 1 cup milk
- 1 cup steel cut oats
- 2½ cups water
- 2 tbsp brown sugar
- 2 tsp vanilla extract

DIRECTIONS:
In a pan that fits your air fryer, mix all ingredients and stir well. Place the pan in your air fryer and cook at 360 degrees F for 17 minutes. Divide into bowls and serve. Enjoy!

NUTRITION:
calories 161, fat 7, fiber 6, carbs 9, protein 6

PEAR AND NUTS OATS
Preparation time: 5 min | Cooking time: 12 min | Servings: 4

INGREDIENTS:

- 1 cup milk
- 1 tbsp butter, softened
- ¼ cups brown sugar
- ½ tsp cinnamon powder
- 1 cup old fashioned oats
- ½ cup walnuts, chopped
- 2 cups pear, peeled and chopped

DIRECTIONS:
In a heat-proof bowl that fits your air fryer, mix all ingredients and stir well. Place in your fryer and cook at 360 degrees F for 12 minutes. Divide into bowls and serve.

NUTRITION:
calories 210, fat 9, fiber 11, carbs 12, protein 5

MILKY ALMOND PUDDING
Preparation time: 5 min | Cooking time: 20 min | Servings: 4

INGREDIENTS:

- 1 cup brown rice
- ½ cup coconut, shredded
- 3 cups almond milk
- ½ cup maple syrup
- ½ cup almonds, chopped

DIRECTIONS:
Put the rice in a pan that fits your air fryer, and add all remaining ingredients; toss. Place pan in your air fryer and cook at 360 degrees F for 20 minutes. Divide into bowls and serve.

NUTRITION:
calories 201, fat 6, fiber 8, carbs 19, protein 6

MUSHROOMS FETA MIX
Preparation time: 5 min | Cooking time: 10 min | Servings: 4

INGREDIENTS:

- 1 red bell pepper, roughly chopped
- 1 cup white mushrooms, sliced
- 1 yellow squash, cubed
- 2 green onions, sliced
- 2 tbsp butter, softened
- ½ cup feta cheese, crumbled

DIRECTIONS:
In a bowl, mix all ingredients except the feta cheese. Transfer to your air fryer and cook at 350 degrees F for 10 minutes, shaking the fryer once. Divide the mixture between plates and serve with feta cheese sprinkled on top.

NUTRITION:
calories 202, fat 12, fiber 4, carbs 7, protein 2

TARRAGON OMELET
Preparation time: 5 min | Cooking time: 15 min | Servings: 4

INGREDIENTS:

- 6 eggs, whisked
- 1 tbsp parsley, chopped
- 1 tbsp tarragon, chopped
- 2 tbsp chives, chopped
- Salt and black pepper to taste
- 2 tbsp parmesan cheese, grated
- 4 tbsp heavy cream

DIRECTIONS:
In a bowl, mix all ingredients—except for the parmesan—and whisk well. Pour this into a pan that fits your air fryer, place it in preheated fryer, and cook at 350 degrees F for 15 minutes. Divide the omelet between plates and serve with the parmesan sprinkled on top.

NUTRITION:
calories 251, fat 8, fiber 4, carbs 15, protein 4

ROTISSERIE CHICKEN AND PARMESAN TORTILLAS
Preparation time: 5 min | Cooking time: 7 min | Servings: 4

INGREDIENTS:

- 4 tortillas
- 4 tbsp butter, softened
- 6 ounces rotisserie chicken, cooked and shredded
- 1 cup zucchini, shredded
- 1 cup mayonnaise
- 2 tbsp mustard
- 1 cup parmesan cheese, grated

DIRECTIONS:
Spread the butter on the tortillas, place them in your air fryer's basket, and heat them up at 400 degrees F for 3 minutes. In a bowl, mix the chicken, zucchini, mayo, and mustard; stir. Divide the mixture between the tortillas, sprinkle with cheese, roll them, and place in your air fryer's basket. Continue to cook at 400 degrees F for 4 minutes more. Serve right away, and enjoy!

NUTRITION:
calories 212, fat 8, fiber 8, carbs 9, protein 4

ENGLISH SANDWICH
Preparation time: 5 min | Cooking time: 6 min | Servings: 1

INGREDIENTS:

- 1 tsp olive oil
- 2 cups kale, torn
- A pinch of salt and black pepper
- 2 tbsp pumpkin seeds
- 1 small shallot, chopped
- 1½ tbsp mayonnaise
- 1 avocado slice
- 1 English muffin, halved

DIRECTIONS:
Heat up your air fryer with the oil at 360 degrees F. Add kale, salt, pepper, pumpkin seeds, and shallots; toss. Cover and cook for 6 minutes, shaking halfway. Spread the mayo on the English muffin halves, add the avocado slice on one half, then add the kale mix, and top with the other muffin half. Serve and enjoy.

NUTRITION:
calories 162, fat 4, fiber 7, carbs 9, protein 4

APPLE PANCAKES
Preparation time: 10 min | Cooking time: 20 min | Servings: 4

INGREDIENTS:

- 1¾ cups white flour
- 2 tbsp sugar
- 2 tsp baking powder
- ¼ tsp vanilla extract
- 2 tsp cinnamon
- 1¼ cups milk
- 1 egg, whisked
- 1 cup apple, peeled, cored and chopped
- Cooking spray

DIRECTIONS:
In a bowl, mix all ingredients (except cooking spray) and stir until you obtain a smooth batter. Grease your air fryer's pan with the cooking spray, and pour in ¼ of the batter; spread it into the pan. Cover and cook at 360 degrees F for 5 minutes, flipping it halfway. Repeat steps 2 and 3 with ¼ of the batter 3 more times, and then serve the pancakes right away.

NUTRITION:
calories 172, fat 4, fiber 4, carbs 8, protein 3

QUINOA ROMANESCO MIX
Preparation time: 10 min | Cooking time: 15 min | Servings: 4

INGREDIENTS:

- 12 ounces firm tofu, cubed
- 3 tbsp maple syrup
- ¼ cup soy sauce
- 2 tbsp olive oil
- 2 tbsp lime juice
- 1 pound fresh romanesco, torn
- 3 carrots, chopped
- 1 red bell pepper, chopped
- 8 ounces baby spinach, torn
- 2 cups red quinoa, cooked

DIRECTIONS:
In your air fryer, mix the tofu with the oil, maple syrup, soy sauce, and lime juice; toss. Cook at 370 degrees F for 15 minutes, shaking halfway, and transfer to a bowl. Add romanesco, carrots, spinach, bell peppers, and quinoa; toss and then divide between bowls. Serve and enjoy.

NUTRITION:
calories 209, fat 7, fiber 6, carbs 8, protein 4

MOZZARELLA BURRITOS
Preparation time: 10 min | Cooking time: 9 min | Servings: 2

INGREDIENTS:

- 2 cups canned black beans, drained
- A drizzle of olive oil
- ½ red bell pepper, sliced
- 1 small avocado, peeled, pitted and sliced
- 2 tbsp mild salsa

- Salt and black pepper to taste
- ⅛ cup mozzarella cheese, shredded
- 2 tortillas

DIRECTIONS:
Grease your air fryer with the oil; then add the beans, bell peppers, salsa, salt, and pepper. Cover and cook at 400 degrees F for 6 minutes. Arrange the tortillas on a working surface, and divide the bean mixture, avocado, and cheese on each; roll the burritos. Put them in your air fryer, and cook at 300 degrees F for 3 minutes more. Divide between plates and serve.

NUTRITION:
calories 189, fat 3, fiber 7, carbs 12, protein 5

VEGGIE CASSEROLE
Preparation time: 10 min | Cooking time: 25 min | Servings: 2

INGREDIENTS:

- 1 yellow onion, chopped
- 1 tsp garlic, minced
- 1 tsp olive oil
- 1 carrot, chopped
- 2 celery stalks, chopped
- ½ cup white mushrooms, chopped
- ½ cup red bell pepper, chopped
- Salt and black pepper to taste
- 1 tsp oregano, dried
- ½ tsp cumin, ground
- 7 ounces firm tofu, cubed
- 1 tbsp lemon juice
- 2 tbsp water
- ½ cup quinoa, already cooked
- 2 tbsp cheddar cheese, grated

DIRECTIONS:
Heat up a pan with the oil over medium heat. Add the garlic and onion, stir, and sauté for 3 minutes. Add bell peppers, celery, carrots, salt, pepper, mushrooms, oregano, and cumin; stir. Cook for 5-6 minutes more and remove from the heat. In your food processor, place the tofu, cheese, lemon juice, quinoa, and water; blend. Add the tofu mixture over the sautéed veggies and toss. Pour everything into your air fryer's pan and cook at 350 degrees F for 15 minutes. Divide between plates and serve.

NUTRITION:
calories 230, fat 11, fiber 7, carbs 14, protein 5

SUGARY YAM PUDDING
Preparation time: 5 min | Cooking time: 8 min | Servings: 4

INGREDIENTS:

- 16 ounces canned candied yams, drained
- ½ tsp cinnamon powder
- ¼ tsp allspice, ground
- ½ cup coconut sugar
- 2 eggs, whisked
- 2 tbsp heavy cream
- ½ cup maple syrup

DIRECTIONS:
In a bowl, mix the yams, cinnamon, and allspice; mash with a fork. Grease your air fryer with cooking spray and heat it up to 400 degrees F. Then spread the yams mixture on the bottom. In another bowl, mix the eggs, cream, and maple syrup, then add to the air fryer; cover and cook for 8 minutes. Divide into bowls and serve.

NUTRITION:
calories 251, fat 11, fiber 7, carbs 9, protein 5

CREAMY CAULIFLOWER BREAKFAST
Preparation time: 5 min | Cooking time: 20 min | Servings: 4

INGREDIENTS:

- 1 big cauliflower head, stems discarded, florets separated and steamed
- 2 tbsp olive oil
- Salt and black pepper to taste
- 1 tbsp hot paprika
- 4 ounces sour cream

DIRECTIONS:
In a pan that fits your air fryer, mix all ingredients and stir well. Put the pan in your air fryer and cook at 360 degrees F for 20 minutes. Divide into bowls and serve; enjoy!

NUTRITION:
calories 150, fat 3, fiber 2, carbs 10, protein 3

NUTMEG FRITTERS
Preparation time: 2 hours | Cooking time: 11 min | Servings: 8

INGREDIENTS:

- 4 ounces mushrooms, chopped
- 1 red onion, chopped
- Salt and black pepper to taste
- ¼ tsp nutmeg, ground
- 2 tbsp olive oil
- 1 tbsp panko breadcrumbs
- 10 ounces milk

DIRECTIONS:
Heat up a pan with 1 tbsp of the oil over medium-high heat, add the onions and mushrooms, and stir / sauté for 3 minutes. Add the milk, salt, pepper, and nutmeg; stir. Remove the mixture from heat and set aside for 2 hours. In a bowl, mix the remaining 1 tbsp of the oil with the panko and stir. Take 1 tbsp of the mushroom mixture, roll in breadcrumbs, flatten with your palms, and put it in your air fryer's basket. Repeat step 5 with the rest of the mushroom mixture and breadcrumbs, and then cook the fritters at 400 degrees F for 8 minutes. Divide between plates and serve.

NUTRITION:
calories 202, fat 8, fiber 1, carbs 11, protein 6

PARSLEY AND TOFU BREAKFAST
Preparation time: 5 min | Cooking time: 10 min | Servings: 8

INGREDIENTS:

- 1 yellow bell pepper, cut into strips
- 1 orange bell pepper, cut into strips
- 1 green bell pepper, cut into strips
- Salt and black pepper to taste
- 3 ounces firm tofu, crumbled
- 1 green onion, chopped
- 2 tbsp parsley, chopped

DIRECTIONS:
In a pan that fits your air fryer, place the bell pepper strips and mix. Then add all remaining ingredients, toss, and place the pan in the air fryer. Cook at 400 degrees F for 10 minutes. Divide between plates and serve.

NUTRITION:
calories 135, fat 2, fiber 2, carbs 8, protein 3

FETA PEPPERS
Preparation time: 5 min | Cooking time: 8 min | Servings: 8

INGREDIENTS:

- 8 small bell peppers, tops cut off and seeds removed
- 1 tbsp avocado oil
- Salt and black pepper to taste
- 3½ ounces feta cheese, cubed

DIRECTIONS:
In a bowl, mix the cheese, salt, pepper, and the oil; toss. Stuff the peppers with the cheese. Place the peppers in your air fryer's basket and cook at 400 degrees F for 8 minutes. Divide the peppers between plates, serve, and enjoy!

NUTRITION:
calories 210, fat 2, fiber 1, carbs 6, protein 5

ROCKET AND LETTUCE MIX
Preparation time: 5 min | Cooking time: 10 min | Servings: 4

INGREDIENTS:

- 1 tbsp lime juice
- 4 red bell peppers
- 1 lettuce head, torn
- 3 tbsp heavy cream
- 2 tbsp olive oil
- 2 ounces rocket leaves

DIRECTIONS:
Place the bell peppers in your air fryer's basket and cook at 400 degrees F for 10 minutes. Remove the peppers, peel, cut them into strips, and put them in a bowl. Add all remaining ingredients, toss, and serve.

NUTRITION:
calories 200, fat 5, fiber 3, carbs 7, protein 6

MOZZARELLA PIE
Preparation time: 15 min | Cooking time: 19 min | Servings: 4

INGREDIENTS:

- 7 ounces white flour
- 7 ounces spinach, torn
- 2 tbsp olive oil
- 2 eggs, whisked
- 2 tbsp milk
- 3 ounces mozzarella cheese, crumbled
- Salt and black pepper to taste
- 1 red onion, chopped

DIRECTIONS:
In your food processor, mix the flour with 1 tbsp of the oil, eggs, milk, salt, and pepper; pulse, then transfer to a bowl. Knead the mixture a bit, cover, and keep in the fridge for 10 minutes. Heat up a pan with the remaining 1 tbsp of oil over medium heat, and then add all remaining ingredients. Stir, cook for 4 minutes, and remove from heat. Divide the dough into 4 pieces, roll each piece, and place in the bottom of a ramekin. Divide the spinach mixture between the ramekins, place them in your air fryer's basket, and cook at 360 degrees F for 15 minutes. Serve and enjoy!

NUTRITION:
calories 200, fat 12, fiber 2, carbs 13, protein 5

TOMATO AND PEPPERS BREAKFAST
Preparation time: 10 min | Cooking time: 45 min | Servings: 4

INGREDIENTS:

- 8 ounces eggplant, sliced
- 8 ounces zucchini, sliced
- 8 ounces bell peppers, chopped
- 2 garlic cloves, minced
- 5 tbsp olive oil
- 2 yellow onions, chopped
- 8 ounces tomatoes, cut into quarters
- Salt and black pepper to taste

DIRECTIONS:
Heat up a pan that fits your air fryer with half of the oil over medium heat. Add the eggplant, salt, and pepper. Stir, cook for 5 minutes, and then transfer to a bowl. Heat up the pan with 1 tbsp of oil, add the zucchini and the bell peppers, cook for 4 minutes, and then add to the eggplant pieces. Heat up the pan with the remaining oil, add onions, stir, and sauté for 3 minutes. Add the tomatoes, garlic, and if desired, more salt and pepper; stir. Transfer the pan to your air fryer and cook at 300 degrees F for 30 minutes. Divide mixture between plates and serve right away.

NUTRITION:
calories 210, fat 1, fiber 3, carbs 14, protein 6

ROSEMARY TOMATOES MIX
Preparation time: 5 min | Cooking time: 20 min | Servings: 2

INGREDIENTS:

- 1 pound cherry tomatoes, halved
- A drizzle of olive oil

- Salt and black pepper to taste
- 1 tsp cilantro, chopped
- 1 tsp basil, chopped
- 1 tsp oregano, chopped
- 1 tsp rosemary, chopped
- 1 cucumber, chopped
- 1 spring onion, chopped

DIRETIONS:
Grease the tomatoes with the oil, season with salt and pepper, and place them in your air fryer's basket. Cook the tomatoes at 320 degrees F for 20 minutes, and then transfer them to a bowl. Add all remaining ingredients, toss, and serve.

NUTRITION:
calories 140, fat 2, fiber 3, carbs 8, protein 4

MILKY PUMPKIN OATS
Preparation time: 5 min | Cooking time: 20 min | Servings: 4

INGREDIENTS:

- 1½ cups milk
- ½ cup pumpkin puree
- 1 tsp pumpkin pie spice
- 3 tbsp sugar
- ½ cup steel cut oats

DIRECTIONS:
In your air fryer's pan, mix all ingredients. Stir, cover, and cook at 360 degrees F for 20 minutes. Divide into bowls and serve.

NUTRITION:
calories 141, fat 4, fiber 7, carbs 8, protein 5

CINNAMON BREAKFAST
Preparation time: 5 min | Cooking time: 15 min | Servings: 6

INGREDIENTS:

- 3 cups almond milk
- 2 apples, cored, peeled and chopped
- 1¼ cups steel cut oats
- ½ tsp cinnamon powder
- ¼ tsp nutmeg, ground
- ¼ tsp allspice, ground
- ¼ tsp ginger powder
- ¼ tsp cardamom, ground
- 2 tsp vanilla extract
- 2 tsp sugar
- Cooking spray

DIRECTIONS:
Spray your air fryer with cooking spray, add all ingredients, and stir. Cover and cook at 360 degrees F for 15 minutes. Divide into bowls and serve.

NUTRITION:
calories 212, fat 5, fiber 7, carbs 14, protein 5

ALMOND OATS
Preparation time: 5 min | Cooking time: 15 min | Ingredients: 4

INGREDIENTS:

- 2 cups almond milk
- ½ cup steel cut oats
- 1 cup carrots, shredded
- 1 tsp cardamom, ground
- 2 tsp sugar
- Cooking spray

DIRECTIONS:
Spray your air fryer with cooking spray, add all ingredients, toss, and cover. Cook at 365 degrees F for 15 minutes. Divide into bowls and serve.

NUTRITION:
calories 172, fat 7, fiber 4, carbs 14, protein 5

VANILLA STRAWBERRY OATS
Preparation time: 5 min | Cooking time: 10 min | Servings: 4

INGREDIENTS:

- 1 cup strawberries, chopped
- 1 cup steel cut oats
- 1 cup almond milk
- 2 tbsp sugar
- ½ tsp vanilla extract
- Cooking spray

DIRECTIONS:
Spray your air fryer with cooking spray and then add all ingredients; toss and cover. Cook at 365 degrees F for 10 minutes. Divide into bowls and serve.

NUTRITION:
calories 172, fat 6, fiber 8, carbs 11, protein 5

PEPPER OATMEAL
Preparation time: 5 min | Cooking time: 15 min | Servings: 2

INGREDIENTS:

- 1 cup steel cut oats
- 2 tbsp canned kidney beans, drained
- 2 red bell peppers, chopped
- 4 tbsp heavy cream
- Salt and black pepper to taste
- ¼ tsp cumin, ground

DIRECTIONS:
Heat up your air fryer at 360 degrees F and add all ingredients; stir. Cover and cook for 15 minutes. Divide into bowls, serve, and enjoy!

NUTRITION:
calories 203, fat 4, fiber 6, carbs 12, protein 4

MAPLE GRANOLA
Preparation time: 5 min | Cooking time: 15 min | Servings: 4

INGREDIENTS:

- ½ cup granola
- ½ cup bran flakes
- 2 green apples, cored, peeled and roughly chopped
- ¼ cup apple juice
- ⅛ cup maple syrup
- 2 tbsp butter
- 1 tsp cinnamon powder
- cinnamon

DIRECTIONS:
In your air fryer, mix all ingredients. Toss,

cover, and cook at 365 degrees F for 15 minutes. Divide into bowls and serve; enjoy!

Nutrition:
calories 208, fat 6, fiber 9, carbs 14, protein

SPINACH EGGS
Preparation time: 10 min | Cooking time: 20 min | Servings: 4

Ingredients:

- 4 eggs
- 1 pound baby spinach, torn
- 7 ounces ham, chopped
- 4 tbsp milk
- 1 tbsp olive oil
- Cooking spray
- Salt and black pepper to the taste

Directions:
Heat up a pan with the oil over medium heat, add baby spinach, stir cook for a couple of minutes and take off heat. Grease 4 ramekins with cooking spray and divide baby spinach and ham in each. Crack an egg in each ramekin, also divide milk, season with salt and pepper, place ramekins in preheated air fryer at 350 degrees F and bake for 20 minutes. Serve baked eggs for breakfast.

Nutrition:
calories 321, fat 6, fiber 8, carbs 15, protein 12

PARMESAN ROLLS
Preparation time: 10 min | Cooking time: 20 min | Servings: 4

Ingredients:

- 4 dinner rolls
- 4 tbsp heavy cream
- 4 eggs
- 4 tbsp mixed chives and parsley
- Salt and black pepper to the taste
- 4 tbsp parmesan, grated

Directions:
Arrange dinner rolls on a baking sheet and crack an egg in each. Divide heavy cream, mixed herbs in each roll and season with salt and pepper. Sprinkle parmesan on top of your rolls, place them in your air fryer and cook at 350 degrees F for 20 minutes. Divide your bread bowls between plates and serve for breakfast.

Nutrition:
calories 238, fat 4, fiber 7, carbs 14, protein 7

CHILI SOUFFLÉ
Preparation time: 10 min | Cooking time: 8 min | Servings: 4

Ingredients:

- 4 eggs, whisked
- 4 tbsp heavy cream
- A pinch of red chili pepper, crushed
- 2 tbsp parsley, chopped
- 2 tbsp chives, chopped

Directions:
In a bowl, mix eggs with salt, pepper, heavy cream, red chili pepper, parsley and chives, stir well and divide into 4 soufflé dishes. Arrange dishes in your air fryer and cook souffles at 350 degrees F for 8 minutes. Serve them hot.

Nutrition:
calories 300, fat 7, fiber 9, carbs 15, protein 6

ENGLISH FRIED SANDWICH
Preparation time: 10 min | Cooking time: 6 min | Servings: 2

Ingredients:

- 2 English muffins, halved
- 2 eggs
- 2 bacon strips

Directions:
Crack eggs in your air fryer, add bacon on top, cover and cook at 392 degrees F for 6 minutes. Heat up your English muffin halves in your microwave for a few seconds, divide eggs into 2 halves, add bacon on top, season with salt and pepper, cover with the other 2 English muffins and serve for breakfast.

Nutrition:
calories 261, fat 5, fiber 8, carbs 12, protein 4

CHIPOLATAS BREAKFAST
Preparation time: 10 min | Cooking time: 13 min | Servings: 4

Ingredients:

- 7 ounces baby spinach
- 8 chestnuts mushrooms, halved
- 8 tomatoes, halved
- 1 garlic clove, minced
- 4 chipolatas
- 4 bacon slices, chopped
- Salt and black pepper to the taste
- 4 eggs
- Cooking spray

Directions:
Grease a cooking pan with the oil and add tomatoes, garlic and mushrooms. Add bacon and chipolatas, also add spinach and crack eggs at the end. Season with salt and pepper, place pan in the cooking basket of your air fryer and cook for 13 minutes at 350 degrees F. Divide among plates and serve for breakfast.

Nutrition:
calories 312, fat 6, fiber 8, carbs 15, protein 5

PARMESAN MUFFINS
Preparation time: 10 min | Cooking time: 15 min | Servings: 4

Ingredients:

- 1 egg
- 2 tbsp olive oil
- 3 tbsp milk
- 3.5 ounces white flour
- 1 tbsp baking powder
- 2 ounces parme-

san, grated
- A splash of Worcestershire sauce

DIRECTIONS:
In a bowl, mix egg with flour, oil, baking powder, milk, Worcestershire and parmesan, whisk well and divide into 4 silicone muffin cups. Arrange cups in your air fryer's cooking basket, cover and cook at 392 degrees F for 15 minutes.

NUTRITION:
calories 251, fat 6, fiber 8, carbs 9, protein 3

CORNMEAL BITES
Preparation time: 10 min | Cooking time: 20 min | Servings: 4

INGREDIENTS:

- For the polenta:
- 1 tbsp butter
- 1 cup cornmeal
- 3 cups water
- Salt and black pepper to the taste
- For the polenta bites:
- 2 tbsp powdered sugar
- Cooking spray

DIRECTIONS:
In a pan, mix water with cornmeal, butter, salt and pepper, stir, bring to a boil over medium heat, cook for 10 minutes, take off heat, whisk one more time and keep in the fridge until it's cold. Scoop 1 tbsp of polenta, shape a ball and place on a working surface. Repeat with the rest of the polenta, arrange all the balls in the cooking basket of your air fryer, spray them with cooking spray, cover and cook at 380 degrees F for 8 minutes. Arrange polenta bites on plates, sprinkle sugar all over and serve for breakfast.

NUTRITION:
calories 231, fat 7, fiber 8, carbs 12, protein 4

PEPPER POTATOES
Preparation time: 10 min | Cooking time: 35 min | Servings: 4

Ingredients:

- 2 tbsp olive oil
- 3 potatoes, cubed
- 1 yellow onion, chopped
- 1 red bell pepper, chopped
- Salt and black pepper to the taste
- 1 tsp garlic powder
- 1 tsp sweet paprika
- 1 tsp onion powder

DIRECTIONS:
Grease your air fryer's basket with olive oil, add potatoes, toss and season with salt and pepper. Add onion, bell pepper, garlic powder, paprika and onion powder, toss well, cover and cook at 370 degrees F for 30 minutes. Divide potatoes mix into plates and serve for breakfast.

NUTRITION:
calories 214, fat 6, fiber 8, carbs 15, protein 4

SUGARY VANILLA TOASTS
Preparation time: 10 min | Cooking time: 5 min | Servings: 6

INGREDIENTS:

- 1 stick butter, soft
- 12 bread slices
- ½ cup sugar
- 1 and ½ tsp vanilla extract
- 1 and ½ tsp cinnamon powder

DIRECTIONS:
In a bowl, mix soft butter with sugar, vanilla and cinnamon and whisk well. Spread this on bread slices, place them in your air fryer and cook at 400 degrees F for 5 minutes, Divide between plates and serve for breakfast.

NUTRITION:
calories 221, fat 4, fiber 7, carbs 12, protein 8

THYME POTATO HASH
Preparation time: 10 min | Cooking time: 25 min | Servings: 4

INGREDIENTS:

- 1 and ½ potatoes, cubed
- 1 yellow onion, chopped
- 2 tsp olive oil
- 1 green bell pepper, chopped
- Salt and black pepper to the taste
- ½ tsp thyme, dried
- 2 eggs

DIRECTIONS:
Heat up your air fryer at 350 degrees F, add oil, heat it up, add onion, bell pepper, salt and pepper, stir and cook for 5 minutes. Add potatoes, thyme and eggs, stir, cover and cook at 360 degrees F for 20 minutes. Divide between plates and serve for breakfast.

NUTRITION:
calories 241, fat 4, fiber 7, carbs 12, protein 7

CREAMY CASSEROLE
Preparation time: 10 min | Cooking time: 30 min | Servings: 4

INGREDIENTS:

- 3 tbsp brown sugar
- 4 tbsp butter
- 2 tbsp white sugar
- ½ tsp cinnamon powder
- ½ cup flour
- For the casserole:
- 2 eggs
- 2 tbsp white sugar
- 2 and ½ cups white flour
- 1 tsp baking soda
- 1 tsp baking powder
- 2 eggs
- ½ cup milk
- 2 cups buttermilk
- 4 tbsp butter
- Zest of 1 lemon, grated
- 1 and 2/3 cup blueberries

DIRECTIONS:
In a bowl, mix eggs with 2 tbsp white sugar, 2 and ½ cups white flour, baking powder, baking soda, 2 eggs, milk, buttermilk, 4 tbsp butter, lemon zest and blueberries, stir and pour into a pan that fits your air fryer. In

another bowl, mix 3 tbsp brown sugar with 2 tbsp white sugar, 4 tbsp butter, ½ cup flour and cinnamon, stir until you obtain a crumble and spread over blueberries mix. Place in preheated air fryer and bake at 300 degrees F for 30 minutes. Divide between plates and serve for breakfast.

Nutrition:
calories 214, fat 5, fiber 8, carbs 12, protein 5

TURKEY CASSEROLE
Preparation time: 10 min | Cooking time: 25 min | Servings: 6

Ingredients:

- 1 pound turkey, ground
- 1 tbsp olive oil
- ½ tsp chili powder
- 12 eggs
- 1 sweet potato, cubed
- 1 cup baby spinach
- Salt and black pepper to the taste
- 2 tomatoes, chopped for serving

Directions:
In a bowl, mix eggs with salt, pepper, chili powder, potato, spinach, turkey and sweet potato and whisk well. Heat up your air fryer at 350 degrees F, add oil and heat it up. Add eggs mix, spread into your air fryer, cover and cook for 25 minutes. Divide between plates and serve for breakfast.

Nutrition:
calories 300, fat 5, fiber 8, carbs 13, protein 6

CHEDDAR BREAKFAST
Preparation time: 10 min | Cooking time: 20 min | Servings: 4

Ingredients:

- 10 ounces sausages, cooked and crumbled
- 1 cup cheddar cheese, shredded
- 1 cup mozzarella cheese, shredded
- 8 eggs, whisked
- 1 cup milk
- Salt and black pepper to the taste
- Cooking spray

Directions:
In a bowl, mix sausages with cheese, mozzarella, eggs, milk, salt and pepper and whisk well. Heat up your air fryer at 380 degrees F, spray cooking oil, add eggs and sausage mix and cook for 20 minutes. Divide between plates and serve.

Nutrition:
calories 320, fat 6, fiber 8, carbs 12, protein 5

Milky Bake
Preparation time: 10 min | Cooking time: 20 min | Servings: 4

Ingredients:

- 4 bacon slices, cooked and crumbled
- 2 cups milk
- 2 and ½ cups cheddar cheese, shredded
- 1 pound breakfast sausage, casings removed and chopped
- 2 eggs
- ½ tsp onion powder
- Salt and black pepper to the taste
- 3 tbsp parsley, chopped
- Cooking spray

Directions:
In a bowl, mix eggs with milk, cheese, onion powder, salt, pepper and parsley and whisk well. Grease your air fryer with cooking spray, heat it up at 320 degrees F and add bacon and sausage. Add eggs mix, spread and cook for 20 minutes. Divide between plates and serve.

Nutrition:
calories 214, fat 5, fiber 8, carbs 12, protein 12

SAUSAGE CASSEROLE
Preparation time: 10 min | Cooking time: 15 min | Servings: 8

Ingredients:

- 12 ounces biscuits, quartered
- 3 tbsp flour
- ½ pound sausage, chopped
- A pinch of salt and black pepper
- 2 and ½ cups milk
- Cooking spray

Directions:
Grease your air fryer with cooking spray and heat it over 350 degrees F. Add biscuits on the bottom and mix with sausage. Add flour, milk, salt and pepper, toss a bit and cook for 15 minutes. Divide between plates and serve for breakfast.

Nutrition:
calories 321, fat 4, fiber 7, carbs 12, protein 5

BELL PEPPERS BURRITO
Preparation time: 10 min | Cooking time: 10 min | Servings: 2

Ingredients:

- 4 slices turkey breast already cooked
- ½ red bell pepper, sliced
- 2 eggs
- 1 small avocado, peeled, pitted and sliced
- 2 tbsp salsa
- Salt and black pepper to the taste
- 1/8 cup mozzarella cheese, grated
- Tortillas for serving

Directions:
In a bowl, whisk eggs with salt and pepper to the taste, pour them into a pan and place it in the air fryer's basket. Cook at 400 degrees F for 5 minutes, take pan out of the fryer and transfer eggs to a plate. Arrange tortillas on a working surface divide eggs on them, also divide turkey meat, bell pepper, cheese, salsa and avocado. Roll your burritos and place them in your air fryer after you've lined it with some tin foil. Heat up the burritos at 300 degrees F for 3 min.
Nutrition: calories 349, fat 23, fiber 11, carbs 20, protein 21

BROCCOLI BREAKFAST SCRAMBLE

Preparation time: 5 min | Cooking time: 30 min | Servings: 4

INGREDIENTS:

- 2 tbsp soy sauce
- 1 tofu block, cubed
- 1 tsp turmeric, ground
- 2 tbsp extra virgin olive oil
- 4 cups broccoli florets
- ½ tsp onion powder
- ½ tsp garlic powder
- 2 and ½ cup red potatoes, cubed
- ½ cup yellow onion, chopped
- Salt and black pepper to the taste

DIRECTIONS:

Mix tofu with 1 tbsp oil, salt, pepper, soy sauce, garlic powder, onion powder, turmeric and onion in a bowl, stir and leave aside. In a separate bowl, combine potatoes with the rest of the oil, a pinch of salt and pepper and toss to coat. Put potatoes in your air fryer at 350 degrees F and bake for 15 minutes, shaking once. Add tofu and its marinade to your air fryer and bake for 15 minutes. Add broccoli to the fryer and cook everything for 5 minutes more. Serve right away.

NUTRITION:
calories 140, fat 4, fiber 3, carbs 10, protein 14

FRUIT CASSEROLE

Preparation time: 10 min | Cooking time: 20 min | Servings: 8

INGREDIENTS:

- 2 cups rolled oats
- 1 tsp baking powder
- 1/3 cup brown sugar
- 1 tsp cinnamon powder
- ½ cup chocolate chips
- 2/3 cup blueberries
- 1 banana, peeled and mashed
- 2 cups milk
- 1 eggs
- 2 tbsp butter
- 1 tsp vanilla extract
- Cooking spray

DIRECTIONS:

In a bowl, mix sugar with baking powder, cinnamon, chocolate chips, blueberries and banana and stir. In a separate bowl, mix eggs with vanilla extract and butter and stir. Heat up your air fryer at 320 degrees F, grease with cooking spray and add oats on the bottom. Add cinnamon mix and eggs mix, toss and cook for 20 minutes. Stir one more time, divide into bowls and serve for breakfast.

NUTRITION:
calories 300, fat 4, fiber 7, carbs 12, protein 10

CHEESE HASH BROWNS

Preparation time: 10 min | Cooking time: 20 min | Servings: 6

INGREDIENTS:

- 2 pounds hash browns
- 1 cup whole milk
- 8 bacon slices, chopped
- 9 ounces cream cheese
- 1 yellow onion, chopped
- 1 cup cheddar cheese, shredded
- 6 green onions, chopped
- Salt and black pepper to the taste
- 6 eggs
- Cooking spray

DIRECTIONS:

Heat up your air fryer at 350 degrees F and grease it with cooking spray. In a bowl, mix eggs with milk, cream cheese, cheddar cheese, bacon, onion, salt and pepper and whisk well. Add hash browns to your air fryer, add eggs mix over them and cook for 20 minutes. Divide between plates and serve.

NUTRITION:
calories 261, fat 6, fiber 9, carbs 8, protein 12

CINNAMON TOASTS

Preparation time: 10 min | Cooking time: 20 min | Servings: 6

INGREDIENTS:

- 1 cup blackberry jam, warm
- 12 ounces bread loaf, cubed
- 8 ounces cream cheese, cubed
- 4 eggs
- 1 tsp cinnamon powder
- 2 cups half and half
- ½ cup brown sugar
- 1 tsp vanilla extract
- Cooking spray

DIRECTIONS:

Grease your air fryer with cooking spray and heat it up at 300 degrees F. Add blueberry jam on the bottom, layer half of the bread cubes, then add cream cheese and top with the rest of the bread. In a bowl, mix eggs with half and half, cinnamon, sugar and vanilla, whisk well and add over bread mixture. Cook for 20 minutes, divide between plates and serve for breakfast.

NUTRITION:
calories 215, fat 6, fiber 9, carbs 16, protein 6

SMOKED BREAKFAST

Preparation time: 10 min | Cooking time: 30 min | Servings: 4

INGREDIENTS:

- 1 and ½ pounds smoked sausage, chopped and browned
- A pinch of salt and black pepper
- 1 and ½ cups grits
- 4 and ½ cups water
- 16 ounces cheddar cheese, shredded
- 1 cup milk
- ¼ tsp garlic powder
- 1 and ½ tsp thyme, chopped
- Cooking spray
- 4 eggs, whisked

DIRECTIONS:
Put the water in a pot, bring to a boil over medium heat, add grits, stir, cover, cook for 5 minutes and take off heat. Add cheese, stir until it melts and mix with milk, thyme, salt, pepper, garlic powder and eggs and whisk really well. Heat up your air fryer at 300 degrees F, grease with cooking spray and add browned sausage. Add grits mix, spread and cook for 25 minutes. Divide between plates and serve for breakfast.

NUTRITION:
calories 321, fat 6, fiber 7, carbs 17, protein 4

ROASTED PARMESAN FRITTATA
Preparation time: 10 min | Cooking time: 20 min | Servings: 6

INGREDIENTS:

- 6 ounces jarred roasted red bell peppers, chopped
- 12 eggs, whisked
- ½ cup parmesan, grated
- 3 garlic cloves, minced
- 2 tbsp parsley, chopped
- Salt and black pepper to the taste
- 2 tbsp chives, chopped
- 16 potato wedges
- 6 tbsp ricotta cheese
- Cooking spray

DIRECTIONS:
In a bowl, mix eggs with red peppers, garlic, parsley, salt, pepper and ricotta and whisk well. Heat up your air fryer at 300 degrees F and grease it with cooking spray. Add half of the potato wedges on the bottom and sprinkle half of the parmesan all over. Add half of the egg mix, add the rest of the potatoes and the rest of the parmesan. Add the rest of the eggs mix, sprinkle chives and cook for 20 minutes. Divide between plates and serve for breakfast.

NUTRITION:
calories 312, fat 6, fiber 9, carbs 16, protein 5

ASPARAGUS OMELET
Preparation time: 10 min | Cooking time: 5 min | Servings: 2

INGREDIENTS:

- 4 eggs, whisked
- 2 tbsp parmesan, grated
- 4 tbsp milk
- Salt and black pepper to the taste
- 10 asparagus tips, steamed
- Cooking spray

DIRECTIONS:
In a bowl, mix eggs with parmesan, milk, salt and pepper and whisk well. Heat up your air fryer at 400 degrees F and grease with cooking spray. Add asparagus, add eggs mix, toss a bit and cook for 5 minutes. Divide frittata between plates.

NUTRITION:
calories 312, fat 5, fiber 8, carbs 14, protein 2

CREAM CHEESE CASSEROLE
Preparation time: 10 min | Cooking time: 8 min | Servings: 5

INGREDIENTS:

- 1/3 cup milk
- 3 tsp sugar
- 2 eggs, whisked
- ¼ tsp nutmeg, ground
- ¼ cup blueberries
- 4 tbsp cream cheese, whipped
- 1 and ½ cups corn flakes, crumbled
- 5 bread slices

DIRECTIONS:
In a bowl, mix eggs with sugar, nutmeg and milk and whisk well. In another bowl, mix cream cheese with blueberries and whisk well. Put corn flakes in a third bowl. Spread blueberry mix on each bread slice, then dip in eggs mix and dredge in corn flakes at the end. Place bread in your air fryer's basket, heat up at 400 degrees F and bake for 8 minutes. Divide between plates and serve for breakfast.

NUTRITION:
calories 300, fat 5, fiber 7, carbs 16, protein 4

MUSTARD BRIE BREAKFAST
Preparation time: 10 min | Cooking time: 25 min | Servings: 6

INGREDIENTS:

- 1 yellow onion, sliced
- 1 red bell pepper, chopped
- 1 gold potato, chopped
- 2 tbsp olive oil
- 8 ounces brie, trimmed and cubed
- 12 ounces sourdough bread, cubed
- 4 ounces parmesan, grated
- 8 eggs
- 2 tbsp mustard
- 3 cups milk
- Salt and black pepper to the taste

DIRECTIONS:
Heat up your air fryer at 350 degrees F, add oil, onion, potato and bell pepper and cook for 5 minutes. In a bowl, mix eggs with milk, salt, pepper and mustard and whisk well. Add bread and brie to your air fryer, add half of the eggs mix and add half of the parmesan as well. Add the rest of the bread and parmesan, toss just a little bit and cook for 20 minutes. Divide between plates and serve for breakfast.

NUTRITION:
calories 231, fat 5, fiber 10, carbs 20, protein 12

PAPRIKA EGGS
Preparation time: 10 min | Cooking time: 10 min | Servings: 2

INGREDIENTS:

- 2 eggs
- 2 tbsp butter
- Salt and black pepper to the taste
- 1 red bell pepper, chopped
- A pinch of sweet paprika

DIRECTIONS:
In a bowl, mix eggs with salt, pepper, paprika and red bell pepper and whisk well. Heat up your air fryer at 140 degrees F, add butter and melt it. Add eggs mix, stir and cook for 10 minutes. Divide scrambled eggs on plates and serve for breakfast.

NUTRITION:
calories 200, fat 4, fiber 7, carbs 10, protein 3

PARMESAN TOMATOES
Preparation time: 5 min | Cooking time: 10 min | Servings: 4

INGREDIENTS:

- 4 eggs
- 2 ounces milk
- 2 tbsp parmesan, grated
- Salt and black pepper to the taste
- 8 cherry tomatoes, halved
- Cooking spray

DIRECTIONS:
Grease your air fryer with cooking spray and heat it up at 200 degrees F. In a bowl, mix eggs with cheese, milk, salt and pepper and whisk. Add this mix to your air fryer and cook for 6 minutes. Add tomatoes, cook your scrambled eggs for 3 minutes, divide between plates and serve.

NUTRITION:
calories 200, fat 4, fiber 7, carbs 12, protein 3

GOUDA CHEESE QUICHE
Preparation time: 10 min | Cooking time: 30 min | Servings: 1

INGREDIENTS:

- 2 tbsp yellow onion, chopped
- 2 eggs
- ¼ cup milk
- ½ cup gouda cheese, shredded
- ¼ cup tomatoes, chopped
- Salt and black pepper to the taste
- Cooking spray

DIRECTIONS:
Grease a ramekin with cooking spray. Crack eggs, add onion, milk, cheese, tomatoes, salt and pepper and stir. Add this to your air fryer's pan and cook at 340 degrees F for 30 minutes. Serve hot.

NUTRITION:
calories 241, fat 6, fiber 8, carbs 14, protein 6

SWISS QUICHE
Preparation time: 10 min | Cooking time: 10 min | Servings: 4

INGREDIENTS:

- 1 tbsp flour
- 1 tbsp butter, soft
- 9 inch pie dough
- 2 button mushrooms, chopped
- 2 tbsp ham, chopped
- 3 eggs
- 1 small yellow onion, chopped
- 1/3 cup heavy cream
- A pinch of nutmeg, ground
- Salt and black pepper to the taste
- ½ tsp thyme, dried
- ¼ cup Swiss cheese, grated

DIRECTIONS:
Dust a working surface with the flour and roll the pie dough. Press in on the bottom of the pie pan your air fryer has. In a bowl, mix butter with mushrooms, ham, onion, eggs, heavy cream, salt, pepper, thyme and nutmeg and whisk well. Add this over pie crust, spread, sprinkle Swiss cheese all over and place pie pan in your air fryer. Cook your quiche at 400 degrees F for 10 minutes. Slice and serve for breakfast.

NUTRITION:
calories 212, fat 4, fiber 6, carbs 7, protein 7

TOFU BREAKFAST
Preparation time: 10 min | Cooking time: 12 min | Servings: 2

INGREDIENTS:

- 1 tofu block, pressed and cubed
- Salt and black pepper to the taste
- 1 tbsp smoked paprika
- ¼ cup cornstarch
- Cooking spray

DIRECTIONS:
Grease your air fryer's basket with cooking spray and heat the fryer at 370 degrees F. In a bowl, mix tofu with salt, pepper, smoked paprika and cornstarch and toss well. Add tofu to you air fryer's basket and cook for 12 minutes shaking the fryer every 4 minutes. Divide into bowls and serve for breakfast.

NUTRITION:
calories 172, fat 4, fiber 7, carbs 12, protein 4

CHEDDAR BROCCOLI QUICHE
Preparation time: 10 min | Cooking time: 20 min | Servings: 2

INGREDIENTS:

- 1 broccoli head, florets separated and steamed
- 1 tomato, chopped
- 3 carrots, chopped and steamed
- 2 ounces cheddar cheese, grated
- 2 eggs
- 2 ounces milk
- 1 tsp parsley, chopped
- 1 tsp thyme, chopped
- Salt and black pepper to the taste

DIRECTIONS:
In a bowl, mix eggs with milk, parsley, thyme, salt and pepper and whisk well. Put broccoli, carrots and tomato in your air fryer. Add eggs mix on top, spread cheddar cheese, cover and cook at 350 degrees F for 20 minutes. Divide between plates and serve for breakfast.

NUTRITION:
calories 214, fat 4, fiber 7, carbs 12, protein 3

SMOKED PAPRIKA EGGS
Preparation time: 10 min | Cooking time: 12

min | Servings: 4

INGREDIENTS:

- 2 tsp butter, soft
- 2 ham slices
- 4 eggs
- 2 tbsp heavy cream
- Salt and black pepper to the taste
- 3 tbsp parmesan, grated
- 2 tsp chives, chopped
- A pinch of smoked paprika

DIRECTIONS:
Grease your air fryer's pan with the butter, line it with the ham and add it to your air fryer's basket. In a bowl, mix 1 egg with heavy cream, salt and pepper, whisk well and add over ham. Crack the rest of the eggs in the pan, sprinkle parmesan and cook your mix for 12 minutes at 320 degrees F. Sprinkle paprika and chives all over, divide between plates and serve for breakfast.

NUTRITION:
calories 263, fat 5, fiber 8, carbs 12, protein 5

CHEESY AIR FRIED TOASTS

Preparation time: 10 min | Cooking time: 8 min | Servings: 3

INGREDIENTS:

- 6 bread slices
- 5 tbsp butter, melted
- 3 garlic cloves, minced
- 6 tsp sun dried tomato pesto
- 1 cup mozzarella cheese, grated

DIRECTIONS:
Arrange bread slices on a working surface. Spread butter all over, divide tomato paste, garlic and top with grated cheese. Add bread slices to your heated air fryer and cook them at 350 degrees F for 8 minutes. Divide between plates and serve for breakfast.

NUTRITION:
calories 187, fat 5, fiber 6, carbs 8, protein 5

HONEY BREAD PUDDING

Preparation time: 10 min | Cooking time: 22 min | Servings: 4

INGREDIENTS:

- ½ pound white bread, cubed
- ¾ cup milk
- ¾ cup water
- 2 tsp cornstarch
- ½ cup apple, peeled, cored and roughly chopped
- 5 tbsp honey
- 1 tsp vanilla extract
- 2 tsp cinnamon powder
- 1 and 1/3 cup flour
- 3/5 cup brown sugar
- 3 ounces soft butter

DIRECTIONS:
In a bowl, mix bread with apple, milk with water, honey, cinnamon, vanilla and cornstarch and whisk well. In a separate bowl, mix flour with sugar and butter and stir until you obtain a crumbled mixture. Press half of the crumble mix on the bottom of your air fryer, add bread and apple mix, add the rest of the crumble and cook everything at 350 degrees F for 22 minutes. Divide bread pudding between plates and serve.

NUTRITION:
calories 261, fat 7, fiber 7, carbs 8, protein 5

MAPLE BISCUITS

Preparation time: 10 min | Cooking time: 8 min | Servings: 4

INGREDIENTS:

- 1 and ¼ cup white flour
- ½ cup self-rising flour
- ¼ tsp baking soda
- ½ tsp baking powder
- 1 tsp sugar
- 4 tbsp butter, cold and cubed+ 1 tbsp melted butter
- ¾ cup buttermilk
- Maple syrup for serving

DIRECTIONS:
In a bowl, mix white flour with self-rising flour, baking soda, baking powder and sugar and stir. Add cold butter and stir using your hands. Add buttermilk, stir until you obtain a dough and transfer to a floured working surface. Roll your dough and cut 10 pieces using a round cutter Arrange biscuits in your air fryer's cake pan, brush them with melted butter and cook at 400 degrees F for 8 minutes. Serve them for breakfast with some maple syrup on top.

NUTRITION:
calories 192, fat 6, fiber 9, carbs 12, protein 3

CORIANDER ROLLS

Preparation time: 10 min | Cooking time: 12 min | Servings: 4

INGREDIENTS:

- 5 potatoes, boiled, peeled and mashed
- 8 bread slices, white parts only
- 1 coriander bunch, chopped
- 2 green chilies, chopped
- 2 small yellow onions, chopped
- ½ tsp turmeric powder
- 2 curry leaf sprigs
- ½ tsp mustard seeds
- 2 tbsp olive oil
- Salt and black pepper to the taste

DIRECTIONS:
Heat up a pan with 1 tsp oil, add mustard seeds, onions, curry leaves and turmeric, stir and cook for a few seconds. Add mashed potatoes, salt, pepper, coriander and chilies, stir well, take off heat and cool it down. Divide potatoes mix into 8 parts and shape ovals using your wet hands. Wet bread slices with water, press in order to drain excess water and keep one slice in your palm. Add a potato oval over bread slice and wrap it around it. Repeat with the rest of the potato mix and bread. Heat up your air fryer at 400 degrees F, add the rest of the oil, add

bread rolls, cook them for 12 minutes. Divide bread rolls between plates and serve for breakfast.

NUTRITION:
calories 261, fat 6, fiber 9, carbs 12, protein 7

CORN OMELET
Preparation time: 10 min | Cooking time: 10 min | Servings: 4

INGREDIENTS:
- 3 eggs
- ½ chorizo, chopped
- 1 potato, peeled and cubed
- ½ cup corn
- 1 tbsp olive oil
- 1 tbsp parsley, chopped
- 1 tbsp feta cheese, crumbled
- Salt and black pepper to the taste

DIRECTIONS:
Heat up your air fryer at 350 degrees F and add oil. Add chorizo and potatoes, stir and brown them for a few seconds. In a bowl, mix eggs with corn, parsley, cheese, salt and pepper and whisk. Pour this over chorizo and potatoes, spread and cook for 5 minutes. Divide omelet between plates and serve for breakfast.

NUTRITION:
calories 300, fat 6, fiber 9, carbs 12, protein 6

CHIVES OMELET
Preparation time: 10 min | Cooking time: 15 min | Servings: 4

INGREDIENTS:
- 1 cup egg whites
- ¼ cup tomato, chopped
- 2 tbsp skim milk
- ¼ cup mushrooms, chopped
- 2 tbsp chives, chopped
- Salt and black pepper to the taste

DIRECTIONS:
In a bowl, mix egg whites with tomato, milk, mushrooms, chives, salt and pepper, whisk well and pour into your air fryer's pan. Cook at 320 degrees F for 15 minutes, cool omelet down, slice, divide between plates and serve.

NUTRITION:
calories 100, fat 3, fiber 6, carbs 7, carbs 4

OREGANO FRITTATA
Preparation time: 10 min | Cooking time: 15 min | Servings: 6

INGREDIENTS:
- 3 canned artichokes hearts
- 2 tbsp olive oil
- ½ tsp oregano, dried
- Salt and black pepper to the taste
- 6 eggs, whisked

DIRECTIONS:
In a bowl, mix artichokes with oregano, salt, pepper and eggs and whisk well. Add the oil to your air fryer's pan, add eggs mix and cook at 320 degrees F for 15 minutes. Divide frittata between plates and serve for breakfast.

NUTRITION:
calories 136, fat 6, fiber 6, carbs 9, protein 4

BEEF MUSTARD BURGER
Preparation time: 10 min | Cooking time: 45 min | Servings: 4

INGREDIENTS:
- 1 pound beef, ground
- 1 yellow onion, chopped
- 1 tsp tomato puree
- 1 tsp garlic, minced
- 1 tsp mustard
- 1 tsp basil, dried
- 1 tsp parsley, chopped
- 1 tbsp cheddar cheese, grated
- Salt and black pepper to the taste
- 4 bread buns, for serving

DIRECTIONS:
In a bowl, mix beef with onion, tomato puree, garlic, mustard, basil, parsley, cheese, salt and pepper, stir well and shape 4 burgers out of this mix. Heat up your air fryer at 400 degrees F, add burgers and cook them for 25 minutes. Reduce temperature to 350 degrees F and bake burgers for 20 minutes more. Arrange them on bread buns and serve for a quick breakfast.

NUTRITION:
calories 234, fat 5, fiber 8, carbs 12, protein 4

POTATOES FRITTATA
Preparation time: 10 min | Cooking time: 20 min | Servings: 6

INGREDIENTS:
- 10 eggs, whisked
- 1 tbsp olive oil
- 1 pound small potatoes, chopped
- 2 yellow onions, chopped
- Salt and black pepper to the taste
- 1 ounce cheddar cheese, grated
- ½ cup sour cream

DIRECTIONS:
In a large bowl, mix eggs with potatoes, onions, salt, pepper, cheese and sour cream and whisk well. Grease your air fryer's pan with the oil, add eggs mix, place in air fryer and cook for 20 minutes at 320 degrees F. Slice frittata, divide between plates and serve for breakfast.

NUTRITION:
calories 231, fat 5, fiber 7, carbs 8, protein 4

MOZZARELLA SAUSAGE FRITTATA
Preparation time: 10 min | Cooking time: 20 min | Servings: 4

INGREDIENTS:
- 2 tbsp olive oil
- ½ pounds chicken sausage, casings removed and chopped

- 1 sweet onion, chopped
- 1 red bell pepper, chopped
- 1 orange bell pepper, chopped
- 1 green bell pepper, chopped
- Salt and black pepper to the taste
- 8 eggs, whisked
- ½ cup mozzarella cheese, shredded
- 2 tsp oregano, chopped

DIRECTIONS:
Add 1 tbsp oil to your air fryer, add sausage, heat up at 320 degrees F and brown for 1 minute. Add the rest of the oil, onion, red bell pepper, orange and green one, stir and cook for 2 minutes more. Add oregano, salt, pepper and eggs, stir and cook for 15 minutes. Add mozzarella, leave frittata aside for a few minutes, divide among plates and serve.

NUTRITION:
calories 212, fat 4, fiber 6, carbs 8, protein 12

CHEDDAR SANDWICH

Preparation time: 10 min | Cooking time: 8 min | Servings: 1

INGREDIENTS:

- 2 bread slices
- 2 tsp butter
- 2 cheddar cheese slices
- A pinch of sweet paprika

DIRECTIONS:
Spread butter on bread slices, add cheddar cheese on one, sprinkle paprika, top with the other bread slices, cut into 2 halves, arrange them in your air fryer and cook at 370 degrees F for 8 minutes, flipping them once, arrange on a plate and serve.

NUTRITION:
calories 130, fat 3, fiber 5, carbs 9, protein 3

LONG BEANS OMELET

Preparation time: 10 min | Cooking time: 10 min | Servings: 3

INGREDIENTS:

- ½ tsp soy sauce
- 1 tbsp olive oil
- 3 eggs, whisked
- A pinch of salt and black pepper
- 4 garlic cloves, minced
- 4 long beans, trimmed and sliced

DIRECTIONS:
In a bowl, mix eggs with a pinch of salt, black pepper and soy sauce and whisk well. Heat up your air fryer at 320 degrees F, add oil and garlic, stir and brown for 1 minute. Add long beans and eggs mix, spread and cook for 10 minutes. Divide omelet between plates and serve for breakfast.

NUTRITION:
calories 200, fat 3, fiber 7, carbs 9, protein 3

FRENCH BEANS AND EGG BREAKFAST MIX

Preparation time: 10 min | Cooking time: 10 min | Servings: 3

INGREDIENTS:

- 2 eggs, whisked
- ½ tsp soy sauce
- 1 tbsp olive oil
- 4 garlic cloves, minced
- 3 ounces French beans, trimmed and sliced diagonally
- Salt and white pepper to the taste

DIRECTIONS:
In a bowl, mix eggs with soy sauce, salt and pepper and whisk well. Heat up your air fryer at 320 degrees F, add oil and heat it up as well. Add garlic and brown for 1 minute. Add French beans and egg mix, toss and cook for 10 minutes. Divide among plates and serve for breakfast.

NUTRITION:
calories 182, fat 3, fiber 6, carbs 8, protein 3

BREAKFAST DOUGHNUTS

Preparation time: 10 min | Cooking time: 18 min | Servings: 6

INGREDIENTS:

- 4 tbsp butter, soft
- 1 and ½ tsp baking powder
- 2 a ¼ cups white flour
- ½ cup sugar
- 1/3 cup caster sugar
- 1 tsp cinnamon powder
- 2 egg yolks
- ½ cup sour cream

DIRECTIONS:
In a bowl, mix 2 tbsp butter with simple sugar and egg yolks and whisk well. Add half of the sour cream and stir. In another bowl, mix flour with baking powder, stir and also add to eggs mix. Stir well until you obtain a dough, transfer it to a floured working surface, roll it out and cut big circles with smaller ones in the middle. Brush doughnuts with the rest of the butter, heat up your air fryer at 360 degrees F, place doughnuts inside and cook them for 8 minutes. In a bowl, mix cinnamon with caster sugar and stir. Arrange doughnuts on plates and dip them in cinnamon and sugar before serving.

NUTRITION:
calories 182, fat 3, fiber 7, carbs 8, protein 3

GREEK BREAKFAST TOFU

Preparation time: 15 min | Cooking time: 20 min | Servings: 4

INGREDIENTS:

- 1 block firm tofu, pressed and cubed
- 1 tsp rice vinegar
- 2 tbsp soy sauce
- 2 tsp sesame oil
- 1 tbsp potato starch
- 1 cup Greek yogurt

DIRECTIONS:
In a bowl, mix tofu cubes with vinegar, soy

sauce and oil, toss, and leave aside for 15 minutes. Dip tofu cubes in potato starch, toss, transfer to your air fryer, heat up at 370 degrees F and cook for 20 minutes shaking halfway. Divide into bowls and serve for breakfast with some Greek yogurt on the side.

NUTRITION:
calories 110, fat 4, fiber 5, carbs 8, protein 4

BROCCOLI BURRITOS

Preparation time: 10 min | Cooking time: 10 min | Servings: 4

INGREDIENTS:

- 2 tbsp cashew butter
- 2 tbsp tamari
- 2 tbsp water
- 2 tbsp liquid smoke
- 4 rice papers
- ½ cup sweet potatoes, steamed and cubed
- ½ small broccoli head, florets separated and steamed
- 7 asparagus stalks
- 8 roasted red peppers, chopped
- A handful kale, chopped

DIRECTIONS:
In a bowl, mix cashew butter with water, tamari and liquid smoke and whisk well. Wet rice papers and arrange them on a working surface. Divide sweet potatoes, broccoli, asparagus, red peppers and kale, wrap burritos and dip each in cashew mix. Arrange burritos in your air fryer and cook them at 350 degrees F for 10 minutes. Divide veggie burritos between plates d serve.

NUTRITION:
calories 172, fat 4, fiber 7, carbs 8, protein 3

CORN FISH TACOS

Preparation time: 10 min | Cooking time: 13 min | Servings: 4

INGREDIENTS:

- 4 big tortillas
- 1 red bell pepper, chopped
- 1 yellow onion, chopped
- 1 cup corn
- 4 white fish fillets, skinless and boneless
- ½ cup salsa
- A handful mixed romaine lettuce, spinach and radicchio
- 4 tbsp parmesan, grated

DIRECTIONS:
Put fish fillets in your air fryer and cook at 350 degrees F for 6 minutes. Meanwhile, heat up a pan over medium high heat, add bell pepper, onion and corn, stir and cook for 1-2 minutes. Arrange tortillas on a working surface, divide fish fillets, spread salsa over them, divide mixed veggies and mixed greens and spread parmesan on each at the end. Roll your tacos, place them in preheated air fryer and cook at 350 degrees F for 6 minutes more. Divide fish tacos between plates and serve for breakfast.

NUTRITION:
calories 200, fat 3, fiber 7, carbs 9, protein 5

SPINACH CREAMY PARCELS

Preparation time: 10 min | Cooking time: 4 min | Servings: 2

INGREDIENTS:

- 4 sheets filo pastry
- 1 pound baby spinach leaves, roughly chopped
- ½ pound ricotta cheese
- 2 tbsp pine nuts
- 1 eggs, whisked
- Zest from 1 lemon, grated
- Greek yogurt for serving
- Salt and black pepper to the taste

DIRECTIONS:
In a bowl, mix spinach with cheese, egg, lemon zest, salt, pepper and pine nuts and stir. Arrange filo sheets on a working surface, divide spinach mix, fold diagonally to shape your parcels and place them in your preheated air fryer at 400 degrees F. Bake parcels for 4 minutes, divide them between plates and serve them with Greek yogurt on the side.

NUTRITION:
calories 182, fat 4, fiber 8, carbs 9, protein 5

MONTEREY FRITTATA

Preparation time: 10 min | Cooking time: 15 min | Servings: 4

INGREDIENTS:

- 4 eggs
- ½ tsp basil, dried
- Cooking spray
- Salt and black pepper to the taste
- ½ cup rice, cooked
- ½ cup shrimp, cooked, peeled, deveined and chopped
- ½ cup baby spinach, chopped
- ½ cup Monterey jack cheese, grated

DIRECTIONS:
In a bowl, mix eggs with salt, pepper and basil and whisk. Grease your air fryer's pan with cooking spray and add rice, shrimp and spinach. Add eggs mix, sprinkle cheese all over and cook in your air fryer at 350 degrees F for 10 minutes. Divide among plates and serve for breakfast.

NUTRITION:
calories 162, fat 6, fiber 5, carbs 8, protein 4

SHRIMP WHEAT SANDWICHES

Preparation time: 10 min | Cooking time: 5 min | Servings: 4

INGREDIENTS:

- 1 and ¼ cups cheddar, shredded
- 6 ounces canned tiny shrimp, drained
- 3 tbsp mayonnaise
- 2 tbsp green onions, chopped
- 4 whole wheat bread slices
- 2 tbsp butter, soft

DIRECTIONS:
In a bowl, mix shrimp with cheese, green onion and mayo and stir well. Spread this

on half of the bread slices, top with the other bread slices, cut into halves diagonally and spread butter on top. Place sandwiches in your air fryer and cook at 350 degrees F for 5 minutes. Divide shrimp sandwiches between plates and serve them for breakfast.

Nutrition:
calories 162, fat 3, fiber 7, carbs 12, protein 4

CREAMY PEA TORTILLA

Preparation time: 10 min | Cooking time: 7 min | Servings: 8

Ingredients:

- ½ pound baby peas
- 4 tbsp butter
- 1 and ½ cup yogurt
- 8 eggs
- ½ cup mint, chopped
- Salt and black pepper to the taste

Directions:
Heat up a pan that fits your air fryer with the butter over medium heat, add peas, stir and cook for a couple of minutes. Meanwhile, in a bowl, mix half of the yogurt with salt, pepper, eggs and mint and whisk well. Pour this over the peas, toss, introduce in your air fryer and cook at 350 degrees F for 7 minutes. Spread the rest of the yogurt over your tortilla, slice and serve.

Nutrition:
calories 192, fat 5, fiber 4, carbs 8, protein 7

CHEESE ROLLS

Preparation time: 30 min | Cooking time: 20 min | Servings: 6

Ingredients:

- 1 cup milk
- 4 tbsp butter
- 3 and ¼ cups flour
- 2 tsp yeast
- ¼ cup sugar
- 1 egg
- For the filling:
- 8 ounces cream cheese, soft
- 12 ounces raspberries
- 1 tsp vanilla extract
- 5 tbsp sugar
- 1 tbsp cornstarch
- Zest from 1 lemon, grated

Directions:
In a bowl, mix flour with sugar and yeast and stir. Add milk and egg, stir until you obtain a dough, leave it aside to rise for 30 minutes, transfer dough to a working surface and roll well. In a bowl, mix cream cheese with sugar, vanilla and lemon zest, stir well and spread over dough. In another bowl, mix raspberries with cornstarch, stir and spread over cream cheese mix. Roll your dough, cut into medium pieces, place them in your air fryer, spray them with cooking spray and cook them at 350 degrees F for 30 minutes. Serve your rolls for breakfast.

Nutrition:
calories 261, fat 5, fiber 8, carbs 9, protein 6

GOLD POTATO FRITTATA

Preparation time: 10 min | Cooking time: 18 min | Servings: 4

Ingredients:

- 2 gold potatoes, boiled, peeled and chopped
- 2 tbsp butter
- 2 leeks, sliced
- Salt and black pepper to the taste
- ¼ cup whole milk
- 10 eggs, whisked
- 5 ounces fromage blanc, crumbled

Directions:
Heat up a pan that fits your air fryer with the butter over medium heat, add leeks, stir and cook for 4 minutes. Add potatoes, salt, pepper, eggs, cheese and milk, whisk well, cook for 1 minute more, introduce in your air fryer and cook at 350 degrees F for 13 minutes. Slice frittata, divide among plates and serve.

Nutrition:
calories 271, fat 6, fiber 8, carbs 12, protein 6

MILK ESPRESSO OATS

Preparation time: 10 min | Cooking time: 17 min | Servings: 4

Ingredients:

- 1 cup milk
- 1 cup steel cut oats
- 2 and ½ cups water
- 2 tbsp sugar
- 1 tsp espresso powder
- 2 tsp vanilla extract

Directions:
In a pan that fits your air fryer, mix oats with water, sugar, milk and espresso powder, stir, introduce in your air fryer and cook at 360 degrees F for 17 minutes. Add vanilla extract, stir, leave everything aside for 5 minutes, divide into bowls and serve for breakfast.

Nutrition:
calories 261, fat 7, fiber 6, carbs 39, protein 6

GOUDA OATMEAL

Preparation time: 10 min | Cooking time: 20 min | Servings: 4

Ingredients:

- 1 small yellow onion, chopped
- 1 cup steel cut oats
- 2 garlic cloves, minced
- 2 tbsp butter
- ½ cup water
- 14 ounces canned chicken stock
- 3 thyme sprigs,
- chopped
- 2 tbsp extra virgin olive oil
- ½ cup gouda cheese, grated
- 8 ounces mushroom, sliced
- Salt and black pepper to the taste

Directions:
Heat up a pan that fits your air fryer with the butter over medium heat, add onions

and garlic, stir and cook for 4 minutes. Add oats, water, salt, pepper, stock and thyme, stir, introduce in your air fryer and cook at 360 degrees F for 16 minutes. Meanwhile, heat up a pan with the olive oil over medium heat, add mushrooms, cook them for 3 minutes, add to oatmeal and cheese, stir, divide into bowls and serve for breakfast.

Nutrition:
calories 284, fat 8, fiber 8, carbs 20, protein 17

PEAR OATMEAL
Preparation time: 5 min | Cooking time: 12 min | Servings: 4

Ingredients:

- 1 cup water
- 1 tbsp butter, soft
- ¼ cups brown sugar
- ½ tsp cinnamon powder
- 1 cup rolled oats
- ½ cup walnuts, chopped
- 2 cups pear, peeled and chopped
- ½ cup raisins

Directions:
In a heat proof dish that fits your air fryer, mix milk with sugar, butter, oats, cinnamon, raisins, pears and walnuts, stir, introduce in your fryer and cook at 360 degrees F for 12 minutes. Divide into bowls and serve.

Nutrition:
calories 230, fat 6, fiber 11, carbs 20, protein 5

Cream Cheese Oatmeal
Preparation time: 10 min | Cooking time: 25 min | Servings: 4

Ingredients:

- 1 cup steel oats
- 3 cups milk
- 1 tbsp butter
- ¾ cup raisins
- 1 tsp cinnamon powder
- ¼ cup brown sugar
- 2 tbsp white sugar
- 2 ounces cream cheese, soft

Directions:
Heat up a pan that fits your air fryer with the butter over medium heat, add oats, stir and toast them for 3 minutes. Add milk and raisins, stir, put in your air fryer and cook at 350 degrees F for 20 minutes. In a bowl, mix cinnamon with brown sugar and stir. In a second bowl, mix white sugar with cream cheese and whisk. Top each with cinnamon and cream cheese.

Nutrition:
calories 152, fat 6, fiber 6, carbs 25, protein 7

CHERRIES RISOTTO
Preparation time: 10 min | Cooking time: 12 min | Servings: 4

Ingredients:

- 1 and ½ cups Arborio rice
- 1 and ½ tsp cinnamon
- 1/3 cup brown sugar
- 2 tbsp butter
- 2 apples, cored and sliced
- 1 cup apple juice
- 3 cups milk
- ½ cup cherries, dried

Directions:
Heat up a pan that fist your air fryer with the butter over medium heat, add rice, stir and cook for 4-5 minutes. Add sugar, apples, apple juice, milk, cinnamon and cherries, stir, introduce in your air fryer and cook at 350 degrees F for 8 minutes. Divide into bowls and serve for breakfast.

Nutrition:
calories 162, fat 12, fiber 6, carbs 23, protein 8

RICE, ALMONDS AND RAISINS PUDDING
Preparation time: 5 min | Cooking time: 8 min | Servings: 4

Ingredients:

- 1 cup brown rice
- ½ cup coconut chips
- 1 cup milk
- 2 cups water
- ½ cup maple syrup
- ¼ cup raisins
- ¼ cup almonds
- A pinch of cinnamon powder

Directions:
Put the rice in a pan that fits your air fryer, add the water, heat up on the stove over medium high heat, cook until rice is soft and drain. Add milk, coconut chips, almonds, raisins, cinnamon and maple syrup, stir well, introduce in your air fryer and cook at 360 degrees F for 8 minutes. Divide rice pudding in bowls and serve.

Nutrition:
calories 251, fat 6, fiber 8, carbs 39, protein 12

DATES AND MILLET PUDDING
Preparation time: 10 min | Cooking time: 15 min | Servings: 4

Ingredients:

- 14 ounces milk
- 7 ounces water
- 2/3 cup millet
- 4 dates, pitted
- Honey for serving

Directions:
Put the millet in a pan that fits your air fryer, add dates, milk and water, stir, introduce in your air fryer and cook at 360 degrees F for 15 minutes. Divide among plates, drizzle honey on top and serve for breakfast.

Nutrition:
calories 231, fat 6, fiber 6, carbs 18, protein 6

AIR FRYER LUNCH RECIPES

GREEK SANDWICHES

Preparation time: 5 min | Cooking time: 6 min | Servings: 4

INGREDIENTS:

- 1 cup barbecue sauce
- 2 tbsp honey
- 8 bacon slices, cooked and cut into thirds
- 2 red bell peppers, sliced
- 3 pita pockets, halved
- 1¼ cups lettuce, torn
- 2 tomatoes, sliced

DIRECTIONS:
In a bowl, mix the barbecue sauce with honey, whisk, and then brush the bacon and bell peppers with this mix. Place the bacon and bell peppers in your air fryer and cook at 350 degrees F for 6 minutes, shaking once. Stuff pita pockets with the bacon and bell peppers mix, and then add tomatoes and lettuce. Garnish with the rest of the barbecue sauce and honey, serve, and enjoy!

NUTRITION:
calories 206, fat 6, fiber 9, carbs 14, protein 5

CHICKEN PIE

Preparation time: 10 min | Cooking time: 10 min | Servings: 4

INGREDIENTS:

- 1 large chicken breast, boneless, skinless and cubed
- 1 carrot, chopped
- 1 yellow onion, chopped
- 6 white mushrooms, chopped
- 1 tsp soy sauce
- Salt and black pepper to taste
- 1 tsp Italian seasoning
- ½ tsp garlic powder
- 1 tsp Worcestershire sauce
- 1 tbsp white flour
- 1 tbsp milk
- 2 puff pastry sheets
- 2 tbsp olive oil

DIRECTIONS:
Heat up a pan with half of the oil over medium-high heat, and then add the carrots and onions; stir and cook for 2 minutes. Add the chicken, mushrooms, salt, soy sauce, pepper, Italian seasoning, garlic powder, Worcestershire sauce, flour, and milk. Stir really well and remove from the heat. Place 1 puff pastry sheet on the bottom of your air fryer's pan, add the chicken mix, and top with the other puff pastry sheet. Brush the pastry with the rest of the oil, and then place the pan in the fryer; cook at 360 degrees F for 8 minutes. Slice, serve, and enjoy.

NUTRITION:
calories 270, fat 5, fiber 7, carbs 14, protein 5

PARMESAN PIZZA ROLLS

Preparation time: 10 min | Cooking time: 30 min | Servings: 4

INGREDIENTS:

- 2 tsp olive oil
- 1 yellow onion, sliced
- 2 chicken breasts, skinless, boneless and sliced
- Salt and black pepper to taste
- 1 tbsp Worcestershire sauce
- 14 ounces pizza dough
- 1½ cups parmesan cheese, grated
- ½ cup tomato sauce

DIRECTIONS:
Preheat your air fryer at 400 degrees F, and add the onion and half of olive oil. Fry for 8 minutes, shaking the fryer halfway. Add the chicken, Worcestershire sauce, salt and pepper; toss and fry for 8 minutes more, stirring once, and then transfer to a bowl. Roll the pizza dough on a working surface and shape into a rectangle. Spread the cheese all over, then the chicken and onion mix, then the tomato sauce. Roll the dough, place it in your air fryer's basket, and brush the roll with the rest of the oil. Cook at 370 degrees F for 14 minutes, flipping the roll halfway. Slice your roll and serve.

NUTRITION:
calories 270, fat 8, fiber 17, carbs 16, protein 6

OLD BAY CHICKEN WINGS

Preparation time: 5 min | Cooking time: 45 min | Servings: 4

INGREDIENTS:

- 3 pounds chicken wings
- ½ cup butter, melted
- 1 tbsp Old Bay seasoning
- ¾ cup potato starch
- 1 tsp lemon juice

DIRECTIONS:
In a bowl, mix the chicken wings with the starch and Old Bay seasoning, toss, and then place the pieces in your air fryer's basket. Cook at 360 degrees F for 35 minutes, shaking the fryer from time to time. Increase temperature to 400 degrees F, and cook chicken wings for 10 minutes more. Divide the wings between plates and serve with the melted butter mixed with the lemon juice drizzled all over.

NUTRITION:
calories 261, fat 6, fiber 8, carbs 18, protein 13

DIJON HOT DOGS

Preparation time: 5 min | Cooking time: 8 min | Servings: 2

INGREDIENTS:

- 2 hot dog buns
- 2 hot dogs
- 1 tbsp Dijon mustard
- 2 tbsp parmesan cheese, grated

DIRECTIONS:
Put hot dogs in preheated air fryer and cook them at 390 degrees F for 5 minutes. Place

the hot dogs into the buns, spread the mustard all over, and sprinkle with the parmesan. Air fry the hot dogs at 390 degrees F for 3 minutes more. Serve and enjoy!

NUTRITION:
calories 251, fat 7, fiber 8, carbs 16, protein 7

SPINACH LUNCH CAKES
Preparation time: 10 min | Cooking time: 10 min | Servings: 2

INGREDIENTS:

- 1 cup canned yellow lentils, drained
- 1 hot chili pepper, chopped
- 1 tsp ginger, grated
- ½ tsp turmeric powder
- 1 tsp garam masala
- 1 tsp baking powder
- Salt and black pepper to taste
- 2 tsp olive oil
- 1 cup water
- ½ cup cilantro, chopped
- 1½ cups baby spinach, chopped
- 4 garlic cloves, minced
- ¾ cup yellow onion, chopped

DIRECTIONS:
In your blender, add all ingredients and blend well. From the mixture, shape 2 medium cakes. Place the lentils cakes in your preheated air fryer at 400 degrees F and cook for 10 minutes. Place lentils cakes on plates, serve, and enjoy.

NUTRITION:
calories 182, fat 2, fiber 8, carbs 16, protein 4

BEEF TOMATO MEATBALLS
Preparation time: 10 min | Cooking time: 15 min | Servings: 4

INGREDIENTS:

- 1 pound lean ground beef
- 1 red onion, chopped
- 2 garlic cloves, minced
- 1 egg yolk
- ¼ cup panko breadcrumbs
- Salt and black pepper to taste
- 1 tbsp olive oil
- 16 ounces tomato sauce

DIRECTIONS:
In a bowl, mix all ingredients except for the tomato sauce and olive oil. Stir well and then shape into medium-sized meatballs. Grease the meatballs with oil, place them in your air fryer, and cook at 400 degrees F for 10 minutes. Heat up a pan over medium heat; add the tomato sauce and heat it up for 2 minutes. Add the meatballs, toss a bit, and cook for 3 minutes more. Divide the meatballs between plates and serve.

NUTRITION:
calories 270, fat 8, fiber 9, carbs 16, protein 4

BEEF MEATBALL BAGUETTES
Preparation time: 10 min | Cooking time: 22 min | Servings: 4

INGREDIENTS:

- 3 baguettes, sliced halfway
- 14 ounces beef, minced
- 7 ounces tomato sauce
- 1 yellow onion, chopped
- 1 egg, whisked
- 1 tbsp breadcrumbs
- 2 tbsp parmesan cheese, grated
- 1 tbsp oregano, chopped
- 1 tbsp olive oil
- Salt and black pepper to taste
- 1 tsp fresh basil, chopped

DIRECTIONS:
In a bowl, mix all ingredients except the tomato sauce, oil, and baguettes; stir and then shape into medium-sized meatballs. Heat up your air fryer with the oil at 375 degrees F, add the meatballs, and cook them for 12 minutes, flipping them halfway. Add the tomato sauce, and cook for 10 minutes more. Divide the meatballs and sauce on half of the baguette halves, top with the other baguette halves, and serve.

NUTRITION:
calories 280, fat 9, fiber 6, carbs 16, protein 15

COD AND GRAPES SALAD
Preparation time: 10 min | Cooking time: 10 min | Servings: 2

INGREDIENTS:

- 2 black cod fillets, boneless
- 2 tbsp olive oil + 1 tsp
- Salt and black pepper to taste
- 1 fennel bulb, thinly sliced
- 1 cup grapes, halved
- 3 cups kale leaves, shredded
- ½ cup pecans
- 2 tsp balsamic vinegar

DIRECTIONS:
Put the fish in your air fryer's basket, and add salt and pepper. Drizzle 1 tsp of the olive oil over the fish, and cook at 400 degrees F for 10 minutes. Divide fish between plates. In a bowl, mix the fennel, grapes, kale, pecans, vinegar, and 2 tbsp of oil; toss. Divide the salad next to the fish, serve, and enjoy.

NUTRITION:
calories 240, fat 4, fiber 2, carbs 15, protein 12

TURKEY LUNCH
Preparation time: 10 min | Cooking time: 1 hour | Servings: 6

- Ingredients:

- 1 whole turkey breast
- 2 tsp olive oil
- ½ tsp sweet paprika
- 1 tsp thyme, dried
- Salt and black pepper to taste
- 1 tbsp butter, melted
- 2 tbsp mustard
- ¼ cup maple syrup

DIRECTIONS:
Brush the turkey breast with the oil, and then season with salt, pepper, paprika, and thyme; rub seasoning into turkey breast. Place the turkey in your air fryer and cook at 350 degrees F for 25 minutes. Flip the turkey breast and cook for 12 minutes more. Flip again and cook another 12 minutes. In a bowl, mix the butter, mustard, and maple syrup; whisk. Brush the turkey breast with the maple syrup mix and cook for another 5 minutes. Transfer the meat to a cutting board, slice, and, if desired, serve with a side salad.

NUTRITION:
calories 230, fat 13, fiber 3, carbs 16, protein 11

HERBED MEATBALLS
Preparation time: 10 min | Cooking time: 12 min | Servings: 4

INGREDIENTS:

- 3 tbsp fresh cilantro, minced
- 1 pound cod, skinless and chopped
- 1 yellow onion, chopped
- 1 egg
- Salt and black pepper to taste
- 2 garlic cloves, minced
- ½ tsp sweet paprika
- ¼ cup panko breadcrumbs
- ½ tsp oregano, ground
- A drizzle of olive oil

DIRECTIONS:
In your food processor, mix all ingredients except the oil; blend, and then shape medium-sized meatballs out of this mix. Place the meatballs in your air fryer's basket, grease them with oil, and cook at 320 degrees F for 12 minutes, shaking halfway. Divide the meatballs between plates and, if desired, serve with a side salad.

NUTRITION:
calories 230, fat 9, fiber 3, carbs 10, protein 15

BEEF STEW
Preparation time: 10 min | Cooking time: 25 min | Servings: 4

INGREDIENTS:

- 2 pounds beef stew meat, cubed
- 1 carrot, sliced
- 4 gold potatoes, cubed
- Salt and black pepper to taste
- 1 quart beef stock
- ½ tsp smoked paprika
- A handful of cilantro, chopped
- 4 tbsp Worcestershire sauce

DIRECTIONS:
In a pan that fits your air fryer, mix all the ingredients except the cilantro and,; toss. Place in your air fryer and cook at 375 degrees F for 25 minutes. Divide into bowls, sprinkle the cilantro on top and serve right away.

NUTRITION:
calories 250, fat 8, fiber 1, carbs 20, protein 17

SEAFOOD PASTA
Preparation time: 10 min | Cooking time: 15 min | Servings: 4

INGREDIENTS:

- 5 ounces spaghetti, cooked
- 8 ounces shrimp, peeled and deveined
- Salt and black pepper to taste
- 5 garlic cloves, minced
- 1 tsp chili powder
- 1 tbsp butter, melted
- 2 tbsp olive oil

DIRECTIONS:
Put 1 tbsp of the oil, along with the butter, in your air fryer. Preheat the air fryer at 350 degrees F, add the shrimp, and cook for 10 minutes. Add all other ingredients, including the remaining 1 tbsp of oil, toss, and cook for 5 minutes more. Divide between plates, serve, and enjoy.

NUTRITION:
calories 270, fat 7, fiber 4, carbs 15, protein 6

MARINARA RAVIOLI
Preparation time: 5 min | Cooking time: 5 min | Servings: 6

INGREDIENTS:

- 15 ounces cheese ravioli
- 10 ounces marinara sauce
- 1 tsp butter, melted
- 1 cup buttermilk
- 2 cups breadcrumbs
- ¼ cup cheddar cheese, grated

DIRECTIONS:
Put the buttermilk in one bowl, and the breadcrumbs in another. Dip each ravioli in buttermilk, then in breadcrumbs. Put the ravioli in your air fryer's basket, brush them with the melted butter, and cook at 400 degrees F for 5 minutes. Divide the ravioli between plates, sprinkle the cheddar cheese on top, and serve.

NUTRITION:
calories 260, fat 12, fiber 4, carbs 14, protein 11

MILKY CURRY
Preparation time: 10 min | Cooking time: 15 min | Servings: 4

INGREDIENTS:

- 4 cod fillets, skinless, boneless and cubed
- 1½ cups milk, heated up
- 2 tsp curry paste
- 2 tbsp cilantro, chopped
- 2 tsp ginger, grated
- Salt and black pepper to taste

DIRECTIONS:
In a bowl, mix the milk, curry paste, ginger, salt, and pepper; whisk. Put the fish in a pan that fits your air fryer, and then add the milk and curry mix; toss gently. Place the pan in the fryer and cook at 400 degrees F for 15 minutes, shaking halfway. Divide the curry into bowls, sprinkle the cilantro on top, and serve.

NUTRITION:
calories 260, fat 8, fiber 3, carbs 13, protein 9

MONTEREY JACK CASSEROLE
Preparation time: 15 min | Cooking time: 25 min | Servings: 6

INGREDIENTS:

- 2 tbsp butter, melted
- 1 cup yogurt
- 12 ounces cream cheese, softened
- 2 cups chicken meat, cooked and cubed
- 2 tsp curry powder
- 4 scallions, chopped
- 6 ounces Monterey jack cheese, grated
- ¼ cup cilantro, chopped
- ½ cup almonds, sliced
- Salt and black pepper to taste
- ½ cup chutney

DIRECTIONS:
In a baking dish that fits your air fryer, add all ingredients except the Monterey jack cheese; mix well. Sprinkle the Monterey jack cheese all over chicken mixture, put the dish in your air fryer, and cook at 350 degrees F for 25 minutes. Divide between plates and serve.

NUTRITION:
calories 280, fat 10, fiber 2, carbs 24, protein 15

CAJUN POTATO LUNCH
Preparation time: 10 min | Cooking time: 17 min | Servings: 4

INGREDIENTS:

4 gold potatoes, cut into medium wedges
- Salt and black pepper to taste
- 2 eggs
- ¼ cup sour cream
- 1 tsp olive oil
- 1½ tsp sweet paprika
- 1 tsp garlic powder
- ½ tsp Cajun seasoning

DIRECTIONS:
In a bowl, mix the eggs with the sour cream, paprika, garlic powder, Cajun seasoning, salt, and pepper; whisk well. Take a pan that fits your air fryer and grease with the oil. Arrange the potatoes on the bottom of the pan, and spread the sour cream mix all over. Place the pan in the fryer and cook at 370 degrees F for 17 minutes. Divide between plates and serve.

NUTRITION:
calories 290, fat 8, fiber 2, carbs 15, protein 7

GARLIC BEEF AND CABBAGE MIX
Preparation time: 10 min | Cooking time: 10 min | Servings: 4

INGREDIENTS:

- ½ pound sirloin steak, cut into strips
- 1 tbsp olive oil
- 1 tsp soy sauce
- 2 cups green cabbage, shredded
- 1 yellow bell pepper, chopped
- 2 green onions, chopped
- 2 garlic cloves, minced
- Salt and black pepper to taste

DIRECTIONS:
In a pan that fits your air fryer, mix the cabbage, salt, pepper, and oil; toss. Put the pan in your air fryer and cook at 370 degrees F for 4 minutes. Add the steak, green onions, bell peppers, soy sauce, and garlic; then toss, cover, and cook for another 6 minutes. Divide into bowls and serve.

NUTRITION:
calories 262, fat 9, fiber 8, carbs 14, protein 11

CORN BREAD PUDDING
Preparation time: 10 min | Cooking time: 30 min | Servings: 6

INGREDIENTS:

- 1 tbsp butter, softened
- 2 cups corn
- 1 yellow onion, chopped
- ¼ cup celery, chopped
- 2 red bell peppers, chopped
- 1 tsp thyme, chopped
- 2 tsp garlic, minced
- Salt and black pepper to taste
- ½ cup heavy cream
- 1½ cups milk
- 3 eggs, whisked
- 3 cups bread, cubed
- 4 tbsp cheddar cheese, grated

DIRECTIONS:
Use the butter to grease a baking dish that fits your air fryer. Add all other ingredients—except the cheddar cheese—and toss. Sprinkle the cheese all over, place the dish in the fryer, and cook at 360 degrees F for 30 minutes. Divide between plates, serve, and enjoy.

NUTRITION:
calories 286, fat 10, fiber 2, carbs 16, protein 11

COCONUT VEGGIES MIX
Preparation time: 5 min | Cooking time: 16 min | Servings: 8

INGREDIENTS:

- 1 cup veggie stock
- 2 tbsp olive oil
- 8 zucchinis, cut in medium wedges
- 2 yellow onions, chopped
- 1 cup coconut cream

- Salt and black pepper to taste
- 1 tbsp soy sauce
- ¼ tsp thyme, dried
- ¼ tsp rosemary, dried
- ½ tsp basil, chopped

DIRECTIONS:
Take a pan that fits your air fryer and grease it with the oil. Add all other ingredients to the pan, and toss. Place the pan in the fryer and cook at 360 degrees F for 16 minutes. Divide the mix between plates, serve, and enjoy.

NUTRITION:
calories 181, fat 4, fiber 4, carbs 10, protein 5

CHICKEN AND MUSHROOM MIX
Preparation time: 5 min | Cooking time: 20 min | Servings: 6

INGREDIENTS:

- 1 bunch kale, torn
- Salt and black pepper to taste
- 2 tbsp chicken stock
- ¼ cup tomato sauce
- 1 cup chicken
- 1½ cups shiitake

DIRECTIONS:
In a pan that fits your air fryer, mix all ingredients and then toss. Place the pan in the fryer and cook at 350 degrees F for 20 minutes. Divide between plates and serve.

NUTRITION:
calories 210, fat 7, fiber 2, carbs 14, protein 5

CHICKEN AND MOZZARELLA BOWLS
Preparation time: 10 min | Cooking time: 20 min | Servings: 6

INGREDIENTS:

- 3 cups chicken
- 24 ounces canned black beans
- ½ cup cilantro, chopped
- 6 kale leaves, chopped
- ½ cup green onions, chopped
- 2 cups salsa
- A drizzle of olive oil
- 2 tsp chili powder
- 2 tsp cumin, ground
- 3 cups mozzarella cheese, shredded
- 1 tbsp garlic powder

DIRECTIONS:
Take a baking dish that fits your air fryer and grease it with the oil. Add all other ingredients—except the cheese—to the baking dish; then sprinkle the cheese all over. Place the dish in the air fryer and cook at 350 degrees F for 20 minutes.

NUTRITION:
calories 285, fat 12, fiber 6, carbs 22, protein 15

COD AND FENNEL MIX
Preparation time: 10 min | Cooking time: 12 min | Servings: 2

INGREDIENTS:

- 4 tbsp butter, softened
- 1 fennel bulb, sliced
- 2 tbsp dill, chopped
- 8 cherry tomatoes, halved
- 2 cod fillets, boneless
- Salt and black pepper to taste
- ¼ cup vermouth, dry

DIRECTIONS:
Divide the butter onto 2 parchment paper pieces. Place the fennel, tomatoes, dill, salt, pepper, and the vermouth in a bowl and toss a bit; then divide between the 2 parchment papers as well. Top this mix with the cod fillets and fold the packets. Place the packets in your preheated air fryer and cook at 400 degrees F for 12 minutes. Unwrap the packets, place on plates, serve, and enjoy!

NUTRITION:
calories 200, fat 9, fiber 2, carbs 9, protein 12

CHICKEN AND TOMATO BAKE
Preparation time: 5 min | Cooking time: 25 min | Servings: 4

INGREDIENTS:

- 2 chicken breasts, skinless, boneless and cubed
- 1 tbsp olive oil
- 1 cup cauliflower florets
- 1 cup tomato sauce
- 1 tsp sweet paprika
- Salt and black pepper to taste

DIRECTIONS:
In a baking dish that fits your air fryer, mix all ingredients. Place the dish in the fryer and bake at 370 degrees F for 25 minutes. Divide between plates and serve.

NUTRITION:
calories 270, fat 8, fiber 12, carbs 17, protein 12

SEA BASS STEW
Preparation time: 10 min | Cooking time: 20 min | Servings: 4

INGREDIENTS:

- 5 ounces white rice
- 2 ounces peas
- 1 red bell pepper, chopped
- 14 ounces white wine
- 3 ounces water
- 1½ pounds sea bass fillets, skinless, boneless and cubed
- 4 shrimp
- Salt and black pepper to taste
- 1 tbsp olive oil

DIRECTIONS:
In your air fryer's pan, mix all ingredients and toss. Place the pan in your air fryer and cook at 400 degrees F for 20 minutes, stirring halfway. Divide into bowls, serve, and enjoy.

NUTRITION:
calories 280, fat 12, fiber 2, carbs 16, protein

COLBY JACK LUNCH BURGER

Preparation time: 10 min | Cooking time: 30 min | Servings: 2

INGREDIENTS:

- 2 tbsp brown sugar
- 1 tbsp bourbon
- 3 maple bacon strips, halved
- 1 pound lean ground beef
- 1 tbsp onion, chopped
- 2 tbsp barbecue sauce
- A pinch of salt and black pepper
- 2 Colby jack cheese slices
- 2 Kaiser rolls
- For the sauce:
- 2 tbsp mayonnaise
- 2 tbsp barbecue sauce
- ¼ tsp sweet paprika

DIRECTIONS:

In a bowl, mix the brown sugar with the bourbon and whisk. Place the bacon strips in your air fryer's basket, brush them with the bourbon mix, and cook at 390 degrees F for 4 minutes on each side. Meanwhile, in a bowl, mix the beef with 2 tbsp of barbecue sauce, salt, pepper, and onions; stir, and then shape 2 burgers out of this mix. Place the burgers in your air fryer's basket and cook them at 370 degrees F for 20 minutes, flipping them halfway. Top each burger with a Colby jack cheese slice and leave them in the fryer for 1-2 minutes more. In a bowl, mix all sauce ingredients and stir well. Spread this sauce on the inside of the Kaiser rolls, place the burgers on the rolls, top with the bourbon bacon, and serve.

NUTRITION:

calories 251, fat 14, fiber 8, carbs 16, protein 8

ROSEMARY LAMB

Preparation time: 10 min | Cooking time: 30 min | Servings: 4

INGREDIENTS:

- 1 tbsp olive oil
- 1 garlic clove, minced
- 2 tbsp macadamia nuts
- 1 tbsp breadcrumbs
- 1 tbsp rosemary, chopped
- 1 egg, whisked
- 1½ pounds rack of lamb
- Salt and black pepper to taste

DIRECTIONS:

In a bowl, mix the oil and garlic; whisk. Brush the rack of lamb with this mix, and season with salt and pepper. In a bowl (can use same as for oil and garlic), mix the egg with salt and pepper. In another bowl, mix the breadcrumbs and rosemary; stir. Dip the lamb in the egg and then in the breadcrumbs, place it in your air fryer's basket, and cook at 400 degrees F for 30 minutes. Serve right away, and enjoy!

NUTRITION:

calories 251, fat 8, fiber 6, carbs 16, protein 9

LEMON BROCCOLI MIX

Preparation time: 5 min | Cooking time: 20 min | Servings: 4

INGREDIENTS:

- 2 broccoli heads, florets separated
- 2 tsp sweet paprika
- Juice of ½ lemon
- 1 tbsp olive oil
- Salt and black pepper to taste
- 1 tbsp sesame seeds
- 3 garlic cloves, minced
- ½ cup bacon, cooked and crumbled

DIRECTIONS:

In your air fryer's pan, mix all ingredients except the bacon, toss, cover, and cook at 360 degrees F for 15 minutes. Add the bacon and cook for 5 more minutes. Divide between plates and serve.

NUTRITION:

calories 251, fat 7, fiber 4, carbs 9, protein 5

BELL PEPPERS LUNCH STEW

Preparation time: 5 min | Cooking time: 20 min | Servings: 5

INGREDIENTS:

- 1 cup okra, sliced
- 1 red bell pepper, chopped
- 2 garlic cloves, minced
- 3 celery ribs, chopped
- 1 yellow onion, chopped
- 20 ounces canned tomatoes, roughly cubed
- ½ cup veggie stock
- Salt and black pepper to taste
- ½ tsp sweet paprika

DIRECTIONS:

In your air fryer, mix all ingredients, cover, and cook at 360 degrees F for 20 minutes. Divide into bowls and serve; enjoy!

NUTRITION:

calories 251, fat 9, fiber 5, carbs 14, protein 4

ZUCCHINI STEW

Preparation time: 10 min | Cooking time: 20 min | Servings: 6

INGREDIENTS:

- 2 tomatoes, roughly chopped
- 2 yellow onions, roughly chopped
- 4 zucchinis, halved lengthwise and sliced
- 1 eggplant, cubed
- 1 tsp oregano, dried
- 1 tsp sugar
- 2 green bell peppers, cut into strips
- 2 garlic cloves, minced
- 1 tsp basil, dried
- Salt and black pepper to taste
- 7 ounces tomato paste
- 2 tbsp olive oil
- 2 tbsp cilantro, chopped

DIRECTIONS:

In a pan that fits your air fryer, combine all

ingredients—except the cilantro—and toss well. Place the pan in the air fryer and cook the stew at 360 degrees F for 20 minutes. Divide the stew into bowls, sprinkle the cilantro on top, and serve.

Nutrition:
calories 200, fat 4, fiber 5, carbs 16, protein

BLACK BEANS AND RICE
Preparation time: 10 min | Cooking time: 25 min | Servings: 6

Ingredients:

- 30 ounces canned black beans, drained
- 1 cup veggie stock
- 1 tbsp olive oil
- 1 yellow onion, chopped
- 1 jalapeno, chopped
- 1 red bell pepper, chopped
- 2 garlic cloves, minced
- 1 tsp ginger, grated
- ½ tsp cumin, ground
- ½ tsp oregano, dried
- Salt and black pepper to taste
- ½ tsp allspice, ground
- 3 cups brown rice, cooked

Directions:
In a pan that fits your air fryer, mix all ingredients except the rice; toss. Place the pan in your air fryer and cook at 360 degrees F for 25 minutes. Add the rice and toss again. Divide into bowls, serve, and enjoy.

Nutrition:
calories 200, fat 8, fiber 4, carbs 8, protein 3

GREEN PEPPERS AND QUINOA STEW
Preparation time: 10 min | Cooking time: 15 min | Servings: 4

Ingredients:

- 30 ounces canned black beans, drained
- 1 cup quinoa
- 30 ounces canned tomatoes, chopped
- 2 sweet potatoes, cubed
- 1 yellow onion, chopped
- 1 green bell pepper, chopped
- 1 tbsp chili powder
- 2 tsp cumin, ground
- ¼ tsp sweet paprika
- Salt and black pepper to taste
- 2 tbsp cocoa powder

Directions:
Place all ingredients in a pan that fits your air fryer, and stir well. Then put the pan in the air fryer and cook at 400 degrees F for 15 minutes. Divide into bowls and serve right away.

Nutrition:
calories 200, fat 8, fiber 4, carbs 9, protein 4

CHICKPEAS STEW
Preparation time: 5 min | Cooking time: 15 min | Servings: 4

Ingredients:

- 15 ounces canned chickpeas, drained
- 1 red onion, chopped
- 2 garlic cloves, minced
- 1 tbsp olive oil
- 2 tsp sweet paprika
- Salt and black pepper to taste
- 28 ounces canned tomatoes, chopped

Directions:
Place all ingredients into a pan that fits your air fryer, and stir / mix well. Then put the pan in the air fryer and cook at 370 degrees F for 15 minutes. Divide the stew into bowls and serve.

Nutrition:
calories 200, fat 8, fiber 3, carbs 15, protein 5

LENTILS GINGER CURRY
Preparation time: 5 min | Cooking time: 15 min | Servings: 6

Ingredients:

- 2 cups canned lentils, drained
- 1 tbsp garlic, minced
- 10 ounces baby spinach
- 15 ounces canned tomatoes, drained and chopped
- 1 tsp ginger, grated
- 1 red onion, chopped
- ½ tsp cumin, ground
- 2 tsp sugar
- ½ tsp coriander, ground
- 1 tbsp lemon juice
- 2 tbsp curry paste
- 2 tbsp cilantro, chopped
- Salt and black pepper to taste

Directions:
In a pan that fits your air fryer, mix all the ingredients except the cilantro and lemon juice; stir. Place the pan in the air fryer and cook at 370 degrees F for 15 minutes. Add the cilantro and the lemon juice, and toss. Divide into bowls, serve, and enjoy!

Nutrition:
calories 251, fat 6, fiber 8, carbs 16, protein 7

CUMIN EGGPLANT STEW
Preparation time: 5 min | Cooking time: 15 min | Servings: 4
Ingredients:

- 1 red onion, chopped
- 25 ounces canned tomatoes, chopped
- 2 tsp cumin, ground
- 1 tsp sweet paprika
- Salt and black pepper to taste
- 3 eggplants, cubed
- 2 red bell peppers, cubed
- 1 tbsp cilantro, chopped
- Juice of ½ lime

Directions:
In a pan that fits your air fryer, add all ingredients except the lime juice and cilantro and mix. Place the pan in the fryer and cook at 370 degrees F for 15 minutes. Then add the lime juice and cilantro, and stir. Divide the

stew between bowls and serve.

NUTRITION:
calories 251, fat 7, fiber 6, carbs 14, protein 9

TOMATOES CORN SALAD
Preparation time: 5 min | Cooking time: 15 min | Servings: 4

INGREDIENTS:

- 15 ounces okra, sliced
- 2 cups corn
- 1 red bell pepper, chopped
- 1 red onion, chopped
- 2 garlic cloves, minced
- 1 tsp sweet paprika
- 1 tsp thyme, dried
- 1 tsp oregano, dried
- 1 tsp rosemary, dried
- Salt and black pepper to taste
- 12 ounces canned tomatoes, chopped

DIRECTIONS:
Place all ingredients in a pan that fits your air fryer; toss well. Place the pan in the fryer and cook at 370 degrees F for 15 minutes. Divide the salad into bowls and serve cold.

NUTRITION:
calories 181, fat 7, fiber 4, carbs 9, protein 6

LUNCH VEGGIES CASSEROLE
Preparation time: 5 min | Cooking time: 20 min | Servings: 4

INGREDIENTS:

- 1 tsp olive oil
- 3 cups green beans, trimmed and halved
- 2 red chilies, chopped
- ½ tsp black mustard seeds
- ½ cup yellow onion, chopped
- ¼ tsp fenugreek seeds
- ½ tsp turmeric powder
- Salt and black pepper to taste
- 2 tomatoes, chopped
- 3 garlic cloves, minced
- 2 tsp tamarind paste
- 2 tsp coriander powder
- 1 tbsp cilantro, chopped

DIRECTIONS:
Use the oil to grease a heat-proof dish that fits your air fryer, then add all the ingredients and toss. Place the dish in the fryer and cook at 370 degrees F for 20 minutes. Divide between plates, serve, and enjoy.

NUTRITION:
calories 251, fat 7, fiber 7, carbs 14, protein 6

TOMATO CHICKEN MIX
Preparation time: 10 min | Cooking time: 20 min | Servings: 4

INGREDIENTS:

- 1 cup chicken stock
- Salt and black pepper to taste
- 8 chicken drumsticks, bone-in
- 1 tsp garlic powder
- 1 yellow onion, chopped
- 28 ounces canned tomatoes, chopped
- 1 tsp oregano, dried
- ½ cup black olives, pitted and sliced

DIRECTIONS:
Add all the ingredients to a baking dish that fits your air fryer and toss. Place the dish in your air fryer and cook at 380 degrees F for 20 minutes. Divide the mix into bowls and serve.

NUTRITION:
calories 261, fat 7, fiber 4, carbs 9, protein 15

SWEET CHICKEN THIGHS
Preparation time: 10 min | Cooking time: 25 min | Servings: 4

INGREDIENTS:

- 1½ pounds chicken thighs, skinless and boneless
- Salt and black pepper to taste
- ¾ cup honey
- ½ cup chicken stock
- 2 tsp sweet paprika
- ½ tsp basil, dried

DIRECTIONS:
In a bowl, make a mixture with all the ingredients except the chicken thighs; whisk well. Add the chicken thighs to this mix and toss until the wings are coated. Put the chicken in your air fryer's basket and cook at 380 degrees F for 25 minutes. Divide between plates, serve, and enjoy.

NUTRITION:
calories 200, fat 7, fiber 6, carbs 16, protein 14

BUTTER BABY CARROTS
Preparation time: 5 min | Cooking time: 15 min | Servings: 4

INGREDIENTS:

- 16 ounces baby carrots
- Salt and black pepper to taste
- 2 tbsp butter, melted
- 4 ounces chicken stock
- 2 tbsp dill, chopped

DIRECTIONS:
In a pan that fits your air fryer, mix all the ingredients and toss. Place the pan in the fryer and cook at 380 degrees F for 15 minutes. Divide between bowls and serve.

NUTRITION:
calories 100, fat 3, fiber 3, carbs 8, protein 8

APPLE AND QUINOA PESTO MIX
Preparation time: 5 min | Cooking time: 15 min | Servings: 4

INGREDIENTS:

- 1 cup quinoa, cooked
- 3 tbsp chicken stock
- ¾ cup jarred spinach pesto

41

- 1 green apple, chopped
- ¼ cup celery, chopped

DIRECTIONS:
Mix all the ingredients in a pan that fits your air fryer; toss. Place the pan in your fryer and cook at 370 degrees F for 15 minutes. Divide into bowls and serve right away.

NUTRITION:
calories 200, fat 6, fiber 9, carbs 11, protein 6

FETA AND QUINOA SALAD
Preparation time: 10 min | Cooking time: 15 min | Servings: 6

INGREDIENTS:

- 1½ cups quinoa, cooked
- 1 tbsp olive oil
- Salt and black pepper to taste
- 1 tbsp balsamic vinegar
- 1 cup cherry tomatoes, halved
- 2 green onions, chopped
- 2 ounces feta cheese, crumbled
- ½ cup Kalamata olives, pitted and chopped
- A handful of basil leaves, chopped
- A handful of parsley leaves, chopped

DIRECTIONS:
Add all the ingredients—except the feta cheese—to a pan that fits your air fryer and toss. Sprinkle the cheese on top, and then place the pan in the air fryer and cook at 370 degrees F for 15 minutes. Divide into bowls and serve.

NUTRITION:
calories 251, fat 8, fiber 4, carbs 14, protein 7

QUINOA AND OLIVES MIX
Preparation time: 10 min | Cooking time: 15 min | Servings: 4

INGREDIENTS:

- ½ cups quinoa, cooked
- 1 red bell pepper, chopped
- 3 celery stalks, chopped
- Salt and black pepper to taste
- 4 cups spinach, torn
- 2 tomatoes, chopped
- ½ cup chicken stock
- ½ cup black olives, pitted and chopped
- ½ cup feta cheese, crumbled
- 1 cup basil pesto
- ¼ cup almonds, sliced

DIRECTIONS:
In a pan that fits your air fryer, combine the quinoa, bell peppers, celery, salt, pepper, spinach, tomatoes, chicken stock, olives, and basil pesto. Sprinkle the almonds and the cheese on top, and then place the pan in the air fryer and cook at 380 degrees F for 15 minutes. Divide between plates and serve.

NUTRITION:
calories 251, fat 8, fiber 5, carbs 20, protein 6

CHICKEN AND CHILI CURRY
Preparation time: 10 min | Cooking time: 30 min | Servings: 3

INGREDIENTS:

- 1½ pounds chicken thighs, boneless
- 1 green cabbage, shredded
- 1 tbsp olive oil
- Salt and black pepper to taste
- 2 chili peppers, chopped
- 1 yellow onion, chopped
- 4 garlic cloves, minced
- 3 tbsp curry paste
- ½ cup white wine
- 10 ounces coconut milk
- 1 tbsp soy sauce

DIRECTIONS:
Use the oil to grease a baking dish and then add all ingredients; toss. Place the pan in the fryer and cook at 380 degrees F for 30 minutes. Divide between bowls and serve.

NUTRITION:
calories 251, fat 11, fiber 4, carbs 17, protein 5

CHICKEN AND BEANS MIX
Preparation time: 10 min | Cooking time: 17 min | Servings: 4

INGREDIENTS:

- 4 chicken breasts, skinless, boneless and cubed
- 2 tbsp olive oil
- 1 onion, chopped
- 3 garlic cloves, minced
- 16 ounces jarred chunky salsa
- 20 ounces canned tomatoes, peeled and chopped
- Salt and black pepper to taste
- 2 tbsp parsley, dried
- 1 tsp garlic powder
- 1 tbsp chili powder
- 12 ounces canned black beans, drained

DIRECTIONS:
Place all ingredients into a pan that fits your air fryer and toss. Put the pan in the fryer and cook at 380 degrees F for 17 minutes. Divide into bowls, serve, and enjoy.

NUTRITION:
calories 251, fat 7, fiber 8, carbs 17, protein 20

LEEKS STEW
Preparation time: 5 min | Cooking time: 15 min | Servings: 4

INGREDIENTS:

- 2 leeks, chopped
- 2 tbsp butter, melted
- 2 tomatoes, cubed
- 2 garlic cloves, minced
- 4 cups corn
- ¼ cup chicken stock
- 1 tsp olive oil
- 4 tarragon sprigs, chopped
- Salt and black pepper to taste
- 1 tbsp chives, chopped

DIRECTIONS:
Grease a pan with the oil, and then add all the ingredients and toss. Place the pan in the fryer and cook at 370 degrees F for 15

minutes. Divide the stew between bowls and serve.

NUTRITION:
calories 265, fat 6, fiber 4, carbs 16, protein 11

CHICKEN AND QUINOA STEW
Preparation time: 10 min | Cooking time: 15 min | Servings: 5

INGREDIENTS:

- 1½ pounds butternut squash, cubed
- ½ cup green onions, chopped
- 3 tbsp butter, melted
- ½ cup carrots, chopped
- ½ cup celery, chopped
- 1 garlic clove, minced
- ½ tsp Italian seasoning
- 15 ounces canned tomatoes, chopped
- Salt and black pepper to taste
- ⅛ tsp red pepper flakes, dried
- 1 cup quinoa, cooked
- 1½ cups heavy cream
- 1 cup chicken meat, already cooked and shredded

DIRECTIONS:
Place all the ingredients in a pan that fits your air fryer and toss. Put the pan into the fryer and cook at 400 degrees F for 15 minutes. Divide the stew between bowls, serve, and enjoy.

NUTRITION:
calories 200, fat 4, fiber 4, carbs 15, protein 8

LUNCH MUSHROOM ROLLS
Preparation time: 10 min | Cooking time: 15 min | Servings: 4

INGREDIENTS:

- ½ cup mushrooms, chopped
- ½ cup carrots, grated
- ½ cup zucchini, grated
- 2 green onions, chopped
- 2 tbsp soy sauce
- 8 egg roll wrappers
- 1 eggs, whisked
- 1 tbsp cornstarch

DIRECTIONS:
In a bowl, mix carrots with mushrooms, zucchini, green onions and soy sauce and stir well. Arrange egg roll wrappers on a working surface, divide veggie mix on each and roll well. In a bowl, mix cornstarch with egg, whisk well and brush eggs rolls with this mix. Seal edges, place all rolls in your preheated air fryer and cook them at 370 degrees F for 15 minutes. Arrange them on a platter and serve them for lunch.

NUTRITION:
calories 172, fat 6, fiber 6, carbs 8, protein 7

GOAT CHEESE TOAST
Preparation time: 10 min | Cooking time: 15 min | Servings: 4

INGREDIENTS:

- 1 red bell pepper, cut into thin strips
- 1 cup cremimi mushrooms, sliced
- 1 yellow squash, chopped
- 2 green onions, sliced
- 1 tbsp olive oil
- 4 bread slices
- 2 tbsp butter, soft
- ½ cup goat cheese, crumbled

DIRECTIONS:
In a bowl, mix red bell pepper with mushrooms, squash, green onions and oil, toss, transfer to your air fryer, cook them at 350 degrees F for 10 minutes, shaking the fryer once and transfer them to a bowl. Spread butter on bread slices, place them in air fryer and cook them at 350 degrees F for 5 minutes. Divide veggie mix on each bread slice, top with crumbled cheese and serve for lunch.

NUTRITION:
calories 152, fat 3, fiber 4, carbs 7, protein 2

STUFFED MUSHROOMS
Preparation time: 10 min | Cooking time: 20 min | Servings: 4

INGREDIENTS:

- 4 big Portobello mushroom caps
- 1 tbsp olive oil
- ¼ cup ricotta cheese
- 5 tbsp parmesan, grated
- 1 cup spinach, torn
- ⅓ cup bread crumbs
- ¼ tsp rosemary, chopped

DIRECTIONS:
Rub mushrooms caps with the oil, place them in your air fryer's basket and cook them at 350 degrees F for 2 minutes. Meanwhile, in a bowl, mix half of the parmesan with ricotta, spinach, rosemary and bread crumbs and stir well. Stuff mushrooms with this mix, sprinkle the rest of the parmesan on top, place them in your air fryer's basket again and cook at 350 degrees F for 10 minutes. Divide them on plates and serve with a side salad for lunch.

NUTRITION:
calories 152, fat 4, fiber 7, carbs 9, protein 5

QUICK LUNCH PIZZAS
Preparation time: 10 min | Cooking time: 7 min | Servings: 4

INGREDIENTS:

- 4 pitas
- 1 tbsp olive oil
- ¾ cup pizza sauce
- 4 ounces jarred mushrooms, sliced
- ½ tsp basil, dried
- 2 green onions, chopped
- 2 cup mozzarella, grated
- 1 cup grape tomatoes, sliced

DIRECTIONS:
Spread pizza sauce on each pita bread, sprinkle green onions and basil, divide

mushrooms and top with cheese. Arrange pita pizzas in your air fryer and cook them at 400 degrees F for 7 minutes. Top each pizza with tomato slices, divide among plates and serve.

NUTRITION:
calories 200, fat 4, fiber 6, carbs 7, protein 3

LUNCH GNOCCHI

Preparation time: 10 min | Cooking time: 17 min | Servings: 4

INGREDIENTS:

- 1 yellow onion, chopped
- 1 tbsp olive oil
- 3 garlic cloves, minced
- 16 ounces gnocchi
- ¼ cup parmesan, grated
- 8 ounces spinach pesto

DIRECTIONS:
Grease your air fryer's pan with olive oil, add gnocchi, onion and garlic, toss, put pan in your air fryer and cook at 400 degrees F for 10 minutes. Add pesto, toss and cook for 7 minutes more at 350 degrees F. Divide among plates and serve for lunch.

NUTRITION:
calories 200, fat 4, fiber 4, carbs 12, protein 4

TUNA AND ZUCCHINI TORTILLAS

Preparation time: 10 min | Cooking time: 10 min | Servings: 4

INGREDIENTS:

- 4 corn tortillas
- 4 tbsp butter, soft
- 6 ounces canned tuna, drained
- 1 cup zucchini, shredded
- 1/3 cup mayonnaise
- 2 tbsp mustard
- 1 cup cheddar cheese, grated

DIRECTIONS:
Spread butter on tortillas, place them in your air fryer's basket and cook them at 400 degrees F for 3 minutes. Meanwhile, in a bowl, mix tuna with zucchini, mayo and mustard and stir. Divide this mix on each tortilla, top with cheese, roll tortillas, place them in your air fryer's basket again and cook them at 400 degrees F for 4 minutes more. Serve for lunch.

NUTRITION:
calories 162, fat 4, fiber 8, carbs 9, protein 4

OREGANO FRITTERS

Preparation time: 10 min | Cooking time: 7 min | Servings: 4

INGREDIENTS:

- 3 ounces cream cheese
- 1 egg, whisked
- ½ tsp oregano, dried
- A pinch of salt and black pepper
- 1 yellow summer squash, grated
- 1/3 cup carrot, grated
- 2/3 cup bread crumbs
- 2 tbsp olive oil

DIRECTIONS:
In a bowl, mix cream cheese with salt, pepper, oregano, egg, breadcrumbs, carrot and squash and stir well. Shape medium patties out of this mix and brush them with the oil. Place squash patties in your air fryer and cook them at 400 degrees F for 7 minutes. Serve them for lunch.

NUTRITION:
calories 200, fat 4, fiber 7, carbs 8, protein 6

BASIL CROQUETTES

Preparation time: 10 min | Cooking time: 8 min | Servings: 4

INGREDIENTS:

- 2/3 pound shrimp, cooked, peeled, deveined and chopped
- 1 and ½ cups bread crumbs
- 1 egg, whisked
- 2 tbsp lemon juice
- 3 green onions, chopped
- ½ tsp basil, dried
- Salt and black pepper to the taste
- 2 tbsp olive oil

DIRECTIONS:
In a bowl, mix half of the bread crumbs with egg and lemon juice and stir well. Add green onions, basil, salt, pepper and shrimp and stir really well. In a separate bowl, mix the rest of the bread crumbs with the oil and toss well. Shape round balls out of shrimp mix, dredge them in bread crumbs, place them in preheated air fryer and cook the for 8 minutes at 400 degrees F. Serve them with a dip for lunch.

NUTRITION:
calories 142, fat 4, fiber 6, carbs 9, protein 4

SALSA PANCAKES

Preparation time: 10 min | Cooking time: 10 min | Servings: 2

INGREDIENTS:

- 1 tbsp butter
- 3 eggs, whisked
- ½ cup flour
- ½ cup milk
- 1 cup salsa
- 1 cup small shrimp, peeled and deveined

DIRECTIONS:
Preheat your air fryer at 400 degrees F, add fryer's pan, add 1 tbsp butter and melt it. In a bowl, mix eggs with flour and milk, whisk well and pour into air fryer's pan, spread, cook at 350 degrees for 12 minutes and transfer to a plate. In a bowl, mix shrimp with salsa, stir and serve your pancake with this on the side.

NUTRITION:
calories 200, fat 6, fiber 8, carbs 12, protein 4

ITALIAN SANDWICHES

Preparation time: 10 min | Cooking time: 10 min | Servings: 4

INGREDIENTS:

- 2 chicken breasts, skinless, boneless and cubed
- 1 red onion, chopped
- 1 red bell pepper, sliced
- ½ cup Italian seasoning
- ½ tsp thyme, dried
- 2 cups butter lettuce, torn
- 4 pita pockets
- 1 cup cherry tomatoes, halved
- 1 tbsp olive oil

DIRECTIONS:
In your air fryer, mix chicken with onion, bell pepper, Italian seasoning and oil, toss and cook at 380 degrees F for 10 minutes. Transfer chicken mix to a bowl, add thyme, butter lettuce and cherry tomatoes, toss well, stuff pita pockets with this mix and serve for lunch.

NUTRITION:
calories 126, fat 4, fiber 8, carbs 14, protein 4

FRESH CHICKEN MIX
Preparation time: 10 min | Cooking time: 22 min | Servings: 4

INGREDIENTS:

- 2 chicken breasts, skinless, boneless and cubed
- 8 button mushrooms, sliced
- 1 red bell pepper, chopped
- 1 tbsp olive oil
- ½ tsp thyme, dried
- 10 ounces alfredo sauce
- 6 bread slices
- 2 tbsp butter, soft

DIRECTIONS:
In your air fryer, mix chicken with mushrooms, bell pepper and oil, toss to coat well and cook at 350 degrees F for 15 minutes. Transfer chicken mix to a bowl, add thyme and alfredo sauce, toss, return to air fryer and cook at 350 degrees F for 4 minutes more. Spread butter on bread slices, add it to the fryer, butter side up and cook for 4 minutes more. Arrange toasted bread slices on a platter, top each with chicken mix and serve for lunch.

NUTRITION:
calories 172, fat 4, fiber 9, carbs 12, protein 4

CAYENNE CHICKEN
Preparation time: 6 hours | Cooking time: 18 min | Servings: 4

INGREDIENTS:

- 1 and ½ pounds chicken thighs
- 2 cups buttermilk
- Salt and black pepper to the taste
- A pinch of cayenne pepper
- 2 cups white flour
- 1 tbsp baking powder
- 1 tbsp sweet paprika
- 1 tbsp garlic powder

DIRECTIONS:
In a bowl, mix chicken thighs with buttermilk, salt, pepper and cayenne, toss and leave aside for 6 hours. In a separate bowl, mix flour with paprika, baking powder and garlic powder and stir. Drain chicken thighs, dredge them in flour mix, arrange them in your air fryer and cook at 360 degrees F for 8 minutes. Flip chicken pieces, cook them for 10 minutes more, arrange on a platter and serve for lunch.

NUTRITION:
calories 200, fat 3, fiber 9, carbs 14, protein 4

SPICY CHICKEN PIE
Preparation time: 10 min | Cooking time: 16 min | Servings: 4

INGREDIENTS:

- 2 chicken thighs, boneless, skinless and cubed
- 1 carrot, chopped
- 1 yellow onion, chopped
- 2 potatoes, chopped
- 2 mushrooms, chopped
- 1 tsp soy sauce
- Salt and black pepper to the taste
- 1 tsp Italian seasoning
- ½ tsp garlic powder
- 1 tsp Worcestershire sauce
- 1 tbsp flour
- 1 tbsp milk
- 2 puff pastry sheets
- 1 tbsp butter, melted

DIRECTIONS:
Heat up a pan over medium high heat, add potatoes, carrots and onion, stir and cook for 2 minutes. Add chicken and mushrooms, salt, soy sauce, pepper, Italians seasoning, garlic powder, Worcestershire sauce, flour and milk, stir really well and take off heat. Place 1 puff pastry sheet on the bottom of your air fryer's pan and trim edge excess. Add chicken mix, top with the other puff pastry sheet, trim excess as well and brush pie with butter. Place in your air fryer and cook at 360 degrees F for 6 minutes. Leave pie to cool down, slice and serve for breakfast.

NUTRITION:
calories 300, fat 5, fiber 7, carbs 14, protein 7

MACARONI AND MOZZARELLA
Preparation time: 10 min | Cooking time: 30 min | Servings: 3

INGREDIENTS:

- 1 and ½ cups favorite macaroni
- Cooking spray
- ½ cup heavy cream
- 1 cup chicken stock
- ¾ cup cheddar cheese, shredded
- ½ cup mozzarella cheese, shredded
- ¼ cup parmesan, shredded
- Salt and black pepper to the taste

DIRECTIONS:
Spray a pan with cooking spray, add macaroni, heavy cream, stock, cheddar cheese, mozzarella and parmesan but also salt and pepper, toss well, place pan in your air fryer's basket and cook for 30 minutes. Divide

among plates and serve for lunch.

NUTRITION:
calories 341, fat 7, fiber 8, carbs 18, protein 4

CHICKEN FAJITAS

Preparation time: 10 min | Cooking time: 10 min | Servings: 4

INGREDIENTS:

- 1 tsp garlic powder
- ¼ tsp cumin, ground
- ½ tsp chili powder
- Salt and black pepper to the taste
- ¼ tsp coriander, ground
- 1 pound chicken breasts, cut into strips
- 1 red bell pepper, sliced
- 1 green bell pepper, sliced
- 1 yellow onion, chopped
- 1 tbsp lime juice
- Cooking spray
- 4 tortillas, warmed up
- Salsa for serving
- Sour cream for serving
- 1 cup lettuce leaves, torn for serving

DIRECTIONS:
In a bowl, mix chicken with garlic powder, cumin, chili, salt, pepper, coriander, lime juice, red bell pepper, green bell pepper and onion, toss, leave aside for 10 minutes, transfer to your air fryer and drizzle some cooking spray all over. Toss and cook at 400 degrees F for 10 minutes. Arrange tortillas on a working surface, divide chicken mix, also add salsa, sour cream and lettuce, wrap and serve for lunch.

NUTRITION:
calories 317, fat 6, fiber 8, carbs 14, protein 4

LUNCH CHICKEN SALAD

Preparation time: 10 min | Cooking time: 20 min | Servings: 4

INGREDIENTS:

- 2 ears of corn, hulled
- 1 pound chicken tenders, boneless
- Olive oil as needed
- Salt and black pepper to the taste
- 1 tsp sweet paprika
- 1 tbsp brown sugar
- ½ tsp garlic powder
- ½ iceberg lettuce head, cut into medium strips
- ½ romaine lettuce head, cut into medium strips
- 1 cup canned black beans, drained
- 1 cup cheddar cheese, shredded
- 3 tbsp cilantro, chopped
- 4 green onions, chopped
- 12 cherry tomatoes, sliced
- ¼ cup ranch dressing
- 3 tbsp BBQ sauce

DIRECTIONS:
Put corn in your air fryer, drizzle some oil, toss, cook at 400 degrees F for 10 minutes, transfer to a plate and leave aside for now. Put chicken in your air fryer's basket, add salt, pepper, brown sugar, paprika and garlic powder, toss, drizzle some more oil, cook at 400 degrees F for 10 minutes, flipping them halfway, transfer tenders to a cutting board and chop them. Cut kernels off the cob, transfer corn to a bowl, add chicken, iceberg lettuce, romaine lettuce, black beans, cheese, cilantro, tomatoes, onions, bbq sauce and ranch dressing, toss well and serve for lunch.

NUTRITION:
calories 372, fat 6, fiber 9, carbs 17, protein 6

FISH AND CHIPS

Preparation time: 10 min | Cooking time: 12 min | Servings: 2

INGREDIENTS:

- 2 medium cod fillets, skinless and boneless
- Salt and black pepper to the taste
- ¼ cup buttermilk
- 3 cups kettle chips, cooked

DIRECTIONS:
In a bowl, mix fish with salt, pepper and buttermilk, toss and leave aside for 5 minutes. Put chips in your food processor, crush them and spread them on a plate. Add fish and press well on all sides. Transfer fish to your air fryer's basket and cook at 400 degrees F for 12 minutes. Serve hot for lunch.

NUTRITION:
calories 271, fat 7, fiber 9, carbs 14, protein 4

HASH BROWN MOZZARELLA FRIES

Preparation time: 10 min | Cooking time: 7 min | Servings: 4

INGREDIENTS:

- 4 hash brown patties, frozen
- 1 tbsp olive oil
- ¼ cup cherry tomatoes, chopped
- 3 tbsp mozzarella, shredded
- 2 tbsp parmesan, grated
- 1 tbsp balsamic vinegar
- 1 tbsp basil, chopped

DIRECTIONS:
Put hash brown patties in your air fryer, drizzle the oil over them and cook them at 400 degrees F for 7 minutes. In a bowl, mix tomatoes with mozzarella, parmesan, vinegar and basil and stir well. Divide hash brown patties on plates, top each with tomatoes mix and serve for lunch.

NUTRITION:
calories 199, fat 3, fiber 8, carbs 12, protein 4

BEEF CUBES WITH RICE

Preparation time: 10 min | Cooking time: 12 min | Servings: 4

INGREDIENTS:

- 1 pound sirloin, cubed
- 16 ounces jarred pasta sauce
- 1 and ½ cups bread crumbs

- 2 tbsp olive oil
- ½ tsp marjoram, dried
- White rice

DIRECTIONS:
In a bowl, mix beef cubes with pasta sauce and toss well. In another bowl, mix bread crumbs with marjoram and oil and stir well. Dip beef cubes in this mix, place them in your air fryer and cook at 360 degrees F for 12 minutes. Divide among plates and serve with white rice on the side.

NUTRITION:
calories 271, fat 6, fiber 9, carbs 18, protein 12

PASTA PEPPERS
Preparation time: 10 min | Cooking time: 12 min | Servings: 6

INGREDIENTS:

- 1 zucchini, sliced in half and roughly chopped
- 1 orange bell pepper, roughly chopped
- 1 green bell pepper, roughly chopped
- 1 red onion, roughly chopped
- 4 ounces brown mushrooms, halved
- Salt and black pepper to the taste
- 1 tsp Italian seasoning
- 1 pound penne rigate, already cooked
- 1 cup cherry tomatoes, halved
- ½ cup kalamata olive, pitted and halved
- ¼ cup olive oil
- 3 tbsp balsamic vinegar
- 2 tbsp basil, chopped

DIRECTIONS:
In a bowl, mix zucchini with mushrooms, orange bell pepper, green bell pepper, red onion, salt, pepper, Italian seasoning and oil, toss well, transfer to preheated air fryer at 380 degrees F and cook them for 12 minutes. In a large salad bowl, mix pasta with cooked veggies, cherry tomatoes, olives, vinegar and basil, toss and serve for lunch.

NUTRITION:
calories 200, fat 5, fiber 8, carbs 10, protein 6

PHILADELPHIA CHICKEN LUNCH
Preparation time: 10 min | Cooking time: 30 min | Servings: 4

INGREDIENTS:

- 1 tsp olive oil
- 1 yellow onion, sliced
- 2 chicken breasts, skinless, boneless and sliced
- Salt and black pepper to the taste
- 1 tbsp Worcestershire sauce
- 14 ounces pizza dough
- 1 and ½ cups cheddar cheese, grated
- ½ cup jarred cheese sauce

DIRECTIONS:
Preheat your air fryer at 400 degrees F, add half of the oil and onions and fry them for 8 minutes, stirring once. Add chicken pieces, Worcestershire sauce, salt and pepper, toss, air fry for 8 minutes more, stirring once and transfer everything to a bowl. Roll pizza dough on a working surface and shape a rectangle. Spread half of the cheese all over, add chicken and onion mix and top with cheese sauce. Roll your dough and shape into a U. Place your roll in your air fryer's basket, brush with the rest of the oil and cook at 370 degrees for 12 minutes, flipping the roll halfway. Slice your roll when it's warm and serve for lunch.

NUTRITION:
calories 300, fat 8, fiber 17, carbs 20, protein 6

BEEF CHEESEBURGERS
Preparation time: 10 min | Cooking time: 20 min | Servings: 2

INGREDIENTS:

- 12 ounces lean beef, ground
- 4 tsp ketchup
- 3 tbsp yellow onion, chopped
- 2 tsp mustard
- Salt and black pepper to the taste
- 4 cheddar cheese slices
- 2 burger buns, halved

DIRECTIONS:
In a bowl, mix beef with onion, ketchup, mustard, salt and pepper, stir well and shape 4 patties out of this mix. Divide cheese on 2 patties and top with the other 2 patties. Place them in preheated air fryer at 370 degrees F and fry them for 20 minutes. Divide cheeseburger on 2 bun halves, top with the other 2 and serve for lunch.

NUTRITION:
calories 261, fat 6, fiber 10, carbs 20, protein 6

FETA KOFTAS
Preparation time: 10 min | Cooking time: 15 min | Servings: 2

INGREDIENTS:

- 1 leek, chopped
- 2 tbsp feta cheese, crumbled
- ½ pound lean beef, minced
- 1 tbsp cumin, ground
- 1 tbsp mint, chopped
- 1 tbsp parsley, chopped
- 1 tsp garlic, minced
- Salt and black pepper to the taste

DIRECTIONS:
In a bowl, mix beef with leek, cheese, cumin, mint, parsley, garlic, salt and pepper, stir well, shape your koftas and place them on sticks. Add koftas to your preheated air fryer at 360 degrees F and cook them for 15 minutes. Serve them with a side salad for lunch.

NUTRITION:
calories 281, fat 7, fiber 8, carbs 17, protein 6

HONEY KABOBS

Preparation time: 10 min | Cooking time: 20 min | Servings: 2

INGREDIENTS:

- 3 orange bell peppers, cut into squares
- ¼ cup honey
- 1/3 cup soy sauce
- Salt and black pepper to the taste
- Cooking spray
- 6 mushrooms, halved
- 2 chicken breasts

DIRECTIONS:
In a bowl, mix chicken with salt, pepper, honey, say sauce and some cooking spray and toss well. Thread chicken, bell peppers and mushrooms on skewers, place them in your air fryer and cook at 338 degrees F for 20 minutes. Divide among plates and serve for lunch.

NUTRITION:
calories 261, fat 7, fiber 9, carbs 12, protein 6

BEEF AND CHEDDAR MEATBALLS

Preparation time: 10 min | Cooking time: 15 min | Servings: 4

INGREDIENTS:

- ½ pound beef, ground
- ½ pound Italian sausage, chopped
- ½ tsp garlic powder
- ½ tsp onion powder
- Salt and black pepper to the taste
- ½ cup cheddar cheese, grated
- Mashed potatoes for serving

DIRECTIONS:
In a bowl, mix beef with sausage, garlic powder, onion powder, salt, pepper and cheese, stir well and shape 16 meatballs out of this mix. Place meatballs in your air fryer and cook them at 370 degrees F for 15 minutes. Serve your meatballs with some mashed potatoes on the side.

NUTRITION:
calories 333, fat 23, fiber 1, carbs 8, protein 20

SOUR-SWEET CHICKEN WINGS

Preparation time: 10 min | Cooking time: 45 min | Servings: 4

INGREDIENTS:

- 3 pounds chicken wings
- ½ cup butter
- 1 tbsp old bay seasoning
- ¾ cup potato starch
- 1 tsp lemon juice
- Lemon wedges for serving

DIRECTIONS:
In a bowl, mix starch with old bay seasoning and chicken wings and toss well. Place chicken wings in your air fryer's basket and cook them at 360 degrees F for 35 minutes shaking the fryer from time to time. Increase temperature to 400 degrees F, cook chicken wings for 10 minutes more and divide them on plates. Heat up a pan over medium heat, add butter and melt it. Add lemon juice, stir well, take off heat and drizzle over chicken wings. Serve them for lunch with lemon wedges on the side.

NUTRITION:
calories 271, fat 6, fiber 8, carbs 18, protein 18

CHEESY HOT DOGS

Preparation time: 10 min | Cooking time: 7 min | Servings: 2

INGREDIENTS:

- 2 hot dog buns
- 2 hot dogs
- 1 tbsp Dijon mustard
- 2 tbsp cheddar cheese, grated

DIRECTIONS:
Put hot dogs in preheated air fryer and cook them at 390 degrees F for 5 minutes. Divide hot dogs into hot dog buns, spread mustard and cheese, return everything to your air fryer and cook for 2 minutes more at 390 degrees F. Serve for lunch.

NUTRITION:
calories 211, fat 3, fiber 8, carbs 12, protein 4

LENTILS FRITTERS

Preparation time: 10 min | Cooking time: 10 min | Servings: 2

INGREDIENTS:

- 1 cup yellow lentils, soaked in water for 1 hour and drained
- 1 hot chili pepper, chopped
- 1 inch ginger piece, grated
- ½ tsp turmeric powder
- 1 tsp garam masala
- 1 tsp baking powder
- Salt and black pepper to the taste
- 2 tsp olive oil
- 1/3 cup water
- ½ cup cilantro, chopped
- 1 and ½ cup spinach, chopped
- 4 garlic cloves, minced
- ¾ cup red onion, chopped
- Mint chutney for serving

DIRECTIONS:
In your blender, mix lentils with chili pepper, ginger, turmeric, garam masala, baking powder, salt, pepper, olive oil, water, cilantro, spinach, onion and garlic, blend well and shape medium balls out of this mix. Place them all in your preheated air fryer at 400 degrees F and cook for 10 minutes. Serve your veggie fritters with a side salad for lunch.

NUTRITION:
calories 142, fat 2, fiber 8, carbs 12, protein 4

BELL PEPPER AND POTATO SALAD

Preparation time: 10 min | Cooking time: 25

min | Servings: 4

INGREDIENTS:

- 2 pound red potatoes, halved
- 2 tbsp olive oil
- Salt and black pepper to the taste
- 2 green onions, chopped
- 1 red bell pepper, chopped
- 1/3 cup lemon juice
- 3 tbsp mustard

DIRECTIONS:

On your air fryer's basket, mix potatoes with half of the olive oil, salt and pepper and cook at 350 degrees F for 25 minutes shaking the fryer once. In a bowl, mix onions with bell pepper and roasted potatoes and toss. In a small bowl, mix lemon juice with the rest of the oil and mustard and whisk really well. Add this to potato salad, toss well and serve for lunch.

NUTRITION:
calories 211, fat 6, fiber 8, carbs 12, protein 4

CREAMY CORN SWISS CASSEROLE

Preparation time: 10 min | Cooking time: 15 min | Servings: 4

INGREDIENTS:

- 2 cups corn
- 3 tbsp flour
- 1 egg
- ¼ cup milk
- ½ cup light cream
- ½ cup Swiss cheese, grated
- 2 tbsp butter
- Salt and black pepper to the taste
- Cooking spray

DIRECTIONS:

In a bowl, mix corn with flour, egg, milk, light cream, cheese, salt, pepper and butter and stir well. Grease your air fryer's pan with cooking spray, pour cream mix, spread and cook at 320 degrees F for 15 minutes. Serve warm for lunch.

NUTRITION:
calories 281, fat 7, fiber 8, carbs 9, protein 6

SAUCE SAUSAGE MIX

Preparation time: 10 min | Cooking time: 10 min | Servings: 4

INGREDIENTS:

- 1 pound sausages, sliced
- 1 red bell pepper, cut into strips
- ½ cup yellow onion, chopped
- 3 tbsp brown sugar
- 1/3 cup ketchup
- 2 tbsp mustard
- 2 tbsp apple cider vinegar
- ½ cup chicken stock

DIRECTIONS:

In a bowl, mix sugar with ketchup, mustard, stock and vinegar and whisk well. In your air fryer's pan, mix sausage slices with bell pepper, onion and sweet and sour mix, toss and cook at 350 degrees F for 10 minutes. Divide into bowls and serve for lunch.

NUTRITION:
calories 162, fat 6, fiber 9, carbs 12, protein 6

BEEF MEATBALLS WITH MUSTARD SAUCE

Preparation time: 10 min | Cooking time: 15 min | Servings: 4

INGREDIENTS:

- 1 pound lean beef, ground
- 3 green onions, chopped
- 2 garlic cloves, minced
- 1 egg yolk
- ¼ cup bread crumbs
- Salt and black pepper to the taste
- 1 tbsp olive oil
- 16 ounces tomato sauce
- 2 tbsp mustard

DIRECTIONS:

In a bowl, mix beef with onion, garlic, egg yolk, bread crumbs, salt and pepper, stir well and shape medium meatballs out of this mix. Grease meatballs with the oil, place them in your air fryer and cook them at 400 degrees F for 10 minutes. In a bowl, mix tomato sauce with mustard, whisk, add over meatballs, toss them and cook at 400 degrees F for 5 minutes more. Divide meatballs and sauce on plates and serve for lunch.

NUTRITION:
calories 300, fat 8, fiber 9, carbs 16, protein 5

BEEF MEATBALLS

Preparation time: 10 min | Cooking time: 10 min | Servings: 4

INGREDIENTS:

- 1/3 cup bread crumbs
- 3 tbsp milk
- 1 tbsp ketchup
- 1 egg
- ½ tsp marjoram, dried
- Salt and black pepper to the taste
- 1 pound lean beef, ground
- 20 cheddar cheese cubes
- 1 tbsp olive oil

DIRECTIONS:

In a bowl, mix bread crumbs with ketchup, milk, marjoram, salt, pepper and egg and whisk well. Add beef, stir and shape 20 meatballs out of this mix. Shape each meatball around a cheese cube, drizzle the oil over them and rub. Place all meatballs in your preheated air fryer and cook at 390 degrees F for 10 minutes. Serve them for lunch with a side salad.

NUTRITION:
calories 200, fat 5, fiber 8, carbs 12, protein 5

SIRLOIN STEAKS WITH VEGGIES

Preparation time: 10 min | Cooking time: 10 min | Servings: 4

Ingredients:

- ½ pound sirloin steak, cut into strips
- 2 tsp cornstarch
- 1 tbsp peanut oil

- 2 cups green cabbage, chopped
- 1 yellow bell pepper, chopped
- 2 green onions, chopped
- 2 garlic cloves, minced

DIRECTIONS:
In a bowl, mix cabbage with salt, pepper and peanut oil, toss, transfer to air fryer's basket, cook at 370 degrees F for 4 minutes and transfer to a bowl. Add steak strips to your air fryer, also add green onions, bell pepper, garlic, salt and pepper, toss and cook for 5 minutes. Add over cabbage, toss, divide among plates and serve for lunch.

NUTRITION:
calories 282, fat 6, fiber 8, carbs 14, protein 6

MAPLE TURKEY BREAST

Preparation time: 10 min | Cooking time: 47 min | Servings: 4

INGREDIENTS:

- 1 big turkey breast
- 2 tsp olive oil
- ½ tsp smoked paprika
- 1 tsp thyme, dried
- ½ tsp sage, dried
- Salt and black pepper to the taste
- 2 tbsp mustard
- ¼ cup maple syrup
- 1 tbsp butter, soft

DIRECTIONS:
Brush turkey breast with the olive oil, season with salt, pepper, thyme, paprika and sage, rub, place in your air fryer's basket and fry at 350 degrees F for 25 minutes. Flip turkey, cook for 10 minutes more, flip one more time and cook for another 10 minutes. Meanwhile, heat up a pan with the butter over medium heat, add mustard and maple syrup, stir well, cook for a couple of minutes and take off heat. Slice turkey breast, divide among plates and serve with the maple glaze drizzled on top.

NUTRITION:
calories 280, fat 2, fiber 7, carbs 16, protein 14

ITALIAN EGGPLANT SANDWICH

Preparation time: 10 min | Cooking time: 16 min | Servings: 2

INGREDIENTS:

- 1 eggplant, sliced
- 2 tsp parsley, dried
- Salt and black pepper to the taste
- ½ cup breadcrumbs
- ½ tsp Italian seasoning
- ½ tsp garlic powder
- ½ tsp onion powder
- 2 tbsp milk
- 4 bread slices
- Cooking spray
- ½ cup mayonnaise
- ¾ cup tomato sauce
- 2 cups mozzarella cheese, grated

DIRECTIONS:
Season eggplant slices with salt and pepper, leave aside for 10 minutes and then pat dry them well. In a bowl, mix parsley with breadcrumbs, Italian seasoning, onion and garlic powder, salt and black pepper and stir. In another bowl, mix milk with mayo and whisk well. Brush eggplant slices with mayo mix, dip them in breadcrumbs, place them in your air fryer's basket, spray with cooking oil and cook them at 400 degrees F for 15 minutes, flipping them after 8 minutes. Brush each bread slice with olive oil and arrange 2 on a working surface. Add mozzarella and parmesan on each, add baked eggplant slices, spread tomato sauce and basil and top with the other bread slices, greased side down. Divide sandwiches on plates, cut them in halves and serve for lunch.

NUTRITION:
calories 324, fat 16, fiber 4, carbs 39, protein 12

THYME CHICKEN STEW

Preparation time: 10 min | Cooking time: 25 min | Servings: 4

INGREDIENTS:

- 1 and ½ cups canned cream of celery soup
- 6 chicken tenders
- Salt and black pepper to the taste
- 2 potatoes, chopped
- 1 bay leaf
- 1 thyme spring, chopped
- 1 tbsp milk
- 1 egg yolk
- ½ cup heavy cream

DIRECTIONS:
In a bowl, mix chicken with cream of celery, potatoes, heavy cream, bay leaf, thyme, salt and pepper, toss, pour into your air fryer's pan and cook at 320 degrees F for 25 minutes. Leave your stew to cool down a bit, discard bay leaf, divide among plates and serve right away.

NUTRITION:
calories 300, fat 11, fiber 2, carbs 23, protein 14

TURKEY CAKES

Preparation time: 10 min | Cooking time: 10 min | Servings: 4

INGREDIENTS:

- 6 mushrooms, chopped
- 1 tsp garlic powder
- 1 tsp onion powder
- Salt and black pepper to the taste
- 1 and ¼ pounds turkey meat, ground
- Cooking spray
- Tomato sauce for serving

DIRECTIONS:
In your blender, mix mushrooms with salt and pepper, pulse well and transfer to a bowl. Add turkey, onion powder, garlic powder, salt and pepper, stir and shape cakes out of this mix Spray them with cooking spray, transfer them to your air fryer and cook at 320 degrees F for 10 minutes.

Serve them with tomato sauce on the side and a tasty side salad.

Nutrition: calories 202, fat 6, fiber 3, carbs 17, protein 10

CHEESE RAVIOLI AND MARINARA SAUCE
Preparation time: 10 min | Cooking time: 8 min | Servings: 6

Ingredients:

- 20 ounces cheese ravioli
- 10 ounces marinara sauce
- 1 tbsp olive oil
- 1 cup buttermilk
- 2 cups bread crumbs
- ¼ cup parmesan, grated

Directions:
Put buttermilk in a bowl and breadcrumbs in another bowl. Dip ravioli in buttermilk, then in breadcrumbs and place them in your air fryer on a baking sheet. Drizzle olive oil over them, cook at 400 degrees F for 5 minutes, divide them on plates, sprinkle parmesan on top and serve for lunch

Nutrition:
calories 270, fat 12, fiber 6, carbs 30, protein 15

BEEF THYME STEW
Preparation time: 10 min | Cooking time: 20 min | Servings: 4

Ingredients:

- 2 pounds beef meat, cut into medium chunks
- 2 carrots, chopped
- 4 potatoes, chopped
- Salt and black pepper to the taste
- 1 quart veggie stock
- ½ tsp smoked paprika
- A handful thyme, chopped

Directions:
In a dish that fits your air fryer, mix beef with carrots, potatoes, stock, salt, pepper, paprika and thyme, stir, place in air fryer's basket and cook at 375 degrees F for 20 minutes. Divide into bowls and serve right away for lunch.

Nutrition:
calories 260, fat 5, fiber 8, carbs 20, protein 22

ONION BAGUETTES WITH MEATBALLS
Preparation time: 10 min | Cooking time: 22 min | Servings: 4

Ingredients:

- 3 baguettes, sliced more than halfway through
- 14 ounces beef, ground
- 7 ounces tomato sauce
- 1 small onion, chopped
- 1 egg, whisked
- 1 tbsp bread crumbs
- 2 tbsp cheddar cheese, grated
- 1 tbsp oregano, chopped
- 1 tbsp olive oil
- Salt and black pepper to the taste
- 1 tsp thyme, dried
- 1 tsp basil, dried

Directions:
In a bowl, combine meat with salt, pepper, onion, breadcrumbs, egg, cheese, oregano, thyme and basil, stir, shape medium meatballs and add them to your air fryer after you've greased it with the oil. Cook them at 375 degrees F for 12 minutes, flipping them halfway. Add tomato sauce, cook meatballs for 10 minutes more and arrange them on sliced baguettes. Serve them right away.

Nutrition:
calories 380, fat 5, fiber 6, carbs 34, protein 20

AIR FRIED RED CABBAGE SALAD
Preparation time: 10 min | Cooking time: 5 min | Servings: 4

Ingredients:

- 1 cup carrots, grated
- 1 cup red cabbage, shredded
- A pinch of salt and black pepper
- A handful cilantro, chopped
- 1 small cucumber, chopped
- Juice from 1 lime
- 2 tsp red curry paste
- 12 big shrimp

Directions:
In a pan that fits your, mix cabbage with carrots, cucumber and shrimp, toss, introduce in your air fryer and cook at 360 degrees F for 5 minutes. Add salt, pepper, cilantro, lime juice and red curry paste, toss again, divide among plates and serve right away.

Nutrition:
calories 172, fat 5, fiber 7, carbs 8, protein 5

SWEET POTATO COCONUT CASSEROLE
Preparation time: 10 min | Cooking time: 50 min | Servings: 6

Ingredients:

- 3 big sweet potatoes, pricked with a fork
- 1 cup chicken stock
- Salt and black pepper to the taste
- A pinch of cayenne pepper
- ¼ tsp nutmeg, ground
- 1/3 cup coconut cream

Directions:
Place sweet potatoes in your air fryer, cook them at 350 degrees F for 40 minutes, cool them down, peel, roughly chop and transfer to a pan that fits your air fryer. Add stock, salt, pepper, cayenne and coconut cream, toss, introduce in your air fryer and cook at 360 degrees F for 10 minutes more. Divide casserole into bowls and serve.

NUTRITION:
calories 245, fat 4, fiber 5, carbs 10, protein 6

HERBED CASSEROLE
Preparation time: 10 min | Cooking time: 16 min | Servings: 8

INGREDIENTS:

- 1 cup veggie stock
- 2 tbsp olive oil
- 2 sweet potatoes, peeled and cut into medium wedges
- 8 zucchinis, cut into medium wedges
- 2 yellow onions, chopped
- 1 cup coconut milk
- Salt and black pepper to the taste
- 1 tbsp soy sauce
- ¼ tsp thyme, dried
- ¼ tsp rosemary, dried
- 4 tbsp dill, chopped
- ½ tsp basil, chopped

DIRECTIONS:
Heat up a pan that fits your air fryer with the oil over medium heat, add onion, stir and cook for 2 minutes. Add zucchinis, thyme, rosemary, basil, potato, salt, pepper, stock, milk, soy sauce and dill, stir, introduce in your air fryer, cook at 360 degrees F for 14 minutes, divide among plates and serve right away.

NUTRITION:
calories 133, fat 3, fiber 4, carbs 10, protein 5

CHICKEN AND LIME CASSEROLE
Preparation time: 10 min | Cooking time: 25 min | Servings: 4

INGREDIENTS:

- 4 lime leaves, torn
- 1 cup veggie stock
- 1 lemongrass stalk, chopped
- 1 inch piece, grated
- 1 pound chicken breast, skinless, boneless and cut into thin strips
- 8 ounces mushrooms, chopped
- 4 Thai chilies, chopped
- 4 tbsp fish sauce
- 6 ounces coconut milk
- ¼ cup lime juice
- ¼ cup cilantro, chopped
- Salt and black pepper to the taste

DIRECTIONS:
Put stock into a pan that fits your air fryer, bring to a simmer over medium heat, add lemongrass, ginger and lime leaves, stir and cook for 10 minutes. Strain soup, return to pan, add chicken, mushrooms, milk, chilies, fish sauce, lime juice, cilantro, salt and pepper, stir, introduce in your air fryer and cook at 360 degrees F for 15 minutes. Divide into bowls and serve.

NUTRITION:
calories 150, fat 4, fiber 4, carbs 6, protein 7

TURKEY AND SHALLOT BURGERS
Preparation time: 10 min | Cooking time: 8 min | Servings: 4

INGREDIENTS:

- 1 pound turkey meat, ground
- 1 shallot, minced
- A drizzle of olive oil
- 1 small jalapeno pepper, minced
- 2 tsp lime juice
- Zest from 1 lime, grated
- Salt and black pepper to the taste
- 1 tsp cumin, ground
- 1 tsp sweet paprika
- Guacamole for serving

DIRECTIONS:
In a bowl, mix turkey meat with salt, pepper, cumin, paprika, shallot, jalapeno, lime juice and zest, stir well, shape burgers from this mix, drizzle the oil over them, introduce in preheated air fryer and cook them at 370 degrees F for 8 minutes on each side. Divide among plates and serve with guacamole on top.

NUTRITION:
calories 200, fat 12, fiber 0, carbs 0, protein 12

SALMON AND ASPARAGUS
Preparation time: 10 min | Cooking time: 23 min | Servings: 4

INGREDIENTS:

- 1 pound asparagus, trimmed
- 1 tbsp olive oil
- A pinch of sweet paprika
- Salt and black pepper to the taste
- A pinch of garlic powder
- A pinch of cayenne pepper
- 1 red bell pepper, cut into halves
- 4 ounces smoked salmon

DIRECTIONS:
Put asparagus spears and bell pepper on a lined baking sheet that fits your air fryer, add salt, pepper, garlic powder, paprika, olive oil, cayenne pepper, toss to coat, introduce in the fryer, cook at 390 degrees F for 8 minutes, flip and cook for 8 minutes more. Add salmon, cook for 5 minutes, more, divide everything on plates and serve.

NUTRITION:
calories 90, fat 1, fiber 1, carbs 1.2, protein 4

SHIITAKE AND POULTRY LUNCH
Preparation time: 10 min | Cooking time: 20 min | Servings: 6

INGREDIENTS:

- 1 bunch kale, chopped
- Salt and black pepper to the taste
- ¼ cup chicken stock
- 1 cup chicken, shredded
- 3 carrots, chopped
- 1 cup shiitake mushrooms, roughly sliced

DIRECTIONS:
In a blender, mix stock with kale, pulse a

few times and pour into a pan that fits your air fryer. Add chicken, mushrooms, carrots, salt and pepper to the taste, toss, introduce in your air fryer and cook at 350 degrees F for 18 minutes.

NUTRITION:
calories 180, fat 7, fiber 2, carbs 10, protein 5

CHICKEN AND COCONUT CASSEROLE
Preparation time: 10 min | Cooking time: 30 min | Servings: 6

INGREDIENTS:
- 1 cup clean chicken stock
- 2 tsp garlic powder
- Salt and black pepper to the taste
- 6 ounces canned coconut milk
- 1 and ½ cups green lentils
- 2 pounds chicken breasts, skinless, boneless and cubed
- 1/3 cup cilantro, chopped
- 3 cups corn
- 3 handfuls spinach
- 3 green onions, chopped

DIRECTIONS:
In a pan that fits your air fryer, mix stock with coconut milk, salt, pepper, garlic powder, chicken and lentils. Add corn, green onions, cilantro and spinach, stir well, introduce in your air fryer and cook at 350 degrees F for 30 minutes.

NUTRITION:
calories 345, fat 12, fiber 10, carbs 20, protein 44

CHICKEN AND KALE MIX
Preparation time: 10 min | Cooking time: 20 min | Servings: 4

INGREDIENTS:
- 4 zucchinis, cut with a spiralizer
- 1 pound chicken breasts, skinless, boneless and cubed
- 2 garlic cloves, minced
- 1 tsp olive oil
- Salt and black pepper to the taste
- 2 cups cherry tomatoes, halved
- ½ cup almonds, chopped
- For the pesto:
- 2 cups basil
- 2 cups kale, chopped
- 1 tbsp lemon juice
- 1 garlic clove
- ¾ cup pine nuts
- ½ cup olive oil
- A pinch of salt

DIRECTIONS:
In your food processor, mix basil with kale, lemon juice, garlic, pine nuts, oil and a pinch of salt, pulse really well and leave aside. Heat up a pan that fits your air fryer with the oil over medium heat, add garlic, stir and cook for 1 minute. Add chicken, salt, pepper, stir, almonds, zucchini noodles, garlic, cherry tomatoes and the pesto you've made at the beginning, stir gently, introduce in preheated air fryer and cook at 360 degrees F for 17 minutes. Divide among plates and serve for lunch.

NUTRITION:
calories 344, fat 8, fiber 7, carbs 12, protein 16

CHICKEN, JALAPENO AND MOZZARELLA CASSEROLE
Preparation time: 10 min | Cooking time: 30 min | Servings: 8

INGREDIENTS:
- 1 cup quinoa, already cooked
- 3 cups chicken breast, cooked and shredded
- 14 ounces canned black beans
- 12 ounces corn
- ½ cup cilantro, chopped
- 6 kale leaves, chopped
- ½ cup green onions, chopped
- 1 cup clean tomato sauce
- 1 cup clean salsa
- 2 tsp chili powder
- 2 tsp cumin, ground
- 3 cups mozzarella cheese, shredded
- 1 tbsp garlic powder
- Cooking spray
- 2 jalapeno peppers, chopped

DIRECTIONS:
Spray a baking dish that fits your air fryer with cooking spray, add quinoa, chicken, black beans, corn, cilantro, kale, green onions, tomato sauce, salsa, chili powder, cumin, garlic powder, jalapenos and mozzarella, toss, introduce in your fryer and cook at 350 degrees F for 17 minutes. Slice and serve warm for lunch.

NUTRITION:
calories 365, fat 12, fiber 6, carbs 22, protein 26

AIR FRYER SIDE DISH RECIPES

SOUR CREAM POTATOES
Preparation time: 5 min | Cooking time: 20 min | Servings: 4

INGREDIENTS:
- 2 gold potatoes, cut into medium pieces
- 1 tbsp olive oil
- Salt and black pepper to taste
- 3 tbsp sour cream

DIRECTIONS:
In a baking dish that fits your air fryer, mix all the ingredients and toss. Place the dish in the air fryer and cook at 370 degrees F for 20 minutes. Divide between plates and serve as a side dish.

NUTRITION:
calories 201, fat 8, fiber 9, carbs 18, protein 5

SWEET POTATO GINGER SALAD
Preparation time: 5 min | Cooking time: 20 min | Servings: 2

INGREDIENTS:

- 2 sweet potatoes, peeled and cut into wedges
- Salt and black pepper to taste
- 2 tbsp avocado oil
- ½ tsp curry powder
- ¼ tsp coriander, ground
- 4 tbsp mayonnaise
- ½ tsp cumin, ground
- A pinch of ginger powder
- A pinch of cinnamon powder

DIRECTIONS:
In your air fryer's basket, mix the sweet potato wedges with salt, pepper, coriander, curry powder, and the oil; toss well. Cook at 370 degrees F for 20 minutes, flipping them once. Transfer the potatoes to a bowl, then add the mayonnaise, cumin, ginger and the cinnamon. Toss and serve as a side salad.

NUTRITION:
calories 190, fat 5, fiber 8, carbs 14, protein 5

GARLIC BRUSSELS SPROUTS
Preparation time: 5 min | Cooking time: 15 min | Servings: 4

INGREDIENTS:

- 1 pound Brussels sprouts
- Salt and black pepper to taste
- 6 tsp olive oil
- ½ cup mayonnaise
- 2 tbsp garlic, minced

DIRECTIONS:
In your air fryer, mix the sprouts, salt, pepper, and oil; toss well. Cook the sprouts at 390 degrees F for 15 minutes. Transfer them to a bowl; then add the mayo and the garlic and toss. Divide between plates and serve as a side dish.

NUTRITION:
calories 202, fat 6, fiber 8, carbs 12, protein 8

WALNUT SHALLOTS
Preparation time: 5 min | Cooking time: 25 min | Servings: 4

INGREDIENTS:

- 1½ pounds green beans, trimmed
- Salt and black pepper to taste
- ½ pound shallots, chopped
- ¼ cup walnuts, chopped
- 2 tbsp olive oil

DIRECTIONS:
In your air fryer, mix all ingredients and toss. Cook at 350 degrees F for 25 minutes. Divide between plates and serve as a side dish.

NUTRITION:
calories 182, fat 3, fiber 6, carbs 11, protein 5

ITALIAN PARMESAN MIX
Preparation time: 5 min | Cooking time: 15 min | Servings: 4

INGREDIENTS:

- 1 pound button mushrooms, halved
- 2 tbsp parmesan cheese, grated
- 1 tsp Italian seasoning
- A pinch of salt and black pepper
- 3 tbsp butter, melted

DIRECTIONS:
In a pan that fits your air fryer, mix all the ingredients and toss. Place the pan in the air fryer and cook at 360 degrees F for 15 minutes. Divide the mix between plates and serve.

NUTRITION:
calories 194, fat 4, fiber 4, carbs 14, protein 7

CORIANDER EGGPLANT MIX
Preparation time: 10 min | Cooking time: 10 min | Servings: 4

INGREDIENTS:

- 8 baby eggplants, cubed
- Salt and black pepper to taste
- 1 green bell pepper, chopped
- 1 tbsp tomato sauce
- 1 bunch coriander, chopped
- ½ tsp garlic powder
- 1 tbsp olive oil
- 1 yellow onion, chopped

DIRECTIONS:
In a pan that fits your air fryer, combine all the ingredients and toss. Place the pan in the fryer and cook at 370 degrees F for 10 minutes. Divide between plates and serve as a side dish.

NUTRITION:
calories 210, fat 5, fiber 7, carbs 12, protein 5

CREOLE TOMATOES
Preparation time: 5 min | Cooking time: 6 min | Servings: 4

INGREDIENTS:

- 1 pound cherry tomatoes, halved
- Salt and black pepper to taste
- A drizzle of olive oil
- 1 cup heavy cream
- ½ tbsp Creole seasoning

DIRECTIONS:
In a pan that fits your air fryer, combine all the ingredients and toss. Place the pan in the fryer and cook at 400 degrees F for 6 minutes. Divide between plates and serve.

NUTRITION:
calories 174, fat 5, fiber 7, carbs 11, protein 4

BREAD ZUCCHINI FRIES
Preparation time: 10 min | Cooking time: 12 min | Servings: 4

INGREDIENTS:

- 2 small zucchinis, cut into fries
- 2 tsp olive oil
- Salt and black pepper to taste
- 2 eggs, whisked

- 1 cup bread-crumbs
- ½ cup white flour

DIRECTIONS:
In a bowl, mix the flour, salt, and pepper; stir. Put the breadcrumbs in another bowl and whisk the eggs in a third bowl. Dredge the zucchini fries in the flour, then in the eggs, and then in the breadcrumbs. Use the oil to grease your air fryer and heat to 400 degrees F. Add the zucchini fries and cook for 12 minutes; serve as a side dish.

NUTRITION:
calories 182, fat 6, fiber 3, carbs 11, protein 5

SMOKED PAPRIKA PEPPERS
Preparation time: 5 min | Cooking time: 20 min | Servings: 4

INGREDIENTS:
- 1 tbsp smoked paprika
- 1 tbsp olive oil
- 4 red bell peppers, cut into medium strips
- 4 green bell peppers, cut in medium strips
- 1 red onion, chopped
- Salt and black pepper to taste

DIRECTIONS:
In your air fryer, mix all ingredients, toss, and cook at 360 degrees F for 20 minutes. Divide the peppers between plates and serve as a side dish.

NUTRITION:
calories 172, fat 5, fiber 4, carbs 7, protein 4

PROVENCE CARROTS MIX
Preparation time: 5 min | Cooking time: 20 min | Servings: 4

INGREDIENTS:
- 1 pound baby carrots, trimmed
- 2 tsp olive oil
- 1 tsp herbs de Provence
- 2 tbsp lime juice

DIRECTIONS:
In a bowl, mix all ingredients well and then transfer to your air fryer's basket. Cook at 320 degrees F for 20 minutes. Divide between plates and serve as a side dish.
Nutrition: calories 132, fat 4, fiber 3, carbs 11, protein 4

MAPLE PARSNIPS MIX
Preparation time: 5 min | Cooking time: 40 min | Servings: 6

INGREDIENTS:
- 2 pounds parsnips, roughly cubed
- 2 tbsp maple syrup
- 1 tbsp cilantro, chopped
- 1 tbsp olive oil

DIRECTIONS:
Preheat your air fryer at 360 degrees F, then add the oil and heat it up. Add the other ingredients, toss, and cook for 40 minutes. Divide between plates and serve as a side dish.

NUTRITION:
calories 174, fat 5, fiber 3, carbs 11, protein 4

AIR FRIED BEETS
Preparation time: 5 min | Cooking time: 35 min | Servings: 6

INGREDIENTS:
- 3 pounds small beets, trimmed and halve
- 4 tbsp maple syrup
- 1 tbsp olive oil

DIRECTIONS:
Heat up your air fryer at 360 degrees F, then add the oil and heat it up. Add the beets and maple syrup, toss, and cook for 35 minutes. Divide the beets between plates and serve as a side dish.

NUTRITION:
calories 171, fat 4, fiber 2, carbs 13, protein 3

CAULIFLOWER AND CHESTNUTS RISOTTO
Preparation time: 10 min | Cooking time: 40 min | Servings: 6

INGREDIENTS:
- 2 tbsp olive oil
- 4 tbsp soy sauce
- 3 garlic cloves, minced
- 1 tbsp ginger, grated
- Juice of 1 lime
- 1 cauliflower head, riced
- 10 ounces water chestnuts, drained
- 15 ounces mushrooms, chopped
- 1 egg, whisked

DIRECTIONS:
In your air fryer, mix the cauliflower rice, oil, soy sauce, garlic, ginger, lime juice, chestnuts, and mushrooms. Stir, cover, and cook at 350 degrees F for 20 minutes. Add the egg, toss, and cook at 360 degrees F for 20 minutes more. Divide between plates and serve.

NUTRITION:
calories 182, fat 3, fiber 2, carbs 8, protein 4

SUMAC EGGPLANTS
Preparation time: 5 min | Cooking time: 20 min | Servings: 6

INGREDIENTS:
- 1½ pounds eggplant, cubed
- 1 tbsp olive oil
- 1 tsp onion powder
- 1 tsp sumac
- 2 tsp za'atar
- Juice of 1 lime

DIRECTIONS:
Place all ingredients in your air fryer and mix well. Cook at 370 degrees F for 20 minutes. Divide between plates and serve as a side dish.

NUTRITION:

calories 182, fat 4, fiber 7, carbs 12, protein 4

SESAME CAULIFLOWER MIX
Preparation time: 5 min | Cooking time: 20 min | Servings: 4

INGREDIENTS:

- 1 tbsp olive oil
- 1 cauliflower head, florets separated
- 3 garlic cloves, minced
- Juice of 1 lime
- 1 tbsp black sesame seeds

DIRECTIONS:
Heat up your air fryer at 350 degrees F, then add the oil and heat it up. Add the cauliflower, garlic, and lime juice; toss and then cook for 20 minutes. Divide between plates, sprinkle the sesame seeds on top, and serve as a side dish.

NUTRITION:
calories 182, fat 4, fiber 3, carbs 11, protein 4

SALTY ROSEMARY POTATOES
Preparation time: 10 min | Cooking time: 30 min | Servings: 4

INGREDIENTS:

- 4 potatoes, thinly sliced
- Salt and black pepper to taste
- 1 tbsp olive oil
- 2 tsp rosemary, chopped

DIRECTIONS:
Place all the ingredients in a bowl, mix well, and then transfer to your air fryer's basket. Cook at 370 degrees F for 30 minutes. Divide between plates and serve as a side dish.

NUTRITION:
calories 190, fat 4, fiber 4, carbs 14, protein 4

PARSNIPS AND THYME FRIES
Preparation time: 5 min | Cooking time: 15 min | Servings: 4

INGREDIENTS:

- 4 parsnips, cut into medium sticks
- 4 carrots, cut into medium sticks
- Salt and black pepper to taste
- 2 tbsp thyme, chopped
- 2 tbsp olive oil
- ½ tsp onion powder

DIRECTIONS:
In a bowl, mix all ingredients and toss. Transfer the fries to your air fryer's basket and cook at 350 degrees F for 15 minutes. Divide between plates and serve as a side dish.

NUTRITION:
calories 160, fat 3, fiber 4, carbs 7, protein 3

PEPPER TOMATOES MIX
Preparation time: 5 min | Cooking time: 15 min | Servings: 6

INGREDIENTS:

- 15 ounces mushrooms, roughly sliced
- 1 red onion, chopped
- Salt and black pepper to taste
- ½ tsp nutmeg, ground
- 2 tbsp olive oil
- 6 ounces canned tomatoes, chopped

DIRECTIONS:
Place all ingredients in a pan that fits your air fryer and mix well. Put the pan in the fryer and cook at 380 degrees F for 15 minutes. Divide the mix between plates and serve as a side dish.

NUTRITION:
calories 202, fat 6, fiber 1, carbs 16, protein 4

YELLOW SQUASH AND ZUCCHINI MIX
Preparation time: 10 min | Cooking time: 35 min | Servings: 4

INGREDIENTS:

- 5 tsp olive oil
- 1 pound zucchinis, sliced
- 1 yellow squash, halved, deseeded, and cut in chunks
- Salt and white pepper to taste
- 1 tbsp cilantro, chopped

DIRECTIONS:
In a bowl, mix all the ingredients, toss well, and transfer them to your air fryer's basket. Cook for 35 minutes at 400 degrees. Divide everything between plates and serve as a side dish.

NUTRITION:
calories 200, fat 4, fiber 1, carbs 15, protein 4

CHEESY MUSHROOM SALAD
Preparation time: 5 min | Cooking time: 15 min | Servings: 3

INGREDIENTS:

- 10 large mushrooms, halved
- 1 tbsp mixed herbs, dried
- 1 tbsp cheddar cheese, grated
- 1 tbsp mozzarella cheese, grated
- A drizzle of olive oil
- 2 tsp parsley flakes
- Salt and black pepper to taste

DIRECTIONS:
Use the oil to grease a pan that fits your air fryer. Add all other ingredients and toss. Place the pan in the fryer and cook at 380 degrees F for 15 minutes. Divide between plates and serve as a side dish.

NUTRITION:
calories 161, fat 7, fiber 1, carbs 12, protein 6

PAPRIKA CORN
Preparation time: 5 min | Cooking time: 15

min | Servings: 2

INGREDIENTS:

- 2 ears of corn, shucked and silk removed
- Salt and black pepper to taste
- 2 tsp olive oil
- Juice of 2 limes
- 2 tsp smoked paprika

DIRECTIONS:
In a bowl, mix the salt with the pepper, oil, lime juice, and paprika and stir well. Rub the corn with this mix and put it in your air fryer's basket. Cook at 400 degrees F for 15 minutes. Divide between plates and serve.

NUTRITION:
calories 180, fat 7, fiber 2, carbs 12, protein 6

SPICY POTATOES

Preparation time: 5 min | Cooking time: 40 min | Servings: 4

INGREDIENTS:

- 4 large potatoes, pricked with a fork
- Salt and black pepper to taste
- 2 tbsp olive oil
- 1 tbsp garlic, minced

DIRECTIONS:
Place all of the ingredients in a bowl and mix well, ensuring the potatoes are coated. Put the potatoes in your air fryer's basket and cook at 400 degrees F for 40 minutes. Peel the potatoes (if desired), cut up, divide between plates, and serve as a side dish.

NUTRITION:
calories 173, fat 3, fiber 2, carbs 16, protein 4

RICE CHICKEN MIX

Preparation time: 5 min | Cooking time: 30 min | Servings: 8

INGREDIENTS:

- 1 shallot, chopped
- 1 tsp garlic, minced
- 1 tsp olive oil
- 1½ cups wild rice
- 4 cups chicken stock
- Salt and black pepper to taste
- 1 tbsp parsley, chopped
- ½ cup hazelnuts, toasted and chopped

DIRECTIONS:
Heat up the oil in a pan that fits your air fryer over medium heat. Add the garlic and the shallots, stir, and cook for 2-3 minutes. Add the rice, stock, salt, and pepper, and stir completely. Place the pan in the air fryer and cook at 380 degrees F for 25 minutes. Add the parsley and the hazelnuts, stir, divide between plates, and serve as a side dish.

NUTRITION:
calories 200, fat 4, fiber 6, carbs 16, protein 4

TURMERIC QUINOA

Preparation time: 5 min | Cooking time: 18 min | Servings: 4

INGREDIENTS:

- 2 cups quinoa
- 2 garlic cloves, minced
- 2 tbsp olive oil
- Salt and black pepper to taste
- 2 tsp turmeric powder
- 3 cups veggie stock
- A handful of parsley, chopped

DIRECTIONS:
Heat the oil up in a pan that fits your air fryer over medium heat. Add the garlic, stir, and cook for 2 minutes. Add the quinoa, salt, pepper, turmeric, and the stock; cover and cook at 360 degrees F for 16 minutes. Add the parsley, stir, and then divide between plates and serve as a side dish.

NUTRITION:
calories 171, fat 4, fiber 8, carbs 16, protein 7

MUSHROOMS RISOTTO

Preparation time: 10 min | Cooking time: 20 min | Servings: 4

INGREDIENTS:

- 2 cups risotto rice
- 4 cups chicken stock, heated up
- 2 garlic cloves, minced
- 1 tbsp olive oil
- 1 yellow onion, chopped
- 8 ounces mushrooms, sliced
- 4 ounces heavy cream
- 2 tbsp parmesan cheese, grated
- 1 tbsp cilantro, chopped

DIRECTIONS:
Add all ingredients—except the cilantro—to a pan that fits your air fryer. Place the pan in the fryer and cook at 360 degrees F for 20 minutes. Add the cilantro, stir, divide between plates, and serve.

NUTRITION:
calories 261, fat 5, fiber 8, carbs 15, protein 5

NUTMEG PUMPKIN RICE

Preparation time: 5 min | Cooking time: 25 min | Servings: 4

INGREDIENTS:

- 2 tbsp olive oil
- 1 small yellow onion, chopped
- 2 garlic cloves, minced
- 12 ounces risotto rice
- 4 cups chicken stock
- 6 ounces pumpkin puree
- ½ tsp nutmeg, ground
- ½ tsp ginger, grated
- ½ tsp cinnamon powder
- ½ tsp allspice
- 4 ounces heavy cream

DIRECTIONS:
In a pan that fits your air fryer, heat up the oil over medium heat. Add the onion and the garlic, stir, and cook for 2 minutes. Add the nutmeg, ginger, cinnamon, and allspice;

stir and cook for 1 more minute. Add the rice, stock, pumpkin puree, and the cream; stir. Place the pan in the fryer and cook at 360 degrees F for 20 minutes. Divide between plates and serve as a side dish.

Nutrition:
calories 251, fat 6, fiber 8, carbs 16, protein 6

MILKY SWEET POTATOES
Preparation time: 10 min | Cooking time: 12 min | Servings: 8

Ingredients:

- 2 garlic cloves
- 3 pounds sweet potatoes, baked, peeled, and chopped
- Salt and black pepper to taste
- ½ tsp parsley, dried
- ¼ tsp sage, dried
- ½ tsp rosemary, dried
- ¼ cup milk
- ½ cup parmesan cheese, grated
- 2 tbsp butter

Directions:
In a pan that fits your air fryer, combine the sweet potatoes, garlic, salt, pepper, parsley, sage, and rosemary; mix well. Place the pan in the fryer and cook at 360 degrees F for 12 minutes. Mash the potatoes, adding the milk, parmesan, and butter; stir well. Divide between plates and serve as a side dish.

Nutrition:
calories 251, fat 6, fiber 5, carbs 16, protein 6

SAFFRON ARBORIO RICE
Preparation time: 5 min | Cooking time: 20 min | Servings: 6

Ingredients:

- 2 tbsp olive oil
- ½ tsp saffron powder
- ½ cup onion, chopped
- 2 tbsp milk, hot
- 1½ cups Arborio rice
- Salt and black pepper to taste
- 3½ cups chicken stock
- 1 tbsp honey
- 1 cup almonds, chopped

Directions:
Add all of the ingredients to a pan that fits your air fryer. Place the pan in the fryer and cook at 360 degrees F for 20 minutes. Divide between plates and serve as a side dish.

Nutrition:
calories 251, fat 4, fiber 3, carbs 13, protein 6

CHERRIES RICE
Preparation time: 10 min | Cooking time: 22 min | Servings: 6

Ingredients:

- 1 tbsp apple cider vinegar
- 1 cup white rice
- 1 tsp lemon juice
- Salt and black pepper to taste
- 3 cups water, hot
- 1 tsp olive oil
- ¼ cup green onions, chopped
- 10 mint leaves, chopped
- 2 cups cherries, pitted and halved

Directions:
In a pan that fits your air fryer, add all of the ingredients and mix well. Place the pan in the fryer and cook at 370 degrees F for 22 minutes. Divide between plates and serve as a side dish.

Nutrition:
calories 200, fat 5, fiber 5, carbs 9, protein 5

CHICKEN FLAVORED RISOTTO
Preparation time: 10 min | Cooking time: 20 min | Servings: 4

Ingredients:

- 2 tbsp olive oil
- Salt and black pepper to taste
- 1 broccoli head, florets separated and roughly chopped
- ½ cup parmesan cheese, grated
- 2 garlic cloves, minced
- 1 cup white rice
- 1 yellow onion, chopped
- 3 cups chicken stock, heated up
- 2 tbsp parsley, chopped
- 1 tbsp butter

Directions:
In a pan that fits your air fryer, mix the oil with the broccoli, salt, pepper, garlic, onions, rice, and stock; stir well. Place the pan in the air fryer and cook at 370 degrees F for 20 minutes. Add the parsley, butter, and the parmesan, and stir. Divide between plates and serve as a side dish.

Nutrition:
calories 200, fat 6, fiber 5, carbs 15, protein 5

PARMESAN RICE
Preparation time: 5 min | Cooking time: 20 min | Servings: 4

Ingredients:

- 1 tbsp olive oil
- 1 cup Arborio rice
- 2 garlic cloves, minced
- 3 cups chicken stock
- 15 ounces canned artichoke hearts, chopped
- 8 ounces cream cheese
- 1 tbsp parmesan cheese, grated
- 1½ tbsp thyme, chopped
- Salt and black pepper to taste

Directions:
In a pan that fits your air fryer, add all the ingredients except the parmesan cheese; stir well. Place the pan in the air fryer and cook at 370 degrees F for 20 minutes. Add the parmesan, stir, divide between plates, and serve as a side dish.

Nutrition:
calories 215, fat 4, fiber 6, carbs 14, protein 4

BEANS MEDLEY
Preparation time: 10 min | Cooking time: 15

min | Servings: 4

Ingredients:

- 1 cup canned garbanzo beans, drained
- 1 cup canned cranberry beans, drained
- 1½ cups green beans, blanched
- 4 cups water
- 1 garlic clove, minced
- 2 celery stalks, chopped
- 1 bunch cilantro, chopped
- 1 small red onion, chopped
- 1 tbsp sugar
- 5 tbsp apple cider vinegar
- 4 tbsp olive oil
- Salt and black pepper to taste

DIRECTIONS:
In a pan that fits your air fryer, mix all ingredients except the cilantro; stir well. Place the pan in the air fryer and cook at 380 degrees F for 15 minutes. Add the cilantro, stir, divide between plates, and serve as a side dish.

NUTRITION:
calories 231, fat 4, fiber 6, carbs 14, protein 6

CUMIN BEANS MIX
Preparation time: 5 min | Cooking time: 15 min | Servings: 6

INGREDIENTS:

- 1 cup canned black beans, drained
- 1 cup water
- Salt and black pepper to taste
- 1 spring onion, chopped
- 2 garlic cloves, minced
- ½ tsp cumin seeds

DIRECTIONS:
Add all ingredients to a pan that fits your air fryer; mix well. Place the pan in the fryer and cook at 370 degrees F for 15 minutes. Divide between plates and serve as a side dish.

NUTRITION:
calories 265, fat 6, fiber 7, carbs 14, protein 6

PINEAPPLE RICE
Preparation time: 5 min | Cooking time: 20 min | Servings: 6

INGREDIENTS:

- 2 cups rice
- 4 cups chicken stock, heated up
- 1 pineapple, peeled and chopped
- Salt and black pepper to taste
- 2 tsp olive oil

DIRECTIONS:
In a pan that fits your air fryer, place all the ingredients and toss. Insert the pan into your preheated air fryer and cook at 370 degrees F for 20 minutes. Divide between plates and serve as a side dish.

NUTRITION:
calories 200, fat 4, fiber 5, carbs 11, protein 4

BEANS AND PEPPERS MIX
Preparation time: 10 min | Cooking time: 25 min | Servings: 6

INGREDIENTS:

- 1 pound canned red kidney beans, drained
- Salt and black pepper to taste
- 1 tsp olive oil
- 1 yellow onion, chopped
- 1 celery stalk, chopped
- 4 garlic cloves, chopped
- 1 green bell pepper, chopped
- 1 tsp thyme, dried
- 2 green onions, minced
- 2 tbsp tomato sauce
- 2 tbsp parsley, minced

DIRECTIONS:
Place all the ingredients—except the parsley—into a pan that fits your air fryer, and stir. Put the pan into your air fryer and cook at 370 degrees F for 25 minutes. Add the parsley, stir, divide between plates, and serve.

NUTRITION:
calories 161, fat 4, fiber 6, carbs 15, protein 6

SPRING CAULIFLOWER PUREE
Preparation time: 5 min | Cooking time: 10 min | Servings: 4

INGREDIENTS:

- 1 cauliflower, florets separated and steamed
- Salt and black pepper to taste
- ½ cup veggie stock, heated up
- ½ tsp turmeric powder
- 1 tbsp butter
- 3 spring onions, chopped

DIRECTIONS:
In a pan that fits your air fryer, mix the cauliflower with the stock, salt, pepper, and turmeric; then stir well. Place the pan in the fryer and cook at 360 degrees F for 10 minutes. Mash the cauliflower mixture using a potato masher, adding the butter and the spring onions. Stir, divide between plates, and serve.

NUTRITION:
calories 140, fat 2, fiber 6, carbs 15, protein 4

CREAMY PARSNIPS
Preparation time: 10 min | Cooking time: 15 min | Servings: 4

INGREDIENTS:

- 4 parsnips, peeled and chopped
- Salt and black pepper to taste
- 1 yellow onion, chopped
- ¼ cup sour cream
- ½ cup chicken stock, heated up

DIRECTIONS:
In a pan that fits your air fryer, place all ingredients except the sour cream; stir well. Place the pan in the air fryer and cook at 370 degrees F for 15 minutes. Mash the parsnip mixture, adding the sour cream; stir well

again. Divide between plates and serve as a side dish.

NUTRITION:
calories 151, fat 3, fiber 6, carbs 11, protein 4

CARROT SOUFFLE
Preparation time: 10 min | Cooking time: 15 min | Servings: 4

INGREDIENTS:

- 1½ pounds carrots, peeled and chopped
- 1 tbsp butter, softened
- Salt and black
- pepper to taste
- 1 cup chicken stock, heated up
- 1 tbsp honey
- 1 tsp brown sugar

DIRECTIONS:
In a pan that fits your air fryer, mix the carrots with the stock, salt, pepper, and sugar; stir well. Put the pan into the fryer and cook at 370 degrees F for 15 minutes. Transfer the carrot mixture to a blender, add the butter and the honey, and pulse well. Divide between plates and serve.

NUTRITION:
calories 100, fat 3, fiber 3, carbs 7, protein 6

BUTTERNUT MASH
Preparation time: 5 min | Cooking time: 20 min | Servings: 4

INGREDIENTS:

- 1 cup veggie stock
- 1 butternut squash, peeled and cut into medium chunks
- 2 tbsp butter, melted
- 1 yellow onion, thinly sliced
- ½ tsp apple pie spice
- Salt and black pepper to taste

DIRECTIONS:
In a pan that fits your air fryer, mix the stock, squash, onion, spice, salt, and pepper; stir well. Place the pan in the fryer and cook at 370 degrees F for 20 minutes. Transfer the squash mixture to a blender, add the butter, and pulse well. Divide between plates and serve as a side dish.

NUTRITION:
calories 200, fat 6, fiber 7, carbs 15, protein 5

CHEESY ASPARAGUS
Preparation time: 5 min | Cooking time: 10 min | Servings: 4

INGREDIENTS:

- 3 garlic cloves, minced
- 1 bunch asparagus, trimmed
- 3 tbsp butter, melted
- 3 tbsp parmesan cheese, grated

DIRECTIONS:
Mix the melted butter with the garlic, and then brush the asparagus with the mixture. Put the asparagus in the air fryer's basket, sprinkle the parmesan on top, and cook at 380 degrees F for 10 minutes. Divide the asparagus between plates and serve.

NUTRITION:
calories 141, fat 4, fiber 4, carbs 8, protein 3

NUTMEG FENNEL
Preparation time: 5 min | Cooking time: 12 min | Servings: 3

INGREDIENTS:

- 2 big fennel bulbs, sliced
- 2 tbsp butter, melted
- A pinch of ground nutmeg
- Salt and black pepper to taste

DIRECTIONS:
Place all of the ingredients into a bowl and toss. Transfer the fennel mixture to your air fryer's basket and cook at 370 degrees F for 12 minutes. Divide between plates and serve as a side dish.

NUTRITION:
calories 151, fat 3, fiber 6, carbs 8, protein 3

FRESH PEAS
Preparation time: 5 min | Cooking time: 12 min | Servings: 4

INGREDIENTS:

- 1 pound fresh peas
- 1 green onion, sliced
- 1 tbsp mint, chopped
- ¼ cup veggie stock
- 1 tbsp butter, melted
- Salt and black pepper to taste

DIRECTIONS:
Place all of the ingredients into a pan that fits your air fryer and mix well. Put the pan in the air fryer and cook at 370 degrees F for 12 minutes. Divide between plates and serve.

NUTRITION:
calories 151, fat 2, fiber 6, carbs 9, protein 5

LUNCH ARTICHOKES
Preparation time: 10 min | Cooking time: 25 min | Servings: 4

INGREDIENTS:

- 2 medium artichokes, trimmed
- Juice of ½ lemon
- A drizzle of olive oil
- Salt to taste

DIRECTIONS:
Brush the artichokes with the oil, season with salt, and put them in your air fryer's basket. Cook at 370 degrees F for 20 minutes.

NUTRITION:
calories 151, fat 3, fiber 7, carbs 8, protein 4

ORANGE CAULIFLOWER MIX

Preparation time: 5 min | Cooking time: 14 min | Servings: 4

INGREDIENTS:

- 2 small cauliflower heads, florets separated
- Juice of 1 orange
- A pinch of hot pepper flakes
- Salt and black pepper to taste
- 4 tbsp olive oil

DIRECTIONS:
Brush the cauliflower with the oil, then season with salt, pepper, and the pepper flakes. Transfer the cauliflower to your air fryer's basket and cook at 380 degrees F for 14 minutes. Divide between plates, drizzle orange juice all over, and serve.

NUTRITION:
calories 151, fat 7, fiber 4, carbs 9, protein

GARLICKY BEETS
Preparation time: 5 min | Cooking time: 20 min | Servings: 4

INGREDIENTS:

- 3 beets, trimmed, peeled, and cut into wedges
- 1 tbsp olive oil
- Salt and black pepper to taste
- 4 garlic cloves, minced
- 1 tsp lemon juice

DIRECTIONS:
Place all the ingredients in a bowl and mix well. Transfer the beets to your air fryer's basket and cook at 400 degrees F for 20 minutes. Divide between plates and serve as a side dish.

NUTRITION:
calories 121, fat 3, fiber 5, carbs 12, protein 4

PARSLEY FAVA BEANS
Preparation time: 10 min | Cooking time: 15 min | Servings: 4

INGREDIENTS:

- 3 pounds fava beans, shelled
- 1 tsp olive oil
- Salt and black pepper to taste
- 4 ounces bacon, cooked and crumbled
- ½ cup white wine
- 1 tbsp parsley, chopped

DIRECTIONS:
Place all of the ingredients into a pan that fits your air fryer and mix well. Put the pan in the air fryer and cook at 380 degrees F for 15 minutes. Divide between plates and serve as a side dish.

NUTRITION:
calories 141, fat 3, fiber 2, carbs 12, protein 3

APPLESAUCE CABBAGE
Preparation time: 10 min | Cooking time: 15 min | Servings: 4

INGREDIENTS:

- 4 garlic cloves, minced
- ½ cup red onion, chopped
- 1 tbsp olive oil
- 6 cups red cabbage, shredded
- 1 tbsp balsamic vinegar
- 3 tbsp applesauce
- Salt and black pepper to taste

DIRECTIONS:
Heat the oil up in a pan that fits your air fryer over medium-high heat. Add the onions and the garlic, stir, and cook for 1-2 minutes. Add the cabbage, vinegar, applesauce, salt, and pepper, and toss. Place the pan in the air fryer and cook at 380 degrees F for 12 minutes. Divide the cabbage mix between plates and serve as a side dish.

NUTRITION:
calories 151, fat 4, fiber 4, carbs 12, protein 3

CREAMY LETTUCE SALAD
Preparation time: 5 min | Cooking time: 15 min | Servings: 4

INGREDIENTS:

- 1 tbsp lemon juice
- 1 red bell pepper
- 1 lettuce head, torn
- Salt and black pepper to taste
- 3 tbsp yogurt
- 2 tbsp olive oil

DIRECTIONS:
In your air fryer, place the bell pepper along with the oil, salt, and pepper; air fry at 400 degrees F for 15 minutes. Cool the bell pepper down, peel, cut it into strips and put it in a bowl. Add lettuce, lemon juice, yogurt, salt, and pepper. Toss well, and serve as a side dish.

NUTRITION:
calories 150, fat 1, fiber 3, carbs 3, protein 2

CHEESY SPINACH
Preparation time: 5 min | Cooking time: 10 min | Servings: 4

INGREDIENTS:

- 14 ounces spinach
- 1 tbsp olive oil
- 2 eggs, whisked
- 2 tbsp milk
- 3 ounces cottage cheese
- Salt and black pepper to taste
- 1 yellow onion, chopped

DIRECTIONS:
In a pan that fits your air fryer, heat up the oil over medium heat, add the onions, stir, and sauté for 2 minutes. Add all other ingredients and toss. Place the pan in the air fryer and cook at 380 degrees F for 8 minutes. Divide the spinach between plates and serve as a side dish.

NUTRITION:
calories 180, fat 4, fiber 2, carbs 13, protein 4

RHUBARB WITH WALNUTS

Preparation time: 10 min | Cooking time: 15 min | Servings: 4

INGREDIENTS:

- 1 pound rhubarb, cut in chunks
- 2 tsp olive oil
- 2 tbsp orange zest
- ½ cup walnuts, chopped
- ½ tsp sugar

DIRECTIONS:
In your air fryer, mix all the listed ingredients, and toss. Cook at 380 degrees F for 15 minutes. Divide the rhubarb between plates and serve as a side dish.

NUTRITION:
calories 180, fat 4, fiber 8, carbs 12, protein 4

OREGANO POTATOES

Preparation time: 10 min | Cooking time: 30 min | Servings: 4

INGREDIENTS:

- 3 large potatoes, peeled and cut into chunks
- 1 tsp parsley, chopped
- 1 tsp chives, chopped
- 1 tsp oregano, chopped
- 1 tbsp garlic, minced
- Salt and black pepper to taste
- 2 tbsp olive oil

DIRECTIONS:
Mix all of the ingredients in your air fryer, and stir well. Cook at 370 degrees F for 30 minutes. Divide between plates and serve as a side dish.

NUTRITION:
calories 160, fat 2, fiber 3, carbs 13, protein 4

TOMATO AND CRANBERRY BEANS SALAD

Preparation time: 10 min | Cooking time: 15 min | Servings: 6

INGREDIENTS:

- 6 garlic cloves, minced
- 2½ cups canned cranberry beans, drained
- 1 yellow onion, chopped
- 2 celery ribs, chopped
- ½ tsp smoked paprika
- ½ tsp red pepper flakes
- 3 tsp basil, chopped
- Salt and black pepper to taste
- 25 ounces canned tomatoes, drained and chopped
- 10 ounces kale

DIRECTIONS:
In a pan that fits your air fryer, add all of the ingredients and mix. Place the pan in the fryer and cook at 370 degrees F for 15 minutes. Divide between plates and serve as a side salad.
Nutrition: calories 190, fat 4, fiber 4, carbs 9, protein 6

SCALLIONS AND CHILI RICE MIX

Preparation time: 5 min | Cooking time: 20 min | Servings: 4

Ingredients:

- 2 scallions, chopped
- 3 garlic cloves, minced
- 1 tbsp olive oil
- Salt and black pepper to taste
- ½ cup white rice
- 1 cup veggie stock
- 1 tsp chili sauce
- 4 endives, trimmed and shredded

DIRECTIONS:
Take the oil and grease a pan that fits your air fryer. Add all other ingredients and toss. Place the pan in the air fryer and cook at 365 degrees F for 20 minutes. Divide everything between plates and serve as a side dish.
Nutrition: calories 200, fat 7, fiber 4, carbs 9, protein 5

TOMATO CABBAGE MIX

Preparation time: 5 min | Cooking time: 12 min | Servings: 4

INGREDIENTS:

1 tbsp olive oil
1 big green cabbage head, shredded
½ cup yellow onion, chopped
2 tsp turmeric powder
Salt and black pepper to taste
4 tbsp tomato sauce

DIRECTIONS:
Take the oil and grease a pan that fits your air fryer. Add all of the other ingredients and toss. Place the pan in the fryer and cook at 365 degrees F for 12 minutes. Divide between plates and serve as a side dish.

NUTRITION:
calories 188, fat 3, fiber 4, carbs 9, protein 7

Sugary Endives Mix
Preparation time: 5 min | Cooking time: 10 min | Servings: 4

INGREDIENTS:

- 8 endives, trimmed
- Juice of 1 lime
- 1 tbsp tomato sauce
- 2 tbsp cilantro, chopped
- 1 tsp sugar
- Salt and black pepper to taste
- 3 tbsp avocado oil

DIRECTIONS:
In a bowl, mix all of the ingredients well, then transfer to your air fryer's basket. Cook at 370 degrees F for 10 minutes. Divide between plates and serve as a side dish.

NUTRITION:
calories 199, fat 6, fiber 6, carbs 9, protein 6

MUNG BEANS MIX

Preparation time: 10 min | Cooking time: 16 min | Servings: 3

INGREDIENTS:

- 1 cup mung beans
- ½ tsp olive oil
- 1 tsp coriander, ground
- ½ tsp turmeric powder
- 1 cup veggie stock
- ½ cup red onion, chopped
- ½ tsp cumin seeds
- 3 tomatoes, chopped
- ½ tsp garam masala
- Salt and black pepper to taste
- 1 tbsp lemon juice
- 4 garlic cloves, minced

Directions:
Place all of the ingredients into a pan that fits your air fryer and toss. Place the pan in the fryer and cook at 365 degrees F for 16 minutes. Divide the mix between plates and serve as a side dish.

Nutrition:
calories 199, fat 6, fiber 4, carbs 12, protein 6

GINGER LENTILS MIX WITH SPINACH
Preparation time: 10 min | Cooking time: 15 min | Servings: 4

Ingredients:
- 1 cup canned brown lentils, drained
- 1 tsp olive oil
- 2 tomatoes, chopped
- 4 garlic cloves, minced
- 1 tsp ginger, grated
- ½ tsp turmeric powder
- ¼ tsp cinnamon powder
- ¼ tsp cardamom powder
- Salt and black pepper to taste
- 8 ounces baby spinach

Directions:
In a pan that fits your air fryer, add all of the listed ingredients and toss. Place the pan the fryer and cook at 370 degrees F for 15 minutes. Divide the lentils between plates and serve as a side dish.

Nutrition:
calories 188, fat 4, fiber 8, carbs 15, protein 7

INDIAN POTATOES WITH CILANTRO
Preparation time: 10 min | Cooking time: 20 min | Servings: 5

Ingredients:
- 2 pounds red potatoes, cubed
- ½ tsp mustard seeds
- 1 tsp garlic, minced
- ¼ cup veggie stock
- ½ cup mint
- ½ cup cilantro
- 1 tsp ginger, grated
- 2 tsp lime juice
- Salt and black pepper to taste

Directions:
In a blender, add the stock, mint, cilantro, ginger, lime juice, salt, and pepper; pulse well. Then place this mint mix into a pan that fits your air fryer, along with the remaining ingredients, and toss. Place the pan in the fryer and cook at 370 degrees F for 20 minutes. Divide the potatoes between plates and serve as a side dish.

Nutrition:
calories 199, fat 4, fiber 7, carbs 12, protein 6

CREAMY POTATO WEDGES
Preparation time: 10 min | Cooking time: 25 min | Servings: 4

Ingredients:
- 2 potatoes, cut into wedges
- 1 tbsp olive oil
- Salt and black pepper to the taste
- 3 tbsp sour cream
- 2 tbsp sweet chili sauce

Directions:
In a bowl, mix potato wedges with oil, salt and pepper, toss well, add to air fryer's basket and cook at 360 degrees F for 25 minutes, flipping them once. Divide potato wedges on plates, drizzle sour cream and chili sauce all over and serve them as a side dish.

Nutrition: calories 171, fat 8, fiber 9, carbs 18, protein 7

MUSHROOM SIDE DISH
Preparation time: 10 min | Cooking time: 8 min | Servings: 4

Ingredients:
- 10 button mushrooms, stems removed
- 1 tbsp Italian seasoning
- Salt and black pepper to the taste
- 2 tbsp cheddar cheese, grated
- 1 tbsp olive oil
- 2 tbsp mozzarella, grated
- 1 tbsp dill, chopped

Directions:
In a bowl, mix mushrooms with Italian seasoning, salt, pepper, oil and dill and rub well. Arrange mushrooms in your air fryer's basket, sprinkle mozzarella and cheddar in each and cook them at 360 degrees F for 8 minutes. Divide them on plates and serve them as a side dish.

Nutrition:
calories 241, fat 7, fiber 8, carbs 14, protein 6

CURRY POTATO FRIES
Preparation time: 10 min | Cooking time: 20 min | Servings: 2

Ingredients:
- 2 sweet potatoes, peeled and cut into medium fries
- Salt and black pepper to the taste
- 2 tbsp olive oil
- ½ tsp curry powder
- ¼ tsp coriander, ground
- ¼ cup ketchup
- 2 tbsp mayonnaise
- ½ tsp cumin, ground
- A pinch of ginger powder
- A pinch of cinnamon powder

DIRECTIONS:
In your air fryer's basket, mix sweet potato fries with salt, pepper, coriander, curry powder and oil, toss well and cook at 370 degrees F for 20 minutes, flipping them once. Meanwhile, in a bowl, mix ketchup with mayo, cumin, ginger and cinnamon and whisk well. Divide fries on plates, drizzle ketchup mix over them and serve as a side dish.

NUTRITION:
calories 200, fat 5, fiber 8, carbs 9, protein 7

CORN WITH PAPRIKA AND FETA
Preparation time: 10 min | Cooking time: 15 min | Servings: 2

INGREDIENTS:

- 2 corns on the cob, husks removed
- A drizzle of olive oil
- ½ cup feta cheese, grated
- 2 tsp sweet paprika
- Juice from 2 limes

DIRECTIONS:
Rub corn with oil and paprika, place in your air fryer and cook at 400 degrees F for 15 minutes, flipping once. Divide corn on plates, sprinkle cheese on top, drizzle lime juice and serve as a side dish.

NUTRITION:
calories 200, fat 5, fiber 2, carbs 6, protein 6

HERBED POTATOES
Preparation time: 10 min | Cooking time: 20 min | Servings: 2

INGREDIENTS:

- 2 potatoes, peeled and thinly sliced almost all the way horizontally
- 2 tbsp olive oil
- 1 tsp garlic, minced
- Salt and black pepper to the taste
- ½ tsp oregano, dried
- ½ tsp basil, dried
- ½ tsp sweet paprika

DIRECTIONS:
In a bowl, mix oil with garlic, salt, pepper, oregano, basil and paprika and whisk really well. Rub potatoes with this mix, place them in your air fryer's basket and fry them at 360 degrees F for 20 minutes. Divide them on plates and serve as a side dish.

NUTRITION:
calories 172, fat 6, fiber 6, carbs 9, protein 6

GARLIC BRUSSELS SPROUTS MIX
Preparation time: 10 min | Cooking time: 15 min | Servings: 4

INGREDIENTS:

- 1 pound Brussels sprouts, trimmed and halved
- Salt and black pepper to the taste
- 6 tsp olive oil
- ½ tsp thyme, chopped
- ½ cup mayonnaise
- 2 tbsp roasted garlic, crushed

DIRECTIONS:
In your air fryer, mix Brussels sprouts with salt, pepper and oil, toss well and cook them at 390 degrees F for 15 minutes. Meanwhile, in a bowl, mix thyme with mayo and garlic and whisk well. Divide Brussels sprouts on plates, drizzle garlic sauce all over and serve as a side dish.

NUTRITION:
calories 172, fat 6, fiber 8, carbs 12, protein 6

CREAMY AIR FRIED POTATO SIDE DISH
Preparation time: 10 min | Cooking time: 1 hour and 20 min | Servings: 2

INGREDIENTS:

- 1 big potato
- 2 bacon strips, cooked and chopped
- 1 tsp olive oil
- 1/3 cup cheddar cheese, shredded
- 1 tbsp green onions, chopped
- Salt and black pepper to the taste
- 1 tbsp butter
- 2 tbsp heavy cream

DIRECTIONS:
Rub potato with oil, season with salt and pepper, place in preheated air fryer and cook at 400 degrees F for 30 minutes. Flip potato, cook for 30 minutes more, transfer to a cutting board, cool it down, slice in half lengthwise and scoop pulp in a bowl. Add bacon, cheese, butter, heavy cream, green onions, salt and pepper, stir well and stuff potato skins with this mix. Return potatoes to your air fryer and cook them at 400 degrees F for 20 minutes. Divide among plates and serve as a side dish.

NUTRITION:
calories 172, fat 5, fiber 7, carbs 9, protein 4

GREEN BEANS AND SHALLOTS MIX
Preparation time: 10 min | Cooking time: 25 min | Servings: 4

INGREDIENTS:

- 1 and ½ pounds green beans, trimmed and steamed for 2 minutes
- Salt and black pepper to the taste
- ½ pound shallots, chopped
- ¼ cup almonds, toasted
- 2 tbsp olive oil

DIRECTIONS:
In your air fryer's basket, mix green beans with salt, pepper, shallots, almonds and oil, toss well and cook at 400 degrees F for 25 minutes. Divide among plates and serve as a side dish.

NUTRITION:
calories 152, fat 3, fiber 6, carbs 7, protein 4

SUGARY AIR FRIED PUMPKIN

Preparation time: 10 min | Cooking time: 12 min | Servings: 4

INGREDIENTS:

- 1 and ½ pound pumpkin, deseeded, sliced and roughly chopped
- 3 garlic cloves, minced
- 1 tbsp olive oil
- A pinch of sea salt
- A pinch of brown sugar
- A pinch of nutmeg, ground
- A pinch of cinnamon powder

DIRECTIONS:

In your air fryer's basket, mix pumpkin with garlic, oil, salt, brown sugar, cinnamon and nutmeg, toss well, cover and cook at 370 degrees F for 12 minutes. Divide among plates and serve as a side dish.

NUTRITION:

calories 200, fat 5, fiber 4, carbs 7, protein 4

CRACKER MUSHROOMS

Preparation time: 10 min | Cooking time: 15 min | Servings: 3

INGREDIENTS:

- 9 button mushroom caps
- 3 cream cracker slices, crumbled
- 1 egg white
- 2 tbsp parmesan, grated
- 1 tsp Italian seasoning
- A pinch of salt and black pepper
- 1 tbsp butter, melted

DIRECTIONS:

In a bowl, mix crackers with egg white, parmesan, Italian seasoning, butter, salt and pepper, stir well and stuff mushrooms with this mix. Arrange mushrooms in your air fryer's basket and cook them at 360 degrees F for 15 minutes. Divide among plates and serve as a side dish.

NUTRITION:

calories 124, fat 4, fiber 4, carbs 7, protein 3

PARMESAN POTATOES

Preparation time: 10 min | Cooking time: 20 min | Servings: 6

INGREDIENTS:

- 2 tbsp parsley, chopped
- 5 garlic cloves, minced
- ½ tsp basil, dried
- ½ tsp oregano, dried
- 3 pounds red potatoes, halved
- 1 tsp thyme, dried
- 2 tbsp olive oil
- Salt and black pepper to the taste
- 2 tbsp butter
- 1/3 cup parmesan, grated

DIRECTIONS:

In a bowl, mix potato halves with parsley, garlic, basil, oregano, thyme, salt, pepper, oil and butter, toss really well and transfer to your air fryer's basket. Cover and cook at 400 degrees F for 20 minutes, flipping them once. Sprinkle parmesan on top, divide potatoes on plates and serve as a side dish.

NUTRITION:

calories 162, fat 5, fiber 5, carbs 7, protein 5

EGGPLANT PEPPER MIX

Preparation time: 10 min | Cooking time: 10 min | Servings: 4

INGREDIENTS:

- 8 baby eggplants, scooped in the center and pulp reserved
- Salt and black pepper to the taste
- A pinch of oregano, dried
- 1 green bell pepper, chopped
- 1 tbsp tomato paste
- 1 bunch coriander, chopped
- ½ tsp garlic powder
- 1 tbsp olive oil
- 1 yellow onion, chopped
- 1 tomato chopped

DIRECTIONS:

Heat up a pan with the oil over medium heat, add onion, stir and cook for 1 minute. Add salt, pepper, eggplant pulp, oregano, green bell pepper, tomato paste, garlic powder, coriander and tomato, stir, cook for 1-2 minutes more, take off heat and cool down. Stuff eggplants with this mix, place them in your air fryer's basket and cook at 360 degrees F for 8 minutes. Divide eggplants on plates and serve them as a side dish.

NUTRITION:

calories 200, fat 3, fiber 7, carbs 12, protein 4

CREAMY CHEDDAR MUSHROOMS

Preparation time: 10 min | Cooking time: 10 min | Servings: 6

INGREDIENTS:

- 2 bacon strips, chopped
- 1 yellow onion, chopped
- 1 green bell pepper, chopped
- 24 mushrooms, stems removed
- 1 carrot, grated
- ½ cup sour cream
- 1 cup cheddar cheese, grated
- Salt and black pepper to the taste

DIRECTIONS:

Heat up a pan over medium high heat, add bacon, onion, bell pepper and carrot, stir and cook for 1 minute. Add salt, pepper and sour cream, stir cook for 1 minute more, take off heat and cool down. Stuff mushrooms with this mix, sprinkle cheese on top and cook at 360 degrees F for 8 minutes. Divide among plates and serve as a side dish.

NUTRITION:

calories 211, fat 4, fiber 7, carbs 8, protein 3

EGGPLANT FRIES

Preparation time: 10 min | Cooking time: 5 min | Servings: 4

INGREDIENTS:

INGREDIENTS:

- Cooking spray
- 1 eggplant, peeled
- 2 tbsp milk
- 1 egg, whisked
- 2 cups panko bread crumbs
- ½ cup Italian cheese, shredded
- A pinch of salt and black pepper

DIRECTIONS:
In a bowl, mix egg with milk, salt and pepper and whisk well. In another bowl, mix panko with cheese and stir. Dip eggplant fries in egg mix, then coat in panko mix, place them in your air fryer greased with cooking spray and cook at 400 degrees F for 5 minutes. Divide among plates and serve as a side dish.

NUTRITION:
calories 162, fat 5, fiber 5, carbs 7, protein 6

BUTTERMILK TOMATOES

Preparation time: 10 min | Cooking time: 5 min | Servings: 4

INGREDIENTS:

- 2 green tomatoes, sliced
- Salt and black pepper to the taste
- ½ cup flour
- 1 cup buttermilk
- 1 cup panko bread crumbs
- ½ tbsp Creole seasoning
- Cooking spray

DIRECTIONS:
Season tomato slices with salt and pepper. Put flour in a bowl, buttermilk in another and panko crumbs and Creole seasoning in a third one. Dredge tomato slices in flour, then in buttermilk and panko bread crumbs, place them in your air fryer's basket greased with cooking spray and cook them at 400 degrees F for 5 minutes. Divide among plates and serve as a side dish.

NUTRITION:
calories 124, fat 5, fiber 7, carbs 9, protein 4

CAULIFLOWER RICE PARMESAN CAKES

Preparation time: 10 min | Cooking time: 10 min | Servings: 6

INGREDIENTS:

- 3 and ½ cups cauliflower rice
- 2 eggs
- ¼ cup white flour
- ½ cup parmesan, grated
- Salt and black pepper to the taste
- Cooking spray

DIRECTIONS:
In a bowl, mix cauliflower rice with salt and pepper, stir and squeeze excess water. Transfer cauliflower to another bowl, add eggs, salt, pepper, flour and parmesan, stir really well and shape your cakes. Grease your air fryer with cooking spray, heat it up at 400 degrees, add cauliflower cakes and cook them for 10 minutes flipping them halfway. Divide cakes on plates and serve as a side dish.

NUTRITION:
calories 125, fat 2, fiber 6, carbs 8, protein 3

BRUSSELS SPROUTS WITH CREAM

Preparation time: 10 min | Cooking time: 25 min | Servings: 8

INGREDIENTS:

- 3 pounds Brussels sprouts, halved
- A drizzle of olive oil
- 1 pound bacon, chopped
- Salt and black pepper to the taste
- 4 tbsp butter
- 3 shallots, chopped
- 1 cup milk
- 2 cups heavy cream
- ¼ tsp nutmeg, ground
- 3 tbsp prepared horseradish

DIRECTIONS:
Preheated you air fryer at 370 degrees F, add oil, bacon, salt and pepper and Brussels sprouts and toss. Add butter, shallots, heavy cream, milk, nutmeg and horseradish, toss again and cook for 25 minutes. Divide among plates and serve as a side dish.

NUTRITION:
calories 214, fat 5, fiber 8, carbs 12, protein 5

BUTTERMILK AND CHEESE BISCUITS

Preparation time: 10 min | Cooking time: 20 min | Servings: 8

INGREDIENTS:

- 2 and 1/3 cup self-rising flour
- ½ cup butter+ 1 tbsp, melted
- 2 tbsp sugar
- ½ cup cheddar cheese, grated
- 1 and 1/3 cup buttermilk
- 1 cup flour

DIRECTIONS:
In a bowl, mix self-rising flour with ½-cup butter, sugar, cheddar cheese and buttermilk and stir until you obtain a dough. Spread 1 cup flour on a working surface, roll dough, flatten it, cut 8 circles with a cookie cutter and coat them with flour. Line your air fryer's basket with tin foil, add biscuits, brush them with melted butter and cook them at 380 degrees F for 20 minutes. Divide among plates and serve as a side.

NUTRITION:
calories 221, fat 3, fiber 8, carbs 12, protein 4

CRISPY ZUCCHINI FRIES

Preparation time: 10 min | Cooking time: 12 min | Servings: 4

INGREDIENTS:

- 1 zucchini, cut into medium sticks
- A drizzle of olive oil
- Salt and black pepper to the taste
- 2 eggs, whisked
- 1 cup bread crumbs
- ½ cup flour

DIRECTIONS:
Put flour in a bowl and mix with salt and pepper and stir. Put breadcrumbs in another bowl. In a third bowl mix eggs with a pinch of salt and pepper. Dredge zucchini fries in flour, then in eggs and in bread crumbs at the end. Grease your air fryer with some olive oil, heat up at 400 degrees F, add zucchini fries and cook them for 12 minutes. Serve them as a side dish.

NUTRITION:
calories 172, fat 3, fiber 3, carbs 7, protein 3

THYME TOMATOES
Preparation time: 10 min | Cooking time: 15 min | Servings: 4

INGREDIENTS:

- 4 big tomatoes, halved and insides scooped out
- Salt and black pepper to the taste
- 1 tbsp olive oil
- 2 garlic cloves, minced
- ½ tsp thyme, chopped

DIRECTIONS:
In your air fryer, mix tomatoes with salt, pepper, oil, garlic and thyme, toss and cook at 390 degrees F for 15 minutes. Divide among plates and serve them as a side dish.

NUTRITION:
calories 112, fat 1, fiber 3, carbs 4, protein 4

SWEET PAPRIKA PEPPERS
Preparation time: 10 min | Cooking time: 20 min | Servings: 4

INGREDIENTS:

- 1 tbsp sweet paprika
- 1 tbsp olive oil
- 4 red bell peppers, cut into medium strips
- 4 green bell peppers, cut into medium strips
- 4 yellow bell peppers, cut into medium strips
- 1 yellow onion, chopped
- Salt and black pepper to the taste

DIRECTIONS:
In your air fryer, mix red bell peppers with green and yellow ones. Add paprika, oil, onion, salt and pepper, toss and cook at 350 degrees F for 20 minutes. Divide among plates and serve as a side dish.

NUTRITION:
calories 142, fat 4, fiber 4, carbs 7, protein 4

GREEK ENDIVES
Preparation time: 10 min | Cooking time: 10 min | Servings: 6

INGREDIENTS:

- 6 endives, trimmed and halved
- 1 tsp garlic powder
- ½ cup Greek yogurt
- ½ tsp curry powder
- Salt and black pepper to the taste
- 3 tbsp lemon juice

DIRECTIONS:
In a bowl, mix endives with garlic powder, yogurt, curry powder, salt, pepper and lemon juice, toss, leave aside for 10 minutes and transfer to your preheated air fryer at 350 degrees F. Cook endives for 10 minutes, divide them on plates and serve as a side dish.

NUTRITION:
calories 100, fat 2, fiber 2, carbs 7, protein 4

PROVENCE CARROTS
Preparation time: 10 min | Cooking time: 20 min | Servings: 4

INGREDIENTS:

- 1 pound baby carrots
- 2 tsp olive oil
- 1 tsp herbs de Provence
- 4 tbsp orange juice

DIRECTIONS:
In your air fryer's basket, mix carrots with herbs de Provence, oil and orange juice, toss and cook at 320 degrees F for 20 minutes. Divide among plates and serve as a side dish.

NUTRITION:
calories 112, fat 2, fiber 3, carbs 4, protein 3

VERMOUTH MUSHROOMS
Preparation time: 10 min | Cooking time: 25 min | Servings: 4

INGREDIENTS:

- 1 tbsp olive oil
- 2 pounds white mushrooms
- 2 tbsp white vermouth
- 2 tsp herbs de Provence
- 2 garlic cloves, minced

DIRECTIONS:
In your air fryer, mix oil with mushrooms, herbs de Provence and garlic, toss and cook at 350 degrees F for 20 minutes. Add vermouth, toss and cook for 5 minutes more. Divide among plates and serve as a side dish.

NUTRITION:
calories 121, fat 2, fiber 5, carbs 7, protein 4

MAPLE PARSNIPS
Preparation time: 10 min | Cooking time: 40 min | Servings: 6

INGREDIENTS:

- 2 pounds parsnips, peeled and cut into medium chunks
- 2 tbsp maple syrup
- 1 tbsp parsley flakes, dried
- 1 tbsp olive oil

DIRECTIONS:
Preheat your air fryer at 360 degrees F, add oil and heat it up as well. Add parsnips, parsley flakes and maple syrup, toss and

cook them for 40 minutes. Divide among plates and serve as a side dish.

NUTRITION:
calories 124, fat 3, fiber 3, carbs 7, protein 4

HERBED RISOTTO
Preparation time: 10 min | Cooking time: 30 min | Servings: 8

INGREDIENTS:

- 5 cups veggie stock
- 3 tbsp olive oil
- 2 yellow onions, chopped
- 2 garlic cloves, minced
- ¾ pound barley
- 3 ounces mushrooms, sliced
- 2 ounces skim milk
- 1 tsp thyme, dried
- 1 tsp tarragon, dried
- Salt and black pepper to the taste
- 2 pounds sweet potato

DIRECTIONS:
Put stock in a pot, add barley, stir, bring to a boil over medium heat and cook for 15 minutes. Heat up your air fryer at 350 degrees F, add oil and heat it up. Add barley, onions, garlic, mushrooms, milk, salt, pepper, tarragon and sweet potato, stir and cook for 15 minutes more. Divide among plates and serve as a side dish.

NUTRITION:
calories 124, fat 4, fiber 4, carbs 6, protein 4

SWEET BEETS
Preparation time: 10 min | Cooking time: 40 min | Servings: 8

INGREDIENTS:

- 3 pounds small beets, trimmed
- 4 tbsp maple syrup
- 1 tbsp duck fat

DIRECTIONS:
Heat up your air fryer at 360 degrees F, add duck fat and heat it up. Add beets and maple syrup, toss and cook for 40 minutes. Divide among plates and serve as a side dish.

NUTRITION:
calories 121, fat 3, fiber 2, carbs 3, protein 4

CHICKEN AND BEER RISOTTO
Preparation time: 10 min | Cooking time: 30 min | Servings: 4

INGREDIENTS:

- 2 tbsp olive oil
- 2 yellow onions, chopped
- 1 cup mushrooms, sliced
- 1 tsp basil, dried
- 1 tsp oregano, dried
- 1 and ½ cups rice
- 2 cups beer
- 2 cups chicken stock
- 1 tbsp butter
- ½ cup parmesan, grated

DIRECTIONS:

In a dish that fits your air fryer, mix oil with onions, mushrooms, basil and oregano and stir. Add rice, beer, butter, stock and butter, stir again, place in your air fryer's basket and cook at 350 degrees F for 30 minutes. Divide among plates and serve with grated parmesan on top as a side dish.

NUTRITION:
calories 142, fat 4, fiber 4, carbs 6, protein 4

SOY RICE
Preparation time: 10 min | Cooking time: 40 min | Servings: 8

INGREDIENTS:

- 1 tbsp peanut oil
- 1 tbsp sesame oil
- 4 tbsp soy sauce
- 3 garlic cloves, minced
- 1 tbsp ginger, grated
- Juice from ½ lemon
- 1 cauliflower head, riced
- 9 ounces water chestnuts, drained
- ¾ cup peas
- 15 ounces mushrooms, chopped
- 1 egg, whisked

DIRECTIONS:
In your air fryer, mix cauliflower rice with peanut oil, sesame oil, soy sauce, garlic, ginger and lemon juice, stir, cover and cook at 350 degrees F for 20 minutes. Add chestnuts, peas, mushrooms and egg, toss and cook at 360 degrees F for 20 minutes more. Divide among plates and serve for breakfast.

NUTRITION:
calories 142, fat 3, fiber 2, carbs 6, protein 4

WALNUT CARROTS MIX
Preparation time: 10 min | Cooking time: 40 min | Servings: 4

INGREDIENTS:

- 1 pound baby carrots
- 2 tsp walnut oil
- 1 pound rhubarb, roughly chopped
- 1 orange, peeled, cut into medium segments and zest grated
- ½ cup walnuts, halved
- ½ tsp stevia

DIRECTIONS:
Put the oil in your air fryer, add carrots, toss and fry them at 380 degrees F for 20 minutes. Add rhubarb, orange zest, stevia and walnuts, toss and cook for 20 minutes more. Add orange segments, toss and serve as a side dish.

NUTRITION:
calories 172, fat 2, fiber 3, carbs 4, protein 4

ROASTED EGGPLANT
Preparation time: 10 min | Cooking time: 20 min | Servings: 6

INGREDIENTS:

- 1 and ½ pounds eggplant, cubed
- 1 tbsp olive oil
- 1 tsp garlic pow-

der
- 1 tsp onion powder
- 1 tsp sumac
- 2 tsp za'atar
- Juice from ½ lemon
- 2 bay leaves

DIRECTIONS:
In your air fryer, mix eggplant cubes with oil, garlic powder, onion powder, sumac, za'atar, lemon juice and bay leaves, toss and cook at 370 degrees F for 20 minutes. Divide among plates and serve as a side dish.

NUTRITION:
calories 172, fat 4, fiber 7, carbs 12, protein 3

LEMONY BROCCOLI
Preparation time: 10 min | Cooking time: 20 min | Servings: 4

INGREDIENTS:

- 1 tbsp duck fat
- 1 broccoli head, florets separated
- 3 garlic cloves, minced
- Juice from ½ lemon
- 1 tbsp sesame seeds

DIRECTIONS:
Heat up your air fryer at 350 degrees F, add duck fat and heat as well. Add broccoli, garlic, lemon juice and sesame seeds, toss and cook for 20 minutes. Divide among plates and serve as a side dish.

NUTRITION:
calories 132, fat 3, fiber 3, carbs 6, protein 4

CRISPY ONION RINGS
Preparation time: 10 min | Cooking time: 10 min | Servings: 3

INGREDIENTS:

- 1 onion cut into medium slices and rings separated
- 1 and ¼ cups white flour
- A pinch of salt
- 1 egg
- 1 cup milk
- 1 tsp baking powder
- ¾ cup bread crumbs

DIRECTIONS:
In a bowl, mix flour with salt and baking powder, stir, dredge onion rings in this mix and place them on a separate plate. Add milk and egg to flour mix and whisk well. Dip onion rings in this mix, dredge them in breadcrumbs, put them in your air fryer's basket and cook them at 360 degrees F for 10 minutes. Divide among plates and serve as a side dish for a steak.

NUTRITION:
calories 140, fat 8, fiber 20, carbs 12, protein 3

PARMESAN POTATO PATTIES
Preparation time: 10 min | Cooking time: 8 min | Servings: 4

INGREDIENTS:

- 4 potatoes, cubed, boiled and mashed
- 1 cup parmesan, grated
- Salt and black pepper to the taste
- A pinch of nutmeg
- 2 egg yolks
- 2 tbsp white flour
- 3 tbsp chives, chopped
- For the breading:
- ¼ cup white flour
- 3 tbsp vegetable oil
- 2 eggs, whisked
- ¼ cup bread crumbs

DIRECTIONS:
In a bowl, mix mashed potatoes with egg yolks, salt, pepper, nutmeg, parmesan, chives and 2 tbsp flour, stir well, shape medium cakes and place them on a plate. In another bowl, mix vegetable oil with bread crumbs and stir. Put whisked eggs in a third bowl and ¼ cup flour in a forth one. Dip cakes in flour, then in eggs and in breadcrumbs at the end, place them in your air fryer's basket, cook them at 390 degrees F for 8 minutes, divide among plates and serve as a side dish.

NUTRITION:
calories 140, fat 3, fiber 4, carbs 17, protein 4

ROSEMARY FRIED POTATO CHIPS
Preparation time: 30 min | Cooking time: 30 min | Servings: 4

INGREDIENTS:

- 4 potatoes, scrubbed, peeled into thin chips, soaked in water for 30 minutes, drained
- and pat dried
- Salt the taste
- 1 tbsp olive oil
- 2 tsp rosemary, chopped

DIRECTIONS:
In a bowl, mix potato chips with salt and oil toss to coat, place them in your air fryer's basket and cook at 330 degrees F for 30 minutes. Divide among plates, sprinkle rosemary all over and serve as a side dish.

NUTRITION:
calories 200, fat 4, fiber 4, carbs 14, protein 5

AVOCADO CRISPY FRIES
Preparation time: 10 min | Cooking time: 10 min | Servings: 4

Ingredients:

1 avocado, pitted, peeled, sliced and cut into medium fries
Salt and black pepper to the taste
½ cup panko bread crumbs
1 tbsp lemon juice
1 egg, whisked
1 tbsp olive oil

DIRECTIONS:
In a bowl, mix panko with salt and pepper and stir. In another bowl, mix egg with a pinch of salt and whisk. In a third bowl, mix avocado fries with lemon juice and oil and toss. Dip fries in egg, then in panko, place them in your air fryer's basket and cook at 390 degrees F for 10 minutes, shaking half-

way. Divide among plates and serve as a side dish.

NUTRITION:
calories 130, fat 11, fiber 3, carbs 16, protein 4

VEGGIE FRIES
Preparation time: 10 min | Cooking time: 30 min | Servings: 4

INGREDIENTS:

- 4 parsnips, cut into medium sticks
- 2 sweet potatoes cut into medium sticks
- 4 mixed carrots cut into medium sticks
- Salt and black pepper to the taste
- 2 tbsp rosemary, chopped
- 2 tbsp olive oil
- 1 tbsp flour
- ½ tsp garlic powder

DIRECTIONS:
Put veggie fries in a bowl, add oil, garlic powder, salt, pepper, flour and rosemary and toss to coat. Put sweet potatoes in your preheated air fryer, cook them for 10 minutes at 350 degrees F and transfer them to a platter. Put parsnip fries in your air fryer, cook for 5 minutes and transfer over potato fries. Put carrot fries in your air fryer, cook for 15 minutes at 350 degrees F and transfer to the platter with the other fries. Divide veggie fries on plates and serve them as a side dish.

NUTRITION:
calories 100, fat 0, fiber 4, carbs 7, protein 4

GREEN CREAMY CABBAGE
Preparation time: 10 min | Cooking time: 20 minute | Servings: 4

INGREDIENTS:

- 1 green cabbage head, chopped
- 1 yellow onion, chopped
- Salt and black pepper to the taste
- 4 bacon slices, chopped
- 1 cup whipped cream
- 2 tbsp cornstarch

DIRECTIONS:
Put cabbage, bacon and onion in your air fryer. In a bowl, mix cornstarch with cream, salt and pepper, stir and add over cabbage. Toss, cook at 400 degrees F for 20 minutes, divide among plates and serve as a side dish.

NUTRITION:
calories 208, fat 10, fiber 3, carbs 16, protein 5

SPICY PAPRIKA CHIPS
Preparation time: 10 min | Cooking time: 6 min | Servings: 4

INGREDIENTS:

- 8 corn tortillas, cut into triangles
- Salt and black pepper to the taste
- 1 tbsp olive oil
- A pinch of garlic powder
- A pinch of sweet paprika

DIRECTIONS:
In a bowl, mix tortilla chips with oil, add salt, pepper, garlic powder and paprika, toss well, place them in your air fryer's basket and cook them at 400 degrees F for 6 minutes. Serve them as a side for a fish dish.

NUTRITION:
calories 53, fat 1, fiber 1, carbs 6, protein 4

ZUCCHINI CROQUETTES
Preparation time: 10 min | Cooking time: 10 min | Servings: 4

INGREDIENTS:

- 1 carrot, grated
- 1 zucchini, grated
- 2 slices of bread, crumbled
- 1 egg
- Salt and black pepper to the taste
- ½ tsp sweet paprika
- 1 tsp garlic, minced
- 2 tbsp parmesan cheese, grated
- 1 tbsp corn flour

DIRECTIONS:
Put zucchini in a bowl, add salt, leave aside for 10 minutes, squeeze excess water and transfer them to another bowl. Add carrots, salt, pepper, paprika, garlic, flour, parmesan, egg and bread crumbs, stir well, shape 8 croquettes, place them in your air fryer and cook at 360 degrees F for 10 minutes. Divide among plates and serve as a side dish

NUTRITION:
calories 100, fat 3, fiber 1, carbs 7, protein 4

GREEK SALTY POTATOES
Preparation time: 10 min | Cooking time: 20 min | Servings: 4
Ingredients:

- 1 and ½ pounds potatoes, peeled and cubed
- 2 tbsp olive oil
- Salt and black pepper to the taste
- 1 tbsp hot paprika
- 1 cup Greek yogurt

DIRECTIONS:
Put potatoes in a bowl, add water to cover, leave aside for 10 minutes, drain, pat dry them, transfer to another bowl, add salt, pepper, paprika and half of the oil and toss them well. Put potatoes in your air fryer's basket and cook at 360 degrees F for 20 minutes. In a bowl, mix yogurt with salt, pepper and the rest of the oil and whisk. Divide potatoes on plates, drizzle yogurt dressing all over, toss them and serve as a side dish.

NUTRITION:
calories 170, fat 3, fiber 5, carbs 20, protein 5

NUTMEG MUSHROOM CAKES
Preparation time: 10 min | Cooking time: 8 min | Servings: 8

INGREDIENTS:

- 4 ounces mushrooms, chopped
- 1 yellow onion, chopped
- Salt and black pepper to the taste
- ½ tsp nutmeg, ground
- 2 tbsp olive oil
- 1 tbsp butter
- 1 and ½ tbsp flour
- 1 tbsp bread crumbs
- 14 ounces milk

DIRECTIONS:
Heat up a pan with the butter over medium high heat, add onion and mushrooms, stir, cook for 3 minutes, add flour, stir well again and take off heat. Add milk gradually, salt, pepper and nutmeg, stir and leave aside to cool down completely. In a bowl, mix oil with bread crumbs and whisk. Take spoonfuls of the mushroom filling, add to breadcrumbs mix, coat well, shape patties out of this mix, place them in your air fryer's basket and cook at 400 degrees F for 8 minutes. Divide among plates and serve as a side for a steak.

NUTRITION:
calories 192, fat 2, fiber 1, carbs 16, protein 6

ROASTED GREEK PEPPERS DISH

Preparation time: 10 min | Cooking time: 10 min | Servings: 4

INGREDIENTS:

- 1 tbsp lemon juice
- 1 red bell pepper
- 1 green bell pepper
- 1 yellow bell pepper
- 1 lettuce head, cut into strips
- 1 ounce rocket leaves
- Salt and black pepper to the taste
- 3 tbsp Greek yogurt
- 2 tbsp olive oil

DIRECTIONS:
Place bell peppers in your air fryer's basket, cook at 400 degrees F for 10 minutes, transfer to a bowl, leave aside for 10 minutes, peel them, discard seeds, cut them in strips, transfer to a larger bowl, add rocket leaves and lettuce strips and toss. In a bowl, mix oil with lemon juice, yogurt, salt and pepper and whisk well. Add this over bell peppers mix, toss to coat, divide among plates and serve as a side salad.

NUTRITION:
calories 170, fat 1, fiber 1, carbs 2, protein 6

HERBED VEGGIE MIX

Preparation time: 10 min | Cooking time: 45 min | Servings: 4

INGREDIENTS:

- 1 eggplant, sliced
- 1 zucchini, sliced
- 2 red bell peppers, chopped
- 2 garlic cloves, minced
- 3 tbsp olive oil
- 1 bay leaf
- 1 thyme spring, chopped
- 2 onions, chopped
- 4 tomatoes, cut into quarters
- Salt and black pepper to the taste

DIRECTIONS:
In your air fryer's pan, mix eggplant slices with zucchini ones, bell peppers, garlic, oil, bay leaf, thyme, onions, tomatoes, salt and pepper, toss and cook them at 300 degrees F for 35 minutes. Divide among plates and serve as a side dish.

NUTRITION:
calories 200, fat 1, fiber 3, carbs 7, protein 6

AIR FRIED ZUCCHINI MIX

Preparation time: 10 min | Cooking time: 35 min | Servings: 4

INGREDIENTS:

- 6 tsp olive oil
- 1 pound zucchinis, sliced
- ½ pound carrots, cubed
- 1 yellow squash, halved, deseeded and cut into chunks
- Salt and white pepper to the taste
- 1 tbsp tarragon, chopped

DIRECTIONS:
In your air fryer's basket, mix zucchinis with carrots, squash, salt, pepper and oil, toss well and cook at 400 degrees F for 25 minutes. Divide them on plates and serve as a side dish with tarragon sprinkled on top.

NUTRITION:
calories 160, fat 2, fiber 1, carbs 5, protein 5

GINGER CAULIFLOWER

Preparation time: 10 min | Cooking time: 10 min | Servings: 4

Ingredients:

- 12 cauliflower florets, steamed
- Salt and black pepper to the taste
- ¼ tsp turmeric powder
- 1 and ½ tsp red chili powder
- 1 tbsp ginger, grated
- 2 tsp lemon juice
- 3 tbsp white flour
- 2 tbsp water
- Cooking spray
- ½ tsp corn flour

DIRECTIONS:
In a bowl, mix chili powder with turmeric powder, ginger paste, salt, pepper, lemon juice, white flour, corn flour and water, stir, add cauliflower, toss well and transfer them to your air fryer's basket. Coat them with cooking spray, cook them at 400 degrees F for 10 minutes, divide among plates and serve as a side dish.

NUTRITION:
calories 70, fat 1, fiber 2, carbs 12, protein 3

CHEDDAR CHEESY POTATOES

Preparation time: 10 min | Cooking time: 20 min | Servings: 4

INGREDIENTS:

- 2 eggs, whisked
- Salt and black pepper to the taste
- 1 tbsp cheddar cheese, grated
- 1 tbsp flour
- 2 potatoes, sliced
- 4 ounces coconut cream

Directions:
Place potato slices in your air fryer's basket and cook at 360 degrees F for 10 minutes. Meanwhile, in a bowl, mix eggs with coconut cream, salt, pepper and flour. Arrange potatoes in your air fryer's pan, add coconut cream mix over them, sprinkle cheese, return to air fryer's basket and cook at 400 degrees F for 10 minutes more. Divide among plates and serve as a side dish.

Nutrition:
calories 170, fat 4, fiber 1, carbs 15, protein 17

CAJUN ONION WEDGES
Preparation time: 10 min | Cooking time: 15 min | Servings: 4

Ingredients:

- 2 big white onions, cut into wedges
- Salt and black pepper to the taste
- 2 eggs
- ¼ cup milk
- 1/3 cup panko
- A drizzle of olive oil
- 1 and ½ tsp paprika
- 1 tsp garlic powder
- ½ tsp Cajun seasoning

Directions:
In a bowl, mix panko with Cajun seasoning and oil and stir. In another bowl, mix egg with milk, salt and pepper and stir. Sprinkle onion wedges with paprika and garlic powder, dip them in egg mix, then in bread crumbs mix, place in your air fryer's basket, cook at 360 degrees F for 10 minutes, flip and cook for 5 minutes more. Divide among plates and serve as a side dish.

Nutrition:
calories 200, fat 2, fiber 2, carbs 14, protein 7

FARRO AND RICE PILAF
Preparation time: 10 min | Cooking time: 25 min | Servings: 12

Ingredients:

- 1 shallot, chopped
- 1 tsp garlic, minced
- A drizzle of olive oil
- 1 cup farro
- ¾ cup wild rice
- 4 cups chicken stock
- Salt and black pepper to the taste
- 1 tbsp parsley, chopped
- ½ cup hazelnuts, toasted and chopped
- ¾ cup cherries, dried
- Chopped chives for serving

Directions:
In a dish that fits your air fryer, mix shallot with garlic, oil, faro, wild rice, stock, salt, pepper, parsley, hazelnuts and cherries, stir, place in your air fryer's basket and cook at 350 degrees F for 25 minutes. Divide among plates and serve as a side dish.
Nutrition: calories 142, fat 4, fiber 4, carbs 16, protein 4

CINNAMON RICE
Preparation time: 5 min | Cooking time: 30 min | Servings: 4

Ingredients:

- 2 tbsp olive oil
- 1 small yellow onion, chopped
- 2 garlic cloves, minced
- 12 ounces white rice
- 4 cups chicken stock
- 6 ounces pumpkin puree
- ½ tsp nutmeg
- 1 tsp thyme, chopped
- ½ tsp ginger, grated
- ½ tsp cinnamon powder
- ½ tsp allspice
- 4 ounces heavy cream

Directions:
In a dish that fits your air fryer, mix oil with onion, garlic, rice, stock, pumpkin puree, nutmeg, thyme, ginger, cinnamon, allspice and cream, stir well, place in your air fryer's basket and cook at 360 degrees F for 30 minutes. Divide among plates and serve as a side dish.

Nutrition:
calories 261, fat 6, fiber 7, carbs 29, protein 4

HERBED BASMATI RICE
Preparation time: 10 min | Cooking time: 25 min | Servings: 4
Ingredients:

- 2 cups basmati rice
- 1 cup mixed carrots, peas, corn and green beans
- 2 cups water
- ½ tsp green chili, minced
- ½ tsp ginger, grated
- 3 garlic cloves, minced
- 2 tbsp butter
- 1 tsp cinnamon powder
- 1 tbsp cumin seeds
- 2 bay leaves
- 3 whole cloves
- 5 black peppercorns
- 2 whole cardamoms
- 1 tbsp sugar
- Salt to the taste

Directions:
Put the water in a heat proof dish that fits your air fryer, add rice, mixed veggies, green chili, grated ginger, garlic cloves, cinnamon, cloves, butter, cumin seeds, bay leaves, cardamoms, black peppercorns, salt and sugar, stir, put in your air fryer's basket and cook at 370 degrees F for 25 minutes. Divide among plates and serve as a side dish.

Nutrition:
calories 283, fat 4, fiber 8, carbs 34, protein 14

POTATO CASSEROLE

Preparation time: 15 min | Cooking time: 40 min | Servings: 4

INGREDIENTS:

- 3 pounds sweet potatoes, scrubbed
- ¼ cup milk
- ½ tsp nutmeg, ground
- 2 tbsp white flour
- ¼ tsp allspice, ground
- Salt to the taste
- For the topping:
- ½ cup almond flour
- ½ cup walnuts, soaked, drained and ground
- ¼ cup pecans, soaked, drained and ground
- ¼ cup coconut, shredded
- 1 tbsp chia seeds
- ¼ cup sugar
- 1 tsp cinnamon powder
- 5 tbsp butter

DIRECTIONS:
Place potatoes in your air fryer's basket, prick them with a fork and cook at 360 degrees F for 30 minutes. Meanwhile, in a bowl, mix almond flour with pecans, walnuts, ¼ cup coconut, ¼ cup sugar, chia seeds, 1 tsp cinnamon and the butter and stir everything. Transfer potatoes to a cutting board, cool them, peel and place them in a baking dish that fits your air fryer. Add milk, flour, salt, nutmeg and allspice and stir. Add crumble mix you've made earlier on top, place dish in your air fryer's basket and cook at 400 degrees F for 8 minutes. Divide among plates and serve as a side dish.

NUTRITION:
calories 162, fat 4, fiber 8, carbs 18, protein 4

AIR FRIED ARTICHOKES

Preparation time: 10 min | Cooking time: 15 min | Servings: 4

INGREDIENTS:

- 2 medium artichokes, trimmed and halved
- Cooking spray
- 2 tbsp lemon juice
- Salt and black pepper to the taste

DIRECTIONS:
Grease your air fryer with cooking spray, add artichokes, drizzle lemon juice and sprinkle salt and black pepper and cook them at 380 degrees F for 15 minutes. Divide them between plates and serve as a side dish.

NUTRITION:
calories 121, fat 3, fiber 6, carbs 9, protein 4

ZESTY CAULIFLOWER

Preparation time: 10 min | Cooking time: 7 min | Servings: 4

INGREDIENTS:

- 2 cauliflower heads, florets separated and steamed
- 1 broccoli head, florets separated and steamed
- Zest from 1 orange, grated
- Juice from 1 orange
- A pinch of hot pepper flakes
- 4 anchovies
- 1 tbsp capers, chopped
- Salt and black pepper to the taste
- 4 tbsp olive oil

DIRECTIONS:
In a bowl, mix orange zest with orange juice, pepper flakes, anchovies, capers salt, pepper and olive oil and whisk well. Add broccoli and cauliflower, toss well, transfer them to your air fryer's basket and cook at 400 degrees F for 7 minutes. Divide between plates and serve as a side dish with some of the orange vinaigrette drizzled on top.

NUTRITION:
calories 300, fat 4, fiber 7, carbs 28, protein 4

GARLIC BEETS

Preparation time: 10 min | Cooking time: 15 min | Servings: 4

INGREDIENTS:

- 4 beets, washed, peeled and cut into large wedges
- 1 tbsp olive oil
- Salt and black to the taste
- 2 garlic cloves, minced
- 1 tsp lemon juice

DIRECTIONS:
In a bowl, mix beets with oil, salt, pepper, garlic and lemon juice, toss well, transfer to your air fryer's basket and cook them at 400 degrees F for 15 minutes. Divide beets wedges between plates and serve as a side dish.

NUTRITION:
calories 182, fat 6, fiber 3, carbs 8, protein 2

FRIED RED CABBAGE

Preparation time: 10 min | Cooking time: 15 min | Servings: 4

INGREDIENTS:

- 4 garlic cloves, minced
- ½ cup yellow onion, chopped
- 1 tbsp olive oil
- 6 cups red cabbage, chopped
- 1 cup veggie stock
- 1 tbsp apple cider vinegar
- 1 cup applesauce
- Salt and black pepper to the taste

DIRECTIONS:
In a heat proof dish that fits your air fryer, mix cabbage with onion, garlic, oil, stock, vinegar, applesauce, salt and pepper, toss well, place the dish in your air fryer's basket and cook at 380 degrees F for 15 minutes. Divide between plates and serve as a side dish.

NUTRITION:
calories 172, fat 7, fiber 7, carbs 14, protein 5

LEMONY ARTICHOKES SAUCE

Preparation time: 10 min | Cooking time: 18 min | Servings: 4

INGREDIENTS:

- 4 artichokes, trimmed
- 2 tbsp tarragon, chopped
- 2 tbsp chicken stock
- Lemon zest from 2 lemons, grated
- 2 tbsp lemon juice
- 1 celery stalk, chopped
- ½ cup olive oil
- Salt to the taste

DIRECTIONS
In your food processor, mix tarragon, chicken stock, lemon zest, lemon juice, celery, salt and olive oil and pulse very well. In a bowl, mix artichokes with tarragon and lemon sauce, toss well, transfer them to your air fryer's basket and cook at 380 degrees F for 18 minutes. Divide artichokes on plates, drizzle the rest of the sauce all over.

NUTRITION:
calories 215, fat 3, fiber 8, carbs 28, protein 6

PINE BRUSSELS SPROUTS SIDE DISH
Preparation time: 5 min | Cooking time: 10 min | Servings: 4

INGREDIENTS:

- 1 pound Brussels sprouts, trimmed and halved
- Salt and black pepper to the taste
- 1 cup pomegranate seeds
- ¼ cup pine nuts, toasted
- 1 tbsp olive oil
- 2 tbsp veggie stock

DIRECTIONS:
In a heat proof dish that fits your air fryer, mix Brussels sprouts with salt, pepper, pomegranate seeds, pine nuts, oil and stock, stir, place in your air fryer's basket and cook at 390 degrees F for 10 minutes.

NUTRITION:
calories 152, fat 4, fiber 7, carbs 12, protein 3

CRISPY BUTTERED POTATOES
Preparation time: 10 min | Cooking time: 8 min | Servings: 4

INGREDIENTS:

- 1 and ½ pounds Brussels sprouts, washed and trimmed
- 1 cup new potatoes, chopped
- 1 and ½ tbsp bread crumbs
- Salt and black pepper to the taste
- 1 and ½ tbsp butter

DIRECTIONS:
Put Brussels sprouts and potatoes in your air fryer's pan, add bread crumbs, salt, pepper and butter, toss well and cook at 400 degrees F for 8 minutes. Divide between plates and serve as a side dish.

NUTRITION:
calories 152, fat 3, fiber 7, carbs 17, protein 4

AIR FRYER SNACK AND APPETIZER RECIPES

PEANUT BUTTER BANANA CHIPS
Preparation time: 5 min | Cooking time: 5 min | Servings: 8

INGREDIENTS:

- ¼ cup peanut butter, soft
- 1 banana, peeled and sliced into 16 pieces
- 1 tbsp vegetable oil

DIRECTIONS:
Put the banana slices in your air fryer's basket and drizzle the oil over them. Cook at 360 degrees F for 5 minutes. Transfer to bowls and serve them dipped in peanut butter.

NUTRITION:
calories 100, fat 4, fiber 1, carbs 10, protein 4

CARAMEL APPLE BITES
Preparation time: 5 min | Cooking time: 5 min | Servings: 4

INGREDIENTS:

- 3 big apples, cored, peeled and cubed
- 2 tsp lemon juice
- ½ cup caramel sauce

DIRECTIONS:
In your air fryer, mix all the ingredients; toss well. Cook at 340 degrees F for 5 minutes. Divide into cups and serve as a snack.

NUTRITION:
calories 180, fat 4, fiber 3, carbs 10, protein 3

GARLIC ZUCCHINI BALLS
Preparation time: 10 min | Cooking time: 12 min | Servings: 8

INGREDIENTS:

- Cooking spray
- ½ cup dill, chopped
- 1 egg
- ½ cup white flour
- Salt and black pepper to taste
- 2 garlic cloves, minced
- 3 zucchinis, grated

DIRECTIONS:
In a bowl, mix all the ingredients and stir. Shape the mix into medium balls and place them into your air fryer's basket. Cook at 375 degrees F for 12 minutes, flipping them halfway. Serve them as a snack right away.

NUTRITION:
calories 120, fat 1, fiber 2, carbs 5, protein 3

BASIL BUTTER CRACKERS
Preparation time: 10 min | Cooking time: 16 min | Servings: 6

INGREDIENTS:

- ½ tsp baking powder

- Salt and black pepper to taste
- 1¼ cups flour
- 1 garlic clove, minced
- 2 tbsp basil, minced
- 2 tbsp cilantro, minced
- 4 tbsp butter, melted

DIRECTIONS:
Add all of the ingredients to a bowl and stir until you obtain a dough. Spread this on a lined baking sheet that fits your air fryer. Place the baking sheet in the fryer at 325 degrees F and cook for 16 minutes. Cool down, cut, and serve.

NUTRITION:
calories 171, fat 9, fiber 1, carbs 8, protein 4

BALSAMIC ZUCCHINI SLICES
Preparation time: 5 min | Cooking time: 50 min | Servings: 6

INGREDIENTS:

- 3 zucchinis, thinly sliced
- Salt and black pepper to taste
- 2 tbsp avocado oil
- 2 tbsp balsamic vinegar

DIRECTIONS:
Add all of the ingredients to a bowl and mix. Put the zucchini mixture in your air fryer's basket and cook at 220 degrees F for 50 minutes. Serve as a snack and enjoy!

NUTRITION:
calories 40, fat 3, fiber 7, carbs 3, protein 7

AIR FRIED TURMERIC CARROTS
Preparation time: 5 min | Cooking time: 25 min | Servings: 4

INGREDIENTS:

- 4 carrots, thinly sliced
- Salt and black pepper to taste
- ½ tsp turmeric powder
- ½ tsp chaat masala
- 1 tsp olive oil

DIRECTIONS:
Place all ingredients in a bowl and toss well. Put the mixture in your air fryer's basket and cook at 370 degrees F for 25 minutes, shaking the fryer from time to time. Serve as a snack.

NUTRITION:
calories 161, fat 1, fiber 2, carbs 5, protein 3

RADISH CHIVES
Preparation time: 5 min | Cooking time: 10 min | Servings: 4

INGREDIENTS:

- 16 radishes, sliced
- A drizzle of olive oil
- Salt and black pepper to taste
- 1 tbsp chives, chopped

DIRECTIONS:
In a bowl, mix the radishes, salt, pepper, and oil; toss well. Place the radishes in your air fryer's basket and cook at 350 degrees F for 10 minutes. Divide into bowls and serve with chives sprinkled on top.

NUTRITION:
calories 100, fat 1, fiber 2, carbs 4, protein 1

PAPRIKA LENTILS SNACK
Preparation time: 5 min | Cooking time: 12 min | Servings: 4

INGREDIENTS:

- 15 ounces canned lentils, drained
- ½ tsp cumin, ground
- 1 tbsp olive oil
- 1 tsp sweet paprika
- Salt and black pepper to taste

DIRECTIONS:
Place all ingredients in a bowl and mix well. Transfer the mixture to your air fryer and cook at 400 degrees F for 12 minutes. Divide into bowls and serve as a snack.

NUTRITION:
calories 151, fat 1, fiber 6, carbs 10, protein 6

BUTTERED CORN
Preparation time: 5 min | Cooking time: 10 min | Servings: 4

INGREDIENTS:

- 2 tbsp corn kernels
- 2½ tbsp butter

DIRECTIONS:
In a pan that fits your air fryer, mix the corn with the butter. Place the pan in the fryer and cook at 400 degrees F for 10 minutes. Serve as a snack and enjoy!

NUTRITION:
calories 70, fat 2, fiber 2, carbs 7, protein 3

AIR FRIED COCONUT SHRIMPS
Preparation time: 10 min | Cooking time: 12min | Servings: 4

INGREDIENTS:

- 12 large shrimp, deveined and peeled
- 2 eggs, whisked
- 2 cups coconut, shredded
- 1 cup white flour
- Salt and black pepper to taste

DIRECTIONS:
Put the coconut in one bowl, the flour in a second one, and the eggs in a third. Season the shrimp with the salt and pepper, then dredge them in the flour, then the eggs, and then the coconut. Place the shrimp in your air fryer's basket and cook at 360 degrees F for 12 minutes, flipping them halfway. Divide the shrimp into bowls and serve as a snack (or an appetizer, or even an entrée!).

NUTRITION:
calories 150, fat 4, fiber 3, carbs 13, protein 4

CRUNCHY CHICKEN STICKS

Preparation time: 10 min | Cooking time: 16 min | Servings: 4

INGREDIENTS:

- ¾ cup white flour
- 1 pound chicken breast, skinless, boneless and cut in medium sticks
- 1 cup breadcrumbs
- 1 egg, whisked
- Salt and black pepper to taste
- ½ tbsp olive oil

DIRECTIONS:
Combine the flour, salt, and pepper in a bowl. Put the egg in another bowl and the breadcrumbs in a third one. Dredge the chicken pieces in the flour, then the egg, and then the breadcrumbs. Place the chicken pieces in your air fryer's basket, drizzle the oil over them, and cook at 400 degrees F for 16 minutes, flipping them halfway.

NUTRITION:
calories 181, fat 4, fiber 7, carbs 15, protein 18

CHEESY BEEF MEATBALLS

Preparation time: 10 min | Cooking time: 8 min | Servings: 8

INGREDIENTS:

- 4 ounces beef meat, minced
- Salt and black pepper to taste
- 1 tbsp breadcrumbs
- 2 tbsp feta cheese, crumbled
- ½ tbsp lemon peel, grated
- 1 tbsp oregano, chopped

DIRECTIONS:
Place all of the ingredients in a bowl and stir well. Shape medium meatballs out of this mix. Place the meatballs in your air fryer's basket and cook at 400 degrees F for 8 minutes. Serve as an appetizer, or even as an entrée.

NUTRITION:
calories 194, fat 9, fiber 2, carbs 11, protein 15

BELL PEPPER FETA ROLLS

Preparation time: 10 min | Cooking time: 10 min | Servings: 8

INGREDIENTS:

- 1 yellow bell pepper, deseeded and halved
- 1 orange bell pepper, deseeded and halved
- Salt and black pepper to taste
- 4 ounces feta cheese, crumbled
- 1 green onion, chopped
- 2 tbsp oregano, chopped

DIRECTIONS:
Place the bell pepper halves in your air fryer's basket and cook at 400 degrees F for 10 minutes. Transfer the bell peppers to a cutting board, cool down, peel, and arrange them on a working surface. In a bowl, mix the cheese, salt, pepper, cilantro, and green onions; stir well. Spread the cheese mixture on each pepper half, roll the peppers, and secure them with toothpicks. Serve as an appetizer, or even as a great side.

NUTRITION:
calories 150, fat 1, fiber 2, carbs 7, protein 5

ITALIAN CHEESY STICKS

Preparation time: 10 min | Cooking time: 8 min | Servings: 12

INGREDIENTS:

- 2 eggs, whisked
- Salt and black pepper to taste
- 8 mozzarella cheese strings, halved
- 1 cup parmesan cheese, grated
- 1 tbsp Italian seasoning
- A drizzle of olive oil

DIRECTIONS:
In a bowl, mix the parmesan, salt, pepper, and Italian seasoning; stir. Put the whisked eggs in another bowl. Dip the mozzarella sticks in the egg mixture, then in the parmesan mix. Dip the sticks one more time in egg and parmesan and place them in your air fryer's basket. Drizzle the oil over them, and cook at 390 degrees F for 8 minutes, flipping them halfway. Serve as an appetizer.

NUTRITION:
calories 200, fat 5, fiber 3, carbs 13, protein 4

FLAX CRACKERS

Preparation time: 10 min | Cooking time: 20 min | Servings: 6

INGREDIENTS:

- 4 cups flax seed, soaked overnight, drained and ground
- 4 bunches kale, chopped
- 1 bunch basil, chopped
- 4 garlic cloves, minced
- 1/2 cup avocado oil

DIRECTIONS:
Place all ingredients in your food processor and pulse well. Spread the mixture in your air fryer's pan and cut into medium crackers. Cook in the air fryer cook at 380 degrees F for 20 minutes. Cool and serve as a snack.

NUTRITION:
calories 153, fat 1, fiber 2, carbs 11, protein 5

SALTY POTATO CHIPS

Preparation time: 5 min | Cooking time: 12 min | Servings: 4

INGREDIENTS:

- 4 potatoes, thinly sliced
- Salt and black pepper to taste
- 1 tbsp olive oil
- Sour cream for serving

DIRECTIONS:
Brush the potato slices with the oil and place them in your air fryer's basket. Cook at 400 degrees F for 12 minutes, flipping them halfway. Serve as a snack along with the sour cream.

NUTRITION:
calories 143, fat 4, fiber 1.5, carbs 10, protein 5

GARLICKY BROCCOLI BITES
Preparation time: 5 min | Cooking time: 15 min | Servings: 6

INGREDIENTS:

- 1 broccoli head, florets separated
- Salt and black pepper to taste
- 1 tsp olive oil
- 2 tsp garlic powder
- 1 tsp butter, melted

DIRECTIONS:
Spread the broccoli florets on a lined baking sheet that fits your air fryer; then add all other ingredients and toss. Cook at 450 degrees F for 15 minutes. Divide into bowls and serve as a snack (or as a side).

NUTRITION:
calories 138, fat 2, fiber 2, carbs 11, protein 2

CREAMY ENDIVES SIDE DISH
Preparation time: 10 min | Cooking time: 10 min | Servings: 4

INGREDIENTS:

- 6 endives, halved lengthwise
- Salt and black pepper to taste
- ½ cup yogurt
- 1 tsp garlic powder
- 3 tbsp lemon juice

DIRECTIONS:
In a bowl, mix all ingredients except the endives; whisk. Now add the endives, toss, and set them aside for 10 minutes. Place the endives in your air fryer's basket and cook at 360 degrees F for 10 minutes.

NUTRITION:
calories 179, fat 6, fiber 12, carbs 11, protein 4

CORIANDER BITES
Preparation time: 10 min | Cooking time: 20 min | Servings: 4

INGREDIENTS:

- 12 ounces tofu, cubed
- 1 tsp sweet paprika
- 2 tsp olive oil
- 1 tbsp coriander paste
- 2 tbsp soy sauce
- 2 tbsp fish sauce

DIRECTIONS:
In a bowl, mix the tofu, paprika, 1 tsp of the oil, coriander paste, soy sauce, and fish sauce; toss and set aside for 10 minutes. Transfer the coriander tofu bites to your air fryer's basket, drizzle the remaining tsp of the oil over them, and cook at 350 degrees F for 20 minutes, shaking halfway. Serve as a snack.

NUTRITION:
calories 100, fat 4, fiber 1, carbs 11, protein 1

BEEF TOMATOES DIP
Preparation time: 10 min | Cooking time: 30 min | Servings: 6

INGREDIENTS:

- 2 pounds ground beef, browned
- 2 carrots, chopped
- 4 garlic cloves, minced
- 2 celery ribs, chopped
- 28 ounces canned tomatoes, crushed
- ¼ cup beef stock
- 1 yellow onion, chopped
- 1 tbsp olive oil
- A pinch of basil, dried
- A pinch of oregano, dried
- A splash of red wine
- Salt and black pepper to taste

DIRECTIONS:
Place all the ingredients in a pan that fits your air fryer and whisk. Put the pan in the fryer and cook at 380 degrees F for 30 minutes. Divide into bowls and serve as a snack or appetizer.

NUTRITION:
calories 251, fat 14, fiber 5, carbs 23, protein 17

RED LENTILS WITH TOMATOES
Preparation time: 5 min | Cooking time: 20 min | Servings: 4

INGREDIENTS:

- 30 ounces canned tomatoes, crushed
- 3 garlic cloves, minced
- 2 cups canned red lentils, drained
- Salt and black pepper to taste
- 1 cup chicken stock

DIRECTIONS:
Add all of the ingredients to a pan that fits your air fryer and stir. Place the pan into the fryer and cook at 370 degrees F for 20 minutes. Blend the mix with an immersion blender. Divide into bowls and serve as a snack or an appetizer.

NUTRITION:
calories 171, fat 6, fiber 4, carbs 12, protein 5

HERBED DIP
Preparation time: 10 min | Cooking time: 12 min | Servings: 4

INGREDIENTS:

- 6 ancho chilies, dried, seedless and chopped
- 2 garlic cloves, minced
- Salt and black

pepper to taste
- 1 cup water
- 1½ tsp sugar
- ½ tsp oregano, dried
- 2 tbsp apple cider vinegar

DIRECTIONS:
Mix all the ingredients together in a pan that fits your air fryer; stir well. Place the pan in the air fryer and cook at 380 degrees F for 12 minutes. Transfer the mixture to a blender and pulse. Divide into bowls and serve as a dip.

NUTRITION:
calories 72, fat 1, fiber 0, carbs 2, protein 3

Tabasco Veggie Dip
Preparation time: 5 min | Cooking time: 10 min | Servings: 4

Ingredients:

- 1 tbsp olive oil
- 1 cup tomato puree
- 1 yellow onion, chopped
- 4 tbsp white vinegar
- 4 tbsp honey
- Salt and black pepper to taste
- 2 garlic cloves, minced
- 1 tsp liquid smoke
- 1 tsp Tabasco sauce
- ⅛ tsp cumin powder

DIRECTIONS:
Place all the ingredients in a pan that fits your air fryer and mix well. Put the pan into the fryer and cook at 370 degrees F for 10 minutes. Whisk well, divide into bowls, and serve as a dip.

NUTRITION:
calories 72, fat 1, fiber 3, carbs 7, protein 4

ONION AND ZUCCHINI SPREAD
Preparation time: 10 min | Cooking time: 12 min | Servings: 4

INGREDIENTS:

- 1 yellow onion, chopped
- 1 tbsp olive oil
- 1½ pounds zucchini, chopped
- Salt and white pepper to taste
- ½ cup veggie stock
- 1 bunch mint, chopped
- 2 garlic cloves, minced

DIRECTIONS:
Over medium heat, heat up the oil in a pan that fits your air fryer. Add the onions and garlic, stir, and cook for 1-2 minutes. Add the remaining ingredients; stir well. Place the pan in the air fryer and cook at 380 degrees F for 10 minutes. Blend using an immersion blender, and serve as an appetizer or party spread.

NUTRITION:
calories 87, fat 6, fiber 2, carbs 5, protein 2

VEGGIE DIP

Preparation time: 10 min | Cooking time: 25 min | Servings: 6

INGREDIENTS:

- 1 yellow onion, chopped
- 2 tbsp olive oil
- 8 carrots, chopped
- 2 butternut squash, chopped
- 8 garlic cloves, minced
- 1 cup veggie stock
- ¼ cup lemon juice
- 1 bunch basil, chopped
- Salt and black pepper to taste

DIRECTIONS:
In a pan that fits your air fryer, mix all the ingredients except the lemon juice. Place the pan in the fryer and cook at 380 degrees F for 25 minutes. Transfer the entire mixture to a blender, add the lemon juice, and pulse well. Divide into bowls and serve as a party dip or an appetizer.

NUTRITION:
calories 141, fat 4, fiber 3, carbs 11, protein 4

SALTY MUSHROOM MIX
Preparation time: 10 min | Cooking time: 25 min | Servings: 6

INGREDIENTS:

- 1 yellow onion, chopped
- ¼ cup olive oil
- Salt and black pepper to taste
- 1 tbsp thyme, chopped
- 3 garlic cloves, minced
- 1 cup chicken stock
- 10 ounces shiitake mushrooms, chopped
- 10 ounces cremini mushrooms, chopped
- 10 ounces Portobello mushrooms, chopped
- ¼ cup coconut cream
- 1 ounce parmesan cheese, grated
- 1 tbsp parsley, minced

DIRECTIONS:
In a pan that fits your air fryer, heat up the oil over medium heat. Add the onions, garlic, thyme, salt, and pepper; stir and cook for 3-4 minutes. Add the stock and the mushrooms; stir and cook for 1-2 minutes more. Place the pan in the air fryer and cook at 350 degrees F for 20 minutes. Add the cream, parmesan, and parsley, and stir well. Divide into bowls and serve as an appetizer.

NUTRITION:
calories 200, fat 5, fiber 6, carbs 15, protein

BUTTERY CAULIFLOWER SIDE DISH
Preparation time: 5 min | Cooking time: 15 min | Servings: 6

INGREDIENTS:

- 2 tbsp butter, melted
- 8 garlic cloves, minced
- 3 cups veggie stock
- 6 cups cauliflower florets
- A handful of mint, chopped

- Salt and black pepper to taste

DIRECTIONS:
Place all the ingredients into a pan that fits your air fryer; mix well. Put the pan into the air fryer and cook at 370 degrees F for 15 minutes. Blend using an immersion blender, divide into bowls, and serve.

NUTRITION:
calories 161, fat 5, fiber 9, carbs 14, protein 6

FAST MANGO DIP
Preparation time: 5 min | Cooking time: 20 min | Servings: 4

INGREDIENTS:

- 1 shallot, chopped
- 1 tbsp avocado oil
- 2 tbsp ginger, minced
- ½ tsp cinnamon powder
- 2 mangos, chopped
- 2 red hot chilies, chopped
- 1¼ cups sugar
- 1¼ cups apple cider vinegar

DIRECTIONS:
In a pan that fits your air fryer, mix all the ingredients well. Place the pan in the fryer and cook at 350 degrees F for 20 minutes. Transfer the contents to a blender and pulse. Divide into bowls and serve as a party dip.

NUTRITION:
calories 100, fat 1, fiber 0, carbs 6, protein 2

HOT PEPPER DIP
Preparation time: 5 min | Cooking time: 5 min | Servings: 6

Ingredients:

- 12 ounces hot peppers, chopped
- Salt and black pepper to taste
- 1¼ cups apple cider vinegar

DIRECTIONS:
Add the ingredients to a pan that fits your air fryer and mix. Place the pan in the fryer and cook at 380 degrees F for 5 minutes. Blend using an immersion blender, divide into bowls, and serve.

NUTRITION:
calories 20, fat 0, fiber 2, carbs 3, protein 1

HERBED PARTY MIX
Preparation time: 5 min | Cooking time: 13 min | Servings: 6

INGREDIENTS:

- 3 pounds tomatoes, roughly cubed
- 1 cup balsamic vinegar
- 1 tbsp ginger, grated
- 3 garlic cloves, minced
- 2 onions, chopped
- ¼ cup raisins
- ¾ tsp cinnamon powder
- ½ tsp coriander, ground
- ¼ tsp nutmeg powder
- 1 tsp sweet paprika
- 1 tsp chili powder

DIRECTIONS:
Add all the ingredients to a pan that fits your air fryer and toss. Place the pan in the air fryer and cook at 360 degrees F for 13 minutes. Remove, place in a bowl, and chill. Serve cold as an appetizer or snack.

NUTRITION:
calories 151, fat 8, fiber 4, carbs 11, protein 5

TOMATOES AND SULTANAS DIP
Preparation time: 5 min | Cooking time: 15 min | Servings: 12

INGREDIENTS:

- 1½ pounds tomatoes, peeled and cubed
- 1 apple, cored and cubed
- 1 yellow onion, chopped
- 6 ounces sultanas, chopped
- 3 ounces dates, roughly chopped
- Salt and black pepper to taste
- 1 tbsp balsamic vinegar
- 1 tsp whole spice
- ½ tbsp brown sugar

DIRECTIONS:
In a pan that fits your air fryer, add and toss all the ingredients. Place the pan in the fryer and cook at 370 degrees F for 15 minutes. Remove the salsa, place in a bowl, and chill. Serve the salsa cold as a snack or appetizer.

NUTRITION:
calories 131, fat 7, fiber 4, carbs 9, protein 3

SWEET CHILI SALSA
Preparation time: 5 min | Cooking time: 10 min | Servings: 12

INGREDIENTS:

- 1½ pounds green tomatoes, cubed
- 1 white onion, chopped
- ¼ cup currants
- 4 red chili peppers, chopped
- 2 tbsp ginger, grated
- 1 tbsp brown sugar
- 1 tbsp balsamic vinegar

DIRECTIONS:
Mix all the ingredients in a pan that fits your air fryer and toss. Place the pan in the fryer and cook at 370 degrees F for 10 minutes. Put the salsa into a bowl and chill. Serve cold as a party salsa or as an appetizer.

NUTRITION:
calories 100, fat 1, fiber 3, carbs 7, protein 4

ONION SAUCE
Preparation time: 10 min | Cooking time: 30 min | Servings: 8

INGREDIENTS:

6 tbsp butter, softened
- 2½ pounds red onions, chopped
- Salt and black pepper to taste

- ½ tsp baking soda

DIRECTIONS:
Place the butter into a pan that fits your air fryer and heat over medium heat. Add the onions and the baking soda, stir, and sauté for 5 minutes. Transfer the pan to your air fryer and cook at 370 degrees F for 25 minutes. Serve warm as a party dip.

NUTRITION:
calories 151, fat 2, fiber 4, carbs 9, protein 4

CRANBERRY CHILI DIP
Preparation time: 10 min | Cooking time: 30 min | Servings: 10

INGREDIENTS:

- 4 garlic cloves, minced
- 2 red onions, chopped
- 4 red chili peppers, seeded and chopped
- 17 ounces cranberries
- 4 ounces sugar
- 1 tsp olive oil
- Black pepper to taste
- 2 tbsp balsamic vinegar

DIRECTIONS:
In a pan that fits your air fryer, place all the ingredients and mix well. Place the pan in the air fryer and cook at 370 degrees F for 30 minutes. Blend using an immersion blender and cool. Serve cold as a party dip or appetizer.

NUTRITION:
calories 121, fat 1, fiber 3, carbs 7, protein 3

SWEET ONION DIP
Preparation time: 5 min | Cooking time: 20 min | Servings: 6

INGREDIENTS:

- 5 ounces red chilies, seeded and chopped
- 4 ounces red onion, chopped
- 3 tbsp sugar
- 12 garlic cloves, minced
- 2 ounces distilled vinegar
- 2 ounces water

DIRECTIONS:
Place all the ingredients into a pan that fits your air fryer and mix well. Put the pan into the air fryer and cook at 370 degrees F for 20 minutes. Blend using an immersion blender, divide into bowls, and serve as a party dip.

NUTRITION:
calories 100, fat 1, fiber 2, carbs 7, protein 4

EGGPLANT AND GARLIC SPREAD
Preparation time: 10 min | Cooking time: 25 min | Servings: 6

INGREDIENTS:

- 15 ounces canned tomatoes, chopped
- 5 garlic cloves, minced
- 3 ounces canned tomato paste
- 1 sweet onion, chopped
- 3 small eggplants, chopped
- ½ cup olive oil
- ½ tsp turmeric powder
- 1 cup beef stock
- 1 tbsp apple cider vinegar
- Salt and black pepper to taste
- ¼ cup parsley, chopped

DIRECTIONS:
In a pan that fits your air fryer, place all the ingredients except the parsley; stir well. Put the pan in the fryer and cook at 380 degrees F for 25 minutes. Blend a bit using an immersion blender, add the parsley, and stir. Put into a bowl, chill, and serve cold.

NUTRITION:
calories 151, fat 8, fiber 6, carbs 11, protein

COCONUT VEGGIE SPREAD
Preparation time: 10 min | Cooking time: 15 min | Servings: 4

INGREDIENTS:

- 1½ cups veggie stock
- 3 cups broccoli florets
- 2 garlic cloves, minced
- Salt and black pepper to taste
- ½ cup coconut milk
- 1 tbsp white wine vinegar
- 1 tbsp olive oil

DIRECTIONS:
In a pan that fits your air fryer, mix all the ingredients except the coconut milk. Place the pan in the fryer and cook at 390 degrees F for 15 minutes. Add the coconut milk and blend using an immersion blender. Put the spread into a bowl and chill. Serve cold as an appetizer.

NUTRITION:
calories 151, fat 4, fiber 7, carbs 12, protein 5

BUTTERY CAYENNE DIP
Preparation time: 10 min | Cooking time: 15 min | Servings: 6

INGREDIENTS:

- 4 tbsp butter, melted
- 2 cups carrots, grated
- Salt and black pepper to taste
- A pinch of cayenne pepper
- 1 tbsp chives

DIRECTIONS:
Add all ingredients to a pan that fits your air fryer and mix. Place the pan in the fryer and cook at 380 degrees F for 15 minutes. Blend a bit using an immersion blender, and then divide into bowls. Serve as a dip.

NUTRITION:
calories 151, fat 4, fiber 5, carbs 13, protein 5

APPLE AND DATES DIP
Preparation time: 5 min | Cooking time: 19 min | Servings: 6

INGREDIENTS:

- 2 cups apples, cored, peeled and grated
- ¼ cup apple juice
- 2 cups dates, dried
- 1 tbsp lemon juice

DIRECTIONS:
In a pan that fits your air fryer, mix all the ingredients. Place the pan in the fryer and cook at 380 degrees F for 19 minutes. Blend a bit using an immersion blender, then place in a bowl and chill. Serve cold as a dip.

NUTRITION:
calories 100, fat 1, fiber 3, carbs 9, protein 3

FENNEL AND TOMATO DIP

Preparation time: 10 min | Cooking time: 16 min | Servings: 6

INGREDIENTS:

- 1 fennel bulb, chopped
- 2 pints grape tomatoes, chopped
- ¼ cup dry white wine
- 3 tbsp olive oil
- Salt and black pepper to taste

DIRECTIONS:
In a pan that fits your air fryer, mix all the ingredients. Place the pan in the fryer and cook at 390 degrees F for 16 minutes. Stir well, divide into bowls, and serve as a dip.

NUTRITION:
calories 100, fat 2, fiber 2, carbs 11, protein 4

CREAMY LEEK DIP

Preparation time: 5 min | Cooking time: 15 min | Servings: 6

INGREDIENTS:

- 3 leeks, roughly chopped
- 2 tbsp butter, melted
- ½ cup whipping cream
- 3 tbsp lemon juice
- Salt and pepper to taste

DIRECTIONS:
In a pan that fits your air fryer, mix the leeks, butter, lemon juice, salt, and pepper; stir well. Put the pan into the fryer and cook at 380 degrees F for 15 minutes. Transfer the mixture to a blender, add the cream, and pulse. Divide into bowls and serve cold.

NUTRITION:
calories 161, fat 8, fiber 2, carbs 14, protein 6

FAST PARSLEY SAUCE

Preparation time: 5 min | Cooking time: 8 min | Servings: 6

INGREDIENTS:

- ¼ cup chicken stock
- 1 yellow onion, chopped
- 2 tbsp butter, melted
- 3 tbsp whole milk
- 6 tbsp parsley, chopped
- ¼ cup heavy cream
- Salt and white pepper to taste

DIRECTIONS:
Place all of the ingredients—except the cream—into a pan that fits your air fryer; mix well. Put the pan into the fryer and cook at 370 degrees F for 8 minutes. Transfer to a blender, add the cream, and pulse. Put the mixture into a bowl and chill. Serve cold.

NUTRITION:
calories 100, fat 2, fiber 5, carbs 11, protein 3

CHILI SCALLIONS DIP

Preparation time: 5 min | Cooking time: 15 min | Servings: 6

INGREDIENTS:

- 3 garlic cloves, minced
- 1 tbsp olive oil
- 2 red chilies, minced
- 3 shallots, minced
- 3 scallions, chopped
- 1 tomato, chopped
- Salt and black pepper to taste
- 2 tbsp cilantro, chopped
- 3½ tbsp veggie stock

DIRECTIONS:
In a pan that fits your air fryer, add all the ingredients and toss. Place the pan in the fryer and cook at 390 degrees F for 15 minutes. Blend a bit using an immersion blender, then put in a bowl and chill. Serve cold as a snack or appetizer; enjoy!

NUTRITION:
calories 131, fat 5, fiber 4, carbs 14, protein 3

CORN AND WINE DIP

Preparation time: 5 min | Cooking time: 18 min | Servings: 4

INGREDIENTS:

- 1 yellow onion, chopped
- 1 tbsp olive oil
- 1 cup chicken stock
- 2 tbsp white wine
- 2 cups corn kernels
- Salt and black pepper to taste
- 2 tsp butter, melted
- 1 tsp thyme, chopped

DIRECTIONS:
Put a pan that fits your air fryer over medium heat and add the oil and the butter; heat up. Add the onion; stir, and sauté for 3 minutes. Add the corn, stock, wine, salt, pepper, and thyme; stir. Place the pan in the fryer and cook at 390 degrees F for 15 minutes. Blend a bit using an immersion blender, divide into bowls, and serve as a party dip or appetizer.

NUTRITION:
calories 151, fat 2, fiber 5, carbs 14, protein 4

CRUNCHY CHICKEN BITES

Preparation time: 10 min | Cooking time: 13 min | Servings: 4

INGREDIENTS:

- 2 tsp garlic powder
- 2 eggs
- Salt and black pepper to the taste
- ¾ cup panko bread crumbs
- ¾ cup coconut, shredded
- Cooking spray
- 8 chicken tenders

DIRECTIONS:
In a bowl, mix eggs with salt, pepper and garlic powder and whisk well. In another bowl, mix coconut with panko and stir well. Dip chicken tenders in eggs mix and then coat in coconut one well. Spray chicken bites with cooking spray, place them in your air fryer's basket and cook them at 350 degrees F for 10 minutes. Arrange them on a platter and serve as an appetizer.

NUTRITION:
calories 252, fat 4, fiber 2, carbs 14, protein 24

BUFFALO VEGGIE SNACK
Preparation time: 10 min | Cooking time: 15 min | Servings: 4

INGREDIENTS:

- 4 cups cauliflower florets
- 1 cup panko bread crumbs
- ¼ cup butter, melted
- ¼ cup buffalo sauce
- Mayonnaise for serving

DIRECTIONS:
In a bowl, mix buffalo sauce with butter and whisk well. Dip cauliflower florets in this mix and coat them in panko bread crumbs. Place them in your air fryer's basket and cook at 350 degrees F for 15 minutes. Arrange them on a platter and serve with mayo on the side.

NUTRITION:
calories 241, fat 4, fiber 7, carbs 8, protein 4

SWEET CHICKEN WINGS
Preparation time: 1 hour and 10 min | Cooking time: 12 min | Servings: 8

INGREDIENTS:

- 16 chicken wings, halved
- 2 tbsp soy sauce
- 2 tbsp honey
- Salt and black pepper to the taste
- 2 tbsp lime juice

DIRECTIONS:
In a bowl, mix chicken wings with soy sauce, honey, salt, pepper and lime juice, toss well and keep in the fridge for 1 hour. Transfer chicken wings to your air fryer and cook them at 360 degrees F for 12 minutes, flipping them halfway. Arrange them on a platter and serve as an appetizer.

NUTRITION:
calories 211, fat 4, fiber 7, carbs 14, protein 3

CRUNCHY SALMON PATTIES
Preparation time: 10 min | Cooking time: 22 min | Servings: 4

INGREDIENTS:

- 3 big potatoes, boiled, drained and mashed
- 1 big salmon fillet, skinless, boneless
- 2 tbsp parsley, chopped
- 2 tbsp dill, chopped
- Salt and black pepper to the taste
- 1 egg
- 2 tbsp bread crumbs
- Cooking spray

DIRECTIONS:
Place salmon in your air fryer's basket and cook for 10 minutes at 360 degrees F. Transfer salmon to a cutting board, cool it down, flake it and put it in a bowl. Add mashed potatoes, salt, pepper, dill, parsley, egg and bread crumbs, stir well and shape 8 patties out of this mix. Place salmon patties in your air fryer's basket, spry them with cooking oil, cook at 360 degrees F for 12 minutes, flipping them halfway, transfer them to a platter and serve as an appetizer.

NUTRITION:
calories 231, fat 3, fiber 7, carbs 14, protein 4

SALTY BANANA CHIPS
Preparation time: 10 min | Cooking time: 15 min | Servings: 4

INGREDIENTS:

- 4 bananas, peeled and sliced
- A pinch of salt
- ½ tsp turmeric powder
- ½ tsp chaat masala
- 1 tsp olive oil

DIRECTIONS:
In a bowl, mix banana slices with salt, turmeric, chaat masala and oil, toss and leave aside for 10 minutes. Transfer banana slices to your preheated air fryer at 360 degrees F and cook them for 15 minutes flipping them once. Serve as a snack.

NUTRITION:
calories 121, fat 1, fiber 2, carbs 3, protein 3

CABBAGE ROLLS
Preparation time: 10 min | Cooking time: 25 min | Servings: 8

INGREDIENTS:

- 2 cups green cabbage, shredded
- 2 yellow onions, chopped
- 1 carrot, grated
- ½ chili pepper, minced
- 1 tbsp ginger, grated
- 3 garlic cloves, minced
- 1 tsp sugar
- Salt and black pepper to the taste
- 1 tsp soy sauce
- 2 tbsp olive oil
- 10 spring roll sheets

- 2 tbsp corn flour
- 2 tbsp water

DIRECTIONS:
Heat up a pan with the oil over medium heat, add cabbage, onions, carrots, chili pepper, ginger, garlic, sugar, salt, pepper and soy sauce, stir well, cook for 2-3 minutes, take off heat and cool down. Cut spring roll sheets into squares, divide cabbage mix on each and roll them. In a bowl, mix corn flour with water, stir well and seal spring rolls with this mix. Place spring rolls in your air fryer's basket and cook them at 360 degrees F for 10 minutes. Flip roll and cook them for 10 minutes more. Arrange on a platter and serve them as an appetizer.

NUTRITION:
calories 214, fat 4, fiber 4, carbs 12, protein 4

CHIVES AND RADISH CHIPS

Preparation time: 10 min | Cooking time: 10 min | Servings: 4

INGREDIENTS:
- Cooking spray
- 15 radishes, sliced
- Salt and black pepper to the taste
- 1 tbsp chives, chopped

DIRECTIONS:
Arrange radish slices in your air fryer's basket, spray them with cooking oil, season with salt and black pepper to the taste, cook them at 350 degrees F for 10 minutes, flipping them halfway, transfer to bowls and serve with chives sprinkled on top.

NUTRITION:
calories 80, fat 1, fiber 1, carbs 1, protein 1

AIR FRIED PAPRIKA PICKLES

Preparation time: 10 min | Cooking time: 5 min | Servings: 4

INGREDIENTS:
- 16 ounces jarred dill pickles, cut into wedges and pat dried
- ½ cup white flour
- 1 egg
- ¼ cup milk
- ½ tsp garlic powder
- ½ tsp sweet paprika
- Cooking spray
- ¼ cup ranch sauce

DIRECTIONS:
In a bowl, combine milk with egg and whisk well. In a second bowl, mix flour with salt, garlic powder and paprika and stir as well Dip pickles in flour, then in egg mix and again in flour and place them in your air fryer. Grease them with cooking spray, cook pickle wedges at 400 degrees F for 5 minutes, transfer to a bowl and serve with ranch sauce on the side.

NUTRITION:
calories 109, fat 2, fiber 2, carbs 10, protein 4

CHICKPEAS PAPRIKA SNACK

Preparation time: 10 min | Cooking time: 10 min | Servings: 4

INGREDIENTS:
- 15 ounces canned chickpeas, drained
- ½ tsp cumin, ground
- 1 tbsp olive oil
- 1 tsp smoked paprika
- Salt and black pepper to the taste

DIRECTIONS:
In a bowl, mix chickpeas with oil, cumin, paprika, salt and pepper, toss to coat, place them in your fryer's basket and cook at 390 degrees F for 10 minutes. Divide into bowls and serve as a snack.

NUTRITION:
calories 140, fat 1, fiber 6, carbs 20, protein 6

YOGURT CHICKEN DIP

Preparation time: 10 min | Cooking time: 25 min | Servings: 10

INGREDIENTS:
- 3 tbsp butter, melted
- 1 cup yogurt
- 12 ounces cream cheese
- 2 cups chicken meat, cooked and shredded
- 2 tsp curry powder
- 4 scallions, chopped
- 6 ounces Monterey jack cheese, grated
- 1/3 cup raisins
- ¼ cup cilantro, chopped
- ½ cup almonds, sliced
- Salt and black pepper to the taste
- ½ cup chutney

DIRECTIONS:
In a bowl mix cream cheese with yogurt and whisk using your mixer. Add curry powder, scallions, chicken meat, raisins, cheese, cilantro, salt and pepper and stir everything. Spread this into a baking dish that fist your air fryer, sprinkle almonds on top, place in your air fryer, bake at 300 degrees for 25 minutes, divide into bowls, top with chutney and serve as an appetizer.

NUTRITION:
calories 240, fat 10, fiber 2, carbs 24, protein 12

SUGARY POPCORN

Preparation time: 5 min | Cooking time: 10 min | Servings: 4

INGREDIENTS:
- 2 tbsp corn kernels
- 2 and ½ tbsp butter
- 2 ounces brown sugar

DIRECTIONS:
Put corn kernels in your air fryer's pan, cook at 400 degrees F for 6 minutes, transfer to a tray, spread and leave aside for now. Heat up a pan over low heat, add butter, melt it, add sugar and stir until it dissolves.

Add popcorn, toss to coat, take off heat and spread on the tray again. Cool down, divide into bowls and serve as a snack.

NUTRITION:
calories 70, fat 0.2, fiber 0, carbs 1, protein 1

APPLE CHIPS
Preparation time: 10 min | Cooking time: 10 min | Servings: 2

INGREDIENTS:

- 1 apple, cored and sliced
- A pinch of salt
- ½ tsp cinnamon powder
- 1 tbsp white sugar

DIRECTIONS:
In a bowl, mix apple slices with salt, sugar and cinnamon, toss, transfer to your air fryer's basket, cook for 10 minutes at 390 degrees F flipping once. Divide apple chips in bowls and serve as a snack.

NUTRITION:
calories 70, fat 0, fiber 4, carbs 3, protein 1

CINNAMON PASTRY STICKS
Preparation time: 10 min | Cooking time: 10 min | Servings: 2

INGREDIENTS:

- 4 bread slices, each cut into 4 sticks
- 2 eggs
- ¼ cup milk
- 1 tsp cinnamon powder
- 1 tbsp honey
- ¼ cup brown sugar
- A pinch of nutmeg

DIRECTIONS:
In a bowl, mix eggs with milk, brown sugar, cinnamon, nutmeg and honey and whisk well. Dip bread sticks in this mix, place them in your air fryer's basket and cook at 360 degrees F for 10 minutes. Divide bread sticks into bowls and serve as a snack.

NUTRITION:
calories 140, fat 1, fiber 4, carbs 8, protein 4

COCONUT SHRIMP
Preparation time: 10 min | Cooking time: 5 min | Servings: 4

INGREDIENTS:

- 12 big shrimp, deveined and peeled
- 2 egg whites
- 1 cup coconut, shredded
- 1 cup panko bread crumbs
- 1 cup white flour
- Salt and black pepper to the taste

DIRECTIONS:
In a bowl, mix panko with coconut and stir. Put flour, salt and pepper in a second bowl and whisk egg whites in a third one. Dip shrimp in flour, egg whites mix and coconut, place them all in your air fryer's basket, cook at 350 degrees F for 10 minutes flipping halfway. Arrange on a platter and serve as an appetizer.

NUTRITION:
calories 140, fat 4, fiber 0, carbs 3, protein 4

TIGER SHRIMP APPETIZER
Preparation time: 10 min | Cooking time: 5 min | Servings: 2

INGREDIENTS:

20 tiger shrimp, peeled and deveined
Salt and black pepper to the taste
½ tsp old bay seasoning
1 tbsp olive oil
¼ tsp smoked paprika

DIRECTIONS:
In a bowl, mix shrimp with oil, salt, pepper, old bay seasoning and paprika and toss to coat. Place shrimp in your air fryer's basket and cook at 390 degrees F for 5 minutes. Arrange them on a platter and serve as an appetizer.

NUTRITION:
calories 162, fat 6, fiber 4, carbs 8, protein 14

WHITE FISH STICKS
Preparation time: 10 min | Cooking time: 12 min | Servings: 2

INGREDIENTS:

- 4 ounces bread crumbs
- 4 tbsp olive oil
- 1 egg, whisked
- 4 white fish filets, boneless, skinless and cut into medium sticks
- Salt and black pepper to the taste

DIRECTIONS:
In a bowl, mix bread crumbs with oil and stir well. Put egg in a second bowl, add salt and pepper and whisk well. Dip fish stick in egg and them in bread crumb mix, place them in your air fryer's basket and cook at 360 degrees F for 12 minutes. Arrange fish sticks on a platter and serve as an appetizer.

NUTRITION:
calories 160, fat 3, fiber 5, carbs 12, protein 3

CRUNCHY FISH NUGGETS
Preparation time: 10 min | Cooking time: 12 min | Servings: 4

INGREDIENTS:

- 28 ounces fish fillets, skinless and cut into medium pieces
- Salt and black pepper to the taste
- 5 tbsp flour
- 1 egg, whisked
- 5 tbsp water
- 3 ounces panko bread crumbs
- 1 tbsp garlic powder
- 1 tbsp smoked paprika
- 4 tbsp homemade mayonnaise
- Lemon juice from ½ lemon
- 1 tsp dill, dried
- Cooking spray

DIRECTIONS:

In a bowl, mix flour with water and stir well. Add egg, salt and pepper and whisk well. In a second bowl, mix panko with garlic powder and paprika and stir well. Dip fish pieces in flour and egg mix and then in panko mix, place them in your air fryer's basket, spray them with cooking oil and cook at 400 degrees F for 12 minutes. Meanwhile, in a bowl mix mayo with dill and lemon juice and whisk well. Arrange fish nuggets on a platter and serve with dill mayo on the side.

Nutrition:
calories 332, fat 12, fiber 6, carbs 17, protein 15

SHRIMP AND MUSHROOM ROLLS
Preparation time: 10 min | Cooking time: 15 min | Servings: 4

Ingredients:

- ½ pound already cooked shrimp, chopped
- 8 ounces water chestnuts, chopped
- ½ pounds shiitake mushrooms, chopped
- 2 cups cabbage, chopped
- 2 tbsp olive oil
- 1 garlic clove, minced
- 1 tsp ginger, grated
- 3 scallions, chopped
- Salt and black pepper to the taste
- 1 tbsp water
- 1 egg yolk
- 6 spring roll wrappers

Directions:
Heat up a pan with the oil over medium high heat, add cabbage, shrimp, chestnuts, mushrooms, garlic, ginger, scallions, salt and pepper, stir and cook for 2 minutes. In a bowl, mix egg with water and stir well. Arrange roll wrappers on a working surface, divide shrimp and veggie mix on them, seal edges with egg wash, place them all in your air fryer's basket, cook at 360 degrees F for 15 minutes, transfer to a platter and serve as an appetizer.

Nutrition:
calories 140, fat 3, fiber 1, carbs 12, protein 3

SEAFOOD APPETIZER
Preparation time: 10 min | Cooking time: 25 min | Servings: 4

Ingredients:

- ½ cup yellow onion, chopped
- 1 cup green bell pepper, chopped
- 1 cup celery, chopped
- 1 cup baby shrimp, peeled and deveined
- 1 cup crab meat, flaked
- 1 cup homemade mayonnaise
- 1 tsp Worcestershire sauce
- Salt and black pepper to the taste
- 2 tbsp bread crumbs
- 1 tbsp butter
- 1 tsp sweet paprika

Directions:
In a bowl, mix shrimp with crab meat, bell pepper, onion, mayo, celery, salt and pepper and stir. Add Worcestershire sauce, stir again and pour everything into a baking dish that fits your air fryer. Sprinkle bread crumbs and add butter, introduce in your air fryer and cook at 320 degrees F for 25 minutes, shaking halfway. Divide into bowl and serve with paprika sprinkled on top as an appetizer.

Nutrition:
calories 200, fat 1, fiber 2, carbs 5, protein 1

SALMON CILANTRO MEATBALLS
Preparation time: 10 min | Cooking time: 12 min | Servings: 4

Ingredients:

- 3 tbsp cilantro, minced
- 1 pound salmon, skinless and chopped
- 1 small yellow onion, chopped
- 1 egg white
- Salt and black pepper to the taste
- 2 garlic cloves, minced
- ½ tsp paprika
- ¼ cup panko
- ½ tsp oregano, ground
- Cooking spray

Directions:
In your food processor, mix salmon with onion, cilantro, egg white, garlic cloves, salt, pepper, paprika and oregano and stir well. Add panko, blend again and shape meatballs from this mix using your palms. Place them in your air fryer's basket, spray them with cooking spray and cook at 320 degrees F for 12 minutes shaking the fryer halfway. Arrange meatballs on a platter and serve them as an appetizer.

Nutrition:
calories 289, fat 12, fiber 3, carbs 22, protein 23

GARLICKY CHICKEN WINGS
Preparation time: 10 min | Cooking time: 1 hours | Servings: 2

Ingredients:

- 16 pieces chicken wings
- Salt and black pepper to the taste
- ¼ cup butter
- ¾ cup potato starch
- ¼ cup honey
- 4 tbsp garlic, minced

Directions:
In a bowl, mix chicken wings with salt, pepper and potato starch, toss well, transfer to your air fryer's basket, cook them at 380 degrees F for 25 minutes and at 400 degrees F for 5 minutes more. Meanwhile, heat up a pan with the butter over medium high heat, melt it, add garlic, stir, cook for 5 minutes and then mix with salt, pepper and honey. Whisk well, cook over medium heat for 20 minutes and take off heat. Arrange chicken wings on a platter, drizzle honey sauce all over and serve as an appetizer.

NUTRITION: calories 244, fat 7, fiber 3, carbs 19, protein 8

MOZZARELLA CHICKEN ROLLS

Preparation time: 10 min | Cooking time: 22 min | Servings: 4

INGREDIENTS:

- 2 cups baby spinach
- 4 chicken breasts, boneless and skinless
- 1 cup sun dried tomatoes, chopped
- Salt and black pepper to the taste
- 1 and ½ tbsp Italian seasoning
- 4 mozzarella slices
- A drizzle of olive oil

DIRECTIONS:
Flatten chicken breasts using a meat tenderizer, divide tomatoes, mozzarella and spinach, season with salt, pepper and Italian seasoning, roll and seal them. Place them in your air fryer's basket, drizzle some oil over them and cook at 375 degrees F for 17 minutes, flipping once. Arrange chicken rolls on a platter and serve them as an appetizer.

NUTRITION: calories 300, fat 1, fiber 4, carbs 7, protein 10

CRISPY CHICKEN BREAST STICKS

Preparation time: 10 min | Cooking time: 16 min | Servings: 4

INGREDIENTS:

- ¾ cup white flour
- 1 pound chicken breast, skinless, boneless and cut into medium sticks
- 1 tsp sweet paprika
- 1 cup panko bread crumbs
- 1 egg, whisked
- Salt and black pepper to the taste
- ½ tbsp olive oil
- Zest from 1 lemon, grated

DIRECTIONS:
In a bowl, mix paprika with flour, salt, pepper and lemon zest and stir. Put whisked egg in another bowl and the panko breadcrumbs in a third one. Dredge chicken pieces in flour, egg and panko and place them in your lined air fryer's basket, drizzle the oil over them, cook at 400 degrees F for 8 minutes, flip and cook for 8 more minutes. Arrange them on a platter and serve as a snack.

NUTRITION: calories 254, fat 4, fiber 7, carbs 20, protein 22

PROVOLONE BEEF ROLLS

Preparation time: 10 min | Cooking time: 14 min | Servings: 4

INGREDIENTS:

- 2 pounds beef steak, opened and flattened with a meat tenderizer
- Salt and black pepper to the taste
- 1 cup baby spinach
- 3 ounces red bell pepper, roasted and chopped
- 6 slices provolone cheese
- 3 tbsp pesto

DIRECTIONS:
Arrange flattened beef steak on a cutting board, spread pesto all over, add cheese in a single layer, add bell peppers, spinach, salt and pepper to the taste. Roll your steak, secure with toothpicks, season again with salt and pepper, place roll in your air fryer's basket and cook at 400 degrees F for 14 minutes, rotating roll halfway. Leave aside to cool down, cut into 2 inch smaller rolls, arrange on a platter and serve them as an appetizer.

NUTRITION: calories 230, fat 1, fiber 3, carbs 12, protein 10

BEEF EMPANADAS

Preparation time: 10 min | Cooking time: 25 min | Servings: 4

INGREDIENTS:

- 1 package empanada shells
- 1 tbsp olive oil
- 1 pound beef meat, ground
- 1 yellow onion, chopped
- Salt and black pepper to the taste
- 2 garlic cloves, minced
- ½ tsp cumin, ground
- ¼ cup tomato salsa
- 1 egg yolk whisked with 1 tbsp water
- 1 green bell pepper, chopped

DIRECTIONS:
Heat up a pan with the oil over medium high heat, add beef and brown on all sides. Add onion, garlic, salt, pepper, bell pepper and tomato salsa, stir and cook for 15 minutes. Divide cooked meat in empanada shells, brush them with egg wash and seal. Place them in your air fryer's steamer basket and cook at 350 degrees F for 10 minutes. Arrange on a platter and serve as an appetizer.

NUTRITION: calories 274, fat 17, fiber 14, carbs 20, protein 7

GREEK FETA MEATBALLS

Preparation time: 10 min | Cooking time: 8 min | Servings: 10

INGREDIENTS:

- 4 ounces lamb meat, minced
- Salt and black pepper to the taste
- 1 slice of bread, toasted and crumbled
- 2 tbsp feta cheese, crumbled
- ½ tbsp lemon peel, grated
- 1 tbsp oregano, chopped

DIRECTIONS:
In a bowl, combine meat with bread crumbs,

salt, pepper, feta, oregano and lemon peel, stir well, shape 10 meatballs and place them in you air fryer. Cook at 400 degrees F for 8 minutes, arrange them on a platter and serve as an appetizer.

NUTRITION:
calories 234, fat 12, fiber 2, carbs 20, protein 30

BEEF AND SAGE ROLLS
Preparation time: 10 min | Cooking time: 15 min | Servings: 4

INGREDIENTS:

- 14 ounces beef stock
- 7 ounces white wine
- 4 beef cutlets
- Salt and black pepper to the taste
- 8 sage leaves
- 4 ham slices
- 1 tbsp butter, melted

DIRECTIONS:
Heat up a pan with the stock over medium high heat, add wine, cook until it reduces, take off heat and divide into small bowls. Season cutlets with salt and pepper, cover with sage and roll each in ham slices. Brush rolls with butter, place them in your air fryer's basket and cook at 400 degrees F for 15 minutes. Arrange rolls on a platter and serve them with the gravy on the side.

NUTRITION:
calories 260, fat 12, fiber 1, carbs 22, protein 21

BEEF AND HAM PATTIES
Preparation time: 10 min | Cooking time: 8 min | Servings: 4

INGREDIENTS:

- 14 ounces beef, minced
- 2 tbsp ham, cut into strips
- 1 leek, chopped
- 3 tbsp bread crumbs
- Salt and black pepper to the taste
- ½ tsp nutmeg, ground

DIRECTIONS:
In a bowl, mix beef with leek, salt, pepper, ham, breadcrumbs and nutmeg, stir well and shape small patties out of this mix. Place them in your air fryer's basket, cook at 400 degrees F for 8 minutes, arrange on a platter and serve as an appetizer.

NUTRITION:
calories 260, fat 12, fiber 3, carbs 12, protein 21

BELL PEPPERS AND FETA ROLLS
Preparation time: 10 min | Cooking time: 10 min | Servings: 8

INGREDIENTS:

- 1 yellow bell pepper, halved
- 1 orange bell pepper, halved
- Salt and black pepper to the taste
- 4 ounces feta cheese, crumbled
- 1 green onion, chopped
- 2 tbsp oregano, chopped

DIRECTIONS:
In a bowl, mix cheese with onion, oregano, salt and pepper and whisk well. Place bell pepper halves in your air fryer's basket, cook at 400 degrees F for 10 minutes, transfer to a cutting board, cool down and peel. Divide cheese mix on each bell pepper half, roll, secure with toothpicks, arrange on a platter and serve as an appetizer.

NUTRITION:
calories 170, fat 1, fiber 2, carbs 8, protein 5

GOAT CHEESE PEPPERS
Preparation time: 10 min | Cooking time: 8 min | Servings: 8

INGREDIENTS:

8 small bell peppers, tops cut off and seeds removed
1 tbsp olive oil
Salt and black pepper to the taste
3.5 ounces goat cheese, cut into 8 pieces

DIRECTIONS:
In a bowl, mix cheese with oil with salt and pepper and toss to coat. Stuff each pepper with goat cheese, place them in your air fryer's basket, cook at 400 degrees F for 8 minutes, arrange on a platter and serve as an appetizer.

NUTRITION:
calories 120, fat 1, fiber 1, carbs 12, protein 8

PARSLEY TOMATOES APPETIZER
Preparation time: 10 min | Cooking time: 20 min | Servings: 2

INGREDIENTS:

- 2 tomatoes, halved
- Cooking spray
- Salt and black pepper to the taste
- 1 tsp parsley, dried
- 1 tsp basil, dried
- 1 tsp oregano, dried
- 1 tsp rosemary, dried

DIRECTIONS:
Spray tomato halves with cooking oil, season with salt, pepper, parsley, basil, oregano and rosemary over them. Place them in your air fryer's basket and cook at 320 degrees F for 20 minutes. Arrange them on a platter and serve as an appetizer.

NUTRITION:
calories 100, fat 1, fiber 1, carbs 4, protein 1

CREAMY JALAPENO BALLS
Preparation time: 10 min | Cooking time: 4 min | Servings: 3

INGREDIENTS:

- 3 bacon slices, cooked and crumbled
- 3 ounces cream cheese
- ¼ tsp onion powder
- Salt and black pepper to the taste
- 1 jalapeno pepper, chopped
- ½ tsp parsley, dried
- ¼ tsp garlic powder

DIRECTIONS:
In a bowl, mix cream cheese with jalapeno pepper, onion and garlic powder, parsley, bacon salt and pepper and stir well. Shape small balls out of this mix, place them in your air fryer's basket, cook at 350 degrees F for 4 minutes, arrange on a platter and serve as an appetizer.

NUTRITION:
calories 172, fat 4, fiber 1, carbs 12, protein 5

MINTY SHRIMP
Preparation time: 10 min | Cooking time: 8 min | Servings: 16

INGREDIENTS:

- 2 tbsp olive oil
- 10 ounces already cooked shrimp, peeled and deveined
- 1 tbsp mint, chopped
- 1/3 cup blackberries, ground
- 11 prosciutto sliced
- 1/3 cup red wine

DIRECTIONS:
Wrap each shrimp in a prosciutto slices, drizzle the oil over them, rub well, place in your preheated air fryer at 390 degrees F and fry them for 8 minutes. Meanwhile, heat up a pan with ground blackberries over medium heat, add mint and wine, stir, cook for 3 minutes and take off heat. Arrange shrimp on a platter, drizzle blackberries sauce over them and serve as an appetizer.

NUTRITION:
calories 224, fat 12, fiber 2, carbs 12, protein 14

CHEDDAR VEGGIE PATTIES
Preparation time: 10 min | Cooking time: 10 min | Servings: 12

INGREDIENTS:

- 4 cups broccoli florets
- 1 and ½ cup almond flour
- 1 tsp paprika
- Salt and black pepper to the taste
- 2 eggs
- ¼ cup olive oil
- 2 cups cheddar cheese, grated
- 1 tsp garlic powder
- ½ tsp apple cider vinegar
- ½ tsp baking soda

DIRECTIONS:
Put broccoli florets in your food processor, add salt and pepper, blend well and transfer to a bowl. Add almond flour, salt, pepper, paprika, garlic powder, baking soda, cheese, oil, eggs and vinegar, stir well and shape 12 patties out of this mix. Place them in your preheated air fryer's basket and cook at 350 degrees F for 10 minutes. Arrange patties on a platter and serve as an appetizer.

NUTRITION:
calories 203, fat 12, fiber 2, carbs 14, protein 2

STUFFED PEPPERS MEDLEY
Preparation time: 10 min | Cooking time: 20 min | Servings: 6

INGREDIENTS:

- 1 pound mini bell peppers, halved
- Salt and black pepper to the taste
- 1 tsp garlic powder
- 1 tsp sweet paprika
- ½ tsp oregano, dried
- ¼ tsp red pepper flakes
- 1 pound beef meat, ground
- 1 and ½ cups cheddar cheese, shredded
- 1 tbsp chili powder
- 1 tsp cumin, ground
- Sour cream for serving

DIRECTIONS:
In a bowl, mix chili powder with paprika, salt, pepper, cumin, oregano, pepper flakes and garlic powder and stir. Heat up a pan over medium heat, add beef, stir and brown for 10 minutes. Add chili powder mix, stir, take off heat and stuff pepper halves with this mix. Sprinkle cheese all over, place peppers in your air fryer's basket and cook them at 350 degrees F for 6 minutes. Arrange peppers on a platter and serve them with sour cream on the side.

NUTRITION:
calories 170, fat 22, fiber 3, carbs 6, protein 27

MOZZARELLA AND ZUCCHINI SNACK
Preparation time: 10 min | Cooking time: 8 min | Servings: 4

INGREDIENTS:

- 1 cup mozzarella, shredded
- ¼ cup tomato sauce
- 1 zucchini, sliced
- Salt and black pepper to the taste
- A pinch of cumin
- Cooking spray

DIRECTIONS:
Arrange zucchini slices in your air fryer's basket, spray them with cooking oil, spread tomato sauce all over, them, season with salt, pepper, cumin, sprinkle mozzarella at the end and cook them at 320 degrees F for 8 minutes. Arrange them on a platter and serve as a snack.

NUTRITION:
calories 150, fat 4, fiber 2, carbs 12, protein 4

CREAMY SPINACH BALLS

Preparation time: 10 min | Cooking time: 7 min | Servings: 30

INGREDIENTS:

- 4 tbsp butter, melted
- 2 eggs
- 1 cup flour
- 16 ounces spinach
- 1/3 cup feta cheese, crumbled
- ¼ tsp nutmeg, ground
- 1/3 cup parmesan, grated
- Salt and black pepper to the taste
- 1 tbsp onion powder
- 3 tbsp whipping cream
- 1 tsp garlic powder

DIRECTIONS:
In your blender, mix spinach with butter, eggs, flour, feta cheese, parmesan, nutmeg, whipping cream, salt, pepper, onion and garlic pepper, blend very well and keep in the freezer for 10 minutes. Shape 30 spinach balls, place them in your air fryer's basket and cook at 300 degrees F for 7 minutes.

NUTRITION:
calories 60, fat 5, fiber 1, carbs 1, protein 2

MUSHROOMS APPETIZER

Preparation time: 10 min | Cooking time: 10 min | Servings: 4

INGREDIENTS:

- ¼ cup mayonnaise
- 1 tsp garlic powder
- 1 small yellow onion, chopped
- 24 ounces white mushroom caps
- Salt and black pepper to the taste
- 1 tsp curry powder
- 4 ounces cream cheese, soft
- ¼ cup sour cream
- ½ cup Mexican cheese, shredded
- 1 cup shrimp, cooked, peeled, deveined and chopped

DIRECTIONS:
In a bowl, mix mayo with garlic powder, onion, curry powder, cream cheese, sour cream, Mexican cheese, shrimp, salt and pepper to the taste and whisk well. Stuff mushrooms with this mix, place them in your air fryer's basket and cook at 300 degrees F for 10 minutes. Arrange on a platter and serve as an appetizer.

NUTRITION:
calories 200, fat 20, fiber 3, carbs 16, protein 14

PARMESAN WINGS

Preparation time: 10 min | Cooking time: 12 min | Servings: 6

INGREDIENTS:

- 6 pound chicken wings, halved
- Salt and black pepper to the taste
- ½ tsp Italian seasoning
- 2 tbsp butter
- ½ cup parmesan cheese, grated
- A pinch of red pepper flakes, crushed
- 1 tsp garlic powder
- 1 egg

DIRECTIONS:
Arrange chicken wings in your air fryer's basket and cook at 390 degrees F and cook for 9 minutes. Meanwhile, in your blender, mix butter with cheese, egg, salt, pepper, pepper flakes, garlic powder and Italian seasoning and blend very well. Take chicken wings out, pour cheese sauce over them, toss to coat well and cook in your air fryer's basket at 390 degrees F for 3 minutes. Serve them as an appetizer.

NUTRITION:
calories 204, fat 8, fiber 1, carbs 18, protein 14

CHEESY PEPPER STICKS

Preparation time: 1 hour and 10 min | Cooking time: 8 min | Servings: 16

INGREDIENTS:

- 2 eggs, whisked
- Salt and black pepper to the taste
- 8 mozzarella cheese strings, cut into halves
- 1 cup parmesan, grated
- 1 tbsp Italian seasoning
- Cooking spray
- 1 garlic clove, minced

DIRECTIONS:
In a bowl, mix parmesan with salt, pepper, Italian seasoning and garlic and stir well. Put whisked eggs in another bowl. Dip mozzarella sticks in egg mixture, then in cheese mix. Dip them again in egg and in parmesan mix and keep them in the freezer for 1 hour. Spray cheese sticks with cooking oil, place them in your air fryer's basket and cook at 390 degrees F for 8 minutes flipping them halfway. Arrange them on a platter and serve as an appetizer.

NUTRITION:
calories 140, fat 5, fiber 1, carbs 3, protein 4

BLUE CHICKEN ROLLS

Preparation time: 2 hours and 10 min | Cooking time: 10 min | Servings: 12

Ingredients:

- 4 ounces blue cheese, crumbled
- 2 cups chicken, cooked and chopped
- Salt and black pepper to the taste
- 2 green onions, chopped
- 2 celery stalks, finely chopped
- ½ cup tomato sauce
- 12 egg roll wrappers
- Cooking spray

DIRECTIONS:
In a bowl, mix chicken meat with blue cheese, salt, pepper, green onions, celery and tomato sauce, stir well and keep in the fridge for 2 hours. Place egg wrappers on a working surface, divide chicken mix on them, roll and seal edges. Place rolls in your air fryer's basket, spray them with cooking

oil and cook at 350 degrees F for 10 minutes, flipping them halfway.

NUTRITION:
calories 220, fat 7, fiber 2, carbs 14, protein 10

BASIL FLAX CRACKERS

Preparation time: 10 min | Cooking time: 20 min | Servings: 6

INGREDIENTS:

- 2 cups flax seed, ground
- 2 cups flax seed, soaked overnight and drained
- 4 bunches kale, chopped
- 1 bunch basil, chopped
- ½ bunch celery, chopped
- 4 garlic cloves, minced
- 1/3 cup olive oil

DIRECTIONS:
In your food processor mix ground flaxseed with celery, kale, basil and garlic and blend well. Add oil and soaked flaxseed and blend again, spread in your air fryer's pan, cut into medium crackers and cook them at 380 degrees F for 20 minutes. Divide into bowls and serve as an appetizer.

NUTRITION:
calories 143, fat 1, fiber 2, carbs 8, protein 4

PARMESAN CHIPS

Preparation time: 5 min | Cooking time: 8 min | Servings: 2

INGREDIENTS:

- ½ tbsp water
- 2 tbsp parmesan, shredded
- 4 eggs whites
- Salt and black pepper to the taste

DIRECTIONS:
In a bowl, mix egg whites with salt, pepper and water and whisk well. Spoon this into a muffin pan that fits your air fryer, sprinkle cheese on top, introduce in your air fryer and cook at 350 degrees F for 8 minutes. Arrange egg white chips on a platter and serve as a snack.

NUTRITION:
calories 180, fat 2, fiber 1, carbs 12, protein 7

PEPPER TUNA CAKES

Preparation time: 10 min | Cooking time: 10 min | Servings: 12

INGREDIENTS:

- 15 ounces canned tuna, drain and flaked
- 3 eggs
- ½ tsp dill, dried
- 1 tsp parsley, dried
- ½ cup red onion, chopped
- 1 tsp garlic powder
- Salt and black pepper to the taste
- Cooking spray

DIRECTIONS:
In a bowl, mix tuna with salt, pepper, dill, parsley, onion, garlic powder and eggs, stir well and shape medium cakes out of this mix. Place tuna cakes in your air fryer's basket, spray them with cooking oil and cook at 350 degrees F for 10 minutes, flipping them halfway. Arrange them on a platter and serve as an appetizer.

NUTRITION:
calories 140, fat 2, fiber 1, carbs 8, protein 6

SEAFOOD SNACK

Preparation time: 10 min | Cooking time: 20 min | Servings: 1

INGREDIENTS:

- 8 ounces calamari, cut into medium rings
- 7 ounces shrimp, peeled and deveined
- 1 eggs
- 3 tbsp white flour
- 1 tbsp olive oil
- 2 tbsp avocado, chopped
- 1 tsp tomato paste
- 1 tbsp mayonnaise
- A splash of Worcestershire sauce
- 1 tsp lemon juice
- Salt and black pepper to the taste
- ½ tsp turmeric powder

DIRECTIONS:
In a bowl, whisk egg with oil, add calamari rings and shrimp and toss to coat. In another bowl, mix flour with salt, pepper and turmeric and stir. Dredge calamari and shrimp in this mix, place them in your air fryer's basket and cook at 350 degrees F for 9 minutes, flipping them once. Meanwhile, in a bowl, mix avocado with mayo and tomato paste and mash using a fork. Add Worcestershire sauce, lemon juice, salt and pepper and stir well. Arrange calamari and shrimp on a platter and serve with the sauce on the side.

NUTRITION:
calories 288, fat 23, fiber 3, carbs 10, protein 15

AIR FRYER FISH AND SEAFOOD RECIPES

SWEET COD FILLETS

Preparation time: 10 min | Cooking time: 15 min | Servings: 4

Ingredients:

- 4 cod fillets, boneless
- Salt and black pepper to taste
- 1 cup water
- 4 tbsp light soy sauce
- 1 tbsp sugar
- 3 tbsp olive oil + a drizzle
- 4 ginger slices
- 3 spring onions, chopped
- 2 tbsp coriander, chopped

DIRECTIONS:

Season the fish with salt and pepper, then drizzle some oil over it and rub well. Put the fish in your air fryer and cook at 360 degrees F for 12 minutes. Put the water in a pot and heat up over medium heat; add the soy sauce and sugar, stir, bring to a simmer, and remove from the heat. Heat up a pan with the olive oil over medium heat; add the ginger and green onions, stir, cook for 2-3 minutes, and remove from the heat. Divide the fish between plates and top with ginger, coriander, and green onions. Drizzle the soy sauce mixture all over, serve, and enjoy!

NUTRITION:

calories 270, fat 12, fiber 8, carbs 16, protein 14

PECAN COD

Preparation time: 10 min | Cooking time: 15 min | Servings: 2

INGREDIENTS:

- 2 black cod fillets, boneless
- 1 tbsp olive oil
- Salt and black pepper to taste
- 2 leeks, sliced
- ½ cup pecans, chopped

DIRECTIONS:

In a bowl, mix the cod with the oil, salt, pepper, and the leeks; toss / coat well. Transfer the cod to your air fryer and cook at 360 degrees F for 15 minutes. Divide the fish and leeks between plates, sprinkle the pecans on top, and serve immediately.

NUTRITION:

calories 280, fat 4, fiber 2, carbs 12, protein 15

BALSAMIC COD

Preparation time: 5 min | Cooking time: 12 min | Servings: 2

INGREDIENTS:

- 2 cod fillets, boneless
- 2 tablespoons lemon juice
- Salt and black pepper to taste
- ½ teaspoon garlic powder
- 1 cup water
- 1 cup balsamic vinegar
- 3 shallots, chopped
- 2 tbsp olive oil

DIRECTIONS:

In a bowl, toss the cod with the salt, pepper, lemon juice, garlic powder, water, vinegar, and oil; coat well. Transfer the fish to your fryer's basket and cook at 360 degrees F for 12 minutes, flipping them halfway. Divide the fish between plates, sprinkle the shallots on top, and serve.

NUTRITION:

calories 271, fat 12, fiber 10, carbs 16, protein 20

GARLIC SALMON FILLETS

Preparation time: 5 min | Cooking time: 8 min | Servings: 2

INGREDIENTS:

- 2 salmon fillets, boneless
- Salt and black pepper to taste
- 3 red chili peppers, chopped
- 2 tbsp lemon juice
- 2 tbsp olive oil
- 2 tbsp garlic, minced

DIRECTIONS:

In a bowl, combine the ingredients, toss, and coat fish well. Transfer everything to your air fryer and cook at 365 degrees F for 8 minutes, flipping the fish halfway. Divide between plates and serve right away.

NUTRITION:

calories 280, fat 4, fiber 8, carbs 15, protein 20

SHRIMP AND VEGGIE MIX

Preparation time: 10 min | Cooking time: 20 min | Servings: 4

INGREDIENTS:

- ½ cup red onion, chopped
- 1 cup red bell pepper, chopped
- 1 cup celery, chopped
- 1 pound shrimp, peeled and deveined
- 1 tsp Worcestershire sauce
- Salt and black pepper to taste
- 1 tbsp butter, melted
- 1 tsp sweet paprika

DIRECTIONS:

Add all the ingredients to a bowl and mix well. Transfer everything to your air fryer and cook 320 degrees F for 20 minutes, shaking halfway. Divide between plates and serve.

NUTRITION:

calories 220, fat 14, fiber 9, carbs 17, protein 20

WHITE FISH WITH PEAS AND BASIL

Preparation time: 10 min | Cooking time: 12 min | Servings: 4

INGREDIENTS:

- 4 white fish fillets, boneless
- 2 tbsp cilantro, chopped
- 2 cups peas, cooked and drained
- 4 tbsp veggie stock
- ½ tsp basil, dried
- ½ tsp sweet paprika
- 2 garlic cloves, minced
- Salt and pepper to taste

DIRECTIONS:

In a bowl, mix the fish with all ingredients except the peas; toss to coat the fish well. Transfer everything to your air fryer and cook at 360 degrees F for 12 minutes. Add the peas, toss, and divide everything between plates. Serve and enjoy.

NUTRITION:

calories 241, fat 8, fiber 12, carbs 15, protein 18

COD AND CHIVES

Preparation time: 5 min | Cooking time: 12 min | Servings: 4

INGREDIENTS:

- 4 cod fillets, boneless
- Salt and black pepper to taste
- 3 tsp lime zest
- 2 tsp lime juice
- 3 tbsp chives, chopped
- 6 tbsp butter, melted
- 2 tbsp olive oil

DIRECTIONS:

Season the fish with the salt and pepper, rub it with the oil, and then put it in your air fryer. Cook at 360 degrees F for 10 minutes, flipping once. Heat up a pan with the butter over medium heat, and then add the chives, salt, pepper, lime juice, and zest, whisk; cook for 1-2 minutes. Divide the fish between plates, drizzle the lime sauce all over, and serve immediately.

NUTRITION:

calories 280, fat 12, fiber 9, carbs 17, protein 15

PAPRIKA SALMON FILLETS

Preparation time: 5 min | Cooking time: 12 min | Servings: 4

Ingredients:

- 4 salmon fillets, boneless
- 1 tbsp olive oil
- Salt and black pepper to taste
- 1 tsp cumin, ground
- 1 tsp sweet paprika
- ½ tsp chili powder
- 1 tsp garlic powder
- Juice of 1 lime

Directions:

In a bowl, mix the salmon with the other ingredients, rub / coat well, and transfer to your air fryer. Cook at 350 degrees F for 6 minutes on each side. Divide the fish between plates and serve right away with a side salad.

NUTRITION:

calories 280, fat 14, fiber 4, carbs 18, protein 20

THYME TUNA

Preparation time: 10 min | Cooking time: 8 min | Servings: 4

INGREDIENTS:

- ½ cup cilantro, chopped
- 1 cup olive oil
- 1 small red onion, chopped
- 3 tbsp balsamic vinegar
- 2 tbsp parsley, chopped
- 2 tbsp basil, chopped
- 1 jalapeno pepper, chopped
- 4 sushi tuna steaks
- Salt and black pepper to taste
- 1 tsp red pepper flakes
- 1 tsp thyme, chopped
- 3 garlic cloves, minced

DIRECTIONS:

Place all ingredients except the fish into a bowl and stir well. Add the fish and toss, coating it well. Transfer everything to your air fryer and cook at 360 degrees F for 4 minutes on each side. Divide the fish between plates and serve.

NUTRITION:

calories 306, fat 8, fiber 1, carbs 14, protein 16

Buttery Shrimp
Preparation time: 5 min | Cooking time: 10 min | Servings: 2

INGREDIENTS:

- 1 tbsp butter, melted
- A drizzle of olive oil
- 1 pound shrimp, peeled and deveined
- ¼ cup heavy cream
- 8 ounces mushrooms, roughly sliced
- A pinch of red pepper flakes
- Salt and black pepper to taste
- 2 garlic cloves, minced
- ½ cup beef stock
- 1 tbsp parsley, chopped
- 1 tbsp chives, chopped

DIRECTIONS:

Season the shrimp with salt and pepper and grease with the oil. Place the shrimp in your air fryer, cook at 360 degrees F for 7 minutes, and divide between plates. Heat up a pan with the butter over medium heat, add the mushrooms, stir, and cook for 3-4 minutes. Add all remaining ingredients; stir and then cook for a few minutes more. Drizzle the butter / garlic mixture over the shrimp and serve.

NUTRITION:

calories 305, fat 13, fiber 4, carbs 14, protein 11

MAPLE SALMON
Preparation time: 5 min | Cooking time: 10 min | Servings: 2

INGREDIENTS:
- 2 salmon fillets, boneless
- Salt and black pepper to taste
- 2 tbsp mustard
- 1 tbsp olive oil
- 1 tbsp maple syrup

DIRECTIONS:
In a bowl, mix the mustard with the oil and the maple syrup; whisk well and brush the salmon with this mix. Place the salmon in your air fryer and cook it at 370 degrees F for 5 minutes on each side.

NUTRITION:
calories 290, fat 7, fiber 14, carbs 18, protein 17

BALSAMIC ORANGE SALMON
Preparation time: 5 min | Cooking time: 15 min | Servings: 4

INGREDIENTS:
- 4 salmon fillets, boneless and cubed
- 2 lemons, sliced
- ¼ cup balsamic vinegar
- ¼ cup orange juice
- A pinch of salt and black pepper

DIRECTIONS:
In a pan that fits your air fryer, mix all ingredients except the fish; whisk. Heat the mixture up over medium-high heat for 5 minutes and add the salmon. Toss gently, and place the pan in the air fryer and cook at 360 degrees F for 10 minutes. Divide between plates and serve right away with a side salad.

NUTRITION:
calories 227, fat 9, fiber 12, carbs 14, protein 11

CRUNCHY PISTACHIO COD
Preparation time: 10 min | Cooking time: 10 min | Servings: 4

INGREDIENTS:
- 1 cup pistachios, chopped
- 4 cod fillets, boneless
- ¼ cup lime juice
- 2 tbsp honey
- 1 tsp parsley, chopped
- Salt and black pepper to taste
- 1 tbsp mustard

DIRECTIONS:
Place all the ingredients except the fish into a bowl; whisk. Spread the mixture over the fish fillets, put them in your air fryer, and cook at 350 degrees F for 10 minutes. Divide the fish between plates and serve immediately with a side salad.

NUTRITION:
calories 270, fat 17, fiber 12, carbs 20, protein 12

ROASTED PARSLEY COD
Preparation time: 10 min | Cooking time: 10 min | Servings: 4

INGREDIENTS:
- 3 tbsp parsley, chopped
- 4 medium cod filets, boneless
- ¼ cup butter, melted
- 2 garlic cloves, minced
- 2 tbsp lemon juice
- 1 shallot, chopped
- Salt and black pepper to taste

DIRECTIONS:
In a bowl, mix all ingredients except the fish; whisk well. Spread this mixture over the cod fillets. Put them in your air fryer and cook at 390 degrees F for 10 minutes. Divide the fish between plates and serve.

NUTRITION:
calories 280, fat 4, fiber 7, carbs 12, protein 15

SALMON WITH ALMONDS
Preparation time: 10 min | Cooking time: 20 min | Servings: 4

INGREDIENTS:
- 2 red onions, chopped
- 2 tbsp olive oil
- 2 small fennel bulbs, trimmed and sliced
- ¼ cup almonds, toasted and sliced
- Salt and black pepper to taste
- 4 salmon fillets, boneless
- 5 tsp fennel seeds, toasted

DIRECTIONS:
Season the fish with salt and pepper, grease it with 1 tbsp of the oil, and place in your air fryer's basket. Cook at 350 degrees F for 5-6 minutes on each side and divide between plates. Heat up a pan with the remaining tbsp of oil over medium-high heat; add the onions, stir, and sauté for 2 minutes. Add the fennel bulbs and seeds, almonds, salt, and pepper, and cook for 2-3 minutes more. Spread the mixture over the fish and serve right away; enjoy!

NUTRITION:
calories 284, fat 7, fiber 10, carbs 17, protein 16

PINEAPPLE SALMON FILLETS
Preparation time: 5 min | Cooking time: 10 min | Servings: 2

INGREDIENTS:
- 20 ounces canned pineapple pieces
- ½ tsp ginger, grated
- A drizzle of olive oil
- 2 tsp garlic powder
- 1 tbsp balsamic vinegar
- 2 medium salmon fillets, boneless
- Salt and black pepper to taste

DIRECTIONS:
Grease a pan that fits your air fryer with the

oil and add the fish inside. Add the remaining ingredients and place the pan in the air fryer. Cook at 350 degrees F for 10 minutes.

Nutrition:
calories 236, fat 8, fiber 12, carbs 17, protein 16

EASY SALMON FILLETS AND BELL PEPPERS
Preparation time: 5 min | Cooking time: 15 min | Servings: 6

Ingredients:

- 1 cup green olives, pitted
- 3 red bell peppers, cut into medium pieces
- ½ tsp smoked paprika
- Salt and black pepper to taste
- 3 tbsp olive oil
- 6 medium salmon fillets, skinless and boneless
- 2 tbsp cilantro, chopped

Directions:
In a baking dish that fits your air fryer, mix all the ingredients and toss gently. Place the baking dish in your air fryer and cook at 360 degrees F for 15 minutes. Divide the fillets between plates and serve.

Nutrition:
calories 281, fat 8, fiber 14, carbs 17, protein 16

GINGER AIR FRIED COD
Preparation time: 5 min | Cooking time: 10 min | Servings: 4

Ingredients:

- 4 medium cod fillets, boneless
- Salt and black pepper to taste
- ½ cup coconut milk
- A drizzle of olive oil
- 1 tsp ginger, grated
- ½ cup parsley, chopped
- 2 garlic cloves, chopped
- ½ jalapeno, chopped

Directions:
Place all ingredients except the fish in your blender; pulse well. In a baking dish that fits your air fryer, place the fish along with the coconut milk mixture and toss gently. Place the dish in your air fryer and cook at 380 degrees F for 10 minutes. Divide between plates and serve hot.

Nutrition:
calories 250, fat 5, fiber 6, carbs 15, protein 18

SALMON AND MUSTARD MIX
Preparation time: 5 min | Cooking time: 10 min | Servings: 2

Ingredients:

- 2 salmon fillets, boneless
- Zest of ½ orange
- Juice of ½ orange
- A pinch of salt and black pepper
- 2 tbsp mustard
- 2 tsp honey
- 2 tbsp olive oil
- 1 tbsp dill, chopped
- 2 tbsp parsley, chopped

Directions:
In a bowl, mix the orange zest with the orange juice, salt, pepper, mustard, honey, oil, dill, and parsley, and whisk well. Add the salmon to this mix, toss, and transfer the fish to your air fryer. Cook at 350 degrees F for 10 minutes, flipping halfway. Divide the fish between plates, drizzle the orange vinaigrette all over, and serve.

Nutrition:
calories 272, fat 8, fiber 12, carbs 15, protein 16

PAELLA MARINERA
Preparation time: 10 min | Cooking time: 25 min | Servings: 4

Ingredients:

- 5 ounces wild rice
- 2 ounces peas
- 1 red bell pepper, deseeded and chopped
- 14 ounces dry white wine
- 3½ ounces chicken stock
- 1 pound sea bass fillets, cubed
- 6 scallops
- 8 shrimp, peeled and deveined
- Salt and black pepper to taste
- A drizzle of olive oil

Directions:
In a heatproof dish that fits your air fryer, place all the ingredients and toss. Place the dish in your air fryer and cook at 380 degrees F and cook for 25 minutes, stirring halfway. Divide between plates and serve.

Nutrition:
calories 290, fat 12, fiber 2, carbs 16, protein 19

PARSLEY COCONUT SHRIMP
Preparation time: 5 min | Cooking time: 10 min | Servings: 4

Ingredients:

- 12 large shrimp, deveined and peeled
- 1 cup coconut cream
- 1 tbsp cornstarch
- 1 tbsp parsley, chopped
- Salt and black pepper to taste

Directions:
Add all ingredients to a pan that fits your air fryer and toss. Place the pan in the fryer and cook at 360 degrees F for 10 minutes. Serve hot and enjoy!

Nutrition:
calories 272, fat 4, fiber 3, carbs 14, protein 4

TIGER SHRIMP MIX
Preparation time: 5 min | Cooking time: 10 min | Servings: 2

INGREDIENTS:

- 20 tiger shrimp, peeled and deveined
- Salt and black pepper to taste
- ½ tsp Italian seasoning
- 1 tbsp extra virgin olive oil
- ¼ tsp smoked paprika

DIRECTIONS:
Add all the ingredients to a bowl and toss. Put the shrimp in the air fryer's basket and cook at 380 degrees F for 10 minutes. Divide into bowls and serve.

NUTRITION:
calories 219, fat 6, fiber 4, carbs 14, protein 15

PAPRIKA AND TABASCO SHRIMP MIX

Preparation time: 2 hours | Cooking time: 10 min | Servings: 4

INGREDIENTS:

- 1 pound large shrimp, peeled and deveined
- 1 tsp red pepper flakes
- 2 tbsp olive oil
- 1 tsp Tabasco sauce
- 2 tbsp water
- 1 tsp basil, dried
- Salt and black pepper to taste
- 1 tbsp parsley, chopped
- ½ tsp garlic powder
- ½ tsp sweet paprika

DIRECTIONS:
In a bowl, mix the shrimp with all other ingredients except the parsley; toss to coat the shrimp well. Place shrimp in the fridge for 2 hours. Transfer the shrimp to your air fryer's basket and cook at 370 degrees F for 10 minutes. Divide into bowls, sprinkle with parsley, and serve with a side salad.

NUTRITION:
calories 210, fat 7, fiber 6, carbs 13, protein 8

ROSEMARY SHRIMPS

Preparation time: 5 min | Cooking time: 10 min | Servings: 2

INGREDIENTS:

- 8 large shrimp
- 4 garlic cloves, minced
- Salt and black pepper to taste
- 1 tbsp rosemary, chopped
- 2 tbsp butter, melted

DIRECTIONS:
Add all the ingredients to a bowl and toss. Transfer the shrimp to your air fryer and cook at 360 degrees F for 10 minutes. Divide into bowls, serve, and enjoy!

Nutrition:
calories 210, fat 11, fiber 12, carbs 16, protein 9

PEPPERY SALMON

Preparation time: 5 min | Cooking time: 12 min | Servings: 4

INGREDIENTS:

- 4 salmon fillets, boneless
- 1 tbsp capers, drained
- 1 tbsp dill,
- chopped
- Salt and black pepper to taste
- Juice of 1 lemon
- 2 tsp olive oil

DIRECTIONS:
In your air fryer, mix the capers, dill, salt, pepper, and the oil, and then rub the fish gently with this mixture. Cook at 360 degrees F for 6 minutes on each side. Divide the fish between plates, drizzle the lemon juice all over, and serve.

NUTRITION:
calories 280, fat 11, fiber 1, carbs 12, protein 18

OLIVES SNAPPER

Preparation time: 5 min | Cooking time: 15 min | Servings: 4

INGREDIENTS:

- 8 garlic cloves, minced
- 1 tbsp lemon zest
- 1 cup olive oil
- 4 medium snapper fillets, boneless
- 1½ tbsp green olives, pitted and sliced
- Juice of 2 limes
- Salt and black pepper to taste

DIRECTIONS:
Add all the ingredients except the fish to a baking dish that fits your air fryer; mix well. Add the fish and toss gently, then place in the fryer. Cook at 360 degrees F for 15 minutes. Divide everything between plates and serve.

NUTRITION:
calories 191, fat 2, fiber 3, carbs 18, protein 12

GARLIC TROUT

Preparation time: 10 min | Cooking time: 13 min | Servings: 2

INGREDIENTS:

- 2 trout fillets, boneless
- Salt and black pepper to taste
- 1 red chili pepper, chopped
- 1 tbsp lemon juice
- 1 tbsp olive oil
- 1 tbsp garlic, minced

DIRECTIONS:
Put the trout in your air fryer and add all other ingredients; rub the trout gently. Cook at 360 degrees F for 13 minutes. Divide between plates and serve.

NUTRITION:
calories 271, fat 4, fiber 2, carbs 15, protein 11

CILANTRO TROUT FILLETS

Preparation time: 5 min | Cooking time: 12 min | Servings: 4

INGREDIENTS:

- 4 trout fillets, boneless
- 4 garlic cloves, minced
- 1 cup black olives, pitted and chopped
- 3 tbsp cilantro, chopped
- 1 tbsp olive oil

DIRECTIONS:
Add all of the ingredients to your air fryer and mix well. Cook at 360 degrees F for 6 minutes on each side. Divide everything between plates and serve.

Nutrition: calories 251, fat 7, fiber 3, carbs 16, protein 12

RICE WITH SALMON

Preparation time: 5 min | Cooking time: 30 min | Servings: 2

INGREDIENTS:

- 2 wild salmon fillets, boneless
- Salt and black pepper to taste
- ½ cup jasmine rice
- 1 cup chicken stock
- 1 tbsp butter, melted
- ¼ tsp saffron

DIRECTIONS:
Add all ingredients except the fish to a pan that fits your air fryer; toss well. Place the pan in the air fryer and cook at 360 degrees F for 15 minutes. Add the fish, cover, and cook at 360 degrees F for 12 minutes more. Divide everything between plates and serve right away.

NUTRITION:
calories 271, fat 8, fiber 9, carbs 15, protein 8

VEGGIE SALMON

Preparation time: 5 min | Cooking time: 20 min | Servings: 2

INGREDIENTS:

- 2 salmon fillets, boneless
- 3 garlic cloves, minced
- 1 tbsp olive oil
- ¼ cup veggie stock
- 1 cup baby carrots
- Salt and black pepper to taste

Directions:
In your air fryer, mix all the ingredients. Cook at 370 degrees F for 20 minutes. Divide everything between plates and serve.

Nutrition: calories 200, fat 6, fiber 6, carbs 18, protein 11

CHILI COD

Preparation time: 5 min | Cooking time: 10 min | Servings: 4

INGREDIENTS:

- 4 cod fillets, boneless
- 2 tbsp assorted chili peppers
- Juice of 1 lemon
- 1 lemon, sliced
- Salt and black pepper to taste

DIRECTIONS:
In your air fryer, mix the cod with the chili pepper, lemon juice, salt, and pepper. Arrange the lemon slices on top and cook at 360 degrees F for 10 minutes. Divide the fillets between plates and serve.

NUTRITION:
calories 200, fat 4, fiber 8, carbs 16, protein 7

HERBED SALMON

Preparation time: 10 min | Cooking time: 12 min | Servings: 4

INGREDIENTS:

- 4 salmon fillets, boneless
- 1 lemon, sliced
- 1 white onion, chopped
- 3 tomatoes, sliced
- 4 thyme sprigs, chopped
- 4 cilantro sprigs, chopped
- 3 tbsp olive oil
- Salt and black pepper to taste

DIRECTIONS:
In your air fryer, mix the salmon with the oil, onions, tomatoes, thyme, cilantro, salt, and pepper. Top with the lemon slices and cook at 360 degrees F for 12 minutes. Divide everything between plates and serve.

NUTRITION:
calories 200, fat 5, fiber 5, carbs 16, protein 15

GARLIC SALMON STEAK

Preparation time: 5 min | Cooking time: 15 min | Servings: 6

INGREDIENTS:

- 6 salmon steaks
- 2 tbsp olive oil
- 2 garlic cloves, minced
- 2 tbsp parsley, chopped
- 1 cup clam juice
- 2 tbsp lemon juice
- Salt and white pepper to taste
- 1 tsp sherry
- 1 cup dill, chopped

DIRECTIONS:
In a pan that fits your air fryer, mix the salmon with all the other ingredients. Place the pan in the fryer and cook at 370 degrees F for 15 minutes. Divide everything between plates and serve.

NUTRITION:
calories 261, fat 8, fiber 6, carbs 15, protein 14

CHINESE TROUT BITES

Preparation time: 5 min | Cooking time: 12 min | Servings: 4

INGREDIENTS:

- 1 pound trout fillets, boneless and cut into cubes
- 1 garlic clove, crushed
- 1 shallot, sliced
- 1-inch ginger piece, chopped
- 1 cup sake
- 1 cup mirin
- ¼ cup miso
- 1 sweet onion, chopped
- 2 celery stalks, sliced
- 1 tbsp rice vinegar
- 1 tsp mustard
- 1 tsp sugar

DIRECTIONS:
Add all ingredients to a pan that fits your air fryer and toss. Place the pan in the fryer and cook at 370 degrees F for 12 minutes. Divide into bowls and serve.

NUTRITION:
calories 271, fat 11, fiber 7, carbs 16, protein 6

CRUNCHY TROUT
Preparation time: 5 min | Cooking time: 20 min | Servings: 4

INGREDIENTS:

- 4 whole trout
- 3 ounces bread-crumbs
- Juice of 1 lemon
- 1 tbsp chives, chopped
- Salt and black pepper to taste
- 1 egg, whisked
- 1 tbsp butter
- 1 tbsp olive oil

DIRECTIONS:
In a bowl, combine the breadcrumbs, lemon juice, salt, pepper, egg, and chives; stir very well. Coat the trout with the breadcrumb mix. Heat up your air fryer with the oil and the butter at 370 degrees F; add the trout and cook for 10 minutes on each side. Divide between plates and serve with a side salad.

NUTRITION:
calories 214, fat 8, fiber 8, carbs 17, protein 7

SPICY MUSSELS
Preparation time: 5 min | Cooking time: 12 min | Servings: 4

INGREDIENTS:

- 2 pounds mussels, scrubbed
- 12 ounces black beer
- 1 tbsp olive oil
- 1 yellow onion, chopped
- 8 ounces spicy sausage, chopped
- 1 tbsp paprika

DIRECTIONS:
Combine all the ingredients in a pan that fits your air fryer. Place the pan in the air fryer and cook at 400 degrees F for 12 minutes. Divide the mussels into bowls, serve, and enjoy!

NUTRITION:
calories 201, fat 6, fiber 7, carbs 17, protein 7

SEAFOOD MEDLEY
Preparation time: 10 min | Cooking time: 15 min | Servings: 4

INGREDIENTS:

- 12 mussels
- 1½ pounds large shrimp, peeled and deveined
- 2 tbsp butter, melted
- 2 yellow onions, chopped
- 3 garlic cloves, minced
- ½ cup parsley, chopped
- 20 ounces canned tomatoes, chopped
- 8 ounces clam juice
- ½ tsp marjoram, dried
- 1 tbsp basil, dried
- Salt and black pepper to taste

DIRECTIONS:
Place all the ingredients in a pan that fits your air fryer; toss well. Put the pan into the fryer and cook at 380 degrees F for 15 minutes.

NUTRITION:
calories 261, fat 7, fiber 7, carbs 16, protein 8

CLAMS AND POTATOES
Preparation time: 5 min | Cooking time: 15 min | Servings: 4

INGREDIENTS:

- 15 small clams, shucked
- 2 chorizo links, sliced
- 1 pound baby red potatoes, scrubbed
- 1 yellow onion, chopped
- 10 ounces beer
- 2 tbsp cilantro, chopped
- 1 tsp olive oil

DIRECTIONS:
In a pan that fits your air fryer, add all of the ingredients and toss. Place the pan in the fryer and cook at 390 degrees F for 15 minutes. Divide into bowls and serve.

NUTRITION:
calories 231, fat 6, fiber 8, carbs 16, protein 16

CREAMY CLAMS
Preparation time: 10 min | Cooking time: 12 min | Servings: 4

INGREDIENTS:

- 24 clams, shucked
- 3 garlic cloves, minced
- 4 tbsp butter, softened
- ¼ cup parsley, chopped
- ¼ cup parmesan cheese, grated
- 1 tsp oregano, dried
- 1 cup bread-crumbs

DIRECTIONS:
In a bowl, combine the breadcrumbs, parmesan, oregano, parsley, butter, and garlic; mix well. Divide the breadcrumb mixture into the exposed clams. Put the clams in your air fryer and cook at 380 degrees F for 12 minutes. Serve and enjoy!

NUTRITION:
calories 100, fat 7, fiber 4, carbs 15, protein 6

PARSLEY SHRIMP MIX

Preparation time: 10 min | Cooking time: 8 min | Servings: 4

INGREDIENTS:

- 20 shrimp, peeled and deveined
- 2 tbsp butter, melted
- Salt and black pepper to taste
- ¼ cup parsley, chopped
- ½ tsp saffron powder
- Juice of 1 lemon
- 4 garlic cloves, minced

DIRECTIONS:

In a pan that fits your air fryer, mix the shrimp with all the other ingredients; toss well. Place the pan in the fryer and cook at 380 degrees F for 8 minutes. Divide between plates and serve hot.

NUTRITION:

calories 261, fat 7, fiber 9, carbs 16, protein 7

RED PEPPER SHRIMPS

Preparation time: 10 min | Cooking time: 10 min | Servings: 4
Ingredients:

- 1½ pounds shrimp, peeled and deveined
- 2 cups corn
- A drizzle of olive oil
- ¼ cup chicken stock
- 1 tbsp old bay seasoning
- Salt and black pepper to taste
- 1 tsp red pepper flakes, crushed
- 2 sweet onions, cut into wedges
- 8 garlic cloves, crushed

DIRECTIONS:

Grease a pan that fits your air fryer with the oil. Add all other ingredients to the oiled pan and toss well. Place the pan in the fryer and cook at 390 degrees F for 10 minutes. Divide everything into bowls and serve.

NUTRITION:

calories 261, fat 7, fiber 6, carbs 17, protein 11

RED ONION SHRIMPS

Preparation time: 10 min | Cooking time: 10 min | Servings: 4

INGREDIENTS:

- 1 pound shrimp, peeled and deveined
- 2 tbsp olive oil
- 1 tbsp red onion, chopped
- 1 cup chicken stock

DIRECTIONS:

In a pan that fits your air fryer, mix all the ingredients. Place the pan in the fryer and cook at 380 degrees F for 10 minutes. Divide into bowls and serve.
Nutrition: calories 261, fat 6, fiber 8, carbs 16, protein 6

SHRIMP AND TOMATOES

Preparation time: 10 min | Cooking time: 15 min | Servings: 4

INGREDIENTS:

- 2 pounds shrimp, peeled and deveined
- 1 pound tomatoes, peeled and chopped
- ¼ cup veggie stock
- Salt and black pepper to taste
- 4 tbsp olive oil
- 4 onions, chopped
- 1 tsp coriander, ground
- Juice of 1 lemon

DIRECTIONS:

In a pan that fits your air fryer, mix all the ingredients well. Place the pan in the fryer and cook at 360 degrees F for 15 minutes. Divide into bowls and serve; enjoy!

NUTRITION:

calories 161, fat 1, fiber 6, carbs 17, protein 7

TOMATO VINEGAR SHRIMP

Preparation time: 10 min | Cooking time: 10 min | Servings: 4

INGREDIENTS:

- 1 pound shrimp, peeled and deveined
- ½ tsp sugar
- 2 tsp vinegar
- 1 cup tomato juice
- Salt and black pepper to taste
- 1 tsp chili powder
- 1 yellow onion, chopped
- 2 tbsp olive oil

DIRECTIONS:

Place all of the ingredients into a pan that fits your air fryer and mix well. Put the pan in the fryer and cook at 370 degrees F for 10 minutes. Divide into bowls and serve.

NUTRITION:

calories 251, fat 7, fiber 7, carbs 18, protein 11

SHRIMP AND PEAS MIX

Preparation time: 10 min | Cooking time: 8 min | Servings: 4:

- 1 pound shrimp, peeled and deveined
- 2 tbsp soy sauce
- ½ pound pea pods
- 3 tbsp balsamic vinegar
- ¾ cup pineapple juice
- 3 tbsp sugar

DIRECTIONS:

In a pan that fits your air fryer, mix all the ingredients. Place the pan in the fryer and cook at 380 degrees F for 8 minutes. Divide into bowls and serve.

NUTRITION:

calories 251, fat 4, fiber 3, carbs 14, protein 5

CHILI SHRIMP MIX

Preparation time: 10 min | Cooking time: 10 min | Servings: 4

INGREDIENTS:

- 18 ounces shrimp, peeled and deveined
- Salt and black pepper to taste

- ½ tbsp mustard seeds
- 1 tbsp olive oil
- 1 tsp turmeric powder
- 2 green chilies, minced
- 2 onions, chopped
- 4 ounces curd, beaten
- 1-inch ginger, chopped

DIRECTIONS:
In a pan that fits your air fryer, place and mix all the ingredients. Place the pan in the fryer and cook at 380 degrees F for 10 minutes. Divide into bowls and serve.

NUTRITION:
calories 251, fat 3, fiber 7, carbs 15, protein 8

OREGANO SHRIMP AND SPAGHETTI

Preparation time: 10 min | Cooking time: 10 min | Servings: 4

INGREDIENTS:

- 1 pound shrimp, cooked, peeled and deveined
- 2 tbsp olive oil
- 1 garlic clove, minced
- 10 ounces canned tomatoes, chopped
- ¼ tsp oregano, dried
- 1 tbsp parsley, finely chopped
- 1 cup parmesan cheese, grated
- 12 ounces spaghetti, cooked

DIRECTIONS:
In a pan that fits your air fryer, add the shrimp with the oil, garlic, tomatoes, oregano, and parsley; toss well. Place the pan in the fryer and cook at 380 degrees F for 10 minutes. Add the spaghetti and the parmesan; toss well. Divide between plates, serve, and enjoy!

NUTRITION:
calories 271, fat 12, fiber 4, carbs 14, protein 5

BUTTER FLOUNDER FILLETS

Preparation time: 5 min | Cooking time: 12 min | Servings: 4

INGREDIENTS:

- 2 pounds flounder fillets
- 4 tbsp butter, melted
- Salt and black pepper to taste
- Juice of 1 lime

DIRECTIONS:
Put the flounder fillets in your air fryer, and then add the melted butter, salt, pepper, and lime juice. Cook at 390 degrees F for 6 minutes on each side. Divide between plates, serve with a side salad, and enjoy.

NUTRITION:
calories 191, fat 6, fiber 7, carbs 15, protein 7

PARMESAN SHRIMP

Preparation time: 10 min | Cooking time: 12 min | Servings: 4

INGREDIENTS:

- 2 tbsp olive oil
- 2 garlic cloves, minced
- 1 yellow onion, chopped
- 2 tbsp dry white wine
- ½ cup chicken stock
- Salt and black pepper to taste
- 1 pound shrimp, peeled and deveined
- ¾ cup parmesan cheese, grated
- ¼ cup tarragon, chopped

DIRECTIONS:
In a pan that fits your air fryer, add all ingredients except the parmesan cheese and stir well. Place the pan in the air fryer and cook at 380 degrees F for 12 minutes. Add the parmesan and toss. Divide everything between plates and serve.

NUTRITION:
calories 271, fat 8, fiber 8, carbs 17, protein 11

GINGER SQUID

Preparation time: 10 min | Cooking time: 25 min | Servings: 4

INGREDIENTS:

- 1 pound squid, cleaned and cut into small pieces
- 10 garlic cloves, minced
- 1 tsp ginger piece, grated
- 2 green chilies, chopped
- 2 yellow onions, chopped
- ½ tbsp lemon juice
- 1 tbsp coriander powder
- ¾ tbsp chili powder
- Salt and black pepper to taste
- 1 tsp mustard seeds, toasted
- ½ cup chicken stock
- 3 tbsp olive oil

DIRECTIONS:
Place all ingredients into a pan that fits your air fryer and toss. Put the pan in the air fryer and cook at 380 degrees F for 25 minutes. Divide between plates and serve.

NUTRITION:
calories 251, fat 6, fiber 5, carbs 15, protein 14

SHRIMP AND MUSHROOMS MIX

Preparation time: 10 min | Cooking time: 15 min | Servings: 4

INGREDIENTS:

- ½ pound shrimp, peeled and deveined
- 8 ounces water chestnuts, chopped
- ½ pound shiitake mushrooms, sliced
- 2 tbsp olive oil
- 1 garlic clove, minced
- 1 tsp ginger, minced
- 3 scallions, chopped
- Salt and black pepper to taste

DIRECTIONS:
In your air fryer, add all the ingredients and mix. Cook at 380 degrees F for 15 minutes. Serve hot and enjoy!

NUTRITION:
calories 190, fat 3, fiber 4, carbs 12, protein 4

MAYO SHRIMP SALAD
Preparation time: 10 min | Cooking time: 12 min | Servings: 4

INGREDIENTS:

- ½ cup yellow onion, chopped
- 1 cup green bell pepper, chopped
- 1 cup red bell pepper, chopped
- 1 pound baby shrimp, peeled and deveined
- 1 cup mayonnaise
- Salt and black pepper to taste
- 1 tbsp olive oil
- 1 tsp sweet paprika

DIRECTIONS:
In a pan that fits your air fryer, add all the ingredients except the mayo; toss well. Place the pan in the fryer and cook at 380 degrees F for 12 minutes. Cool the mixture down, and then add the mayo. Toss and serve.

NUTRITION:
calories 210, fat 8, fiber 2, carbs 15, protein 5

TROUT AND SOY SAUCE
Preparation time: 10 min | Cooking time: 15 min | Servings: 5
Ingredients:

- 4 trout fillets, boneless
- Cooking spray
- Salt and black pepper to taste
- For the sauce:
- 1 cup almond butter
- 4 tsp soy sauce
- ¼ cup lemon juice
- 1 tsp almond oil
- ¼ cup water

DIRECTIONS:
Put the fish fillets in your air fryer, season with salt and pepper, and grease with the cooking spray. Cook at 380 degrees F for 5 minutes on each side and divide between plates. Heat up a pan with the almond butter over medium heat; then add the soy sauce, lemon juice, almond oil, and the water. Whisk the sauce well and cook for 2-3 minutes. Drizzle the almond butter sauce over the fish and serve.

NUTRITION:
calories 280, fat 7, fiber 3, carbs 18, protein 11

HERBED BAKED COD
Preparation time: 5 min | Cooking time: 12 min | Servings: 4

INGREDIENTS:

- 4 cod fillets, boneless
- Salt and black pepper to taste
- 2 tbsp parsley, chopped
- A drizzle of olive oil
- ¾ tsp sweet paprika
- ½ tsp oregano, dried
- ½ tsp thyme, dried
- ½ tsp basil, dried
- Juice of 1 lemon
- 2 tbsp butter, melted

DIRECTIONS:
Add all ingredients to a bowl and toss gently. Transfer the fish to your air fryer and cook at 380 degrees F for 6 minutes on each side. Serve right away.

NUTRITION:
calories 216, fat 7, fiber 3, carbs 14, protein 9

LIME BAKED SALMON
Preparation time: 5 min | Cooking time: 12 min | Servings: 6

INGREDIENTS:

- 2 salmon fillets, boneless
- 1 lime, sliced
- Juice of 1 lime
- ½ cup butter, melted
- ½ cup olive oil
- 3 garlic cloves, minced
- 2 shallots, chopped
- Salt and black pepper to taste
- 6 green onions, chopped

DIRECTIONS:
In a bowl, mix the salmon with the lime juice, butter, oil, garlic, shallots, salt, pepper, and the green onions; rub well. Transfer the fish to your air fryer, top with the lime slices, and cook at 380 degrees F for 6 minutes on each side. Serve with a side salad.

NUTRITION:
calories 270, fat 4, fiber 2, carbs 12, protein 6

SALMON AND BERRY DIP
Preparation time: 5 min | Cooking time: 12 min | Servings: 2

INGREDIENTS:

- 2 salmon fillets, boneless
- 1 tbsp honey
- ½ cup blackberries
- 1 tbsp olive oil
- Juice of ½ lemon
- Salt and black pepper to taste

DIRECTIONS:
In a blender, mix the blackberries with the honey, oil, lemon juice, salt, and pepper; pulse well. Spread the blackberry mixture over the salmon, and then place the fish in your air fryer's basket. Cook at 380 degrees F for 12 minutes, flipping the fish halfway. Serve hot, and enjoy!

NUTRITION:
calories 210, fat 8, fiber 4, carbs 14, protein 11

SHRIMP AND TOMATO SAUCE
Preparation time: 10 min | Cooking time: 8 min | Servings: 4

INGREDIENTS:

- 2 red onions, cut into chunks
- 3 zucchinis, cut in medium chunks
- 1 pound shrimp, peeled and deveined
- 2 tbsp olive oil
- ¼ cup tomato

sauce
- Salt and black pepper to taste
- 1 garlic clove, minced
- 1 tbsp lemon juice
- ½ cup parsley, chopped

DIRECTIONS:
In a baking dish that fits your air fryer, mix all the ingredients except the parsley; toss well. Place the baking dish into the fryer and cook at 400 degrees F for 8 minutes. Add the parsley and stir. Divide everything between plates and serve.

NUTRITION:
calories 210, fat 7, fiber 4, carbs 15, protein 9

FRIED GINGER COD
Preparation time: 10 min | Cooking time: 12 min | Servings: 4

INGREDIENTS:

- 2 cod fish, 7 ounces each
- A drizzle of sesame oil
- Salt and black pepper to the taste
- 1 cup water
- 1 tsp dark soy sauce
- 4 tbsp light soy sauce
- 1 tbsp sugar
- 3 tbsp olive oil
- 4 ginger slices
- 3 spring onions, chopped
- 2 tbsp coriander, chopped

DIRECTIONS:
Season fish with salt, pepper, drizzle sesame oil, rub well and leave aside for 10 minutes. Add fish to your air fryer and cook at 356 degrees F for 12 minutes. Meanwhile, heat up a pot with the water over medium heat, add dark and light soy sauce and sugar, stir, bring to a simmer and take off heat. Heat up a pan with the olive oil over medium heat, add ginger and green onions, stir, cook for a few minutes and take off heat. Divide fish on plates, top with ginger and green onions, drizzle soy sauce mix, sprinkle coriander and serve right away.

NUTRITION:
calories 300, fat 17, fiber 8, carbs 20, protein 22

PAPRIKA CATFISH
Preparation time: 10 min | Cooking time: 20 min | Servings: 4

INGREDIENTS:

- 4 cat fish fillets
- Salt and black pepper to the taste
- A pinch of sweet paprika
- 1 tbsp parsley, chopped
- 1 tbsp lemon juice
- 1 tbsp olive oil

DIRECTIONS:
Season catfish fillets with salt, pepper, paprika, drizzle oil, rub well, place in your air fryer's basket and cook at 400 degrees F for 20 minutes, flipping the fish after 10 minutes. Divide fish on plates, drizzle lemon juice all over, sprinkle parsley and serve.

NUTRITION:
calories 253, fat 6, fiber 12, carbs 26, protein 22

FENNEL COD FILLETS
Preparation time: 10 min | Cooking time: 15 min | Servings: 2

INGREDIENTS:

- 2 black cod fillets, boneless
- 1 tbsp olive oil
- Salt and black pepper to the taste
- 1 fennel bulb, thinly sliced
- 1 cup grapes, halved
- ½ cup pecans

DIRECTIONS:
Drizzle half of the oil over fish fillets, season with salt and pepper, rub well, place fillets in your air fryer's basket, cook for 10 minutes at 400 degrees F and transfer to a plate. In a bowl, mix pecans with grapes, fennel, the rest of the oil, salt and pepper, toss to coat, add to a pan that fits your air fryer and cook at 400 degrees F for 5 minutes. Divide cod on plates, add fennel and grapes mix on the side and serve.

NUTRITION:
calories 300, fat 4, fiber 2, carbs 32, protein 22

SQUID AND GUACAMOLE
Preparation time: 10 min | Cooking time: 6 min | Servings: 2

INGREDIENTS:

- 2 medium squids, tentacles separated and tubes scored lengthwise
- 1 tbsp olive oil
- Juice from 1 lime
- Salt and black pepper to the taste

For the guacamole:

- 2 avocados, pitted, peeled and chopped
- 1 tbsp coriander, chopped
- 2 red chilies, chopped
- 1 tomato, chopped
- 1 red onion, chopped
- Juice from 2 limes

DIRECTIONS:
Season squid and squid tentacles with salt, pepper, drizzle the olive oil all over, put in your air fryer's basket and cook at 360 degrees F for 3 minutes on each side. Transfer squid to a bowl, drizzle lime juice all over and toss. Meanwhile, put avocado in a bowl, mash with a fork, add coriander, chilies, tomato, onion and juice from 2 limes and toss. Divide squid on plates, top with guacamole and serve.

NUTRITION:
calories 500, fat 43, fiber 6, carbs 7, protein 20

SPICY SHRIMP
Preparation time: 10 min | Cooking time: 10 min | Servings: 4

INGREDIENTS:

- 1 pound shrimp, peeled and deveined
- 1 tsp red pepper flakes
- 2 tbsp olive oil
- 1 tsp Tabasco sauce
- 2 tbsp water
- 1 tsp oregano, dried
- Salt and black pepper to the taste
- ½ tsp parsley, dried
- ½ tsp smoked paprika

DIRECTIONS:
In a bowl, mix oil with water, Tabasco sauce, pepper flakes, oregano, parsley, salt, pepper, paprika and shrimp and toss well to coat. Transfer shrimp to your preheated air fryer at 370 degrees F and cook for 10 minutes shaking the fryer once. Divide shrimp on plates and serve with a side salad.

NUTRITION:
calories 200, fat 5, fiber 6, carbs 13, protein 8

BELL PEPPER SHRIMP SKEWERS

Preparation time: 10 min | Cooking time: 6 min | Servings: 2

INGREDIENTS:

- 8 shrimps, peeled and deveined
- 4 garlic cloves, minced
- Salt and black pepper to the taste
- 8 green bell pepper slices
- 1 tbsp rosemary, chopped
- 1 tbsp butter, melted

DIRECTIONS:
In a bowl, mix shrimp with garlic, butter, salt, pepper, rosemary and bell pepper slices, toss to coat and leave aside for 10 minutes. Arrange 2 shrimp and 2 bell pepper slices on a skewer and repeat with the rest of the shrimp and bell pepper pieces. Place them all in your air fryer's basket and cook at 360 degrees F for 6 minutes. Divide among plates and serve right away.

NUTRITION:
calories 140, fat 1, fiber 12, carbs 15, protein 7

HONEY SALMON

Preparation time: 1 hour | Cooking time: 15 min | Servings: 2

INGREDIENTS:

- 2 medium salmon fillets
- 6 tbsp light soy sauce
- 3 tsp mirin
- 1 tsp water
- 6 tbsp honey

DIRECTIONS:
In a bowl, mix soy sauce with honey, water and mirin, whisk well, add salmon, rub well and leave aside in the fridge for 1 hour. Transfer salmon to your air fryer and cook at 360 degrees F for 15 minutes, flipping them after 7 minutes. Meanwhile, put the soy marinade in a pan, heat up over medium heat, whisk well, cook for 2 minutes and take off heat. Divide salmon on plates, drizzle marinade all over and serve.

NUTRITION:
calories 300, fat 12, fiber 8, carbs 13, protein 24

HERBED COD STEAKS

Preparation time: 10 min | Cooking time: 20 min | Servings: 2
Ingredients:

- 2 big cod steaks
- Salt and black pepper to the taste
- ½ tsp garlic powder
- ½ tsp ginger
- ¼ tsp turmeric powder
- 1 tbsp plum sauce
- Cooking spray

DIRECTIONS:
Season cod steaks with salt and pepper, spray them with cooking oil, add garlic powder, ginger powder and turmeric powder and rub well. Place cod steaks in your air fryer and cook at 360 degrees F for 15 minutes, flipping them after 7 minutes. Heat up a pan over medium heat, add plum sauce, stir and cook for 2 minutes. Divide cod steaks on plates, drizzle plum sauce all over and serve.

NUTRITION:
calories 250, fat 7, fiber 1, carbs 14, protein 12

FLAVORED AIR FRIED SALMON

Preparation time: 1 hour | Cooking time: 8 min | Servings: 2

INGREDIENTS:

- 2 salmon fillets
- 2 tbsp lemon juice
- Salt and black pepper to the taste
- ½ tsp garlic powder
- 1/3 cup water
- 1/3 cup soy sauce
- 3 scallions, chopped
- 1/3 cup brown sugar
- 2 tbsp olive oil

DIRECTIONS:
In a bowl, mix sugar with water, soy sauce, garlic powder, salt, pepper, oil and lemon juice, whisk well, add salmon fillets, toss to coat and leave aside in the fridge for 1 hour. Transfer salmon fillets to the fryer's basket and cook at 360 degrees F for 8 minutes flipping them halfway. Divide salmon on plates, sprinkle scallions on top and serve right away.

NUTRITION:
calories 300, fat 12, fiber 10, carbs 23, protein 20

SALMON WITH POTATOES

Preparation time: 10 min | Cooking time: 20 min | Servings: 4

INGREDIENTS:

- 4 salmon fillets, skinless and bone-

less
- 1 tbsp capers, drained
- Salt and black pepper to the taste
- Juice from 1 lemon
- 2 tsp olive oil

For the potato mash:
- 2 tbsp olive oil
- 1 tbsp dill, dried
- 1 pound potatoes, chopped
- ½ cup milk

DIRECTIONS:
Put potatoes in a pot, add water to cover, add some salt, bring to a boil over medium high heat, cook for 15 minutes, drain, transfer to a bowl, mash with a potato masher, add 2 tbsp oil, dill, salt, pepper and milk, whisk well and leave aside for now. Season salmon with salt and pepper, drizzle 2 tsp oil over them, rub, transfer to your air fryer's basket, add capers on top, cook at 360 degrees F and cook for 8 minutes. Divide salmon and capers on plates, add mashed potatoes on the side, drizzle lemon juice all over and serve.

NUTRITION:
calories 300, fat 17, fiber 8, carbs 12, protein 18

SABA FISH

Preparation time: 10 min | Cooking time: 8 min | Servings: 1

INGREDIENTS:

- 4 Saba fish fillet, boneless
- Salt and black pepper to the taste
- 3 red chili pepper, chopped
- 2 tbsp lemon juice
- 2 tbsp olive oil
- 2 tbsp garlic, minced

DIRECTIONS:
Season fish fillets with salt and pepper and put in a bowl. Add lemon juice, oil, chili and garlic toss to coat, transfer fish to your air fryer and cook at 360 degrees F for 8 minutes, flipping halfway. Divide among plates and serve with some fries.

NUTRITION:
calories 300, fat 4, fiber 8, carbs 15, protein 15

SPICY SWEET HALIBUT

Preparation time: 30 min | Cooking time: 10 min | Servings: 3

INGREDIENTS:

- 1 pound halibut steaks
- 2/3 cup soy sauce
- ¼ cup sugar
- 2 tbsp lime juice
- ½ cup mirin
- ¼ tsp red pepper flakes, crushed
- ¼ cup orange juice
- ¼ tsp ginger, grated
- 1 garlic clove, minced

DIRECTIONS:
Put soy sauce in a pan, heat up over medium heat, add mirin, sugar, lime and orange juice, pepper flakes, ginger and garlic, stir well, bring to a boil and take off heat. Transfer half of the marinade to a bowl, add halibut, toss to coat and leave aside in the fridge for 30 minutes. Transfer halibut to your air fryer and cook at 390 degrees F for 10 minutes, flipping once. Divide halibut steaks on plates, drizzle the rest of the marinade all over and serve hot.

NUTRITION:
calories 286, fat 5, fiber 12, carbs 14, protein 23

COD AND VEGGIES MEDLEY

Preparation time: 10 min | Cooking time: 15 min | Servings: 4

INGREDIENTS:

- 4 cod fillets, skinless and boneless
- 12 cherry tomatoes, halved
- 8 black olives, pitted and roughly chopped
- 2 tbsp lemon juice
- Salt and black pepper to the taste
- 2 tbsp olive oil
- Cooking spray
- 1 bunch basil, chopped

DIRECTIONS:
Season cod with salt and pepper to the taste, place in your air fryer's basket and cook at 360 degrees F for 10 minutes, flipping after 5 minutes. Meanwhile, heat up a pan with the oil over medium heat, add tomatoes, olives and lemon juice, stir, bring to a simmer, add basil, salt and pepper, stir well and take off heat. Divide fish on plates and serve with the vinaigrette drizzled on top.

NUTRITION:
calories 300, fat 5, fiber 8, carbs 12, protein 8

SEAFOOD MIX

Preparation time: 10 min | Cooking time: 40 min | Servings: 6

INGREDIENTS:

- 6 tbsp butter
- 2 ounces mushrooms, chopped
- 1 small green bell pepper, chopped
- 1 celery stalk, chopped
- 2 garlic cloves, minced
- 1 small yellow onion, chopped
- Salt and black pepper to the taste
- 4 tbsp flour
- ½ cup white wine
- 1 and ½ cups milk
- ½ cup heavy cream
- 4 sea scallops, sliced
- 4 ounces haddock, skinless, boneless and cut into small pieces
- 4 ounces lobster meat, already cooked and cut into small pieces
- ½ tsp mustard powder
- 1 tbsp lemon juice
- 1/3 cup bread crumbs
- Salt and black pepper to the taste
- 3 tbsp cheddar cheese, grated
- A handful parsley, chopped
- 1 tsp sweet paprika

DIRECTIONS:
Heat up a pan with 4 tbsp butter over medium high heat, add bell pepper, mushrooms,

celery, garlic, onion and wine, stir and cook for 10 minutes Add flour, cream and milk, stir well and cook for 6 minutes. Add lemon juice, salt, pepper, mustard powder, scallops, lobster meat and haddock, stir well, take off heat and transfer to a pan that fits your air fryer. In a bowl, mix the rest of the butter with bread crumbs, paprika and cheese and sprinkle over seafood mix. Transfer pan to your air fryer and cook at 360 degrees F for 16 minutes. Divide among plates and serve with parsley sprinkled on top.

Nutrition:
calories 270, fat 32, fiber 14, carbs 15, protein 23

ORANGE TROUT

Preparation time: 10 min | Cooking time: 10 min | Servings: 4

Ingredients:

- 4 trout fillets, skinless and boneless
- 4 spring onions, chopped
- 1 tbsp olive oil
- 1 tbsp ginger, minced
- Salt and black pepper to the taste
- Juice and zest from 1 orange

Directions:
Season trout fillets with salt, pepper, rub them with the olive oil, place in a pan that fits your air fryer, add ginger, green onions, orange zest and juice, toss well, place in your air fryer and cook at 360 degrees F for 10 minutes. Divide fish and sauce on plates and serve right away.

Nutrition:
calories 239, fat 10, fiber 7, carbs 18, protein 23

PARSLEY COD FILLETS

Preparation time: 10 min | Cooking time: 10 min | Servings: 4

Ingredients:

- 4 cod fillets, boneless
- 2 tbsp parsley, chopped
- 2 cups peas
- 4 tbsp wine
- ½ tsp oregano, dried
- ½ tsp sweet paprika
- 2 garlic cloves, minced
- Salt and pepper to the taste

Directions:
In your food processor mix garlic with parsley, salt, pepper, oregano, paprika and wine and blend well. Rub fish with half of this mix, place in your air fryer and cook at 360 degrees F for 10 minutes. Meanwhile, put peas in a pot, add water to cover, add salt, bring to a boil over medium high heat, cook for 10 minutes, drain and divide among plates. Also divide fish on plates, spread the rest of the herb dressing all over and serve.

Nutrition:
calories 261, fat 8, fiber 12, carbs 20, protein 22

THYME AND PARSLEY SALMON

Preparation time: 10 min | Cooking time: 15 min | Servings: 4

Ingredients:

- 4 salmon fillets, boneless
- Juice from 1 lemon
- 1 yellow onion, chopped
- 3 tomatoes, sliced
- 4 thyme sprigs
- 4 parsley sprigs
- 3 tbsp extra virgin olive oil
- Salt and black pepper to the taste

Directions:
Drizzle 1 tbsp oil in a pan that fits your air fryer, add a layer of tomatoes, salt and pepper, drizzle 1 more tbsp oil, add fish, season them with salt and pepper, drizzle the rest of the oil, add thyme and parsley sprigs, onions, lemon juice, salt and pepper, place in your air fryer's basket and cook at 360 degrees F for 12 minutes shaking once. Divide everything on plates and serve right away.

Nutrition:
calories 242, fat 9, fiber 12, carbs 20, protein 31

BUTTER TROUT AND LEMON SAUCE

Preparation time: 10 min | Cooking time: 10 min | Servings: 4

Ingredients:

- 4 trout fillets, boneless
- Salt and black pepper to the taste
- 3 tsp lemon zest, grated
- 3 tbsp chives, chopped
- 6 tbsp butter
- 2 tbsp olive oil
- 2 tsp lemon juice

Directions:
Season trout with salt and pepper, drizzle the olive oil, rub, transfer to your air fryer and cook at 360 degrees F for 10 minutes, flipping once. Meanwhile, heat up a pan with the butter over medium heat, add salt, pepper, chives, lemon juice and zest, whisk well, cook for 1-2 minutes and take off heat Divide fish fillets on plates, drizzle butter sauce all over and serve.

Nutrition:
calories 300, fat 12, fiber 9, carbs 27, protein 24

CHEDDAR SALMON

Preparation time: 10 min | Cooking time: 10 min | Servings: 4

Ingredients:

- 4 salmon fillets, boneless
- 1 tbsp olive oil
- Salt and black pepper to the taste
- 1/3 cup cheddar cheese, grated
- 1 and ½ tsp mustard
- ½ cup coconut cream

DIRECTIONS:
Season salmon with salt and pepper, drizzle the oil and rub well. In a bowl, mix coconut cream with cheddar, mustard, salt and pepper and stir well. Transfer salmon to a pan that fits your air fryer, add coconut cream mix, introduce in your air fryer and cook at 320 degrees F for 10 minutes. Divide among plates and serve.

NUTRITION:
calories 200, fat 6, fiber 14, carbs 17, protein 20

SALMON AND PEPPERY SALSA
Preparation time: 30 min | Cooking time: 10 min | Servings: 4

INGREDIENTS:

- 4 salmon fillets
- 1 tbsp olive oil
- Salt and black pepper to the taste
- 1 tsp cumin, ground
- 1 tsp sweet paprika
- ½ tsp chili powder
- 1 tsp garlic powder

For the salsa:
- 1 small red onion, chopped
- 1 avocado, pitted, peeled and chopped
- 2 tbsp cilantro, chopped
- Juice from 2 limes
- Salt and black pepper to the taste

DIRECTIONS:
In a bowl, mix salt, pepper, chili powder, onion powder, paprika and cumin, stir, rub salmon with this mix, drizzle the oil, rub again, transfer to your air fryer and cook at 350 degrees F for 5 minutes on each side. Meanwhile, in a bowl, mix avocado with red onion, salt, pepper, cilantro and lime juice and stir. Divide fillets on plates, top with avocado salsa and serve.

NUTRITION:
calories 300, fat 14, fiber 4, carbs 18, protein 16

ITALIAN BARRAMUNDI AND OLIVES MIX
Preparation time: 10 min | Cooking time: 8 min | Servings: 4

INGREDIENTS:

- 2 barramundi fillets, boneless
- 1 tbsp olive oil+ 2 tsp
- 2 tsp Italian seasoning
- ¼ cup green olives, pitted and chopped
- ¼ cup cherry tomatoes, chopped
- ¼ cup black olives, chopped
- 1 tbsp lemon zest
- 2 tbsp lemon zest
- Salt and black pepper to the taste
- 2 tbsp parsley, chopped

DIRECTIONS:
Rub fish with salt, pepper, Italian seasoning and 2 tsp olive oil, transfer to your air fryer and cook at 360 degrees F for 8 minutes, flipping them halfway. In a bowl, mix tomatoes with black olives, green olives, salt, pepper, lemon zest and lemon juice, parsley and 1 tbsp olive oil and toss well. Divide fish on plates, add tomato salsa on top and serve.

NUTRITION:
calories 270, fat 4, fiber 2, carbs 18, protein 27

CREAMY SHRIMP AND VEGGIES
Preparation time: 10 min | Cooking time: 30 min | Servings: 4

INGREDIENTS:

- 8 ounces mushrooms, chopped
- 1 asparagus bunch, cut into medium pieces
- 1 pound shrimp, peeled and deveined
- Salt and black pepper to the taste
- 1 spaghetti squash, cut into halves
- 2 tbsp olive oil
- 2 tsp Italian seasoning
- 1 yellow onion, chopped
- 1 tsp red pepper flakes, crushed
- ¼ cup butter, melted
- 1 cup parmesan cheese, grated
- 2 garlic cloves, minced
- 1 cup heavy cream

DIRECTIONS:
Place squash halves in you air fryer's basket, cook at 390 degrees F for 17 minutes, transfer to a cutting board, scoop insides and transfer to a bowl. Put water in a pot, add some salt, bring to a boil over medium heat, add asparagus, steam for a couple of minutes, transfer to a bowl filled with ice water, drain and leave aside as well. Heat up a pan that fits your air fryer with the oil over medium heat, add onions and mushrooms, stir and cook for 7 minutes. Add pepper flakes, Italian seasoning, salt, pepper, squash, asparagus, shrimp, melted butter, cream, parmesan and garlic, toss and cook in your air fryer at 360 degrees F for 6 minutes. Divide everything on plates and serve.

NUTRITION:
calories 325, fat 6, fiber 5, carbs 14, protein 13

TUNA STEAK AND ARUGULA
Preparation time: 10 min | Cooking time: 8 min | Servings: 4

INGREDIENTS:

- ½ cup cilantro, chopped
- 1/3 cup olive oil+ 2 tbsp
- 1 small red onion, chopped
- 3 tbsp balsamic vinegar
- 2 tbsp parsley, chopped
- 2 tbsp basil, chopped
- 1 jalapeno pepper, chopped
- 1 pound sushi tuna steak
- Salt and black pepper to the taste
- 1 tsp red pepper flakes
- 1 tsp thyme, chopped

- 3 garlic cloves, minced
- 2 avocados, pitted, peeled and sliced
- 6 ounces baby arugula

DIRECTIONS:
In a bowl, mix 1/3 cup oil with jalapeno, vinegar, onion, cilantro, basil, garlic, parsley, pepper flakes, thyme, salt and pepper, whisk well and leave aside for now. Season tuna with salt and pepper, rub with the rest of the oil, place in your air fryer and cook at 360 degrees F for 3 minutes on each side. Mix arugula with half of the chimichuri mix you've made and toss to coat. Divide arugula on plates, slice tuna and also divide among plates, top with the rest of the chimichuri and serve.

NUTRITION:
calories 276, fat 3, fiber 1, carbs 14, protein 20

AIR FRIED SHRIMPS AND CAULIFLOWER

Preparation time: 10 min | Cooking time: 12 min | Servings: 2

INGREDIENTS:

- 1 tbsp butter
- Cooking spray
- 1 cauliflower head, riced
- 1 pound shrimp, peeled and deveined
- ¼ cup heavy cream
- 8 ounces mushrooms, roughly chopped
- A pinch of red pepper flakes
- Salt and black pepper to the taste
- 2 garlic cloves, minced
- 4 bacon slices, cooked and crumbled
- ½ cup beef stock
- 1 tbsp parsley, finely chopped
- 1 tbsp chives, chopped

DIRECTIONS:
Season shrimp with salt and pepper, spray with cooking oil, place in your air fryer and cook at 360 degrees F for 7 minutes. Meanwhile, heat up a pan with the butter over medium heat, add mushrooms, stir and cook for 3-4 minutes. Add garlic, cauliflower rice, pepper flakes, stock, cream, chives, parsley, salt and pepper, stir, cook for a few minutes and take off heat. Divide shrimp on plates, add cauliflower mix on the side, sprinkle bacon on top and serve.

NUTRITION:
calories 245, fat 7, fiber 4, carbs 6, protein 20

MUSHROOM-STUFFED SALMON

Preparation time: 10 min | Cooking time: 20 min | Servings: 2

INGREDIENTS:

- 2 salmon fillets, skinless and boneless
- 1 tbsp olive oil
- 5 ounces tiger shrimp, peeled, deveined and chopped
- 6 mushrooms, chopped
- 3 green onions, chopped
- 2 cups spinach, torn
- ¼ cup macadamia nuts, toasted and chopped
- Salt and black pepper to the taste

DIRECTIONS:
Heat up a pan with half of the oil over medium high heat, add mushrooms, onions, salt and pepper, stir and cook for 4 minutes. Add macadamia nuts, spinach and shrimp, stir, cook for 3 minutes and take off heat. Make an incision lengthwise in each salmon fillet, season with salt and pepper, divide spinach, shrimp mix into incisions, and rub with the rest of the olive oil. Place in your air fryer's basket and cook at 360 degrees F and cook for 10 minutes, flipping halfway. Divide stuffed salmon on plates and serve.

NUTRITION:
calories 290, fat 15, fiber 3, carbs 12, protein 31

MAPLE SALMON

Preparation time: 10 min | Cooking time: 10 min | Servings: 1

INGREDIENTS:

- 1 big salmon fillet, boneless
- Salt and black pepper to the taste
- 2 tbsp mustard
- 1 tbsp coconut oil
- 1 tbsp maple extract

DIRECTIONS:
In a bowl, mix maple extract with mustard, whisk well, season salmon with salt and pepper and brush salmon with this mix. Spray some cooking spray over fish, place in your air fryer and cook at 370 degrees F for 10 minutes, flipping halfway. Serve with a tasty side salad.

NUTRITION:
calories 300, fat 7, fiber 14, carbs 16, protein 20

JAMAICAN SALMON WITH ARUGULA

Preparation time: 10 min | Cooking time: 10 min | Servings: 4

INGREDIENTS:

- 2 tsp sriracha sauce
- 4 tsp sugar
- 3 scallions, chopped
- Salt and black pepper to the taste
- 2 tsp olive oil
- 4 tsp apple cider vinegar
- 3 tsp avocado oil
- 4 medium salmon fillets, boneless
- 4 cups baby arugula
- 2 cups cabbage, shredded
- 1 and ½ tsp Jamaican jerk seasoning
- ¼ cup pepitas, toasted
- 2 cups radish, julienned

DIRECTIONS:
In a bowl, mix sriracha with sugar, whisk and transfer 2 tsp to another bowl. Combine 2 tsp sriracha mix with the avocado oil, olive oil, vinegar, salt and pepper and whisk

well. Sprinkle jerk seasoning over salmon, rub with sriracha and sugar mix and season with salt and pepper. Transfer to your air fryer and cook at 360 degrees F for 10 minutes, flipping once. In a bowl, mix radishes with cabbage, arugula, salt, pepper, sriracha and vinegar mix and toss well. Divide salmon and radish mix on plates, sprinkle pepitas and scallions on top and serve.

Nutrition:
calories 290, fat 6, fiber 12, carbs 17, protein 10

SWORDFISH AND SPICY FRUIT SALSA
Preparation time: 10 min | Cooking time: 6 min | Servings: 2

Ingredients:

- 2 medium swordfish steaks
- Salt and black pepper to the taste
- 2 tsp avocado oil
- 1 tbsp cilantro, chopped
- 1 mango, chopped
- 1 avocado, pitted, peeled and chopped
- A pinch of cumin
- A pinch of onion powder
- A pinch of garlic powder
- 1 orange, peeled and sliced
- ½ tbsp balsamic vinegar

Directions:
Season fish steaks with salt, pepper, garlic powder, onion powder and cumin and rub with half of the oil, place in your air fryer and cook at 360 degrees F for 6 minutes, flipping halfway. Meanwhile, in a bowl, mix avocado with mango, cilantro, balsamic vinegar, salt, pepper and the rest of the oil and stir well. Divide fish on plates, top with mango salsa and serve with orange slices on the side.

Nutrition:
calories 200, fat 7, fiber 2, carbs 14, protein 14

SALMON AND CITRIC MARMALADE
Preparation time: 10 min | Cooking time: 15 min | Servings: 4

Ingredients:

- 1 pound wild salmon, skinless, boneless and cubed
- 2 lemons, sliced
- ¼ cup balsamic vinegar
- ¼ cup orange juice
- 1/3 cup orange marmalade
- A pinch of salt and black pepper

Directions:
Heat up a pot with the vinegar over medium heat, add marmalade and orange juice, stir, bring to a simmer, cook for 1 minute and take off heat. Thread salmon cubes and lemon slices on skewers, season with salt and black pepper, brush them with half of the orange marmalade mix, arrange in your air fryer's basket and cook at 360 degrees F for 3 minutes on each side. Brush skewers with the rest of the vinegar mix, divide among plates and serve right away with a side salad.

Nutrition:
calories 240, fat 9, fiber 12, carbs 14, protein 10

CHILI SALMON
Preparation time: 10 min | Cooking time: 15 min | Servings: 12

Ingredients:

- 1 and ¼ cups coconut, shredded
- 1 pound salmon, cubed
- 1/3 cup flour
- A pinch of salt and black pepper
- 1 egg
- 2 tbsp olive oil
- ¼ cup water
- 4 red chilies, chopped
- 3 garlic cloves, minced
- ¼ cup balsamic vinegar
- ½ cup honey

Directions:
In a bowl, mix flour with a pinch of salt and stir. In another bowl, mix egg with black pepper and whisk. Put coconut in a third bowl. Dip salmon cubes in flour, egg and coconut, put them in your air fryer's basket, cook at 370 degrees F for 8 minutes, shaking halfway and divide among plates. Heat up a pan with the water over medium high heat, add chilies, cloves, vinegar and honey, stir very well, bring to a boil, simmer for a couple of minutes, drizzle over salmon and serve.

Nutrition:
calories 220, fat 12, fiber 2, carbs 14, protein 13

SALMON WITH CITRIC RELISH
Preparation time: 10 min | Cooking time: 30 min | Servings: 2
Ingredients:

- 2 salmon fillets, boneless
- Salt and black pepper to the taste
- 1 tbsp olive oil
- For the relish:
- 1 tbsp lemon juice
- 1 shallot, chopped
- 1 Meyer lemon, cut into wedges and then sliced
- 2 tbsp parsley, chopped
- ¼ cup olive oil

Directions:
Season salmon with salt and pepper, rub with 1 tbsp oil, place in your air fryer's basket and cook at 320 degrees F for 20 minutes, flipping the fish halfway. Meanwhile, in a bowl, mix shallot with the lemon juice, a pinch of salt and black pepper, stir and leave aside for 10 minutes. In a separate bowl, mix marinated shallot with lemon slices, salt, pepper, parsley and ¼ cup oil and whisk well. Divide salmon on plates, top with lemon relish and serve.

Nutrition:
calories 200, fat 3, fiber 3, carbs 23, protein 19

SALMON AND COCONUT DIP

Preparation time: 10 min | Cooking time: 10 min | Servings: 4

INGREDIENTS:

- 1 avocado, pitted, peeled and chopped
- 4 salmon fillets, boneless
- ¼ cup cilantro, chopped
- 1/3 cup coconut milk
- 1 tbsp lime juice
- 1 tbsp lime zest, grated
- 1 tsp onion powder
- 1 tsp garlic powder
- Salt and black pepper to the taste

DIRECTIONS:

Season salmon fillets with salt, black pepper and lime zest, rub well, put in your air fryer, cook at 350 degrees F for 9 minutes, flipping once and divide among plates. In your food processor, mix avocado with cilantro, garlic powder, onion powder, lime juice, salt, pepper and coconut milk, blend well, drizzle over salmon and serve right away.

NUTRITION:

calories 260, fat 7, fiber 20, carbs 28, protein 18

CRUNCHY SALMON

Preparation time: 10 min | Cooking time: 10 min | Servings: 4

INGREDIENTS:

- 1 cup pistachios, chopped
- 4 salmon fillets
- ¼ cup lemon juice
- 2 tbsp honey
- 1 tsp dill, chopped
- Salt and black pepper to the taste
- 1 tbsp mustard

DIRECTIONS:

In a bowl, mix pistachios with mustard, honey, lemon juice, salt, black pepper and dill, whisk and spread over salmon. Put in your air fryer and cook at 350 degrees F for 10 minutes. Divide among plates and serve with a side salad.

NUTRITION:

calories 300, fat 17, fiber 12, carbs 20, protein 22

MAPLE SALMON AND CHIVES MEDLEY

Preparation time: 10 min | Cooking time: 12 min | Servings: 4

INGREDIENTS:

- 2 tbsp dill, chopped
- 4 salmon fillets, boneless
- 2 tbsp chives, chopped
- 1/3 cup maple syrup
- 1 tbsp olive oil
- 3 tbsp balsamic vinegar
- Salt and black pepper to the taste

DIRECTIONS:

Season fish with salt and pepper, rub with the oil, place in your air fryer and cook at 350 degrees F for 8 minutes, flipping once. Heat up a small pot with the vinegar over medium heat, add maple syrup, chives and dill, stir and cook for 3 minutes. Divide fish on plates and serve with chives vinaigrette on top.

NUTRITION:

calories 270, fat 3, fiber 13, carbs 25, protein 10

ROSEMARY HALIBUT AND TOMATOES

Preparation time: 10 min | Cooking time: 10 min | Servings: 2

INGREDIENTS:

- 2 medium halibut fillets
- 2 garlic cloves, minced
- 2 tsp olive oil
- Salt and black pepper to the taste
- 6 sun dried tomatoes, chopped
- 2 small red onions, sliced
- 1 fennel bulb, sliced
- 9 black olives, pitted and sliced
- 4 rosemary sprigs, chopped
- ½ tsp red pepper flakes, crushed

DIRECTIONS:

Season fish with salt, pepper, rub with garlic and oil and put in a heat proof dish that fits your air fryer. Add onion slices, sun dried tomatoes, fennel, olives, rosemary and sprinkle pepper flakes, transfer to your air fryer and cook at 380 degrees F for 10 minutes. Divide fish and veggies on plates and serve.

NUTRITION:

calories 300, fat 12, fiber 9, carbs 18, protein 30

COD FILLET AND PLUM SAUCE

Preparation time: 10 min | Cooking time: 15 min | Servings: 2

INGREDIENTS:

- 1 egg white
- ½ cup red quinoa, already cooked
- 2 tsp whole wheat flour
- 4 tsp lemon juice
- ½ tsp smoked paprika
- 1 tsp olive oil
- 2 medium black cod fillets, skinless and boneless
- 1 red plum, pitted and chopped
- 2 tsp raw honey
- ¼ tsp black peppercorns, crushed
- 2 tsp parsley
- ¼ cup water

DIRECTIONS:

In a bowl, mix 1 tsp lemon juice with egg white, flour and ¼ tsp paprika and whisk well. Put quinoa in a bowl and mix it with 1/3 of egg white mix. Put the fish into the bowl with the remaining egg white mix and toss to coat. Dip fish in quinoa mix, coat well and leave aside for 10 minutes. Heat up a pan with 1 tsp oil over medium heat, add peppercorns, honey and plum, stir, bring to a simmer and cook for 1 minute. Add the rest of the lemon juice, the rest of the paprika and the water, stir well and simmer for 5 minutes. Add parsley, stir, take sauce off heat and leave aside for now. Put fish in your air fryer and cook at 380 degrees F for 10 minutes. Arrange fish on plates, drizzle plum sauce on top and serve.

NUTRITION:
calories 324, fat 14, fiber 22, carbs 27, protein 22

SEA BASS WITH COUSCOUS
Preparation time: 10 min | Cooking time: 15 min | Servings: 4

INGREDIENTS:

- 2 red onions, chopped
- Cooking spray
- 2 small fennel bulbs, cored and sliced
- ¼ cup almonds, toasted and sliced
- Salt and black pepper to the taste
- 2 and ½ pounds sea bass, gutted
- 5 tsp fennel seeds
- ¾ cup whole wheat couscous, cooked

DIRECTIONS:
Season fish with salt and pepper, spray with cooking spray, place in your air fryer and cook at 350 degrees F for 10 minutes. Meanwhile, spray a pan with some cooking oil and heat it up over medium heat. Add fennel seeds to this pan, stir and toast them for 1 minute. Add onion, salt, pepper, fennel bulbs, almonds and couscous, stir, cook for 2-3 minutes and divide among plates. Add fish next to couscous mix and serve right away.

NUTRITION:
calories 354, fat 7, fiber 10, carbs 20, protein 30

PEANUT COD
Preparation time: 10 min | Cooking time: 10 min | Servings: 2

INGREDIENTS:

- 2 medium cod fillets, boneless
- 1 tsp peanuts, crushed
- 2 tsp garlic powder
- 1 tbsp light soy sauce
- ½ tsp ginger, grated

DIRECTIONS:
Put fish fillets in a heat proof dish that fits your air fryer, add garlic powder, soy sauce and ginger, toss well, put in your air fryer and cook at 350 degrees F for 10 minutes. Divide fish on plates, sprinkle peanuts on top and serve.

NUTRITION:
calories 254, fat 10, fiber 11, carbs 14, protein 23

COD WITH PEARL ONIONS
Preparation time: 10 min | Cooking time: 15 min | Servings: 2

INGREDIENTS:

- 14 ounces pearl onions
- 2 medium cod fillets
- 1 tbsp parsley, dried
- 1 tsp thyme, dried
- Black pepper to the taste
- 8 ounces mushrooms, sliced

DIRECTIONS:
Put fish in a heat proof dish that fits your air fryer, add onions, parsley, mushrooms, thyme and black pepper, toss well, put in your air fryer and cook at 350 degrees F and cook for 15 minutes. Divide everything on plates and serve.

NUTRITION:
calories 270, fat 14, fiber 8, carbs 14, protein 22

HAWAIIAN PINEAPPLE SALMON
Preparation time: 10 min | Cooking time: 10 min | Servings: 2

INGREDIENTS:

- 20 ounces canned pineapple pieces and juice
- ½ tsp ginger, grated
- 2 tsp garlic powder
- 1 tsp onion powder
- 1 tbsp balsamic vinegar
- 2 medium salmon fillets, boneless
- Salt and black pepper to the taste

DIRECTIONS:
Season salmon with garlic powder, onion powder, salt and black pepper, rub well, transfer to a heat proof dish that fits your air fryer, add ginger and pineapple chunks and toss them really gently. Drizzle the vinegar all over, put in your air fryer and cook at 350 degrees F for 10 minutes. Divide everything on plates and serve.

NUTRITION:
calories 200, fat 8, fiber 12, carbs 17, protein 20

SALMON AND HERBED SALAD
Preparation time: 10 min | Cooking time: 20 min | Servings: 4

INGREDIENTS:

- 2 medium salmon fillets
- ¼ cup melted butter
- 4 ounces mushrooms, sliced
- Sea salt and black pepper to the taste
- 12 cherry tomatoes, halved
- 2 tbsp olive oil
- 8 ounces lettuce leaves, torn
- 1 avocado, pitted, peeled and cubed
- 1 jalapeno pepper, chopped
- 5 cilantro sprigs, chopped
- 2 tbsp white wine vinegar
- 1 ounce feta

DIRECTIONS:

Place salmon on a lined baking sheet, brush with 2 tbsp melted butter, season with salt and pepper, broil for 15 minutes over medium heat and then keep warm. Meanwhile, heat up a pan with the rest of the butter over medium heat, add mushrooms, stir and cook for a few minutes. Put tomatoes in a bowl, add salt, pepper and 1 tbsp olive oil and toss to coat. In a salad bowl, mix salmon with mushrooms, lettuce, avocado, tomatoes, jalapeno and cilantro. Add the rest of the oil, vinegar, salt and pepper, sprinkle cheese on top and serve.

NUTRITION:
calories 230, fat 9, fiber 8, carbs 14, protein 22

SALMON AND GREEK SALSA

Preparation time: 10 min | Cooking time: 20 min | Servings: 2

INGREDIENTS:

- 2 medium salmon fillets
- 1 tbsp basil, chopped
- 6 lemon slices
- Sea salt and black pepper to the taste
- 1 cup Greek yogurt
- 2 tsp curry powder
- A pinch of cayenne pepper
- 1 garlic clove, minced
- ½ tsp cilantro, chopped
- ½ tsp mint, chopped

DIRECTIONS:

Place each salmon fillet on a parchment paper piece, make 3 splits in each and stuff them with basil. Season with salt and pepper, top each fillet with 3 lemon slices, fold parchment, seal edges, introduce in the oven at 400 degrees F and bake for 20 minutes. Meanwhile, in a bowl, mix yogurt with cayenne pepper, salt to the taste, garlic, curry, mint and cilantro and whisk well. Transfer fish to plates, drizzle the yogurt sauce you've just prepared on top and serve right away!

NUTRITION:
calories 242, fat 1, fiber 2, carbs 3, protein 3

BEETS SALMON

Preparation time: 10 min | Cooking time: 25 min | Servings: 4

INGREDIENTS:

- 1 pound medium beets, sliced
- 6 tbsp olive oil
- 1 and ½ pounds salmon fillets, skinless and boneless
- Salt and pepper to the taste
- 1 tbsp chives, chopped
- 1 tbsp parsley, chopped
- 1 tbsp fresh tarragon, chopped
- 3 tbsp shallots, chopped
- 1 tbsp grated lemon zest
- ¼ cup lemon juice
- 4 cups mixed baby greens

DIRECTIONS:

In a bowl, mix beets with ½ tbsp oil and toss to coat. Season them with salt and pepper, arrange them on a baking sheet, introduce in the oven at 450 degrees F and bake for 20 minutes. Take beets out of the oven, add salmon on top, brush it with the rest if the oil and season with salt and pepper. In a bowl, mix chives with parsley and tarragon and sprinkle 1 tbsp of this mix over salmon. Introduce in the oven again and bake for 15 minutes. Meanwhile, in a boil with shallots with lemon peel, salt, pepper and lemon juice and the rest of the herbs mixture and stir gently. Combine 2 tbsp of shallots dressing with mixed greens and toss gently. Take salmon out of the oven, arrange on plates, add beets and greens on the side, drizzle the rest of the shallot dressing on top and serve right away.

NUTRITION:
calories 312, fat 2, fiber 2, carbs 2, protein 4

SPANISH SALMON

Preparation time: 10 min | Cooking time: 15 min | Servings: 6

INGREDIENTS:

- 2 cups bread croutons
- 3 red onions, cut into medium wedges
- ¾ cup green olives, pitted
- 3 red bell peppers, cut into medium wedges
- ½ tsp smoked paprika
- Salt and black pepper to the taste
- 5 tbsp olive oil
- 6 medium salmon fillets, skinless and boneless
- 2 tbsp parsley, chopped

DIRECTIONS:

In a heat proof dish that fits your air fryer, mix bread croutons with onion wedges, bell pepper ones, olives, salt, pepper, paprika and 3 tbsp olive oil, toss well, place in your air fryer and cook at 356 degrees F for 7 minutes. Rub salmon with the rest of the oil, add over veggies and cook at 360 degrees F for 8 minutes. Divide fish and veggie mix on plates, sprinkle parsley all over and serve.

NUTRITION:
calories 321, fat 8, fiber 14, carbs 27, protein 22

HERBED SALMON

Preparation time: 1 hour | Cooking time: 20 min | Servings: 6

INGREDIENTS:

- 1 whole salmon
- 1 tbsp dill, chopped
- 1 tbsp tarragon, chopped
- 1 tbsp garlic, minced
- Juice from 2 lemons
- 1 lemon, sliced
- A pinch of salt and black pepper

DIRECTIONS:
In a large fish, mix fish with salt, pepper and lemon juice, toss well and keep in the fridge for 1 hour. Stuff salmon with garlic and lemon slices, place in your air fryer's basket and cook at 320 degrees F for 25 minutes. Divide among plates and serve with a tasty coleslaw on the side.

NUTRITION:
calories 300, fat 8, fiber 9, carbs 19, protein 27

RED SNAPPER WITH OKRA

Preparation time: 30 min | Cooking time: 15 min | Servings: 4

INGREDIENTS:

- 1 big red snapper, cleaned and scored
- Salt and black pepper to the taste
- 3 garlic cloves, minced
- 1 jalapeno, chopped
- ¼ pound okra, chopped
- 1 tbsp butter
- 2 tbsp olive oil
- 1 red bell pepper, chopped
- 2 tbsp white wine
- 2 tbsp parsley, chopped

DIRECTIONS:
In a bowl, mix jalapeno, wine with garlic, stir well and rub snapper with this mix. Season fish with salt and pepper and leave it aside for 30 minutes. Meanwhile, heat up a pan with 1 tbsp butter over medium heat, add bell pepper and okra, stir and cook for 5 minutes. Stuff red snapper's belly with this mix, also add parsley and rub with the olive oil. Place in preheated air fryer and cook at 400 degrees F for 15 minutes, flipping the fish halfway. Divide among plates and serve.

NUTRITION:
calories 261, fat 7, fiber 18, carbs 28, protein 18

SNAPPER WITH PEPPERS

Preparation time: 10 min | Cooking time: 14 min | Servings: 2

INGREDIENTS:

- 2 red snapper fillets, boneless
- 1 tbsp olive oil
- ½ cup red bell pepper, chopped
- ½ cup green bell pepper, chopped
- ½ cup leeks, chopped
- Salt and black pepper to the taste
- 1 tsp tarragon, dried
- A splash of white wine

DIRECTIONS:
In a heat proof dish that fits your air fryer, mix fish fillets with salt, pepper, oil, green bell pepper, red bell pepper, leeks, tarragon and wine, toss well everything, introduce in preheated air fryer at 350 degrees F and cook for 14 minutes, flipping fish fillets halfway. Divide fish and veggies on plates and serve warm.

NUTRITION:
calories 300, fat 12, fiber 8, carbs 29, protein 12

CITRIC BRANZINO

Preparation time: 10 min | Cooking time: 10 min | Servings: 4

INGREDIENTS:

- Zest from 1 lemon, grated
- Zest from 1 orange, grated
- Juice from ½ lemon
- Juice from ½ orange
- Salt and black pepper to the taste
- 4 medium branzino fillets, boneless
- ½ cup parsley, chopped
- 2 tbsp olive oil
- A pinch of red pepper flakes, crushed

DIRECTIONS:
In a large bowl, mix fish fillets with lemon zest, orange zest, lemon juice, orange juice, salt, pepper, oil and pepper flakes, toss really well, transfer fillets to your preheated air fryer at 350 degrees F and bake for 10 minutes, flipping fillets once. Divide fish on plates, sprinkle with parsley and serve.

NUTRITION:
calories 261, fat 8, fiber 12, carbs 21, protein 12

LEMON SOLE WITH CHARD MIX

Preparation time: 10 min | Cooking time: 14 min | Servings: 4

INGREDIENTS:

- 1 tsp lemon zest, grated
- 4 white bread slices, quartered
- ¼ cup walnuts, chopped
- ¼ cup parmesan, grated
- 4 tbsp olive oil
- 4 sole fillets, boneless
- Salt and black pepper to the taste
- 4 tbsp butter
- ¼ cup lemon juice
- 3 tbsp capers
- 2 garlic cloves, minced
- 2 bunches Swiss chard, chopped

DIRECTIONS:
In your food processor, mix bread with walnuts, cheese and lemon zest and pulse well. Add half of the olive oil, pulse really well again and leave aside for now. Heat up a pan with the butter over medium heat, add lemon juice, salt, pepper and capers, stir well, add fish and toss it. Transfer fish to your preheated air fryer's basket, top with bread mix you've made at the beginning and cook at 350 degrees F for 14 minutes. Meanwhile, heat up another pan with the rest of the oil, add garlic, Swiss chard, salt and pepper, stir gently, cook for 2 minutes and take off heat. Divide fish on plates and serve with sautéed chard on the side.

NUTRITION:
calories 321, fat 7, fiber 18, carbs 27, protein 12

SALMON AND SWEET BERRY GLAZE

Preparation time: 10 min | Cooking time: 33 min | Servings: 4

INGREDIENTS:

- 1 cup water
- 1 inch ginger piece, grated
- Juice from ½ lemon
- 12 ounces blackberries
- 1 tbsp olive oil
- ¼ cup sugar
- 4 medium salmon fillets, skinless
- Salt and black pepper to the taste

DIRECTIONS:
Heat up a pot with the water over medium high heat, add ginger, lemon juice and blackberries, stir, bring to a boil, cook for 4-5 minutes, take off heat, strain into a bowl, return to pan and combine with sugar. Stir this mix, bring to a simmer over medium low heat and cook for 20 minutes. Leave blackberry sauce to cool down, brush salmon with it, season with salt and pepper, drizzle olive oil all over and rub fish well. Place fish in your preheated air fryer at 350 degrees F and cook for 10 minutes, flipping fish fillets once. Divide among plates, drizzle some of the remaining blackberry sauce all over and serve.

NUTRITION:
calories 312, fat 4, fiber 9, carbs 19, protein 14

ORIENTAL FISH

Preparation time: 10 min | Cooking time: 12 min | Servings: 4

INGREDIENTS:

- 2 pounds red snapper fillets, boneless
- Salt and black pepper to the taste
- 3 garlic cloves, minced
- 1 yellow onion, chopped
- 1 tbsp tamarind paste
- 1 tbsp oriental sesame oil
- 1 tbsp ginger, grated
- 2 tbsp water
- ½ tsp cumin, ground
- 1 tbsp lemon juice
- 3 tbsp mint, chopped

DIRECTIONS:
In your food processor, mix garlic with onion, salt, pepper, tamarind paste, sesame oil, ginger, water and cumin, pulse well and rub fish with this mix. Place fish in your preheated air fryer at 320 degrees F and cook for 12 minutes, flipping fish halfway. Divide fish on plates, drizzle lemon juice all over, sprinkle mint and serve right away.

NUTRITION:
calories 241, fat 8, fiber 16, carbs 17, protein 12

FRENCH COD WITH TOMATOES

Preparation time: 10 min | Cooking time: 22 min | Servings: 4

INGREDIENTS:

- 2 tbsp olive oil
- 1 yellow onion, chopped
- ½ cup white wine
- 2 garlic cloves, minced
- 14 ounces canned tomatoes, stewed
- 3 tbsp parsley, chopped
- 2 pounds cod, boneless
- Salt and black pepper to the taste
- 2 tbsp butter

DIRECTIONS:
Heat up a pan with the oil over medium heat, add garlic and onion, stir and cook for 5 minutes. Add wine, stir and cook for 1 minute more. Add tomatoes, stir, bring to a boil, cook for 2 minutes, add parsley, stir again and take off heat. Pour this mix into a heat proof dish that fits your air fryer, add fish, season it with salt and pepper and cook in your fryer at 350 degrees F for 14 minutes. Divide fish and tomatoes mix on plates and serve.

NUTRITION:
calories 231, fat 8, fiber 12, carbs 26, protein 14

WORCESTERSHIRE CATFISH FILLETS

Preparation time: 10 min | Cooking time: 12 min | Servings: 4

INGREDIENTS:

- 2 catfish fillets
- ½ tsp garlic, minced
- 2 ounces butter
- 4 ounces Worcestershire sauce
- ½ tsp jerk seasoning
- 1 tsp mustard
- 1 tbsp balsamic vinegar
- ¾ cup catsup
- Salt and black pepper to the taste
- 1 tbsp parsley, chopped

DIRECTIONS:
Heat up a pan with the butter over medium heat, add Worcestershire sauce, garlic, jerk seasoning, mustard, catsup, vinegar, salt and pepper, stir well, take off heat and add fish fillets. Toss well, leave aside for 10 minutes, drain fillets, transfer them to your preheated air fryer's basket at 350 degrees F and cook for 8 minutes, flipping fillets halfway. Divide among plates, sprinkle parsley on top and serve right away.

NUTRITION:
calories 351, fat 8, fiber 16, carbs 27, protein 17

GINGER TILAPIA

Preparation time: 10 min | Cooking time: 10 min | Servings: 4

INGREDIENTS:

- 4 medium tilapia fillets
- Salt and black pepper to the taste
- ½ cup coconut milk
- 1 tsp ginger, grated
- ½ cup cilantro, chopped

- 2 garlic cloves, chopped
- ½ tsp garam masala
- Cooking spray
- ½ jalapeno, chopped

DIRECTIONS:
In your food processor, mix coconut milk with salt, pepper, cilantro, ginger, garlic, jalapeno and garam masala and pulse really well. Spray fish with cooking spray, spread coconut mix all over, rub well, transfer to your air fryer's basket and cook at 400 degrees F for 10 minutes. Divide among plates and serve hot.

NUTRITION:
calories 200, fat 5, fiber 6, carbs 25, protein 26

GREEK TILAPIA

Preparation time: 10 min | Cooking time: 8 min | Servings: 4

INGREDIENTS:

- 4 medium tilapia fillets
- Cooking spray
- Salt and black pepper to the taste
- 2 tsp honey
- ¼ cup Greek yogurt
- Juice from 1 lemon
- 2 tbsp chives, chopped

DIRECTIONS:
Season fish with salt and pepper, spray with cooking spray, place in preheated air fryer 350 degrees F and cook for 8 minutes, flipping halfway. Meanwhile, in a bowl, mix yogurt with honey, salt, pepper, chives and lemon juice and whisk really well. Divide air fryer fish on plates, drizzle yogurt sauce all over and serve right away.

NUTRITION:
calories 261, fat 8, fiber 18, carbs 24, protein 21

CITRIC SEA BASS

Preparation time: 10 min | Cooking time: 10 min | Servings: 2

INGREDIENTS:

- 2 sea bass fillets
- Zest from ½ orange, grated
- Juice from ½ orange
- A pinch of salt and black pepper
- 2 tbsp mustard
- 2 tsp honey
- 2 tbsp olive oil
- ½ pound canned lentils, drained
- A small bunch of dill, chopped
- 2 ounces watercress
- A small bunch of parsley, chopped

DIRECTIONS:
Season fish fillets with salt and pepper, add orange zest and juice, rub with 1 tbsp oil, with honey and mustard, rub, transfer to your air fryer and cook at 350 degrees F for 10 minutes, flipping halfway. Meanwhile, put lentils in a small pot, warm it up over medium heat, add the rest of the oil, watercress, dill and parsley, stir well and divide among plates. Add fish fillets and serve right away.

NUTRITION:
calories 212, fat 8, fiber 12, carbs 9, protein 17

TASTY POLLOCK

Preparation time: 10 min | Cooking time: 15 min | Servings: 6

INGREDIENTS:

- ½ cup sour cream
- 4 Pollock fillets, boneless
- ¼ cup parmesan, grated
- 2 tbsp butter, melted
- Salt and black pepper to the taste
- Cooking spray

DIRECTIONS:
In a bowl, mix sour cream with butter, parmesan, salt and pepper and whisk well. Spray fish with cooking spray and season with salt and pepper. Spread sour cream mix on one side of each Pollock fillet, arrange them in your preheated air fryer at 320 degrees F and cook them for 15 minutes. Divide Pollock fillets on plates and serve with a tasty side salad.

NUTRITION:
calories 300, fat 13, fiber 3, carbs 14, protein 44

AIR FRYER POULTRY RECIPES

GINGER CHICKEN LEGS

Preparation time: 5 min | Cooking time: 20 min | Servings: 4

INGREDIENTS:

- 4 chicken legs
- 5 tsp turmeric powder
- 2 tbsp ginger, grated
- Salt and black pepper to taste
- 4 tbsp heavy cream

DIRECTIONS:
Place all ingredients in a bowl and mix well. Transfer the chicken to your air fryer and cook at 380 degrees F for 20 minutes. Divide between plates and serve.

NUTRITION:
calories 300, fat 4, fiber 12, carbs 22, protein 20

ROSEMARY TURKEY BREAST

Preparation time: 10 min | Cooking time: 50 min | Servings: 4

INGREDIENTS:

- 2 turkey breasts, skinless, boneless and halved
- Salt and black pepper to taste
- 1 tsp garlic powder
- 1 tsp onion powder
- ½ tsp thyme, dried
- 1 tsp rosemary, dried
- 1 tbsp lemon juice
- 2 tbsp olive oil

DIRECTIONS:
In a bowl, mix all the ingredients and rub the turkey well. Transfer to your air fryer's basket and cook at 370 degrees F for 25 minutes on each side. Serve hot with a side salad.

NUTRITION:
calories 271, fat 10, fiber 5, carbs 18, protein 15

SALSA VERDE CHICKEN BREAST

Preparation time: 10 min | Cooking time: 20 min | Servings: 4

INGREDIENTS:

- 16 ounces salsa Verde
- 1 tbsp avocado oil
- Salt and black pepper to taste
- 1 pound chicken breast, boneless and skinless
- 1½ cups cheddar cheese, grated
- ¼ cup parsley, chopped
- 1 tsp sweet paprika

DIRECTIONS:
In a baking dish that fits your air fryer, place all ingredients except the cheese; toss well. Put the pan into the fryer and cook at 380 degrees F for 17 minutes. Sprinkle with the cheese and cook for 3-4 minutes more. Divide between plates and serve.

NUTRITION:
calories 280, fat 18, fiber 9, carbs 17, protein 14

CHEESY CHICKEN THIGHS

Preparation time: 10 min | Cooking time: 20 min | Servings: 4

INGREDIENTS:

- 5 chicken thighs
- 1 tbsp olive oil
- 2 garlic cloves, minced
- 1 tbsp rosemary
- ½ cup heavy cream
- ¾ cup chicken stock
- 1 tsp chili powder
- ¼ cup cheddar cheese, grated
- ½ cup tomatoes, chopped
- 2 tbsp basil, chopped
- Salt and black pepper to taste

DIRECTIONS:
Season the chicken with salt and pepper and rub it with ½ tbsp of the oil. Put the chicken in your air fryer's basket and cook at 350 degrees F for 4 minutes. Heat up a pan that fits your air fryer with the remaining ½ tbsp of oil over medium heat. Add rosemary, garlic, chili powder, tomatoes, cream, stock, cheese, salt, and pepper; stir / combine. Bring the mixture to a simmer, take off the heat, and then add the chicken thighs and toss everything. Place the pan in the air fryer and cook at 340 degrees F for 12 minutes. Divide between plates, sprinkle the basil on top, serve, and enjoy.

NUTRITION:
calories 232, fat 9, fiber 12, carbs 27, protein 16

SOY CHICKEN

Preparation time: 10 min | Cooking time: 30 min | Servings: 4

INGREDIENTS:

- 4 chicken thighs
- 2 green chilies, chopped
- 1 tbsp olive oil
- 1 bunch spring onions, chopped
- 1 tbsp ginger, grated
- 1 tbsp fish sauce
- 1 tbsp soy sauce
- 1 tsp sesame oil
- 14 ounces water
- 1 tbsp rice wine

DIRECTIONS:
Heat up a pan that fits your air fryer with the olive and sesame oil over medium heat. Add the chilies, onions, ginger, fish sauce, soy sauce, rice wine, and the water; whisk, bring to a simmer, cook for 3-4 minutes, and then take off the heat. Add the chicken thighs and toss everything. Place the pan into the air fryer and cook at 370 degrees F for 25 minutes. Divide between plates and serve.

NUTRITION:
calories 280, fat 12, fiber 12, carbs 20, protein 13

SWEET PAPRICA CHICKEN THIGHS

Preparation time: 5 min | Cooking time: 30 min | Servings: 4

INGREDIENTS:

- 8 chicken thighs
- 2 tbsp olive oil
- 4 tsp oregano, chopped
- ½ tsp sweet paprika
- Salt and black pepper to taste
- 2 garlic cloves, minced
- 1 red onion, chopped

DIRECTIONS:

In a baking dish that fits your air fryer, place all of the ingredients and mix well. Transfer the dish to your air fryer and cook at 400 degrees F for 30 minutes, shaking halfway. Divide between plates and serve.

NUTRITION:

calories 264, fat 14, fiber 13, carbs 21, protein 15

SPICY CHICKEN

Preparation time: 5 min | Cooking time: 30 min | Servings: 8

INGREDIENTS:

- 8 chicken thighs
- Salt and black pepper to taste
- 3 garlic cloves, minced
- 3 tbsp butter, melted
- 1 cup chicken stock
- ¼ cup heavy cream
- ½ tsp basil, dried
- ½ tsp thyme, dried
- ½ tsp oregano, dried
- 1 tbsp mustard
- ¼ cup cheddar cheese, grated

DIRECTIONS:

In a baking dish that fits your air fryer, place all ingredients except the cheddar cheese; mix well. Transfer the dish to your air fryer and cook at 370 degrees F for 25 minutes. Sprinkle the cheese on top and cook for 5 more minutes. Divide everything between plates and serve.

NUTRITION:

calories 280, fat 11, fiber 13, carbs 22, protein 14

SWEET DUCK BREAST

Preparation time: 10 min | Cooking time: 20 min | Servings: 6

INGREDIENTS:

- 6 duck breasts, boneless
- 4 tbsp soy sauce
- 1 tsp olive oil
- 2 tbsp honey
- Salt and black pepper to taste
- 20 ounces chicken stock
- 1 tbsp ginger, grated
- 4 tbsp hoisin sauce

DIRECTIONS:

Place all of the ingredients in a bowl and toss well. Put the bowl in the fridge for 10 minutes. Transfer the duck breasts to your air fryer's basket and cook at 400 degrees F for 10 minutes on each side. Divide between plates and serve with a side salad.

NUTRITION:

calories 286, fat 9, fiber 1, carbs 20, protein 17

DUCK AND CRANBERRIES

Preparation time: 5 min | Cooking time: 25 min | Servings: 4

INGREDIENTS:

- 2 duck breasts, skin scored
- Salt and black pepper to taste
- 1 tbsp sugar
- 1 tbsp olive oil
- 2 tbsp cranberries
- 8 ounces white wine
- 1 tbsp garlic, minced
- 2 tbsp heavy cream

DIRECTIONS:

Season the duck breasts with salt and pepper and put them in preheated air fryer. Cook at 350 degrees F for 10 minutes on each side and divide between plates. Heat up a pan with the oil over medium heat, and add the cranberries, sugar, wine, garlic, and the cream; whisk well. Cook for 3-4 minutes, drizzle over the duck, and serve.

Nutrition: calories 280, fat 11, fiber 32, carbs 19, protein 20

WINE CHICKEN WINGS

Preparation time: 10 min | Cooking time: 30 min | Servings: 4

INGREDIENTS:

- 8 chicken wings, halved
- 6 endives, shaved
- 1 tbsp olive oil
- 2 garlic cloves, minced
- ¼ cup white wine
- Salt and black pepper to taste
- 1 tbsp rosemary, chopped
- 1 tsp cumin, ground

DIRECTIONS:

Season the chicken wings with the salt, pepper, cumin, and rosemary. Place the wings in your air fryer's basket and cook at 360 degrees F for 10 minutes on each side; divide between plates. Heat up a pan with the oil over medium heat, and then add the garlic, endives, salt, pepper, and the wine; bring to a simmer. Cook for 8 minutes, spread over the chicken, and serve.

Nutrition: calories 270, fat 8, fiber 12, carbs 20, protein 22

TURKEY AND PARSLEY PESTO

Preparation time: 35 min | Cooking time: 35 min | Servings: 4

INGREDIENTS:

- 1 cup parsley, chopped
- ½ cup olive oil
- ¼ cup red wine
- 4 garlic cloves
- A pinch of salt

and black pepper
- A drizzle of maple syrup
- 2 turkey breasts, boneless, skinless and halved

DIRECTIONS:
In a blender, mix the parsley, garlic, salt, pepper, oil, wine, and maple syrup; pulse to make a parsley pesto and then transfer to a bowl. Add the turkey breasts to the bowl and toss well. Then place the bowl in the fridge for 30 minutes. Drain the turkey breasts (retaining the parsley pesto), put them in your air fryer's basket and cook at 380 degrees F for 35 minutes, flipping the meat halfway. Divide the turkey between plates, drizzle the parsley pesto, all over and serve.

NUTRITION:
calories 274, fat 10, fiber 12, carbs 20, protein 17

MUSHROOM CHICKEN BREASTS
Preparation time: 10 min | Cooking time: 20 min | Servings: 4

INGREDIENTS:

- 2 pounds chicken breasts, skinless and boneless
- 2 tbsp olive oil
- 1 red onion, chopped
- 2 garlic cloves, minced
- Salt and black pepper to taste
- 12 brown mushrooms, halved
- 1 red bell pepper, chopped
- 1 green bell pepper, roughly chopped
- 2 tbsp cheddar cheese, shredded

DIRECTIONS:
Season the chicken breasts with salt and pepper, and then rub with the garlic and 1 tbsp of the oil. Place the chicken breasts in your preheated air fryer's basket, cook at 390 degrees F for 6 minutes on each side, and divide between plates. Heat up a pan with the remaining 1 tbsp of the oil over medium heat; add the onions, stir, and cook for 2 minutes. Add the mushrooms and bell peppers, stir, and cook for 5-6 minutes more. Divide this next to the chicken, sprinkle the cheese all over, and serve.

NUTRITION:
calories 285, fat 12, fiber 11, carbs 20, protein 22

CHICKEN DRUMSTICKS AND COCONUT SAUCE
Preparation time: 10 min | Cooking time: 16 min | Servings: 4

INGREDIENTS:

- 10 green onions, roughly chopped
- 1 tbsp ginger, grated
- 4 garlic cloves, minced
- 2 tbsp oyster sauce
- 3 tbsp soy sauce
- 1 tsp Chinese five spice
- 10 chicken drumsticks
- 1 cup coconut milk
- Salt and black pepper to taste
- 1 tsp olive oil
- ¼ cup parsley, chopped
- 1 tbsp lemon juice

DIRECTIONS:
In a blender, mix the green onions with the ginger, garlic, soy sauce, oyster sauce, five spice, salt, pepper, oil, and coconut milk; pulse well. In a baking dish that fits your air fryer, mix the chicken with the green sauce, toss, and then place the dish in the air fryer. Cook at 370 degrees F for 16 minutes, shaking the fryer once. Divide between plates, sprinkle the parsley on top, drizzle the lemon juice all over, and serve.

NUTRITION:
calories 281, fat 11, fiber 12, carbs 22, protein 16

PARTY CHICKEN THIGHS
Preparation time: 5 min | Cooking time: 16 min | Servings: 6

INGREDIENTS:

- 8 chicken thighs
- 1 tbsp turmeric powder
- 1 tbsp coriander, ground
- 1 tbsp ginger, grated
- 1 tbsp sweet paprika
- Salt and black pepper to taste
- 2 tbsp olive oil
- 1 tbsp lime juice

DIRECTIONS:
Place all the ingredients in a bowl and toss well. Transfer the chicken thighs to your air fryer's basket and cook at 370 degrees F for 8 minutes on each side. Divide between plates and serve with a side salad.

NUTRITION:
calories 270, fat 11, fiber 11, carbs 17, protein 11

CHICKEN BREASTS DELIGHT
Preparation time: 5 min | Cooking time: 25 min | Servings: 6

INGREDIENTS:

- 1 tbsp olive oil
- 3½ pounds chicken breasts
- 1 cup chicken stock
- 1¼ cups yellow onion, chopped
- 1 tbsp lime juice
- 2 tsp sweet paprika
- 1 tsp red pepper flakes
- 2 tbsp green onions, chopped
- Salt and black pepper to taste

DIRECTIONS:
Heat the oil up in a pan that fits your air fryer over medium heat. Add the onions, lime juice, paprika, green onions, pepper flakes, salt, and pepper. Stir the onion mixture and cook for 8 minutes. Add the chicken and the stock, toss, and simmer for 1 more minute. Transfer the pan to your air fryer and cook at 370 degrees F for 12 minutes. Divide between plates and serve.

NUTRITION:

calories 280, fat 11, fiber 13, carbs 27, protein 16

MOZZARELLA CHICKEN MIX

Preparation time: 10 min | Cooking time: 20 min | Servings: 6

INGREDIENTS:

- 14 ounces tomato sauce
- 1 tbsp olive oil
- 4 medium chicken breasts, skinless and boneless
- Salt and black pepper to taste
- 1 tsp oregano, dried
- 6 ounces mozzarella cheese, grated
- 1 tsp garlic powder

DIRECTIONS:
Put the chicken in your air fryer and season with salt, pepper, garlic powder, and the oregano. Cook the chicken at 360 degrees F for 5 minutes; then transfer to a pan that fits your air fryer, greased with the oil. Add the tomato sauce, sprinkle the mozzarella on top, place the pan in the fryer, and cook at 350 degrees F for 15 minutes more. Divide between plates and serve.

NUTRITION:
calories 270, fat 10, fiber 16, carbs 16, protein 18

CHICKEN AND VEGGIE MEDLEY

Preparation time: 10 min | Cooking time: 25 min | Servings: 4

INGREDIENTS:

- 1 red onion, chopped
- 1 carrot, chopped
- 3 garlic cloves, minced
- 4 chicken breasts, boneless and skinless
- 1 celery stalk,
- chopped
- 1 cup chicken stock
- 2 tbsp olive oil
- ½ tsp rosemary, dried
- 1 tsp sage, dried
- Salt and black pepper to taste

DIRECTIONS:
In a pan that fits your air fryer, place all ingredients and toss well. Put the pan in the fryer and cook at 360 degrees F for 25 minutes. Divide everything between plates, serve, and enjoy!

NUTRITION:
calories 292, fat 12, fiber 16, carbs 19, protein 15

SWEET AND SOUR CHICKEN THIGHS

Preparation time: 10 min | Cooking time: 30 min | Servings: 5

INGREDIENTS:

- 2 pounds chicken thighs
- Salt and black pepper to taste
- 5 spring onions, chopped
- 2 tbsp olive oil
- 1 tbsp sherry wine
- ½ tsp white vinegar
- 1 tbsp soy sauce
- ¼ tsp sugar

DIRECTIONS:
Season the chicken with salt and pepper, rub with 1 tbsp of the oil, and put it in the air fryer's basket. Cook at 360 degrees F for 10 minutes on each side and divide between plates. Heat up a pan with the remaining tbsp of oil over medium-high heat, and add the spring onions, sherry wine, vinegar, soy sauce, and sugar; whisk. Cook for 10 minutes, drizzle over the chicken, and serve.

NUTRITION:
calories 271, fat 8, fiber 12, carbs 26, protein 17

WHOLE CHICKEN

Preparation time: 10 min | Cooking time: 20 min | Servings: 8

INGREDIENTS:

- 1 whole chicken, cut into medium pieces
- 3 tbsp white wine
- 2 carrots, chopped
- 1 cup chicken stock
- 1 tbsp ginger, grated
- Salt and black pepper to taste

DIRECTIONS:
In a pan that fits your air fryer, mix all of the ingredients. Put the pan in the air fryer and cook at 370 degrees F for 20 minutes. Divide between plates and serve.

NUTRITION:
calories 220, fat 10, fiber 8, carbs 20, protein 16

ITALIAN CHICKEN THIGHS

Preparation time: 5 min | Cooking time: 30 min | Servings: 4

INGREDIENTS:

- 3 carrots, chopped
- 2 pounds chicken thighs, boneless and skinless
- ¼ cup red wine vinegar
- 4 garlic cloves, minced
- Salt and black pepper to taste
- 4 tbsp olive oil
- 1 tbsp garlic powder
- 1 tbsp Italian seasoning
- 1 cup white rice
- 1 tsp turmeric powder
- 2 cups chicken stock

DIRECTIONS:
In a pan that fits your air fryer, mix all of the ingredients and toss. Place the pan in the fryer and cook at 370 degrees F for 30 minutes. Divide between plates and serve.

NUTRITION:
calories 280, fat 12, fiber 12, carbs 16, protein 13

GLAZED CHICKEN AND APPLES

Preparation time: 10 min | Cooking time: 20 min | Servings: 4

INGREDIENTS:

- 3 apples, cored and sliced
- 2 tbsp olive oil
- 1 tbsp rosemary, chopped
- Salt and black pepper to taste
- 6 chicken thighs, skin-on
- 1 cup apple cider
- 1 tbsp mustard
- 2 tbsp honey

DIRECTIONS:
Heat up a pan that fits your air fryer with 1 tbsp of the oil over medium heat. Add the cider, honey, and mustard; whisk. Bring to a simmer and take off the heat. Add the chicken, apples, salt, pepper, and rosemary; toss. Place the pan in your air fryer and cook at 390 degrees F for 17 minutes. Divide between plates and serve.

NUTRITION:
calories 281, fat 11, fiber 12, carbs 28, protein 19

CITRIC CHICKEN AND ZUCCHINI

Preparation time: 5 min | Cooking time: 15 min | Servings: 4

INGREDIENTS:

- 2 tbsp olive oil
- Juice of 1 lemon
- 1 tsp oregano, dried
- 3 garlic cloves, minced
- 1 pound chicken thighs
- Salt and black pepper to taste
- ½ pound asparagus, trimmed and halved
- 1 zucchini, roughly cubed
- 1 lemon, sliced

DIRECTIONS:
In a pan that fits your air fryer, mix all of the ingredients. Place the pan in your air fryer and cook at 380 degrees F for 15 minutes. Divide between plates and serve.

NUTRITION:
calories 280, fat 8, fiber 12, carbs 20, protein 15

TURKEY WITH FRUIT SAUCE

Preparation time: 10 min | Cooking time: 30 min | Servings: 4

INGREDIENTS:

- 2 turkey breasts, halved
- 1 tbsp olive oil
- ½ tsp garlic powder
- ¼ tsp sweet paprika
- Salt and black pepper to taste
- 1 cup chicken stock
- 3 tbsp butter, melted
- 1 shallot, chopped
- ½ cup red wine
- 4 tbsp figs, chopped
- 1 tbsp white flour

DIRECTIONS:
Heat up a pan with the olive oil and 1½ tbsp of the butter over medium-high heat. Add the shallots, stir, and cook for 2 minutes. Add the garlic powder, paprika, stock, salt, pepper, wine, and the figs; stir and cook for 7-8 minutes. Next add the flour, stir well, and cook the sauce for 1-2 minutes more; take off heat. Season the turkey with salt and pepper, and drizzle the remaining 1½ tbsp of butter over them. Place the turkey in your air fryer's basket, and cook at 380 degrees F for 15 minutes, flipping them halfway. Divide between plates, drizzle the sauce all over, and serve.

NUTRITION:
calories 246, fat 12, fiber 4, carbs 22, protein 16

GARLIC AND LEMON PEPPER CHICKEN

Preparation time: 10 min | Cooking time: 15 min | Servings: 4

INGREDIENTS:

- 4 chicken breasts, skinless and boneless
- 4 garlic heads, peeled, cloves separated and cut into quarters
- 2 tbsp lemon juice
- Salt and black pepper to taste
- ½ tsp lemon pepper
- 1½ tbsp avocado oil

DIRECTIONS:
In a bowl, mix all of the ingredients and toss well. Transfer the chicken mixture to your air fryer and cook at 360 degrees F for 15 minutes. Divide between plates and serve with a side salad.

NUTRITION:
calories 240, fat 7, fiber 1, carbs 17, protein 18

TARRAGON CHICKEN BREASTS

Preparation time: 10 min | Cooking time: 15 min | Servings: 2

INGREDIENTS:

- 2 chicken breasts, skinless and boneless
- 1 cup white wine
- ¼ cup soy sauce
- 2 garlic cloves, minced
- 8 tarragon sprigs, chopped
- Salt and black pepper to taste
- 1 tbsp butter, melted

DIRECTIONS:
In a bowl, mix the chicken with the wine, soy sauce, garlic, tarragon, salt, pepper, and the butter; toss well and set aside for 10 minutes. Transfer the chicken and its marinade to a baking dish that fits your air fryer and cook at 370 degrees F for 15 minutes, shaking the fryer halfway. Divide everything between plates and serve.

NUTRITION:
calories 271, fat 12, fiber 3, carbs 17, protein 15

CHICKEN BREASTS AND PEAR JELLY

Preparation time: 10 min | Cooking time: 20 min | Servings: 6

INGREDIENTS:

- 3 cups ketchup
- 1 cup pear jelly
- ¼ cup honey
- ½ tsp smoked paprika
- 1 tsp chili powder
- 1 tsp mustard powder
- Salt and black pepper to taste
- 1 tsp garlic powder
- 6 chicken breasts, skinless and boneless

Directions:
Season the chicken with salt and pepper, put it in preheated air fryer, and cook at 350 degrees F for 10 minutes. Heat up a pan with the ketchup over medium heat, add the pear jelly, honey, smoked paprika, chili powder, mustard powder, garlic powder, salt, and pepper; whisk and cook for 5-6 minutes. Add the chicken, toss, and cook for 4 minutes more. Divide everything between plates and serve.

Nutrition:
calories 283, fat 13, fiber 7, carbs 19, protein 17

SWEET CHICKEN AND DATES MIX
Preparation time: 10 min | Cooking time: 25 min | Servings: 6

Ingredients:

- 1 whole chicken, cut into medium pieces
- ¾ cup water
- 1 cup honey
- Salt and black pepper to taste
- ¼ cup olive oil
- 4 dates, chopped

Directions:
Put the water in a pot, bring to a simmer over medium heat. Add the honey, whisk, and take off the heat. Rub the chicken with the oil, season with salt and pepper, and place in your air fryer's basket. Add the dates and cook at 350 degrees F for 10 minutes. Brush the chicken with some of the honey mix, cook for 6 minutes more, flip again, brush one more time with the honey mix, and cook for 7 minutes more. Divide the chicken and the dates between plates and serve.

Nutrition:
calories 270, fat 14, fiber 3, carbs 15, protein 20

CHICKEN THIGHS AND LEEKS
Preparation time: 10 min | Cooking time: 30 min | Servings: 4

Ingredients:

- 4 chicken thighs, bone-in
- Salt and black pepper to taste
- 1 tbsp olive oil
- 1 cup chicken stock
- 3 leeks, sliced
- 3 carrots, cut into thin sticks
- 2 tbsp chives, chopped

Directions:
Heat up a pan that fits your air fryer over medium heat, add the stock, leeks and carrots, cover, and simmer for 20 minutes. Rub the chicken with olive oil, season with salt and pepper, put it in your air fryer, and cook at 350 degrees F for 4 minutes. Add the chicken to the leeks mix, place the pan in your air fryer, and cook for 6 minutes more. Divide between plates, serve, and enjoy!

Nutrition:
calories 237, fat 10, fiber 4, carbs 19, protein 16

CHICKEN AND BELL PEPPERS MIX
Preparation time: 1 hour | Cooking time: 15 min | Servings: 4

Ingredients:

- 17 ounces chicken meat, boneless and cubed
- 1 red bell pepper, deseeded and cubed
- 1 green bell pepper, deseeded and cubed
- 1 yellow bell pepper, deseeded and cubed
- 14 ounces yogurt
- Salt and black pepper to taste
- 3½ ounces cherry tomatoes, halved
- 1 tbsp ginger, grated
- 2 tbsp red chili powder
- 2 tbsp coriander powder
- 2 tsp olive oil
- 1 tsp turmeric powder
- 2 tbsp cumin powder
- 3 mint leaves, torn

Directions:
In a bowl, mix all of the ingredients, toss well, and place in the fridge for 1 hour. Transfer the whole mix to a pan that fits your air fryer and cook at 400 degrees F for 15 minutes, shaking the pan halfway.

Nutrition:
calories 245, fat 4, fiber 5, carbs 17, protein 16

AIR FRIED CHICKEN WINGS
Preparation time: 10 min | Cooking time: 45 min | Servings: 4

Ingredients:

- 16 chicken wings
- Salt and black pepper to taste
- ¼ cup butter, melted
- ¼ cup clover honey
- 4 tbsp garlic, minced

Directions:
Put the chicken wings in your air fryer's basket and season with salt and pepper. Cook at 380 degrees F for 25 minutes, then at 400 degrees F for 5 minutes and put it in a bowl. Melt the butter in a pan over medium-high heat; then add the garlic, stir, and sauté for 5 minutes. Add salt, pepper, the air fried chicken and the honey; stir, and simmer for 10 minutes more over medium heat. Divide the chicken wings and the sauce between plates and serve.

Nutrition:
calories 274, fat 11, fiber 3, carbs 19, protein 15

TURKEY BREASTS AND SPRING ONIONS

Preparation time: 10 min | Cooking time: 30 min | Servings: 2

Ingredients:

- 2 small turkey breasts, boneless and skinless
- 2 red chilies, chopped
- 1 tbsp olive oil
- 1 bunch spring onions, chopped
- 1 tbsp oyster sauce
- 1 tbsp soy sauce
- 1 cup chicken stock
- 1 tbsp Chinese rice wine

Directions:

Add the oil to a pan that fits your air fryer and place it over medium heat. Then add the chilies, spring onions, oyster sauce, soy sauce, stock, and rice wine; whisk, and simmer for 3-4 minutes. Add the turkey, toss, and place the pan in the air fryer and cook at 380 degrees F for 30 minutes. Divide everything between plates and serve.

Nutrition:

calories 280, fat 12, fiber 5, carbs 16, protein 14

SOY AND GINGER CHICKEN

Preparation time: 10 min | Cooking time: 40 min | Servings: 6

Ingredients:

- 1 whole chicken, cut into pieces
- 1 tbsp ginger, grated
- 1 chili pepper, minced
- 2 tsp soy sauce
- 1 tsp sesame oil
- Salt and black pepper to taste

Directions:

In a bowl, mix the chicken with all the other ingredients and rub well. Transfer the chicken pieces to your air fryer's basket. Cook at 400 degrees F for 30 minutes, and then at 380 degrees F for 10 minutes more. Divide everything between plates and serve

Nutrition:

calories 270, fat 8, fiber 4, carbs 20, protein 17

PARMESAN CHICKEN

Preparation time: 10 min | Cooking time: 30 min | Servings: 4

Ingredients:

- 4 chicken breasts, boneless and skinless
- ¼ cup butter, melted
- ½ cup parmesan cheese, grated
- 1 cup corn flakes, crushed
- Salt and black pepper to taste
- 1 tbsp olive oil

Directions:

In a bowl, mix all the ingredients and toss. Place the chicken in your air fryer's basket and cook at 360 degrees F for 15 minutes on each side. Divide between plates and serve.

Nutrition:

calories 271, fat 9, fiber 4, carbs 19, protein 15

DUCK AND GOLD POTATOES

Preparation time: 10 min | Cooking time: 30 min | Servings: 2

Ingredients:

- 1 duck breast, halved and scored
- 2 gold potatoes, cubed
- Salt and black pepper to taste
- 2 tbsp butter, melted
- 1 ounce red wine

Directions:

Season the duck pieces with salt and pepper, put them in a pan, and heat up over medium-high heat. Cook for 4 minutes on each side, transfer to your air fryer's basket, and cook at 360 degrees F for 8 minutes. Put the butter in a pan and heat it up over medium heat; then add the potatoes, salt, pepper, and the wine, and cook for 8 minutes. Add the duck pieces, toss, and cook everything for 3-4 minutes more. Divide all between plates and serve.

Nutrition:

calories 290, fat 13, fiber 4, carbs 10, protein 16

CHEESY CHICKEN

Preparation time: 10 min | Cooking time: 20 min | Servings: 4

Ingredients:

- 1 yellow onion, minced
- 4 chicken breasts, skinless and boneless
- ¼ cup balsamic vinegar
- 12 ounces canned tomatoes, chopped
- Salt and black pepper to taste
- ¼ cup cheddar cheese, grated
- ¼ tsp garlic powder

Directions:

In a baking dish that fits your air fryer, mix the chicken with the onions, vinegar, tomatoes, salt, pepper, and garlic powder. Sprinkle the cheese on top and place the pan in the air fryer; cook at 400 degrees F for 20 minutes. Divide between plates and serve.

Nutrition:

calories 280, fat 11, fiber 2, carbs 19, protein 16

SIMPLE LEMONGRASS CHICKEN

Preparation time: 10 min | Cooking time: 30 min | Servings: 4

Ingredients:

- 1 bunch lemongrass, trimmed
- 1 tbsp ginger, chopped
- 4 garlic cloves, minced
- 2 tbsp fish sauce
- 3 tbsp soy sauce
- 10 chicken drumsticks
- 1 cup coconut milk

- Salt and black pepper to taste
- 1 tsp butter, melted
- ¼ cup parsley, chopped
- 1 yellow onion, chopped
- 1 tbsp lemon juice

DIRECTIONS:
In a blender, combine the lemongrass, ginger, garlic, soy sauce, fish sauce, and coconut milk; pulse well. Put the butter in a pan that fits your air fryer and heat it up over medium heat; add the onions, stir, and cook for 2-3 minutes. Add the chicken, salt, pepper, and the lemongrass mix; toss well. Place the pan in the fryer and cook at 380 degrees F for 25 minutes. Add the lemon juice and the parsley and toss. Divide everything between plates and serve.

NUTRITION:
calories 251, fat 8, fiber 14, carbs 19, protein 6

HERBED CHICKEN
Preparation time: 10 min | Cooking time: 25 min | Servings: 4

INGREDIENTS:

- 6 chicken thighs, boneless
- 2 tbsp olive oil
- ½ tsp coriander, ground
- ½ tsp cumin, ground
- ½ tsp ginger powder
- ½ tsp turmeric, ground
- ½ tsp cinnamon, ground
- 1 tsp sweet paprika
- 2 yellow onions, chopped
- 5 garlic cloves, chopped
- ¼ cup white wine
- 1 cup chicken stock
- ¼ cup cranberries, dried
- Juice of 1 lemon
- ½ cup cilantro, chopped

DIRECTIONS:
Heat up the oil in a pan that fits your air fryer over medium heat. Add all other ingredients except the chicken, lemon juice, and cilantro; stir and cook for 5 minutes. Then add the chicken and toss. Place the pan in the fryer and cook at 380 degrees F for 20 minutes. Add the lemon juice and the cilantro and toss. Divide between plates, serve, and enjoy!

NUTRITION:
calories 261, fat 12, fiber 7, carbs 15, protein 25

TURKEY WITH LENTILS
Preparation time: 10 min | Cooking time: 25 min | Servings: 4

INGREDIENTS:

- 1 pound turkey meat, cubed and browned
- Salt and black pepper to taste
- 15 ounces canned lentils, drained
- 1 yellow onion, chopped
- 1 green bell pepper, chopped
- 3 garlic cloves, chopped
- 2½ tbsp chili powder
- 1½ tsp cumin, ground
- 12 ounces veggie stock

DIRECTIONS:
Add all of the ingredients to a pan that fits your air fryer and mix well. Place the pan in the fryer and cook at 380 degrees F for 25 minutes. Divide into bowls and serve hot.

NUTRITION:
calories 251, fat 8, fiber 8, carbs 15, protein 17

MEXICAN TURKEY AND MUSHROOMS
Preparation time: 5 min | Cooking time: 20 min | Servings: 4

INGREDIENTS:

- 1 pound turkey meat, ground
- Salt and black pepper to taste
- 2 tbsp olive oil
- 10 ounces tomato sauce
- 4 ounces mushrooms, sliced
- 1 tbsp oregano, dried
- 1 tsp garlic, minced
- 1 tsp basil, dried
- 1 yellow onion, chopped
- 1 cup cheddar cheese, grated

DIRECTIONS:
Heat up the oil in a pan that fits your air fryer over medium heat. Add the turkey, oregano, garlic, basil, and the onions; toss, and cook for 2-3 minutes. Then add the mushrooms and tomato sauce, toss, and cook for 2 minutes more. Place the pan in the fryer and cook at 370 degrees F for 16 minutes. Sprinkle the cheese all over, divide the mix between plates, and serve.

NUTRITION:
calories 261, fat 8, fiber 6, carbs 16, protein 16

BALSAMIC CHICKEN
Preparation time: 5 min | Cooking time: 20 min | Servings: 4

INGREDIENTS:

- 8 chicken thighs, boneless
- Salt and black pepper to taste
- ½ cup balsamic vinegar
- 1 tsp black peppercorns
- 4 garlic cloves, minced
- ½ cup soy sauce

DIRECTIONS:
In a pan that fits your air fryer, mix the chicken with all the other ingredients and toss. Place the pan in the fryer and cook at 380 degrees F for 20 minutes. Divide everything between plates and serve.

NUTRITION:
calories 261, fat 7, fiber 5, carbs 15, protein 16

PARMESAN TURKEY MEATBALLS

Preparation time: 10 min | Cooking time: 15 min | Servings: 8

INGREDIENTS:

- 1 pound turkey meat, ground
- 1 yellow onion, minced
- ¼ cup parmesan cheese, grated
- ½ cup panko breadcrumbs
- 4 garlic cloves, minced
- ¼ cup parsley, chopped
- Salt and black pepper to taste
- 1 tsp oregano, dried
- 1 egg, whisked
- ¼ cup milk
- 2 tsp soy sauce
- 1 tsp fish sauce
- Cooking spray

DIRECTIONS:
In a bowl, mix together all of the ingredients (except the cooking spray), stir well, and then shape into medium-sized meatballs. Place the meatballs in your air fryer's basket, grease them with cooking spray, and cook at 380 degrees F for 15 minutes. Serve the meatballs with a side salad.

NUTRITION:
calories 261, fat 7, fiber 6, carbs 15, protein 18

GARLIC CHICKEN BREASTS

Preparation time: 10 min | Cooking time: 25 min | Servings: 4

INGREDIENTS:

- 4 garlic cloves, chopped
- 2 chicken breasts, skinless, boneless and halved
- 1 yellow onion, sliced
- 1 tsp rosemary, dried
- 1 tbsp fresh rosemary, chopped
- 1 cup chicken stock
- 1 tbsp soy sauce
- Salt and black pepper to taste
- 2 tbsp cornstarch mixed with 2½ tbsp water
- 2 tbsp butter, melted

DIRECTIONS:
Heat up the butter in a pan that fits your air fryer over medium heat. Add the onions, garlic, dried and fresh rosemary, stock, soy sauce, salt, and pepper; stir, and simmer for 2-3 minutes. Add the cornstarch mixture, whisk, cook for 2 minutes more, and take off the heat. Add the chicken, toss gently, and place the pan in the fryer; cook at 370 degrees F for 20 minutes. Divide between plates and serve hot.

NUTRITION:
calories 281, fat 8, fiber 5, carbs 15, protein 20

CHICKEN AND SMOKED PANCETTA

Preparation time: 10 min | Cooking time: 25 min | Servings: 4

INGREDIENTS:

- 2 chicken breasts, skinless, boneless, cubed
- 4 ounces smoked pancetta, chopped
- ½ cup chicken stock
- 2 scallions, chopped
- ½ bunch thyme, chopped
- Salt and black pepper to taste
- ½ bunch rosemary, chopped
- ½ fennel bulb, cut into matchsticks
- 4 carrots, cut into thin matchsticks
- Juice of 1 lemon
- A drizzle of olive oil

DIRECTIONS:
Heat up the oil in a pan that fits your air fryer over medium heat. Add the scallions, pancetta, thyme, rosemary, salt, pepper, fennel, and carrots; toss and cook for 5 minutes. Add the lemon juice and the chicken, toss, and cook for 5 more minutes. Place the pan in the fryer and cook at 380 degrees F for 15 minutes. Divide everything between plates and serve.

NUTRITION:
calories 281, fat 11, fiber 5, carbs 17, protein 20

TURKEY WINGS WITH CRANBERRIES

Preparation time: 10 min | Cooking time: 35 min | Servings: 4

INGREDIENTS:

- 2 turkey wings
- 2 tbsp butter, melted
- 1½ cups cranberries
- Salt and black pepper to taste
- 1 yellow onion, sliced
- 1 cup orange juice
- 1 bunch thyme, roughly chopped

DIRECTIONS:
Place the butter in a pan that fits your air fryer and heat up over medium-high heat. Add the cranberries, salt, pepper, onions, and orange juice; whisk, and cook for 3 minutes. Add the turkey wings, toss, and cook for 3-4 minutes more. Transfer the pan to your air fryer and cook at 380 degrees F for 25 minutes. Add the thyme, toss, and divide everything between plates. Serve, and enjoy!

NUTRITION:
calories 291, fat 12, fiber 7, carbs 20, protein 22

SPICY CHICKEN MIX

Preparation time: 10 min | Cooking time: 35 min | Servings: 8

INGREDIENTS:

- 1 whole chicken, cut into pieces
- 1 tbsp olive oil
- 1½ tbsp lemon zest
- 1 cup chicken stock
- 1½ tsp cinnamon powder
- Salt and black pepper to taste
- 2 tsp garlic powder
- 1 tbsp coriander

Place all of the ingredients in a bowl and mix well. Transfer the chicken to your air fryer's basket and cook at 370 degrees F for 35 minutes, shaking the fryer from time to time. Divide the chicken between plates and serve with a side salad.

NUTRITION:
calories 281, fat 7, fiber 8, carbs 20, protein 28

HONEY WINGS
Preparation time: 10 min | Cooking time: 17 min | Servings: 6

INGREDIENTS:
- 12 chicken wings, cut into 24 pieces
- ¼ cup honey
- 4 tbsp hot sauce
- Salt and black pepper to taste
- ¼ cup tomato sauce
- 1 tbsp cilantro, chopped

DIRECTIONS:
In a bowl, mix the chicken wings with the hot sauce, honey, salt, pepper, and tomato sauce; toss well. Transfer the chicken wings to your air fryer's basket and cook at 400 degrees F for 17 minutes. Divide between plates, sprinkle the cilantro on top, and serve.

NUTRITION:
calories 271, fat 7, fiber 6, carbs 14, protein 20

CHICKEN AND TOMATOES MIX
Preparation time: 5 min | Cooking time: 30 min | Servings: 4

INGREDIENTS:
- 6 chicken thighs
- 1 tsp olive oil
- Salt and black pepper to taste
- 1 yellow onion, chopped
- ½ pound baby carrots, halved
- ½ tsp thyme, dried
- 2 tbsp tomato paste
- ½ cup white wine
- 15 ounces canned tomatoes, chopped
- 1 cup chicken stock

DIRECTIONS:
Put the oil into a pan that fits your air fryer and heat up over medium heat. Add the chicken thighs and brown them for 1-2 minutes on each side. Add all the remaining ingredients, toss, and cook for 4-5 minutes more. Place the pan in the air fryer and cook at 380 degrees F for 22 minutes. Divide the chicken and carrots mix between plates and serve.

NUTRITION:
calories 271, fat 11, fiber 7, carbs 17, protein 20

CAJUN CHICKEN WITH VEGGIES
Preparation time: 10 min | Cooking time: 30 min | Servings: 4

INGREDIENTS:
- 1 tbsp olive oil
- 1 pound chicken thighs, halved
- Salt and black pepper to taste
- 1 tbsp Cajun spice
- 1 red bell pepper, chopped
- 1 yellow onion, chopped
- 4 garlic cloves, minced
- 1 cup chicken stock
- ½ pound okra

DIRECTIONS:
Add the oil to a pan that fits your air fryer and heat up over medium heat. Then add the chicken and brown for 2-3 minutes. Next, add all remaining ingredients, toss, and cook for 3-4 minutes more. Place the pan into the air fryer and cook at 380 degrees F for 22 minutes. Divide everything between plates and serve.

NUTRITION:
calories 261, fat 11, fiber 6, carbs 19, protein 17

SWEET CHICKEN AND GREEN CHILIES
Preparation time: 10 min | Cooking time: 30 min | Servings: 4

INGREDIENTS:
- 1½ cups canned kidney beans, drained
- 1 yellow onion, minced
- 2 garlic cloves, minced
- Salt and black pepper to taste
- 1 pound chicken meat, ground
- 1 tbsp olive oil
- 2 carrots, chopped
- 4 ounces canned green chilies, chopped
- 1 tsp brown sugar
- 15 ounces canned tomatoes, chopped
- A handful of cilantro, chopped

DIRECTIONS:
Heat up the oil in a pan that fits your air fryer oil over medium heat; then add the onion and the garlic. Stir and cook for 2-3 minutes. Add the chicken, salt, pepper, carrots, chilies, sugar, and the tomatoes. Stir, bring to a simmer, and cook for 2-3 minutes more. Add the beans, toss, and place the pan in the air fryer. Cook at 370 degrees F for 25 minutes. Divide into bowls, sprinkle the cilantro on top, and serve.

NUTRITION:
calories 300, fat 14, fiber 11, carbs 18, protein 22

CHICKEN DRUMSTICKS AND BEER
Preparation time: 10 min | Cooking time: 30 min | Servings: 4

INGREDIENTS:
- 1 yellow onion, minced
- 4 chicken drumsticks
- 1 tbsp balsamic vinegar
- 1 chili pepper, chopped

- 15 ounces beer
- Salt and black pepper to taste
- 2 tbsp olive oil

DIRECTIONS:
Put the oil in a pan that fits your air fryer and heat up over medium heat. Add the onion and the chili pepper, stir, and cook for 2 minutes. Add the vinegar, beer, salt, and pepper; stir, and cook for 3 more minutes. Add the chicken, toss, and put the pan in the fryer and cook at 370 degrees F for 20 minutes. Divide everything between plates and serve.

NUTRITION:
calories 291, fat 11, fiber 7, carbs 18, protein 22

CHICKEN CREAMY CURRY

Preparation time: 10 min | Cooking time: 30 min | Servings: 4

INGREDIENTS:

- 15 ounces chicken breast, skinless, boneless, cubed
- 1 tbsp olive oil
- 1 yellow onion, sliced
- Salt and black pepper to taste
- 6 potatoes, peeled and cubed
- 5 ounces heavy cream
- 1 tsp curry powder
- ½ bunch coriander, chopped

DIRECTIONS:
Heat up the oil in a pan that fits your air fryer over medium heat. Add the chicken, toss, and brown for 2 minutes. Then add the onions, curry powder, salt, and pepper; toss, and cook for 3 minutes. Next add the potatoes and the cream; toss well. Place the pan in the air fryer and cook at 370 degrees F for 20 minutes. Add the coriander and stir. Divide the curry into bowls and serve.

NUTRITION:
calories 221, fat 8, fiber 11, carbs 17, protein 20

MARINARA CHEDDAR CHICKEN

Preparation time: 10 min | Cooking time: 25 min | Servings: 6

INGREDIENTS:

- 1 tbsp olive oil
- 2 pounds chicken breasts, skinless, boneless and cubed
- Salt and black pepper to taste
- ¾ cup yellow onion, diced
- 1 cup green bell pepper, chopped
- ¾ cup marinara sauce
- ½ cup cheddar cheese, grated

DIRECTIONS:
Heat up a pan that fits your air fryer with the oil over medium heat. Add the chicken, toss, and brown for 3 minutes. Add the salt, pepper, onions, bell peppers, and the marinara sauce; stir, and cook for 3 minutes more. Place the pan in the air fryer and cook at 370 degrees F for 15 minutes. Sprinkle the cheese on top, divide the mix between plates, and serve.

NUTRITION:
calories 283, fat 11, fiber 5, carbs 15, protein 16

BUFFALO CHICKEN MIX

Preparation time: 10 min | Cooking time: 20 min | Servings: 4

INGREDIENTS:

- 1 pound chicken breasts, skinless, boneless and cut into thin strips
- 1 small yellow onion, sliced
- ½ cup buffalo sauce
- ½ cup chicken stock
- ¼ cup bleu cheese, crumbled

DIRECTIONS:
In a pan that fits your air fryer, mix the chicken with the onions, buffalo sauce, and the stock. Toss everything and then place the pan in the fryer; cook at 370 degrees F for 20 minutes. Sprinkle the cheese on top, divide everything between plates, and serve.

NUTRITION:
calories 261, fat 11, fiber 8, carbs 14, protein 18

CHICKEN AND GOLD POTATOES

Preparation time: 5 min | Cooking time: 20 min | Servings: 4

INGREDIENTS:

- 4 gold potatoes, cut into medium chunks
- 1 yellow onion, thinly sliced
- 1 pound chicken thighs, boneless
- ½ cup chicken stock
- Salt and black pepper to taste

DIRECTIONS:
In a pan that fits your air fryer, mix the chicken with the salt, pepper, onions, and the stock. Place the pan in the fryer and cook at 380 degrees F for 10 minutes. Add the potatoes, put the pan in the fryer again, and cook at 400 degrees F for 10 minutes more. Divide between plates and serve.

NUTRITION:
calories 281, fat 11, fiber 7, carbs 20, protein 16

CARROTS CHICKEN AND CHICKPEAS

Preparation time: 10 min | Cooking time: 25 min | Servings: 4

INGREDIENTS:

- 5 ounces bacon, cooked and crumbled
- 2 tbsp olive oil
- 1 cup yellow onion, chopped
- 8 ounces canned chickpeas, drained
- 2 carrots, chopped
- 1 tbsp parsley, chopped
- Salt and black

pepper to taste
- 2 pounds chicken thighs, boneless
- 1 cup chicken stock
- 1 tsp balsamic vinegar

DIRECTIONS:
Heat up a pan that fits your air fryer with the oil over medium heat. Add the onions, carrots, salt and pepper; stir, and sauté for 3-4 minutes. Add the chicken, stock, vinegar, and chickpeas; then toss. Place the pan in the fryer and cook at 380 degrees F for 20 minutes. Add the bacon and the parsley and toss again. Divide everything between plates and serve.

NUTRITION:
calories 300, fat 8, fiber 11, carbs 20, protein 22

CHICKEN DRUMSTICKS AND SQUASH
Preparation time: 10 min | Cooking time: 25 min | Servings: 4

INGREDIENTS:

- 3 garlic cloves, minced
- 2 tbsp olive oil
- 2 red chilies, minced
- 2 tbsp green curry paste
- A pinch of cumin, ground
- ¼ tsp coriander, ground
- 14 ounces coconut milk
- 6 cups squash, cubed
- 8 chicken drumsticks
- Salt and black pepper to taste
- ½ cup cilantro, chopped
- ½ cup basil, chopped

DIRECTIONS:
Heat up a pan that fits your air fryer with the oil over medium heat. Add the garlic, chilies, curry paste, cumin, coriander, salt, and pepper; stir, and cook for 3-4 minutes. Add the chicken pieces and the coconut milk, and stir. Place the pan in the fryer and cook at 380 degrees F for 15 minutes. Add the squash, cilantro, and basil; toss, and cook for 5-6 minutes more. Divide into bowls and serve. Enjoy!

NUTRITION:
calories 299, fat 11, fiber 6, carbs 18, protein 20

INDIAN CHICKEN WITH TOMATOES
Preparation time: 10 min | Cooking time: 30 min | Servings: 4

INGREDIENTS:

- 1 yellow onion, chopped
- 2 tbsp butter, melted
- 4 garlic cloves, minced
- 1 tbsp ginger, grated
- 1½ tsp paprika
- 1½ tsp coriander, ground
- 1 tsp turmeric powder
- Salt and black pepper to taste
- 15 ounces canned tomatoes, crushed
- ¼ cup lemon juice
- 1 pound spinach, chopped
- 1½ pounds chicken drumsticks
- ½ cup cilantro, chopped
- ½ cup chicken stock
- ½ cup heavy cream

DIRECTIONS:
Place the butter in a pan that fits your air fryer and heat over medium heat. Add the onions and the garlic, stir, and cook for 3 minutes. Add the ginger, paprika, coriander, turmeric, salt, pepper, and the chicken; toss, and cook for 4 minutes more. Add the tomatoes and the stock, and stir. Place the pan in the fryer and cook at 370 degrees F for 15 minutes. Add the spinach, lemon juice, cilantro, and the cream; stir, and cook for 5-6 minutes more. Divide everything into bowls and serve.

NUTRITION:
calorie 281, fat 9, fiber 7, carbs 17, protein 20

SESAME AND SOY SAUCE CHICKEN
Preparation time: 10 min | Cooking time: 20 min | Servings: 4

INGREDIENTS:

- 2 pounds chicken breasts, skinless, boneless and cubed
- ½ cup yellow onion, chopped
- Salt and black pepper to taste
- 1 tbsp olive oil
- 2 garlic cloves, minced
- ½ cup soy sauce
- 2 tsp sesame oil
- ½ cup honey
- ¼ tsp red pepper flakes
- 1 tbsp sesame seeds, toasted

DIRECTIONS:
Heat up the oil in a pan that fits your air fryer oil over medium heat. Add the chicken, toss, and brown for 3 minutes. Add the onions, garlic, salt, and pepper; stir, and cook for 2 minutes more. Add the soy sauce, sesame oil, honey, and pepper flakes; toss well. Place the pan in the fryer and cook at 380 degrees F for 15 minutes. Top with the sesame seeds and toss. Divide between plates and serve.

NUTRITION:
calories 240, fat 11, fiber 5, carbs 18, protein 16

MARJORAM CHICKEN
Preparation time: 10 min | Cooking time: 30 min | Servings: 6

INGREDIENTS:

- 2 pounds chicken thighs
- Salt and black pepper to taste
- 1 tbsp olive oil
- ½ tsp sweet paprika
- ¼ cup white wine
- 1 tsp marjoram, dried
- ¼ cup chicken stock

Directions:

Heat up a pan that fits your air fryer with the oil over medium heat. Add the chicken pieces and brown them for 5 minutes. Add all remaining ingredients and toss well. Place the pan in the fryer and cook at 390 degrees F for 25 minutes. Divide between plates and serve.

Nutrition:
calories 231, fat 7, fiber 6, carbs 18, protein 20

COCONUT CHICKEN

Preparation time: 2 hours | Cooking time: 25 min | Servings: 4

Ingredients:

- 4 big chicken legs
- 5 tsp turmeric powder
- 2 tbsp ginger, grated
- Salt and black pepper to the taste
- 4 tbsp coconut cream

Directions:
In a bowl, mix cream with turmeric, ginger, salt and pepper, whisk, add chicken pieces, toss them well and leave aside for 2 hours. Transfer chicken to your preheated air fryer, cook at 370 degrees F for 25 minutes, divide among plates and serve with a side salad.

Nutrition:
calories 300, fat 4, fiber 12, carbs 22, protein 20

LIME CHICKEN WINGS

Preparation time: 2 hours | Cooking time: 15 min | Servings: 6

Ingredients:

- 16 chicken wings
- 2 tbsp honey
- 2 tbsp soy sauce
- Salt and black pepper to the taste
- ¼ tsp white pepper
- 3 tbsp lime juice

Directions:
In a bowl, mix honey with soy sauce, salt, black and white pepper and lime juice, whisk well, add chicken pieces, toss to coat and keep in the fridge for 2 hours. Transfer chicken to your air fryer, cook at 370 degrees F for 6 minutes on each side, increase heat to 400 degrees F and cook for 3 minutes more. Serve hot.

Nutrition:
calories 372, fat 9, fiber 10, carbs 37, protein 24

THYME CHICKEN

Preparation time: 30 min | Cooking time: 40 min | Servings: 4

Ingredients:

- 1 whole chicken
- Salt and black pepper to the taste
- 1 tsp garlic powder
- 1 tsp onion powder
- ½ tsp thyme, dried
- 1 tsp rosemary, dried
- 1 tbsp lemon juice
- 2 tbsp olive oil

Directions:
Season chicken with salt and pepper, rub with thyme, rosemary, garlic powder and onion powder, rub with lemon juice and olive oil and leave aside for 30 minutes. Put chicken in your air fryer and cook at 360 degrees F for 20 minutes on each side. Leave chicken aside to cool down, carve and serve.

Nutrition:
calories 390, fat 10, fiber 5, carbs 22, protein 20

CHICKEN MOZZARELLA

Preparation time: 10 min | Cooking time: 15 min | Servings: 4

Ingredients:

- 2 cups panko bread crumbs
- ¼ cup parmesan, grated
- ½ tsp garlic powder
- 2 cups white flour
- 1 egg, whisked
- 1 and ½ pounds chicken cutlets, skinless and boneless
- Salt and black pepper to the taste
- 1 cup mozzarella, grated
- 2 cups tomato sauce
- 3 tbsp basil, chopped

Directions:
In a bowl, mix panko with parmesan and garlic powder and stir. Put flour in a second bowl and the egg in a third. Season chicken with salt and pepper, dip in flour, then in egg mix and in panko. Put chicken pieces in your air fryer and cook them at 360 degrees F for 3 minutes on each side. Transfer chicken to a baking dish that fits your air fryer, add tomato sauce and top with mozzarella, introduce in your air fryer and cook at 375 degrees F for 7 minutes. Divide among plates, sprinkle basil on top and serve.

Nutrition:
calories 304, fat 12, fiber 11, carbs 22, protein 15

CHICKEN VERDE

Preparation time: 10 min | Cooking time: 20 min | Servings: 4

Ingredients:

- 16 ounces salsa verde
- 1 tbsp olive oil
- Salt and black pepper to the taste
- 1 pound chicken breast, boneless and skinless
- 1 and ½ cup Monterey Jack cheese, grated
- ¼ cup cilantro, chopped
- 1 tsp garlic powder

Directions:
Pour salsa verde in a baking dish that fits your air fryer, season chicken with salt, pepper, garlic powder, brush with olive oil and place it over your salsa verde. Introduce in

your air fryer and cook at 380 degrees F for 20 minutes. Sprinkle cheese on top and cook for 2 minutes more. Divide among plates and serve hot.

NUTRITION:
calories 340, fat 18, fiber 14, carbs 32, protein 18

CHICKEN AND CREAMY RICE

Preparation time: 10 min | Cooking time: 30 min | Servings: 4

INGREDIENTS:

- 1 pound chicken breasts, skinless, boneless and cut into quarters
- 1 cup white rice, already cooked
- Salt and black pepper to the taste
- 1 tbsp olive oil
- 3 garlic cloves, minced
- 1 yellow onion, chopped
- ½ cup white wine
- ¼ cup heavy cream
- 1 cup chicken stock
- ¼ cup parsley, chopped
- 2 cups peas, frozen
- 1 and ½ cups parmesan, grated

DIRECTIONS:
Season chicken breasts with salt and pepper, drizzle half of the oil over them, rub well, put in your air fryer's basket and cook them at 360 degrees F for 6 minutes. Heat up a pan with the rest of the oil over medium high heat, add garlic, onion, wine, stock, salt, pepper and heavy cream, stir, bring to a simmer and cook for 9 minutes. Transfer chicken breasts to a heat proof dish that fits your air fryer, add peas, rice and cream mix over them, toss, sprinkle parmesan and parsley all over, place in your air fryer and cook at 420 degrees F for 10 minutes. Divide among plates and serve hot.

NUTRITION:
calories 313, fat 12, fiber 14, carbs 27, protein 44

ITALIAN CHICKEN WITH PARMESAN

Preparation time: 10 min | Cooking time: 16 min | Servings: 4

INGREDIENTS:

- 5 chicken thighs
- 1 tbsp olive oil
- 2 garlic cloves, minced
- 1 tbsp thyme, chopped
- ½ cup heavy cream
- ¾ cup chicken stock
- 1 tsp red pepper flakes, crushed
- ¼ cup parmesan, grated
- ½ cup sun dried tomatoes
- 2 tbsp basil, chopped
- Salt and black pepper to the taste

DIRECTIONS:
Season chicken with salt and pepper, rub with half of the oil, place in your preheated air fryer at 350 degrees F and cook for 4 minutes. Meanwhile, heat up a pan with the rest of the oil over medium high heat, add thyme garlic, pepper flakes, sun dried tomatoes, heavy cream, stock, parmesan, salt and pepper, stir, bring to a simmer, take off heat and transfer to a dish that fits your air fryer. Add chicken thighs on top, introduce in your air fryer and cook at 320 degrees F for 12 minutes. Divide among plates and serve with basil sprinkled on top.

NUTRITION:
calories 272, fat 9, fiber 12, carbs 37, protein 23

MUSTARD DUCK BREASTS

Preparation time: 10 min | Cooking time: 22 min | Servings: 2

INGREDIENTS:

- 1 smoked duck breast, halved
- 1 tsp honey
- 1 tsp tomato paste
- 1 tbsp mustard
- ½ tsp apple vinegar

DIRECTIONS:
In a bowl, mix honey with tomato paste, mustard and vinegar, whisk well, add duck breast pieces, toss to coat well, transfer to your air fryer and cook at 370 degrees F for 15 minutes. Take duck breast out of the fryer, add to honey mix, toss again, return to air fryer and cook at 370 degrees F for 6 minutes more. Divide among plates and serve with a side salad.

NUTRITION:
calories 274, fat 11, fiber 13, carbs 22, protein 13

SOUR-SWEET DUCK LEGS

Preparation time: 10 min | Cooking time: 36 min | Servings: 2

INGREDIENTS:

- 2 duck legs
- 2 dried chilies, chopped
- 1 tbsp olive oil
- 2 star anise
- 1 bunch spring onions, chopped
- 4 ginger slices
- 1 tbsp oyster sauce
- 1 tbsp soy sauce
- 1 tsp sesame oil
- 14 ounces water
- 1 tbsp rice wine

DIRECTIONS:
Heat up a pan with the oil over medium high heat, add chili, star anise, sesame oil, rice wine, ginger, oyster sauce, soy sauce and water, stir and cook for 6 minutes. Add spring onions and duck legs, toss to coat, transfer to a pan that fits your air fryer, put in your air fryer and cook at 370 degrees F for 30 minutes. Divide among plates and serve.

NUTRITION:
calories 300, fat 12, fiber 12, carbs 26, protein 18

YUM-STUFFED CHICKEN

Preparation time: 10 min | Cooking time: 35 min | Servings: 8

INGREDIENTS:

- 1 whole chicken
- 10 wolfberries
- 2 red chilies, chopped
- 4 ginger slices
- 1 yam, cubed
- 1 tsp soy sauce
- Salt and white pepper to the taste
- 3 tsp sesame oil

DIRECTIONS:
Season chicken with salt, pepper, rub with soy sauce and sesame oil and stuff with wolfberries, yam cubes, chilies and ginger. Place in your air fryer, cook at 400 degrees F for 20 minutes and then at 360 degrees F for 15 minutes. Carve chicken, divide among plates and serve.

NUTRITION:
calories 320, fat 12, fiber 17, carbs 22, protein 12

EASY CHICKEN THIGHS AND BABY POTATOES
Preparation time: 10 min | Cooking time: 30 min | Servings: 4

INGREDIENTS:

- 8 chicken thighs
- 2 tbsp olive oil
- 1 pound baby potatoes, halved
- 2 tsp oregano, dried
- 2 tsp rosemary, dried
- ½ tsp sweet paprika
- Salt and black pepper to the taste
- 2 garlic cloves, minced
- 1 red onion, chopped
- 2 tsp thyme, chopped

DIRECTIONS:
In a bowl, mix chicken thighs with potatoes, salt, pepper, thyme, paprika, onion, rosemary, garlic, oregano and oil. Toss to coat, spread everything in a heat proof dish that fits your air fryer and cook at 400 degrees F for 30 minutes, shaking halfway. Divide among plates and serve.

NUTRITION:
calories 364, fat 14, fiber 13, carbs 21, protein 34

BUTTER CHICKEN AND CAPERS
Preparation time: 10 min | Cooking time: 20 min | Servings: 2

INGREDIENTS:

- 4 chicken thighs
- 3 tbsp capers
- 4 garlic cloves, minced
- 3 tbsp butter, melted
- Salt and black pepper to the taste
- ½ cup chicken stock
- 1 lemon, sliced
- 4 green onions, chopped

DIRECTIONS:
Brush chicken with butter, sprinkle salt and pepper to the taste, place them in a baking dish that fits your air fryer. Also add capers, garlic, chicken stock and lemon slices, toss to coat, introduce in your air fryer and cook at 370 degrees F for 20 minutes, shaking halfway. Sprinkle green onions, divide among plates and serve.

NUTRITION:
calories 200, fat 9, fiber 10, carbs 17, protein 7

CHICKEN AND OREGANO MUSHROOMS
Preparation time: 10 min | Cooking time: 30 min | Servings: 8

INGREDIENTS:

- 8 chicken thighs
- Salt and black pepper to the taste
- 8 ounces cremini mushrooms, halved
- 3 garlic cloves, minced
- 3 tbsp butter, melted
- 1 cup chicken stock
- ¼ cup heavy cream
- ½ tsp basil, dried
- ½ tsp thyme, dried
- ½ tsp oregano, dried
- 1 tbsp mustard
- ¼ cup parmesan, grated

DIRECTIONS:
Rub chicken pieces with 2 tbsp butter, season with salt and pepper, put in your air fryer's basket, cook at 370 degrees F for 5 minutes and leave aside in a bowl for now. Meanwhile, heat up a pan with the rest of the butter over medium high heat, add mushrooms and garlic, stir and cook for 5 minutes. Add salt, pepper, stock, oregano, thyme and basil, stir well and transfer to a heat proof dish that fits your air fryer. Add chicken, toss everything, put in your air fryer and cook at 370 degrees F for 20 minutes. Add mustard, parmesan and heavy cream, toss everything again, cook for 5 minutes more, divide among plates and serve.

NUTRITION:
calories 340, fat 10, fiber 13, carbs 22, protein 12

DUCK BREASTS AND BEEF SAUCE
Preparation time: 10 min | Cooking time: 32 min | Servings: 2

INGREDIENTS:

- 2 duck breasts
- 1 tbsp butter, melted
- 1 star anise
- 1 tbsp olive oil
- 1 shallot, chopped
- 9 ounces red plumps, stoned, cut into small wedges
- 2 tbsp sugar
- 2 tbsp red wine
- 1 cup beef stock

DIRECTIONS:
Heat up a pan with the olive oil over medium heat, add shallot, stir and cook for 5 minutes. Add sugar and plums, stir and cook until sugar dissolves. Add stock and wine, stir, cook for 15 minutes, take off heat and keep warm for now. Score duck breasts, season with salt and pepper, rub with melted butter, transfer to a heat proof dish that fits your air fryer, add star anise and plum

sauce, introduce in your air fryer and cook at 360 degrees F for 12 minutes. Divide everything on plates and serve.

Nutrition:
calories 400, fat 25, fiber 12, carbs 29, protein 44

JAPANESE DUCK WITH HONEY
Preparation time: 10 min | Cooking time: 20 min | Servings: 6

Ingredients:

- 6 duck breasts, boneless
- 4 tbsp soy sauce
- 1 and ½ tsp five spice powder
- 2 tbsp honey
- Salt and black pepper to the taste
- 20 ounces chicken stock
- 4 ginger slices
- 4 tbsp hoisin sauce
- 1 tsp sesame oil

Directions:
In a bowl, mix five spice powder with soy sauce, salt, pepper and honey, whisk, add duck breasts, toss to coat and leave aside for now. Heat up a pan with the stock over medium high heat, hoisin sauce, ginger and sesame oil, stir well, cook for 2-3 minutes more, take off heat and leave aside. Put duck breasts in your air fryer and cook them at 400 degrees F for 15 minutes. Divide among plates, drizzle hoisin and ginger sauce all over them and serve.

Nutrition:
calories 336, fat 12, fiber 1, carbs 25, protein 33

MUSHROOM DUCK BREASTS
Preparation time: 10 min | Cooking time: 40 min | Servings: 6

Ingredients:

- 6 duck breasts, halved
- Salt and black pepper to the taste
- 3 tbsp flour
- 6 tbsp butter, melted
- 2 cups chicken stock
- ½ cup white wine
- ¼ cup parsley, chopped
- 2 cups mushrooms, chopped

Directions:
Season duck breasts with salt and pepper, place them in a bowl, add melted butter, toss and transfer to another bowl. Combine melted butter with flour, wine, salt, pepper and chicken stock and stir well. Arrange duck breasts in a baking dish that fits your air fryer, pour the sauce over them, add parsley and mushrooms, introduce in your air fryer and cook at 350 degrees F for 40 minutes. Divide among plates and serve.

Nutrition:
calories 320, fat 28, fiber 12, carbs 12, protein 42

DUCK BREASTS WITH ENDIVES
Preparation time: 10 min | Cooking time: 25 min | Servings: 4

Ingredients:

- 2 duck breasts
- Salt and black pepper to the taste
- 1 tbsp sugar
- 1 tbsp olive oil
- 6 endives, julienned
- 2 tbsp cranberries
- 8 ounces white wine
- 1 tbsp garlic, minced
- 2 tbsp heavy cream

Directions:
Score duck breasts and season them with salt and pepper, put in preheated air fryer and cook at 350 degrees F for 20 minutes, flipping them halfway. Meanwhile, heat up a pan with the oil over medium heat, add sugar and endives, stir and cook for 2 minutes. Add salt, pepper, wine, garlic, cream and cranberries, stir and cook for 3 minutes. Divide duck breasts on plates, drizzle the endives sauce all over and serve.

Nutrition:
calories 400, fat 12, fiber 32, carbs 29, protein 28

CHICKEN BREASTS WITH TOMATO
Preparation time: 10 min | Cooking time: 20 min | Servings: 4

Ingredients:

- 1 red onion, chopped
- 4 chicken breasts, skinless and boneless
- ¼ cup balsamic vinegar
- 14 ounces canned tomatoes, chopped
- Salt and black pepper to the taste
- ¼ cup parmesan, grated
- ¼ tsp garlic powder
- Cooking spray

Directions:
Spray a baking dish that fits your air fryer with cooking oil, add chicken, season with salt, pepper, balsamic vinegar, garlic powder, tomatoes and cheese, toss, introduce in your air fryer and cook at 400 degrees F for 20 minutes. Divide among plates and serve hot.

Nutrition:
calories 250, fat 12, fiber 12, carbs 19, protein 28

ROSEMARY CHICKEN AND ASPARAGUS
Preparation time: 10 min | Cooking time: 20 min | Servings: 4

Ingredients:

- 8 chicken wings, halved
- 8 asparagus spears
- Salt and black pepper to the taste
- 1 tbsp rosemary, chopped
- 1 tsp cumin, ground

Directions:
Pat dry chicken wings, season with salt, pepper, cumin and rosemary, put them in your air fryer's basket and cook at 360 de-

grees F for 20 minutes. Meanwhile, heat up a pan over medium heat, add asparagus, add water to cover, steam for a few minutes, transfer to a bowl filled with ice water, drain and arrange on plates. Add chicken wings on the side and serve.

Nutrition:
calories 270, fat 8, fiber 12, carbs 24, protein 22

MAPLE CHICKEN IN SYRUP

Preparation time: 12 hours | Cooking time: 30 min | Servings: 4

Ingredients:

- 8 chicken thighs, bone in and skin on
- Salt and black pepper to the taste
- 1 tbsp apple cider vinegar
- 3 tbsp onion, chopped
- 1 tbsp ginger, grated
- ½ tsp thyme, dried
- 3 apples, cored and cut into quarters
- ¾ cup apple juice
- ½ cup maple syrup

Directions:
In a bowl, mix chicken with salt, pepper, vinegar, onion, ginger, thyme, apple juice and maple syrup, toss well, cover and keep in the fridge for 12 hours. Transfer this whole mix to a baking dish that fits your air fryer, add apple pieces, place in your air fryer and cook at 350 degrees F for 30 minutes. Divide among plates and serve warm.

Nutrition:
calories 314, fat 8, fiber 11, carbs 34, protein 22

OREGANO CHICKEN AND MAPLE SAUCE

Preparation time: 30 min | Cooking time: 25 min | Servings: 6

Ingredients:

- 1 cup parsley, chopped
- 1 tsp oregano, dried
- ½ cup olive oil
- ¼ cup red wine
- 4 garlic cloves
- A pinch of salt
- A drizzle of maple syrup
- 12 chicken thighs

Directions:
In your food processor, mix parsley with oregano, garlic, salt, oil, wine and maple syrup and pulse really well. In a bowl, mix chicken with parsley sauce, toss well and keep in the fridge for 30 minutes. Drain chicken, transfer to your air fryer's basket and cook at 380 degrees F for 25 minutes, flipping chicken once. Divide chicken on plates, drizzle parsley sauce all over and serve.

Nutrition:
calories 354, fat 10, fiber 12, carbs 22, protein 17

CHEDDAR CHICKEN AND LENTILS

Preparation time: 10 min | Cooking time: 1 hour | Servings: 8

Ingredients:

- 1 and ½ cups green lentils
- 3 cups chicken stock
- 2 pound chicken breasts, skinless, boneless and chopped
- Salt and cayenne pepper to the taste
- 3 tsp cumin, ground
- Cooking spray
- 5 garlic cloves, minced
- 1 yellow onion, chopped
- 2 red bell peppers, chopped
- 14 ounces canned tomatoes, chopped
- 2 cups corn
- 2 cups Cheddar cheese, shredded
- 2 tbsp jalapeno pepper, chopped
- 1 tbsp garlic powder
- 1 cup cilantro, chopped

Directions:
Put the stock in a pot, add some salt, add lentils, stir, bring to a boil over medium heat, cover and simmer for 35 minutes. Meanwhile, spray chicken pieces with some cooking spray, season with salt, cayenne pepper and 1 tsp cumin, put them in your air fryer's basket and cook them at 370 degrees for 6 minutes, flipping half way. Transfer chicken to a heat proof dish that fits your air fryer, add bell peppers, garlic, tomatoes, onion, salt, cayenne and 1 tsp cumin. Drain lentils and add them to the chicken mix as well. Add jalapeno pepper, garlic powder, the rest of the cumin, corn, half of the cheese and half of the cilantro, introduce in your air fryer and cook at 320 degrees F for 25 minutes. Sprinkle the rest of the cheese and the remaining cilantro, divide chicken casserole on plates and serve.

Nutrition:
calories 344, fat 11, fiber 12, carbs 22, protein 33

MOZZARELLA FRIED CHICKEN

Preparation time: 10 min | Cooking time: 20 min | Servings: 8

Ingredients:

- 3 pounds chicken breasts, skinless and boneless
- 1 yellow onion, chopped
- 1 garlic clove, minced
- Salt and black pepper to the taste
- 10 white mushrooms, halved
- 1 tbsp olive oil
- 1 red bell pepper, chopped
- 1 green bell pepper
- 2 tbsp mozzarella cheese, shredded
- Cooking spray

Directions:
Season chicken with salt and pepper, rub with garlic, spray with cooking spray, place in your preheated air fryer and cook at 390 degrees F for 12 minutes. Meanwhile, heat up a pan with the oil over medium heat, add onion, stir and sauté for 2 minutes.

Add mushrooms, garlic and bell peppers, stir and cook for 8 minutes. Divide chicken on plates, add mushroom mix on the side, sprinkle cheese while chicken is still hot and serve right away.

NUTRITION:
calories 305, fat 12, fiber 11, carbs 26, protein 32

CHICKEN SALAD
Preparation time: 10 min | Cooking time: 10 min | Servings: 4

INGREDIENTS:

- 1 pound chicken breast, boneless, skinless and halved
- Cooking spray
- Salt and black pepper to the taste
- ½ cup feta cheese, cubed
- 2 tbsp lemon juice
- 1 and ½ tsp mustard
- 1 tbsp olive oil
- 1 and ½ tsp red wine vinegar
- ½ tsp anchovies, minced
- ¾ tsp garlic, minced
- 1 tbsp water
- 8 cups lettuce leaves, cut into strips
- 4 tbsp parmesan, grated

DIRECTIONS:
Spray chicken breasts with cooking oil, season with salt and pepper, introduce in your air fryer's basket and cook at 370 degrees F for 10 minutes, flipping halfway. Transfer chicken beasts to a cutting board, shred using 2 forks, put in a salad bowl and mix with lettuce leaves. In your blender, mix feta cheese with lemon juice, olive oil, mustard, vinegar, garlic, anchovies, water and half of the parmesan and blend very well. Add this over chicken mix, toss, sprinkle the rest of the parmesan and serve.

NUTRITION:
calories 312, fat 6, fiber 16, carbs 22, protein 26

COCONUT CHICKEN AND GREEN SAUCE
Preparation time: 10 min | Cooking time: 16 min | Servings: 4

INGREDIENTS:

- 10 green onions, roughly chopped
- 1 inch piece ginger root, chopped
- 4 garlic cloves, minced
- 2 tbsp fish sauce
- 3 tbsp soy sauce
- 1 tsp Chinese five spice
- 10 chicken drumsticks
- 1 cup coconut milk
- Salt and black pepper to the taste
- 1 tsp butter, melted
- ¼ cup cilantro, chopped
- 1 tbsp lime juice

DIRECTIONS:
In your food processor, mix green onions with ginger, garlic, soy sauce, fish sauce, five spice, salt, pepper, butter and coconut milk and pulse well. In a bowl, mix chicken with green onions mix, toss well, transfer everything to a pan that fits your air fryer and cook at 370 degrees F for 16 minutes, shaking the fryer once. Divide among plates, sprinkle cilantro on top, drizzle lime juice and serve with a side salad.

NUTRITION:
calories 321, fat 12, fiber 12, carbs 22, protein 20

TOMATOES AND CHICKEN CACCIATORE
Preparation time: 10 min | Cooking time: 20 min | Servings: 4

INGREDIENTS:

- Salt and black pepper to the taste
- 8 chicken drumsticks, bone-in
- 1 bay leaf
- 1 tsp garlic powder
- 1 yellow onion, chopped
- 28 ounces canned tomatoes and juice, crushed
- 1 tsp oregano, dried
- ½ cup black olives, pitted and sliced

DIRECTIONS:
In a heat proof dish that fits your air fryer, mix chicken with salt, pepper, garlic powder, bay leaf, onion, tomatoes and juice, oregano and olives, toss, introduce in your preheated air fryer and cook at 365 degrees F for 20 minutes. Divide among plates and serve.

NUTRITION:
calories 300, fat 12, fiber 8, carbs 20, protein 24

CHICKEN WINGS AND MINT SAUCE
Preparation time: 20 min | Cooking time: 16 min | Servings: 6

INGREDIENTS:

- 18 chicken wings, halved
- 1 tbsp turmeric powder
- 1 tbsp cumin, ground
- 1 tbsp ginger, grated
- 1 tbsp coriander, ground
- 1 tbsp sweet paprika
- Salt and black pepper to the taste
- 2 tbsp olive oil
- For the mint sauce:
- Juice from ½ lime
- 1 cup mint leaves
- 1 small ginger piece, chopped
- ¾ cup cilantro
- 1 tbsp olive oil
- 1 tbsp water
- Salt and black pepper to the taste
- 1 Serrano pepper, chopped

DIRECTIONS:
In a bowl, mix 1 tbsp ginger with cumin, coriander, paprika, turmeric, salt, pepper, cayenne and 2 tbsp oil and stir well. Add chicken wings pieces to this mix, toss to coat well and keep in the fridge for 10 minutes. Transfer chicken to your air fryer's basket and cook at 370 degrees F for 16 minutes,

flipping them halfway. In your blender, mix mint with cilantro, 1 small ginger pieces, juice from ½ lime, 1 tbsp olive oil, salt, pepper, water and Serrano pepper and blend very well. Divide chicken wings on plates, drizzle mint sauce all over and serve.

NUTRITION:
calories 300, fat 15, fiber 11, carbs 27, protein 16

CITRIC CHICKEN

Preparation time: 10 min | Cooking time: 30 min | Servings: 6

INGREDIENTS:

- 1 whole chicken, cut into medium pieces
- 1 tbsp olive oil
- Salt and black pepper to the taste
- Juice from 2 lemons
- Zest from 2 lemons, grated

DIRECTIONS:
Season chicken with salt, pepper, rub with oil and lemon zest, drizzle lemon juice, put in your air fryer and cook at 350 degrees F for 30 minutes, flipping chicken pieces halfway. Divide among plates and serve with a side salad.

NUTRITION:
calories 334, fat 24, fiber 12, carbs 26, protein 20

CHICKEN BREASTS AND COCONUT

Preparation time: 10 min | Cooking time: 12 min | Servings: 6

INGREDIENTS:

- 1 tbsp olive oil
- 3 and ½ pounds chicken breasts
- 1 cup chicken stock
- 1 and ¼ cups yellow onion, chopped
- 1 tbsp lime juice
- ¼ cup coconut milk
- 2 tsp sweet paprika
- 1 tsp red pepper flakes
- 2 tbsp green onions, chopped
- Salt and black pepper to the taste

DIRECTIONS:
Heat up a pan that fits your air fryer with the oil over medium high heat, add onions, stir and cook for 4 minutes. Add stock, coconut milk, pepper flakes, paprika, lime juice, salt and pepper and stir well. Add chicken to the pan, add more salt and pepper, toss, introduce in your air fryer and cook at 360 degrees F for 12 minutes. Divide chicken and sauce on plates and serve.

NUTRITION:
calories 320, fat 13, fiber 13, carbs 32, protein 23

GARLIC CHICKEN AND BLACK OLIVES

Preparation time: 10 min | Cooking time: 8 min | Servings: 2

INGREDIENTS:

- 1 chicken breast cut into 4 pieces
- 2 tbsp olive oil
- 3 garlic cloves, minced
- For the sauce:
- 1 cup black olives, pitted
- Salt and black pepper to the taste
- 2 tbsp olive oil
- ¼ cup parsley, chopped
- 1 tbsp lemon juice

DIRECTIONS:
In your food processor, mix olives with salt, pepper, 2 tbsp olive oil, lemon juice and parsley, blend very well and transfer to a bowl. Season chicken with salt and pepper, rub with the oil and garlic, place in your preheated air fryer and cook at 370 degrees F for 8 minutes. Divide chicken on plates, top with olives sauce and serve.

NUTRITION:
calories 270, fat 12, fiber 12, carbs 23, protein 22

CRISPY CRUSTED CHICKEN

Preparation time: 10 min | Cooking time: 15 min | Servings: 4

INGREDIENTS:

- 4 bacon slices, cooked and crumbled
- 4 chicken breasts, skinless and boneless
- 1 tbsp water
- ½ cup avocado oil
- 1 egg, whisked
- Salt and black pepper to the taste
- 1 cup asiago cheese, shredded
- ¼ tsp garlic powder
- 1 cup parmesan cheese, grated

DIRECTIONS:
In a bowl, mix parmesan with garlic, salt and pepper and stir. In another bowl, mix egg with water and whisk well. Season chicken with salt and pepper and dip each pieces into egg and then into cheese mix. Add chicken to your air fryer and cook at 320 degrees F for 15 minutes. Divide chicken on plates, sprinkle bacon and asiago cheese on top and serve.

NUTRITION:
calories 400, fat 22, fiber 12, carbs 32, protein 47

PEPPERONI CHICKEN

Preparation time: 10 min | Cooking time: 22 min | Servings: 6

INGREDIENTS:

- 14 ounces tomato paste
- 1 tbsp olive oil
- 4 medium chicken breasts, skinless and boneless
- Salt and black pepper to the taste
- 1 tsp oregano, dried
- 6 ounces mozzarella, sliced
- 1 tsp garlic powder
- 2 ounces pepperoni, sliced

DIRECTIONS:
In a bowl, mix chicken with salt, pepper, garlic powder and oregano and toss. Put chicken in your air fryer, cook at 350 degrees F for 6 minutes and transfer to a pan that fits your air fryer. Add mozzarella slices on top, spread tomato paste, top with pepperoni slices, introduce in your air fryer and cook at 350 degrees F for 15 minutes more. Divide among plates and serve.

NUTRITION:
calories 320, fat 10, fiber 16, carbs 23, protein 27

CHICKEN AND CREAMY MUSHROOMS MIX
Preparation time: 10 min | Cooking time: 30 min | Servings: 6

INGREDIENTS:

- 2 cups whipping cream
- 40 ounces chicken pieces, boneless and skinless
- 3 tbsp butter, melted
- ½ cup yellow onion, chopped
- ¾ cup red peppers, chopped
- 29 ounces chicken stock
- Salt and black pepper to the taste
- 1 bay leaf
- 8 ounces mushrooms, chopped
- 17 ounces asparagus, trimmed
- 3 tsp thyme, chopped

DIRECTIONS:
Heat up a pan with the butter over medium heat, add onion and peppers, stir and cook for 3 minutes. Add stock, bay leaf, salt and pepper, bring to a boil and simmer for 10 minutes. Add asparagus, mushrooms, chicken, cream, thyme, salt and pepper to the taste, stir, introduce in your air fryer and cook at 360 degrees F for 15 minutes. Divide chicken and veggie mix on plates and serve.

NUTRITION:
calories 360, fat 27, fiber 13, carbs 24, protein 47

TURKEY QUARTERS AND HERBS
Preparation time: 10 min | Cooking time: 34 min | Servings: 4

INGREDIENTS:

- 1 yellow onion, chopped
- 1 carrot, chopped
- 3 garlic cloves, minced
- 2 pounds turkey quarters
- 1 celery stalk, chopped
- 1 cup chicken stock
- 2 tbsp olive oil
- 2 bay leaves
- ½ tsp rosemary, dried
- ½ tsp sage, dried
- ½ tsp thyme, dried
- Salt and black pepper to the taste

DIRECTIONS:
Rub turkey quarters with salt, pepper, half of the oil, thyme, sage, rosemary and thyme, put in your air fryer and cook at 360 degrees F for 20 minutes. In a pan that fits your air fryer, mix onion with carrot, garlic, celery, the rest of the oil, stock, bay leaves, salt and pepper and toss. Add turkey, introduce everything in your air fryer and cook at 360 degrees F for 14 minutes more. Divide everything on plates and serve.

NUTRITION:
calories 362, fat 12, fiber 16, carbs 22, protein 17

CHICKEN AND GARLIC SAUCE
Preparation time: 10 min | Cooking time: 20 min | Servings: 4

INGREDIENTS:

- 1 tbsp butter, melted
- 4 chicken breasts, skin on and bone-in
- 1 tbsp olive oil
- Salt and black pepper to the taste
- 40 garlic cloves, peeled and chopped
- 2 thyme sprigs
- ¼ cup chicken stock
- 2 tbsp parsley, chopped
- ¼ cup dry white wine

DIRECTIONS:
Season chicken breasts with salt and pepper, rub with the oil, place in your air fryer, cook at 360 degrees F for 4 minutes on each side and transfer to a heat proof dish that fits your air fryer. Add melted butter, garlic, thyme, stock, wine and parsley, toss, introduce in your air fryer and cook at 350 degrees F for 15 minutes more. Divide everything on plates and serve.

NUTRITION:
calories 227, fat 9, fiber 13, carbs 22, protein 12

TURKEY BREASTS WITH CELERY
Preparation time: 10 min | Cooking time: 20 min | Servings: 4

INGREDIENTS:

- 2 pounds turkey breasts, skinless, boneless
- Salt and black pepper to the taste
- 1 yellow onion, chopped
- 1 celery stalk, chopped
- ½ cup peas
- 1 cup chicken stock
- 1 cup cream of mushrooms soup
- 1 cup bread cubes

DIRECTIONS:
In a pan that fits your air fryer, mix turkey with salt, pepper, onion, celery, peas and stock, introduce in your air fryer and cook at 360 degrees F for 15 minutes. Add bread cubes and cream of mushroom soup, stir toss and cook at 360 degrees F for 5 minutes more. Divide among plates and serve hot.

NUTRITION:
calories 271, fat 9, fiber 9, carbs 16, protein 7

SALTY CHICKEN THIGHS
Preparation time: 10 min | Cooking time: 20 min | Servings: 6

INGREDIENTS:

- 2 and ½ pounds chicken thighs
- Salt and black pepper to the taste
- 5 green onions, chopped
- 2 tbsp sesame oil
- 1 tbsp sherry wine
- ½ tsp white vinegar
- 1 tbsp soy sauce
- ¼ tsp sugar

DIRECTIONS:
Season chicken with salt and pepper, rub with half of the sesame oil, add to your air fryer and cook at 360 degrees F for 20 minutes. Meanwhile, heat up a pan with the rest of the oil over medium high heat, add green onions, sherry wine, vinegar, soy sauce and sugar, toss, cover and cook for 10 minutes. Shred chicken using 2 forks divide among plates, drizzle sauce all over and serve.

NUTRITION:
calories 321, fat 8, fiber 12, carbs 36, protein 24

CHICKEN TENDERS AND PAPRIKA

Preparation time: 10 min | Cooking time: 10 min | Servings: 6

INGREDIENTS:

- 1 tsp chili powder
- 2 tsp garlic powder
- 1 tsp onion powder
- 1 tsp sweet paprika
- Salt and black pepper to the taste
- 2 tbsp butter
- 2 tbsp olive oil
- 2 pounds chicken tenders
- 2 tbsp cornstarch
- ½ cup chicken stock
- 2 cups heavy cream
- 2 tbsp water
- 2 tbsp parsley, chopped

DIRECTIONS:
In a bowl, mix garlic powder with onion powder, chili, salt, pepper and paprika, stir, add chicken and toss. Rub chicken tenders with oil, place in your air fryer and cook at 360 degrees F for 10 minutes. Meanwhile, heat up a pan with the butter over medium high heat, add cornstarch, stock, cream, water and parsley, stir, cover and cook for 10 minutes. Divide chicken on plates, drizzle sauce all over and serve.

NUTRITION:
calories 351, fat 12, fiber 9, carbs 20, protein 17

GINGER DUCK

Preparation time: 10 min | Cooking time: 20 min | Servings: 8

INGREDIENTS:

- 1 duck, chopped in medium pieces
- 3 cucumbers, chopped
- 3 tbsp white wine
- 2 carrots, chopped
- 1 cup chicken stock
- 1 small ginger piece, grated
- Salt and black pepper to the taste

DIRECTIONS:
In a pan that fits your air fryer, mix duck pieces with cucumbers, wine, carrots, ginger, stock, salt and pepper, toss, introduce in your air fryer and cook at 370 degrees F for 20 minutes. Divide everything on plates and serve.

NUTRITION:
calories 200, fat 10, fiber 8, carbs 20, protein 22

MARJORAM CHICKEN AND APRICOT DIP

Preparation time: 10 min | Cooking time: 20 min | Servings: 4

INGREDIENTS:

- 1 whole chicken, cut into medium pieces
- Salt and black pepper to the taste
- 1 tbsp olive oil
- ½ tsp smoked paprika
- ¼ cup white wine
- ½ tsp marjoram, dried
- ¼ cup chicken stock
- 2 tbsp white vinegar
- ¼ cup apricot preserves
- 1 and ½ tsp ginger, grated
- 2 tbsp honey

DIRECTIONS:
Season chicken with salt, pepper, marjoram and paprika, toss to coat, add oil, rub well, place in your air fryer and cook at 360 degrees F for 10 minutes. Transfer chicken to a pan that fits your air fryer, add stock, wine, vinegar, ginger, apricot preserves and honey, toss, put in your air fryer and cook at 360 degrees F for 10 minutes more. Divide chicken and apricot dip on plates and serve.

NUTRITION:
calories 200, fat 7, fiber 19, carbs 20, protein 14

TURMERIC CHICKEN AND CAULIFLOWER RICE

Preparation time: 10 min | Cooking time: 20 min | Servings: 6

INGREDIENTS:

- 3 bacon slices, chopped
- 3 carrots, chopped
- 3 pounds chicken thighs, boneless and skinless
- 2 bay leaves
- ¼ cup red wine vinegar
- 4 garlic cloves, minced
- Salt and black pepper to the taste
- 4 tbsp olive oil
- 1 tbsp garlic powder
- 1 tbsp Italian seasoning
- 24 ounces cauliflower rice
- 1 tsp turmeric powder
- 1 cup beef stock

DIRECTIONS:
Heat up a pan that fits your air fryer over medium high heat, add bacon, carrots, onion and garlic, stir and cook for 8 minutes. Add chicken, oil, vinegar, turmeric, garlic

powder, Italian seasoning and bay leaves, stir, introduce in your air fryer and cook at 360 degrees F for 12 minutes. Add cauliflower rice and stock, stir, cook for 6 minutes more, divide among plates and serve.

Nutrition:
calories 340, fat 12, fiber 12, carbs 16, protein 8

PARSLEY CHICKEN AND BABY SPINACH
Preparation time: 10 min | Cooking time: 12 min | Servings: 2

Ingredients:

- 2 tsp parsley, dried
- 2 chicken breasts, skinless and boneless
- ½ tsp onion powder
- 2 tsp sweet paprika
- ½ cup lemon juice
- Salt and black pepper to the taste
- 5 cups baby spinach
- 8 strawberries, sliced
- 1 small red onion, sliced
- 2 tbsp balsamic vinegar
- 1 avocado, pitted, peeled and chopped
- ¼ cup olive oil
- 1 tbsp tarragon, chopped

Directions:
Put chicken in a bowl, add lemon juice, parsley, onion powder and paprika and toss. Transfer chicken to your air fryer and cook at 360 degrees F for 12 minutes. In a bowl, mix spinach, onion, strawberries and avocado and toss. In another bowl, mix oil with vinegar, salt, pepper and tarragon, whisk well, add to the salad and toss. Divide chicken on plates, add spinach salad on the side and serve.

Nutrition:
calories 240, fat 5, fiber 13, carbs 25, protein 22

BALSAMIC CHICKEN AND WATER CHESTNUTS
Preparation time: 10 min | Cooking time: 12 min | Servings: 2

Ingredients:

- ½ pound chicken pieces
- 1 small yellow onion, chopped
- 2 tsp garlic, minced
- A pinch of ginger, grated
- A pinch of allspice, ground
- 4 tbsp water chestnuts
- 2 tbsp soy sauce
- 2 tbsp chicken stock
- 2 tbsp balsamic vinegar
- 2 tortillas for serving

Directions:
In a pan that fits your air fryer, mix chicken meat with onion, garlic, ginger, allspice, chestnuts, soy sauce, stock and vinegar, stir, transfer to your air fryer and cook at 360 degrees F for 12 minutes. Divide everything on plates and serve.

Nutrition:
calories 301, fat 12, fiber 7, carbs 24, protein 12

ROSEMARY GLAZED CHICKEN
Preparation time: 10 min | Cooking time: 14 min | Servings: 4

Ingredients:

- 1 sweet potato, cubed
- 2 apples, cored and sliced
- 1 tbsp olive oil
- 1 tbsp rosemary, chopped
- Salt and black pepper to the taste
- 6 chicken thighs, bone in and skin on
- 2/3 cup apple cider
- 1 tbsp mustard
- 2 tbsp honey
- 1 tbsp butter

Directions:
Heat up a pan that fits your air fryer with half of the oil over medium high heat, add cider, honey, butter and mustard, whisk well, bring to a simmer, take off heat, add chicken and toss really well. In a bowl, mix potato cubes with rosemary, apples, salt, pepper and the rest of the oil, toss well and add to chicken mix. Place pan in your air fryer and cook at 390 degrees F for 14 minutes. Divide everything on plates and serve.

Nutrition:
calories 241, fat 7, fiber 12, carbs 28, protein 22

ITALIAN CHICKEN BREASTS
Preparation time: 10 min | Cooking time: 15 min | Servings: 4

Ingredients:

- 4 chicken breasts, skinless and boneless
- 2 tbsp olive oil
- Salt and black pepper to the taste
- 1 zucchini, chopped
- 1 tsp Italian seasoning
- 2 yellow bell peppers, chopped
- 3 tomatoes, chopped
- 1 red onion, chopped
- 1 cup mozzarella, shredded

Directions:
Mix a slit on each chicken breast creating a pocket, season with salt and pepper and rub them with olive oil. In a bowl, mix zucchini with Italian seasoning, bell peppers, tomatoes and onion and stir. Stuff chicken breasts with this mix, sprinkle mozzarella over them, place them in your air fryer's basket and cook at 350 degrees F for 15 minutes. Divide among plates and serve.

Nutrition:
calories 300, fat 12, fiber 7, carbs 22, protein 18

ZUCCHINI CHICKEN
Preparation time: 10 min | Cooking time: 15 min | Servings: 4

INGREDIENTS:

- 2 tbsp olive oil
- Juice from 1 lemon
- 1 tsp oregano, dried
- 3 garlic cloves, minced
- 1 pound chicken thighs
- Salt and black pepper to the taste
- ½ pound asparagus, trimmed
- 1 zucchini, roughly chopped
- 1 lemon sliced

DIRECTIONS:
In a heat proof dish that fits your air fryer, mix chicken pieces with oil, lemon juice, oregano, garlic, salt, pepper, asparagus, zucchini and lemon slices, toss, introduce in preheated air fryer and cook at 380 degrees F for 15 minutes. Divide everything on plates and serve.

NUTRITION:
calories 300, fat 8, fiber 12, carbs 20, protein 18

RED WINE DUCK AND ORANGE SAUCE

Preparation time: 10 min | Cooking time: 35 min | Servings: 4

INGREDIENTS:

- ½ cup honey
- 2 cups orange juice
- 4 cups red wine
- 2 tbsp sherry vinegar
- 2 cups chicken stock
- 2 tsp pumpkin pie spice
- 2 tbsp butter
- 2 duck breasts, skin on and halved
- 2 tbsp olive oil
- Salt and black pepper to the taste

DIRECTIONS:
Heat up a pan with the orange juice over medium heat, add honey, stir well and cook for 10 minutes. Add wine, vinegar, stock, pie spice and butter, stir well, cook for 10 minutes more and take off heat. Season duck breasts with salt and pepper, rub with olive oil, place in preheated air fryer at 370 degrees F and cook for 7 minutes on each side. Divide duck breasts on plates, drizzle wine and orange juice all over and serve right away.

NUTRITION:
calories 300, fat 8, fiber 12, carbs 24, protein 11

DUCK WITH FIGS

Preparation time: 10 min | Cooking time: 20 min | Servings: 4

INGREDIENTS:

- 2 duck breasts, skin on, halved
- 1 tbsp olive oil
- ½ tsp thyme, chopped
- ½ tsp garlic powder
- ¼ tsp sweet paprika
- Salt and black pepper to the taste
- 1 cup beef stock
- 3 tbsp butter, melted
- 1 shallot, chopped
- ½ cup port wine
- 4 tbsp fig preserves
- 1 tbsp white flour

DIRECTIONS:
Season duck breasts with salt and pepper, drizzle half of the melted butter, rub well, put in your air fryer's basket and cook at 350 degrees F for 5 minutes on each side. Meanwhile, heat up a pan with the olive oil and the rest of the butter over medium high heat, add shallot, stir and cook for 2 minutes. Add thyme, garlic powder, paprika, stock, salt, pepper, wine and figs, stir and cook for 7-8 minutes. Add flour, stir well, cook until sauce thickens a bit and take off heat. Divide duck breasts on plates, drizzle figs sauce all over and serve.

NUTRITION:
calories 246, fat 12, fiber 4, carbs 22, protein 3

DUCK BREASTS AND RASPBERRY SAUCE

Preparation time: 10 min | Cooking time: 15 min | Servings: 4

INGREDIENTS:

- 2 duck breasts, skin on and scored
- Salt and black pepper to the taste
- Cooking spray
- ½ tsp cinnamon powder
- ½ cup raspberries
- 1 tbsp sugar
- 1 tsp red wine vinegar
- ½ cup water

DIRECTIONS:
Season duck breasts with salt and pepper, spray them with cooking spray, put in preheated air fryer skin side down and cook at 350 degrees F for 10 minutes. Heat up a pan with the water over medium heat, add raspberries, cinnamon, sugar and wine, stir, bring to a simmer, transfer to your blender, puree and return to pan. Add air fryer duck breasts to pan as well, toss to coat, divide among plates and serve right away.

NUTRITION:
calories 456, fat 22, fiber 4, carbs 14, protein 45

DUCK AND CHERRIES

Preparation time: 10 min | Cooking time: 20 min | Servings: 4

Ingredients:

- ½ cup sugar
- ¼ cup honey
- 1/3 cup balsamic vinegar
- 1 tsp garlic, minced
- 1 tbsp ginger, grated
- 1 tsp cumin, ground
- ½ tsp clove, ground
- ½ tsp cinnamon powder
- 4 sage leaves, chopped
- 1 jalapeno, chopped
- 2 cups rhubarb, sliced
- ½ cup yellow onion, chopped
- 2 cups cherries, pitted
- 4 duck breasts, boneless

DIRECTIONS:
Season duck breast with salt and pepper, put in your air fryer and cook at 350 degrees F for 5 minutes on each side. Meanwhile, heat up a pan over medium heat, add sugar, honey, vinegar, garlic, ginger, cumin, clove, cinnamon, sage, jalapeno, rhubarb, onion and cherries, stir, bring to a simmer and cook for 10 minutes. Add duck breasts, toss well, divide everything on plates and serve.

NUTRITION:
calories 456, fat 13, fiber 4, carbs 64, protein 31

LEMONY DUCK BREASTS
Preparation time: 10 min | Cooking time: 15 min | Servings: 4

INGREDIENTS:

- 4 duck breasts, skinless and boneless
- 4 garlic heads, peeled, tops cut off and quartered
- 2 tbsp lemon juice
- Salt and black pepper to the taste
- ½ tsp lemon pepper
- 1 and ½ tbsp olive oil

DIRECTIONS:
In a bowl, mix duck breasts with garlic, lemon juice, salt, pepper, lemon pepper and olive oil and toss everything. Transfer duck and garlic to your air fryer and cook at 350 degrees F for 15 minutes.

NUTRITION:
calories 200, fat 7, fiber 1, carbs 11, protein 17

TEA DUCK
Preparation time: 10 min | Cooking time: 20 min | Servings: 4

INGREDIENTS:

- 2 duck breast halves, boneless
- 2 and ¼ cup chicken stock
- ¾ cup shallot, chopped
- 1 and ½ cup orange juice
- Salt and black pepper to the taste
- 3 tsp earl gray tea leaves
- 3 tbsp butter, melted
- 1 tbsp honey

DIRECTIONS:
Season duck breast halves with salt and pepper, put in preheated air fryer and cook at 360 degrees F for 10 minutes. Meanwhile, heat up a pan with the butter over medium heat, add shallot, stir and cook for 2-3 minutes. Add stock, stir and cook for another minute. Add orange juice, tea leaves and honey, stir, cook for 2-3 minutes more and strain into a bowl. Divide duck on plates, drizzle tea sauce all over and serve.

NUTRITION:
calories 228, fat 11, fiber 2, carbs 20, protein 12

TARRAGON DUCK BREASTS
Preparation time: 1 day | Cooking time: 15 min | Servings: 2

INGREDIENTS:

- 2 duck breasts
- 1 cup white wine
- ¼ cup soy sauce
- 2 garlic cloves, minced
- 6 tarragon sprigs
- Salt and black pepper to the taste
- 1 tbsp butter
- ¼ cup sherry wine

DIRECTIONS:
In a bowl, mix duck breasts with white wine, soy sauce, garlic, tarragon, salt and pepper, toss well and keep in the fridge for 1 day. Transfer duck breasts to your preheated air fryer at 350 degrees F and cook for 10 minutes, flipping halfway. Meanwhile, pour the marinade in a pan, heat up over medium heat, add butter and sherry, stir, bring to a simmer, cook for 5 minutes and take off heat. Divide duck breasts on plates, drizzle sauce all over and serve.

NUTRITION:
calories 475, fat 12, fiber 3, carbs 10, protein 48

PASSION FRUIT CHICKEN
Preparation time: 10 min | Cooking time: 10 min | Servings: 4

INGREDIENTS:

- 4 chicken breasts
- Salt and black pepper to the taste
- 4 passion fruits, halved, deseeded and pulp reserved
- 1 tbsp whiskey
- 2 star anise
- 2 ounces maple syrup
- 1 bunch chives, chopped

DIRECTIONS:
Heat up a pan with the passion fruit pulp over medium heat, add whiskey, star anise, maple syrup and chives, stir well, simmer for 5-6 minutes and take off heat. Season chicken with salt and pepper, put in preheated air fryer and cook at 360 degrees F for 10 minutes, flipping halfway. Divide chicken on plates, heat up the sauce a bit, drizzle it over chicken and serve.
Nutrition: calories 374, fat 8, fiber 22, carbs 34, protein 37

BBQ CHICKEN WITH CHILI
Preparation time: 10 min | Cooking time: 20 min | Servings: 6

INGREDIENTS:

- 2 cups chili sauce
- 2 cups ketchup
- 1 cup pear jelly
- ¼ cup honey
- ½ tsp liquid smoke
- 1 tsp chili powder
- 1 tsp mustard powder
- 1 tsp sweet paprika
- Salt and black pepper to the taste
- 1 tsp garlic powder
- 6 chicken breasts, skinless and boneless

DIRECTIONS:
Season chicken breasts with salt and pepper, put in preheated air fryer and cook at 350 degrees F for 10 minutes. Meanwhile, heat up a pan with the chili sauce over medium heat, add ketchup, pear jelly, honey, liquid smoke, chili powder, mustard powder, sweet paprika, salt, pepper and the garlic powder, stir, bring to a simmer and cook for 10 minutes. Add air fried chicken breasts, toss well, divide among plates and serve.

NUTRITION:
calories 473, fat 13, fiber 7, carbs 39, protein 33

DUCK WITH MANGO SALSA
Preparation time: 1 hour | Cooking time: 10 min | Servings: 4

INGREDIENTS:

- 4 duck breasts
- 1 and ½ tbsp lemongrass, chopped
- 3 tbsp lemon juice
- 2 tbsp olive oil
- Salt and black pepper to the taste
- 3 garlic cloves, minced
- For the mango mix:
- 1 mango, peeled and chopped
- 1 tbsp coriander, chopped
- 1 red onion, chopped
- 1 tbsp sweet chili sauce
- 1 and ½ tbsp lemon juice
- 1 tsp ginger, grated
- ¾ tsp sugar

DIRECTIONS:
In a bowl, mix duck breasts with salt, pepper, lemongrass, 3 tbsp lemon juice, olive oil and garlic, toss well, keep in the fridge for 1 hour, transfer to your air fryer and cook at 360 degrees F for 10 minutes, flipping once. Meanwhile, in a bowl, mix mango with coriander, onion, chili sauce, lemon juice, ginger and sugar and toss well. Divide duck on plates, add mango mix on the side and serve.

NUTRITION:
calories 465, fat 11, fiber 4, carbs 29, protein 38

MILKY CHICKEN CASSEROLE
Preparation time: 10 min | Cooking time: 12 min | Servings: 4

INGREDIENTS:

- 10 ounces spinach, chopped
- 4 tbsp butter
- 3 tbsp flour
- 1 and ½ cups milk
- ½ cup parmesan, grated
- ½ cup heavy cream
- Salt and black pepper to the taste
- 2 cup chicken breasts, skinless, boneless and cubed
- 1 cup bread crumbs

DIRECTIONS:
Heat up a pan with the butter over medium heat, add flour and stir well. Add milk, heavy cream and parmesan, stir well, cook for 1-2 minutes more and take off heat. In a pan that fits your air fryer, spread chicken and spinach. Add salt and pepper and toss. Add cream mix and spread, sprinkle bread crumbs on top, introduce in your air fryer and cook at 350 degrees F for 12 minutes. Divide chicken and spinach mix on plates and serve.

NUTRITION:
calories 321, fat 9, fiber 12, carbs 22, protein 17

PEACH CHICKEN
Preparation time: 10 min | Cooking time: 30 min | Servings: 6

INGREDIENTS:

- 1 whole chicken, cut into medium pieces
- ¾ cup water
- 1/3 cup honey
- Salt and black pepper to the taste
- ¼ cup olive oil
- 4 peaches, halved

DIRECTIONS:
Put the water in a pot, bring to a simmer over medium heat, add honey, whisk really well and leave aside. Rub chicken pieces with the oil, season with salt and pepper, place in your air fryer's basket and cook at 350 degrees F for 10 minutes. Brush chicken with some of the honey mix, cook for 6 minutes more, flip again, brush one more time with the honey mix and cook for 7 minutes more. Divide chicken pieces on plates and keep warm. Brush peaches with what's left of the honey marinade, place them in your air fryer and cook them for 3 minutes. Divide among plates next to chicken pieces and serve.

NUTRITION:
calories 430, fat 14, fiber 3, carbs 15, protein 20

BLACK TEA CHICKEN
Preparation time: 10 min | Cooking time: 30 min | Servings: 6

INGREDIENTS:

- ½ cup apricot preserves
- ½ cup pineapple preserves
- 6 chicken legs
- 1 cup hot water
- 6 black tea bags
- 1 tbsp soy sauce
- 1 onion, chopped
- ¼ tsp red pepper flakes
- 1 tbsp olive oil
- Salt and black pepper to the taste
- 6 chicken legs

DIRECTIONS:
Put the hot water in a bowl, add tea bags, leave aside covered for 10 minutes, discard bags at the end and transfer tea to another bowl. Add soy sauce, pepper flakes, apricot and pineapple preserves, whisk really well and take off heat. Season chicken with salt and pepper, rub with oil, put in your air fryer and cook at 350 degrees F for 5 minutes.

Spread onion on the bottom of a baking dish that fits your air fryer, add chicken pieces, drizzle the tea glaze on top, introduce in your air fryer and cook at 320 degrees F for 25 minutes. Divide everything on plates and serve.

Nutrition:
calories 298, fat 14, fiber 1, carbs 14, protein 30

CHICKEN AND RADISH MIX

Preparation time: 10 min | Cooking time: 30 min | Servings: 4

Ingredients:

- 4 chicken things, bone-in
- Salt and black pepper to the taste
- 1 tbsp olive oil
- 1 cup chicken stock
- 6 radishes, halved
- 1 tsp sugar
- 3 carrots, cut into thin sticks
- 2 tbsp chives, chopped

Directions:
Heat up a pan that fits your air fryer over medium heat, add stock, carrots, sugar and radishes, stir gently, reduce heat to medium, cover pot partly and simmer for 20 minutes. Rub chicken with olive oil, season with salt and pepper, put in your air fryer and cook at 350 degrees F for 4 minutes. Add chicken to radish mix, toss, introduce everything in your air fryer, cook for 4 minutes more, divide among plates and serve.

Nutrition:
calories 237, fat 10, fiber 4, carbs 19, protein 29

AIR FRYER MEAT RECIPES

GARLIC PORK CHOPS

Preparation time: 5 min | Cooking time: 15 min | Servings: 4

Ingredients:

- 4 medium pork chops
- Salt and black pepper to taste
- 1 tbsp olive oil
- 2 tbsp sweet paprika
- 2 tbsp onion powder
- 2 tbsp garlic powder
- 2 tbsp oregano, dried
- 1 tbsp cumin, ground
- 1 tbsp rosemary, dried

Directions:
In a bowl, mix all of the ingredients and rub the pork chops well. Put the pork chops in your air fryer's basket and cook at 400 degrees F for 15 minutes, flipping them halfway. Divide between plates, serve, and enjoy.

Nutrition:
calories 281, fat 8, fiber 7, carbs 17, protein 19

BROCCOLI PORK AND SOY SAUCE

Preparation time: 5 min | Cooking time: 15 min | Servings: 4

Ingredients:

- 1 pound pork stew meat, cut into strips
- 1 pound broccoli florets
- 1 cup oyster sauce
- 2 tsp olive oil
- 1 tsp soy sauce
- 1 garlic clove, minced

Directions:
In a bowl, mix the pork with all the other ingredients and toss well. Put the mixture into your air fryer and cook at 390 degrees F for 15 minutes. Divide into bowls and serve.

Nutrition:
calories 281, fat 12, fiber 7, carbs 19, protein 20

PROVENCE BEEF MIX

Preparation time: 5 min | Cooking time: 15 min | Servings: 2

Ingredients:

- 1 red onion, sliced
- 1 green bell pepper, cut in strips
- Salt and black pepper to taste
- 2 tsp Provencal herbs
- ½ tbsp mustard
- 1 tbsp olive oil
- 7 ounces beef fillets, cut into strips

Directions:
Place all the ingredients in a baking dish that fits your air fryer and mix well. Put the pan in the fryer and cook at 400 degrees F for 15 minutes. Divide the mixture between bowls and serve.

NUTRITION:
calories 291, fat 8, fiber 7, carbs 19, protein 20

SOY BEEF AND MUSHROOMS
Preparation time: 5 min | Cooking time: 17 min | Servings: 2

INGREDIENTS:

- 2 beef steaks, cut into strips
- Salt and black pepper to taste
- 8 ounces white mushrooms, sliced
- 1 yellow onion, chopped
- 2 tbsp dark soy sauce
- 1 tsp olive oil

DIRECTIONS:
In a baking dish that fits your air fryer, combine all ingredients; toss well. Place the pan in the fryer and cook at 390 degrees F for 17 minutes. Divide everything between plates and serve.

NUTRITION:
calories 285, fat 8, fiber 2, carbs 18, protein 20

OREGANO PORK CHOPS
Preparation time: 5 min | Cooking time: 15 min | Servings: 4

INGREDIENTS:

- 2 tbsp olive oil
- 4 pork chops
- Salt and black pepper to taste
- 4 garlic cloves, minced
- 2 tbsp oregano, chopped

DIRECTIONS:
Place all of the ingredients in a bowl and toss / mix well. Transfer the chops to your air fryer's basket and cook at 400 degrees F for 15 minutes. Serve with a side salad and enjoy!

NUTRITION:
calories 301, fat 7, fiber 5, carbs 19, protein 22

CRUSTED RACK OF MACADAMIA LAMB
Preparation time: 10 min | Cooking time: 20 min | Servings: 4

INGREDIENTS:

- 2 tbsp macadamia nuts, toasted and crushed
- 1 tbsp vegetable oil
- 2 garlic cloves, minced
- 28 ounces rack of lamb
- Salt and black pepper to taste
- 1 egg, whisked
- 1 tbsp oregano, chopped

DIRECTIONS:
In a bowl, mix the lamb with the salt, pepper, garlic, and the oil; rub the lamb well. In another bowl, mix the macadamia nuts with the oregano, salt, and pepper; stir. Put the egg in a third bowl. Dredge the lamb in the egg, then in the macadamia nuts mix. Place the lamb in your air fryer's basket and cook at 380 degrees F for 10 minutes on each side. Divide between plates and serve with a side salad.

NUTRITION:
calories 280, fat 12, fiber 8, carbs 20, protein 19

COCONUT AND GINGER PORK
Preparation time: 5 min | Cooking time: 15 min | Servings: 4

INGREDIENTS:

- 1 tsp ginger, grated
- 2 tsp chili paste
- 2 garlic cloves, minced
- 14 ounces pork chops, cut into strips
- 1 shallot, chopped
- 7 ounces coconut milk
- 2 tbsp olive oil
- 3 tbsp soy sauce
- Salt and black pepper to taste

DIRECTIONS:
In a baking dish that fits your air fryer, mix the pork with the ginger, chili paste, garlic, shallots, oil soy sauce, salt, and pepper; toss well. Place the pan in the fryer and cook at 400 degrees F for 12 minutes, shaking the fryer halfway. Add the coconut milk, toss, and cook for 3-4 minutes more. Divide everything into bowls and serve.

NUTRITION:
calories 283, fat 11, fiber 9, carbs 22, protein 14

ROSEMARY PORK AND BRUSSELS SPROUTS
Preparation time: 10 min | Cooking time: 25 min | Servings: 4

INGREDIENTS:

- 1 pound pork tenderloin, cubed
- 2 tbsp olive oil
- 2 tbsp rosemary, chopped
- Salt and black pepper to taste
- 1 garlic clove, minced
- 1½ pounds Brussels sprouts, trimmed
- ½ cup sour cream
- Salt and black pepper to taste

DIRECTIONS:
In a pan that fits your air fryer, mix the pork with the oil, rosemary, salt, pepper, garlic, salt, and pepper; toss well. Place the pan in the fryer and cook at 400 degrees F for 17 minutes. Next add the sprouts and the sour cream and toss. Place the pan in the fryer and cook for 8 more minutes. Divide everything into bowls and serve.

NUTRITION:
calories 280, fat 13, fiber 9, carbs 22, protein 18

TARRAGON PORK AND MUSTARD
Preparation time: 10 min | Cooking time: 22

min | Servings: 6

INGREDIENTS:

- 1 cup mayonnaise
- 2 garlic cloves, minced
- 1 pound pork tenderloin, cubed
- 2 tbsp chives, chopped
- 2 tbsp mustard
- ¼ cup tarragon, chopped
- Salt and black pepper to taste

DIRECTIONS:
Place all ingredients except the mayo into a pan that fits your air fryer; mix well. Put the pan in the fryer and cook at 400 degrees F for 15 minutes. Add the mayo and toss. Put the pan in the fryer for 7 more minutes. Divide into bowls and serve.

NUTRITION:
calories 280, fat 12, fiber 2, carbs 17, protein 14

BEEF IN WINE

Preparation time: 10 min | Cooking time: 40 min | Servings: 6

INGREDIENTS:

- 2 tbsp butter, melted
- 3 garlic cloves, minced
- Salt and black pepper to taste
- 1 tbsp mustard
- 3 pounds beef roast
- 1¾ cups beef stock
- ¾ cup red wine

DIRECTIONS:
In a bowl, mix the beef with the butter, mustard, garlic, salt, and pepper; rub the meat thoroughly. Put the beef roast in your air fryer's basket and cook at 400 degrees F for 15 minutes. Heat up a pan over medium-high heat and add the stock and the wine. Then add the beef roast and place the pan in the fryer; cook at 380 degrees F for 25 minutes more. Divide into bowls and serve.

NUTRITION:
calories 300, fat 11, fiber 4, carbs 18, protein 22

CREAMY LAMB CHOPS

Preparation time: 10 min | Cooking time: 20 min | Servings: 6

INGREDIENTS:

- 1 pound lamb chops
- 2 yellow onions, chopped
- 1 tbsp olive oil
- 1 garlic clove, minced
- 3 cups chicken stock
- 2 tbsp sweet paprika
- Salt and black pepper to taste
- 1½ cups heavy cream
- 2 tbsp dill, chopped

DIRECTIONS:
Put the lamb chops in your air fryer and season with the salt, pepper, garlic, and paprika; rub the chops thoroughly. Cook at 380 degrees F for 10 minutes. Transfer the lamb to a baking dish that fits your air fryer. Then add the onions, stock, cream, and dill, and toss. Place the pan in the fryer and cook everything for 7-8 minutes more. Divide everything between plates and serve hot.

NUTRITION:
calories 310, fat 8, fiber 10, carbs 19, protein 25

SWEET PAPRIKA PORK CHOPS

Preparation time: 10 min | Cooking time: 15 min | Servings: 6

INGREDIENTS:

- 2 pork chops
- ¼ cup olive oil
- 2 garlic cloves, minced
- 1 tbsp mustard
- 1 tsp sweet paprika
- Salt and black pepper to taste

DIRECTIONS:
Place all of the ingredients in a bowl, and coat the pork chops well. Transfer the pork chops to your air fryer's basket and cook at 400 degrees F for 15 minutes. Divide the chops between plates and serve

NUTRITION:
calories 284, fat 14, fiber 4, carbs 17, protein 28

BEEF WITH GRAPES

Preparation time: 10 min | Cooking time: 40 min | Servings: 4

INGREDIENTS:

- 1 pound beef roast meat, cubed
- 3 tbsp olive oil
- Salt and black pepper to taste
- 1½ cups chicken stock
- ½ cup dry white wine
- 2 garlic cloves, minced
- 1 tsp thyme, chopped
- ½ red onion, chopped
- ½ pound red grapes

DIRECTIONS:
Heat up the oil in a pan that fits your air fryer over medium-high heat. Add the beef, salt, and pepper; toss, and brown for 5 minutes. Add the stock, wine, garlic, thyme, and onions; toss and cook for 5 minutes more. Transfer the pan to your air fryer and cook at 390 degrees F for 25 minutes. Add the grapes, toss gently, and cook everything for 5-6 minutes more. Divide between plates and serve right away.

NUTRITION:
calories 290, fat 12, fiber 5, carbs 19, protein 28

SMOKED PAPRIKA PORK MIX

Preparation time: 10 min | Cooking time: 50 min | Servings: 6

INGREDIENTS:

- 2½ pounds pork loin, boneless and cubed
- ¾ cup beef stock
- 2 tbsp olive oil
- ½ tbsp smoked paprika
- 3 tsp sage, dried
- ½ tbsp garlic powder
- 1 tsp basil, dried
- 1 tsp oregano, dried
- Salt and black pepper to taste

DIRECTIONS:
In a pan that fits your air fryer, heat up the oil over medium heat. Add the pork, toss, and brown for 5 minutes. Add the paprika, sage, garlic powder, basil, oregano, salt, and pepper; toss and cook for 2 more minutes. Next add the stock and toss. Place the pan in the fryer and cook at 360 degrees F for 40 minutes. Divide everything between plates and serve.

NUTRITION:
calories 290, fat 11, fiber 6, carbs 20, protein 29

GARLIC BEEF ROAST
Preparation time: 10 min | Cooking time: 55 min | Servings: 4

INGREDIENTS:

- 3 tbsp garlic, minced
- 1 tbsp smoked paprika
- 3 tbsp olive oil
- 2 pounds beef roast
- Salt and black pepper to taste

DIRECTIONS:
In a bowl, combine all the ingredients and coat the roast well. Place the roast in your air fryer and cook at 390 degrees F for 55 minutes. Slice the roast, divide it between plates, and serve with a side salad.

NUTRITION:
calories 291, fat 12, fiber 9, carbs 20, protein 26

GARLIC PORK LOIN
Preparation time: 10 min | Cooking time: 55 min | Servings: 6

INGREDIENTS:

- 3 pounds pork loin roast, trimmed
- Salt and black pepper to taste
- 3 garlic cloves, minced
- 2 tbsp tarragon, chopped
- 2 tsp sweet paprika
- ¼ cup olive oil

DIRECTIONS:
In a bowl, mix the roast with all the other ingredients and rub well. Transfer the roast to your air fryer and cook at 390 degrees F for 55 minutes. Slice the roast, divide it between plates, and serve.

NUTRITION:
calories 290, fat 14, fiber 9, carbs 19, protein 22

CELERY BEEF AND TOMATOES
Preparation time: 10 min | Cooking time: 55 min | Servings: 6

INGREDIENTS:

- 1 pound yellow onion, chopped
- 3 pounds beef roast
- 1 pound celery, chopped
- Salt and black pepper to taste
- 3 cups beef stock
- 16 ounces canned tomatoes, chopped
- 2 tbsp olive oil

DIRECTIONS:
Place all the ingredients into a baking dish that fits your air fryer and mix well. Put the pan in the fryer and cook at 390 degrees F for 55 minutes. Slice the roast, and then divide it and the celery mix between plates. Serve, and enjoy!

NUTRITION:
calories 300, fat 12, fiber 4, carbs 18, protein 20

SESAME BEEF MIX
Preparation time: 5 min | Cooking time: 20 min | Servings: 4

INGREDIENTS:

- 1 cup green onion, chopped
- 1 cup soy sauce
- ¼ cup sesame seeds, toasted
- 5 garlic cloves,
- Black pepper to taste
- 1 pound beef stew meat, cut into strips

DIRECTIONS:
In a pan that fits your air fryer, place all ingredients and mix well. Place the pan in the fryer and cook at 390 degrees F for 20 minutes. Divide everything into bowls and serve.

NUTRITION:
calories 289, fat 8, fiber 12, carbs 20, protein 19

PORK AND BELL PEPPERS
Preparation time: 5 min | Cooking time: 20 min | Servings: 4

INGREDIENTS:

- 1 pound pork, cut into strips
- 4 garlic cloves, minced
- 2 tbsp olive oil
- 2 red bell peppers, cut in strips
- A pinch of salt and black pepper
- 2 tbsp fish sauce
- ½ cup beef stock
- 4 shallots, chopped

DIRECTIONS:
In a pan that fits your air fryer, place all the ingredients and toss. Place the pan in the fryer and cook at 400 degrees F for 20 minutes, shaking the fryer halfway. Divide everything between plates and serve.

NUTRITION:
calories 293, fat 12, fiber 12, carbs 20, protein 29

LAMB AND BEANS

Preparation time: 5 min | Cooking time: 30 min | Servings: 4

INGREDIENTS:

- 1 carrot, chopped
- 1 yellow onion, sliced
- ½ tbsp olive oil
- 3 ounces canned kidney beans, drained
- 8 ounces lamb loin, cubed
- 1 garlic clove, minced
- Salt and black pepper to taste
- 1 tbsp ginger, grated
- 3 tbsp soy sauce

DIRECTIONS:
In baking dish that fits your air fryer, place all of the ingredients and mix well. Place the dish in the fryer and cook at 390 degrees F for 30 minutes. Divide everything into bowls and serve.

NUTRITION:
calories 275, fat 3, fiber 7, carbs 20, protein 18

PORK CHOPS WITH PESTO

Preparation time: 5 min | Cooking time: 15 min | Servings: 4

INGREDIENTS:

- 2 pork chops
- Salt and black pepper to taste
- 2 cups baby spinach
- 3 tbsp spinach pesto
- ¼ cup beef stock

DIRECTIONS:
Place the pork chops, salt, pepper, and spinach pesto in a bowl; toss well. Place the pork chops in the air fryer and cook at 400 degrees F for 4 minutes on each side. Transfer the chops to a pan that fits your air fryer, and add the stock and the baby spinach. Put the pan in the fryer and cook at 400 degrees F for 7 minutes more. Divide everything between plates and serve.

NUTRITION:
calories 290, fat 11, fiber 9, carbs 22, protein 19

GROUND CUMIN BEEF WITH PEPPERS

Preparation time: 5 min | Cooking time: 20 min | Servings: 4

INGREDIENTS:

- 1 tbsp olive oil
- 1 pound ground beef
- 1 yellow onion, chopped
- Salt and black pepper to taste
- 2 garlic cloves, minced
- ½ tsp cumin
- ¼ cup tomato salsa
- 1 green bell pepper, chopped

DIRECTIONS:
Heat up the oil in a pan that fits your air fryer over medium heat. Add the onion, garlic, bell peppers, and the cumin; stir, and sauté for 3 minutes. Add the meat, toss, cook for 3 minutes more, and take off the heat. Add the salsa, toss, and place the pan in the fryer; cook at 380 degrees F for 14 minutes more. Divide everything into bowls and serve.

NUTRITION:
calories 264, fat 11, fiber 4, carbs 20, protein 16

PAPRIKA PORK ROAST

Preparation time: 5 min | Cooking time: 55 min | Servings: 4

INGREDIENTS:

- 2 pounds pork loin roast
- Salt and black pepper to taste
- 1 tbsp olive oil
- 3 tbsp smoked paprika
- 1 tsp liquid smoke
- 1 tbsp brown sugar
- 2 tbsp oregano, chopped

DIRECTIONS:
Place all ingredients into a bowl, mix well, and be sure the pork is thoroughly coated. Transfer the roast to your air fryer and cook at 370 degrees F for 55 minutes. Slice the roast, divide it between plates, and serve.

NUTRITION:
calories 300, fat 12, fiber 9, carbs 22, protein 18

SOY PORK AND CAULIFLOWER

Preparation time: 5 min | Cooking time: 22 min | Servings: 4

INGREDIENTS:

- 1 pound pork stew meat, cubed
- 1 cauliflower head, florets separated
- 2 tbsp olive oil
- 1 tsp soy sauce
- 1 tsp sugar
- 1 cup balsamic vinegar
- 1 garlic clove, minced

DIRECTIONS:
Place all the ingredients in a pan that fits your air fryer and mix well. Put the pan into the fryer and cook at 390 degrees F for 22 minutes. Divide into bowls, serve, and enjoy.

NUTRITION:
calories 270, fat 9, fiber 7, carbs 23, protein 20

PORK AND BELL PEPPERS

Preparation time: 10 min | Cooking time: 22 min | Servings: 2

INGREDIENTS:

- 1 sweet onion, chopped
- 1 red bell pepper, cut into strips

- 1 green bell pepper, cut into strips
- 1 yellow bell pepper, cut in strips
- Salt and black pepper to taste
- 1 tbsp olive oil
- 7 ounces pork tenderloin, cut into strips

DIRECTIONS:
Place all of the ingredients into a pan that fits your air fryer, and toss well. Put the pan in the fryer and cook at 390 degrees F for 22 minutes. Divide the mix between plates and serve.

NUTRITION:
calories 280, fat 13, fiber 7, carbs 21, protein 19

BEEF STEAKS WITH PEAS

Preparation time: 5 min | Cooking time: 25 min | Servings: 2

INGREDIENTS:

- 2 beef steaks, cut into strips
- Salt and black pepper to taste
- 14 ounces snow peas
- 2 tbsp soy sauce
- 1 tbsp olive oil

DIRECTIONS:
Put all of the ingredients into a pan that fits your air fryer; toss well. Place the pan in the fryer and cook at 390 degrees F for 25 minutes. Divide everything between plates and serve.

NUTRITION:
calories 265, fat 11, fiber 4, carbs 22, protein 19

FENNEL PORK MIX

Preparation time: 5 min | Cooking time: 15 min | Servings: 4

INGREDIENTS:

- 3 tbsp olive oil
- 2 pork chops
- Salt and black pepper to taste
- 1 tsp fennel seeds, roasted
- 1 tbsp rosemary, chopped

DIRECTIONS:
In a bowl, mix the pork chops with the oil, salt, pepper, fennel, and the rosemary; toss and make sure the pork chops are coated well. Transfer the chops to your air fryer and cook at 400 degrees F for 15 minutes. Divide the chops between plates and serve.

NUTRITION:
calories 281, fat 11, fiber 8, carbs 17, protein 20

LAMB MEATBALLS

Preparation time: 10 min | Cooking time: 12 min | Servings: 8

INGREDIENTS:

- 4 ounces lamb meat, minced
- Salt and black pepper to taste
- 1 egg, whisked
- ½ tbsp lemon zest
- 1 tbsp oregano, chopped
- Cooking spray

DIRECTIONS:
In a bowl, combine all of the ingredients except the cooking spray and stir well. Shape medium-sized meatballs out of this mix. Place the meatballs in your air fryer's basket, grease them with cooking spray, and cook at 400 degrees F for 12 minutes. Divide between plates and serve.

NUTRITION:
calories 294, fat 12, fiber 2, carbs 22, protein 19

CHORIZO MEATLOAF

Preparation time: 5 min | Cooking time: 20 min | Servings: 4

INGREDIENTS:

- 1 pound ground pork meat
- 3 tbsp breadcrumbs
- Cooking spray
- 1 egg, whisked
- 1 ounce chorizo, chopped
- Salt and black pepper to taste
- 1 tbsp thyme, chopped
- 1 yellow onion, chopped

DIRECTIONS:
Place all of the ingredients (except the cooking spray) in a bowl and stir / combine well. Transfer the mixture to a loaf pan, greased with cooking spray that fits your air fryer. Place the pan in the fryer and cook at 390 degrees F for 20 minutes. Slice and serve.

NUTRITION:
calories 290, fat 12, fiber 1, carbs 19, protein 26

PAPRIKA PORK STEAKS

Preparation time: 5 min | Cooking time: 14 min | Servings: 4

INGREDIENTS:

- 1 tbsp sweet paprika
- 4 pork steaks
- Salt and black pepper to taste
- 1 tbsp butter, melted

DIRECTIONS:
Rub the pork steaks with the salt, pepper, butter, and paprika until thoroughly coated. Transfer the steaks to your air fryer's basket and cook at 390 degrees F for 7 minutes on each side. Divide the steaks between plates and serve.

NUTRITION:
calories 250, fat 12, fiber 5, carbs 18, protein 21

ROSEMARY SAUSAGE MIX

Preparation time: 5 min | Cooking time: 20 min | Servings: 4

INGREDIENTS:

- 6 sausage links, halved
- 1 tbsp olive oil
- Salt and black pepper to taste
- 1 tbsp sweet paprika
- 1 red onion, sliced
- 1 tbsp rosemary, chopped
- 2 garlic cloves, minced

DIRECTIONS:
In a pan that fits your air fryer, mix all of the ingredients and toss. Place the pan in the fryer and cook at 360 degrees F for 20 minutes. Divide between plates and serve.

NUTRITION:
calories 280, fat 11, fiber 7, carbs 18, protein 18

CINNAMON PORK MIX
Preparation time: 10 min | Cooking time: 17 min | Servings: 4

INGREDIENTS:

- 1 pound pork tenderloin, cubed
- ½ tsp hot chili powder
- 1 tsp cinnamon powder
- 1 garlic clove, minced
- Salt and black pepper to taste
- 2 tbsp olive oil
- 1 red onion, chopped
- 3 tbsp parsley, chopped

DIRECTIONS:
In a bowl, combine the chili, cinnamon, garlic, salt, pepper, and the oil. Then add the pork and rub it well with the mixture. Transfer the meat to your air fryer and cook at 280 degrees F for 12 minutes. Add the onions and cook for 5 minutes more. Divide everything between plates and serve with the parsley sprinkled on top.

NUTRITION:
calories 264, fat 12, fiber 1, carbs 19, protein 23

TOMATO BEEF WITH LEEKS
Preparation time: 10 min | Cooking time: 12 min | Servings: 4

INGREDIENTS:

- 1 pound ground beef
- 3 leeks, roughly chopped
- Salt and black pepper to taste
- 1 tbsp olive oil
- 2 tbsp tomato paste
- 5 ounces baby arugula

DIRECTIONS:
In a pan that fits your air fryer, mix the beef with the leeks, salt, pepper, oil, and the tomato paste; toss well. Place the pan in the fryer and cook at 380 degrees F for 12 minutes. Add the arugula and toss. Divide into bowls and serve.

NUTRITION:
calories 220, fat 12, fiber 3, carbs 18, protein 15

LOIN ROAST
Preparation time: 5 min | Cooking time: 55 min | Servings: 4

INGREDIENTS:

- 2 tbsp panko breadcrumbs
- 1 tbsp olive oil
- 3 garlic cloves, minced
- 1 pound pork loin roast
- Salt and black pepper to taste
- 1 tbsp rosemary, chopped

DIRECTIONS:
Place all ingredients except the roast into a bowl; stir / mix well. Spread the mixture over the roast. Place the roast in the air fryer and cook at 360 degrees F for 55 minutes. Slice the roast, divide it between plates, and serve with a side salad.

NUTRITION:
calories 300, fat 12, fiber 9, carbs 20, protein 28

PORK CHOPS WITH PEANUTS
Preparation time: 5 min | Cooking time: 15 min | Servings: 4

INGREDIENTS:

- 2 tsp chili paste
- 2 garlic cloves, minced
- 14 ounces pork chops, cubed
- 1 shallot, chopped
- 1 tsp coriander, ground
- 7 ounces coconut milk
- 2 tbsp olive oil
- 3 ounces peanuts, chopped
- Salt and black pepper to taste

DIRECTIONS:
Place all of the ingredients into a pan that fits your air fryer; mix well. Put the pan in the fryer and cook at 400 degrees F for 15 minutes. Divide into bowls and serve.

NUTRITION:
calories 283, fat 11, fiber 8, carbs 22, protein 18

GINGER FLANK STEAKS
Preparation time: 5 min | Cooking time: 14 min | Servings: 4

INGREDIENTS:

- ¼ cup ancho chili powder
- 1 tbsp dry mustard
- 2 tbsp sweet paprika
- Salt and black pepper to taste
- 2 tsp ginger, grated
- 1 tbsp oregano, dried
- 1 tbsp coriander, ground
- 4 flank steaks
- Cooking spray

DIRECTIONS:
In a bowl, mix all of the spices, and then rub the steaks well with the mixture. Put the steaks in your air fryer's basket, grease with cooking spray, and cook at 370 degrees F for 7 minutes on each side. Serve the steaks

with a side salad, and enjoy!

NUTRITION:
calories 290, fat 12, fiber 10, carbs 22, protein 18

COCONUT LAMB

Preparation time: 5 min | Cooking time: 15 min | Servings: 4

INGREDIENTS:

- 1 pound lamb chops
- 2 tbsp olive oil
- 1 tbsp rosemary, chopped
- 1 garlic clove, minced
- 1 tbsp butter, melted
- 1 cup coconut milk
- Salt and black pepper to taste

DIRECTIONS:
Season the lamb chops with salt and pepper, then put them in a pan that fits your air fryer. Add the oil, rosemary, garlic, butter, and milk to the pan; toss well Place the pan in the fryer and cook at 400 degrees F for 15 minutes. Divide the mix between plates and serve.

NUTRITION:
calories 281, fat 13, fiber 9, carbs 22, protein 19

WORCESTERSHIRE BEEF

Preparation time: 5 min | Cooking time: 26 min | Servings: 4

INGREDIENTS:

- 1½ pounds beef fillet
- 3 tsp sweet paprika
- 2 tbsp olive oil
- 1 tbsp tomato paste
- ½ cup beef stock
- 1 tbsp Worcestershire sauce
- 1 red onion, roughly chopped
- Salt and black pepper to taste

DIRECTIONS:
In a bowl, mix the beef with all remaining ingredients; toss well. Transfer the mixture to a pan that fits your air fryer and cook at 400 degrees F for 26 minutes, shaking the air fryer halfway. Divide everything between plates and serve.

NUTRITION:
calories 304, fat 13, fiber 5, carbs 22, protein 18

CHIVES PORK CHOPS

Preparation time: 5 min | Cooking time: 14 min | Servings: 6

INGREDIENTS:

- 3 garlic cloves, minced
- 2 pounds pork chops
- 2 tbsp chives, chopped
- 4 tbsp mustard
- Salt and black pepper to taste

DIRECTIONS:
In a bowl, mix the pork chops with the other ingredients and rub the chops well. Put the pork chops in your air fryer's basket and cook at 400 degrees F for 7 minutes on each side. Serve right away.

NUTRITION:
calories 260, fat 12, fiber 2, carbs 20, protein 19

BEEF IN VINEGAR

Preparation time: 5 min | Cooking time: 55 min | Servings: 6

INGREDIENTS:

- 2 tbsp olive oil
- 2 tbsp chives, minced
- 3 garlic cloves, minced
- Salt and black
- pepper to taste
- 2 pounds beef roast
- 1 cup balsamic vinegar

DIRECTIONS:
In a bowl, mix the oil, vinegar, and spices (all ingredients except for the roast); whisk well. Add the roast and coat with the mixture. Transfer the roast to your air fryer's basket and cook at 390 degrees F for 55 minutes, flipping the roast halfway. Carve and serve right away.

NUTRITION:
calories 300, fat 9, fiber 4, carbs 19, protein 22

CILANTRO BEEF

Preparation time: 5 min | Cooking time: 55 min | Servings: 6

INGREDIENTS:

- 2 pounds beef roast
- Juice of 1 lemon
- 2 garlic cloves, minced
- 2 yellow onions, thinly sliced
- 1 tbsp cilantro, chopped
- 1½ tbsp cinnamon powder
- Salt and black pepper to taste
- 1 cup beef stock

DIRECTIONS:
In a baking dish that fits your air fryer, mix the roast with all other ingredients and toss well. Place the dish in your fryer and cook at 390 degrees F for 55 minutes, flipping the roast halfway. Carve the roast, divide between plates, and serve with the cooking juices drizzled on top; enjoy!

NUTRITION:
calories 261, fat 11, fiber 7, carbs 20, protein 18

BEEF ROAST WITH CARROTS

Preparation time: 5 min | Cooking time: 55 min | Servings: 6

INGREDIENTS:

- 1½ pounds beef roast

- 2 carrots, sliced
- 1 cup beef stock
- 2 garlic cloves, minced
- 1 tbsp basil, dried
- Salt and black pepper to taste

DIRECTIONS:
In a pan that fits your air fryer, combine all ingredients well. Place the pan in the fryer and cook at 390 degrees F for 55 minutes. Slice the roast, divide it and the carrots between plates, and serve with cooking juices drizzled on top.

NUTRITION:
calories 281, fat 7, fiber 9, carbs 20, protein 27

TOMATO BEEF CURRY

Preparation time: 5 min | Cooking time: 35 min | Servings: 4

INGREDIENTS:

- 2 pounds cubed beef
- 2 tbsp olive oil
- 3 potatoes, diced
- 1 tomato, cubed
- 2½ tbsp curry powder
- 2 yellow onions, chopped
- 2 garlic cloves, minced
- 10 ounces coconut milk
- Salt and black pepper to taste

DIRECTIONS:
In a pan that fits your air fryer, heat up the oil over medium heat. Add the meat and brown it for 2-3 minutes. Then add the potatoes, tomato, curry powder, onions, garlic, salt, and pepper; toss, and cook for 2 more minutes. Transfer the pan to your air fryer and cook at 380 degrees F for 25 minutes. Add the coconut milk, toss, and cook for 5 minutes more. Divide everything into bowls, serve, and enjoy.

NUTRITION:
calories 300, fat 14, fiber 8, carbs 16, protein 20

MUSHROOMS BEEF

Preparation time: 10 min | Cooking time: 45 min | Servings: 4

INGREDIENTS:

- 1½ pounds cubed beef
- 1 red onion, chopped
- 2½ tbsp vegetable oil
- 1½ tbsp white flour
- 2 garlic cloves, minced
- 4 ounces brown mushrooms, sliced
- Salt and black pepper to taste
- 8 ounces sour cream
- 1 tbsp cilantro, chopped

DIRECTIONS:
In a bowl, mix the beef with the salt, pepper, and flour; toss. Heat up the oil in a pan that fits your air fryer over medium-high heat. Add the beef, onions, and garlic; stir, and cook for 5 minutes. Add the mushrooms and toss. Place the pan in the fryer and cook at 380 degrees F for 35 minutes. Add the sour cream and cilantro and toss; cook for 5 minutes more. Divide everything between plates and serve.

NUTRITION:
calories 300, fat 12, fiber 6, carbs 20, protein 13

JALAPENO PEPPERS BEEF

Preparation time: 5 min | Cooking time: 40 min | Servings: 6

INGREDIENTS:

- 1½ pounds ground beef
- 1 red onion, chopped
- Salt and black pepper to taste
- 16 ounces canned white beans, drained
- 20 ounces canned tomatoes, chopped
- 1 cup beef stock
- 6 garlic cloves, chopped
- 7 jalapeno peppers, diced
- 2 tbsp olive oil
- 3 tbsp chili powder

DIRECTIONS:
Heat up the oil in a pan that fits your air fryer over medium heat. Add the beef and the onions, stir, and cook for 2 minutes. Add all remaining ingredients and stir; cook for 3 minutes more. Place the pan in the air fryer and cook at 380 degrees F for 35 minutes. Divide everything into bowls and serve.

NUTRITION:
calories 300, fat 8, fiber 6, carbs 20, protein 17

CUMIN BEEF MIX

Preparation time: 5 min | Cooking time: 35 min | Servings: 4

INGREDIENTS:

- 1 pound ground beef
- 1 yellow onion, chopped
- 2 tbsp olive oil
- Salt and black pepper to taste
- 2 garlic cloves, minced
- 4 ounces canned kidney beans, drained
- 8 ounces canned tomatoes, chopped
- 2 tsp cumin, ground

DIRECTIONS:
Heat up the oil in a pan that fits your air fryer over medium heat. Add the onion and the beef, stir, and cook for 2-3 minutes. Then add the garlic, salt, pepper, beans, tomatoes, and the cumin; toss, and cook for another 2 minutes. Transfer the pan to your air fryer and cook at 380 degrees F for 30 minutes. Divide everything into bowls and serve.

NUTRITION:
calories 281, fat 11, fiber 7, carbs 20, protein 15

LAMB AND CARROTS MIX

Preparation time: 10 min | Cooking time: 30 min | Servings: 6

INGREDIENTS:

- 1½ pounds ground lamb
- ½ tbsp olive oil
- Salt and black pepper to taste
- 1 cup beef stock
- 1 tbsp red wine
- ½ tsp smoked paprika
- 1 yellow onion, chopped
- 4 garlic cloves, minced
- 4 carrots, grated

DIRECTIONS:
Heat up a pan that fits your air fryer with the oil over medium heat; add the lamb, stir, and brown for 1-2 minutes. Add all remaining ingredients and toss well; cook for 2 more minutes. Transfer the pan to your air fryer and cook at 380 degrees F for 25 minutes. Divide the mix into bowls and serve.

NUTRITION:
calories 271, fat 12, fiber 6, carbs 17, protein 16

PORK AND CELERY MIX
Preparation time: 10 min | Cooking time: 35 min | Servings: 4

INGREDIENTS:

- 3 ounces white mushrooms, sliced
- 1½ pounds pork stew meat, cubed
- 2 ounces canned tomatoes, cubed
- 16 ounces shallots, chopped
- ½ cup beef stock
- 2 ounces white wine
- 2 garlic cloves, minced
- 2 tbsp chives, chopped
- Salt and black pepper to taste
- 2 tbsp olive oil
- 1 tbsp cilantro, chopped

DIRECTIONS:
Heat up a pan that fits your air fryer with the oil over medium heat. Add the meat, stir, and brown for 2 minutes. Next, add the shallots, garlic, chives, salt, pepper, and mushrooms; toss, and cook for 2 minutes more. Then add the mushrooms, tomatoes, wine, and stock; stir well. Simmer for about 1 minute, and then transfer the pan to your air fryer; cook at 380 degrees F for 30 minutes. Add the cilantro and toss. Divide everything into bowls and serve.

NUTRITION:
calories 271, fat 11, fiber 4, carbs 19, protein 24

PORK AND CHIVES MIX
Preparation time: 5 min | Cooking time: 35 min | Servings: 4

INGREDIENTS:

- 2 tbsp olive oil
- 1½ pounds pork stew meat, cubed
- 1 yellow onion, chopped
- 2 tbsp red wine
- 2 garlic cloves, minced
- 2 cups beef stock
- ¼ cup tomato sauce
- Salt and black pepper to taste
- 3 celery stalks, chopped
- ½ bunch parsley

DIRECTIONS:
In a pan that fits your air fryer, heat up the oil over medium heat. Add the pork and brown for 2-3 minutes. Next, add the onions, garlic, wine, salt, pepper, tomato sauce, and celery; stir, and cook for 2 minutes more. Place the pan in the fryer and cook at 380 degrees F for 30 minutes. Divide between plates and serve with the parsley sprinkled on top.

NUTRITION:
calories 291, fat 8, fiber 8, carbs 20, protein 16

MOZZARELLA BEEF CASSEROLE
Preparation time: 10 min | Cooking time: 35 min | Servings: 4

INGREDIENTS:

- 17 ounces small pasta, cooked
- 1 pound ground beef, browned
- 13 ounces mozzarella cheese, shredded
- 16 ounces tomato puree
- 1 celery stalk, chopped
- 1 yellow onion, chopped
- 1 carrot, chopped
- Cooking spray

DIRECTIONS:
Grease a baking dish that fits your air fryer with the cooking spray and spread the pasta on the bottom. Next layer the beef, tomato puree, celery, onion, and carrots. Season with salt and pepper and sprinkle the mozzarella on top. Place the dish in the air fryer and cook at 380 degrees F for 35 minutes. Divide between plates and serve.

NUTRITION:
calories 261, fat 11, fiber 7, carbs 18, protein 22

BEEF STEAK AND TOFU
Preparation time: 10 min | Cooking time: 30 min | Servings: 6

INGREDIENTS:

- 1 cup beef stock
- 2 pounds beef steak, cut into thin strips and browned
- Salt and black pepper to taste
- 1 yellow onion, thinly sliced
- 12 ounces extra firm tofu, cubed
- 1 chili pepper, sliced
- 1 scallion, chopped

DIRECTIONS:
Mix all of the ingredients in a pan that fits your air fryer; toss well. Place the pan in the fryer and cook at 380 degrees F for 30 minutes. Divide between plates and serve.

NUTRITION:
calories 237, fat 8, fiber 6, carbs 18, protein 20

CHUCK ROAST BEEF
Preparation time: 10 min | Cooking time: 20

min | Servings: 4

INGREDIENTS:

- 3 pounds chuck roast, cut into thin strips
- 1 tbsp olive oil
- ½ cup soy sauce
- ½ cup black soy sauce
- 2 tbsp fish sauce
- 5 garlic cloves, minced
- 3 red peppers, dried and crushed

DIRECTIONS:
In a bowl, combine the beef with all ingredients; toss well and place in the fridge for 10 minutes. Transfer the beef to your air fryer's basket and cook at 380 degrees F for 20 minutes. Serve with a side salad.

NUTRITION:
calories 281, fat 11, fiber 6, carbs 17, protein 11

PORK AND RED CABBAGE

Preparation time: 10 min | Cooking time: 35 min | Servings: 6

INGREDIENTS:

- 2½ pounds pork stew meat, cubed
- 2 tsp olive oil
- 2 bay leaves
- 3 garlic cloves, chopped
- 4 carrots, chopped
- 1 red cabbage head, shredded
- Salt and black pepper to taste
- ½ cup tomato sauce

DIRECTIONS:
Heat up a pan that fits your air fryer with the oil over medium-high heat, add the meat, and brown it for 5 minutes. Add all remaining ingredients and toss. Place the pan in the fryer and cook at 380 degrees F for 30 minutes. Divide the mix between plates and serve.

NUTRITION:
calories 300, fat 12, fiber 6, carbs 19, protein 20

TOMATO PORK CHOPS

Preparation time: 5 min | Cooking time: 20 min | Servings: 4

INGREDIENTS:

- 4 pork chops
- 2 tbsp olive oil
- 2 tbsp white flour
- 1 yellow onion, minced
- 2 garlic cloves, minced
- 2 tbsp tomato paste
- 1 tsp oregano, dried
- 4 ounces red wine
- Salt and black pepper to taste

DIRECTIONS:
In a bowl, mix the pork chops with the flour, salt, and pepper; coat the chops well. Heat up the oil in a pan that fits your air fryer over medium heat. Add the pork chops and brown for 2-3 minutes. Add the onions, garlic, oregano, and wine; stir and cook for 2 more minutes. Add the tomato paste, toss, and then place the pan into the fryer. Cook at 380 degrees F for 14 minutes, and then divide between plates. Serve with a side salad, and enjoy!

NUTRITION:
calories 271, fat 11, fiber 5, carbs 19, protein 17

SALTY LAMB RIBS

Preparation time: 5 min | Cooking time: 14 min | Servings: 4

INGREDIENTS:

- 4 lamb ribs
- 4 garlic cloves, minced
- 1 cup veggie stock
- ½ tsp chili powder
- ¼ tsp smoked paprika
- 2 tbsp extra virgin olive oil
- Salt and black pepper to taste

DIRECTIONS:
In a bowl, combine all of the ingredients—except the ribs—and mix well. Then add the ribs and rub them thoroughly with the mixture. Transfer the ribs to your air fryer's basket and cook at 390 degrees F for 7 minutes on each side. Serve with a side salad.

NUTRITION:
calories 281, fat 7, fiber 9, carbs 17, protein 15

OLIVE LAMB CHOPS

Preparation time: 10 min | Cooking time: 14 min | Servings: 4

INGREDIENTS:

- 4 lamb chops
- 1 tbsp white flour
- 2 tbsp olive oil
- Salt and black pepper to taste
- 1 tsp marjoram, dried
- 3 garlic cloves, minced
- 1 tsp thyme, dried
- ½ cup veggie stock
- 1 cup green olives, pitted and sliced

DIRECTIONS:
Place all ingredients—except the olives—in a bowl and mix well. Then put in the fridge for 10 minutes. Transfer the lamb chops to your air fryer's basket and cook at 390 degrees F for 7 minutes on each side. Divide the lamb chops between plates, sprinkle the olives on top, and serve.

NUTRITION:
calories 271, fat 4, fiber 8, carbs 18, protein 11

CREAMY PORK MIX

Preparation time: 5 min | Cooking time: 30 min | Servings: 4

INGREDIENTS:

- 1 pound pork stew meat, cubed
- 2 ounces coconut cream
- 3 tbsp pure cream
- 3 tbsp curry powder
- 2 tbsp olive oil

- 1 yellow onion, chopped
- 1 tbsp cilantro, chopped
- Salt and black pepper to taste

Directions:
In a bowl, mix the pork with the curry powder, salt, and pepper. Heat up a pan that fits your air fryer with the oil over medium-high heat; add the pork, toss, and brown for 3 minutes. Add the coconut cream, pure cream, and onions; toss. Place the pan in the fryer and cook at 380 degrees F for 25 minutes. Add the cilantro and toss. Divide everything into bowls and serve.

Nutrition:
calories 271, fat 7, fiber 6, carbs 18, protein 18

TOMATO AND GARLIC LAMB CHOPS
Preparation time: 5 min | Cooking time: 15 min | Servings: 4

Ingredients:

- 4 lamb chops
- Salt and black pepper to taste
- 2 tbsp flour
- 2 tbsp olive oil
- 3 ounces red wine
- 2 garlic cloves, crushed
- 2 tbsp tomato sauce
- 2 tbsp bbq sauce
- 14 ounces canned tomatoes, chopped
- 2 tbsp cilantro, chopped

Directions:
In a bowl, mix the lamb chops with salt, pepper, and the flour; toss and coat the lamb chops well. Heat up a pan that fits your air fryer with the oil over medium heat; add the lamb, toss, and brown for 2-3 minutes. Add the garlic, wine, tomato sauce, bbq sauce, and tomatoes; toss again. Place the pan in the fryer and cook at 400 degrees F for 12 minutes. Divide between plates and serve.

Nutrition:
calories 261, fat 9, fiber 9, carbs 18, protein 20

BEEF AND PLUMS MIX
Preparation time: 10 min | Cooking time: 40 min | Servings: 6

Ingredients:

- 1½ pounds beef stew meat, cubed
- 3 tbsp honey
- 2 tbsp olive oil
- 9 ounces plums, pitted and halved
- 8 ounces beef stock
- 2 yellow onions, chopped
- 2 garlic cloves, minced
- Salt and black pepper to tastes
- 1 tsp turmeric powder
- 1 tsp ginger powder
- 1 tsp cinnamon powder

Directions:
In a pan that fits your air fryer, heat up the oil over medium heat. Add the beef, stir, and brown for 2 minutes. Add the honey, onions, garlic, salt, pepper, turmeric, ginger, and cinnamon; toss, and cook for 2-3 minutes more. Add the plums and the stock; toss again. Place the pan in the fryer and cook at 380 degrees for 30 minutes. Divide everything into bowls and serve.

Nutrition:
calories 271, fat 11, fiber 6, carbs 19, protein 20

FRENCH LAMB MIX
Preparation time: 10 min | Cooking time: 20 min | Servings: 4

Ingredients:

- 1½ pounds lamb chops
- ½ pounds mushrooms, sliced
- 4 tomatoes, chopped
- 1 small yellow onion, chopped
- 6 garlic cloves, minced
- 2 tbsp tomato paste
- 1 tsp olive oil
- Salt and black pepper to taste
- 1 tsp oregano, dried
- ½ tsp mint, dried
- A handful of cilantro, chopped

Directions:
Heat up a pan that fits your air fryer with the oil over medium heat. Add the lamb chops, salt, pepper, oregano, and mint; toss, and brown for 2-3 minutes. Add the mushrooms, onions, garlic, tomatoes, and tomato paste, toss and cook for 2 more minutes. Place the pan in the fryer and cook at 400 degrees F for 12 minutes more. Add the cilantro and toss. Divide everything between plates and serve.

Nutrition:
calories 271, fat 11, fiber 9, carbs 19, protein 12

SUGARY RIB EYE STEAK
Preparation time: 10 min | Cooking time: 20 min | Servings: 4

Ingredients:

- 2 pounds rib eye steak
- Salt and black pepper to the taste
- 1 tbsp olive oil
- For the rub:
- 3 tbsp sweet paprika
- 2 tbsp onion powder
- 2 tbsp garlic powder
- 1 tbsp brown sugar
- 2 tbsp oregano, dried
- 1 tbsp cumin, ground
- 1 tbsp rosemary, dried

Directions:
In a bowl, mix paprika with onion and garlic powder, sugar, oregano, rosemary, salt, pepper and cumin, stir and rub steak with this mix. Season steak with salt and pepper, rub again with the oil, put in your air fryer and cook at 400 degrees F for 20 minutes, flipping them halfway. Transfer steak to a cutting board, slice and serve with a side salad.

NUTRITION:
calories 320, fat 8, fiber 7, carbs 22, protein 21

SESAME STEAK AND FLORETS

Preparation time: 45 min | Cooking time: 12 min | Servings: 4

INGREDIENTS:

- ¾ pound round steak, cut into strips
- 1 pound broccoli florets
- 1/3 cup oyster sauce
- 2 tsp sesame oil
- 1 tsp soy sauce
- 1 tsp sugar
- 1/3 cup sherry
- 1 tbsp olive oil
- 1 garlic clove, minced

DIRECTIONS:
In a bowl, mix sesame oil with oyster sauce, soy sauce, sherry and sugar, stir well, add beef, toss and leave aside for 30 minutes. Transfer beef to a pan that fits your air fryer, also add broccoli, garlic and oil, toss everything and cook at 380 degrees F for 12 minutes. Divide among plates and serve.

NUTRITION:
calories 330, fat 12, fiber 7, carbs 23, protein 23

FRENCH PORK

Preparation time: 10 min | Cooking time: 15 min | Servings: 2

INGREDIENTS:

- 1 red onion, sliced
- 1 yellow bell pepper, cut into strips
- 1 green bell pepper, cut into strips
- Salt and black pepper to the taste
- 2 tsp Provencal herbs
- ½ tbsp mustard
- 1 tbsp olive oil
- 7 ounces pork tenderloin

DIRECTIONS:
In a baking dish that fits your air fryer, mix yellow bell pepper with green bell pepper, onion, salt, pepper, Provencal herbs and half of the oil and toss well. Season pork with salt, pepper, mustard and the rest of the oil, toss well and add to veggies. Introduce everything in your air fryer, cook at 370 degrees F for 15 minutes, divide among plates and serve.

NUTRITION:
calories 300, fat 8, fiber 7, carbs 21, protein 23

BEEF STRIPS WITH SNOW PEAS AND MUSHROOMS

Preparation time: 10 min | Cooking time: 22 min | Servings: 2

INGREDIENTS:

- 2 beef steaks, cut into strips
- Salt and black pepper to the taste
- 7 ounces snow peas
- 8 ounces white mushrooms, halved
- 1 yellow onion, cut into rings
- 2 tbsp soy sauce
- 1 tsp olive oil

DIRECTIONS:
In a bowl, mix olive oil with soy sauce, whisk, add beef strips and toss. In another bowl, mix snow peas, onion and mushrooms with salt, pepper and the oil, toss well, put in a pan that fits your air fryer and cook at 350 degrees F for 16 minutes. Add beef strips to the pan as well and cook at 400 degrees F for 6 minutes more. Divide everything on plates and serve.

NUTRITION:
calories 235, fat 8, fiber 2, carbs 22, protein 24

HERBED LAMB CHOPS

Preparation time: 10 min | Cooking time: 10 min | Servings: 4

INGREDIENTS:

- 3 tbsp olive oil
- 8 lamb chops
- Salt and black pepper to the taste
- 4 garlic cloves, minced
- 1 tbsp oregano, chopped
- 1 tbsp coriander, chopped

DIRECTIONS:
In a bowl, mix oregano with salt, pepper, oil, garlic and lamb chops and toss to coat. Transfer lamb chops to your air fryer and cook at 400 degrees F for 10 minutes. Divide lamb chops on plates and serve with a side salad.

NUTRITION:
calories 231, fat 7, fiber 5, carbs 14, protein 23

CRUSTY LAMB

Preparation time: 10 min | Cooking time: 30 min | Servings: 4

INGREDIENTS:

- 1 tbsp bread crumbs
- 2 tbsp macadamia nuts, toasted and crushed
- 1 tbsp olive oil
- 1 garlic clove, minced
- 28 ounces rack of lamb
- Salt and black pepper to the taste
- 1 egg
- 1 tbsp rosemary, chopped

DIRECTIONS:
In a bowl, mix oil with garlic and stir well. Season lamb with salt, pepper and brush with the oil. In another bowl, mix nuts with breadcrumbs and rosemary. Put the egg in a separate bowl and whisk well. Dip lamb in egg, then in macadamia mix, place them in your air fryer's basket, cook at 360 degrees F and cook for 25 minutes, increase heat to 400 degrees F and cook for 5 minutes more.

NUTRITION:
calories 230, fat 2, fiber 2, carbs 10, protein 12

INDIAN PORK DISH

Preparation time: 35 min | Cooking time: 10 min | Servings: 4

Ingredients:

- 1 tsp ginger powder
- 2 tsp chili paste
- 2 garlic cloves, minced
- 14 ounces pork chops, cubed
- 1 shallot, chopped
- 1 tsp coriander, ground
- 7 ounces coconut milk
- 2 tbsp olive oil
- 3 ounces peanuts, ground
- 3 tbsp soy sauce
- Salt and black pepper to the taste

Directions:

In a bowl, mix ginger with 1 tsp chili paste, half of the garlic, half of the soy sauce and half of the oil, whisk, add meat, toss and leave aside for 10 minutes. Transfer meat to your air fryer's basket and cook at 400 degrees F for 12 minutes, turning halfway. Meanwhile, heat up a pan with the rest of the oil over medium high heat, add shallot, the rest of the garlic, coriander, coconut milk, the rest of the peanuts, the rest of the chili paste and the rest of the soy sauce, stir and cook for 5 minutes. Divide pork on plates, spread coconut mix on top and serve.

Nutrition:

calories 423, fat 11, fiber 4, carbs 42, protein 18

CREAMY LAMB AND SPROUTS

Preparation time: 10 min | Cooking time: 1 hour and 10 min | Servings: 4

Ingredients:

- 2 pounds leg of lamb, scored
- 2 tbsp olive oil
- 1 tbsp rosemary, chopped
- 1 tbsp lemon thyme, chopped
- 1 garlic clove, minced
- 1 and ½ pounds Brussels sprouts, trimmed
- 1 tbsp butter, melted
- ½ cup sour cream
- Salt and black pepper to the taste

Directions:

Season leg of lamb with salt, pepper, thyme and rosemary, brush with oil, place in your air fryer's basket, cook at 300 degrees F for 1 hour, transfer to a plate and keep warm. In a pan that fits your air fryer, mix Brussels sprouts with salt, pepper, garlic, butter and sour cream, toss, put in your air fryer and cook at 400 degrees F for 10 minutes. Divide lamb on plates, add Brussels sprouts on the side and serve.

Nutrition:

calories 440, fat 23, fiber 0, carbs 2, protein 49

BEEF WITH MAYO

Preparation time: 10 min | Cooking time: 40 min | Servings: 8

Ingredients:

- 1 cup mayonnaise
- 1/3 cup sour cream
- 2 garlic cloves, minced
- 3 pounds beef fillet
- 2 tbsp chives, chopped
- 2 tbsp mustard
- 2 tbsp mustard
- ¼ cup tarragon, chopped
- Salt and black pepper to the taste

Directions:

Season beef with salt and pepper to the taste, place in your air fryer, cook at 370 degrees F for 20 minutes, transfer to a plate and leave aside for a few minutes. In a bowl, mix garlic with sour cream, chives, mayo, some salt and pepper, whisk and leave aside. In another bowl, mix mustard with Dijon mustard and tarragon, whisk, add beef, toss, return to your air fryer and cook at 350 degrees F for 20 minutes more. Divide beef on plates, spread garlic mayo on top and serve.

Nutrition:

calories 400, fat 12, fiber 2, carbs 27, protein 19

MARINATED PEPPER BEEF

Preparation time: 10 min | Cooking time: 45 min | Servings: 6

Ingredients:

- 6 bacon strips
- 2 tbsp butter
- 3 garlic cloves, minced
- Salt and black pepper to the taste
- 1 tbsp horseradish
- 1 tbsp mustard
- 3 pounds beef roast
- 1 and ¾ cup beef stock
- ¾ cup red wine

Directions:

In a bowl, mix butter with mustard, garlic, salt, pepper and horseradish, whisk and rub beef with this mix. Arrange bacon strips on a cutting board, place beef on top, fold bacon around beef, transfer to your air fryer's basket, cook at 400 degrees F for 15 minutes and transfer to a pan that fits your fryer. Add stock and wine to beef, introduce pan in your air fryer and cook at 360 degrees F for 30 minutes more. Carve beef, divide among plates and serve with a side salad.

Nutrition:

calories 500, fat 9, fiber 4, carbs 29, protein 36

SWEET PAPRIKA PORK

Preparation time: 10 min | Cooking time: 22 min | Servings: 6

Ingredients:

- 2 pounds pork meat, boneless and cubed
- 2 yellow onions, chopped
- 1 tbsp olive oil
- 1 garlic clove, minced
- 3 cups chicken stock
- 2 tbsp sweet paprika

- Salt and black pepper to the taste
- 2 tbsp white flour
- 1 and ½ cups sour cream
- 2 tbsp dill, chopped

Directions:
In a pan that fits your air fryer, mix pork with salt, pepper and oil, toss, introduce in your air fryer and cook at 360 degrees F for 7 minutes. Add onion, garlic, stock, paprika, flour, sour cream and dill, toss and cook at 370 degrees F for 15 minutes more. Divide everything on plates and serve right away.

Nutrition:
calories 300, fat 4, fiber 10, carbs 26, protein 34

MARINATED CAYENNE PORK
Preparation time: 24 hours | Cooking time: 25 min | Servings: 6

Ingredients:
- 2 pork chops
- ¼ cup olive oil
- 2 yellow onions, sliced
- 2 garlic cloves, minced
- 2 tsp mustard
- 1 tsp sweet paprika
- Salt and black pepper to the taste
- ½ tsp oregano, dried
- ½ tsp thyme, dried
- A pinch of cayenne pepper

Directions:
In a bowl, mix oil with garlic, mustard, paprika, black pepper, oregano, thyme and cayenne and whisk well. Combine onions with meat and mustard mix, toss to coat, cover and keep in the fridge for 1 day. Transfer meat and onions mix to a pan that fits your air fryer and cook at 360 degrees F for 25 minutes. Divide everything on plates and serve.

Nutrition:
calories 384, fat 4, fiber 4, carbs 17, protein 25

SIMPLE PORK IN WINE
Preparation time: 40 min | Cooking time: 40 min | Servings: 4

Ingredients:
- 2 pounds pork loin roast, boneless and cubed
- 4 tbsp butter, melted
- Salt and black pepper to the taste
- 2 cups chicken stock
- ½ cup dry white wine
- 2 garlic cloves, minced
- 1 tsp thyme, chopped
- 1 thyme spring
- 1 bay leaf
- ½ yellow onion, chopped
- 2 tbsp white flour
- ½ pound red grapes

Directions:
Season pork cubes with salt and pepper, rub with 2 tbsp melted butter, put in your air fryer and cook at 370 degrees F for 8 minutes. Meanwhile, heat up a pan that fits your air fryer with 2 tbsp butter over medium high heat, add garlic and onion, stir and cook for 2 minutes. Add wine, stock, salt, pepper, thyme, flour and bay leaf, stir well, bring to a simmer and take off heat. Add pork cubes and grapes, toss, introduce in your air fryer and cook at 360 degrees F for 30 minutes more. Divide everything on plates and serve.

Nutrition:
calories 320, fat 4, fiber 5, carbs 29, protein 38

OREGANO COUSCOUS PORK
Preparation time: 10 min | Cooking time: 35 min | Servings: 6

Ingredients:
- 2 and ½ pounds pork loin, boneless and trimmed
- ¾ cup chicken stock
- 2 tbsp olive oil
- ½ tbsp sweet paprika
- 2 and ¼ tsp sage, dried
- ½ tbsp garlic powder
- ¼ tsp rosemary, dried
- ¼ tsp marjoram, dried
- 1 tsp basil, dried
- 1 tsp oregano, dried
- Salt and black pepper to the taste
- 2 cups couscous, cooked

Directions:
In a bowl, mix oil with stock, paprika, garlic powder, sage, rosemary, thyme, marjoram, oregano, salt and pepper to the taste, whisk well, add pork loin, toss well and leave aside for 1 hour. Transfer everything to a pan that fits your air fryer and cook at 370 degrees F for 35 minutes. Divide among plates and serve with couscous on the side.

Nutrition:
calories 310, fat 4, fiber 6, carbs 37, protein 34

AIR FRIED PORK
Preparation time: 30 min | Cooking time: 1 hour and 20 min | Servings: 6

Ingredients:
- 3 tbsp garlic, minced
- 3 tbsp olive oil
- 4 pounds pork shoulder
- Salt and black pepper to the taste

Directions:
In a bowl, mix olive oil with salt, pepper and oil, whisk well and brush pork shoulder with this mix. Place in preheated air fryer and cook at 390 degrees F for 10 minutes. Reduce heat to 300 degrees F and roast pork for 1 hour and 10 minutes. Slice pork shoulder, divide among plates and serve with a side salad.

Nutrition:
calories 221, fat 4, fiber 4, carbs 7, protein 10

FENNEL PORK LOIN

Preparation time: 10 min | Cooking time: 1 hour | Servings: 10

INGREDIENTS:

- 5 and ½ pounds pork loin roast, trimmed
- Salt and black pepper to the taste
- 3 garlic cloves, minced
- 2 tbsp rosemary, chopped
- 1 tsp fennel, ground
- 1 tbsp fennel seeds
- 2 tsp red pepper, crushed
- ¼ cup olive oil

DIRECTIONS:

In your food processor mix garlic with fennel seeds, fennel, rosemary, red pepper, some black pepper and the olive oil and blend until you obtain a paste. Spread 2 tbsp garlic paste on pork loin, rub well, season with salt and pepper, introduce in your preheated air fryer and cook at 350 degrees F for 30 minutes. Reduce heat to 300 degrees F and cook for 15 minutes more. Slice pork, divide among plates and serve.

NUTRITION:

calories 300, fat 14, fiber 9, carbs 26, protein 22

BEEF BRISKET WITH TOMATOES

Preparation time: 10 min | Cooking time: 2 hours | Servings: 6

INGREDIENTS:

- 1 pound yellow onion, chopped
- 4 pounds beef brisket
- 1 pound carrot, chopped
- 8 earl grey tea bags
- ½ pound celery, chopped
- Salt and black pepper to the taste
- 4 cups water
- For the sauce:
- 16 ounces canned tomatoes, chopped
- ½ pound celery, chopped
- 1 ounce garlic, minced
- 4 ounces vegetable oil
- 1 pound sweet onion, chopped
- 1 cup brown sugar
- 8 earl grey tea bags
- 1 cup white vinegar

DIRECTIONS:

Put the water in a heat proof dish that fits your air fryer, add 1 pound onion, 1 pound carrot, ½ pound celery, salt and pepper, stir and bring to a simmer over medium high heat. Add beef brisket and 8 tea bags, stir, transfer to your air fryer and cook at 300 degrees F for 1 hour and 30 minutes. Meanwhile, heat up a pan with the vegetable oil over medium high heat, add 1 pound onion, stir and sauté for 10 minutes. Add garlic, ½ pound celery, tomatoes, sugar, vinegar, salt, pepper and 8 tea bags, stir, bring to a simmer, cook for 10 minutes and discard tea bags. Transfer beef brisket to a cutting board, slice, divide among plates, drizzle onion sauce all over and serve.

NUTRITION:

calories 400, fat 12, fiber 4, carbs 38, protein 34

SESAME BEEF AND ONIONS

Preparation time: 10 min | Cooking time: 20 min | Servings: 4

INGREDIENTS:

- 1 cup green onion, chopped
- 1 cup soy sauce
- ½ cup water
- ¼ cup brown sugar
- ¼ cup sesame seeds
- 5 garlic cloves, minced
- 1 tsp black pepper
- 1 pound lean beef

DIRECTIONS:

In a bowl, mix onion with soy sauce, water, sugar, garlic, sesame seeds and pepper, whisk, add meat, toss and leave aside for 10 minutes. Drain beef, transfer to your preheated air fryer and cook at 390 degrees F for 20 minutes. Slice, divide among plates and serve with a side salad.

NUTRITION:

calories 329, fat 8, fiber 12, carbs 26, protein 22

GARLIC BEEF

Preparation time: 30 min | Cooking time: 30 min | Servings: 4

INGREDIENTS:

- 11 ounces steak fillets, sliced
- 4 garlic cloves, minced
- 2 tbsp olive oil
- 1 red bell pepper, cut into strips
- Black pepper to the taste
- 1 tbsp sugar
- 2 tbsp fish sauce
- 2 tsp corn flour
- ½ cup beef stock
- 4 green onions, sliced

DIRECTIONS:

In a pan that fits your air fryer mix beef with oil, garlic, black pepper and bell pepper, stir, cover and keep in the fridge for 30 minutes. Put the pan in your preheated air fryer and cook at 360 degrees F for 14 minutes. In a bowl, mix sugar with fish sauce, stir well, pour over beef and cook at 360 degrees F for 7 minutes more. Add stock mixed with corn flour and green onions, toss and cook at 370 degrees F for 7 minutes more. Divide everything on plates and serve.

NUTRITION:

calories 343, fat 3, fiber 12, carbs 26, protein 38

MARINATED LAMB AND VEGGIES

Preparation time: 10 min | Cooking time: 30 min | Servings: 4

INGREDIENTS:

- 1 carrot, chopped
- 1 onion, sliced
- ½ tbsp olive oil
- 3 ounces bean sprouts
- 8 ounces lamb

loin, sliced
- For the marinade:
- 1 garlic clove, minced
- ½ apple, grated
- Salt and black pepper to the taste
- 1 small yellow onion, grated
- 1 tbsp ginger, grated
- 5 tbsp soy sauce
- 1 tbsp sugar
- 2 tbsp orange juice

DIRECTIONS:
In a bowl, mix 1 grated onion with the apple, garlic, 1 tbsp ginger, soy sauce, orange juice, sugar and black pepper, whisk well, add lamb and leave aside for 10 minutes. Heat up a pan that fits your air fryer with the olive oil over medium high heat, add 1 sliced onion, carrot and bean sprouts, stir and cook for 3 minutes. Add lamb and the marinade, transfer pan to your preheated air fryer and cook at 360 degrees F for 25 minutes. Divide everything into bowls and serve.

NUTRITION:
calories 265, fat 3, fiber 7, carbs 18, protein 22

CREAMY LAMB
Preparation time: 1 day | Cooking time: 1 hour | Servings: 8

INGREDIENTS:
- 5 pounds leg of lamb
- 2 cups low fat buttermilk
- 2 tbsp mustard
- ½ cup butter
- 2 tbsp basil, chopped
- 2 tbsp tomato paste
- 2 garlic cloves, minced
- Salt and black pepper to the taste
- 1 cup white wine
- 1 tbsp cornstarch mixed with 1 tbsp water
- ½ cup sour cream

DIRECTIONS:
Put lamb roast in a big dish, add buttermilk, toss to coat, cover and keep in the fridge for 24 hours. Pat dry lamb and put in a pan that fits your air fryer. In a bowl, mix butter with tomato paste, mustard, basil, rosemary, salt, pepper and garlic, whisk well, spread over lamb, introduce everything in your air fryer and cook at 300 degrees F for 1 hour. Slice lamb, divide among plates, leave aside for now and heat up cooking juices from the pan on your stove. Add wine, cornstarch mix, salt, pepper and sour cream, stir, take off heat, drizzle this sauce over lamb and serve.

NUTRITION:
calories 287, fat 4, fiber 7, carbs 19, protein 25

CORIANDER LAMB SHANKS
Preparation time: 10 min | Cooking time: 45 min | Servings: 4

INGREDIENTS:
- 4 lamb shanks
- 1 yellow onion, chopped
- 1 tbsp olive oil
- 4 tsp coriander seeds, crushed
- 2 tbsp white flour
- 4 bay leaves
- 2 tsp honey
- 5 ounces dry sherry
- 2 and ½ cups chicken stock
- Salt and pepper to the taste

DIRECTIONS:
Season lamb shanks with salt and pepper, rub with half of the oil, put in your air fryer and cook at 360 degrees F for 10 minutes. Heat up a pan that fits your air fryer with the rest of the oil over medium high heat, add onion and coriander, stir and cook for 5 minutes. Add flour, sherry, stock, honey and bay leaves, salt and pepper, stir, bring to a simmer, add lamb, introduce everything in your air fryer and cook at 360 degrees F for 30 minutes. Divide everything on plates and serve.

NUTRITION:
calories 283, fat 4, fiber 2, carbs 17, protein 26

ROSEMARY LAMB ROAST
Preparation time: 10 min | Cooking time: 45 min | Servings: 6

INGREDIENTS:
- 4 pounds lamb roast
- 1 spring rosemary
- 3 garlic cloves, minced
- 6 potatoes, halved
- ½ cup lamb stock
- 4 bay leaves
- Salt and black pepper to the taste

DIRECTIONS:
Put potatoes in a dish that fits your air fryer, add lamb, garlic, rosemary spring, salt, pepper, bay leaves and stock, toss, introduce in your air fryer and cook at 360 degrees F for 45 minutes. Slice lamb, divide among plates and serve with potatoes and cooking juices.

NUTRITION:
calories 273, fat 4, fiber 12, carbs 25, protein 29

LAMB LEG IN HERBS
Preparation time: 10 min | Cooking time: 1 hour | Servings: 6

INGREDIENTS:
- 4 pounds lamb leg
- 2 tbsp olive oil
- 2 sprigs rosemary, chopped
- 2 tbsp parsley, chopped
- 2 tbsp oregano, chopped
- Salt and black pepper to the taste
- 1 tbsp lemon rind, grated
- 3 garlic cloves, minced
- 2 tbsp lemon juice
- 2 pounds baby potatoes
- 1 cup beef stock

DIRECTIONS:
Make small cuts all over lamb, insert rosemary sprigs and season with salt and pepper. In a bowl, mix 1 tbsp oil with oregano, parsley, garlic, lemon juice and rind, stir and rub lamb with this mix. Heat up a pan

that fits your air fryer with the rest of the oil over medium high heat, stir and cook for 3 minutes. Add lamb and stock, stir, introduce in your air fryer and cook at 360 degrees F for 1 hour. Divide everything on plates and serve.

Nutrition:
calories 264, fat 4, fiber 12, carbs 27, protein 32

BEEF WINE CURRY

Preparation time: 10 min | Cooking time: 45 min | Servings: 4

Ingredients:

- 2 pounds beef steak, cubed
- 2 tbsp olive oil
- 3 potatoes, cubed
- 1 tbsp wine mustard
- 2 and ½ tbsp curry powder
- 2 yellow onions, chopped
- 2 garlic cloves, minced
- 10 ounces canned coconut milk
- 2 tbsp tomato sauce
- Salt and black pepper to the taste

Directions:
Heat up a pan that fits your air fryer with the oil over medium high heat, add onions and garlic, stir and cook for 4 minutes. Add potatoes and mustard, stir and cook for 1 minute. Add beef, curry powder, salt, pepper, coconut milk and tomato sauce, stir, transfer to your air fryer and cook at 360 degrees F for 40 minutes. Divide into bowls and serve.

Nutrition:
calories 432, fat 16, fiber 4, carbs 20, protein 27

BEEF ROAST WITH SMOKED PAPRIKA

Preparation time: 10 min | Cooking time: 45 min | Servings: 6

Ingredients:

- 3 pounds beef roast
- Salt and black pepper to the taste
- 17 ounces beef stock
- 3 ounces red wine
- ½ tsp chicken salt
- ½ tsp smoked paprika
- 1 yellow onion, chopped
- 4 garlic cloves, minced
- 3 carrots, chopped
- 5 potatoes, chopped

Directions:
In a bowl, mix salt, pepper, chicken salt and paprika, stir, rub beef with this mix and put it in a big pan that fits your air fryer. Add onion, garlic, stock, wine, potatoes and carrots, introduce in your air fryer and cook at 360 degrees F for 45 minutes. Divide everything on plates and serve.

Nutrition:
calories 304, fat 20, fiber 7, carbs 20, protein 32

GARLIC BEEF AND CABBAGE

Preparation time: 10 min | Cooking time: 40 min | Servings: 6

Ingredients:

- 2 and ½ pounds beef brisket
- 1 cup beef stock
- 2 bay leaves
- 3 garlic cloves, chopped
- 4 carrots, chopped
- 1 cabbage head, cut into medium wedges
- Salt and black pepper to the taste
- 3 turnips, cut into quarters

Directions:
Put beef brisket and stock in a large pan that fits your air fryer, season beef with salt and pepper, add garlic and bay leaves, carrots, cabbage, potatoes and turnips, toss, introduce in your air fryer and cook at 360 degrees F and cook for 40 minutes. Divide among plates and serve.

Nutrition:
calories 353, fat 16, fiber 7, carbs 20, protein 24

ONION LAMB SHANKS AND TOMATOES

Preparation time: 10 min | Cooking time: 45 min | Servings: 4

Ingredients:

- 4 lamb shanks
- 2 tbsp olive oil
- 1 yellow onion, finely chopped
- 6 carrots, roughly chopped
- 2 garlic cloves, minced
- 2 tbsp tomato paste
- 1 tsp oregano, dried
- 1 tomato, roughly chopped
- 2 tbsp water
- 4 ounces red wine
- Salt and black pepper to the taste

Directions:
Season lamb with salt and pepper, rub with oil, put in your air fryer and cook at 360 degrees F for 10 minutes. In a pan that fits your air fryer, mix onion with carrots, garlic, tomato paste, tomato, oregano, wine and water and toss. Add lamb, toss, introduce in your air fryer and cook at 370 degrees F for 35 minutes. Divide everything on plates and serve.

Nutrition:
calories 432, fat 17, fiber 8, carbs 17, protein 43

VEGGIE LAMB RIBS

Preparation time: 15 min | Cooking time: 40 min | Servings: 8

Ingredients:

- 8 lamb ribs
- 4 garlic cloves, minced
- 2 carrots, chopped
- 2 cups veggie stock
- 1 tbsp rosemary, chopped
- 2 tbsp extra virgin olive oil

- Salt and black pepper to the taste
- 3 tbsp white flour

DIRECTIONS:
Season lamb ribs with salt and pepper, rub with oil and garlic, put in preheated air fryer and cook at 360 degrees F for 10 minutes. In a heat proof dish that fits your fryer, mix stock with flour and whisk well. Add rosemary, carrots and lamb ribs, place in your air fryer and cook at 350 degrees F for 30 minutes. Divide lamb mix on plates and serve hot.

NUTRITION:
calories 302, fat 7, fiber 2, carbs 22, protein 27

ORIENTAL LAMB
Preparation time: 10 min | Cooking time: 42 min | Servings: 8

INGREDIENTS:

- 2 and ½ pounds lamb shoulder, chopped
- 3 tbsp honey
- 3 ounces almonds, peeled and chopped
- 9 ounces plumps, pitted
- 8 ounces veggie stock
- 2 yellow onions, chopped
- 2 garlic cloves, minced
- Salt and black pepper to the tastes
- 1 tsp cumin powder
- 1 tsp turmeric powder
- 1 tsp ginger powder
- 1 tsp cinnamon powder
- 3 tbsp olive oil

DIRECTIONS:
In a bowl, mix cinnamon powder with ginger, cumin, turmeric, garlic, olive oil and lamb, toss to coat, place in your preheated air fryer and cook at 350 degrees F for 8 minutes. Transfer meat to a dish that fits your air fryer, add onions, stock, honey and plums, stir, introduce in your air fryer and cook at 350 degrees F for 35 minutes. Divide everything on plates and serve with almond sprinkled on top.

NUTRITION:
calories 432, fat 23, fiber 6, carbs 30, protein 20

RIBS AND WINE SAUCE
Preparation time: 10 min | Cooking time: 36 min | Servings: 4

INGREDIENTS:

- 2 green onions, chopped
- 1 tsp vegetable oil
- 3 garlic cloves, minced
- 3 ginger slices
- 4 pounds short ribs
- ½ cup water
- ½ cup soy sauce
- ¼ cup rice wine
- ¼ cup pear juice
- 2 tsp sesame oil

DIRECTIONS:
Heat up a pan that fits your air fryer with the oil over medium heat, add green onions, ginger and garlic, stir and cook for 1 minute. Add ribs, water, wine, soy sauce, sesame oil and pear juice, stir, introduce in your air fryer and cook at 350 degrees F for 35 minutes. Divide ribs and sauce on plates and serve.

NUTRITION:
calories 321, fat 12, fiber 4, carbs 20, protein 14

SHORT RIBS IN BEER
Preparation time: 15 min | Cooking time: 45 min | Servings: 6

INGREDIENTS:

- 4 pounds short ribs, cut into small pieces
- 1 yellow onion, chopped
- Salt and black pepper to the taste
- ¼ cup tomato paste
- 1 cup dark beer
- 1 cup chicken stock
- 1 bay leaf
- 6 thyme sprigs, chopped
- 1 Portobello mushroom, dried

DIRECTIONS:
Heat up a pan that fits your air fryer over medium heat, add tomato paste, onion, stock, beer, mushroom, bay leaves and thyme and bring to a simmer. Add ribs, introduce in your air fryer and cook at 350 degrees F for 40 minutes. Divide everything on plates and serve.

NUTRITION:
calories 300, fat 7, fiber 8, carbs 18, protein 23

PORK BELLY AND APPLES
Preparation time: 10 min | Cooking time: 40 min | Servings: 6

INGREDIENTS:

- 2 tbsp sugar
- 1 tbsp lemon juice
- 1 quart water
- 17 ounces apples, cored and cut into wedges
- 2 pounds pork belly, scored
- Salt and black pepper to the taste
- A drizzle of olive oil

DIRECTIONS:
In your blender, mix water with apples, lemon juice and sugar, pulse well, transfer to a bowl, add meat, toss well, drain, put in your air fryer and cook at 400 degrees F for 40 minutes. Pour the sauce in a pot, heat up over medium heat and simmer for 15 minutes. Slice pork belly, divide among plates, drizzle the sauce all over and serve.

NUTRITION:
calories 456, fat 34, fiber 4, carbs 10, protein 25

CITRIC PORK STEAKS
Preparation time: 10 min | Cooking time: 20 min | Servings: 4

INGREDIENTS:

- Zest from 2 limes, grated
- Zest from 1 orange, grated
- Juice from 1 orange
- Juice from 2 limes
- 4 tsp garlic, minced
- ¾ cup olive oil
- 1 cup cilantro, chopped
- 1 cup mint, chopped
- 1 tsp oregano, dried
- Salt and black pepper to the taste
- 2 tsp cumin, ground
- 4 pork loin steaks
- 2 pickles, chopped
- 4 ham slices
- 6 Swiss cheese slices
- 2 tbsp mustard

DIRECTIONS:
In your food processor, mix lime zest and juice with orange zest and juice, garlic, oil, cilantro, mint, oregano, cumin, salt and pepper and blend well. Season steaks with salt and pepper, place them into a bowl, add marinade and toss to coat. Place steaks on a working surface, divide pickles, cheese, mustard and ham on them, roll and secure with toothpicks. Put stuffed pork steaks in your air fryer and cook at 340 degrees F for 20 minutes. Divide among plates and serve with a side salad.

NUTRITION:
calories 270, fat 7, fiber 2, carbs 13, protein 20

PORK AND MUSHROOM MAYO

Preparation time: 10 min | Cooking time: 40 min | Servings: 3

INGREDIENTS:

- 8 ounces mushrooms, sliced
- 1 tsp garlic powder
- 1 yellow onion, chopped
- 1 cup mayonnaise
- 3 pork chops, boneless
- 1 tsp nutmeg
- 1 tbsp balsamic vinegar
- ½ cup olive oil

DIRECTIONS:
Heat up a pan that fits your air fryer with the oil over medium heat, add mushrooms and onions, stir and cook for 4 minutes. Add pork chops, nutmeg and garlic powder and brown on both sides. Introduce pan your air fryer at 330 degrees F and cook for 30 minutes. Add vinegar and mayo, stir, divide everything on plates and serve.

NUTRITION:
calories 600, fat 10, fiber 1, carbs 8, protein 30

SQUASH WITH BEEF

Preparation time: 10 min | Cooking time: 40 min | Servings: 2

INGREDIENTS:

1 spaghetti squash, pricked
- 1 pound beef, ground
- Salt and black pepper to the taste
- 3 garlic cloves, minced
- 1 yellow onion, chopped
- 1 Portobello mushroom, sliced
- 28 ounces canned tomatoes, chopped
- 1 tsp oregano, dried
- ¼ tsp cayenne pepper
- ½ tsp thyme, dried
- 1 green bell pepper, chopped

DIRECTIONS:
Put spaghetti squash in your air fryer, cook at 350 degrees F for 20 minutes, transfer to a cutting board, cut into halves and discard seeds. Heat up a pan over medium high heat, add meat, garlic, onion and mushroom, stir and cook until meat browns. Add salt, pepper, thyme, oregano, cayenne, tomatoes and green pepper, stir and cook for 10 minutes. Stuff squash with this beef mix, introduce in the fryer and cook at 360 degrees F for 10 minutes. Divide among plates and serve.

NUTRITION:
calories 260, fat 7, fiber 2, carbs 14, protein 10

GREEK BEEF SALAD

Preparation time: 10 min | Cooking time: 10 min | Servings: 6

INGREDIENTS:

- ¼ cup milk
- 17 ounces beef, ground
- 1 yellow onion, grated
- 5 bread slices, cubed
- 1 egg, whisked
- ¼ cup parsley, chopped
- Salt and black pepper to the taste
- 2 garlic cloves, minced
- ¼ cup mint, chopped
- 2 and ½ tsp oregano, dried
- 1 tbsp olive oil
- Cooking spray
- 7 ounces cherry tomatoes, halved
- 1 cup baby spinach
- 1 and ½ tbsp lemon juice
- 7 ounces Greek yogurt

DIRECTIONS:
Put torn bread in a bowl, add milk, soak for a few minutes, squeeze and transfer to another bowl Add beef, egg, salt, pepper, oregano, mint, parsley, garlic and onion, stir and shape medium meatballs out of this mix. Spray them with cooking spray, place them in your air fryer and cook at 370 degrees F for 10 minutes. In a salad bowl, mix spinach with cucumber and tomato. Add meatballs, the oil, some salt, pepper, lemon juice and yogurt, toss and serve.

NUTRITION:
calories 200, fat 4, fiber 8, carbs 13, protein 27

BEEF PATTIES AND CREAMY SAUCE

Preparation time: 10 min | Cooking time: 25 min | Servings: 6

INGREDIENTS:

- 2 pounds beef, ground
- Salt and black pepper to the taste
- ½ tsp garlic powder
- 1 tbsp soy sauce
- ¼ cup beef stock
- ¾ cup flour
- 1 tbsp parsley, chopped
- 1 tbsp onion flakes
- For the sauce:
- 1 cup yellow onion, chopped
- 2 cups mushrooms, sliced
- 2 tbsp bacon fat
- 2 tbsp butter
- ½ tsp soy sauce
- ¼ cup sour cream
- ½ cup beef stock
- Salt and black pepper to the taste

DIRECTIONS:
In a bowl, mix beef with salt, pepper, garlic powder, 1 tbsp soy sauce, ¼ cup beef stock, flour, parsley and onion flakes, stir well, shape 6 patties, place them in your air fryer and cook at 350 degrees F for 14 minutes. Meanwhile, heat up a pan with the butter and the bacon fat over medium heat, add mushrooms, stir and cook for 4 minutes. Add onions, stir and cook for 4 minutes more. Add ½ tsp soy sauce, sour cream and ½ cup stock, stir well, bring to a simmer and take off heat. Divide beef patties on plates and serve with mushroom sauce on top.

NUTRITION:
calories 435, fat 23, fiber 4, carbs 6, protein 32

WORCESTERSHIRE BEEF CASSEROLE

Preparation time: 30 min | Cooking time: 35 min | Servings: 12

INGREDIENTS:

- 1 tbsp olive oil
- 2 pounds beef, ground
- 2 cups eggplant, chopped
- Salt and black pepper to the taste
- 2 tsp mustard
- 2 tsp gluten free Worcestershire sauce
- 28 ounces canned tomatoes, chopped
- 2 cups mozzarella, grated
- 16 ounces tomato sauce
- 2 tbsp parsley, chopped
- 1 tsp oregano, dried

DIRECTIONS:
In a bowl, mix eggplant with salt, pepper and oil and toss to coat. In another bowl, mix beef with salt, pepper, mustard and Worcestershire sauce, stir well and spread on the bottom of a pan that fits your air fryer. Add eggplant mix, tomatoes, tomato sauce, parsley, oregano and sprinkle mozzarella at the end. Introduce in your air fryer and cook at 360 degrees F for 35 minutes Divide among plates and serve hot.

NUTRITION:
calories 200, fat 12, fiber 2, carbs 16, protein 15

CARDAMOM LAMB AND SPINACH

Preparation time: 10 min | Cooking time: 35 min | Servings: 6

INGREDIENTS:

- 2 tbsp ginger, grated
- 2 garlic cloves, minced
- 2 tsp cardamom, ground
- 1 red onion, chopped
- 1 pound lamb meat, cubed
- 2 tsp cumin
- powder
- 1 tsp garam masala
- ½ tsp chili powder
- 1 tsp turmeric
- 2 tsp coriander, ground
- 1 pound spinach
- 14 ounces canned tomatoes, chopped

DIRECTIONS:
In a heat proof dish that fits your air fryer, mix lamb with spinach, tomatoes, ginger, garlic, onion, cardamom, cloves, cumin, garam masala, chili, turmeric and coriander, stir, introduce in preheated air fryer and cook at 360 degrees F for 35 minutes. Divide into bowls and serve.

NUTRITION:
calories 160, fat 6, fiber 3, carbs 17, protein 20

LAMB AND CITRIC FLAVOR

Preparation time: 10 min | Cooking time: 30 min | Servings: 4

INGREDIENTS:

- 2 lamb shanks
- Salt and black pepper to the taste
- 2 garlic cloves, minced
- 4 tbsp olive oil
- Juice from ½ lemon
- Zest from ½ lemon
- ½ tsp oregano, dried

DIRECTIONS:
Season lamb with salt, pepper, rub with garlic, put in your air fryer and cook at 350 degrees F for 30 minutes. Meanwhile, in a bowl, mix lemon juice with lemon zest, some salt and pepper, the olive oil and oregano and whisk very well. Shred lamb, discard bone, divide among plates, drizzle the lemon dressing all over and serve.

NUTRITION:
calories 260, fat 7, fiber 3, carbs 15, protein 12

LAMB AND PARSLEY

Preparation time: 1 hour | Cooking time: 45 min | Servings: 4

INGREDIENTS:

- 1 cup parsley
- 1 cup mint
- 1 small yellow onion, roughly chopped
- 1/3 cup pistachios, chopped
- 1 tsp lemon zest, grated
- 5 tbsp olive oil
- Salt and black pepper to the taste
- 2 pounds lamb riblets
- ½ onion, chopped
- 5 garlic cloves, minced
- Juice from 1 orange

DIRECTIONS:
In your food processor, mix parsley with mint, onion, pistachios, lemon zest, salt, pepper and oil and blend very well. Rub lamb with this mix, place in a bowl, cover and leave in the fridge for 1 hour. Transfer lamb to a baking dish that fits your air fryer, also add garlic, drizzle orange juice and cook in your air fryer at 300 degrees F for 45 minutes. Divide lamb on plates and serve.

NUTRITION:
calories 200, fat 4, fiber 6, carbs 15, protein 7

FENNEL LAMB RACKS
Preparation time: 10 min | Cooking time: 16 min | Servings: 4

INGREDIENTS:

- 12 ounces lamb racks
- 2 fennel bulbs, sliced
- Salt and black pepper to the taste
- 2 tbsp olive oil
- 4 figs, cut into halves
- 1/8 cup apple cider vinegar
- 1 tbsp brown sugar

DIRECTIONS:
In a bowl, mix fennel with figs, vinegar, sugar and oil, toss to coat well, transfer to a baking dish that fits your air fryer, introduce in your air fryer and cook at 350 degrees F for 6 minutes. Season lamb with salt and pepper, add to the baking dish with the fennel mix and air fry for 10 minutes more. Divide everything on plates and serve.

NUTRITION:
calories 240, fat 9, fiber 3, carbs 15, protein 12

BURGUNDY BEEF AND TOMATOES
Preparation time: 10 min | Cooking time: 1 hour | Servings: 7

INGREDIENTS:

- 2 pounds beef chuck roast, cubed
- 15 ounces canned tomatoes, chopped
- 4 carrots, chopped
- Salt and black pepper to the taste
- ½ pounds mushrooms, sliced
- 2 celery ribs, chopped
- 2 yellow onions, chopped
- 1 cup beef stock
- 1 tbsp thyme, chopped
- ½ tsp mustard powder
- 3 tbsp almond flour
- 1 cup water

DIRECTIONS:
Heat up a heat proof pot that fits your air fryer over medium high heat, add beef, stir and brown them for a couple of minutes. Add tomatoes, mushrooms, onions, carrots, celery, salt, pepper mustard, stock and thyme and stir. In a bowl mix water with flour, stir well, add this to the pot, toss, introduce in your air fryer and cook at 300 degrees F for 1 hour. Divide into bowls and serve.

NUTRITION:
calories 275, fat 13, fiber 4, carbs 17, protein 28

MEXICAN BEEF MIX
Preparation time: 10 min | Cooking time: 1 hour and 10 min | Servings: 8

INGREDIENTS:

- 2 yellow onions, chopped
- 2 tbsp olive oil
- 2 pounds beef roast, cubed
- 2 green bell peppers, chopped
- 1 habanero pepper, chopped
- 4 jalapenos, chopped
- 14 ounces canned tomatoes, chopped
- 2 tbsp cilantro,
- 6 garlic cloves, minced
- ½ cup water
- Salt and black pepper to the taste
- 1 and ½ tsp cumin, ground
- ½ cup black olives, pitted and chopped
- 1 tsp oregano, dried

DIRECTIONS:
In a pan that fits your air fryer, combine beef with oil, green bell peppers, onions, jalapenos, habanero pepper, tomatoes, garlic, water, cilantro, oregano, cumin, salt and pepper, stir, put in your air fryer and cook at 300 degrees F for 1 hour and 10 minutes. Add olives, stir, divide into bowls and serve.

NUTRITION:
calories 305, fat 14, fiber 4, carbs 18, protein 25

CHEDDAR HAM AND CAULIFLOWER
Preparation time: 10 min | Cooking time: 1 hour | Servings: 6

INGREDIENTS:

- 8 ounces cheddar cheese, grated
- 4 cups ham, cubed
- 14 ounces chicken stock
- ½ tsp garlic powder
- ½ tsp onion powder
- Salt and black pepper to the taste
- 4 garlic cloves, minced
- ¼ cup heavy cream
- 16 ounces cauliflower florets

DIRECTIONS:
In a pot that fits your air fryer, mix ham with stock, cheese, cauliflower, garlic powder, onion powder, salt, pepper, garlic and heavy cream, stir, put in your air fryer and cook at 300 degrees F for 1 hour. Divide into bowls and serve.

NUTRITION:
calories 320, fat 20, fiber 3, carbs 16, protein 23

PORTOBELLO MIX
Preparation time: 10 min | Cooking time: 40 min | Servings: 6

INGREDIENTS:

- 3 red bell peppers, chopped
- 2 pounds pork sausage, sliced
- Salt and black pepper to the taste
- 2 pounds Portobello mushrooms, sliced
- 2 sweet onions, chopped
- 1 tbsp brown sugar
- 1 tsp olive oil

DIRECTIONS:
In a baking dish that fits your air fryer, mix sausage slices with oil, salt, pepper, bell pepper, mushrooms, onion and sugar, toss, introduce in your air fryer and cook at 300 degrees F for 40 minutes. Divide among plates and serve right away.

NUTRITION:
calories 130, fat 12, fiber 1, carbs 13, protein 18

HOT SAUSAGE AND PEPPERS
Preparation time: 10 min | Cooking time: 20 min | Servings: 4

INGREDIENTS:

- 1 cup yellow onion, chopped
- 1 and ½ pound Italian pork sausage, sliced
- ½ cup red bell pepper, chopped
- Salt and black pepper to the taste
- 5 pounds kale, chopped
- 1 tsp garlic, minced
- ¼ cup red hot chili pepper, chopped
- 1 cup water

DIRECTIONS:
In a pan that fits your air fryer, mix sausage with onion, bell pepper, salt, pepper, kale, garlic, water and chili pepper, toss, introduce in preheated air fryer and cook at 300 degrees F for 20 minutes. Divide everything on plates and serve.

NUTRITION:
calories 150, fat 4, fiber 1, carbs 12, protein 14

SIRLOIN STEAKS AND TOMATO SAUCE
Preparation time: 10 min | Cooking time: 10 min | Servings: 4

INGREDIENTS:

- 2 tbsp chili powder
- 4 medium sirloin steaks
- 1 tsp cumin, ground
- ½ tbsp sweet paprika
- 1 tsp onion powder
- 1 tsp garlic powder
- Salt and black pepper to the taste
- For the Pico de gallo:
- 1 small red onion, chopped
- 2 tomatoes, chopped
- 2 garlic cloves, minced
- 2 tbsp lime juice
- 1 small green bell pepper, chopped
- 1 jalapeno, chopped
- ¼ cup cilantro, chopped
- ¼ tsp

DIRECTIONS:
In a bowl, mix chili powder with a pinch of salt, black pepper, onion powder, garlic powder, paprika and 1 tsp cumin, stir well, season steaks with this mix, put them in your air fryer and cook at 360 degrees F for 10 minutes. In a bowl, mix red onion with tomatoes, garlic, lime juice, bell pepper, jalapeno, cilantro, black pepper to the taste and ¼ tsp cumin and toss. Top steaks with this mix and serve right away

NUTRITION:
calories 200, fat 12, fiber 4, carbs 15, protein 18

COFFEE RIB EYE STEAKS
Preparation time: 10 min | Cooking time: 15 min | Servings: 4

INGREDIENTS:

- 1 and ½ tbsp coffee, ground
- 4 rib eye steaks
- ½ tbsp sweet paprika
- 2 tbsp chili powder
- 2 tsp garlic powder
- 2 tsp onion powder
- ¼ tsp ginger, ground
- ¼ tsp, coriander, ground
- A pinch of cayenne pepper
- Black pepper to the taste

DIRECTIONS:
In a bowl, mix coffee with paprika, chili powder, garlic powder, onion powder, ginger, coriander, cayenne and black pepper, stir, rub steaks with this mix, put in preheated air fryer and cook at 360 degrees F for 15 minutes. Divide steaks on plates and serve with a side salad.

NUTRITION:
calories 160, fat 10, fiber 8, carbs 14, protein 12

FILET MIGNON AND COCONUT SAUCE
Preparation time: 10 min | Cooking time: 25 min | Servings: 4

INGREDIENTS:

- 12 mushrooms, sliced
- 1 shallot, chopped
- 4 fillet mignons
- 2 garlic cloves, minced
- 2 tbsp olive oil
- ¼ cup Dijon mustard
- ¼ cup wine
- 1 and ¼ cup coconut cream
- 2 tbsp parsley, chopped
- Salt and black pepper to the taste

DIRECTIONS:
Heat up a pan with the oil over medium high heat, add garlic and shallots, stir and cook for 3 minutes. Add mushrooms, stir and cook for 4 minutes more. Add wine, stir and cook until it evaporates. Add coconut cream, mustard, parsley, a pinch of salt and black pepper to the taste, stir, cook for 6

minutes more and take off heat. Season fillets with salt and pepper, put them in your air fryer and cook at 360 degrees F for 10 minutes. Divide fillets on plates and serve with the mushroom sauce on top.

NUTRITION:
calories 340, fat 12, fiber 1, carbs 14, protein 23

BEEF AND ZUCCHINI KABOBS

Preparation time: 10 min | Cooking time: 10 min | Servings: 4

INGREDIENTS:

- 2 red bell peppers, chopped
- 2 pounds sirloin steak, cut into medium pieces
- 1 red onion, chopped
- 1 zucchini, sliced
- Juice form 1 lime
- 2 tbsp chili powder
- 2 tbsp hot sauce
- ½ tbsp cumin, ground
- ¼ cup olive oil
- ¼ cup salsa
- Salt and black pepper to the taste

DIRECTIONS:
In a bowl, mix salsa with lime juice, oil, hot sauce, chili powder, cumin, salt and black pepper and whisk well. Divide meat bell peppers, zucchini and onion on skewers, brush kabobs with the salsa mix you made earlier, put them in your preheated air fryer and cook them for 10 minutes at 370 degrees F flipping kabobs halfway. Divide among plates and serve with a side salad.

NUTRITION:
calories 170, fat 5, fiber 2, carbs 13, protein 16

MEDITERRANEAN SCALLOPS

Preparation time: 10 min | Cooking time: 14 min | Servings: 2

INGREDIENTS:

- 10 sea scallops
- 2 beef steaks
- 4 garlic cloves, minced
- 1 shallot, chopped
- 2 tbsp lemon juice
- 2 tbsp parsley, chopped
- 2 tbsp basil, chopped
- 1 tsp lemon zest
- ¼ cup butter
- ¼ cup veggie stock
- Salt and black pepper to the taste

DIRECTIONS:
Season steaks with salt and pepper, put them in your air fryer, cook at 360 degrees F for 10 minutes and transfer to a pan that fits the fryer. Add shallot, garlic, butter, stock, basil, lemon juice, parsley, lemon zest and scallops, toss everything gently and cook at 360 degrees F for 4 minutes more. Divide steaks and scallops on plates and serve.

NUTRITION:
calories 150, fat 2, fiber 2, carbs 14, protein 17

BEEF CHILI MEDALLIONS

Preparation time: 2 hours | Cooking time: 10 min | Servings: 4

INGREDIENTS:

- 2 tsp chili powder
- 1 cup tomatoes, crushed
- 4 beef medallions
- 2 tsp onion powder
- 2 tbsp soy sauce
- Salt and black pepper to the taste
- 1 tbsp hot pepper
- 2 tbsp lime juice

DIRECTIONS:
In a bowl, mix tomatoes with hot pepper, soy sauce, chili powder, onion powder, a pinch of salt, black pepper and lime juice and whisk well. Arrange beef medallions in a dish, pour sauce over them, toss and leave them aside for 2 hours. Discard tomato marinade, put beef in your preheated air fryer and cook at 360 degrees F for 10 minutes. Divide steaks on plates and serve with a side salad.

NUTRITION:
calories 230, fat 4, fiber 1, carbs 13, protein 14

BALSAMIC BEEF

Preparation time: 10 min | Cooking time: 1 hour | Servings: 6

INGREDIENTS:

- 1 medium beef roast
- 1 tbsp Worcestershire sauce
- ½ cup balsamic vinegar
- 1 cup beef stock
- 1 tbsp honey
- 1 tbsp soy sauce
- 4 garlic cloves, minced

DIRECTIONS:
In a heat proof dish that fits your air fryer, mix roast with roast with Worcestershire sauce, vinegar, stock, honey, soy sauce and garlic, toss well, introduce in your air fryer and cook at 370 degrees F for 1 hour. Slice roast, divide among plates, drizzle the sauce all over and serve.

NUTRITION:
calories 311, fat 7, fiber 12, carbs 20, protein 16

ROASTED PORK CHOPS AND PAPRIKA

Preparation time: 10 min | Cooking time: 16 min | Servings: 4

INGREDIENTS:

- 3 tbsp olive oil
- 3 tbsp lemon juice
- 1 tbsp smoked paprika
- 2 tbsp thyme, chopped
- 3 garlic cloves, minced
- 4 pork chops, bone in
- Salta and black pepper to the taste
- 2 roasted bell peppers, chopped

DIRECTIONS:
In a pan that fits your air fryer, mix pork chops with oil, lemon juice, smoked pa-

prika, thyme, garlic, bell peppers, salt and pepper, toss well, introduce in your air fryer and cook at 400 degrees F for 16 minutes. Divide pork chops and peppers mix on plates and serve right away.

Nutrition:
calories 321, fat 6, fiber 8, carbs 14, protein 17

SAGE PORK CHOPS AND BEANS

Preparation time: 10 min | Cooking time: 15 min | Servings: 4

Ingredients:

- 4 pork chops, bone in
- 2 tbsp olive oil
- 1 tbsp sage, chopped
- Salt and black pepper to the taste
- 16 ounces green beans
- 3 garlic cloves, minced
- 2 tbsp parsley, chopped

Directions:
In a pan that fits your air fryer, mix pork chops with olive oil, sage, salt, pepper, green beans, garlic and parsley, toss, introduce in your air fryer and cook at 360 degrees F for 15 minutes. Divide everything on plates and serve.

Nutrition:
calories 261, fat 7, fiber 9, carbs 14, protein 20

BUTTERED PORK CHOPS

Preparation time: 10 min | Cooking time: 15 min | Servings: 2

Ingredients:

- 2 pork chops
- Salt and black pepper to the taste
- 1 tbsp olive oil
- 2 tbsp butter
- 1 shallot, sliced
- 1 handful sage, chopped
- 1 tsp lemon juice

Directions:
Season pork chops with salt and pepper, rub with the oil, put in your air fryer and cook at 370 degrees F for 10 minutes, flipping them halfway. Meanwhile, heat up a pan with the butter over medium heat, add shallot, stir and cook for 2 minutes. Add sage and lemon juice, stir well, cook for a few more minutes and take off heat. Divide pork chops on plates, drizzle sage sauce all over and serve.

Nutrition:
calories 265, fat 6, fiber 8, carbs 19, protein 12

ONION HAM AND COLLARD GREENS

Preparation time: 10 min | Cooking time: 16 min | Servings: 8

Ingredients:

- 2 tbsp olive oil
- 4 cups ham, chopped
- 2 tbsp flour
- 3 cups chicken stock
- 5 ounces onion, chopped
- 16 ounces collard greens, chopped
- 14 ounces canned black eyed peas, drained
- ½ tsp red pepper, crushed

Directions:
Drizzle the oil in a pan that fits your air fryer, add ham, stock and flour and whisk. Also add onion, black eyed peas, red pepper and collard greens, introduce in your air fryer and cook at 390 degrees F for 16 minutes. Divide everything on plates and serve.

Nutrition:
calories 322, fat 6, fiber 8, carbs 12, protein 5

AIR FRIED HAM MIX

Preparation time: 10 min | Cooking time: 20 min | Servings: 6

Ingredients:

- ¼ cup butter
- ¼ cup flour
- 3 cups milk
- ½ tsp thyme, dried
- 2 cups ham, chopped
- 6 ounces sweet peas
- 4 ounces mushrooms, halved
- 1 cup baby carrots

Directions:
Heat up a large pan that fits your air fryer with the butter over medium heat, melt it, add flour and whisk well. Add milk and, well again and take off heat. Add thyme, ham, peas, mushrooms and baby carrots, toss, put in your air fryer and cook at 360 degrees F for 20 minutes. Divide everything on plates and serve.

Nutrition:
calories 311, fat 6, fiber 8, carbs 12, protein 7

AIR FRYER VEGETABLE RECIPES

CREAMY SPINACH MIX
Preparation time: 5 min | Cooking time: 8 min | Servings: 4

Ingredients:

- 14 ounces baby spinach
- 1 tbsp olive oil
- 2 tbsp milk
- 3 ounces cream cheese, softened
- Salt and black pepper to taste
- 1 yellow onion, chopped

Directions:
In a pan that fits your air fryer, mix all ingredients and toss gently. Place the pan in the air fryer and cook at 260 degrees F for 8 minutes. Divide between plates and serve.

Nutrition:
calories 190, fat 4, fiber 2, carbs 13, protein 9

BALSAMIC LIME ASPARAGUS
Preparation time: 5 min | Cooking time: 5 min | Servings: 4

Ingredients:

- 1 asparagus bunch, trimmed and halved
- Salt and black pepper to taste
- 2 tbsp lime juice
- 2 tbsp olive oil
- 2 tsp balsamic vinegar
- 1 tsp oregano, dried

Directions:
In a bowl, combine all ingredients and toss. Put the asparagus in your air fryer's basket and cook at 400 degrees F for 5 minutes. Divide the asparagus between plates and serve.

Nutrition:
calories 190, fat 3, fiber 6, carbs 8, protein 4

CHEESY ASPARAGUS
Preparation time: 5 min | Cooking time: 6 min | Servings: 6

Ingredients:

- 14 ounces asparagus, trimmed
- 8 ounces cream cheese, softened
- 16 ounces cheddar cheese, grated
- ½ cup sour cream
- 3 garlic cloves, minced
- 1 tsp garlic powder

Directions:
In a pan that fits your air fryer, the mix asparagus with the cream cheese, sour cream, garlic powder, and garlic; toss. Sprinkle the cheddar cheese on top, and then place the pan in the fryer. Cook at 400 degrees F for 6 minutes. Divide between plates and serve.

Nutrition:
calories 191, fat 8, fiber 2, carbs 12, protein 8

SIMPLE FENNEL MIX
Preparation time: 10 min | Cooking time: 12 min | Servings: 2

Ingredients:

- 2 fennel bulbs, trimmed and halved
- A drizzle of olive oil
- 2 garlic cloves, minced
- 1 tbsp lime juice
- 1 tsp sweet paprika

Directions:
In a bowl, combine all ingredients and toss. Put the fennel in your air fryer's basket and cook at 400 degrees F for 12 minutes. Divide between plates and serve.

Nutrition:
calories 131, fat 4, fiber 7, carbs 10, protein 8

BEETS IN CILANTRO
Preparation time: 5 min | Cooking time: 20 min | Servings: 4

Ingredients:

- 4 beets, peeled and cut into wedges
- 2 tbsp balsamic vinegar
- 1 tbsp cilantro, chopped
- Salt and black pepper to taste
- 1 tbsp olive oil
- 2 tbsp capers

Directions:
Put the beet wedges in your air fryer's basket and cook at 400 degrees F for 20 minutes. Transfer the beet wedges to a salad bowl, and then add the remaining ingredients. Toss, serve, and enjoy.

Nutrition:
calories 70, fat 1, fiber 1, carbs 6, protein 4

SESAME BEETS
Preparation time: 10 min | Cooking time: 20 min | Servings: 6

Ingredients:

- 6 beets, peeled and quartered
- Salt and black pepper to taste
- 1 tbsp sesame seeds, toasted
- 1 tbsp red wine vinegar
- 1 tbsp olive oil

Directions:
Put the beets in your air fryer's basket and cook at 400 degrees F for 20 minutes. Transfer the beets to a bowl, and add all remaining ingredients. Toss and serve.

Nutrition:
calories 100, fat 2, fiber 4, carbs 7, protein 5

BEETS AND SCALLIONS MIX
Preparation time: 5 min | Cooking time: 20 min | Servings: 4

Ingredients:

- 1½ pounds beets, peeled and quar-

- tered
- 1 tbsp olive oil
- 2 tbsp balsamic vinegar
- ½ cup orange juice
- Salt and black pepper to taste
- 2 scallions, chopped
- 2 cups kale leaves

DIRECTIONS:
Put the beets in your air fryer's basket and cook at 400 degrees F for 15 minutes. Add the kale leaves and cook for another 5 minutes. Transfer the beets and kale to a bowl and add all remaining ingredients. Toss, serve, and enjoy.

NUTRITION:
calories 151, fat 2, fiber 3, carbs 9, protein 4

CHERRY TOMATO SALAD
Preparation time: 5 min | Cooking time: 25 min | Servings: 6

INGREDIENTS:

- 8 small beets, trimmed, peeled and cut into wedges
- 1 red onion, sliced
- 1 tbsp balsamic vinegar
- Salt and black pepper to taste
- 1 pint mixed cherry tomatoes, halved
- 2 ounces pecans, chopped
- 2 tbsp olive oil

DIRECTIONS:
Put the beets in your air fryer's basket, and add the salt, pepper, and 1 tbsp of the oil. Cook at 400 degrees F for 15 minutes. Transfer the beets to a pan that fits your air fryer, and add the onions, tomatoes, pecans, and remaining 1 tbsp of the oil; toss well. Cook at 400 degrees F for 10 more minutes. Divide between plates and serve.

NUTRITION:
calories 144, fat 7, fiber 5, carbs 8, protein 6

CAULIFLOWER PEANUT MIX
Preparation time: 5 min | Cooking time: 7 min | Servings: 4

INGREDIENTS:

- 1 cauliflower head, florets separated
- 1 tbsp peanut oil
- 6 garlic cloves, minced
- 1 tbsp Chinese rice wine vinegar
- Salt and black pepper to taste

DIRECTIONS:
Mix all ingredients in a bowl. Put the mixture in the fryer and cook at 400 degrees F for 7 minutes. Divide between plates and serve.

NUTRITION:
calories 141, fat 3, fiber 4, carbs 4, protein 2

BROCCOLI AND SCALLIONS
Preparation time: 5 min | Cooking time: 7 min | Servings: 4

INGREDIENTS:

- 1 broccoli head, florets separated
- Salt and black pepper to taste
- 6 cherry tomatoes, halved
- ¼ cup scallions, chopped
- 1 tbsp olive oil

DIRECTIONS:
Put the broccoli florets in your air fryer's basket, and add the salt, pepper, and ½ tbsp of the oil; toss well. Cook at 380 degrees F for 7 minutes. Transfer the broccoli to a bowl, and add the tomatoes, scallions, salt, pepper, and the remaining ½ tbsp of oil. Toss and serve.

NUTRITION:
calories 111, fat 4, fiber 4, carbs 9, protein 2

CILANTRO BRUSSELS SPROUTS
Preparation time: 5 min | Cooking time: 15 min | Servings: 4

INGREDIENTS:

- 1 pound Brussels sprouts, trimmed
- Salt and black pepper to taste
- 1 tbsp mustard
- 1 tbsp olive oil
- 2 tbsp cilantro, chopped

DIRECTIONS:
In a bowl, mix the sprouts with the salt, pepper, mustard, and the oil; toss well. Transfer the sprouts to your air fryer's basket and cook at 380 degrees F for 15 minutes. Divide the sprouts between plates, sprinkle the cilantro on top, and serve.

NUTRITION:
calories 122, fat 2, fiber 2, carbs 9, protein 4

CHEESE BROCCOLI
Preparation time: 5 min | Cooking time: 8 min | Servings: 4

INGREDIENTS:

- 1 broccoli head, florets separated
- Juice of 1 lime
- Salt and black pepper to taste
- 2 tbsp olive oil
- 3 tbsp parmesan cheese, grated

DIRECTIONS:
Put the broccoli in your air fryer's basket; add the salt, pepper, and the oil, and toss. Cook at 400 degrees F for 8 minutes. Transfer the broccoli to a bowl, add the lime juice and parmesan, toss, and serve.

NUTRITION:
calories 122, fat 3, fiber 6, carbs 8, protein 9

BALSAMIC RED CABBAGE
Preparation time: 5 min | Cooking time: 8 min | Servings: 4

INGREDIENTS:

- 1 red cabbage head, shredded
- 1 tbsp olive oil
- 1 carrot, grated
- ¼ cup balsamic vinegar
- Salt and black pepper to taste

DIRECTIONS:
Place all ingredients in a pan that fits your air fryer, and mix well. Put the pan in the fryer and cook at 380 degrees F for 8 minutes. Divide between plates and serve.

NUTRITION:
calories 100, fat 4, fiber 2, carbs 7, protein 2

BUTTER CARROTS
Preparation time: 5 min | Cooking time: 15 min | Servings: 4

INGREDIENTS:

- 1 pound carrots, cut into wedges
- A pinch of salt and black pepper
- 1 tsp sweet paprika
- ½ tbsp butter, melted

DIRECTIONS:
In a bowl, combine all of the ingredients and toss well. Put the carrots in your air fryer and cook at 350 degrees F for 15 minutes. Divide between plates and serve.

NUTRITION:
calories 90, fat 2, fiber 3, carbs 4, protein 4

GARLIC BEANS MIX
Preparation time: 5 min | Cooking time: 6 min | Servings: 4

INGREDIENTS:

- 1 pound green beans, trimmed
- 2 tbsp olive oil
- 3 garlic cloves, minced
- Salt and black pepper to taste
- 1 tbsp balsamic vinegar

DIRECTIONS:
Place all of the ingredients in a bowl, except the vinegar, and mix well. Put the beans in your air fryer and cook at 400 degrees F for 6 minutes. Divide the green beans between plates, drizzle the vinegar all over, and serve.

NUTRITION:
calories 101, fat 3, fiber 3, carbs 4, protein 2

CHILI KALE MIX
Preparation time: 5 min | Cooking time: 12 min | Servings: 6

INGREDIENTS:

- 2 tbsp olive oil
- 3 garlic cloves, minced
- 2½ pounds kale leaves
- Salt and black pepper to taste
- 2 tbsp balsamic vinegar
- 1 tbsp chili powder
- ½ tsp crushed red pepper

DIRECTIONS:
In a bowl, mix the kale with salt, pepper, oil, red pepper, and chili powder; toss well. Transfer the kale to your air fryer and cook at 250 degrees F for 12 minutes. Put the kale leaves in a bowl, add the garlic and the vinegar, and toss. Serve, and enjoy!

NUTRITION:
calories 102, fat 4, fiber 8, carbs 4, protein 2

OREGANO EGGPLANTS MIX
Preparation time: 5 min | Cooking time: 15 min | Servings: 4

INGREDIENTS:

- 4 eggplants, roughly cubed
- 2 tbsp lime juice
- Salt and black pepper to taste
- 1 tsp oregano, dried
- 2 tbsp olive oil

DIRECTIONS:
Place all of the ingredients in a pan that fits your air fryer and mix / toss well. Put the pan into the fryer and cook at 400 degrees F for 15 minutes. Divide the eggplants between plates and serve.

NUTRITION:
calories 125, fat 5, fiber 2, carbs 11, protein 5

CREAMY GREEK POTATOES
Preparation time: 5 min | Cooking time: 15 min | Servings: 4

INGREDIENTS:

- 1½ pounds potatoes, peeled and cubed
- 1 tbsp olive oil
- Salt and black pepper to taste
- 1 tbsp hot paprika
- 2 tbsp black olives, pitted and sliced
- 1 cup Greek yogurt

DIRECTIONS:
In a bowl, mix the potatoes with the oil, salt, pepper, and paprika; toss well. Put the potatoes in your air fryer's basket and cook at 400 degrees F for 15 minutes. Place the potatoes in a serving dish, and add the yogurt and the black olives. Toss, serve, and enjoy.

NUTRITION:
calories 140, fat 3, fiber 4, carbs 10, protein 4

COCONUT MIX
Preparation time: 5 min | Cooking time: 8 min | Servings: 8

INGREDIENTS:

- 1 pound brown mushrooms, halved
- 1 small yellow onion, chopped
- Salt and black pepper to taste
- 2 tbsp olive oil
- 14 ounces coconut milk

DIRECTIONS:
Add all ingredients to a pan that fits your air fryer and mix well. Place the pan in the fryer and cook at 400 degrees F for 8 minutes. Divide between plates and serve.

NUTRITION:
calories 202, fat 4, fiber 1, carbs 13, protein 4

SPICY PEARL ONIONS

Preparation time: 5 min | Cooking time: 10 min | Servings: 8

INGREDIENTS:

- 1 pound pearl onions, trimmed
- 3 ounces feta cheese, crumbled
- 1 tbsp olive oil
- A pinch of salt and black pepper
- 2 tbsp oregano, chopped

DIRECTIONS:
In a bowl, mix the onions with the salt, pepper, and oil. Transfer the contents to your air fryer and cook at 400 degrees F for 10 minutes. Transfer the onions to a bowl, add the oregano and the cheese, toss, and serve.

NUTRITION:
calories 140, fat 4, fiber 2, carbs 9, protein 5

GOAT CHEESE SPROUTS

Preparation time: 5 min | Cooking time: 15 min | Servings: 8

INGREDIENTS:

- 1 pound Brussels sprouts, trimmed
- 1 tbsp olive oil
- Salt and black pepper to taste
- 3 ounces goat cheese, crumbled

DIRECTIONS:
In a bowl, mix the sprouts with the oil, salt, and pepper; toss well. Put the sprouts in your air fryer's basket and cook at 380 degrees F for 15 minutes. Divide between plates, sprinkle the cheese on top, and serve.

NUTRITION:
calories 150, fat 3, fiber 4, carbs 4, protein 6

TARRAGON GREEN BEANS
Preparation time: 5 min | Cooking time: 7 min | Servings: 4

INGREDIENTS:

- 1 pound green beans, trimmed
- 1 tbsp tarragon, chopped
- Zest of 2 lemons
- 1 tbsp olive oil
- Salt and black pepper to taste

DIRECTIONS:
In a bowl, mix the green beans with the lemon zest, oil, salt, and pepper; toss well. Put the beans in your air fryer and cook at 400 degrees F for 7 minutes. Divide the beans between plates, sprinkle the tarragon on top, and serve.

NUTRITION:
calories 181, fat 7, fiber 4, carbs 9, protein 3

OREGANO AND ZUCCHINI MIX

Preparation time: 5 min | Cooking time: 12 min | Servings: 4

INGREDIENTS:

- 4 zucchinis, sliced
- Salt and black pepper to taste
- 2 tbsp lime juice
- 2 tbsp olive oil
- 2 tsp balsamic vinegar
- 1 tsp oregano, dried

DIRECTIONS:
In a pan that fits your air fryer, mix all the ingredients well. Place the pan in the fryer and cook at 400 degrees F for 12 minutes. Divide the mix between plates and serve.

NUTRITION:
calories 100, fat 1, fiber 3, carbs 8, protein 4

ARTICHOKES AND PARMESAN MAYO

Preparation time: 5 min | Cooking time: 15 min | Servings: 6
Ingredients:

- 14 ounces canned artichoke hearts
- A drizzle of olive oil
- 16 ounces parmesan cheese, grated
- 3 garlic cloves, minced
- ½ cup mayonnaise
- 1 tsp garlic powder

DIRECTIONS:
In a pan that fits your air fryer, mix the artichokes with the oil, garlic, and garlic powder, and then toss well. Place the pan in the fryer and cook at 350 degrees F for 15 minutes. Cool the mix down, add the mayo, and toss. Divide between plates, sprinkle the parmesan on top, and serve.

NUTRITION:
calories 200, fat 11, fiber 3, carbs 9, protein 4

ARTICHOKES WITH COCONUT

Preparation time: 5 min | Cooking time: 15 min | Servings: 2

INGREDIENTS:

- 2 artichokes, washed, trimmed and halved
- 2 garlic cloves, minced
- ¼ cup coconut, shredded
- Juice of 1 lemon
- 1 tbsp coconut oil, melted

DIRECTIONS:

In a bowl, mix the artichokes with the garlic, oil, and lemon juice; toss well. Put the artichokes into your air fryer and cook at 360 degrees F for 15 minutes. Divide the artichokes between plates, sprinkle the coconut on top, and serve. Enjoy!

NUTRITION:
calories 213, fat 8, fiber 6, carbs 13, protein 6

ASPARAGUS AND PROSCIUTTO

Preparation time: 5 min | Cooking time: 5 min | Servings: 4

INGREDIENTS:

- 8 asparagus spears, trimmed
- 8 ounces prosciutto slices
- A pinch of salt and black pepper

DIRECTIONS:
Wrap the asparagus in prosciutto slices and then season with salt and pepper. Put all in your air fryer's basket and cook at 400 degrees F for 5 minutes. Divide between plates and serve.

NUTRITION:
calories 100, fat 2, fiber 5, carbs 8, protein 4

CAJUN ASPARAGUS
Preparation time: 5 min | Cooking time: 5 min | Servings: 4

INGREDIENTS:

- 1 tsp extra virgin olive oil
- 1 bunch asparagus, trimmed
- ½ tbsp Cajun seasoning

DIRECTIONS:
In a bowl, mix the asparagus with the oil and Cajun seasoning; coat the asparagus well. Put the asparagus in your air fryer and cook at 400 degrees F for 5 minutes. Divide between plates and serve.

NUTRITION:
calories 151, fat 3, fiber 4, carbs 9, protein 4

BUTTERNUT SQUASH SALAD
Preparation time: 5 min | Cooking time: 12 min | Servings: 4

INGREDIENTS:

- 1 butternut squash, cubed
- 2 tbsp balsamic vinegar
- 1 bunch cilantro, chopped
- Salt and black pepper to taste
- 1 tbsp olive oil

DIRECTIONS:
Put the squash in your air fryer, and add the salt, pepper, and oil; toss well. Cook at 400 degrees F for 12 minutes. Transfer the squash to a bowl, add the vinegar and cilantro, and toss. Serve and enjoy!

NUTRITION:
calories 151, fat 4, fiber 7, carbs 11, protein 8

SOUR CREAM SQUASH MIX
Preparation time: 5 min | Cooking time: 12 min | Servings: 6

INGREDIENTS:

- 1 big butternut squash, roughly cubed
- 1 cup sour cream
- Salt and black pepper to taste
- 1 tbsp parsley, chopped
- A drizzle of olive oil

DIRECTIONS:
Put the squash in your air fryer, add the salt and pepper, and rub with the oil. Cook at 400 degrees F for 12 minutes. Transfer the squash to a bowl, and add the cream and the parsley. Toss and serve.

NUTRITION:
calories 200, fat 7, fiber 6, carbs 11, protein 7

ZESTY CARROTS
Preparation time: 5 min | Cooking time: 15 min | Servings: 4

INGREDIENTS:

- 1½ pounds baby carrots
- 2 tsp orange zest
- 2 tbsp cider vinegar
- ½ cup orange juice
- A handful of parsley, chopped
- A drizzle of olive oil

DIRECTIONS:
Put the baby carrots in your air fryer's basket, add the orange zest and oil, and rub the carrots well. Cook at 350 degrees F for 15 minutes. Transfer the carrots to a bowl, and then add the vinegar, orange juice, and parsley. Toss, serve, and enjoy!

NUTRITION:
calories 151, fat 6, fiber 6, carbs 11, protein 5

CHERRY TOMATOES AND FETA SALAD
Preparation time: 5 min | Cooking time: 5 min | Servings: 8

INGREDIENTS:

- 1 red onion, sliced
- 2 ounces feta cheese, crumbled
- Salt and black pepper to taste
- 1 pint mixed cherry tomatoes, halved
- 2 ounces pecans
- 2 tbsp olive oil

DIRECTIONS:
In your air fryer, mix the tomatoes with the salt, pepper, onions, and the oil. Cook at 400 degrees F for 5 minutes. Transfer to a bowl and add the pecans and the cheese. Toss and serve.

NUTRITION:
calories 151, fat 4, fiber 6, carbs 9, protein 4

GREEN BEANS AND CHILI SALAD
Preparation time: 5 min | Cooking time: 6 min | Servings: 4

INGREDIENTS:

- 1 pound green beans, trimmed and halved
- 2 green onions, chopped
- 5 ounces canned green chilies, chopped
- 1 jalapeno pepper, chopped
- A drizzle of olive oil
- 2 tsp chili powder
- 1 tsp garlic powder
- Salt and black pepper to taste
- 8 cherry tomatoes, halved

DIRECTIONS:
Place all ingredients in a pan that fits your air fryer, and mix / toss. Put the pan in the fryer and cook at 400 degrees F for 6 minutes. Divide the mix between plates and serve hot.

NUTRITION:
calories 200, fat 4, fiber 7, carbs 12, protein 6

BELL PEPPERS AND KALE LEAVES
Preparation time: 5 min | Cooking time: 15 min | Servings: 4

INGREDIENTS:

- 2 red bell peppers, cut into strips
- 2 green bell peppers, cut into strips
- ½ pound kale leaves
- Salt and black pepper to taste
- 2 yellow onions, roughly chopped
- ¼ cup veggie stock
- 2 tbsp tomato sauce

DIRECTIONS:
Add all ingredients to a pan that fits your air fryer; mix well. Place the pan in the fryer and cook at 360 degrees F for 15 minutes. Divide between plates, serve, and enjoy!

NUTRITION:
calories 161, fat 7, fiber 6, carbs 12, protein 7

GARLIC PARSNIPS
Preparation time: 5 min | Cooking time: 15 min | Servings: 4

INGREDIENTS:

- 1 pound parsnips, cut into chunks
- 1 tbsp olive oil
- 6 garlic cloves, minced
- 1 tbsp balsamic vinegar
- Salt and black pepper to taste

DIRECTIONS:
Add all of the ingredients to a bowl and mix well. Place them in the air fryer and cook at 380 degrees F for 15 minutes. Divide between plates and serve.

NUTRITION:
calories 121, fat 3, fiber 6, carbs 12, protein 6

FLORETS AND POMEGRANATE
Preparation time: 5 min | Cooking time: 7 min | Servings: 4

Ingredients:

- 1 broccoli head, florets separated
- Salt and black pepper to taste
- 1 pomegranate, seeds separated
- A drizzle of olive oil

DIRECTIONS:
In a bowl, mix the broccoli with the salt, pepper, and oil; toss. Put the florets in your air fryer and cook at 400 degrees F for 7 minutes. Divide between plates, sprinkle the pomegranate seeds all over, and serve.

NUTRITION:
calories 141, fat 3, fiber 4, carbs 11, protein 4

BACON AND CAULIFLOWER MIX
Preparation time: 5 min | Cooking time: 12 min | Servings: 4

INGREDIENTS:

- 1 cauliflower head, florets separated
- 1 tbsp olive oil
- Salt and black pepper to taste
- ½ cup bacon, cooked and chopped
- 2 tbsp dill, chopped

DIRECTIONS:
Put the cauliflower in your air fryer and add the salt, pepper, and oil; toss well. Cook at 400 degrees F for 12 minutes. Divide the cauliflower between plates, sprinkle the bacon and the dill on top, and serve.

NUTRITION:
calories 200, fat 7, fiber 5, carbs 17, protein 7

LIME BROCCOLI
Preparation time: 5 min | Cooking time: 6 min | Servings: 4

INGREDIENTS:

- 1 broccoli head, florets separated
- 1 tbsp lime juice
- Salt and black pepper to taste
- 2 tbsp butter, melted

DIRECTIONS:
In a bowl, mix well all of the ingredients. Put the broccoli mixture in your air fryer and cook at 400 degrees F for 6 minutes. Serve hot.

NUTRITION:
calories 151, fat 4, fiber 7, carbs 12, protein 6

NEW POTATOES DISH
Preparation time: 5 min | Cooking time: 15 min | Servings: 4

INGREDIENTS:

- 1 pound new potatoes, halved
- Salt and black pepper to taste
- 1½ tbsp butter, melted
- 1 tbsp dill, chopped

DIRECTIONS:
Put the potatoes in your air fryer's basket, and add the salt, pepper, and butter; toss well. Cook at 400 degrees F for 15 minutes. Divide between plates, sprinkle the dill on top, and serve.

NUTRITION:
calories 171, fat 5, fiber 6, carbs 15, protein 8

NUTMEG NAPA CABBAGE
Preparation time: 5 min | Cooking time: 12 min | Servings: 4

INGREDIENTS:

- 1 napa cabbage, shredded
- 1 yellow onion, chopped
- 2 tbsp tomato sauce
- ¼ tsp nutmeg, ground
- Salt and black pepper to taste
- 1 tbsp parsley, chopped

DIRECTIONS:
Add all of the ingredients to a pan that fits your air fryer and mix well. Place the pan in the fryer and cook at 300 degrees F for 12 minutes. Divide between plates and serve.

NUTRITION:
calories 154, fat 4, fiber 4, carbs 12, protein 5

SWEET PAPRIKA CABBAGE MIX
Preparation time: 5 min | Cooking time: 12 min | Servings: 8

INGREDIENTS:

- 1 green cabbage head, shredded
- ¼ cup butter, melted
- 1 tbsp sweet paprika
- 1 tbsp dill, chopped

DIRECTIONS:
Mix all of the ingredients in a pan that fits your air fryer. Place the pan in the fryer and cook at 320 degrees F for 12 minutes. Divide everything between plates, serve, and enjoy!

NUTRITION:
calories 181, fat 4, fiber 6, carbs 15, protein 5

TURMERIC MIX
Preparation time: 5 min | Cooking time: 12 min | Servings: 2

INGREDIENTS:

- 3 tbsp butter, melted
- 2 cups kale leaves
- Salt and black pepper to taste
- ½ cup yellow onion, chopped
- 2 tsp turmeric powder

DIRECTIONS:
Place all ingredients in a pan that fits your air fryer and mix well. Put the pan in the fryer and cook at 250 degrees F for 12 minutes. Divide between plates and serve.

NUTRITION:
calories 151, fat 4, fiber 5, carbs 15, protein 6

GREEN CAYENNE CABBAGE
Preparation time: 5 min | Cooking time: 12 min | Servings: 4

INGREDIENTS:

- 1 green cabbage head, shredded
- 1 tbsp olive oil
- 1 tsp cayenne pepper
- A pinch of salt and black pepper
- 2 tsp sweet paprika

DIRECTIONS:
Mix all of the ingredients in a pan that fits your fryer. Place the pan in the fryer and cook at 320 degrees F for 12 minutes. Divide between plates and serve right away.

NUTRITION:
calories 124, fat 6, fiber 6, carbs 16, protein 7

EASY CELERY ROOT MIX
Preparation time: 5 min | Cooking time: 15 min | Servings: 4

Ingredients:

- 2 cups celery root, roughly cubed
- A pinch of salt
- and black pepper
- ½ tbsp butter, melted

DIRECTIONS:
Put all of the ingredients in your air fryer and toss. Cook at 350 degrees F for 15 minutes. Divide between plates and serve.

NUTRITION:
calories 124, fat 1, fiber 4, carbs 6, protein 6

MAPLE CORN
Preparation time: 5 min | Cooking time: 6 min | Servings: 4

INGREDIENTS:

- 4 ears of corn
- 1 tbsp maple syrup
- Black pepper to taste
- 1 tbsp butter, melted

DIRECTIONS:
Combine the black pepper, butter, and the maple syrup in a bowl. Rub the corn with the mixture, and then put it in your air fryer. Cook at 390 degrees F for 6 minutes. Divide the corn between plates and serve.

NUTRITION:
calories 100, fat 2, fiber 3, carbs 8, protein 3

DILL BUTTERY CORN
Preparation time: 5 min | Cooking time: 6 min | Servings: 4

INGREDIENTS:

- 4 ears of corn
- Salt and black pepper to taste
- 2 tbsp butter, melted
- 2 tbsp dill, chopped

DIRECTIONS:
In a bowl, combine the salt, pepper, and the butter. Rub the corn with the butter mixture, and then put it in your air fryer. Cook at 390 degrees F for 6 minutes. Divide the corn between plates, sprinkle the dill on top, and serve.

NUTRITION:
calories 100, fat 2, fiber 5, carbs 9, protein 6

FETTUCCHINE CASSEROLE

Preparation time: 5 min | Cooking time: 15 min | Servings: 4

INGREDIENTS:

- 2 tbsp butter, melted
- 6 cups broccoli florets
- 2 garlic cloves, minced
- 1 cup chicken stock
- Salt and black pepper to taste
- 1 pound fettuccine pasta, cooked
- 2 green onions, chopped
- 1 tbsp parmesan cheese, grated
- 3 tomatoes, chopped

DIRECTIONS:

Use the butter to grease a baking dish that fits your air fryer. Add the broccoli, garlic, stock, salt, pepper, pasta, onions, and tomatoes; toss gently. Place the dish in the fryer and cook at 390 degrees F for 15 minutes. Sprinkle the parmesan on top, divide everything between plates, and serve.

NUTRITION:

calories 151, fat 6, fiber 5, carbs 12, protein 4

COLLARD GREENS MIX

Preparation time: 5 min | Cooking time: 12 min | Servings: 6

INGREDIENTS:

- 1 pound collard greens, trimmed
- ¼ pound bacon, cooked and chopped
- A drizzle of olive oil
- Salt and black pepper to taste
- ½ cup veggie stock

DIRECTIONS:

Place all ingredients in a pan that fits your air fryer and mix well. Put the pan in the fryer and cook at 260 degrees F for 12 minutes. Divide everything between plates and serve.

NUTRITION:

calories 161, fat 4, fiber 5, carbs 14, protein 3

TOMATO AND BALSAMIC GREENS

Preparation time: 5 min | Cooking time: 12 min | Servings: 4

INGREDIENTS:

- 1 bunch mustard greens, trimmed
- 2 tbsp olive oil
- ½ cup chicken stock
- 2 tbsp tomato puree
- 3 garlic cloves, minced
- Salt and black pepper to taste
- 1 tbsp balsamic vinegar

DIRECTIONS:

Combine all ingredients in a pan that fits your air fryer and toss well. Place the pan in the fryer and cook at 260 degrees F for 12 minutes. Divide everything between plates, serve, and enjoy!

NUTRITION:

calories 151, fat 2, fiber 4, carbs 14, protein 4

LIME ENDIVES

Preparation time: 5 min | Cooking time: 10 min | Servings: 4

INGREDIENTS:

- 4 endives, trimmed and halved
- Salt and black pepper to taste
- 1 tbsp lime juice
- 1 tbsp butter, melted

DIRECTIONS:

Put the endives in your air fryer, and add the salt, pepper, lemon juice, and butter. Cook at 360 degrees F for 10 minutes. Divide between plates and serve.

NUTRITION:

calories 100, fat 3, fiber 4, carbs 8, protein 4

NUTMEG ENDIVES AND BACON

Preparation time: 5 min | Cooking time: 10 min | Servings: 4

INGREDIENTS:

- 4 endives, trimmed and halved
- Salt and black pepper to taste
- 1 tbsp olive oil
- 2 tbsp bacon, cooked and crumbled
- ½ tsp nutmeg, ground

DIRECTIONS:

Put the endives in your air fryer's basket, and add the salt, pepper, oil, and nutmeg; toss gently. Cook at 360 degrees F for 10 minutes. Divide the endives between plates, sprinkle the bacon on top, and serve.

NUTRITION:

calories 151, fat 6, fiber 8, carbs 14, protein 6

SPINACH MILKY PIE

Preparation time: 10 min | Cooking time: 15 min | Servings: 4

INGREDIENTS:

- 7 ounces flour
- 2 tbsp butter
- 7 ounces spinach
- 1 tbsp olive oil
- 2 eggs
- 2 tbsp milk
- 3 ounces cottage cheese
- Salt and black pepper to the taste
- 1 yellow onion, chopped

DIRECTIONS:

In your food processor, mix flour with butter, 1 egg, milk, salt and pepper, blend well, transfer to a bowl, knead, cover and leave for 10 minutes. Heat up a pan with the oil over medium high heat, add onion and spinach, stir and cook for 2 minutes. Add salt, pepper, the remaining egg and cottage cheese, stir well and take off heat. Divide dough in 4 pieces, roll each piece, place on the bottom of a ramekin, add spinach filling over dough, place ramekins in your air fryer's basket and cook at 360 degrees F for 15 minutes. Serve warm,

NUTRITION:
calories 250, fat 12, fiber 2, carbs 23, protein 12

OREGANO ARTICHOKES

Preparation time: 10 min | Cooking time: 7 min | Servings: 4

INGREDIENTS:

- 4 big artichokes, trimmed
- Salt and black pepper to the taste
- 2 tbsp lemon juice
- ¼ cup extra virgin olive oil
- 2 tsp balsamic vinegar
- 1 tsp oregano, dried
- 2 garlic cloves, minced

DIRECTIONS:
Season artichokes with salt and pepper, rub them with half of the oil and half of the lemon juice, put them in your air fryer and cook at 360 degrees F for 7 minutes. Meanwhile, in a bowl, mix the rest of the lemon juice with vinegar, the remaining oil, salt, pepper, garlic and oregano and stir very well. Arrange artichokes on a platter, drizzle the balsamic vinaigrette over them and serve.

NUTRITION:
calories 200, fat 3, fiber 6, carbs 12, protein 4

MOZZARELLA ARTICHOKES

Preparation time: 10 min | Cooking time: 6 min | Servings: 6

INGREDIENTS:

- 14 ounces canned artichoke hearts
- 8 ounces cream cheese
- 16 ounces parmesan cheese, grated
- 10 ounces spinach
- ½ cup chicken stock
- 8 ounces mozzarella, shredded
- ½ cup sour cream
- 3 garlic cloves, minced
- ½ cup mayonnaise
- 1 tsp onion powder

DIRECTIONS:
In a pan that fits your air fryer, mix artichokes with stock, garlic, spinach, cream cheese, sour cream, onion powder and mayo, toss, introduce in your air fryer and cook at 350 degrees F for 6 minutes. Add mozzarella and parmesan, stir well and serve.

NUTRITION:
calories 261, fat 12, fiber 2, carbs 12, protein 15

ARTICHOKES AND COCONUT SAUCE

Preparation time: 10 min | Cooking time: 6 min | Servings: 2

INGREDIENTS:

- 2 artichokes, trimmed
- A drizzle of olive oil
- 2 garlic cloves, minced
- 1 tbsp lemon juice
- For the sauce:
- ¼ cup coconut oil
- ¼ cup extra virgin olive oil
- 3 anchovy fillets
- 3 garlic cloves

DIRECTIONS:
In a bowl, mix artichokes with oil, 2 garlic cloves and lemon juice, toss well, transfer to your air fryer, cook at 350 degrees F for 6 minutes and divide among plates. In your food processor, mix coconut oil with anchovy, 3 garlic cloves and olive oil, blend very well, drizzle over artichokes and serve.

NUTRITION:
calories 261, fat 4, fiber 7, carbs 20, protein 12

BEET SALAD AND CAPERS

Preparation time: 10 min | Cooking time: 14 min | Servings: 4

INGREDIENTS:

- 4 beets
- 2 tbsp balsamic vinegar
- A bunch of parsley, chopped
- Salt and black pepper to the taste
- 1 tbsp extra virgin olive oil
- 1 garlic clove, chopped
- 2 tbsp capers

DIRECTIONS:
Put beets in your air fryer and cook them at 360 degrees F for 14 minutes. Meanwhile, in a bowl, mix parsley with garlic, salt, pepper, olive oil and capers and stir very well. Transfer beets to a cutting board, leave them to cool down, peel them, slice put them in a salad bowl. Add vinegar, drizzle the parsley dressing all over and serve.

NUTRITION:
calories 70, fat 2, fiber 1, carbs 6, protein 4

BLUE BEETS AND CHEESE SALAD

Preparation time: 10 min | Cooking time: 14 min | Servings: 6

INGREDIENTS:

- 6 beets, peeled and quartered
- Salt and black pepper to the taste
- ¼ cup blue cheese, crumbled
- 1 tbsp olive oil

DIRECTIONS:
Put beets in your air fryer, cook them at 350 degrees F for 14 minutes and transfer them to a bowl. Add blue cheese, salt, pepper and oil, toss and serve.

NUTRITION:
calories 100, fat 4, fiber 4, carbs 10, protein 5

SWEET BEETS AND ARUGULA

Preparation time: 10 min | Cooking time: 10 min | Servings: 4

INGREDIENTS:

- 1 and ½ pounds beets, peeled and quartered
- A drizzle of olive oil
- 2 tsp orange zest, grated
- 2 tbsp cider vinegar
- ½ cup orange juice
- 2 tbsp brown sugar
- 2 scallions, chopped
- 2 tsp mustard
- 2 cups arugula

DIRECTIONS:
Rub beets with the oil and orange juice, place them in your air fryer and cook at 350 degrees F for 10 minutes. Transfer beet quarters to a bowl, add scallions, arugula and orange zest and toss. In a separate bowl, mix sugar with mustard and vinegar, whisk well, add to salad, toss and serve.

NUTRITION:
calories 121, fat 2, fiber 3, carbs 11, protein 4

GOAT CHEESE AND VEGGIES MIX

Preparation time: 30 min | Cooking time: 14 min | Servings: 8

INGREDIENTS:

- 8 small beets, trimmed, peeled and halved
- 1 red onion, sliced
- 4 ounces goat cheese, crumbled
- 1 tbsp balsamic vinegar
- Salt and black pepper to the taste
- 2 tbsp sugar
- 1 pint mixed cherry tomatoes, halved
- 2 ounces pecans
- 2 tbsp olive oil

DIRECTIONS:
Put beets in your air fryer, season them with salt and pepper, cook at 350 degrees F for 14 minutes and transfer to a salad bowl. Add onion, cherry tomatoes and pecans and toss. In another bowl, mix vinegar with sugar and oil, whisk well until sugar dissolves and add to salad. Also add goat cheese, toss and serve.

NUTRITION:
calories 124, fat 7, fiber 5, carbs 12, protein 6

BROCCOLI FLORETS SALAD

Preparation time: 10 min | Cooking time: 8 min | Servings: 4

INGREDIENTS:

- 1 broccoli head, florets separated
- 1 tbsp peanut oil
- 6 garlic cloves, minced
- 1 tbsp Chinese rice wine vinegar
- Salt and black pepper to the taste

DIRECTIONS:
In a bowl, mix broccoli with salt, pepper and half of the oil, toss, transfer to your air fryer and cook at 350 degrees F for 8 minutes, shaking the fryer halfway. Transfer broccoli to a salad bowl, add the rest of the peanut oil, garlic and rice vinegar, toss really well and serve.

Nutrition: calories 121, fat 3, fiber 4, carbs 4, protein 4

GREEN BRUSSELS SPROUTS MIX

Preparation time: 5 min | Cooking time: 10 min | Servings: 4

INGREDIENTS:

- 1 pound Brussels sprouts, trimmed
- Salt and black pepper to the taste
- 6 cherry tomatoes, halved
- ¼ cup green onions, chopped
- 1 tbsp olive oil

DIRECTIONS:
Season Brussels sprouts with salt and pepper, put them in your air fryer and cook at 350 degrees F for 10 minutes. Transfer them to a bowl, add salt, pepper, cherry tomatoes, green onions and olive oil, toss well and serve.

NUTRITION:
calories 121, fat 4, fiber 4, carbs 11, protein 4

SPROUTS AND MUSTARD SAUCE

Preparation time: 4 min | Cooking time: 10 min | Servings: 4

INGREDIENTS:

- 1 pound Brussels sprouts, trimmed
- Salt and black pepper to the taste
- ½ cup bacon, cooked and chopped
- 1 tbsp mustard
- 1 tbsp butter
- 2 tbsp dill, finely chopped

DIRECTIONS:
Put Brussels sprouts in your air fryer and cook them at 350 degrees F for 10 minutes. Heat up a pan with the butter over medium high heat, add bacon, mustard and dill and whisk well. Divide Brussels sprouts on plates, drizzle butter sauce all over and serve.

NUTRITION:
calories 162, fat 8, fiber 8, carbs 14, protein 5

PARMESAN BRUSSELS SPROUTS

Preparation time: 10 min | Cooking time: 8 min | Servings: 4

INGREDIENTS:

- 1 pound Brussels sprouts, washed
- Juice of 1 lemon
- Salt and black pepper to the taste
- 2 tbsp butter
- 3 tbsp parmesan, grated

DIRECTIONS:
Put Brussels sprouts in your air fryer, cook them at 350 degrees F for 8 minutes and transfer them to a bowl. Heat up a pan with the butter over medium heat, add lemon juice, salt and pepper, whisk well and add to Brussels sprouts. Add parmesan, toss until parmesan melts and serve.

NUTRITION:
calories 152, fat 6, fiber 6, carbs 8, protein 12

SPICY CABBAGE AND CARROTS

Preparation time: 10 min | Cooking time: 8 min | Servings: 4

INGREDIENTS:

- 1 cabbage, cut into 8 wedges
- 1 tbsp sesame seed oil
- 1 carrots, grated
- ¼ cup apple cider vinegar
- ¼ cups apple juice
- ½ tsp cayenne pepper
- 1 tsp red pepper flakes, crushed

DIRECTIONS:
In a pan that fits your air fryer, combine cabbage with oil, carrot, vinegar, apple juice, cayenne and pepper flakes, toss, introduce in preheated air fryer and cook at 350 degrees F for 8 minutes. Divide cabbage mix on plates and serve.

NUTRITION:
calories 100, fat 4, fiber 2, carbs 11, protein 7

SUGARY BABY CARROTS

Preparation time: 10 min | Cooking time: 10 min | Servings: 4

INGREDIENTS:

- 2 cups baby carrots
- A pinch of salt and black pepper
- 1 tbsp brown sugar
- ½ tbsp butter, melted

DIRECTIONS:
In a dish that fits your air fryer, mix baby carrots with butter, salt, pepper and sugar, toss, introduce in your air fryer and cook at 350 degrees F for 10 minutes. Divide among plates and serve.

NUTRITION:
calories 100, fat 2, fiber 3, carbs 7, protein 4

BALSAMIC GREENS MIX

Preparation time: 10 min | Cooking time: 10 min | Servings: 4

INGREDIENTS:

- 1 bunch collard greens, trimmed
- 2 tbsp olive oil
- 2 tbsp tomato puree
- 1 yellow onion, chopped
- 3 garlic cloves, minced
- Salt and black pepper to the taste
- 1 tbsp balsamic vinegar
- 1 tsp sugar

DIRECTIONS:
In a dish that fits your air fryer, mix oil, garlic, vinegar, onion and tomato puree and whisk. Add collard greens, salt, pepper and sugar, toss, introduce in your air fryer and cook at 320 degrees F for 10 minutes. Divide collard greens mix on plates and serve.

NUTRITION:
calories 121, fat 3, fiber 3, carbs 7, protein 3

GARLIC GREENS AND TURKEY

Preparation time: 10 min | Cooking time: 20 min | Servings: 6

INGREDIENTS:

- 1 sweet onion, chopped
- 2 smoked turkey wings
- 2 tbsp olive oil
- 3 garlic cloves, minced
- 2 and ½ pounds collard greens, chopped
- Salt and black pepper to the taste
- 2 tbsp apple cider vinegar
- 1 tbsp brown sugar
- ½ tsp crushed red pepper

DIRECTIONS:
Heat up a pan that fits your air fryer with the oil over medium high heat, add onions, stir and cook for 2 minutes. Add garlic, greens, vinegar, salt, pepper, crushed red pepper, sugar and smoked turkey, introduce in preheated air fryer and cook at 350 degrees F for 15 minutes. Divide greens and turkey on plates and serve.

NUTRITION:
calories 262, fat 4, fiber 8, carbs 12, protein 4

HERBED ZUCCHINIS AND EGGPLANT MIX

Preparation time: 10 min | Cooking time: 8 min | Servings: 4

INGREDIENTS:

1 eggplant, roughly cubed
3 zucchinis, roughly cubed
2 tbsp lemon juice
Salt and black pepper to the taste
1 tsp thyme, dried
1 tsp oregano, dried
3 tbsp olive oil

DIRECTIONS:
Put eggplant in a dish that fits your air fryer, add zucchinis, lemon juice, salt, pepper, thyme, oregano and olive oil, toss, introduce in your air fryer and cook at 360 degrees F for 8 minutes. Divide among plates and serve right away.

NUTRITION:
calories 152, fat 5, fiber 7, carbs 19, protein 5

PARMESAN FENNEL

Preparation time: 10 min | Cooking time: 8 min | Servings: 4

INGREDIENTS:

- 2 fennel bulbs, cut into quarters
- 3 tbsp olive oil
- Salt and black pepper to the taste
- 1 garlic clove, minced
- 1 red chili pepper, chopped
- ¾ cup veggie stock
- Juice from ½ lemon
- ¼ cup white wine

- ¼ cup parmesan, grated

DIRECTIONS:
Heat up a pan that fits your air fryer with the oil over medium high heat, add garlic and chili pepper, stir and cook for 2 minutes. Add fennel, salt, pepper, stock, wine, lemon juice, and parmesan, toss to coat, introduce in your air fryer and cook at 350 degrees F for 6 minutes. Divide among plates and serve right away.

NUTRITION:
calories 100, fat 4, fiber 8, carbs 4, protein 4

OKRA AND CORN SALAD
Preparation time: 10 min | Cooking time: 12 min | Servings: 6

INGREDIENTS:

- 1 pound okra, trimmed
- 6 scallions, chopped
- 3 green bell peppers, chopped
- Salt and black pepper to the taste
- 2 tbsp olive oil
- 1 tsp sugar
- 28 ounces canned tomatoes, chopped
- 1 cup con

DIRECTIONS:
Heat up a pan that fits your air fryer with the oil over medium high heat, add scallions and bell peppers, stir and cook for 5 minutes. Add okra, salt, pepper, sugar, tomatoes and corn, stir, introduce in your air fryer and cook at 360 degrees F for 7 minutes. Divide okra mix on plates and serve warm.

NUTRITION:
calories 152, fat 4, fiber 3, carbs 18, protein 4

AIR FRIED LEEKS
Preparation time: 10 min | Cooking time: 7 min | Servings: 4

INGREDIENTS:

- 4 leeks, washed, ends cut off and halved
- Salt and black pepper to the taste
- 1 tbsp butter, melted
- 1 tbsp lemon juice

DIRECTIONS:
Rub leeks with melted butter, season with salt and pepper, put in your air fryer and cook at 350 degrees F for 7 minutes. Arrange on a platter, drizzle lemon juice all over and serve.

NUTRITION:
calories 100, fat 4, fiber 2, carbs 6, protein 2

CRUNCHY GOLD POTATOES AND PARSLEY
Preparation time: 10 min | Cooking time: 10 min | Servings: 4

INGREDIENTS:

- 1 pound gold potatoes, cut into wedges
- Salt and black pepper to the taste
- 2 tbsp olive
- Juice from ½ lemon
- ¼ cup parsley leaves, chopped

DIRECTIONS:
Rub potatoes with salt, pepper, lemon juice and olive oil, put them in your air fryer and cook at 350 degrees F for 10 minutes. Divide among plates, sprinkle parsley on top and serve.

NUTRITION:
calories 152, fat 3, fiber 7, carbs 17, protein 4

INDIAN TURMERIC SALAD
Preparation time: 10 min | Cooking time: 12 min | Servings: 4

INGREDIENTS:

- 20 ounces turnips, peeled and chopped
- 1 tsp garlic, minced
- 1 tsp ginger, grated
- 2 yellow onions, chopped
- 2 tomatoes, chopped
- 1 tsp cumin, ground
- 1 tsp coriander, ground
- 2 green chilies, chopped
- ½ tsp turmeric powder
- 2 tbsp butter
- Salt and black pepper to the taste
- A handful coriander leaves, chopped

DIRECTIONS:
Heat up a pan that fits your air fryer with the butter, melt it, add green chilies, garlic and ginger, stir and cook for 1 minute. Add onions, salt, pepper, tomatoes, turmeric, cumin, ground coriander and turnips, stir, introduce in your air fryer and cook at 350 degrees F for 10 minutes. Divide among plates, sprinkle fresh coriander on top and serve.

NUTRITION:
calories 100, fat 3, fiber 6, carbs 12, protein 4

SIMPLE MUSHROOM TOMATOES
Preparation time: 10 min | Cooking time: 15 min | Servings: 4

INGREDIENTS:

- 4 tomatoes, tops cut off and pulp scooped and chopped
- Salt and black pepper to the taste
- 1 yellow onion, chopped
- 1 tbsp butter
- 2 tbsp celery, chopped
- ½ cup mushrooms, chopped
- 1 tbsp bread crumbs
- 1 cup cottage cheese
- ¼ tsp caraway seeds
- 1 tbsp parsley, chopped

DIRECTIONS:
Heat up a pan with the butter over medium heat, melt it, add onion and celery, stir and cook for 3 minutes. Add tomato pulp and mushrooms, stir and cook for 1 minute more. Add salt, pepper, crumbled bread,

cheese, caraway seeds and parsley, stir, cook for 4 minutes more and take off heat. Stuff tomatoes with this mix, place them in your air fryer and cook at 350 degrees F for 8 minutes. Divide stuffed tomatoes on plates and serve.

Nutrition:
calories 143, fat 4, fiber 6, carbs 4, protein 4

INDIAN CHILI POTATOES
Preparation time: 10 min | Cooking time: 12 min | Servings: 4

Ingredients:

- 1 tbsp coriander seeds
- 1 tbsp cumin seeds
- Salt and black pepper to the taste
- ½ tsp turmeric powder
- ½ tsp red chili powder
- 1 tsp pomegranate powder
- 1 tbsp pickled mango, chopped
- 2 tsp fenugreek, dried
- 5 potatoes, boiled, peeled and cubed
- 2 tbsp olive oil

Directions:
Heat up a pan that fits your air fryer with the oil over medium heat, add coriander and cumin seeds, stir and cook for 2 minutes. Add salt, pepper, turmeric, chili powder, pomegranate powder, mango, fenugreek and potatoes, toss, introduce in your air fryer and cook at 360 degrees F for 10 minutes. Divide among plates and serve hot.

Nutrition:
calories 251, fat 7, fiber 4, carbs 12, protein 7

TOMATOES AND FLORETS STEW
Preparation time: 10 min | Cooking time: 20 min | Servings: 4

Ingredients:

- 1 broccoli head, florets separated
- 2 tsp coriander seeds
- 1 tbsp olive oil
- 1 yellow onion, chopped
- Salt and black pepper to the taste
- A pinch of red pepper, crushed
- 1 small ginger piece, chopped
- 1 garlic clove, minced
- 28 ounces canned tomatoes, pureed

Directions:
Heat up a pan that fits your air fryer with the oil over medium heat, add onions, salt, pepper and red pepper, stir and cook for 7 minutes. Add ginger, garlic, coriander seeds, tomatoes and broccoli, stir, introduce in your air fryer and cook at 360 degrees F for 12 minutes. Divide into bowls and serve.

Nutrition:
calories 150, fat 4, fiber 2, carbs 7, protein 12

COLLARD GREENS AND TOMATOES
Preparation time: 10 min | Cooking time: 12 min | Servings: 4

Ingredients:

- 1 pound collard greens
- 3 bacon strips, chopped
- ¼ cup cherry tomatoes, halved
- 1 tbsp apple cider vinegar
- 2 tbsp chicken stock
- Salt and black pepper to the taste

Directions:
Heat up a pan that fits your air fryer over medium heat, add bacon, stir and cook 1-2 minutes. Add tomatoes, collard greens, vinegar, stock, salt and pepper, stir, introduce in your air fryer and cook at 320 degrees F for 10 minutes. Divide among plates and serve.

Nutrition:
calories 120, fat 3, fiber 1, carbs 3, protein 7

SPICY MUSTARD GREENS
Preparation time: 10 min | Cooking time: 11 min | Servings: 4

Ingredients:

- 2 garlic cloves, minced
- 1 pound mustard greens, torn
- 1 tbsp olive oil
- ½ cup yellow onion, sliced
- Salt and black pepper to the taste
- 3 tbsp veggie stock
- ¼ tsp dark sesame oil

Directions:
Heat up a pan that fits your air fryer with the oil over medium heat, add onions, stir and brown them for 5 minutes. Add garlic, stock, greens, salt and pepper, stir, introduce in your air fryer and cook at 350 degrees F for 6 minutes. Add sesame oil.

Nutrition:
calories 120, fat 3, fiber 1, carbs 3, protein 7

PARMESAN RADISH HASH
Preparation time: 10 min | Cooking time: 7 min | Servings: 4

Ingredients:

- ½ tsp onion powder
- 1 pound radishes, sliced
- ½ tsp garlic powder
- Salt and black pepper to the taste
- 4 eggs
- 1/3 cup parmesan, grated

Directions:
In a bowl, mix radishes with salt, pepper, onion and garlic powder, eggs and parmesan and stir well. Transfer radishes to a pan that fits your air fryer and cook at 350 degrees F for 7 minutes. Divide hash on plates and serve.

Nutrition:
calories 80, fat 5, fiber 2, carbs 5, protein 7

OREGANO ZUCCHINI MIX

Preparation time: 10 min | Cooking time: 14 min | Servings: 6

INGREDIENTS:

- 6 zucchinis, halved and then sliced
- Salt and black pepper to the taste
- 1 tbsp butter
- 1 tsp oregano, dried
- ½ cup yellow onion, chopped
- 3 garlic cloves, minced
- 2 ounces parmesan, grated
- ¾ cup heavy cream

DIRECTIONS:

Heat up a pan that fits your air fryer with the butter over medium high heat, add onion, stir and cook for 4 minutes. Add garlic, zucchinis, oregano, salt, pepper and heavy cream, toss, introduce in your air fryer and cook at 350 degrees F for 10 minutes. Add parmesan, stir, divide among plates and serve.

NUTRITION:

calories 160, fat 4, fiber 2, carbs 8, protein 8

SWISS CHARD AND RICOTTA

Preparation time: 10 min | Cooking time: 20 min | Servings: 8

INGREDIENTS:

- 8 cups Swiss chard, chopped
- ½ cup onion, chopped
- 1 tbsp olive oil
- 1 garlic clove, minced
- Salt and black pepper to the taste
- 3 eggs
- 2 cups ricotta cheese
- 1 cup mozzarella, shredded
- A pinch of nutmeg
- ¼ cup parmesan, grated
- 1 pound sausage, chopped

DIRECTIONS:

Heat up a pan that fits your air fryer with the oil over medium heat, add onions, garlic, Swiss chard, salt, pepper and nutmeg, stir, cook for 2 minutes and take off heat. In a bowl, whisk eggs with mozzarella, parmesan and ricotta, stir, pour over Swiss chard mix, toss, introduce in your air fryer and cook at 320 degrees F for 17 minutes. Divide among plates and serve.

NUTRITION:

calories 332, fat 13, fiber 3, carbs 14, protein 23

SWISS CHARD AND PINE NUTS SALAD

Preparation time: 10 min | Cooking time: 13 min | Servings: 4

INGREDIENTS:

- 1 bunch Swiss chard, torn
- 2 tbsp olive oil
- 1 small yellow onion, chopped
- A pinch of red pepper flakes
- ¼ cup pine nuts, toasted
- ¼ cup raisins
- 1 tbsp balsamic vinegar
- Salt and black pepper to the taste

DIRECTIONS:

Heat up a pan that fits your air fryer with the oil over medium heat, add chard and onions, stir and cook for 5 minutes. Add salt, pepper, pepper flakes, raisins, pine nuts and vinegar, stir, introduce in your air fryer and cook at 350 degrees F for 8 minutes. Divide among plates and serve.

NUTRITION:

calories 120, fat 2, fiber 1, carbs 8, protein 8

SPANISH GREENS

Preparation time: 10 min | Cooking time: 8 min | Servings: 4

INGREDIENTS:

- 1 apple, cored and chopped
- 1 yellow onion, sliced
- 3 tbsp olive oil
- ¼ cup raisins
- 6 garlic cloves, chopped
- ¼ cup pine nuts, toasted
- ¼ cup balsamic vinegar
- 5 cups mixed spinach and chard
- Salt and black pepper to the taste
- A pinch of nutmeg

DIRECTIONS:

Heat up a pan that fits your air fryer with the oil over medium high heat, add onion, stir and cook for 3 minutes. Add apple, garlic, raisins, vinegar, mixed spinach and chard, nutmeg, salt and pepper, stir, introduce in preheated air fryer and cook at 350 degrees F for 5 minutes. Divide among plates, sprinkle pine nuts on top and serve.

NUTRITION:

calories 120, fat 1, fiber 2, carbs 3, protein 6

OREGANO AIR FRIED TOMATOES

Preparation time: 10 min | Cooking time: 15 | Servings: 8

INGREDIENTS:

- 1 jalapeno pepper, chopped
- 4 garlic cloves, minced
- 2 pounds cherry tomatoes, halved
- Salt and black pepper to the taste
- ¼ cup olive oil
- ½ tsp oregano, dried
- ¼ cup basil, chopped
- ½ cup parmesan, grated

DIRECTIONS:

In a bowl, mix tomatoes with garlic, jalapeno, season with salt, pepper and oregano and drizzle the oil, toss to coat, introduce in your air fryer and cook at 380 degrees F for 15 minutes Transfer tomatoes to a bowl, add basil and parmesan, toss and serve.

NUTRITION:

calories 140, fat 2, fiber 2, carbs 6, protein 8

ITALIAN STEW

Preparation time: 10 min | Cooking time: 15 min | Servings: 4

INGREDIENTS:

- 1 red onion, chopped
- 2 garlic cloves, chopped
- 1 bunch parsley, chopped
- Salt and black pepper to the taste
- 1 tsp oregano, dried
- 2 eggplants, cut into medium chunks
- 2 tbsp olive oil
- 2 tbsp capers, chopped
- 1 handful green olives, pitted and sliced
- 5 tomatoes, chopped
- 3 tbsp herb vinegar

DIRECTIONS:
Heat up a pan that fits your air fryer with the oil over medium heat, add eggplant, oregano, salt and pepper, stir and cook for 5 minutes. Add garlic, onion, parsley, capers, olives, vinegar and tomatoes, stir, introduce in your air fryer and cook at 360 degrees F for 15 minutes. Divide into bowls and serve.

NUTRITION:
calories 170, fat 13, fiber 3, carbs 5, protein 7

RUTABAGA AND VEGGIE PASTA MIX

Preparation time: 10 min | Cooking time: 15 min | Servings: 4

INGREDIENTS:

- 1 tbsp shallot, chopped
- 1 garlic clove, minced
- ¾ cup cashews, soaked for a couple of hours and drained
- 2 tbsp nutritional yeast
- ½ cup veggie stock
- Salt and black pepper to the taste
- 2 tsp lemon juice
- For the pasta:
- 1 cup cherry tomatoes, halved
- 5 tsp olive oil
- ¼ tsp garlic powder
- 2 rutabagas, peeled and cut into thick noodles

DIRECTIONS:
Place tomatoes and rutabaga noodles into a pan that fits your air fryer, drizzle the oil over them, season with salt, black pepper and garlic powder, toss to coat and cook in your air fryer at 350 degrees F for 15 minutes. Meanwhile, in a food processor, mix garlic with shallots, cashews, veggie stock, nutritional yeast, lemon juice, a pinch of sea salt and black pepper to the taste and blend well. Divide rutabaga pasta on plates, top with tomatoes, drizzle the sauce over them and serve.

NUTRITION:
calories 160, fat 2, fiber 5, carbs 10, protein 8

Garlic Tomatoes with Thyme
Preparation time: 10 min | Cooking time: 15 min | Servings: 4

INGREDIENTS:

- 4 garlic cloves, crushed
- 1 pound mixed cherry tomatoes
- 3 thyme sprigs, chopped
- Salt and black pepper to the taste
- ¼ cup olive oil

DIRECTIONS:
In a bowl, mix tomatoes with salt, black pepper, garlic, olive oil and thyme, toss to coat, introduce in your air fryer and cook at 360 degrees F for 15 minutes. Divide tomatoes mix on plates and serve.

NUTRITION:
calories 100, fat 0, fiber 1, carbs 1, protein 6

CHEDDAR AND GARLIC TART

Preparation time: 10 min | Cooking time: 14 min | Servings: 2

INGREDIENTS:

- 1 bunch basil, chopped
- 4 eggs
- 1 garlic clove, minced
- Salt and black pepper to the taste
- ½ cup cherry tomatoes, halved
- ¼ cup cheddar cheese, grated

DIRECTIONS:
In a bowl, mix eggs with salt, black pepper, cheese and basil and whisk well. Pour this into a baking dish that fits your air fryer, arrange tomatoes on top, introduce in the fryer and cook at 320 degrees F for 14 minutes. Slice and serve right away.

NUTRITION:
calories 140, fat 1, fiber 1, carbs 2, protein 10

ZUCCHINI NOODLES WITH TOMATO SAUCE

Preparation time: 10 min | Cooking time: 20 min | Servings: 6

INGREDIENTS:

- 2 tbsp olive oil
- 3 zucchinis, cut with a spiralizer
- 16 ounces mushrooms, sliced
- ¼ cup sun dried tomatoes, chopped
- 1 tsp garlic, minced
- ½ cup cherry tomatoes, halved
- 2 cups tomatoes sauce
- 2 cups spinach, torn
- Salt and black pepper to the taste
- A handful basil, chopped

Directions:
Put zucchini noodles in a bowl, season salt and black pepper and leave them aside for 10 minutes. Heat up a pan that fits your air fryer with the oil over medium high heat, add garlic, stir and cook for 1 minute. Add mushrooms, sun dried tomatoes, cherry tomatoes, spinach, cayenne, sauce and zucchini noodles, stir, introduce in your air fryer and cook at 320 degrees F for 10 minutes. Divide among plates and serve with basil

sprinkled on top.

NUTRITION:
calories 120, fat 1, fiber 1, carbs 2, protein 9

CHERRY TOMATOES AND ROSEMARY SAUCE
Preparation time: 10 min | Cooking time: 15 min | Servings: 4

INGREDIENTS:

- 2 red bell peppers, chopped
- 2 garlic cloves, minced
- 1 pound cherry tomatoes, halved
- 1 tsp rosemary, dried
- 3 bay leaves
- 2 tbsp olive oil
- 1 tbsp balsamic vinegar
- Salt and black pepper to the taste

DIRECTIONS:
In a bowl mix tomatoes with garlic, salt, black pepper, rosemary, bay leaves, half of the oil and half of the vinegar, toss to coat, introduce in your air fryer and roast them at 320 degrees F for 15 minutes. Meanwhile, in your food processor, mix bell peppers with a pinch of sea salt, black pepper, the rest of the oil and the rest of the vinegar and blend very well. Divide roasted tomatoes on plates, drizzle the bell peppers sauce over them and serve.

NUTRITION:
calories 123, fat 1, fiber 1, carbs 8, protein 10

BALSAMIC CHERRY TOMATOES SKEWERS
Preparation time: 30 min | Cooking time: 6 min | Servings: 4

INGREDIENTS:

- 3 tbsp balsamic vinegar
- 24 cherry tomatoes
- 2 tbsp olive oil
- 3 garlic cloves, minced
- 1 tbsp thyme, chopped
- Salt and black pepper to the taste
- For the dressing:
- 2 tbsp balsamic vinegar
- Salt and black pepper to the taste
- 4 tbsp olive oil

DIRECTIONS:
In a bowl, mix 2 tbsp oil with 3 tbsp vinegar, 3 garlic cloves, thyme, salt and black pepper and whisk well. Add tomatoes, toss to coat and leave aside for 30 minutes. Arrange 6 tomatoes on one skewer and repeat with the rest of the tomatoes. Introduce them in your air fryer and cook at 360 degrees F for 6 minutes. In another bowl, mix 2 tbsp vinegar with salt, pepper and 4 tbsp oil and whisk well. Arrange tomato skewers on plates and serve with the dressing drizzled on top.

NUTRITION:
calories 140, fat 1, fiber 1, carbs 2, protein 7

SPINACH AND PORTOBELLO MUSHROOMS
Preparation time: 10 min | Cooking time: 12 min | Servings: 4

INGREDIENTS:

- 10 basil leaves
- 1 cup baby spinach
- 3 garlic cloves, chopped
- 1 cup almonds, roughly chopped
- 1 tbsp parsley
- ¼ cup olive oil
- 8 cherry tomatoes, halved
- Salt and black pepper to the taste
- 4 Portobello mushrooms, stems removed and chopped

DIRECTIONS:
In your food processor, mix basil with spinach, garlic, almonds, parsley, oil, salt, black pepper to the taste and mushroom stems and blend well. Stuff each mushroom with this mix, place them in your air fryer and cook at 350 degrees F for 12 minutes. Divide mushrooms on plates and serve.

NUTRITION:
calories 145, fat 3, fiber 2, carbs 6, protein 17

MEXICAN SALAD
Preparation time: 10 min | Cooking time: 25 min | Servings: 4

INGREDIENTS:

- 4 bell peppers, tops cut off and seeds removed
- ½ cup tomato juice
- 2 tbsp jarred jalapenos, chopped
- 4 chicken breasts
- 1 cup tomatoes, chopped
- ¼ cup yellow onion, chopped
- ¼ cup green peppers, chopped
- 2 cups tomato sauce
- Salt and black pepper to the taste
- 2 tsp onion powder
- ½ tsp red pepper, crushed
- 1 tsp chili powder
- ½ tsp garlic powder
- 1 tsp cumin, ground

DIRECTIONS:
In a pan that fits your air fryer, mix chicken breasts with tomato juice, jalapenos, tomatoes, onion, green peppers, salt, pepper, onion powder, red pepper, chili powder, garlic powder, oregano and cumin, stir well, introduce in your air fryer and cook at 350 degrees F for 15 minutes. Shred meat using 2 forks, stir, stuff bell peppers with this mix, place them in your air fryer and cook at 320 degrees F for 10 minutes more. Divide stuffed peppers on plates and serve.

NUTRITION:
calories 180, fat 4, fiber 3, carbs 7, protein 14

BEEF-STUFFED PEPPERS
Preparation time: 10 min | Cooking time: 55 min | Servings: 4

INGREDIENTS:

- 1 pound beef, ground
- 1 tsp coriander, ground
- 1 onion, chopped
- 3 garlic cloves, minced
- 2 tbsp olive oil
- 1 tbsp ginger, grated
- ½ tsp cumin, ground
- ½ tsp turmeric powder
- 1 tbsp hot curry powder
- Salt and black pepper to the taste
- 1 egg
- 4 bell peppers, cut into halves and seeds removed
- 1/3 cup raisins
- 1/3 cup walnuts, chopped

DIRECTIONS:
Heat up a pan with the oil over medium high heat, add onion, stir and cook for 4 minutes. Add garlic and beef, stir and cook for 10 minutes. Add coriander, ginger, cumin, curry powder, salt, pepper, turmeric, walnuts and raisins, stir take off heat and mix with the egg. Stuff pepper halves with this mix, introduce them in your air fryer and cook at 320 degrees F for 20 minutes. Divide among plates and serve.

NUTRITION:
calories 170, fat 4, fiber 3, carbs 7, protein 12

STUFFED POBLANO PEPPERS

Preparation time: 10 min | Cooking time: 15 min | Servings: 4

INGREDIENTS:

- 2 tsp garlic, minced
- 1 white onion, chopped
- 10 poblano peppers, tops cut off and deseeded
- 1 tbsp olive oil
- 8 ounces mushrooms, chopped
- Salt and black pepper to the taste
- ½ cup cilantro, chopped

DIRECTIONS:
Heat up a pan with the oil over medium high heat, add onion and mushrooms, stir and cook for 5 minutes. Add garlic, cilantro, salt and black pepper, stir and cook for 2 minutes. Divide this mix into poblanos, introduce them in your air fryer and cook at 350 degrees F for 15 minutes. Divide among plates and serve.

NUTRITION:
calories 150, fat 3, fiber 2, carbs 7, protein 10

BABY PEPPERS WITH SHRIMP

Preparation time: 10 min | Cooking time: 6 min | Servings: 4

INGREDIENTS:

- 12 baby bell peppers, cut into halves lengthwise
- ¼ tsp red pepper flakes, crushed
- 1 pound shrimp, cooked, peeled and deveined
- 6 tbsp jarred basil pesto
- Salt and black pepper to the taste
- 1 tbsp lemon juice
- 1 tbsp olive oil
- A handful parsley, chopped

DIRECTIONS:
In a bowl, mix shrimp with pepper flakes, pesto, salt, black pepper, lemon juice, oil and parsley, whisk very well and stuff bell pepper halves with this mix. Place them in your air fryer and cook at 320 degrees F for 6 minutes, Arrange peppers on plates and serve.

NUTRITION:
calories 130, fat 2, fiber 1, carbs 3, protein 15

EGGPLANT AND GINGER SAUCE

Preparation time: 10 min | Cooking time: 10 min | Servings: 4

INGREDIENTS:

- 2 tbsp olive oil
- 2 garlic cloves, minced
- 3 eggplants, halved and sliced
- 1 red chili pepper, chopped
- 1 green onion stalk, chopped
- 1 tbsp ginger, grated
- 1 tbsp soy sauce
- 1 tbsp balsamic vinegar

DIRECTIONS:
Heat up a pan that fits your air fryer with the oil over medium high heat, add eggplant slices and cook for 2 minutes. Add chili pepper, garlic, green onions, ginger, soy sauce and vinegar, introduce in your air fryer and cook at 320 degrees F for 7 minutes. Divide among plates and serve.

NUTRITION:
calories 130, fat 2, fiber 4, carbs 7, protein 9

EGGPLANT TABASCO HASH

Preparation time: 20 min | Cooking time: 10 min | Servings: 4

INGREDIENTS:

- 1 eggplant, roughly chopped
- ½ cup olive oil
- ½ pound cherry tomatoes, halved
- 1 tsp Tabasco sauce
- ¼ cup basil, chopped
- ¼ cup mint, chopped
- Salt and black pepper to the taste

DIRECTIONS:
Heat up a pan that fits your air fryer with half of the oil over medium high heat, add eggplant pieces, cook for 3 minutes, flip, cook them for 3 minutes more and transfer to a bowl. Heat up the same pan with the rest of the oil over medium high heat, add tomatoes, stir and cook for 1-2 minutes. Return eggplant pieces to the pan, add salt, black pepper, basil, mint and Tabasco sauce, introduce in your air fryer and cook at 320 degrees F for 6 minutes. Divide among plates and serve.

NUTRITION:
calories 120, fat 1, fiber 4, carbs 8, protein 15

CINNAMON POTATOES MIX

Preparation time: 10 min | Cooking time: 15

min | Servings: 4

INGREDIENTS:

- 3 sweet potatoes, cubed
- 4 tbsp olive oil
- 4 garlic cloves, minced
- ½ pound bacon, chopped
- Juice from 1 lime
- Salt and black pepper to the taste
- 2 tbsp balsamic vinegar
- A handful dill, chopped
- 2 green onions, chopped
- A pinch of cinnamon powder
- A pinch of red pepper flakes

DIRECTIONS:
Arrange bacon and sweet potatoes in your air fryer's basket, add garlic and half of the oil, toss well and cook at 350 degrees F and bake for 15 minutes. Meanwhile, in a bowl, mix vinegar with lime juice, olive oil, green onions, pepper flakes, dill, salt, pepper and cinnamon and whisk. Transfer bacon and sweet potatoes to a salad bowl, add salad dressing, toss well and serve right away.

NUTRITION:
calories 170, fat 3, fiber 2, carbs 5, protein 12

GREEK VEGGIES MIX

Preparation time: 10 min | Cooking time: 20 min | Servings: 2

INGREDIENTS:

- 2 medium potatoes, cut into wedges
- 1 yellow onion, chopped
- 2 tbsp butter
- 1 small carrot, roughly chopped
- 1 and ½ tbsp flour
- 1 bay leaf
- ½ cup chicken stock
- 2 tbsp Greek yogurt
- Salt and black pepper to the taste

DIRECTIONS:
Heat up a pan that fits your air fryer with the butter over medium high heat, add onion and carrot, stir and cook for 3-4 minutes. Add potatoes, flour, chicken stock, salt, pepper and bay leaf, stir, introduce in your air fryer and cook at 320 degrees F for 16 minutes. Add Greek yogurt, toss, divide among plates and serve.

NUTRITION:
calories 198, fat 3, fiber 2, carbs 6, protein 8

BROCCOLI HASH

Preparation time: 30 min | Cooking time: 8 min | Servings: 2

INGREDIENTS:

- 10 ounces mushrooms, halved
- 1 broccoli head, florets separated
- 1 garlic clove, minced
- 1 tbsp balsamic vinegar
- 1 yellow onion, chopped
- 1 tbsp olive oil
- Salt and black pepper
- 1 tsp basil, dried
- 1 avocado, peeled and pitted
- A pinch of red pepper flakes

DIRECTIONS:
In a bowl, mix mushrooms with broccoli, onion, garlic and avocado. In another bowl, mix vinegar, oil, salt, pepper and basil and whisk well. Pour this over veggies, toss to coat, leave aside for 30 minutes, transfer to your air fryer's basket and cook at 350 degrees F for 8 minutes, Divide among plates and serve with pepper flakes on top.

NUTRITION:
calories 182, fat 3, fiber 3, carbs 5, protein 8

FETA FRIED ASPARAGUS

Preparation time: 10 min | Cooking time: 15 min | Servings: 4

INGREDIENTS:

- 2 pounds fresh asparagus, trimmed
- ¼ cup olive oil
- Salt and black pepper to the taste
- 1 tsp lemon zest
- 4 garlic cloves, minced
- ½ tsp oregano, dried
- ¼ tsp red pepper flakes
- 4 ounces feta cheese, crumbled
- 2 tbsp parsley, finely chopped
- Juice from 1 lemon

DIRECTIONS:
In a bowl, mix oil with lemon zest, garlic, pepper flakes and oregano and whisk. Add asparagus, cheese, salt and pepper, toss, transfer to your air fryer's basket and cook at 350 degrees F for 8 minutes. Divide asparagus on plates, drizzle lemon juice and sprinkle parsley on top and serve.

NUTRITION:
calories 162, fat 13, fiber 5, carbs 12, protein 8

GREEK STUFFED EGGPLANTS

Preparation time: 10 min | Cooking time: 30 min | Servings: 4

INGREDIENTS:

- 4 small eggplants, halved lengthwise
- Salt and black pepper to the taste
- 10 tbsp olive oil
- 2 and ½ pounds tomatoes, cut into halves and grated
- 1 green bell pepper, chopped
- 1 yellow onion, chopped
- 1 tbsp garlic, minced
- ½ cup cauliflower, chopped
- 1 tsp oregano, chopped
- ½ cup parsley, chopped
- 3 ounces feta cheese, crumbled

DIRECTIONS:
Season eggplants with salt, pepper and 4 tbsp oil, toss, put them in your air fryer and cook at 350 degrees F for 16 minutes. Meanwhile, heat up a pan with 3 tbsp oil over medium high heat, add onion and cook for 5 minutes. Add bell pepper, garlic and cauliflower, stir, cook for 5 minutes, take off heat, add parsley, tomato, salt, pepper,

oregano and cheese and whisk everything. Stuff eggplants with the veggie mix, drizzle the rest of the oil over them, put them in your air fryer and cook at 350 degrees F for 6 minutes more. Divide among plates and serve right away.

Nutrition:
calories 240, fat 4, fiber, 2, carbs 19, protein 2

SALTY BEANS AND PARMESAN

Preparation time: 10 min | Cooking time: 8 min | Servings: 4

Ingredients:

- 12 ounces green beans
- 2 tsp garlic, minced
- 2 tbsp olive oil
- Salt and black pepper to the taste
- 1 egg, whisked
- 1/3 cup parmesan, grated

Directions:
In a bowl, mix oil with salt, pepper, garlic and egg and whisk well. Add green beans to this mix, toss well and sprinkle parmesan all over. Transfer green beans to your air fryer and cook them at 390 degrees F for 8 minutes. Divide green beans on plates and serve them right away.

Nutrition:
calories 120, fat 8, fiber 2, carbs 7, protein 4

MOZZARELLA GREEN BEANS

Preparation time: 10 min | Cooking time: 15 min | Servings: 4

Ingredients:

- ½ cup heavy cream
- 1 cup mozzarella, shredded
- 2/3 cup parmesan, grated
- Salt and black pepper to the taste
- 2 pounds green beans
- 2 tsp lemon zest, grated
- A pinch of red pepper flakes

Directions:
Put the beans in a dish that fits your air fryer, add heavy cream, salt, pepper, lemon zest, pepper flakes, mozzarella and parmesan, toss, introduce in your air fryer and cook at 350 degrees F for 15 minutes. Divide among plates and serve right away.

Nutrition:
calories 231, fat 6, fiber 7, carbs 8, protein 5

GREEN VEGGIES MIX

Preparation time: 10 min | Cooking time: 15 min | Servings: 4

Ingredients:

- 1 pint cherry tomatoes
- 1 pound green beans
- 2 tbsp olive oil
- Salt and black pepper to the taste

Directions:
In a bowl, mix cherry tomatoes with green beans, olive oil, salt and pepper, toss, transfer to your air fryer and cook at 400 degrees F for 15 minutes. Divide among plates and serve right away.

Nutrition:
calories 162, fat 6, fiber 5, carbs 8, protein 9

POTATOES AND BEANS MIX

Preparation time: 10 min | Cooking time: 15 min | Servings: 5

Ingredients:

- 2 pounds green beans
- 6 new potatoes, halved
- Salt and black pepper to the taste
- A drizzle of olive oil
- 6 bacon slices, cooked and chopped

Directions:
In a bowl, mix green beans with potatoes, salt, pepper and oil, toss, transfer to your air fryer and cook at 390 degrees F for 15 minutes. Divide among plates and serve with bacon sprinkled on top.

Nutrition:
calories 374, fat 15, fiber 12, carbs 28, protein 12

FLAVORED GREEN BEANS

Preparation time: 10 min | Cooking time: 15 min | Servings: 4

Ingredients:

- 1 pound red potatoes, cut into wedges
- 1 pound green beans
- 2 garlic cloves, minced
- 2 tbsp olive oil
- Salt and black pepper to the taste
- ½ tsp oregano, dried

Directions:
In a pan that fits your air fryer, combine potatoes with green beans, garlic, oil, salt, pepper and oregano, toss, introduce in your air fryer and cook at 380 degrees F for 15 minutes. Divide among plates and serve.

Nutrition:
calories 211, fat 6, fiber 7, carbs 8, protein 5

POTATOES AND PAPRIKA MIX

Preparation time: 10 min | Cooking time: 16 min | Servings: 4

Ingredients:

- 1 and ½ pounds red potatoes, quartered
- 2 tbsp olive oil
- 1 pint cherry tomatoes
- 1 tsp sweet paprika
- 1 tbsp rosemary, chopped
- Salt and black pepper to the taste
- 3 garlic cloves, minced

DIRECTIONS:
In a bowl, mix potatoes with tomatoes, oil, paprika, rosemary, garlic, salt and pepper, toss, transfer to your air fryer and cook at 380 degrees F for 16 minutes. Divide among plates and serve.

NUTRITION:
calories 192, fat 4, fiber 4, carbs 30, protein 3

BABY BALSAMIC POTATOES
Preparation time: 10 min | Cooking time: 20 min | Servings: 4

INGREDIENTS:

- 1 and ½ pounds baby potatoes, halved
- 2 garlic cloves, chopped
- 2 red onions, chopped
- 9 ounces cherry tomatoes
- 3 tbsp olive oil
- 1 and ½ tbsp balsamic vinegar
- 2 thyme sprigs, chopped
- Salt and black pepper to the taste

DIRECTIONS:
In your food processor, mix garlic with onions, oil, vinegar, thyme, salt and pepper and pulse really well. In a bowl, mix potatoes with tomatoes and balsamic marinade, toss well, transfer to your air fryer and cook at 380 degrees F for 20 minutes. Divide among plates and serve.

NUTRITION:
calories 301, fat 6, fiber 8, carbs 18, protein 6

POTATOES AND OREGANO SAUCE
Preparation time: 10 min | Cooking time: 16 min | Servings: 4

INGREDIENTS:

- 2 pounds potatoes, cubed
- 4 garlic cloves, minced
- 1 yellow onion, chopped
- 1 cup tomato sauce
- 2 tbsp basil, chopped
- 2 tbsp olive oil
- ½ tsp oregano, dried
- ½ tsp parsley, dried

DIRECTIONS:
Heat up a pan that fits your air fryer with the oil over medium heat, add onion, stir and cook for 1-2 minutes. Add garlic, potatoes, parsley, tomato sauce and oregano, stir, introduce in your air fryer and cook at 370 degrees F and cook for 16 minutes. Add basil, toss everything, divide among plates and serve.

NUTRITION:
calories 211, fat 6, fiber 8, carbs 14, protein 6

AIR FRYER DESSERT RECIPES
AVOCADO CAKE
Preparation time: 10 min | Cooking time: 30 min | Servings: 4

INGREDIENTS:

- 1 tbsp butter, melted
- 1 egg, whisked
- 1 cup brown sugar
- 2 avocados, peeled, pitted and mashed
- 1 cup white flour
- 1 tsp baking powder
- ½ tsp cinnamon powder
- Cooking spray

DIRECTIONS:
Place all of the ingredients (except the cooking spray) in a bowl; mix / whisk well. Pour this mixture into a cake pan greased with cooking spray. Place the pan in your air fryer and cook at 350 degrees F for 30 minutes. Cool down, slice, and serve.

NUTRITION:
calories 202, fat 4, fiber 1, carbs 14, protein 7

OREO CHEESECAKE
Preparation time: 10 min | Cooking time: 20 min | Servings: 8

INGREDIENTS:

1 pound cream cheese, softened
½ tsp vanilla extract
2 eggs, whisked
4 tbsp sugar
1 cup Oreo cookies, crumbled
2 tbsp butter, melted

DIRECTIONS:
In a bowl, mix the cookies with the butter, and then press this mixture onto the bottom of a cake pan lined with parchment paper. Place the pan in your air fryer and cook at 350 degrees F for 4 minutes. In a bowl, mix the sugar with the cream cheese, eggs, and vanilla; whisk until combined and smooth and spread this over the crust. Cook the cheesecake in your air fryer at 310 degrees F for 15 minutes. Place the cheesecake in the fridge for a couple of hours before serving.

NUTRITION:
calories 195, fat 12, fiber 4, carbs 20, protein 7

CHERRY AND RAISINS PUDDING
Preparation time: 5 min | Cooking time: 55 min | Servings: 4

INGREDIENTS:

- 2 cups cherries, pitted and halved
- 4 egg yolks
- 1½ cups whipping cream
- ½ cup raisins
- ¼ cup sugar
- ½ cup chocolate chips.

DIRECTIONS:
Place all ingredients in a bowl and mix well.

Transfer the mixture to a greased pan that fits your air fryer. Cook at 310 degrees F for 55 minutes. Cool down and serve.

NUTRITION:
calories 212, fat 8, fiber 2, carbs 13, protein 7

CHOCOLATE AMARETTO CREAM
Preparation time: 5 min | Cooking time: 12 min | Servings: 8

INGREDIENTS:

- 1 cup sugar
- ½ cup butter, melted
- 1 cup heavy cream
- 12 ounces chocolate chips
- 2 tbsp amaretto liqueur

DIRECTIONS:
Place all of the ingredients in a bowl and stir. Pour the mixture into small ramekins and place in the air fryer. Cook at 320 degrees F for 12 minutes. Refrigerate / freeze for a while… best when served really cold.

NUTRITION:
calories 190, fat 2, fiber 1, carbs 6, protein 3

CINNAMON ROLLS
Preparation time: 2 hours | Cooking time: 10 min | Servings: 8

INGREDIENTS:

- 1 pound bread dough
- ¾ cup brown sugar
- 1½ tbsp cinnamon, ground
- ¼ cup butter, melted

DIRECTIONS:

Roll the dough on a floured working surface, shape a rectangle, and brush with the butter. In a bowl, combine the cinnamon and sugar, and then sprinkle this over the dough. Roll the dough into a log, seal, cut into 8 pieces, and leave the rolls to rise for 2 hours. Place the rolls in your air fryer's basket and cook at 350 degrees F for 5 minutes on each side. Serve warm, and enjoy!

NUTRITION:
calories 200, fat 11, fiber 2, carbs 15, protein 4

SWEET AND SPICY PUMPKIN PIE
Preparation time: 10 min | Cooking time: 35 min | Servings: 8

INGREDIENTS:

- 1 pie crust
- 3½ ounces pumpkin flesh, chopped
- 1 tsp nutmeg, ground
- 3 ounces water
- 1 egg, whisked
- 1 tbsp sugar

DIRECTIONS:
Put the water in a pot and bring to a boil over medium-high heat. Add the pumpkin, egg, sugar, and the nutmeg; stir, and allow to boil for 20 minutes. Remove the mixture from the heat and blend using an immersion blender. Put the pie crust in a lined pan that fits your air fryer and spread the pumpkin mix all over. Place the pan in the fryer and cook at 360 degrees F for 15 minutes. Slice and serve warm.

NUTRITION:
calories 212, fat 5, fiber 2, carbs 15, protein 7

CINNAMON PEARS
Preparation time: 5 min | Cooking time: 15 min | Servings: 4

INGREDIENTS:

- 2 pears, halved
- ½ tsp cinnamon powder
- 2 tbsp sugar

DIRECTIONS:
Put the pears in your air fryer, and sprinkle the cinnamon and the sugar all over. Cook at 320 degrees F for 15 minutes. Serve these pears warm, and enjoy!

NUTRITION:
calories 210, fat 2, fiber 1, carbs 12, protein 3

BUTTER DONUTS
Preparation time: 10 min | Cooking time: 15 min | Servings: 4

INGREDIENTS:

- 8 ounces flour
- 1 tbsp brown sugar
- 1 tbsp white sugar
- 1 egg
- 2½ tbsp butter
- 4 ounces whole milk
- 1 tsp baking powder

DIRECTIONS:
Place all of the ingredients in a bowl and mix well. Shape donuts from this mix and place them in your air fryer's basket. Cook at 360 degrees F for 15 minutes. Arrange the donuts on a platter and serve them warm.

NUTRITION:
calories 190, fat 8, fiber 1, carbs 14, protein 3

CINNAMON SUGAR APPLES
Preparation time: 5 min | Cooking time: 15 min | Servings: 4

INGREDIENTS:

- 3 tbsp butter, melted
- 4 apples, peeled, cored and cut into wedges
- 3 tbsp cinnamon sugar

DIRECTIONS:
In a pan that fits your air fryer, mix the apples with the sugar and the butter; toss. Place the pan in the fryer and cook at 370 degrees F for 15 minutes. Serve warm.

NUTRITION:
calories 204, fat 3, fiber 4, carbs 12, protein 4.

LEMON CHOCOLATE CAKE
Preparation time: 5 min | Cooking time: 17 min | Servings: 6

INGREDIENTS:
- 3½ ounces butter, melted
- 3 eggs
- 3 ounces brown sugar
- 3 ounces flour
- 1 tsp dark chocolate, grated
- ½ tsp lemon juice

DIRECTIONS:
Mix all of the ingredients in a bowl. Pour the mixture into a greased cake pan, and place in the fryer. Cook at 360 degrees F for 17 minutes. Let cake cool before serving.

NUTRITION:
calories 220, fat 11, fiber 3, carbs 15, protein 7

GREEK CAKE
Preparation time: 5 min | Cooking time: 30 min | Servings: 8

INGREDIENTS:
- 1½ cups white flour
- 1 tsp baking soda
- ¾ cup sugar
- 1 banana, mashed
- ½ tsp baking powder
- 2 tbsp vegetable oil
- 1 cup Greek yogurt
- 8 ounces canned pumpkin puree
- Cooking spray
- 1 egg
- ½ tsp vanilla extract

DIRECTIONS:
In a bowl, combine all ingredients (except the cooking spray) and stir well. Pour the mixture into a cake pan greased with cooking spray and put it in your air fryer's basket. Cook at 330 degrees F for 30 minutes. Cool down, slice, and serve.

NUTRITION:
calories 192, fat 7, fiber 7, carbs 12, protein 4

ZUCCHINI BREAD
Preparation time: 10 min | Cooking time: 40 min | Servings: 6

INGREDIENTS:
- 3 cups zucchinis, grated
- 1 cup sugar
- 1 tbsp vanilla extract
- 2 eggs, whisked
- 2 cups white flour
- 1 tbsp baking powder
- 1 stick butter, melted

DIRECTIONS:
Add all of the ingredients to a bowl and mix well. Pour the mixture into a lined loaf pan and place in the fryer. and cook at 320 degrees F for 40 minutes. Slice and serve warm.

NUTRITION:
calories 132, fat 6, fiber 7, carbs 11, protein 7

CREAM OF TARTAR BREAD
Preparation time: 10 min | Cooking time: 40 min | Servings: 6

INGREDIENTS:
- ¾ cup sugar
- 1 cup butter
- 1 tsp vanilla extract
- 1 egg
- 2 zucchinis, grated
- 1 tsp baking powder
- 1½ cups flour
- ½ tsp baking soda
- 1 cup milk
- 1½ tsp cream of tartar

DIRECTIONS:
Place all ingredients in a bowl and mix well. Pour the mixture into a lined loaf pan and place the pan in the air fryer. Cook at 320 degrees F for 40 minutes Cool down, slice, and serve.

NUTRITION:
calories 222, fat 7, fiber 8, carbs 14, protein 4

SWEET ORANGE CAKE
Preparation time: 10 min | Cooking time: 20 min | Servings: 3

INGREDIENTS:
- 1 egg
- 4 tbsp sugar
- 2 tbsp vegetable oil
- 4 tbsp milk
- 2 tbsp orange juice
- 4 tbsp flour
- 1 tbsp cocoa powder
- ½ tsp baking powder
- ½ tsp orange zest

DIRECTIONS:
Place all of the ingredients in a bowl and mix well. Divide the mixture between 3 ramekins and place them in your air fryer. Cook at 320 degrees F for 20 minutes. Serve the cakes warm, and enjoy!

NUTRITION:
calories 191, fat 7, fiber 3, carbs 14, protein 4

MAPLE CINNAMON APPLES
Preparation time: 10 min | Cooking time: 10 min | Servings: 4

INGREDIENTS:
- 2 tsp cinnamon powder
- 5 apples, cored and cut into wedges
- ½ tsp nutmeg powder
- 1 tbsp maple syrup
- 4 tbsp butter
- ¼ cup brown sugar

DIRECTIONS:
In a pan that fits your air fryer, mix the apples with the other ingredients and toss. Place the pan in the fryer and cook at 360 degrees F for 10 minutes. Divide into cups and serve.

NUTRITION:
calories 180, fat 6, fiber 8, carbs 19, protein 12

PINEAPPLE AND YOGURT CAKE
Preparation time: 10 min | Cooking time: 45 min | Servings: 6

INGREDIENTS:

- 5 ounces flour
- ¾ tsp baking powder
- ½ tsp baking soda
- ½ tsp cinnamon powder
- 1 egg, whisked
- 3 tbsp yogurt
- ½ cup sugar
- ¼ cup pineapple juice
- 4 tbsp vegetable oil
- 1 cup carrots, grated
- 1 cup coconut flakes, shredded
- Cooking spray

DIRECTIONS:
Place all of the ingredients (except the cooking spray) in a bowl, and mix well. Pour the mixture into a spring form pan, greased with cooking spray that fits your air fryer. Place the pan in your air fryer and cook at 320 degrees F for 45 minutes. Allow the cake to cool before cutting and serving.

NUTRITION:
calories 200, fat 6, fiber 7, carbs 12, protein 4

RUM SUGAR CHEESECAKE
Preparation time: 10 min | Cooking time: 20 min | Servings: 6

INGREDIENTS:

- 2 tsp butter, melted
- ½ cup graham cookies, crumbled
- 16 ounces cream cheese, softened
- 2 eggs
- ½ cup sugar
- 1 tsp rum
- ½ tsp vanilla extract

DIRECTIONS:
Grease a pan with the butter and spread the cookie crumbs on the bottom. In a bowl, mix all the remaining ingredients and whisk well; then spread this mixture over the cookie crumbs. Place the pan in your air fryer and cook at 340 degrees F for 20 minutes. Let the cheesecake cool down, refrigerate, and serve cold.

NUTRITION:
calories 212, fat 12, fiber 6, carbs 12, protein 7

STRAWBERRY CREAM CHEESE
Preparation time: 5 min | Cooking time: 15 min | Servings: 6

INGREDIENTS

- 1 tsp gelatin
- 8 ounces cream cheese
- 4 ounces strawberries
- 2 tbsp water
- ½ tbsp lemon juice
- ¼ tsp sugar
- ½ cup heavy cream

DIRECTIONS:
Place all ingredients in your blender and pulse. Divide the mixture into 6 ramekins and place them in your air fryer. Cook at 330 degrees F for 15 minutes. Refrigerate (or place briefly in freezer) and serve the cream really cold.

NUTRITION:
calories 202, fat 8, fiber 2, carbs 6, protein 7

COFFEE CREAM
Preparation time: 5 min | Cooking time: 10 min | Servings: 6

INGREDIENTS:

- 2 tbsp butter
- 8 ounces cream cheese
- 3 tbsp coffee
- 3 eggs
- 1 cup sugar
- 1 tbsp caramel syrup

DIRECTIONS:
Place all ingredients in your blender and pulse. Divide the mixture between 6 ramekins, and place in the fryer. Cook at 320 degrees F; bake for 10 minutes. Let cool down and then place in the freezer before serving.

NUTRITION:
calories 234, fat 13, fiber 4, carbs 11, protein 5

CREAM CHEESE VANILLA COOKIES
Preparation time: 10 min | Cooking time: 14 min | Servings: 12

INGREDIENTS:

- 6 ounces vegetable oil
- 6 eggs
- 3 ounces cocoa powder
- 2 tsp vanilla extract
- ½ tsp baking powder
- 4 ounces cream cheese
- 5 tbsp sugar

DIRECTIONS:
Add all the ingredients to a blender and pulse a bit. Pour this mixture into a baking dish lined with parchment paper that fits your air fryer. Place the pan in the fryer at 320 degrees F, and bake for 14 minutes. Slice into rectangles and serve.

NUTRITION:
calories 178, fat 11, fiber 3, carbs 3, protein 5

WALNUT AND COCOA COOKIES
Preparation time: 5 min | Cooking time: 17 min | Servings: 4

INGREDIENTS:

- 1 egg
- 1 cup cocoa powder
- 1 cup sugar
- 7 tbsp butter, melted
- ½ tsp vanilla extract
- ¼ cup white flour
- ¼ cup walnuts, chopped
- ½ tsp baking powder

DIRECTIONS:
Place all of the ingredients in a bowl and mix well (preferably using a mixer). Spread the mixture on a baking sheet lined with parch-

ment paper that fits your air fryer. Place the baking sheet in the fryer and bake at 320 degrees F for 17 minutes. Let the cookies cool down, cut, and serve.

NUTRITION:
calories 203, fat 12, fiber 1, carbs 13, protein 6

CREAMY VANILLA AND BLACKBERRY MIX
Preparation time: 5 min | Cooking time: 12 min | Servings: 4

INGREDIENTS:

- 1 cup blackberries
- 2 eggs
- ½ cup heavy cream
- ½ cup butter, melted
- 5 tbsp sugar
- 2 tsp vanilla extract
- 2 tsp baking powder

DIRECTIONS:
Place all of the ingredients in a bowl and whisk well. Divide the mixture between 4 ramekins, and place the ramekins in the fryer. Cook at 320 degrees F for 12 minutes. Refrigerate, and serve cold.

NUTRITION:
calories 230, fat 2, fiber 2, carbs 14, protein 7

CHOCOLATE BROWNIES WITH CHOCOLATE CHIPS
Preparation time: 5 min | Cooking time: 25 min | Servings: 12

INGREDIENTS:

- 1 tsp vanilla extract
- ½ cup butter, melted
- 1 egg
- 4 tbsp sugar
- 2 cups white flour
- ½ cup chocolate chips

DIRECTIONS:
Place all the ingredients in a bowl and mix well. Spread the mixture into a pan that fits your air fryer. Place the pan in the fryer and bake at 330 degrees F for 25 minutes. Cool down, slice, serve, and enjoy!

NUTRITION:
calories 230, fat 12, fiber 2, carbs 12, protein 5

CREAM CHEESE CAKE
Preparation time: 10 min | Cooking time: 30 min | Servings: 10

INGREDIENTS:

- 6 eggs, whisked
- 1 mandarin orange, peeled and pureed
- 1 tsp vanilla extract
- 1 tsp baking powder
- 9 ounces white flour
- 6 tbsp sugar
- 4 ounces cream cheese, softened
- 4 ounces yogurt

DIRECTIONS:
In a food processor, add the mandarin puree, flour, 2 tbsp of sugar, eggs, vanilla extract, and baking powder; pulse. Divide the mixture between 2 cake pans lined with parchment paper cook each in the air fryer at 330 degrees F for 15 minutes. In a bowl, combine the cream cheese, yogurt, and 4 tbsp sugar; whisk well. Place one cake layer on a plate and top with half of the yogurt mix; spread evenly. Add the other cake layer on top of the first with the yogurt mix, and top this layer with the remaining yogurt mix, spreading it well. Slice, serve, and enjoy!

NUTRITION:
calories 231, fat 13, fiber 2, carbs 11, protein 5

CREAMY VANILLA CHEESECAKE
Preparation time: 10 min | Cooking time: 20 min | Servings: 8

INGREDIENTS:

For the crust:

- 4 tbsp butter, melted
- 1½ cups chocolate cookies, crumbled

For the filling:

- 24 ounces cream cheese, softened
- 2 tbsp cornstarch
- 1 cup sugar
- 3 eggs, whisked
- 1 tbsp vanilla extract
- ½ cup heavy cream
- 12 ounces white chocolate, melted

DIRECTIONS:
Place the cookie crumbs and butter in a bowl, and stir well. Spread the cookie crumb mixture on the bottom of a cake pan lined with parchment paper and freeze for now. In another bowl, mix all other ingredients; whisk well. Spread this over the cake crust, put the pan in the fryer, and cook at 320 degrees F for 20 minutes. Let the cake cool down and put in the fridge for 1 hour before serving.

NUTRITION:
calories 261, fat 12, fiber 6, carbs 12, protein 6

GREEK CAKE
Preparation time: 10 min | Cooking time: 25 min | Servings: 8

INGREDIENTS:

- 1 cup white flour
- 1 tsp baking powder
- ¾ tsp pumpkin pie spice
- ¾ cup sugar
- Cooking spray
- ½ cup Greek yogurt
- 8 ounces canned pumpkin puree
- 1 egg, whisked

DIRECTIONS:
Place all ingredients (other than the cooking spray) in a bowl and mix well. Grease a

cake pan with cooking spray, pour the cake batter inside, and spread. Place the pan in the air fryer and cook at 330 degrees F for 25 minutes. Let the cake cool down, slice, and serve.

Nutrition:
calories 214, fat 9, fiber 3, carbs 14, protein 8

BANANA BREAD
Preparation time: 10 min | Cooking time: 40 min | Servings: 6

Ingredients:

- 3 bananas, peeled and mashed
- 1 cup sugar
- 2 eggs, whisked
- 2 cups white flour
- 1 tbsp baking powder
- 1 stick of butter, melted

Directions:
Place all the ingredients in a bowl and stir well. Pour this mixture into a lined loaf pan, and place in the air fryer. Cook at 340 degrees F for 40 minutes. Let the bread cool; then slice, serve, and enjoy!

Nutrition:
calories 200, fat 5, fiber 3, carbs 13, protein 7

PEAR BREAD
Preparation time: 10 min | Cooking time: 40 min | Servings: 6

Ingredients:

- 1 cup sugar
- 1 cup butter, melted
- 1 tsp vanilla extract
- 1 egg, whisked
- 2 pears, peeled and chopped
- 1 tsp baking powder
- 1½ cups flour
- 1 cup almond milk
- Cooking spray

Directions:
Combine all of the ingredients (except the cooking spray) in a bowl and mix well. Spread the mixture into a loaf pan greased with cooking spray, and place the pan in the air fryer. Cook at 340 degrees F for 40 minutes. Cool the bread down, slice, and serve.

Nutrition:
calories 211, fat 4, fiber 6, carbs 14, protein 6

CITRIC CAKE
Preparation time: 10 min | Cooking time: 20 min | Servings: 4

Ingredients:

- 1 egg, whisked
- 4 tbsp sugar
- 2 tbsp butter, melted
- 4 tbsp milk
- 4 tbsp flour
- ½ tsp baking powder
- 1 tsp lemon zest
- 1 tsp lemon juice

Directions:
Mix all the ingredients in a bowl and pour into 4 small ramekins. Place the ramekins in your air fryer and cook at 320 degrees F for 20 minutes. Serve the cakes right away.

Nutrition:
calories 213, fat 5, fiber 5, carbs 15, protein 6

MAPLE PEAR DESSERT
Preparation time: 5 min | Cooking time: 20 min | Servings: 4

Ingredients:

- 2 tsp cinnamon powder
- 4 pears, peeled and roughly cut into cubes
- 1 tbsp maple syrup
- 4 tbsp butter, melted
- ¼ cup brown sugar

Directions:
In a pan that fits your air fryer, place all the ingredients and toss. Place the pan in the air fryer and cook at 300 degrees F for 20 minutes. Divide into cups, refrigerate, and serve cold.

Nutrition:
calories 200, fat 3, fiber 4, carbs 16, protein 4

JUICY ORANGE STEW
Preparation time: 10 min | Cooking time: 20 min | Servings: 3

Ingredients:

- 4 oranges, peeled and cut into segments
- 2¼ cups white sugar
- 2 cups orange juice

Directions:
In a pan that fits your air fryer, mix the oranges with the sugar and orange juice; toss. Place the pan in the fryer and cook at 320 degrees F for 20 minutes. Divide the orange stew into cups, refrigerate, and serve cold.

Nutrition:
calories 171, fat 1, fiber 4, carbs 8, protein 2

BAKED PEARS AND WINE
Preparation time: 5 min | Cooking time: 20 min | Servings: 4

Ingredients:

- 4 pears, peeled and halved
- 1 cup red wine
- ½ cup sugar

Directions:
In a pan that fits your air fryer, mix the pears with the wine and sugar. Place the pan in the fryer and cook at 340 degrees F for 20 minutes. Divide into bowls and serve.

Nutrition:
calories 200, fat 1, fiber 4, carbs 12, protein 3

HEAVY LIQUEUR CHOCOLATE CREAM
Preparation time: 5 min | Cooking time: 12

min | Servings: 4

INGREDIENTS:

- 3½ ounces heavy cream
- 3½ ounces sweet dark chocolate, cut into chunks
- 1 tsp liquor

DIRECTIONS:
In a heat-proof dish, mix the cream with the chocolate and the liqueur. Place the dish in the air fryer and cook at 300 degrees F for 12 minutes. Whisk the cream, divide it into cups, and serve.

NUTRITION:
calories 200, fat 3, fiber 4, carbs 11, protein 3

APRICOT AND GINGER CAKE

Preparation time: 10 min | Cooking time: 30 min | Servings: 4

INGREDIENTS:

- 8 ounces apricots, chopped
- 1 cup white flour
- 3 tsp baking powder
- 1 cup sugar
- 1 tsp ginger powder
- 1 tsp cinnamon powder
- ½ cup butter, softened
- 3 tbsp maple syrup
- 4 eggs, whisked

DIRECTIONS:
Place all the ingredients in a bowl and stir well. Pour the mixture into a cake pan lined with parchment paper, and place the pan in the fryer. Cook at 340 degrees F for 30 minutes. Let the cake cool before slicing and serving. Enjoy!

NUTRITION:
calories 213, fat 3, fiber 6, carbs 15, protein 4

SPICED BANANA PUDDING

Preparation time: 10 min | Cooking time: 25 min | Serving: 6

INGREDIENTS:

- 4 bananas, peeled and mashed
- 2 eggs, whisked
- 1 cup milk
- ¾ cup maple syrup
- 1 tsp cinnamon powder
- ½ tsp ginger powder
- ¼ tsp cloves, ground
- 1 tbsp cornstarch

DIRECTIONS:
In a bowl, mix all the ingredients; whisk well. Pour the mixture into a pudding mould, put it in the air fryer, and cook at 340 degrees F for 25 minutes. Serve the pudding warm; enjoy

NUTRITION:
calories 200, fat 4, fiber 6, carbs 15, protein 4

MILKY TAPIOCA PUDDING

Preparation time: 10 min | Cooking time: 15 min | Servings: 6

INGREDIENTS:

- 2 cups milk
- 1 cup tapioca pearls, rinsed
- ½ cup sugar
- Zest of 1 lime

DIRECTIONS:
Place all ingredients in a heat-proof dish that fits your air fryer; whisk well. Put the dish in the fryer and cook at 320 degrees F for 15 minutes. Set the pudding aside for 10 minutes, divide into bowls, and serve.

NUTRITION:
calories 161, fat 3, fiber 5, carbs 14, protein 4

STRAWBERRY RICOTTA CHEESECAKE

Preparation time: 10 min | Cooking time: 35 min | Servings: 8

INGREDIENTS:

- 1 pound strawberries, chopped
- 1 cup ricotta cheese
- ¼ cup sugar
- 1 tbsp lemon juice
- 1 egg, whisked
- 1 tsp vanilla extract
- 3 tbsp butter, melted
- 1 cup white flour
- 2 tsp baking powder

DIRECTIONS:
Place all of the ingredients in a bowl and whisk well. Pour the mixture into a cake pan lined with parchment paper, and place in the air fryer. Cook at 340 degrees F for 35 minutes. Cool the cake down, slice, and serve.

NUTRITION:
calories 200, fat 4, fiber 4, carbs 16, protein 4

ALMOND AND RICOTTA CAKE

Preparation time: 10 min | Cooking time: 40 min | Servings: 6
Ingredients:

- 1 tsp almond extract
- 1 cup ricotta cheese, softened
- ½ cup cocoa powder
- ½ cup sugar
- 3 tbsp butter, melted
- 1 cup white flour
- 2 eggs, whisked
- 2 tsp baking powder
- ¼ cup almonds, sliced

DIRECTIONS:
Place all of the ingredients in a bowl and stir well. Pour the mixture into a cake pan lined with parchment paper place the pan in the fryer, and cook at 330 degrees F for 40 minutes. Allow the cake to cool, slice, and serve.

NUTRITION:
calories 200, fat 4, fiber 5, carbs 15, protein 5

CREAMY ORANGE PUDDING

Preparation time: 5 min | Cooking time: 25 min | Servings: 6
INGREDIENTS:

- 2 cups fresh cream
- 6 egg yolks, whisked
- 6 tbsp white sugar
- Zest of 1 orange

DIRECTIONS:
Combine all ingredients in a bowl and whisk well. Divide the mixture between 6 small ramekins. Place the ramekins in your air fryer and cook at 340 degrees F for 25 minutes. Place in the fridge for 1 hour before serving.

NUTRITION:
calories 200, fat 3, fiber 5, carbs 15, protein 5

BRIOCHE MILK AND RAISINS PUDDING

Preparation time: 5 min | Cooking time: 30 min | Servings: 4

INGREDIENTS:

- 4 egg yolks, whisked
- 3 cups brioche, cubed
- 2 cups half and half
- ½ tsp vanilla extract
- 1 cup sugar
- 2 tbsp butter, melted
- 2 cups milk
- ½ cup raisins
- Zest of ½ lemon

DIRECTIONS:
In a bowl, add all of the ingredients and whisk well. Pour the mixture into a pudding mould and place it in the air fryer. Cook at 330 degrees F for 30 minutes. Cool down and serveNutrition: calories 251, fat 4, fiber 5, carbs 20, protein 5

APPLE AND WINE SAUCE

Preparation time: 10 min | Cooking time: 30 min | Servings: 6

INGREDIENTS:

- 6 apples, peeled, cored and cut into wedges
- 1 tbsp cinnamon powder
- 1 cup sugar
- 1 cup red wine

DIRECTIONS:
In a pan that fits your air fryer, place all of the ingredients and toss. Place the pan in the fryer and cook at 320 degrees F for 30 minutes. Divide into cups and serve right away.

NUTRITION:
calories 200, fat 4, fiber 4, carbs 15, protein 3

JUICY LEMONS STEW

Preparation time: 5 min | Cooking time: 14 min | Servings: 4

INGREDIENTS:

- 1 pound red grapes
- Juice and zest of 1 lemon
- 26 ounces grape juice

DIRECTIONS:
In a pan that fits your air fryer, add all ingredients and toss. Place the pan in the fryer and cook at 320 degrees F for 14 minutes. Divide into cups, refrigerate, and serve cold.

NUTRITION:
calories 151, fat 4, fiber 5, carbs 8, protein 4

MILKY RICE PUDDING

Preparation time: 5 min | Cooking time: 20 min | Servings: 6

INGREDIENTS:

- 1 tbsp butter, melted
- 7 ounces white rice
- 16 ounces milk
- 1/3 cup sugar
- 1 tbsp heavy cream
- 1 tsp vanilla extract

DIRECTIONS:
Place all ingredients in a pan that fits your air fryer and stir well. Put the pan in the fryer and cook at 360 degrees F for 20 minutes. Stir the pudding, divide it into bowls, refrigerate, and serve cold.

NUTRITION:
calories 230, fat 4, fiber 6, carbs 17, protein 5

VANILLA AND BLACKBERRY PUDDING

Preparation time: 10 min | Cooking time: 30 min | Servings: 6

Ingredients:

- 1 pound ricotta cheese, softened
- 6 ounces blackberries
- 2 ounces honey
- 4 eggs
- ¼ cup sugar
- ¼ tsp vanilla extract
- Zest of ½ orange

DIRECTIONS:
Place all the ingredients in a bowl; whisk well. Divide the mixture between 6 ramekins and place them in the air fryer. Cook at 300 degrees F for 30 minutes.

NUTRITION:
calories 191, fat 3, fiber 6, carbs 13, protein 5

MAPLE RICE PUDDING

Preparation time: 10 min | Cooking time: 20 min | Servings: 6

INGREDIENTS:

- 1 cup brown rice
- 3 cups milk
- 2 bananas, peeled and mashed
- ½ cup maple syrup
- 1 tsp vanilla extract

DIRECTIONS:
Place all the ingredients in a pan that fits your air fryer; stir well. Put the pan in the fryer and cook at 360 degrees F for 20 minutes. Stir the pudding, divide into cups, refrigerate, and serve cold.

NUTRITION:
calories 161, fat 5, fiber 4, carbs 16, protein 5

ZESTY ORANGE MARMALADE

Preparation time: 10 min | Cooking time: 20 min | Servings: 4

INGREDIENTS:

- 4 oranges, peeled and chopped
- 3 cups sugar
- 1½ cups water

DIRECTIONS:
In a pan that fits your air fryer, mix the oranges with the sugar and the water; stir. Place the pan in the fryer and cook at 340 degrees F for 20 minutes. Stir well, divide into cups, refrigerate, and serve cold.

NUTRITION:
calories 161, fat 4, fiber 4, carbs 12, protein 4

POUND JAM

Preparation time: 5 min | Cooking time: 25 min | Servings: 6

INGREDIENTS:

- Juice of 2 limes
- 4 cups sugar
- 1 pound strawberries, chopped
- 2 cups water

DIRECTIONS:
In a pan that fits your air fryer, mix the strawberries with the sugar, lime juice and the water; stir. Place the pan in the fryer and cook at 340 degrees F for 25 minutes. Blend the mix using an immersion blender, divide into cups, refrigerate, and serve cold.

NUTRITION:
calories 161, fat 2, fiber 4, carbs 15, protein 2

CRANBERRY AND CURRANT JAM

Preparation time: 5 min | Cooking time: 20 min | Servings: 8

INGREDIENTS:

- 2 pounds cranberries
- 4 ounces black currant
- 2 pounds sugar
- Zest of 1 lime
- 3 tbsp water

DIRECTIONS:
In a pan that fits your air fryer, add all the ingredients and stir. Place the pan in the fryer and cook at 360 degrees F for 20 minutes. Stir the jam well, divide into cups, refrigerate, and serve cold.

NUTRITION:
calories 176, fat 2, fiber 3, carbs 15, protein 1

SUGARY PLUM STEW

Preparation time: 10 min | Cooking time: 30 min | Servings: 8

INGREDIENTS:

- 1½ pounds plums, pitted and chopped
- 2 tbsp lime juice
- 1 cup white sugar
- ½ cup water

DIRECTIONS:
In a pan that fits your air fryer, mix the plums with the other ingredients; stir. Place the pan in the fryer and cook at 330 degrees F for 30 minutes. Divide the stew into cups, refrigerate, and serve cold.

NUTRITION:
calories 171, fat 1, fiber 3, carbs 16, protein 6

CINNAMON APPLE JAM

Preparation time: 10 min | Cooking time: 20 min | Servings:

INGREDIENTS:

- 8 apples, peeled, cored and blended
- 1 cup apple juice
- 1 tsp cinnamon powder

DIRECTIONS:
In a pan that fits your air fryer, mix the apples with the cinnamon and apple juice; stir. Place the pan in the fryer and cook at 340 degrees F for 20 minutes. Blend using an immersion blender. Divide the jam into cups and serve.

NUTRITION:
calories 141, fat 2, fiber 4, carbs 14, protein 3

HONEY BANANA CAKE

Preparation time: 10 min | Cooking time: 30 min | Servings: 4

INGREDIENTS:

- 1 tbsp butter, soft
- 1 egg
- 1/3 cup brown sugar
- 2 tbsp honey
- 1 banana, peeled and mashed
- 1 cup white flour
- 1 tsp baking powder
- ½ tsp cinnamon powder
- Cooking spray

DIRECTIONS:
Spray a cake pan with some cooking spray and leave aside. In a bowl, mix butter with sugar, banana, honey, egg, cinnamon, baking powder and flour and whisk Pour this into a cake pan greased with cooking spray, introduce in your air fryer and cook at 350 degrees F for 30 minutes. Leave cake to cool down, slice and serve.

NUTRITION:
calories 232, fat 4, fiber 1, carbs 34, protein 4

CREAM CHEESECAKE

Preparation time: 10 min | Cooking time: 15 min | Servings: 15

INGREDIENTS:

- 1 pound cream cheese
- ½ tsp vanilla extract
- 2 eggs
- 4 tbsp sugar
- 1 cup graham crackers, crumbled
- 2 tbsp butter

DIRECTIONS:

In a bowl, mix crackers with butter. Press crackers mix on the bottom of a lined cake pan, introduce in your air fryer and cook at 350 degrees F for 4 minutes. Meanwhile, in a bowl, mix sugar with cream cheese, eggs and vanilla and whisk well. Spread filling over crackers crust and cook your cheesecake in your air fryer at 310 degrees F for 15 minutes. Leave cake in the fridge for 3 hours, slice and serve.

NUTRITION:
calories 245, fat 12, fiber 1, carbs 20, protein 3

DOUGHNUTS PUDDING

Preparation time: 10 min | Cooking time: 1 hour | Servings: 4

INGREDIENTS:

- 6 glazed doughnuts, crumbled
- 1 cup cherries
- 4 egg yolks
- 1 and ½ cups whipping cream
- ½ cup raisins
- ¼ cup sugar
- ½ cup chocolate chips

DIRECTIONS:
In a bowl, mix cherries with egg yolks and whipping cream and stir well. In another bowl, mix raisins with sugar, chocolate chips and doughnuts and stir. Combine the 2 mixtures, transfer everything to a greased pan that fits your air fryer and cook at 310 degrees F for 1 hour. Chill pudding before cutting and serving it.

NUTRITION:
calories 302, fat 8, fiber 2, carbs 23, protein 10

DOUGHY AMARETTO DESSERT

Preparation time: 10 min | Cooking time: 12 min | Servings: 12

INGREDIENTS:

- 1 pound bread dough
- 1 cup sugar
- ½ cup butter, melted
- 1 cup heavy cream
- 12 ounces chocolate chips
- 2 tbsp amaretto liqueur

DIRECTIONS:
Roll dough, cut into 20 slices and then cut each slice in halves. Brush dough pieces with butter, sprinkle sugar, place them in your air fryer's basket after you've brushed it some butter, cook them at 350 degrees F for 5 minutes, flip them, cook for 3 minutes more and transfer to a platter. Heat up a pan with the heavy cream over medium heat, add chocolate chips and stir until they melt. Add liqueur, stir again, transfer to a bowl and serve bread dippers with this sauce.

NUTRITION:
calories 200, fat 1, fiber 0, carbs 6, protein 6

SUGARY ROLLS AND CHEESE DIP

Preparation time: 2 hours | Cooking time: 15 min | Servings: 8

INGREDIENTS:

- 1 pound bread dough
- ¾ cup brown sugar
- 1 and ½ tbsp cinnamon, ground
- ¼ cup butter, melted
- For the cream cheese dip:
- 2 tbsp butter
- 4 ounces cream cheese
- 1 and ¼ cups sugar
- ½ tsp vanilla

DIRECTIONS:
Roll dough on a floured working surface, shape a rectangle and brush with ¼ cup butter. In a bowl, mix cinnamon with sugar, stir, sprinkle this over dough, roll dough into a log, seal well and cut into 8 pieces. Leave rolls to rise for 2 hours, place them in your air fryer's basket, cook at 350 degrees F for 5 minutes, flip them, cook for 4 minutes more and transfer to a platter. In a bowl, mix cream cheese with butter, sugar and vanilla and whisk really well. Serve your cinnamon rolls with this cream cheese dip.

NUTRITION:
calories 200, fat 1, fiber 0, carbs 5, protein 6

SPICY PIE

Preparation time: 10 min | Cooking time: 15 min | Servings: 9

INGREDIENTS:

- 1 tbsp sugar
- 2 tbsp flour
- 1 tbsp butter
- 2 tbsp water
- For the pumpkin pie filling:
- 3.5 ounces pumpkin flesh, chopped
- 1 tsp mixed spice
- 1 tsp nutmeg
- 3 ounces water
- 1 egg, whisked
- 1 tbsp sugar

DIRECTIONS:
Put 3 ounces water in a pot, bring to a boil over medium high heat, add pumpkin, egg, 1 tbsp sugar, spice and nutmeg, stir, boil for 20 minutes, take off heat and blend using an immersion blender. In a bowl, mix flour with butter, 1 tbsp sugar and 2 tbsp water and knead your dough well. Grease a pie pan that fits your air fryer with butter, press dough into the pan, fill with pumpkin pie filling, place in your air fryer's basket and cook at 360 degrees F for 15 minutes. Slice and serve warm.

NUTRITION:
calories 200, fat 5, fiber 2, carbs 5, protein 6

PASTRY PEARS

Preparation time: 10 min | Cooking time: 15 min | Servings: 4

INGREDIENTS:

- 4 puff pastry sheets
- 14 ounces vanilla custard
- 2 pears, halved
- 1 egg, whisked
- ½ tsp cinnamon powder

- 2 tbsp sugar

DIRECTIONS:
Place puff pastry slices on a working surface, add spoonfuls of vanilla custard in the center of each, top with pear halves and wrap. Brush pears with egg, sprinkle sugar and cinnamon, place them in your air fryer's basket and cook at 320 degrees F for 15 minutes. Divide parcels on plates and serve.

NUTRITION:
calories 200, fat 2, fiber 1, carbs 14, protein 3

GLAZED DONUTS
Preparation time: 10 min | Cooking time: 15 min | Servings: 4

INGREDIENTS:

- ounces flour
- 1 tbsp brown sugar
- 1 tbsp white sugar
- 1 egg
- 2 and ½ tbsp butter
- 4 ounces whole milk
- 1 tsp baking powder
- For the strawberry icing:
- 2 tbsp butter
- 3.5 ounces icing sugar
- ½ tsp pink coloring
- ¼ cup strawberries, chopped
- 1 tbsp whipped cream

DIRECTIONS:
In a bowl, mix butter, 1 tbsp brown sugar, 1 tbsp white sugar and flour and stir. In a second bowl, mix egg with 1 and ½ tbsp butter and milk and stir well. Combine the 2 mixtures, stir, shape donuts from this mix, place them in your air fryer's basket and cook at 360 degrees F for 15 minutes. Put 1 tbsp butter, icing sugar, food coloring, whipped cream and strawberry puree and whisk well. Arrange donuts on a platter.

NUTRITION:
calories 250, fat 12, fiber 1, carbs 32, protein 4

CRUNCHY CORN BANANAS
Preparation time: 10 min | Cooking time: 15 min | Servings: 4

INGREDIENTS:

- 3 tbsp butter
- 2 eggs
- 8 bananas, peeled and halved
- ½ cup corn flour
- 3 tbsp cinnamon sugar
- 1 cup panko

DIRECTIONS:
Heat up a pan with the butter over medium high heat, add panko, stir and cook for 4 minutes and then transfer to a bowl. Roll each in flour, eggs and panko mix, arrange them in your fryer's basket, dust with cinnamon sugar and cook at 280 degrees F for 10 minutes. Serve right away.

NUTRITION:
calories 164, fat 1, fiber 4, carbs 32, protein 4

BUTTERY COCOA CAKE
Preparation time: 10 min | Cooking time: 17 min | Servings: 6
Ingredients:

- 3.5 ounces butter, melted
- 3 eggs
- 3 ounces sugar
- 1 tsp cocoa powder
- 3 ounces flour
- ½ tsp lemon juice

DIRECTIONS:
In a bowl, mix 1 tbsp butter with cocoa powder and whisk. In another bowl, mix the rest of the butter with sugar, eggs, flour and lemon juice, whisk well and pour half into a cake pan that fits your air fryer. Add half of the cocoa mix, spread, add the rest of the butter layer and top with the rest of cocoa. Introduce in your air fryer and cook at 360 degrees F for 17 minutes. Cool cake down before slicing and serving.

NUTRITION:
calories 340, fat 11, fiber 3, carbs 25, protein 5

GREEK CHOCO CAKE
Preparation time: 10 min | Cooking time: 30 min | Servings: 12

INGREDIENTS:

- ¾ cup white flour
- ¾ cup whole wheat flour
- 1 tsp baking soda
- ¾ tsp pumpkin pie spice
- ¾ cup sugar
- 1 banana, mashed
- ½ tsp baking powder
- 2 tbsp canola oil
- ½ cup Greek yogurt
- 8 ounces canned pumpkin puree
- Cooking spray
- 1 egg
- ½ tsp vanilla extract
- 2/3 cup chocolate chips

DIRECTIONS:
In a bowl, mix white flour with whole wheat flour, salt, baking soda and powder and pumpkin spice and stir. In another bowl, mix sugar with oil, banana, yogurt, pumpkin puree, vanilla and egg and stir using a mixer. Combine the 2 mixtures, add chocolate chips, stir, pour this into a greased Bundt pan that fits your air fryer. Introduce in your air fryer and cook at 330 degrees F for 30 minutes. Leave the cake to cool down, before cutting and serving it.

NUTRITION:
calories 232, fat 7, fiber 7, carbs 29, protein 4

APPLE SPICED BREAD
Preparation time: 10 min | Cooking time: 40 min | Servings: 6

INGREDIENTS:

- 3 cups apples, cored and cubed
- 1 cup sugar
- 1 tbsp vanilla
- 2 eggs
- 1 tbsp apple pie spice
- 2 cups white flour
- 1 tbsp baking powder

- 1 stick butter
- 1 cup water

DIRECTIONS:
In a bowl mix egg with 1 butter stick, apple pie spice and sugar and stir using your mixer. Add apples and stir again well. In another bowl, mix baking powder with flour and stir. Combine the 2 mixtures, stir and pour into a spring form pan. Put spring form pan in your air fryer and cook at 320 degrees F for 40 minutes. Slice and serve.

NUTRITION:
calories 192, fat 6, fiber 7, carbs 14, protein 7

MILKY BANANA BREAD
Preparation time: 10 min | Cooking time: 40 min | Servings: 6

INGREDIENTS:
- ¾ cup sugar
- 1/3 cup butter
- 1 tsp vanilla extract
- 1 egg
- 2 bananas, mashed
- 1 tsp baking powder
- 1 and ½ cups flour
- ½ tsp baking soda
- 1/3 cup milk
- 1 and ½ tsp cream of tartar
- Cooking spray

DIRECTIONS:
In a bowl, mix milk with cream of tartar, sugar, butter, egg, vanilla and bananas and stir everything. In another bowl, mix flour with baking powder and baking soda. Combine the 2 mixtures, stir well, pour this into a cake pan greased with some cooking spray, introduce in your air fryer and cook at 320 degrees F for 40 minutes. Take bread out, leave aside to cool down, slice and serve it.

NUTRITION:
calories 292, fat 7, fiber 8, carbs 28, protein 4

COCOA LAVA CAKES
Preparation time: 10 min | Cooking time: 20 min | Servings: 3

INGREDIENTS:
- 1 egg
- 4 tbsp sugar
- 2 tbsp olive oil
- 4 tbsp milk
- 4 tbsp flour
- 1 tbsp cocoa powder
- ½ tsp baking powder
- ½ tsp orange zest

DIRECTIONS:
In a bowl, mix egg with sugar, oil, milk, flour, salt, cocoa powder, baking powder and orange zest, stir very well and pour this into greased ramekins. Add ramekins to your air fryer and cook at 320 degrees F for 20 minutes. Serve lava cakes warm.

NUTRITION:
calories 201, fat 7, fiber 8, carbs 23, protein 4

BAKED CINNAMON APPLES
Preparation time: 10 min | Cooking time: 10 min | Servings: 4

INGREDIENTS:
- 2 tsp cinnamon powder
- 5 apples, cored and cut into chunks
- ½ tsp nutmeg powder
- 1 tbsp maple syrup
- ½ cup water
- 4 tbsp butter
- ¼ cup flour
- ¾ cup old fashioned rolled oats
- ¼ cup brown sugar

DIRECTIONS:
Put the apples in a pan that fits your air fryer, add cinnamon, nutmeg, maple syrup and water. In a bowl, mix butter with oats, sugar, salt and flour, stir, drop spoonfuls of this mix on top of apples, introduce in your air fryer and cook at 350 degrees F for 10 minutes. Serve warm.

NUTRITION:
calories 200, fat 6, fiber 8, carbs 29, protein 12

NUTS CAKE
Preparation time: 10 min | Cooking time: 45 min | Servings: 6

INGREDIENTS:
- 5 ounces flour
- ¾ tsp baking powder
- ½ tsp baking soda
- ½ tsp cinnamon powder
- ¼ tsp nutmeg, ground
- ½ tsp allspice
- 1 egg
- 3 tbsp yogurt
- ½ cup sugar
- ¼ cup pineapple juice
- 4 tbsp sunflower oil
- 1/3 cup carrots, grated
- 1/3 cup pecans, toasted and chopped
- 1/3 cup coconut flakes, shredded
- Cooking spray

DIRECTIONS:
In a bowl, mix flour with baking soda and powder, salt, allspice, cinnamon and nutmeg and stir. In another bowl, mix egg with yogurt, sugar, pineapple juice, oil, carrots, pecans and coconut flakes and stir well. Combine the two mixtures and stir well, pour this into a spring form pan that fits your air fryer which you've greased with some cooking spray, transfer to your air fryer and cook on 320 degrees F for 45 minutes. Leave cake to cool down, then cut and serve it.

NUTRITION:
calories 200, fat 6, fiber 20, carbs 22, protein 4

GINGER CREAM CHEESECAKE
Preparation time: 2 hours and 10 min | Cooking time: 20 min | Servings: 6

INGREDIENTS:
- 2 tsp butter, melted
- ½ cup ginger cookies, crumbled
- 16 ounces cream cheese, soft
- 2 eggs
- ½ cup sugar

- 1 tsp rum
- ½ tsp vanilla extract
- ½ tsp nutmeg, ground

DIRECTIONS:
Grease a pan with the butter and spread cookie crumbs on the bottom. In a bowl, beat cream cheese with nutmeg, vanilla, rum and eggs, whisk well and spread over the cookie crumbs. Introduce in your air fryer and cook at 340 degrees F for 20 minutes. Leave cheesecake to cool down and keep in the fridge for 2 hours.

NUTRITION:
calories 412, fat 12, fiber 6, carbs 20, protein 6

COCONUT AND STRAWBERRY PIE
Preparation time: 10 min | Cooking time: 20 min | Servings: 12

INGREDIENTS:

For the crust:
- 1 cup coconut, shredded
- 1 cup sunflower seeds
- ¼ cup butter

For the filling:
- 1 tsp gelatin
- 8 ounces cream cheese
- 4 ounces strawberries
- 2 tbsp water
- ½ tbsp lemon juice
- ¼ tsp stevia
- ½ cup heavy cream
- 8 ounces strawberries, chopped for serving

DIRECTIONS:
In your food processor, mix sunflower seeds with coconut, a pinch of salt and butter, pulse and press this on the bottom of a cake pan that fits your air fryer. Heat up a pan with the water over medium heat, add gelatin, stir until it dissolves, leave aside to cool down, add this to your food processor, mix with 4 ounces strawberries, cream cheese, lemon juice and stevia and blend well. Add heavy cream, stir well and spread this over crust. Top with 8 ounces strawberries, introduce in your air fryer and cook at 330 degrees F for 15 minutes. Keep in the fridge until you serve it.

NUTRITION:
calories 234, fat 23, fiber 2, carbs 6, protein 7

CARAMEL CHEESECAKES
Preparation time: 10 min | Cooking time: 20 min | Servings: 6

INGREDIENTS:

- For the cheesecakes:
- 2 tbsp butter
- 8 ounces cream cheese
- 3 tbsp coffee
- 3 eggs
- 1/3 cup sugar
- 1 tbsp caramel syrup
- For the frosting:
- 3 tbsp caramel syrup
- 3 tbsp butter
- 8 ounces mascarpone cheese, soft
- 2 tbsp sugar

DIRECTIONS:
In your blender, mix cream cheese with eggs, 2 tbsp butter, coffee, 1 tbsp caramel syrup and 1/3 cup sugar and pulse very well, spoon into a cupcakes pan that fits your air fryer, introduce in the fryer and cook at 320 degrees F and bake for 20 minutes. Leave aside to cool down and then keep in the freezer for 3 hours. Meanwhile, in a bowl, mix 3 tbsp butter with 3 tbsp caramel syrup, 2 tbsp sugar and mascarpone, blend well, spoon this over cheesecakes and serve them.

NUTRITION:
calories 254, fat 23, fiber 0, carbs 21, protein 5

COCOA COOKIES
Preparation time: 10 min | Cooking time: 14 min | Servings: 12

INGREDIENTS:

- 6 ounces coconut oil, melted
- 6 eggs
- 3 ounces cocoa powder
- 2 tsp vanilla
- ½ tsp baking powder
- 4 ounces cream cheese
- 5 tbsp sugar

DIRECTIONS:
In a blender, mix eggs with coconut oil, cocoa powder, baking powder, vanilla, cream cheese and swerve and stir using a mixer. Pour this into a lined baking dish that fits your air fryer, introduce in the fryer at 320 degrees F and bake for 14 minutes. Slice cookie sheet into rectangles and serve.

NUTRITION:
calories 178, fat 14, fiber 2, carbs 3, protein 5

WALNUT BROWNIES
Preparation time: 10 minute | Cooking time: 17 min | Servings: 4

INGREDIENTS:

- 1 egg
- 1/3 cup cocoa powder
- 1/3 cup sugar
- 7 tbsp butter
- ½ tsp vanilla extract
- ¼ cup white flour
- ¼ cup walnuts, chopped
- ½ tsp baking powder
- 1 tbsp peanut butter

DIRECTIONS:
Heat up a pan with 6 tbsp butter and the sugar over medium heat, stir, cook for 5 minutes, transfer this to a bowl, add salt, vanilla extract, cocoa powder, egg, baking powder, walnuts and flour, stir the whole thing really well and pour into a pan that fits your air fryer. In a bowl, mix 1 tbsp butter with peanut butter, heat up in your microwave for a few seconds, stir well and drizzle this over brownies mix. Introduce in your air fryer and bake at 320 degrees F and bake for 17 minutes. Leave brownies to cool

down, cut and serve.

NUTRITION:
calories 223, fat 32, fiber 1, carbs 3, protein 6

BERRY SCONES
Preparation time: 10 min | Cooking time: 10 min | Servings: 10

INGREDIENTS:

- 1 cup white flour
- 1 cup blueberries
- 2 eggs
- ½ cup heavy cream
- ½ cup butter
- 5 tbsp sugar
- 2 tsp vanilla extract
- 2 tsp baking powder

DIRECTIONS:
In a bowl, mix flour, salt, baking powder and blueberries and stir. In another bowl, mix heavy cream with butter, vanilla extract, sugar and eggs and stir well. Combine the 2 mixtures, knead until you obtain your dough, shape 10 triangles from this mix, place them on a lined baking sheet that fits your air fryer and cook them at 320 degrees F for 10 minutes. Serve them cold.

NUTRITION:
calories 130, fat 2, fiber 2, carbs 4, protein 3

CHIP COOKIES
Preparation time: 10 min | Cooking time: 25 min | Servings: 12

INGREDIENTS:

- 1 tsp vanilla extract
- ½ cup butter
- 1 egg
- 4 tbsp sugar
- 2 cups flour
- ½ cup unsweetened chocolate chips

DIRECTIONS:
Heat up a pan with the butter over medium heat, stir and cook for 1 minute. In a bowl, mix egg with vanilla extract and sugar and stir well. Add melted butter, flour and half of the chocolate chips and stir everything. Transfer this to a pan that fits your air fryer, spread the rest of the chocolate chips on top, introduce in the fryer at 330 degrees F and bake for 25 minutes. Slice when it's cold and serve.

NUTRITION:
calories 230, fat 12, fiber 2, carbs 4, protein 5

CREAMY ORANGE CAKE
Preparation time: 10 min | Cooking time: 32 min | Servings: 12

INGREDIENTS:

- 6 eggs
- 1 orange, peeled and cut into quarters
- 1 tsp vanilla extract
- 1 tsp baking powder
- 9 ounces flour
- 2 ounces sugar + 2 tbsp
- 2 tbsp orange zest
- 4 ounces cream cheese
- 4 ounces yogurt

DIRECTIONS:
In your food processor, pulse orange very well. Add flour, 2 tbsp sugar, eggs, baking powder, vanilla extract and pulse well again. Transfer this into 2 spring form pans, introduce each in your fryer and cook at 330 degrees F for 16 minutes. Meanwhile, in a bowl, mix cream cheese with orange zest, yogurt and the rest of the sugar and stir well. Place one cake layer on a plate, add half of the cream cheese mix, add the other cake layer and top with the rest of the cream cheese mix. Spread it well, slice and serve.

NUTRITION:
calories 200, fat 13, fiber 2, carbs 9, protein 8

COCONUT MACAROONS
Preparation time: 10 min | Cooking time: 8 min | Servings: 20

INGREDIENTS:

- 2 tbsp sugar
- 4 egg whites
- 2 cup coconut, shredded
- 1 tsp vanilla extract

DIRECTIONS:
In a bowl, mix egg whites with stevia and beat using your mixer. Add coconut and vanilla extract, whisk again, shape small balls out of this mix, introduce them in your air fryer and cook at 340 degrees F for 8 minutes. Serve macaroons cold.

NUTRITION:
calories 55, fat 6, fiber 1, carbs 2, protein 1

LIME CHEESECAKE
Preparation time: 4 hours and 10 min | Cooking time: 4 min | Servings: 10

INGREDIENTS:

- 2 tbsp butter, melted
- 2 tsp sugar
- 4 ounces flour
- ¼ cup coconut, shredded
- For the filling:
- 1 pound cream cheese
- Zest from 1 lime, grated
- Juice form 1 lime
- 2 cups hot water
- 2 sachets lime jelly

DIRECTIONS:
In a bowl, mix coconut with flour, butter and sugar, stir well and press this on the bottom of a pan that fits your air fryer. Meanwhile, put the hot water in a bowl, add jelly sachets and stir until it dissolves. Put cream cheese in a bowl, add jelly, lime juice and zest and whisk really well. Add this over the crust, spread, introduce in the air fryer and cook at 300 degrees F for 4 minutes. Keep in the fridge for 4 hours before serving.

NUTRITION:
calories 260, fat 23, fiber 2, carbs 5, protein 7

COCONUT GRANOLA
Preparation time: 10 min | Cooking time: 35 min | Servings: 4

INGREDIENTS:

- 1 cup coconut, shredded
- ½ cup almonds
- ½ cup pecans, chopped
- 2 tbsp sugar
- ½ cup pumpkin seeds
- ½ cup sunflower seeds
- 2 tbsp sunflower oil
- 1 tsp nutmeg, ground
- 1 tsp apple pie spice mix

DIRECTIONS:
In a bowl, mix almonds and pecans with pumpkin seeds, sunflower seeds, coconut, nutmeg and apple pie spice mix and stir well. Heat up a pan with the oil over medium heat, add sugar and stir well. Pour this over nuts and coconut mix and stir well. Spread this on a lined baking sheet that fits your air fryer, introduce in your air fryer and cook at 300 degrees F and bake for 25 minutes. Leave your granola to cool down, cut and serve.

NUTRITION:
calories 322, fat 7, fiber 8, carbs 12, protein 7

FRUITY COBBLER
Preparation time: 10 min | Cooking time: 25 min | Servings: 6

INGREDIENTS:

- ¾ cup sugar
- 6 cups strawberries, halved
- 1/8 tsp baking powder
- 1 tbsp lemon juice
- ½ cup flour
- A pinch of baking soda
- ½ cup water
- 3 and ½ tbsp vegetable oil
- Cooking spray

DIRECTIONS:
In a bowl, mix strawberries with half of sugar, sprinkle some flour, add lemon juice, whisk and pour into the baking dish that fits your air fryer and greased with cooking spray. In another bowl, mix flour with the rest of the sugar, baking powder and soda and stir well. Add the oil and mix until the whole thing with your hands. Add ½ cup water and spread over strawberries. Introduce in the fryer at 355 degrees F and bake for 25 minutes. Leave cobbler aside to cool down, slice and serve.

NUTRITION:
calories 221, fat 3, fiber 3, carbs 6, protein 9

MILK TEA CAKE
Preparation time: 10 min | Cooking time: 35 min | Servings: 12

INGREDIENTS:

- 6 tbsp black tea powder
- 2 cups milk
- ½ cup butter
- 2 cups sugar
- 4 eggs
- 2 tsp vanilla extract
- ½ cup olive oil
- 3 and ½ cups flour
- 1 tsp baking soda
- 3 tsp baking powder
- For the cream:
- 6 tbsp honey
- 4 cups sugar
- 1 cup butter, soft

DIRECTIONS:
Put the milk in a pot, heat up over medium heat, add tea, stir well, take off heat and leave aside to cool down. In a bowl, mix ½ cup butter with 2 cups sugar, eggs, vegetable oil, vanilla extract, baking powder, baking soda and 3 and ½ cups flour and stir everything really well. Pour this into 2 greased round pans, introduce each in the fryer at 330 degrees F and bake for 25 minutes. In a bowl, mix 1 cup butter with honey and 4 cups sugar and stir really well. Arrange one cake on a platter, spread the cream all over, top with the other cake and keep in the fridge until you serve it.

NUTRITION:
calories 200, fat 4, fiber 4, carbs 6, protein 2

LEMONY PLUM CAKE
Preparation time: 1 hour and 20 min | Cooking time: 36 min | Servings: 8

INGREDIENTS:

- 7 ounces flour
- 1 package dried yeast
- 1 ounce butter, soft
- 1 egg, whisked
- 5 tbsp sugar
- 3 ounces warm milk
- 1 and ¾ pounds plums, pitted and cut into quarters
- Zest from 1 lemon, grated
- 1 ounce almond flakes

DIRECTIONS:
In a bowl, mix yeast with butter, flour and 3 tbsp sugar and stir well. Add milk and egg and whisk for 4 minutes until your obtain a dough. Arrange the dough in a spring form pan that fits your air fryer and which you've greased with some butter, cover and leave aside for 1 hour. Arrange plumps on top of the butter, sprinkle the rest of the sugar, introduce in your air fryer at 350 degrees F, bake for 36 minutes, cool down, sprinkle almond flakes and lemon zest on top, slice and serve.

NUTRITION:
calories 192, fat 4, fiber 2, carbs 6, protein 7

RAISIN COOKIES
Preparation time: 10 min | Cooking time: 15 min | Servings: 36

INGREDIENTS:

- 1 cup water
- 1 cup canned lentils, drained and mashed
- 1 cup white flour
- 1 tsp cinnamon
- 1 cup whole wheat flour
- 1 tsp baking powder
- ½ tsp nutmeg, ground
- 1 cup butter, soft
- ½ cup brown sugar
- ½ cup white sugar
- 1 egg
- 2 tsp almond extract
- 1 cup raisins
- 1 cup rolled oats
- 1 cup coconut, unsweetened, shredded

DIRECTIONS:
In a bowl, mix white and whole wheat flour with salt, cinnamon, baking powder and nutmeg and stir. In another bowl, mix butter with white and brown sugar and stir using your kitchen mixer for 2 minutes. Add egg, almond extract, lentils mix, flour mix, oats, raisins and coconut and stir everything well. Scoop tbsp of dough on a lined baking sheet that fits your air fryer, introduce them in the fryer and cook at 350 degrees F for 15 minutes.

NUTRITION:
calories 154, fat 2, fiber 2, carbs 4, protein 7

LENTILS AND DATES BROWNIES

Preparation time: 10 min | Cooking time: 15 min | Servings: 8

INGREDIENTS:

- 28 ounces canned lentils, rinsed and drained
- 12 dates
- 1 tbsp honey
- 1 banana, peeled and chopped
- ½ tsp baking soda
- 4 tbsp almond butter
- 2 tbsp cocoa powder

DIRECTIONS:
In your food processor, mix lentils with butter, banana, cocoa, baking soda and honey and blend really well. Add dates, pulse a few more times, pour this into a greased pan that fits your air fryer, spread evenly, introduce in the fryer at 360 degrees F and bake for 15 minutes. Take brownies mix out of the oven, cut, arrange on a platter.

NUTRITION:
calories 162, fat 4, fiber 2, carbs 3, protein 4

APPLESAUCE CUPCAKES

Preparation time: 10 min | Cooking time: 20 min | Servings: 4

INGREDIENTS:

- 4 tbsp butter
- 4 eggs
- ½ cup pure applesauce
- 2 tsp cinnamon powder
- 1 tsp vanilla extract
- ½ apple, cored and chopped
- 4 tsp maple syrup
- ¾ cup white flour
- ½ tsp baking powder

DIRECTIONS:
Heat up a pan with the butter over medium heat, add applesauce, vanilla, eggs and maple syrup, stir, take off heat and leave aside to cool down. Add flour, cinnamon, baking powder and apples, whisk, pour in a cupcake pan, introduce in your air fryer at 350 degrees F and bake for 20 minutes. Leave cupcakes them to cool down, transfer to a platter and serve them.

NUTRITION:
calories 150, fat 3, fiber 1, carbs 5, protein 4

SWEET RHUBARB PIE

Preparation time: 30 min | Cooking time: 45 min | Servings: 6

INGREDIENTS:

- 1 and ¼ cups almond flour
- 8 tbsp butter
- 5 tbsp cold water
- 1 tsp sugar
- For the filling:
- 3 cups rhubarb, chopped
- 3 tbsp flour
- 1 and ½ cups sugar
- 2 eggs
- ½ tsp nutmeg, ground
- 1 tbsp butter
- 2 tbsp low fat milk

DIRECTIONS:
In a bowl, mix 1 and ¼ cups flour with 1 tsp sugar, 8 tbsp butter and cold water, stir and knead until you obtain a dough. Transfer dough to a floured working surface, shape a disk, flatten, wrap in plastic, keep in the fridge for about 30 minutes, roll and press on the bottom of a pie pan that fits your air fryer. In a bowl, mix rhubarb with 1 and ½ cups sugar, nutmeg, 3 tbsp flour and whisk. In another bowl, whisk eggs with milk, add to rhubarb mix, pour the whole mix into the pie crust, introduce in your air fryer and cook at 390 degrees F for 45 minutes. Cut and serve it cold.

NUTRITION:
calories 200, fat 2, fiber 1, carbs 6, protein 3

CRISPY LEMON TART

Preparation time: 1 hour | Cooking time: 20 min | Servings: 6

INGREDIENTS:

For the crust:
- 2 tbsp sugar
- 2 cups white flour
- A pinch of salt
For the filling:
- 2 eggs, whisked
- 1 and ¼ cup sugar
- 10 tbsp melted and chilled butter
- 3 tbsp ice water
- 12 tbsp cold butter
- Juice from 2 lemons
- Zest from 2 lemons, grated

DIRECTIONS:
In a bowl, mix 2 cups flour with a pinch of salt and 2 tbsp sugar and whisk. Add 12 tbsp butter and the water, knead until you obtain a dough, shape a ball, wrap in foil and keep in the fridge for 1 hour. Transfer dough to a floured surface, flatten it, arrange on the bottom of a tart pan, prick with a fork, keep in the fridge for 20 minutes, introduce in your air fryer at 360 degrees F and bake for 15 minutes. In a bowl, mix 1 and ¼ cup sugar with eggs, 10 tbsp butter, lemon juice and lemon zest and whisk very well. Pour this into pie crust, spread evenly, introduce in the fryer and cook at 360 degrees F for 20 minutes. Cut and serve it.

NUTRITION:
calories 182, fat 4, fiber 1, carbs 2, protein 3

MANDARIN ALMOND PUDDING

Preparation time: 20 min | Cooking time: 40 min | Servings: 8

INGREDIENTS:

- 1 mandarin, peeled and sliced
- Juice from 2 mandarins
- 2 tbsp brown sugar
- 4 ounces butter, soft
- 2 eggs, whisked
- ¾ cup sugar
- ¾ cup white flour
- ¾ cup almonds, ground
- Honey for serving

DIRECTIONS:

Grease a loaf pan with some butter, sprinkle brown sugar on the bottom and arrange mandarin slices. In a bowl, mix butter with sugar, eggs, almonds, flour and mandarin juice, stir, spoon this over mandarin slices, place pan in your air fryer and cook at 360 degrees F for 40 minutes. Transfer pudding to a plate and serve with honey on top.

NUTRITION:

calories 162, fat 3, fiber 2, carbs 3, protein 6

BUTTERMILK SHORTCAKES

Preparation time: 20 min | Cooking time: 45 min | Servings: 6

INGREDIENTS:

- Cooking spray
- ¼ cup sugar + 4 tbsp
- 1 and ½ cup flour
- 1 tsp baking powder
- ¼ tsp baking soda
- 1/3 cup butter
- 1 cup buttermilk
- 1 egg, whisked
- 2 cups strawberries, sliced
- 1 tbsp rum
- 1 tbsp mint, chopped
- 1 tsp lime zest, grated
- ½ cup whipping cream

DIRECTIONS:

In a bowl, mix flour with ¼ cup sugar, baking powder and baking soda and stir. In another bowl, mix buttermilk with egg, stir, add to flour mix and whisk. Spoon this dough into 6 jars greased with cooking spray, cover with tin foil, arrange them in your air fryer and cook at 360 degrees F for 45 minutes. Meanwhile, in a bowl, mix strawberries with 3 tbsp sugar, rum, mint and lime zest, stir and leave aside in a cold place. In another bowl, mix whipping cream with 1 tbsp sugar and stir. Take jars out, divide strawberry mix and whipped cream on top.

NUTRITION:

calories 164, fat 2, fiber 3, carbs 5, protein 2

SUGARY SPONGE CAKE

Preparation time: 10 min | Cooking time: 20 min | Servings: 12

INGREDIENTS:

- 3 cups flour
- 3 tsp baking powder
- ½ cup cornstarch
- 1 tsp baking soda
- 1 cup olive oil
- 1 and ½ cup milk
- 1 and 2/3 cup sugar
- 2 cups water
- ¼ cup lemon juice
- 2 tsp vanilla extract

DIRECTIONS:

In a bowl, mix flour with cornstarch, baking powder, baking soda and sugar and whisk well. In another bowl, mix oil with milk, water, vanilla and lemon juice and whisk. Combine the two mixtures, stir, pour in a greased baking dish that fits your air fryer, introduce in the fryer and cook at 350 degrees F for 20 minutes. Leave cake to cool down, cut and serve.

NUTRITION:

calories 246, fat 3, fiber 1, carbs 6, protein 2

CITRIC RICOTTA CAKE

Preparation time: 10 min | Cooking time: 1 hour and 10 min | Servings: 4

INGREDIENTS:

- 8 eggs, whisked
- 3 pounds ricotta cheese
- ½ pound sugar
- Zest from 1 lemon, grated
- Zest from 1 orange, grated
- Butter for the pan

DIRECTIONS:

In a bowl, mix eggs with sugar, cheese, lemon and orange zest and stir very well. Grease a baking pan that fits your air fryer with some butter, spread ricotta mixture, introduce in the fryer at 390 degrees F and bake for 30 minutes. Reduce heat at 380 degrees F and bake for 40 more minutes. Take out of the oven, leave cake to cool down and serve!

NUTRITION:

calories 110, fat 3, fiber 2, carbs 3, protein 4

VANILLA CAKE

Preparation time: 10 min | Cooking time: 20 min | Servings: 8

INGREDIENTS:

- ¾ cup sugar
- 2 cups flour
- ¼ cup olive oil
- ½ cup milk
- 1 tsp cider vinegar
- ½ tsp vanilla extract
- Juice and zest from 2 lemons
- Juice and zest from 1 tangerine
- Tangerine segments, for serving

DIRECTIONS:

In a bowl, mix flour with sugar and stir. In another bowl, mix oil with milk, vinegar, vanilla extract, lemon juice and zest and tangerine zest and whisk very well. Add flour, stir well, pour this into a cake pan that fits your air fryer, introduce in the fryer and cook at 360 degrees F for 20 minutes. Serve right away with tangerine segments on top.

NUTRITION:

calories 190, fat 1, fiber 1, carbs 4, protein 4

BLUEBERRY OATMEAL PUDDING

Preparation time: 10 min | Cooking time: 25 min | Servings: 6

Ingredients:

- 2 cups flour
- 2 cups rolled oats
- 8 cups blueberries
- 1 stick butter, melted
- 1 cup walnuts, chopped
- 3 tbsp maple syrup
- 2 tbsp rosemary, chopped

Directions:

Spread blueberries in a greased baking pan and leave aside. In your food processor, mix rolled oats with flour, walnuts, butter, maple syrup and rosemary, blend well, layer this over blueberries, introduce everything in your air fryer and cook at 350 degrees for 25 minutes. Leave dessert to cool down, cut and serve.

Nutrition:

calories 150, fat 3, fiber 2, carbs 7, protein 4

DATE AND ALMOND BARS

Preparation time: 30 min | Cooking time: 4 min | Servings: 6

Ingredients:

- ¼ cup cocoa nibs
- 1 cup almonds, soaked and drained
- 2 tbsp cocoa powder
- ¼ cup hemp seeds
- ¼ cup goji berries
- ¼ cup coconut, shredded
- 8 dates, pitted and soaked

Directions:

Put almonds in your food processor, blend, add hemp seeds, cocoa nibs, cocoa powder, goji, coconut and blend very well. Add dates, blend well again, spread on a lined baking sheet that fits your air fryer and cook at 320 degrees F for 4 minutes. Cut into equal parts and keep in the fridge for 30 minutes before serving.

Nutrition:

calories 140, fat 6, fiber 3, carbs 7, protein 19

POMEGRANATE CHOCO-BARS

Preparation time: 2 hours | Cooking time: 10 min | Servings: 6

Ingredients:

- ½ cup milk
- 1 tsp vanilla extract
- 1 and ½ cups dark chocolate, chopped
- ½ cup almonds, chopped
- ½ cup pomegranate seeds

Directions:

Heat up a pan with the milk over medium low heat, add chocolate, stir for 5 minutes, take off heat add vanilla extract, half of the pomegranate seeds and half of the nuts and stir. Pour this into a lined baking pan, spread, sprinkle a pinch of salt, the rest of the pomegranate arils and nuts, introduce in your air fryer and cook at 300 degrees F for 4 minutes. Keep in the fridge for 2 hours before serving.

Nutrition:

calories 68, fat 1, fiber 4, carbs 6, protein 1

SWEET TOMATO CAKE

Preparation time: 10 min | Cooking time: 30 min | Servings: 4

Ingredients:

- 1 and ½ cups flour
- 1 tsp cinnamon powder
- 1 tsp baking powder
- 1 tsp baking soda
- ¾ cup maple syrup
- 1 cup tomatoes chopped
- ½ cup olive oil
- 2 tbsp apple cider vinegar

Directions:

In a bowl, mix flour with baking powder, baking soda, cinnamon and maple syrup and stir well. In another bowl, mix tomatoes with olive oil and vinegar and stir well. Combine the 2 mixtures, stir well, pour into a greased round pan that fits your air fryer, introduce in the fryer and cook at 360 degrees F for 30 minutes. Leave cake to cool down, slice and serve.

Nutrition:

calories 153, fat 2, fiber 1, carbs 25, protein 4

BERRIES MEDLEY

Preparation time: 5 min | Cooking time: 6 min | Servings: 4

Ingredients:

- 2 tbsp lemon juice
- 1 and ½ tbsp maple syrup
- 1 and ½ tbsp champagne vinegar
- 1 tbsp olive oil
- 1 pound strawberries, halved
- 1 and ½ cups blueberries
- ¼ cup basil leaves, torn

Directions:

In a pan that fits your air fryer, mix lemon juice with maple syrup and vinegar, bring to a boil over medium high heat, add oil, blueberries and strawberries, stir, introduce in your air fryer and cook at 310 degrees F for 6 minutes. Sprinkle basil on top and serve!

Nutrition:

calories 163, fat 4, fiber 4, carbs 10, protein 2.1

PASSION FRUIT MAPLE PUDDING

Preparation time: 10 min | Cooking time: 40 min | Servings: 6

Ingredients:

- 1 cup Paleo passion fruit curd
- 4 passion fruits, pulp and seeds

- 3 and ½ ounces maple syrup
- 3 eggs
- 2 ounces ghee, melted
- 3 and ½ ounces almond milk
- ½ cup almond flour
- ½ tsp baking powder

DIRECTIONS:
In a bowl, mix the half of the fruit curd with passion fruit seeds and pulp, stir and divide into 6 heat proof ramekins. In a bowl, whisked eggs with maple syrup, ghee, the rest of the curd, baking powder, milk and flour and stir well. Divide this into the ramekins as well, introduce in the fryer and cook at 200 degrees F for 40 minutes. Leave puddings to cool down and serve!

NUTRITION:
calories 430, fat 22, fiber 3, carbs 7, protein 8

RAISIN APPLES
Preparation time: 10 min | Cooking time: 17 min | Servings: 4

INGREDIENTS:
- 4 big apples, cored
- A handful raisins
- 1 tbsp cinnamon, ground
- Raw honey to the taste

DIRECTIONS:
Fill each apple with raisins, sprinkle cinnamon, drizzle honey, put them in your air fryer and cook at 367 degrees F for 17 minutes. Leave them to cool down and serve.

NUTRITION:
calories 220, fat 3, fiber 4, carbs 6, protein 10

PUMPKIN COOKIES
Preparation time: 10 min | Cooking time: 15 min | Servings: 24

INGREDIENTS:
- 2 and ½ cups flour
- ½ tsp baking soda
- 1 tbsp flax seed, ground
- 3 tbsp water
- ½ cup pumpkin flesh, mashed
- ¼ cup honey
- 2 tbsp butter
- 1 tsp vanilla extract
- ½ cup dark chocolate chips

DIRECTIONS:
In a bowl, mix flax seed with water, stir and leave aside for a few minutes. In another bowl, mix flour with salt and baking soda. In a third bowl, mix honey with pumpkin puree, butter, vanilla extract and flaxseed. Combine flour with honey mix and chocolate chips and stir. Scoop 1 tbsp of cookie dough on a lined baking sheet that fits your air fryer, repeat with the rest of the dough, introduce them in your air fryer and cook at 350 degrees F for 15 minutes. Leave cookies to cool down and serve.

NUTRITION:
calories 140, fat 2, fiber 2, carbs 7, protein 10

FIGS AND COCONUT BUTTER MIX
Preparation time: 6 min | Cooking time: 4 min | Servings: 3

INGREDIENTS:
- 2 tbsp coconut butter
- 12 figs, halved
- ¼ cup sugar
- 1 cup almonds, toasted and chopped

DIRECTIONS:
Put butter in a pan that fits your air fryer and melt over medium high heat. Add figs, sugar and almonds, toss, introduce in your air fryer and cook at 300 degrees F for 4 minutes. Divide into bowls and serve cold.

NUTRITION:
calories 170, fat 4, fiber 5, carbs 7, protein 9

LEMON BUTTER BARS
Preparation time: 10 min | Cooking time: 25 min | Servings: 6

INGREDIENTS:
- 4 eggs
- 2 and ¼ cups flour
- Juice from 2 lemons
- 1 cup butter, soft
- 2 cups sugar

DIRECTIONS:
In a bowl, mix butter with ½ cup sugar and 2 cups flour, stir well, press on the bottom of a pan that fits your air fryer, introduce in the fryer and cook at 350 degrees F for 10 minutes. In another bowl, mix the rest of the sugar with the rest of the flour, eggs and lemon juice, whisk well and spread over crust. Introduce in the fryer at 350 degrees F for 15 minutes more, leave aside to cool down, cut bars and serve them.

NUTRITION:
calories 125, fat 4, fiber 4, carbs 16, protein 2

MASCARPONE AND ESPRESSO CREAM
Preparation time: 10 min | Cooking time: 30 min | Servings: 4

INGREDIENTS:
- 4 pears, halved and cored
- 2 tbsp lemon juice
- 1 tbsp sugar
- 2 tbsp water
- 2 tbsp butter
- For the cream:
- 1 cup whipping cream
- 1 cup mascarpone
- 1/3 cup sugar
- 2 tbsp espresso, cold

DIRECTIONS:
In a bowl, mix pears halves with lemon juice, 1 tbsp sugar, butter and water, toss well, transfer them to your air fryer and cook at 360 degrees F for 30 minutes. Meanwhile, in a bowl, mix whipping cream with mascarpone, 1/3 cup sugar and espresso, whisk really well and keep in the fridge until pears are done. Divide pears on plates, top with espresso cream and serve them.

NUTRITION:
calories 211, fat 5, fiber 7, carbs 8, protein 7

PASSION FRUIT CREAMY CAKE

Preparation time: 10 min | Cooking time: 30 min | Servings: 6

INGREDIENTS:

- 1 and ¼ cups flour
- 1 tsp baking powder
- ¾ cup sugar
- 1 tbsp orange zest, grated
- 2 tsp lime zest, grated
- ½ cup butter, soft
- 2 eggs, whisked
- ½ tsp vanilla extract
- 2 tbsp poppy seeds
- 1 cup milk
- For the cream:
- 1 cup sugar
- ½ cup passion fruit puree
- 3 tbsp butter, melted
- 4 egg yolks

DIRECTIONS:
In a bowl, mix flour with baking powder, ¾ cup sugar, orange zest and lime zest and stir. Add ½ cup butter, eggs, poppy seeds, vanilla and milk, stir using your mixer, pour into a cake pan that fits your air fryer and cook at 350 degrees F for about 30 minutes. Meanwhile, heat up a pan with 3 tbsp butter over medium heat, add sugar and stir until it dissolves. Take off heat, add passion fruit puree and egg yolks gradually and whisk really well. Take cake out of the fryer, cool it down a bit and cut into halves horizontally. Spread ¼ of passion fruit cream over one half, top with the other cake half and spread ¼ of the cream on top. Serve cold.

NUTRITION:
calories 211, fat 6, fiber 7, carbs 12, protein 6

SUGAR COOKIES

Preparation time: 10 min | Cooking time: 30 min | Servings: 6

INGREDIENTS:

- 1 cup flour
- ½ cup butter, soft
- 1 cup sugar
- ¼ cup powdered sugar
- 2 tsp lemon peel, grated
- 2 tbsp lemon juice
- 2 eggs, whisked
- ½ tsp baking powder

DIRECTIONS:
In a bowl, mix flour with powdered sugar and butter, stir well, press on the bottom of a pan that fits your air fryer, introduce in the fryer and bake at 350 degrees F for 14 minutes. In another bowl, mix sugar with lemon juice, lemon peel, eggs and baking powder, stir using your mixer and spread over baked crust. Bake for 15 minutes more, leave aside to cool down, cut into medium squares and serve cold.

NUTRITION:
calories 100, fat 4, fiber 1, carbs 12, protein 1

PLUM SUGAR BARS

Preparation time: 10 min | Cooking time: 16 min | Servings: 8

INGREDIENTS:

- 2 cups dried plums
- 6 tbsp water
- 2 cup rolled oats
- 1 cup brown sugar
- ½ tsp baking soda
- 1 tsp cinnamon powder
- 2 tbsp butter, melted
- 1 egg, whisked
- Cooking spray

DIRECTIONS:
In your food processor, mix plums with water and blend until you obtain a sticky spread. In a bowl, mix oats with cinnamon, baking soda, sugar, egg and butter and whisk really well. Press half of the oats mix in a baking pan that fits your air fryer sprayed with cooking oil, spread plums mix and top with the other half of the oats mix. Introduce in your air fryer and cook at 350 degrees F for 16 minutes. Leave mix aside to cool down, cut into medium bars and serve.

NUTRITION:
calories 111, fat 5, fiber 6, carbs 12, protein 6

PLUM AND WHITE CURRANT TART

Preparation time: 30 min | Cooking time: 35 min | Servings: 6

INGREDIENTS:

For the crumble:
- ¼ cup almond flour
- ¼ cup millet flour
- 1 cup brown rice flour
- ½ cup cane sugar
- 10 tbsp butter, soft
- 3 tbsp milk

For the filling:
- 1 pound small plums, pitted and halved
- 1 cup white currants
- 2 tbsp cornstarch
- 3 tbsp sugar
- ½ tsp vanilla extract
- ½ tsp cinnamon powder
- ¼ tsp ginger powder
- 1 tsp lime juice

DIRECTIONS:
In a bowl, mix brown rice flour with ½ cup sugar, millet flour, almond flour, butter and milk and stir until you obtain a sand like dough. Reserve ¼ of the dough, press the rest of the dough into a tart pan that fits your air fryer and keep in the fridge for 30 minutes. Meanwhile, in a bowl, mix plums with currants, 3 tbsp sugar, cornstarch, vanilla extract, cinnamon, ginger and lime juice and stir well. Pour this over tart crust, crumble reserved dough on top, introduce in your air fryer and cook at 350 degrees F for 35 minutes. Leave tart to cool down, slice and serve.

NUTRITION:
calories 200, fat 5, fiber 4, carbs 8, protein 6

CREAM CHEESE ORANGE COOKIES

Preparation time: 10 min | Cooking time: 12 min | Servings: 8

INGREDIENTS:

- 2 cups flour
- 1 tsp baking powder
- ½ cup butter, soft
- ¾ cup sugar
- 1 egg, whisked
- 1 tsp vanilla extract
- 1 tbsp orange zest, grated
- For the filling:
- 4 ounces cream cheese, soft
- ½ cup butter
- 2 cups powdered sugar

DIRECTIONS:
In a bowl, mix cream cheese with ½ cup butter and 2 cups powdered sugar, stir well using your mixer and leave aside for now. In another bowl, mix flour with baking powder. In a third bowl, mix ½ cup butter with ¾ cup sugar, egg, vanilla extract and orange zest and whisk well. Combine flour with orange mix, stir well and scoop 1 tbsp of the mix on a lined baking sheet that fits your air fryer. Repeat with the rest of the orange batter, introduce in the fryer and cook at 340 degrees F for 12 minutes. Leave cookies to cool down, spread cream filling on half of them top with the other cookies and serve.

NUTRITION:
calories 124, fat 5, fiber 6, carbs 8, protein 4

CASHEW BARS

Preparation time: 10 min | Cooking time: 15 min | Servings: 6

INGREDIENTS:

- 1/3 cup honey
- ¼ cup almond meal
- 1 tbsp almond butter
- 1 and ½ cups cashews, chopped
- 4 dates, chopped
- ¾ cup coconut, shredded
- 1 tbsp chia seeds

DIRECTIONS:
In a bowl, mix honey with almond meal and almond butter and stir well. Add cashews, coconut, dates and chia seeds and stir well again. Spread this on a lined baking sheet that fits your air fryer and press well. Introduce in the fryer and cook at 300 degrees F for 15 minutes. Leave mix to cool down, cut into medium bars and serve.

NUTRITION:
calories 121, fat 4, fiber 7, carbs 5, protein 6

PECANS COOKIES

Preparation time: 10 min | Cooking time: 10 min | Servings: 6

INGREDIENTS:

- 1 and ½ cups butter
- 2 cups brown sugar
- 2 eggs, whisked
- 3 cups flour
- 2/3 cup pecans, chopped
- 2 tsp vanilla extract
- 1 tsp baking soda
- ½ tsp baking powder

DIRECTIONS:
Heat up a pan with the butter over medium heat, stir until it melts, add brown sugar and stir until this dissolves. In a bowl, mix flour with pecans, vanilla extract, baking soda, baking powder and eggs and stir well. Add brown butter, stir well and arrange spoonfuls of this mix on a lined baking sheet that fits your air fryer. Introduce in the fryer and cook at 340 degrees F for 10 minutes. Leave cookies to cool down and serve.

NUTRITION:
calories 144, fat 5, fiber 6, carbs 19, protein 2

GRAHAM CHEESECAKE

Preparation time: 10 min | Cooking time: 5 min | Servings: 4

INGREDIENTS:

- 4 tbsp butter, melted
- 6 ounces mascarpone, soft
- 8 ounces cream cheese, soft
- 2/3 cup graham crackers, crumbled
- ¾ cup milk
- 1 tsp vanilla extract
- 2/3 cup sweet potato puree
- ¼ tsp cinnamon powder

DIRECTIONS:
In a bowl, mix butter with crumbled crackers, stir well, press on the bottom of a cake pan that fits your air fryer and keep in the fridge for now. In another bowl, mix cream cheese with mascarpone, sweet potato puree, milk, cinnamon and vanilla and whisk really well. Spread this over crust, introduce in your air fryer, cook at 300 degrees F for 4 minutes and keep in the fridge for a few hours before serving.

NUTRITION:
calories 172, fat 4, fiber 6, carbs 8, protein 3

PEACH AND NUTMEG PIE

Preparation time: 10 min | Cooking time: 35 min | Servings: 4

INGREDIENTS:

- 1 pie dough
- 2 and ¼ pounds peaches, pitted and chopped
- 2 tbsp cornstarch
- ½ cup sugar
- 2 tbsp flour
- A pinch of nutmeg, ground
- 1 tbsp dark rum
- 1 tbsp lemon juice
- 2 tbsp butter, melted

DIRECTIONS:
Roll pie dough into a pie pan that fits your air fryer and press well. In a bowl, mix peaches with cornstarch, sugar, flour, nutmeg, rum, lemon juice and butter and stir well. Pour and spread this into pie pan, introduce in your air fryer and cook at 350 degrees F for 35 minutes. Serve warm or cold.

NUTRITION:
calories 231, fat 6, fiber 7, carbs 9, protein 5

CONCLUSION

Cooking with an air fryer gives you a chance on making something unusual with your daily meals. If you are looking for new meal ideas and trying to experiment with your dishes this cookbook is one of the best options you can turn to. You don't have to search for something useful anymore! This cookbook containing 1001 recipes for air fryer will cover all the needs you have on daily cooking in general and air frying in particular.

Best cooking at home means fuss-free foolproof cooking and when we say foolproof we mean cooking with confidence. These everyday recipes you might have already had the chance to look through are foolproof thanks to being tested numbers and numbers of times. Having this cookbook is like having a knowing friend standing beside you and answering the questions you might have along the way.

Recipes offered in this cookbook cover air frying exclusively. An air fryer is a revolutionary kitchen appliance that cooks your food using the circulation of hot air. Succulent on the inside and perfectly cooked on the outside – what else you can wish from food cooked fast and cooked healthy? Cooking pretty much everything you can imagine is a nice possibility to have; air fryer gives you one.

Last but not at least this cookbook taken together with air fryer will help you cook your meals in a much healthier way! This is one of the main reasons why many people all over the world just fell in love with this great and amazing tool. Now it's your turn to become one of them.

If you don't have an air fryer purchase one right away and if you have it already, get your hands on this cooking journal as soon as possible! These recipes will taste so good your family will wonder how is that even possible you made this yourself.

So, let's get started.
Get the book and have fun cooking!

RECIPE INDEX

ALMOND MILK
Milky Almond Pudding, 17
Cinnamon Breakfast, 21
Almond Oats, 21
Vanilla Strawberry Oats, 21
Maple Chicken in Syrup, 130
Passion Fruit Maple Pudding, 200

ALMOND
Rice, Almonds and Raisins Pudding, 33
Salmon with Almonds, 93
Mandarin Almond Pudding, 199

APPLE
Apple Pancakes, 18
Cinnamon Breakfast, 21
Maple Granola, 21
Honey Bread Pudding, 28
Cherries Risotto, 33
Apple and Quinoa Pesto Mix, 41
Caramel Apple Bites, 74
Herbed Dip, 77
Tomatoes and Sultanas Dip, 79
Apple and Dates Dip, 80
Apple Chips, 84
Glazed Chicken and Apples, 117
Rosemary Glazed Chicken, 135
Pork Belly and Apples, 157
Cinnamon Sugar Apples, 184
Maple Cinnamon Apples, 185
Apple and Wine Sauce, 190
Cinnamon Apple Jam, 191
Apple Spiced Bread, 193
Baked Cinnamon Apples, 194
Fruity Cobbler, 197
Applesauce Cupcakes, 198
Raisin Apples, 201

APRICOT
Marjoram Chicken and Apricot Dip, 134
Black Tea Chicken, 138
Apricot and Ginger Cake, 189

ARTICHOKE
Artichoke Omelet, 15
Oregano Frittata, 29
Parmesan Rice, 58
Lunch Artichokes, 60
Air Fried Artichokes, 73
Lemony Artichokes Sauce, 73
Artichokes and Parmesan Mayo, 167
Artichokes with Coconut, 167
Oregano Artichokes, 172
Mozzarella Artichokes, 172
Artichokes and Coconut Sauce, 172

ASPARAGUS
Asparagus Omelet, 26
Salmon and Asparagus, 52
Cheesy Asparagus, 164
Balsamic Lime Asparagus, 164
Asparagus and Prosciutto, 167
Cajun Asparagus, 168
Feta Fried Asparagus, 181

AVOCADO
Avocado Chicken Burrito, 11
Avocado Crispy Fries, 69
Squid and Guacamole, 101
Avocado Cake, 183

BACON
Bacon and Cheese Breakfst, 26
Tomato and Bacon Mix, 11
Bacon Hash Browns, 12
English Fried Sandwich, 22
Greek Sandwiches, 34
Colby Jack Lunch Burger, 39
Lemon Broccoli Mix, 39
Parsley Fava Beans, 61
Creamy Jalapeno Balls, 87
Bacon and Cauliflower Mix, 169

BANANA
Fruit Casserole, 25
Peanut Butter Banana Chips, 74
Salty Banana Chips, 82
Banana Bread, 188
Spiced Banana Pudding, 189
Honey Banana Cake, 191
Milky Banana Bread, 194

BARRAMUNDI
Italian Barramundi and Olives Mix, 105

BEANS
Beans Casserole, 16
Mozzarella Burritos, 18
Long Beans Omelet, 30
French Beans and Egg Breakfast Mix, 30
Black Beans and Rice, 40
Lunch Veggies Casserole, 41
Chicken and Beans Mix, 42
Lunch Chicken Salad, 46
Chicken, Jalapeno and Mozzarella Casserole, 53
Beans Medley, 58
Cumin Beans Mix, 59
Beans and Peppers Mix, 59
Parsley Fava Beans, 114
Tomato and Cranberry Beans Salad, 62
Mung Beans Mix, 62
Green Beans and Shallots Mix, 64
Jalapeno Peppers Beef, 147
Sage Pork Chops and Beans, 163
Garlic Beans Mix, 166]
Green Beans and Chili Salad, 168
Salty Beans and Parmesan, 182
Mozzarella Green Beans, 182
Green Veggies Mix, 182
Potatoes and Beans Mix, 182
Flavored Green Beans, 182

BEEF
Beef Mustard Burger, 29
Beef Tomato Meatballs, 35
Beef Meatball Baguettes, 35
Beef Stew, 36
Garlic Beef and Cabbage Mix, 37
Colby Jack Lunch Burger, 39
Beef Cubes with Rice, 46
Beef Cheeseburgers, 47
Feta Koftas, 47
Beef and Cheddar Meatballs, 48

Beef Meatballs with Mustard Sauce, 49
Beef Meatballs, 49
Sirloin Steaks with Veggies, 49
Beef Thyme Stew, 51
Onion Baguettes with Meatballs, 51
Cheesy Beef Meatballs, 76
Beef Tomatoes Dip, 77
Provolone Beef Rolls, 86
Beef Empanadas, 86
Beef and Sage Rolls, 87
Beef and Ham Patties, 87
Provence Beef Mix, 139
Soy Beef and Mushrooms, 140
Beef in Wine, 141
Beef with Grapes, 141
Garlic Beef Roast, 142
Celery Beef and Tomatoes, 142
Sesame Beef Mix, 142
Ground Cumin Beef with Peppers, 143
Beef Steaks with Peas, 144
Tomato Beef with Leeks, 145
Worcestershire Beef, 146
Beef in Vinegar, 146
Cilantro Beef, 146
Tomato Beef Curry, 147
Mushrooms Beef, 147
Jalapeno Peppers Beef, 147
Cumin Beef Mix, 147
Mozzarella Beef Casserole, 148
Beef Steak and Tofu, 148
Chuck Roast Beef, 148
Beef and Plums Mix, 150
Sugary Rib Eye Steak, 150
Sesame Steak and Florets, 151
Beef Strips with Snow Peas and Mushrooms, 151
Beef with Mayo, 152
Marinated Pepper Beef, 152
Beef Brisket with Tomatoes, 154
Sesame Beef and Onions, 154
Garlic Beef, 154
Beef Wine Curry, 156
Beef Roast with Smoked Paprika, 156
Garlic Beef and Cabbage, 156
Squash with Beef, 158
Greek Beef Salad, 158
Beef Patties and Creamy Sauce, 158
Worcestershire Beef Casserole, 159
Burgundy Beef and Tomatoes, 160
Mexican Beef Mix, 160
Sirloin Steaks and Tomato Sauce, 161
Coffee Rib Eye Steaks, 161
Filet Mignon and Coconut Sauce, 161
Beef and Zucchini Kabobs, 162
Mediterranean Scallops, 162
Beef Chili Medallions, 162
Balsamic Beef, 162
Beef-Stuffed Peppers, 179

Beer
Chicken and Beer Risotto, 68
Chicken Drumsticks and Beer, 123
Short Ribs in Beer, 157

Beets
Air Fried Beets, 55
Garlicky Beets, 61
Sweet Beets, 68
Garlic Beets, 73
Beets Salmon, 110
Beets in Cilantro, 164
Sesame Beets, 164
Beets and Scallions Mix, 164
Beet Salad and Capers, 172
Blue Beets and Cheese Salad, 172
Sweet Beets and Arugula, 172
Goat Cheese and Veggies Mix, 173

Bell Pepper
Hash Brown Breakfast, 11
Parmesan Frittata, 12
Parsley and Tofu Breakfast, 19
Feta Peppers, 19
Tomato and Peppers Breakfast, 20
Pepper Oatmeal, 21
Bell Peppers Burrito, 24
Bell Peppers Lunch Stew, 39
Bell Pepper and Potato Salad, 48
Sauce Sausage Mix, 49
Smoked Paprika Peppers, 55
Beans and Peppers Mix, 59
Sweet Paprika Peppers, 67
Roasted Greek Peppers Side Dish, 71
Bell Pepper Feta Rolls, 76
Bell Peppers and Feta Rolls, 87
Goat Cheese Peppers, 87
Stuffed Peppers Medley, 88
Easy Salmon Fillets and Bell Peppers, 94
Bell Pepper Shrimp Skewers, 102
Snapper with Peppers, 111
Chicken and Bell Peppers Mix, 119
Bell Peppers and Kale Leaves, 169

Biscuits
Green Peppers and Quinoa Stew, 40
Salmon and Berry Dip, 183

Blackberries
Blackberry Breakfast Mix, 12
Cinnamon Toasts, 25
Salmon and Sweet Berry Glaze, 112
Creamy Vanilla and Blackberry Mix, 187
Vanilla and Blackberry Pudding, 332

Branzino
Citric Branzino, 111

Breadcrumbs
Marinara Ravioli, 36
Oregano Fritters, 44
Basil Croquettes, 44
Beef Cubes with Rice, 46
Beef Meatballs with Mustard Sauce, 49
Cheese Ravioli and Marinara Sauce, 51
Bread Zucchini Fries, 54
Eggplant Fries, 65
Buttermilk Tomatoes, 66
Crispy Zucchini Fries, 66
Crispy Onion Rings, 69
Crunchy Chicken Sticks, 76
Crunchy Chicken Bites, 81
Buffalo Veggie Snack, 82
Crispy Chicken Breast Sticks, 86
Creamy Clams, 97

Bread
Tomato and Bacon Mix, 11
Mozzarella Breakfast Toast, 13
Sugary Toasts, 13

Italian Mozzarella Sandwich, 14
Cheddar Bread Pudding, 14
Cheddar Cheese Toasts, 16
Provolone Tuna Sandwiches, 16
Sugary Vanilla Toasts, 23
Cinnamon Toasts, 25
Mustard Brie Breakfast, 26
Cheesy Air Fried Toasts, 28
Honey Bread Pudding, 28
Coriander Rolls, 28
Beef Mustard Burger, 29
Cheddar Sandwich, 30
Shrimp Wheat Sandwiches, 31
Greek Sandwiches, 34
Dijon Hot Dogs, 34
Beef Meatball Baguettes, 35
Corn Bread Pudding, 37
Colby Jack Lunch Burger, 39
Goat Cheese Toast, 43
Italian Sandwiches, 44
Fresh Chicken Mix, 45
Beef Cheeseburgers, 47
Cheesy Hot Dogs, 48
Onion Baguettes with Meatballs, 51
Cinnamon Pastry Sticks, 84
Spanish Salmon, 110
Chicken and Smoked Pancetta, 122
Doughnuts Pudding, 192

Broccoli
Broccoli Breakfast Scramble, 25
Cheddar Broccoli Quiche, 27
Broccoli Burritos, 31
Lemon Broccol Mix, 74
Lemony Broccoli, 69
Zesty Cauliflower, 73
Garlicky Broccoli Bites, 77
Coconut Veggie Spread, 80
Cheddar Veggie Patties, 88
Broccoli and Scallions, 165
Cheese Broccoli, 165
Florets and Pomegranate, 169
Lime Broccoli, 169
Broccoli Florets Salad, 173
Tomatoes and Florets Stew, 176
Broccoli Hash, 181

Brussels Sprouts
Garlic Brussels Sprouts, 54
Garlic Brussels Sprouts Mix, 64
Brussels Sprouts with Cream, 66
Pine Brussels Sprouts Side Dish, 74
Crispy Buttered Potatoes, 74
Creamy Lamb and Sprouts, 152
Cilantro Brussels Sprouts, 165
Green Brussels Sprouts Mix, 173
Sprouts and Mustard Sauce, 173
Parmesan Brussels Sprouts, 173

Buttermilk
Buttermilk Biscuits, 15
Creamy Casserole, 23
Maple Biscuits, 28
Marinara Ravioli, 36
Cayenne Chicken, 45
Cheese Ravioli and Marinara Sauce, 51

Butter
Old Bay Chicken Wings, 34

Sour-Sweet Chicken Wings, 48
Buttery Cocoa Cake, 193

Cabbage
Garlic Beef and Cabbage Mix, 37
Sirloin Steaks with Veggies, 49
Air Fried Red Cabbage Salad, 51
Applesauce Cabbage, 61
Tomato Cabbage Mix, 62
Green Creamy Cabbage, 70
Fried Red Cabbage, 73
Cabbage Rolls, 82
Pork and Red Cabbage, 149
Garlic Beef and Cabbage, 156
Balsamic Red Cabbage, 165
Nutmeg Napa Cabbage, 169
Sweet Paprika Cabbage Mix, 170
Green Cayenne Cabbage, 170

Carrot
Veggie Breakfast Mix, 12
Veggie Casserole, 19
Almond Oats, 21
Cheddar Broccoli Quiche, 27
Beef Stew, 36
Butter Baby Carrots, 41
Lunch Mushroom Rolls, 43
Beef Thyme Stew, 51
Provence Carrots Mix, 55
Parsnips and Thyme Fries, 56
Carrot Souffle, 60
Provence Carrots, 67
Walnut Carrots Mix, 68
Air Fried Zucchini Mix, 71
Air Fried Turmeric Carrots, 75
Buttery Cayenne Dip, 80
Chicken and Veggie Medley, 117
Italian Chicken Thighs, 117
Turkey Quarters and Herbs, 133
Ginger Duck, 134
Lamb and Carrots Mix, 147
Butter Carrots, 166
Zesty Carrots, 168
Spicy Cabbage and Carrots, 174
Sugary Baby Carrots, 174

Cashew
Cashew Bars, 203

CATFISH
Paprika Catfish, 101
Worcestershire Catfish Fillets, 112

Cauliflower
Veggie Breakfast Mix, 12
Creamy Cauliflower Breakfast, 19
Chicken and Tomato Bake, 38
Cauliflower and Chestnuts Risotto, 55
Sesame Cauliflower Mix, 56
Spring Cauliflower Puree, 59
Orange Cauliflower Mix, 60
Cauliflower Rice Parmesan Cakes, 66
Ginger Cauliflower, 71
Zesty Cauliflower, 73
Buttery Cauliflower Side Dish, 78
Buffalo Veggie Snack, 82
Air Fried Shrimps and Cauliflower, 106
Turmeric Chicken and Cauliflower Rice, 134
Cheddar Ham and Cauliflower, 160

Cauliflower Peanut Mix, 165
Bacon and Cauliflower Mix, 169

CELERY
Thyme Chicken Stew, 50
Turkey Breasts with Celery, 133
Pork and Celery Mix, 148
Easy Celery Root Mix, 170

CHEDDAR
Bacon and Cheese Breakfast, 11
Tomato and Bacon Mix, 11
Bacon Hash Browns, 12
Cheese and Mushrooms Pie, 12
Cheddar Peppery Mix, 14
Cheddar Bread Pudding, 14
Cheddar Dough Rolls, 15
Cheddar Cheese Toasts, 16
Cheddar Breakfast, 24
Cheese Hash Browns, 25
Smoked Breakfast, 25
Cheddar Broccoli Quiche, 27
Cheddar Sandwich, 30
Shrimp Wheat Sandwiches, 31
Cherries Risotto, 33
Philadelphia Chicken Lunch, 47
Beef and Cheddar Meatballs, 48
Beef Meatballs, 49
Creamy Air Fried Potato Side Dish, 64
Creamy Cheddar Mushrooms, 65
Buttermilk and Cheese Biscuits, 66
Cheddar Cheesy Potatoes, 71
Cheddar Veggie Patties, 88
Cheesy Chicken Thighs, 114
Marinara Cheddar Chicken, 124
Cheddar Ham and Cauliflower, 282
Cheddar and Garlic Tart, 178

CHERRY
Cherries Rice, 58
Duck and Cherries, 136
Cherry and Raisins Pudding, 183

CHESTNUT
Soy Rice, 68
Shrimp and Mushroom Rolls, 85
Balsamic Chicken and Water Chestnuts, 135

CHICKEN
Chicken Paprika Casserole, 11
Avocado Chicken Burrito, 11
Rotisserie Chicken Parmesan Tortillas, 18
Chipolatas Breakfast, 22
Chicken Pie, 34
Old Bay Chicken Wings, 34
Monterey Jack Casserole, 37
Chicken and Mushroom Mix, 38
Chicken and Mozzarella Bowls, 38
Chicken and Tomato Bake, 38
Tomato Chicken Mix, 41
Sweet Chicken Thighs, 41
Chicken and Chili Curry, 42
Chicken and Beans Mix, 42
Chicken and Quinoa Stew, 43
Italian Sandwiches, 44
Fresh Chicken Mix, 45
Cayenne Chicken, 45
Spicy Chicken Pie, 45
Chicken Fajitas, 46

Lunch Chicken Salad, 46
Philadelphia Chicken Lunch, 47
Honey Kabobs, 48
Sour-Sweet Chicken Wings, 48
Thyme Chicken Stew, 50
Chicken and Lime Casserole, 52
Shiitake and Poultry Lunch, 52
Chicken and Coconut Casserole, 53
Chicken and Kale Mix, 53
Chicken, Jalapeno and Mozzarella Casserole, 53
Chicken Flavored Risotto, 58
Chicken and Beer Risotto, 68
Crunchy Chicken Sticks, 76
Crunchy Chicken Bites, 81
Sweet Chicken Wings, 82
Yogurt Chicken Dip, 83
Garlicky Chicken Wings, 85
Mozzarella Chicken Rolls, 86
Crispy Chicken Breast Sticks, 86
Blue Chicken Rolls, 89
Ginger Chicken Legs, 114
Salsa Verde Chicken Breast, 114
Cheesy Chicken Thighs, 114
Soy Chicken, 114
Sweet Paprika Chicken Thighs, 115
Spicy Chicken, 115
Wine Chicken Wings, 115
Mushroom Chicken Breasts, 116
Chicken Drumsticks and Coconut Sauce, 116
Party Chicken Thighs, 116
Chicken Breasts Delight, 116
Sweet and Sour Chicken Thighs, 117
Chicken and Veggie Medley, 117
Whole Chicken, 117
Italian Chicken Thighs, 117
Glazed Chicken and Apples, 117
Citric Chicken and Zucchini, 117
Garlic and Lemon Pepper Chicken, 118
Tarragon Chicken Breasts, 118
Chicken Breasts and Pear Jelly, 118
Sweet Chicken and Dates Mix, 119
Chicken Thighs and Leeks, 119
Chicken and Bell Peppers Mix, 119
Air Fried Chicken Wings, 119
Soy and Ginger Chicken, 120
Parmesan Chicken, 120
Cheesy Chicken, 120
Simple Lemongrass Chicken, 120
Herbed Chicken, 121
Balsamic Chicken, 121
Garlic Chicken Breasts, 122
Chicken and Smoked Pancetta, 122
Spicy Chicken Mix, 122
Honey Wings, 123
Chicken and Tomatoes Mix, 123
Cajun Chicken with Veggies, 123
Sweet Chicken and Green Chilies, 123
Chicken Drumsticks and Beer, 123
Chicken Creamy Curry, 124
Marinara Cheddar Chicken, 124
Buffalo Chicken Mix, 124
Chicken and Gold Potatoes, 124
Carrots Chicken and Chickpeas, 124
Chicken Drumsticks and Squash, 125
Indian Chicken with Tomatoes, 125
Sesame and Soy Sauce Chicken, 125
Marjoram Chicken, 125
Coconut Chicken, 126
Lime Chicken Wings, 126

Thyme Chicken, 126
Chicken Mozzarella, 126
Chicken and Creamy Rice, 127
Italian Chicken with Parmesan, 127
Yum-Stuffed Chicken, 127
Easy Chicken Thighs and Baby Potatoes, 128
Butter Chicken and Capers, 128
Chicken and Oregano Mushrooms, 128
Chicken Breasts with Tomato, 129
Rosemary Chicken and Asparagus, 129
Maple Chicken in Syrup, 130
Oregano Chicken and Maple Sauce, 130
Cheddar Chicken and Lentils, 130
Chicken Salad, 131
Coconut Chicken and Green Sauce, 131
Tomatoes and Chicken Cacciatore, 131
Chicken Wings and Mint Sauce, 131
Citric Chicken, 132
Chicken Breasts and Coconut, 132
Garlic Chicken and Black Olives, 132
Crispy Crusted Chicken, 132
Pepperoni Chicken, 132
Chicken and Creamy Mushrooms Mix, 133
Chicken and Garlic Sauce, 133
Salty Chicken Thighs, 133
Chicken Tenders and Paprika, 134
Marjoram Chicken and Apricot Dip, 134
Turmeric Chicken and Cauliflower Rice, 134
Parsley Chicken and Baby Spinach, 135
Balsamic Chicken and Water Chestnuts, 135
Rosemary Glazed Chicken, 135
Italian Chicken Breasts, 135
Zucchini Chicken, 135
Passion Fruit Chicken, 137
BBQ Chicken with Chili, 137
Milky Chicken Casserole, 138
Peach Chicken, 138
Black Tea Chicken, 138
Chicken and Radish Mix, 139

Chickpeas
Chickpeas Stew, 40
Chickpeas Paprika Snack, 83
Carrots Chicken and Chickpeas, 124

Chocolate
Chocolate Amaretto Cream, 184
Chocolate Brownies with Chocolate Chips, 187
Heavy Liqueur Chocolate Cream, 188
Chip Cookies, 196
Pomegranate Choco-Bars, 200

Chorizo
Corn Cilantro Omelet, 15

Clams
Creamy Clams, 178

Coconut
Milky Almond Pudding, 17
Bacon and Cheese Breakfst, 26
Coconut Veggies Mix, 37
Chicken and Chili Curry, 42
Sweet Potato Coconut Casserole, 51
Herbed Casserole, 52
Chicken and Coconut Casserole, 53
Air Fried Coconut Shrimp, 75
Coconut Veggie Spread, 80
Coconut Shrimp, 84
Parsley Coconut Shrimp, 94
Chili Salmon, 107
Salmon and Coconut Dip, 108
Chicken Drumsticks and Coconut Sauce, 116
Simple Lemongrass Chicken, 120
Coconut Chicken and Green Sauce, 131
Chicken Breasts and Coconut, 132
Coconut Lamb, 146
Filet Mignon and Coconut Sauce, 161
Coconut Mix, 166
Coconut and Strawberry Pie, 195
Coconut Macaroons, 196
Coconut Granola, 196

Cod
Marine Tortilla, 16
Cod and Grapes Salad, 35
Herbed Meatballs, 36
Milky Curry, 36
Cod and Fennel Mix, 38
Fish and Chips, 46
Sweet Cod Fillets, 91
Pecan Cod, 91
Balsamic Cod, 91
Cod and Chives, 92
Crunchy Pistachio Cod, 93
Roasted Parsley Cod, 93
Ginger Air Fried Cod, 94
Chili Cod, 96
Herbed Baked Cod, 100
Fried Ginger Cod, 101
Fennel Cod Fillets, 101
Herbed Cod Steaks, 102
Cod and Veggies Medley, 103
Parsley Cod Fillets, 104
Cod Fillet and Plum Sauce, 108
Peanut Cod, 109
Cod with Pearl Onions, 109
French Cod with Tomatoes, 112

Collard Greens
Collard Greens Mix, 171
Balsamic Greens Mix, 174
Garlic Greens and Turkey, 174
Collard Greens and Tomatoes, 176
Spicy Mustard Greens, 176

Cornflakes
Cream Cheese Casserole, 26

Cornmeal
Cornmeal Cakes, 13
Cornmeal Bites, 23

Corn
Cheddar Bread Pudding, 14
Corn Cilantro Omelet, 15
Marine Tortilla, 16
Corn Omelet, 29
Corn Fish Tacos, 31
Corn Bread Pudding, 37
Tomatoes Corn Salad, 41
Leeks Stew, 46
Lunch Chicken Salad, 46
Creamy Corn Swiss Casserole, 49
Paprika Corn, 56

Corn with Paprika and Feta, 64
Buttered Corn, 75
Corn and Wine Dip, 81
Sugary Popcorn, 83
Maple Corn, 170
Dill Buttery Corn, 170

Couscous
Sea Bass with Couscous, 109
Oregano Couscous Pork, 153

Crab
Seafood Appetizer, 85

Cranberry
Cranberry Chili Dip, 80
Turkey Wings with Cranberries, 122
Cranberry and Currant Jam, 191

Cream Cheese
Cream Cheese Casserole, 26
Cheese Rolls, 32
Cream Cheese Oatmeal, 64
Monterey Jack Casserole, 37
Oregano Fritters, 44
Creamy Spinach Mix, 164
Oreo Cheesecake, 183
Rum Sugar Cheesecake, 186
Strawberry Cream Cheese, 186
Coffee Cream, 186
Cream Cheese Vanilla Cookies, 186
Cream Cheese Cake, 187
Creamy Vanilla Cheesecake, 187
Cream Cheesecake, 191
Ginger Cream Cheesecake, 194
Caramel Cheesecakes, 195
Cocoa Cookies, 195
Lime Cheesecake, 196
Cream Cheese Orange Cookies, 202
Graham Cheesecake, 203

Cream
Creole Tomatoes, 54
Brussels Sprouts with Cream, 66
Green Creamy Cabbage, 70
Creamy Leek Dip, 81
Fast Parsley Sauce, 81
Chicken and Creamy Rice, 127
Chicken and Creamy Mushrooms Mix, 133
Chicken Tenders and Paprika, 134

Dates
Dates and Millet Pudding, 33
Apple and Dates Dip, 80
Sweet Chicken and Dates Mix, 119
Date and Almond Bars, 200

Dough
Cheese and Mushrooms Pie, 12
Cheddar Dough Rolls, 15
Swiss Quiche, 27
Spinach Creamy Parcels, 31
Chicken Pie, 34
Parmesan Pizza Rolls, 34
Spicy Chicken Pie, 45
Sweet and Spicy Pumpkin Pie, 184
Brioche Milk and Raisins Pudding, 190
Doughy Amaretto Dessert, 192

Sugary Rolls and Cheese Dip, 192

Duck
Sweet Duck Breast, 115
Duck and Cranberries, 115
Duck and Gold Potatoes, 120
Mustard Duck Breasts, 127
Sour-Sweet Duck Legs, 127
Japanese Duck with Honey, 129
Mushroom Duck Breasts, 129
Duck Breasts with Endives, 129
Ginger Duck, 134
Red Wine Duck and Orange Sauce, 136
Duck with Figs, 136
Duck Breasts and Raspberry Sauce, 136
Duck and Cherries, 136
Lemony Duck Breasts, 137
Tea Duck, 137
Tarragon Duck Breasts, 137
Duck with Mango Salsa, 138

Eggplant
Italian Mozzarella Sandwich, 14
Tomato and Peppers Breakfast, 20
Zucchini Stew, 39
Cumin Eggplant Stew, 40
Italian Eggplant Sandwich, 50
Coriander Eggplant Mix, 54
Sumac Eggplants, 55
Eggplant Pepper Mix, 65
Eggplant Fries, 65
Roasted Eggplant, 68
Herbed Veggie Mix, 71
Eggplant and Garlic Spread, 149
Oregano Eggplants Mix, 166
Herbed Zucchinis and Eggplant Mix, 174
Italian Stew, 178
Eggplant and Ginger Sauce, 180
Eggplant Tabasco Hash, 180
Greek Stuffed Eggplants, 181

Eggs
Chicken Paprika Casserole, 11
Parmesan Frittata, 12
Paprika Breakfast, 12
Creamy Eggs Souffle, 13
Cheddar Peppery Mix, 14
Corn Cilantro Omelet, 15
Artichoke Omelet, 15
Parmesan Potato Omelet, 16
Beans Casserole, 16
Yogurt Peas Omelet, 17
Tarragon Omelet, 17
Apple Pancakes, 18
Sugary Yam Pudding, 19
Spinach Eggs, 22
Chili Souffle, 22
English Fried Sandwich, 22
Thyme Potato Hash, 23
Creamy Casserole, 23
Turkey Casserole, 24
Cheddar Breakfast, 24
Roasted Parmesan Frittata, 26
Asparagus Omelet, 26
Mustard Brie Breakfast, 26
Paprika Eggs, 26
Parmesan Tomatoes, 27
Gouda Cheese Quiche, 27
Smoked Paprika Eggs, 27
Corn Omelet, 29

Chives Omelet, 29
Oregano Frittata, 29
Potatoes Frittata, 29
Mozzarella Sausage Frittata, 29
Long Beans Omelet, 30
French Beans and Egg Breakfast Mix, 30
Monterey Frittata, 31
Creamy Pea Tortilla, 32
Gold Potato Frittata, 32
Cajun Potato Lunch, 37

Endives
Greek Endives, 67
Creamy Endives Side Dish, 77
Lime Endives, 171
Nutmeg Endives and Bacon, 171

Farro
Farro and Rice Pilaf, 72

Fennel
Nutmeg Fennel, 60
Fennel and Tomato Dip, 81
Simple Fennel Mix, 164

Feta
Mushrooms Feta Mix, 17
Feta Peppers, 19
Feta and Quinoa Salad, 42
Feta Koftas, 47
Corn with Paprika and Feta, 64
Bell Pepper Feta Rolls, 76
Greek Feta Meatballs, 86
Bell Peppers and Feta Rolls, 87
Creamy Spinach Balls, 88
Cherry Tomatoes and Feta Salad, 168

Figs
Figs and Coconut Butter Mix, 201

Flax
Flax Crackers, 76
Basil Flax Crackers, 90

Flounder
Butter Flounder Fillets, 99

Flour
Worcestershire Muffins, 14
Buttermilk Biscuits, 15
Apple Pancakes, 18
Mozzarella Pie, 20
Parmesan Muffins, 22
Maple Biscuits, 28
Breakfast Doughnuts, 30
Cheese Rolls, 32
Salsa Pancakes, 44
Cayenne Chicken, 45
Buttermilk and Cheese Biscuits, 66
Basil Butter Crackers, 74
Butter Donuts, 184
Lemon Chocolate Cake, 185
Greek Cake, 187
Cream of Tartar Bread, 185
Sweet Orange Cake, 185
Glazed Donuts, 193
Greek Choco Cake, 193
Nuts Cake, 194

Berry Scones, 196
Crispy Lemon Tart, 198
Buttermilk Shortcakes, 199
Sugary Sponge Cake, 199
Vanilla Cake, 199
Blueberry Oatmeal Pudding, 200
Lemon Butter Bars, 201
Passion Fruit Creamy Cake, 202
Sugar Cookies, 202

Gnozzi
Lunch Gnocci, 44

Goat Cheese
Goat Cheese Toast, 43
Goat Cheese Peppers, 87
Goat Cheese Sprouts, 167
Goat Cheese and Veggies Mix, 173

Gouda
Gouda Cheese Quiche, 27
Gouda Oatmeal, 32

Granola
Maple Granola, 21

Grapes
Cod and Grapes Salad, 35
Fennel Cod Fillets, 185
Juicy Lemons Stew, 190

Haddock
Seafood Mix, 103

Halibut
Spicy Sweet Halibut, 103

Half and Half
Cinnamon Toasts, 25

Ham
Mozzarella Pastry, 16
Onion Ham and Collard Greens, 163
Air Fried Ham Mix, 163

Hash Brown
Bacon Hash Browns, 12
Cheese Hash Browns, 25
Hash Brown Mozzarella Fries, 46

Hazelnut
Rice Chicken Mix, 57

Honey
Honey Bread Pudding, 28
Honey Wings, 123

Hot Pepper
Hot Peppers Dip, 147

Kale
English Sandwich, 18
Cod and Grapes Salad, 68
Chicken and Mushroom Mix, 38

Chicken and Kale Mix, 53
Chili Kale Mix, 166
Turmeric Mix, 170

Lamb
Rosemary Lamb, 39
Greek Feta Meatballs, 86
Crusted Rack of Macadamia Lamb, 140
Creamy Lamb Chops, 141
Lamb and Beans, 143
Lamb Meatballs, 144
Coconut Lamb, 258
Lamb and Carrots Mix, 147
Salty Lamb Ribs, 149
Olive Lamb Chops, 149
Tomato and Garlic Lamb Chops, 150
French Lamb Mix, 150
Herbed Lamb Chops, 151
Crusty Lamb, 151
Creamy Lamb and Sprouts, 152
Marinated Lamb and Veggies, 154
Creamy Lamb, 155
Coriander Lamb Shanks, 155
Rosemary Lamb Roast, 155
Lamb Leg in Herbs, 155
Onion Lamb Shanks and Tomatoes, 156
Veggie Lamb Ribs, 156
Oriental Lamb, 157
Ribs and Wine Sauce, 157
Short Ribs In Beer, 157
Cardamom Lamb and Spinach, 159
Lamb and Citric Flavor, 159
Lamb and Parsley, 159
Fennel Lamb Racks, 160

Leek
Leeks Stew, 42
Creamy Leek Dip, 81
Chicken Thighs and Leeks, 119
Air Fried Leeks, 175

Lentils
Spinach Lunch Cakes, 35
Lentils Ginger Curry, 40
Lentils Fritters, 48
Ginger Lentils Mix with Spinach, 63
Paprika Lentils Snack, 75
Red Lentils with Tomatoes, 77
Turkey with Lentils, 121
Cheddar Chicken and Lentils, 130
Lentils and Dates Brownies, 198

Lettuce
Rocket and Lettuce Mix, 20
Greek Sandwiches, 34
Italian Sandwiches, 44
Chicken Fajitas, 46
Creamy Lettuce Salad, 61
Roasted Greek Peppers Side Dish, 71
Chicken Salad, 131
Seafood Mix, 103

Mango
Fast Mango Dip, 79
Duck with Mango Salsa, 138

Mascarpone
Mascarpone and Espresso Cream, 201

Milk
Berry Oats, 11
Blackberry Breakfast Mix, 12
Cheddar Bread Pudding, 14
Milk Oats, 17
Pear and Nuts Oats, 17
Apple Pancakes, 18
Milky Pumpkin Oats, 21
Cheddar Breakfast, 24
Sausage Casserole, 24
Fruit Casserole, 25
Cheese Hash Browns, 25
Smoked Breakfast, 25
Mustard Brie Breakfast, 26
Milk Espresso Oats, 32
Rice, Almonds and Raisins Pudding, 33
Milky Curry, 36
Corn Bread Pudding, 37
Creamy Corn Swiss Casserole, 49
Milky Sweet Potatoes, 58
Nutmeg Mushroom Cakes, 70
Seafood Mix, 103
Milky Tapioca Pudding, 189
Milky Rice Pudding, 190
Maple Rice Pudding, 332
Milk Tea Cake, 197

Millet
Dates and Millet Pudding, 33

Monterey Jack
Tomato and Bacon Mix, 11
Cheese and Mushrooms Pie, 12
Monterey Frittata, 31
Monterey Jack Casserole, 37
Chicken Verde, 227

Mozzarella
Mozzarella Breakfast Toast, 13
Italian Mozzarella Sandwich, 14
Mozzarella Pastry, 16
Mozzarella Burritos, 18
Mozzarella Pie, 20
Cheesy Air Fried Toasts, 28
Mozzarella Sausage Frittata, 29
Chicken and Mozzarella Bowls, 38
Quick Lunch Pizzas, 43
Macaroni and Mozzarella, 45
Italian Eggplant Sandwich, 50
Chicken, Jalapeno and Mozzarella Casserole, 53
Italian Cheesy Sticks, 76
Mozzarella Chicken Rolls, 86
Mozzarella and Zuchini Snack, 88
Cheesy Pepper Sticks, 89
Mozzarella Chicken Mix, 117
Chicken Mozzarella, 126
Mozzarella Fried Chicken, 130
Rosemary Glazed Chicken, 135
Mozzarella Beef Casserole, 148
Worcestershire Beef Casserole, 159
Mozzarella Green Beans, 182

Muffins
English Sandwich, 18
English Fried Sandwich, 22

Mushrooms
Cheese and Mushrooms Pie, 12

Spinach and Mushrooms Mix, 14
Mushrooms Feta Mix, 17
Nutmeg Fritters, 19
Chipolatas Breakfast, 22
Chives Omelet, 29
Gouda Oatmeal, 32
Chicken and Mushroom Mix, 38
Lunch Mushroom Rolls, 43
Goat Cheese Toast, 43
Stuffed Mushrooms, 43
Fresh Chicken Mix, 45
Turkey Cakes, 50
Chicken and Lime Casserole, 52
Shiitake and Poultry Lunch, 52
Italian Parmesan Mix, 54
Cauliflower and Chestnuts Risotto, 55
Pepper Tomatoes Mix, 56
Cheesy Mushroom Salad, 56
Mushrooms Risotto, 57
Mushroom Side Dish, 63
Cracker Mushrooms, 65
Creamy Cheddar Mushrooms, 65
Vermouth Mushrooms, 67
Chicken and Beer Risotto, 68
Nutmeg Mushroom Cakes, 70
Salty Mushroom Mix, 78
Shrimp and Mushroom Rolls, 85
Mushrooms Appetizer, 89
Shrimp and Mushrooms Mix, 99
Mushroom-Stuffed Salmon, 106
Salmon and Herbed Salad, 109
Mushroom Chicken Breasts, 116
Mexican Turkey and Mushrooms, 121
Chicken and Oregano Mushrooms, 128
Mushroom Duck Breasts, 129
Mozzarella Fried Chicken, 130
Chicken and Creamy Mushrooms Mix, 133
Mushrooms Beef, 147
Beef Strips with Snow Peas Mushrooms, 267
Beef Patties and Creamy Sauce, 158
Portobello Mix, 160
Stuffed Poblano Peppers, 180

MUSSELS
Spicy Mussels, 97
Seafood Medley, 87

OATS
Berry Oats, 11
Milk Oats, 17
Pear and Nuts Oats, 17
Milky Pumpkin Oats, 21
Cinnamon Breakfast, 21
Almond Oats, 21
Vanilla Strawberry Oats, 21
Pepper Oatmeal, 21
Fruit Casserole, 25
Milk Espresso Oats, 32
Gouda Oatmeal, 32
Pear Oatmeal, 33
Cream Cheese Oatmeal, 64

OKRA
Tomatoes Corn Salad, 41
Quinoa and Olives Mix, 42
Cajun Chicken with Veggies, 123
Okra and Corn Salad, 175

OLIVES
Garlic Chicken and Black Olives, 132

ONION
Hash Brown Breakfast, 11
Nutmeg Fritters, 19
Crispy Onion Rings, 69
Cajun Onion Wedges, 72
Onion and Zucchini Spread, 78
Onion Sauce, 79
Sweet Onion Dip, 80
Chicken Breasts Delight, 116
Sesame Beef Mix, 142
Sesame Beef and Onions, 272
Spicy Pearl Onions, 167

ORANGE
Honey Kabobs, 48
Orange Cauliflower Mix, 60
Balsamic Orange Salmon, 93
Orange Trout, 104
Juicy Orange Stew, 188
Creamy Orange Pudding, 189
Zesty Orange Marmalade, 191
Creamy Orange Cake, 196

PARMESAN
Parmesan Frittata, 12
Worcestershire Muffins, 14
Parmesan Potato Omelet, 16
Rotisserie Chicken Parmesan Tortillas, 18
Parmesan Rolls, 22
Parmesan Muffins, 22
Roasted Parmesan Frittata, 26
Parmesan Pizza Rolls, 34
Parmesan Potatoes, 65
Parmesan Potato Patties, 69
Italian Cheesy Sticks, 76
Cheesy Pepper Sticks, 89
Parmesan Chips, 90
Creamy Shrimp and Veggies, 105
Parmesan Chicken, 120
Italian Chicken with Parmesan, 127
Crispy Crusted Chicken, 132
Parmesan Fennel, 174

PARSNIP
Maple Parsnips Mix, 55
Parsnips and Thyme Fries, 56
Creamy Parsnips, 59
Maple Parsnips, 67
Veggie Fries, 70
Garlic Parsnips, 169

PARSLEY
Fast Parsley Sauce, 81
Thyme and Parsley Salmon, 104
Turkey and Parsley Pesto, 115
Lamb and Parsley, 280

PASTA
Seafood Pasta, 36
Pasta Peppers, 47
Oregano Shrimp and Spaghetti, 99
Fettucchine Casserole, 171

PASTRY
Mozzarella Pastry, 16

PEACH
Peach and Nutmeg Pie, 203

PEAR
Pear and Nuts Oats, 17
Pear Oatmeal, 33
Chicken Breasts and Pear Jelly, 118
Cinnamon Pears, 184
Baked Pears and Wine, 188
Pastry Pears, 192

PEAS
Yogurt Peas Omelet, 17
Creamy Pea Tortilla, 32
Fresh Peas, 60
White Fish with Peas and Basil, 91
Parsley Cod Fillets, 104
Chicken and Creamy Rice, 127
Air Fried Ham Mix, 163
Maple Pear Dessert, 188

PICKLES
Air Fried Paprika Pickles, 83

PINEAPPLE
Pineapple Rice, 59
Pineapple Salmon Fillets, 93
Hawaiian Pineapple Salmon, 109
Pineapple and Yogurt Cake, 186

PISTACHIO
Crunchy Pistachio Cod, 171
Crunchy Salmon, 108

PLUM
Duck Breasts and Beef Sauce, 128
Sugry Plum Stew, 191
Lemony Plum Cake, 197
Plum Sugar Bars, 202
Plum and White Currant Tart, 202

POLLOCK
Tasty Pollock, 113

POMEGRANATE
Pine Brussels Sprouts Side Dish, 137
Florets and Pomegranate, 169

PORK
Garlic Pork Chops, 139
Broccoli Pork and Soy Sauce, 139
Oregano Pork Chops, 140
Coconut and Ginger Pork, 140
Rosemary Pork and Brussels Sprouts, 140
Tarragon Pork and Mustard, 140
Sweet Paprika Pork Chops, 141
Smoked Paprika Pork Mix, 141
Garlic Pork Loin, 142
Pork and Bell Peppers, 142
Pork Chops with Pesto, 143
Paprika Pork Roast, 143
Soy Pork and Cauliflower, 143
Pork and Peppers, 255
Fennel Pork Mix, 144
Chorizo Meatloaf, 144
Paprika Pork Steaks, 144
Cinnamon Pork Mix, 145
Loin Roast, 145
Pork Chops with Peanuts, 145
Ginger Flank Steaks, 145
Chives Pork Chops, 146
Pork and Celery Mix, 148
Pork and Chives Mix, 148
Pork and Red Cabbage, 149
Tomato Pork Chops, 149
Creamy Pork Mix, 149
French Pork, 151
Indian Pork Dish, 152
Sweet Paprika Pork, 152
Marinated Cayenne Pork, 153
Simple Pork in Wine, 153
Oregano Couscous Pork, 153
Air Fried Pork, 153
Fennel Pork Loin, 154
Pork Belly and Apples, 157
Citric Pork Steaks, 157
Pork and Mushroom Mayo, 158
Roasted Pork Chops and Paprika, 162
Sage Pork Chops and Beans, 163
Buttered Pork Chops, 163

POTATO
Hash Brown Breakfast, 11
Greek Potatoes Breakfast, 15
Parmesan Potato Omelet, 16
Pepper Potatoes, 23
Thyme Potato Hash, 23
Broccoli Breakfast Scramble, 25
Coriander Rolls, 28
Potatoes Frittata, 29
Broccoli Burritos, 31
Gold Potato Frittata, 32
Beef Stew, 36
Cajun Potato Lunch, 37
Bell Pepper and Potato Salad, 48
Sweet Potato Coconut Casserole, 51
Sour Cream Potatoes, 53
Sweet Potato Ginger Salad, 53
Salty Rosemary Potatoes, 56
Spicy Potatoes, 57
Milky Sweet Potatoes, 58
Oregano Potatoes, 62
Indian Potatoes with Cilantro, 63
Creamy Potato Wedges, 63
Curry Potato Fries, 63
Herbed Potatoes, 64
Creamy Air Fried Potato Side Dish, 64
Parmesan Potatoes, 65
Herbed Risotto, 68
Parmesan Potato Patties, 69
Rosemary Fried Potato Chips, 69
Veggie Fries, 70
Greek Salty Potatoes, 70
Cheddar Cheesy Potatoes, 71
Potato Casserole, 73
Crispy Buttered Potatoes, 137
Salty Potato Chips, 76
Clams and Potatoes, 87
Salmon with Potatoes, 102
Duck and Gold Potatoes, 217
Chicken Creamy Curry, 124
Easy Chicken Thighs and Baby Potatoes, 128
Beef Wine Curry, 156
Beef Roast with Smoked Paprika, 156
Creamy Greek Potatoes, 166

New Potatoes Dish, 169
Crunchy Gold Potatoes and Parsley, 175
Indian Chili Potatoes, 176
Cinnamon Potatoes Mix, 180
Greek Veggies Mix, 181
Potatoes and Paprika Mix, 182
Baby Balsamic Potatoes, 183
Potatoes and Oregano Sauce, 183

Provolone
Provolone Tuna Sandwiches, 16

Pumpkin
Milky Pumpkin Oats, 21
Nutmeg Pumpkin Rice, 57
Sugary Air Fried Pumpkin, 65
Cinnamon Rice, 72
Spicy Pie, 192
Pumpkin Cookies, 201

Quinoa
Quinoa Romanesco Mix, 18
Veggie Casserole, 19
Green Peppers and Quinoa Stew, 40
Apple and Quinoa Pesto Mix, 41
Feta and Quinoa Salad, 42
Quinoa and Olives Mix, 42
Chicken and Quinoa Stew, 43
Turmeric Quinoa, 57

Radish
Radish Chives, 75
Chives and Radish Chips, 83
Parmesan Radish Hash, 176

Raisins
Cherry and Raisins Pudding, 183
Raisin Cookies, 197

Raspberries
Cheese Rolls, 32

Ravioli
Marinara Ravioli, 36
Cheese Ravioli and Marinara Sauce, 96

Rhubarb
Rhubarb with Walnuts, 61
Sweet Rhubarb Pie, 198

Rice
Milky Almond Pudding, 17
Cherries Risotto, 33
Rice, Almonds and Raisins Pudding, 33
Sea Bass Stew, 38
Black Beans and Rice, 40
Beef Cubes with Rice, 46
Rice Chicken Mix, 57
Mushrooms Risotto, 57
Saffron Arborio Rice, 58
Cherries Rice, 58
Chicken Flavored Risotto, 58
Parmesan Rice, 58
Pineapple Rice, 111
Scallions and Chili Rice Mix, 62
Cauliflower Rice Parmesan Cakes, 66
Soy Rice, 68
Farro and Rice Pilaf, 72

Cinnamon Rice, 72
Herbed Basmati Rice, 72
Rice with Salmon, 96

Ricotta
Stuffed Mushrooms, 43
Swiss Chard and Ricotta, 177
Strawberry Ricotta Cheesecake, 189
Almond and Ricotta Cake, 189
Citric Ricotta Cake, 199

Rolls
Parmesan Rolls, 22

Romanesco
Quinoa Romanesco Mix, 18

Rutabaga
Rutabaga and Veggie Pasta Mix, 178

Saba
Saba Fish, 103

Salmon
Salmon and Asparagus, 52
Crunchy Salmon Patties, 82
Salmon Cilantro Meatballs, 85
Garlic Salmon Fillets, 91
Paprika Salmon Fillets, 92
Maple Salmon, 92
Balsamic Orange Salmon, 93
Salmon with Almonds, 93
Pineapple Salmon Fillets, 93
Easy Salmon Fillets and Bell Peppers, 172
Salmon and Mustard Mix, 94
Peppery Salmon, 95
Rice with Salmon, 96
Veggie Salmon, 96
Garlic Salmon Steak, 96
Lime Baked Salmon, 100
Salmon and Berry Dip, 100
Honey Salmon, 102
Flavored Air Fried Salmon, 102
Salmon with Potatoes, 102
Thyme and Parsley Salmon, 104
Cheddar Salmon, 104
Salmon and Peppery Salsa, 105
Mushroom-Stuffed Salmon, 106
Maple Salmon, 96
Jamaican Salmon with Arugula, 106
Salmon and Citric Marmalade, 107
Chili Salmon, 107
Salmon with Citric Relish, 107
Salmon and Coconut Dip, 108
Crunchy Salmon, 108
Maple Salmon and Chives Medley, 108
Hawaiian Pineapple Salmon, 109
Salmon and Herbed Salad, 109
Salmon and Greek Salsa, 110
Beets Salmon, 110
Spanish Salmon, 110
Herbed Salmon, 110
Salmon and Sweet Berry Glaze, 112

Salsa
Salsa Pancakes, 44
Salsa Verde Chicken Breast, 114
Chicken Verde, 126

SAUSAGE
Bacon and Cheese Breakfast, 11
Cherry Omelet, 13
Cheddar Dough Rolls, 15
Cheddar Breakfast, 24
Sausage Casserole, 24
Smoked Breakfast, 25
Mozzarella Sausage Frittata, 29
Dijon Hot Dogs, 34
Sea Bass Stew, 38
Cheesy Hot Dogs, 48
Sauce Sausage Mix, 49
Rosemary Sausage Mix, 144
Portobello Mix, 160
Hot Sausage and Peppers, 161

SCALLION
Scallions and Chili Rice Mix, 62
Chili Scallions Dip, 81
Beets and Scallions Mix, 164
Broccoli and Scallions, 165

SCALLOP
Mediterranean Scallops, 162

SEA BASS
Paella Marinera, 94
Sea Bass with Couscous, 109
Citric Sea Bass, 113

SHALLOT
Turkey and Shallot Burgers, 52
Walnut Shallots, 54
Green Beans and Shallots Mix, 64

SHRIMP
Shrimp Wheat Sandwiches, 31
Seafood Pasta, 36
Basil Croquettes, 44
Salsa Pancakes, 44
Macaroni and Mozzarella, 45
Air Fried Red Cabbage Salad, 51
Air Fried Coconut Shrimp, 75
Coconut Shrimp, 84
Tiger Shrimp Appetizer, 84
Seafood Appetizer, 85
Minty Shrimp, 88
Mushrooms Appetizer, 89
Seafood Snack, 90
Shrimp and Veggie Mix, 91
Buttery Shrimp, 170
Paella Marinera, 94
Parsley Coconut Shrimp, 94
Tiger Shrimp Mix, 94
Paprika and Tabasco Shrimp Mix, 95
Rosemary Shrimps, 95
Seafood Medley, 87
Parsley Shrimp Mix, 98
Red Pepper Shrimps, 98
Red Onion Shrimps, 98
Shrimp and Tomatoes, 98
Tomato Vinegar Shrimp, 98
Shrimp and Peas Mix, 98
Chili Shrimp Mix, 98
Oregano Shrimp and Spaghetti, 99
Parmesan Shrimp, 99
Shrimp and Mushrooms Mix, 182
Mayo Shrimp Salad, 100

Shrimp and Tomato Sauce, 100
Spicy Shrimp, 101
Bell Pepper Shrimp Skewers, 102
Creamy Shrimp and Veggies, 105
Air Fried Shrimps and Cauliflower, 106

SNAPPER
Olives Snapper, 95
Red Snapper with Okra, 111
Snapper with Peppers, 111
Oriental Fish, 112

SOLE
Lemon Sole with Chard Mix, 111

SPINACH
Chicken Paprika Casserole, 11
Spinach and Mushrooms Mix, 14
Mozzarella Pie, 20
Spinach Eggs, 22
Chipolatas Breakfast, 22
Turkey Casserole, 24
Spinach Creamy Parcels, 31
Monterey Frittata, 31
Spinach Lunch Cakes, 35
Lentils Ginger Curry, 40
Quinoa and Olives Mix, 42
Lunch Gnocci, 44
Lentils Fritters, 48
Cheesy Spinach, 61
Ginger Lentils Mix with Spinach, 63
Mozzarella Chicken Rolls, 86
Provolone Beef Rolls, 86
Creamy Spinach Balls, 88
Milky Chicken Casserole, 138
Cardamom Lamb and Spinach, 159
Creamy Spinach Mix, 164
Spinach Milky Pie, 171
Spanish Greens, 177
Spinach and Portobello Mushrooms, 179

SQUASH
Chicken and Quinoa Stew, 43
Yellow Squash and Zucchini Mix, 56
Butternut Mash, 60
Veggie Dip, 78
Chicken Drumsticks and Squash, 125
Squash with Beef, 158
Butternut Squash Salad, 168
Sour Cream Squash Mix, 168

SQUID
Ginger Squid, 99
Squid and Guacamole, 101
Pound Jam, 191

STRAWBERRY
Vanilla Strawberry Oats, 21
Coconut Granola, 196
Berries Medley, 200

SUGAR
Sugary Yam Pudding, 19
Sugary Vanilla Toasts, 23
Breakfast Doughnuts, 30
Fast Mango Dip, 79
Chocolate Amaretto Cream, 184
Cinnamon Rolls, 184

Butter Donuts, 184
Walnut and Cocoa Cookies, 186
Pear Bread, 188
Citric Cake, 188
Cocoa Lava Cakes, 194
Pecans Cookies, 203

SWISS CHARD
Swiss Chard and Pine Nuts Salad, 177

SWISS CHEESE
Swiss Quiche, 27
Creamy Corn Swiss Casserole, 49

SWORDFISH
Swordfish and Spicy Fruit Salsa, 107

TILAPIA
Ginger Tilapia, 112
Greek Tilapia, 113

TOFU
Quinoa Romanesco Mix, 18
Veggie Casserole, 19
Parsley and Tofu Breakfast, 19
Tofu Breakfast, 27
Greek Breakfast Tofu, 30
Coriander Bites, 77
Beef Steak and Tofu, 148

TOMATO
Tomato and Bacon Mix, 11
Cherry Omelet, 13
Cheddar Peppery Mix, 14
Tomato and Peppers Breakfast, 20
Rosemary Tomatoes Mix, 20
Parmesan Tomatoes, 27
Beef Tomato Meatballs, 35
Cod and Fennel Mix, 38
Chicken and Tomato Bake, 38
Bell Peppers Lunch Stew, 39
Zucchini Stew, 39
Green Peppers and Quinoa Stew, 40
Chickpeas Stew, 40
Lentils Ginger Curry, 40
Cumin Eggplant Stew, 40
Tomatoes Corn Salad, 41
Tomato Chicken Mix, 41
Feta and Quinoa Salad, 42
Chicken and Beans Mix, 42
Quick Lunch Pizzas, 43
Pasta Peppers, 47
Creole Tomatoes, 54
Pepper Tomatoes Mix, 56
Tomato and Cranberry Beans Salad, 62
Tomato Cabbage Mix, 62
Buttermilk Tomatoes, 66
Thyme Tomatoes, 67
Beef Tomatoes Dip, 77
Herbed Party Mix, 79
Tomatoes and Sultanas Dip, 79
Sweet Chili Salsa, 79
Eggplant and Garlic Spread, 80
Fennel and Tomato Dip, 81
Parsley Tomatoes Appetizer, 87
Seafood Medley, 87
Shrimp and Tomato Sauce, 100
Rosemary Halibut and Tomatoes, 197
French Cod with Tomatoes, 112
Chicken and Tomatoes Mix, 123
Sweet Chicken and Green Chilies, 123
Indian Chicken with Tomatoes, 125
Chicken Breasts with Tomato, 129
Tomatoes and Chicken Cacciatore, 131
Pepperoni Chicken, 132
Tomato Beef Curry, 147
Tomato Pork Chops, 149
Tomato and Garlic Lamb Chops, 150
Beef Brisket with Tomatoes, 154
Burgundy Beef and Tomatoes, 160
Sirloin Steaks and Tomato Sauce, 161
Cherry Tomato Salad, 165
Cherry Tomatoes and Feta Salad, 168
Tomato and Balsamic Greens, 171
Simple Mushroom Tomatoes, 175
Oregano Air Fried Tomatoes, 177
Garlic Tomatoes with Thyme, 179
Cherry Tomatoes and Rosemary Sauce, 179
Balsamic Cherry Tomatoes Skewers, 179
Mexican Salad, 179
Sweet Tomato Cake, 200

TORTILLAS
Marine Tortilla, 16
Tuna and Zucchini Tortillas, 44
Chicken Fajitas, 46
Spicy Paprika Chips, 70

TROUT
Garlic Trout, 95
Cilantro Trout Fillets, 96
Chinese Trout Bites, 96
Crunchy Trout, 97
Trout and Soy Sauce, 100
Orange Trout, 104
Butter Trout and Lemon Sauce, 104

TUNA
Provolone Tuna Sandwiches, 16
Tuna and Zucchini Tortillas, 44
Pepper Tuna Cakes, 90
Thyme Tuna, 92
Tuna Steak and Arugula, 105

TURKEY
Turkey Casserole, 24
Bell Peppers Burrito, 24
Creamy Pea Tortilla, 32
Turkey Lunch, 35
Maple Turkey Breast, 50
Turkey Cakes, 50
Turkey and Shallot Burgers, 52
Rosemary Turkey Breast, 114
Turkey and Parsley Pesto, 115
Turkey with Fruit Sauce, 118
Turkey Breasts and Spring Onions, 120
Turkey with Lentils, 121
Mexican Turkey and Mushrooms, 121
Parmesan Turkey Meatballs, 122
Turkey Wings with Cranberries, 122
Turkey Quarters and Herbs, 133
Turkey Breasts with Celery, 133

TURNIPS
Indian Turmeric Salad, 175

YAM
Sugary Yam Pudding, 19

Yum-Stuffed Chicken, 127

YOGURT
Greek Potatoes Breakfast, 15
Yogurt Peas Omelet, 17
Greek Breakfast Tofu, 30
Monterey Jack Casserole, 37
Greek Salty Potatoes, 131
Salmon and Greek Salsa, 110
Greek Tilapia, 113

Walnuts
Pear and Nuts Oats, 17
Pear Oatmeal, 33
Walnut Shallots, 54
Rhubarb with Walnuts, 61
Walnut Carrots Mix, 68
Potato Casserole, 73
Walnut Brownies, 195

WHITE FISH
Corn Fish Tacos, 31
White Fish Sticks, 84
Crunchy Fish Nuggets, 84
White Fish with Peas and Basil, 91

WINE
Sea Bass Stew, 38
Paella Marinera, 94
Red Wine Duck and Orange Sauce, 136

ZUCCHINI
Rotisserie Chicken Parmesan Tortillas, 18
Coconut Veggies Mix, 37
Zucchini Stew, 39
Lunch Mushroom Rolls, 43
Tuna and Zucchini Tortillas, 44
Pasta Peppers, 47
Herbed Casserole, 52
Bread Zucchini Fries, 54
Yellow Squash and Zucchini Mix, 56
Crispy Zucchini Fries, 66
Zucchini Croquettes, 70
Herbed Veggie Mix, 71
Air Fried Zucchini Mix, 71
Garlic Zucchini Balls, 74
Balsamic Zucchini Slices, 75
Onion and Zucchini Spread, 78
Mozzarella and Zucchini Snack, 88
Zucchini Chicken, 135
Beef and Zucchini Kabobs, 162
Oregano and Zucchini Mix, 167
Herbed Zucchinis and Eggplant Mix, 174

Made in the USA
Coppell, TX
07 May 2020

24274247R00127